A. J.·HOLMAN COMPANY

DAILY DEVOTIONAL BIBLE COMMENTARY

Psalms—Malachi

A. J. HOLMAN COMPANY
NASHVILLE, TENN.

© 1973 Scripture Union
First published 1974
Reprinted 1977

U.S. Library of Congress Cataloging in Publication Data

Daily Bible Commentary: Psalms—Malachi.
  Reprint of the ed. published by Scripture Union,
London.
  1. Bible. O.T.—Commentaries.   I. Cundall,
Arthur Ernest.
BS1151.2.D32   1977   222′.07   76–46493
ISBN–0–87981–069–6

This edition printed
and bound in U.S.A. 1980
Code 4690-32

Contents

Maps, Illustrations and Articles

General Introduction

The overwhelming response to the Scripture Union Bible Study Books, when originally issued during the period 1967–71, has led to the demand for their preservation in a more compact and durable form.

It will be recalled that the original intention of this series was to encourage the daily study of the Bible at greater depth than was possible with the Bible Study Notes. This allowed fuller discussion of introductory, textual and background material, whilst still aiming at devotional warmth, sound exegesis and relevance to daily life. It is heartening to know that this aim has, in considerable measure, been achieved. Moreover, the Bible Study Books have been widely used as the basis for group discussion in homes, colleges and churches, and some volumes have even been used as prescribed texts in Bible colleges! It is hoped that the new format will find an equally encouraging reception.

It remains true, however, that the principal aim of this series is to stimulate personal daily Bible study. Each main section contains material for a three-month period. The one exception to this is the section on the Psalms which contains readings for a four-month period. Where it is suggested that two sections should be read together in order to fit a three or four-month period, they are marked with an asterisk. There is, of course, no obligation to adopt this suggestion. This particular volume, therefore, provides material for a period of approximately sixteen months. The complete series of four volumes will provide for daily readings over a five-year cycle, and will form a complete Bible Commentary. It is appreciated that few students will have the time available for a full consideration of all the questions set for further study. But since these are placed at approximately weekly intervals it would be stimulating and refreshing if time could be set aside once a week for the study of one or more questions.

The authors of the individual sections have been allowed the necessary liberty of approach within the general scope of the series. This provides for a certain variation which we trust will prove stimulating rather than disconcerting. All authors are united within the circle of evangelical, conservative scholarship and are widely respected within this field.

Opportunity has been taken to correct errors which escaped attention in the earlier edition and also to make limited revisions where necessary. The inclusion of further introductory articles, maps, diagrams and charts will, we trust, add to the value of this volume as an aid to the study of God's Word.

List of Standard Abbreviations

AV (KJV)	Authorised Version (King James), 1611.
c. (circa)	about
cf., cp.	compare
e.g.	for example
f.	verse following
ff.	verses following
Gk.	Greek
Heb.	Hebrew
i.e.	that is
J.B.	Jerusalem Bible, 1966.
LXX	Septuagint (Greek Version of the O.T.)
NEB	New English Bible, 1961 and 1970.
NT	New Testament
OT	Old Testament
p.	page
pp.	pages
RSV	Revised Standard Version 1946 and 1952.
RV	Revised Version (American Standard Version) 1885.
s.v.	(*sub voce*) 'under that word'
v.	verse
vs.	verses
viz.	namely

The Psalms

The Psalter is the hymn and prayer book of Solomon's Temple, to which some religious poems and later psalms have been added. The actual bringing together of the psalms and their editing is post-exilic, and we know virtually nothing of the process. It should not be assumed that they are all necessarily suited to Christian worship. Even in the Synagogue only about two-thirds are ever used in public.

All the psalms are in poetry, which in Hebrew is expressed by,

(a) a rhythm the translations seldom try to reproduce;

(b) a special choice of words, which cannot always be brought out in English;

(c) a special structure clearly shown in the RV and RSV. Each verse consists of two or more lines; the thought of the first line is continued, amplified or modified by the second and following. This means that in interpretation we must take the verse and not the line as the unit of expression. The RSV occasionally changes the verse punctuation of the Hebrew where this parallelism of thought seems to demand it.

The psalms, being mostly inspired prayers and hymns for general worship, so generalize the experiences that lie behind them that they can be used by those that pass through similar but different experiences. Very often we can fix their background only through their titles.

Since most of the psalms were sung at Temple services, they contain a number of musical directions. These seldom contribute to our understanding of the text, and there is little agreement about the meaning of most of them, so they are normally ignored in the notes. The Psalter is divided into five books, and a brief introduction is provided for each.

The comments are based on the RSV. Questions of authorship and of the text are referred to only where it seems necessary for better understanding. The AV(KJV) is mentioned only where its rendering is preferable or where it is particularly misleading. The Septuagint is occasionally mentioned: a Greek translation of the Hebrew Old Testament dating from the 1st or 2nd century B.C. It is commonly known by the symbol LXX.

For the ordinary reader looking for more than just devotional exegesis the best commentary is still that by Kirkpatrick in the Cambridge Bible for Schools and Colleges (one-volume edition). Occasionally reference is made to the commentary on the Psalter by Weiser.

7

All these psalms except 1 and 33 are Davidic. For the omission of the title in Psa. 2 see notes; Psa. 10 is part of Psa. 9. This is almost certainly the oldest section of the Psalter. It is worth noting how David repeatedly refers to wicked men. Where we are apt to speak of Satan, he is concerned with his instruments.

Psalm 1 God's Man

The first two psalms are an introduction to the Psalter as a whole. This, the psalm of God's man, represents all those that speak of the joys and sorrows, victories and defeats of the godly. They are not direct predictions of the Messiah, but just as all the godly who have followed Him have shown something of His glory, so those who were before Him prefigured Him to a greater or lesser degree.

The nature of the godly is shown negatively (1), positively (2,3) and by contrast (4–6). On the principle of the unity of thought in a verse, we must not distinguish three downward steps in v. 1, but three different ways in which we can identify ourselves with sinners, by following their advice, by adopting their practices and by sharing their outlook. 'Blessed is the man': better, 'How happy the man'. 'The law (torah) of the LORD' (2) is really 'the instruction of the LORD.' At all times the godly have turned to the Bible to discover its teaching. As we apply it in practice it is meditation (2b). Note that we are not told (3) that all the acts of the godly man prosper, but that he does, whatever the outcome of the acts (cf. Rom. 8.28).

The wicked are used by way of contrast. As a result of the Fall we find it very hard to appreciate goodness in itself; we must contrast it with badness to see it properly. Probably v. 5 refers primarily to human judgement, but if we cannot stand the scrutiny of man, how much less that of God! God's knowledge (6) is not simply intellectual apprehension but an active sharing in, cf. Amos 3.2. For God to withdraw co-operation means speedy downfall. Jesus expressed it briefly by saying, 'Apart from Me—i.e. separated from Me—you can do nothing' (John 15.5). 'Way' (1,6) refers to the manner of life in general, not to a path leading to a chosen goal; hence in v. 1 standing and not walking is used with it, and in v. 6 it perishes. *Thought: The most terrible fate for a man is to be left alone by God.*

Psalm 2 God's King

Though this psalm was known to be Davidic (Acts 4.25), the title was not inserted to show that it here serves as an introduction to the royal psalms. These are normally more directly predictive of the Messiah than those represented by Psa. 1. The king represented God, but all knew he was merely foreshadowing the perfect representative to come. So language was used about him which suited only the coming One.

Psa. 2 was evoked by the promise of 2 Sam. 7.8–16, and it will have been used at the coronation of David's successors, not to hail them as the Messiah, but to remind them whom they prefigured. It consists of four almost equal stanzas, each of three verses. We can picture the anointing priest speaking the first and last, the king the other two.

The first gives the international setting, the rebellion of the world's rulers against God's rule as exercised through His king. The second gives God's reaction to their rebellion. Note that the mere words of God suffice to terrify them. Their challenge (3) is answered by God's fact (4)—'I' is emphatic (6). The third shows the king's confidence based on God's word. Finally we have a call to universal submission, cf. Phil. 2.9,10; the last line is a word for the watching congregation.

'You are My son' (7), cf. 2 Sam. 7.14. Since even the purely human king was God's representative, he occupied a special relationship to God. The New Testament use of this verse is indicated by Acts 13.33; Heb. 1.5 (note the linking with 2 Sam. 7.14); 5.5. The king was officially seen as 'God's son' at his coronation; even so, though He was the Divine Son from all eternity, Jesus Christ was 'designated Son of God in power . . . by His resurrection from the dead' (Rom. 1.4).

It is a pity that some regard 'with trembling kiss his feet' (11,12) as theological modernism. It can never be more than an attractive and plausible emendation, but the AV(KJV) 'kiss the son' is very difficult to accept, and Jerome's 'worship purely' is little better. The Greek 'lay hold of instruction', followed by the Latin, demands a different Hebrew text. Since the Son is clearly mentioned in v. 7, modern scholars have no interest in removing the word from v. 12. Certainly the RSV does not change the basic sense.

Psalms 3 and 4   Morning and Evening I will Trust

There is little obvious order in the Psalter, but the juxtaposition of certain psalms is definitely intentional. Psa. 3 is a morning psalm (5), Psa. 4 an evening one (8). This also explains their position at the head of the collection. Though they are parallel in structure, there is no evidence that they come from the same setting in David's life.

9

Here we meet 'Selah' for the first time. It is a musical direction, the meaning of which was early forgotten, but there is no reasonable doubt that it indicates a pause for music. The worshippers could use it as a moment for thought on what had just been sung, but the words does not mean this. When we read the psalms aloud, Selah should not be read but indicated by a pause. Its irregular distribution through the Psalter shows it was not always copied from the music editions, where it stood.

Psa. 3 contains very little petition; a recitation of the facts of the situation was sufficient. David's sin could remove his glory and make him a man worthy of death (2 Sam. **12.**7 *seq.*), but not so his son's rebellion; even in Jerusalem his sin could put him out of fellowship with God (cf. Psa. **38**), but the fugitive was in closest touch with the hill of Zion (4). In v. 7 a picture is assumed which is often used, e.g. Psa. **22.**20,21. Those in opposition to and rebellion against God's king are compared to wild beasts, whose offensive weapons are their teeth. So David is asking for the disarming of his enemies.

Quite possibly Psa. **4.**1 should be moved into the past, for David is appealing to his experiences, e.g. 'The God of my salvation answered me when I called'. In v. 4 the reference is less to night-time and more to privacy. 'Good' (6) may mean rain, which for most Palestinians was the supreme loving gift of God (cf. v. 7). 'Sleep' (8) is mentioned in both psalms, for when the will is no longer in control we discover whether the heart is really at peace. We cannot will ourselves to sleep. It is easier to accept God's guidance for ourselves than for others; in vs. 4,5 David urges his friends to accept God's treatment of him without rebellious thoughts, even if they are angry about his enemies.

Psalm 5   The Rest of the Righteous

After the two psalms of David's confidence comes one in which he clearly distinguishes himself from the wicked. He, the righteous, expresses his thoughts in v. 1–3,7,8,11,12, while the wicked are described in vs. 4–6,9,10. The purpose of the comparison is largely the same as in Psa. 1.

David wanted to worship; the sacrifice (3) was above all prayer. It was carefully prepared and the answer watched for. Substitute 'musing' for 'groaning' (1) and understand this as referring to all David's words, spoken and unspoken. His confidence was not based on his own goodness, but as he watched the wicked (4–6), he could not deny that he was different through God's grace. So his relative

10

goodness, proof of God's work in him, give him courage to draw near. He would do this by attending morning worship (7), in which v. 8 describes his 'sacrifice' (3). It is a prayer that he and others (11) may be kept from the evil. The 'shield' (12) is not the ordinary fighting one, but the largest size, normally carried by an attendant (1 Sam. 17.7).

So far as we can gather Satan is never allowed to tempt anyone directly, Jesus being the great exception. He has always to find instruments, mainly those who consciously or unconsciously serve him as king (John 12.31; 14.30) and worship him as god (2 Cor. 4.4). Hence, where we pray for deliverance from the evil one, David asks for it from evil men. This is the most characteristic sign of the psalms that bear his name, i.e. preoccupation with evil men.

Though David was not granted to know the fullness of God's grace in Jesus Christ, yet he was aware that he stood in a position of special privilege with God (2 Sam. 7.14; Psa. 2.7). For all that, his approach to God called for preparation. We are children of God, but that does not free us from the obligation of reverence and preparation for prayer. God expects that we should confess our sins (1 John 1.9) and also that we should pray intelligently.

'House' (bayit, 7) is also used of the Patriarch's tents, e.g. Gen. 27.15, and 'temple' (hekal, 7) really means a palace, so the use of these terms does not prove that David was not referring to the tent pitched for the Ark (2 Sam. 6.17,18).

Psalm 6   'O Lord, Heal Me!'

This is the first of the psalms known traditionally to the Church as the Penitential Psalms, viz., 6,32,38,51,102,130,143. This tradition has no basis in the New Testament or Judaism, but that does not mean we should dismiss it out of hand. Evangelicalism, with its rejoicing in sins forgiven, often cannot understand the use of such psalms in public worship or personal piety. This comes from an undue individualism, which forgets that, whatever our personal standing before God, we are caught up inescapably in the sins of Church and nation.

There is a great deal to be said for Delitzsch's view that Pss. 6,38,51,32 in that order form a series after David's adultery with Bathsheba. If that is so, it means that God prepared David for Nathan's rebuke (2 Sam. 12.1–15) by a severe attack of illness. Note that here physical illness has not created a conviction of any particular sin, though 'anger' and 'wrath' (1) are an implicit confession

11

of it. It is peculiarly easy to cloak a particular sin by confessing sin in general.

It was a severe illness, for it penetrated to the depths of his body (2, 'my bones'), distressed his mind (3, 'my soul') and made him expect death (5). The Old Testament does not teach 'soul sleep'—unconsciousness in Sheol, the place of the dead—but an ineffective shadow existence that can neither know what others are doing, nor make known what is being experienced, even to God. This was the common and popular concept. Some of the psalms will point us to something higher. David's physical suffering was aggravated by the joy of his enemies (7).

The psalm ends with an outburst of faith (8–10) based less on his prayer and more on the certainty that his enemies, God's enemies, will be defeated. David's sin with Bathsheba was such a 'natural' one for the time—sexual morality among royalty is a very recent virtue—that they did not realize that they had sinned. But David's act of faith in the midst of illness made it possible for God to proceed with His chastening work.

Question: Do I acknowledge God's hand in all circumstances and troubles?

Psalm 7   The Persecution of the Innocent

This is almost certainly one of the earliest of David's psalms. He is not yet king, and there is nothing to suggest that he is fleeing from Saul. In the period of mounting tension between him and Saul, Cush brought a charge against him calculated to ruin his character.

David turned in trustful desperation to God—'Shiggaion' may mean lament. He sees himself as seeking sanctuary with God from his persecutor—so essentially the AV(KJV) is preferable to the RV and RSV 'pursuers'; the context suggests a minor textual change to the singular, for the Hebrew has the singular in v. 2, cf. AV(KJV) and RV. Then he pictures himself taking a solemn oath of innocence before God (3–5). He almost certainly did so publicly, for this was the recognized way to prove one's innocence, if one could not do it through witnesses, cf. the elaborate example in Job 31.1–40.

Having cleared himself by his oath David turns on his enemies. Cush will have been punished for his false charge, for we have no reason to think the contrary, but he had been only the mouthpiece of many others (6). David realizes that his complete vindication must await God's judgement in 'the Day of the Lord'— we would say 'at the great white throne' or 'the judgement seat of Christ'.

12

This in turn makes him desire the judgement day (9–11) not for his own sake but that evil may come to an end.

The Old Testament shares the New Testament vision that the effect of the final judgement is discernible in advance (cf. Rom. 1.18, where 'wrath' is primarily an eschatological word, as in 1 Thess. 1.10). So David turns to the wicked man and warns him (12–16). Cush's fate probably lies behind the words, but they are general in their application. 'Fiery shafts' (13) are incendiary arrows; the thought is that God destroys not merely the man but also his house. The wicked bring trouble on nearest and dearest as well.

'Righteousness' (17) is conformity to a standard. Man is righteous before man as he conforms to man's law, and before God as he conforms to God's law by faith in Christ. But how and when is God righteous? Scripture means that God will never fall below the highest revelation He has given of Himself. Indeed He is always higher.

Question: Cannot I trust God to vindicate His child's honour?

Psalm 8   Man: God's Representative

With this short psalm read Heb. 2.6–9, which indicates its real meaning. David, king by God's choice, and so His representative, looks on mankind in general, who should be God's rulers and representatives (Gen. 1.27,28; note this is addressed to the woman as well as the man). Though man, thanks to his sin, cannot achieve the functions for which he was made, the image (Gen. 9.6; 1 Cor. 11.7) and likeness (Jas. 3.9) of God are still to be found in him, however marred they may be. So repeatedly the Old Testament foresees the restoration of Edenic conditions, e.g. Joel 3.18; Amos 9.13–15; Isa. 11. 6–9; 35.1,2; 65.25. David is contrasting man's high calling and goal with present realities.

The rendering of v. 2 by the RSV is possible, but it seems preferable to retain the punctuation of the AV(KJV) and RV. Although 'the heavens are telling the glory of God' (Psa. 19.1), He repeatedly delights to defend His honour through 'the mouth of babes and infants', both literally and through those who have become His children (Matt. 18.3).

There is a point at which increase of distance and size have little meaning for the human mind. David knew nothing of the immense distances revealed by modern astronomy, but the contrast between man in his frailty and origin from the dust of the ground, and the wonders of God's work in the heavens, created precisely the same problem for him as modern man in his smallness feels when faced

13

with the vastness of the universe. But David reposed his faith on God-given quality, not quantity. Since man had been made in the image and likeness of God, he is 'little less than God' (5), and his glory is greater than that of inanimate nature, or that of the animals over which he was to rule.

The choice of this psalm for Ascension Day in the Anglican Prayer Book shows deep spiritual wisdom. The Ascension was not primarily the eternal Word returning to where He had been from all eternity, but the victorious Son of man mounting up to be 'crowned with glory and honour' and thereby guaranteeing for those who put their trust in Him, that where He is there they shall be also.

The psalm ends with the opening invocation. At the beginning it breathed David's awe; at the end it indicates his realization of grace beyond the expression of words.

Thought: 'If we endure, we shall also reign with Him.'

Questions for further study and discussion on Psalms 1–8

1. How far do the contents of a modern hymn-book conform to the two categories of psalms suggested by Pss. 1 and 2?
2. How far and in what ways should a Christian prepare his prayers?
3. What place do you consider there should be for penitence in Christian worship?
4. Is there a place for indignation against the wicked in Christian thought and worship?
5. In what way and in what measure can we apply Psa. 8 to man in general?
6. Consider the implications of man's being made in the image and likeness of God.

Psalms 9 and 10 God the Judge

In the Septuagint and the Vulgate these form one psalm. That this is correct is shown by their being tied together by an alphabetic acrostic. The division into two must be early, for scribes have partially obliterated the acrostic. Four letters are missing, one in Psa. 9, and in three cases we must alter the verse divisions to bring it out. Their original unity explains the lack of heading to Psa. 10.

Our interpretation of the whole will depend on our understanding of 9.3,4. The usual one, clearly implied by the RSV, is that David is praising God for victory given. It can also mean that he will praise when his enemies turn back, etc., because it will show that God has maintained his cause. In other words, it is a psalm of confident faith based on the experience of God's acts in the past (5,6), where the conquest of Canaan is probably referred to. This is more probable, because it does justice to the note of distress later.

From the past David deduced certain general truths about God's activity (7–12). But the certainty of God's deliverance does not decrease the reality of present difficulty (13,14). Once again the memory of the past and a jubilant musical interval usher in the certainty of God's triumph (17–20).

There is a naïve belief that considers suffering and apparent defeat a contradiction of true faith in Christ. It is based neither on Scripture nor Church history, where all too often we see,

> *'Truth for ever on the scaffold,*
> *Wrong for ever on the throne.'*

David depicts the reality and triumph of the wicked without God (10.1–11). His own need now pales into insignificance and becomes part of his cry for the setting up of God's kingdom (12–18). A babe in Christ naturally boggles at suffering. As we mature we realize that God triumphs through suffering, not merely that of Christ but also that of His saints, in the Old and New Testaments alike. Do we realize how much there is about suffering in the New Testament, e.g. Acts 9.16; 14.22; Rom. 8.17; 2 Cor. 1.7; Phil. 3.10; Col. 1.24; 1 Pet. 4.1,12,13? We have to go no further than our Lord's command to take up the cross, and John 15.18–20 to realize how far suffering and apparent defeat are built into Christ's will for His Church.

Psalm 11   The Foundations are Destroyed

The problem of the Christian faced by the forces of evil considered in Psa. 10 introduces a whole group of psalms (11–18) where this is considered from various aspects.

Psa. 11 may very well reflect that dark hour in David's life when he abandoned hope and went with his men to Achish, king of Gath (1 Sam. 27.1,2), when he could no longer trust Saul and he did not know from what quarter he might next experience treachery. The temptation was not to imitate the evil around or even to compromise with it, but simply to acquiesce in it and cease to resist it. Many have echoed v. 3 when confronted by the overwhelming might of totalitarian systems. Even in the more elaborate society of today, some have been able to find 'a mountain cleft', where they could let the world go by.

For David to have done so would have meant a denial of God's power to keep him (1). It is never God's will that we should deliberately of our own volition challenge the forces of evil, but it is our duty to stand our ground where He has placed us (Eph. 6.13,14). The heart of the temptation lay in the secrecy of the attack (2). David replies that there are no secrets from God. He knows both what men are doing and what their motives are (4). Hence the arrow in the dark is in full light for Him. Furthermore, however much the character and actions of the righteous are maligned, God knows the truth about them.

Then we come back to the note of judgement (see comments on Psa. 7). That God will judge suffices for David. There is no guarantee that the judgement will come in one's own lifetime, but it will surely come. This is one of the reasons why we must learn to live in the light of the Second Coming.

Presumably for David 'the upright shall behold His face'—not as the AV(KJV)— meant the restoration of the possibility of public worship for the righteous. For us it is the guarantee of glory to come, however much the experience of life down here may seem a denial of it.

Thought: The love of your friends will often create your most subtle temptations.

*Psalm 12 Lying Lips

In Psa. 11 David was concerned with the sudden shaft of malice from the midst of men who outwardly pretended to support righteousness. Here he finds himself surrounded by complete godlessness. Beyond the certainty that he is writing as a spiritually maturer man, we cannot even suggest the place of this psalm in David's life. It is not that men have grown worse, but that he knows them better.

God is a maker and keeper of covenants; His faithfulness to His covenant is one of His outstanding characteristics. The man who is unfaithful to those to whom he is bound by the obligations of family relationships, national ties and common faith is automatically godless, because he is going against this basic feature of God's nature—this is one of the main points in Hosea's message.

This faithlessness was and is shown above all by lying in all its forms (cf. Rev. 21.8,27; 22.15). True speech is part of the dowry of the image and likeness of God. By it, as by nothing else, we can bind men together and exalt them. It is the only method by which I and another can really become one. In lying I create a barrier between me and others; I declare my lack of love for and trust in them. That is one reason why a Christian should have little to do with modern empty and slipshod phrases that would hide rather than reveal reality.

Lying brings its own nemesis. The greater the liar the more he becomes convinced of the truth of his lies (4). In the religious sphere we accustom ourselves to half-truths and clichés, which gradually convince us that we and our denomination are all right, or at least as right as can reasonably be expected. We become so besotted by our lies and half-truths, that we no longer recognize the true and good when we see it, but rather vilify and persecute it. That is why God promises His intervention (5).

Unlike those of the godless, God's promises (6) (literally, 'words') are true and mean exactly what they say. There is nothing to quarrel with, when someone suggests that one of God's promises is even greater than its literal meaning. It is quite other, when, because it does not suit his theology or his convenience, someone maintains that God cannot mean what He has promised.

*Psalm 13   'How Long, O Lord?'

If the language of Psa. 13 seems strange to us, let us, without leaving our own time, think of the believers in Russia, persecuted by the State Church down to 1917, and along with it ever since; of Protestants in lands like Spain and Colombia; of Christians generally in Communist countries; of the Confessing Church in Nazi Germany, and of the martyrs of the mission field. We must always resist the popular idea that true spirituality must normally walk in the sunshine.

The specific form of David's complaints comes from the fact that the one from whom he had specially to suffer—my enemy (2,4; Saul?)—was God's enemy, so his apparent triumph suggested the failure of God's promise. David could not, dared not suggest that God could be false to His promises, but perhaps He had more important things to concern Himself with (1)—Job has a similar thought in 7.7,21; 10.9, etc. Though we do not use David's language, there are many who are fond of stressing their insignificance, meaning thereby that they cannot expect too much from God. God understood David's wild language (1,2), as He did Job's, so He gave a measure of peace to him, which allowed him to pray more quietly (3,4).

How instructive people's eyes can be! The truly vivacious sparkle (3) does nor come from bodily health alone but reveals the mind behind them. In praying for the lightening of his eyes David is asking for the removal of the clouds over his soul, not for deliverance. He has come to an understanding of what was most important.

We must imagine a pause before v. 5, filled most probably with a

17

musical interlude, though there is no Selah, which seems not always to have been copied from the music edition. Suddenly David realizes that the very vehemence of his prayer came not from doubt but from trust in God's covenant loyalty. He foresees the moment when the joy of salvation will sweep his heart (5). He proceeds to seeing himself bring his sacrifice of thanksgiving—not merely singing is implied in v. 6. The last step is the most important. Not merely does he express God's goodness as a certainty by the use of the past, but the past shows that he had realized that the suffering also was part of the bounty.

Thought: 'In all things God works for good to them that love Him.'

Psalm 14 The Atheist

The AV(KJV) translates five different Hebrew words as 'fool'; the RSV eliminates only one of them and rarely looks for a synonym. An attempt to separate their meanings belongs rather to a study of *Proverbs*. For us it is important to realize that none of the Hebrew words translated 'fool' really represents the main idea of the English word. In every case mental and moral culpability is suggested. Our sense is really suggested by words translated 'simple', 'brutish', etc.

In other words the 'fool' is one who deliberately sees and thinks crookedly. He eliminates the testimony borne to God by nature and history, and so he reaches the point where his whole life is lived in an ignoring of God. He is a practical atheist, not a theoretical one—the latter exists, but he is rare and the Bible does not know him. The elimination of God from thought automatically brings elimination of good from life (1). This is true of the theoretical atheist, the humanist, as well, but there it will show itself more slowly.

Probably vs. 2,3 refer primarily to Gentiles, cf. Rom. 1.18–32. In v. 4, however, the Israelite 'fool' who wants to oppress his fellow-countrymen is emphatically ranged alongside the Gentiles. His elimination of God leads to his own elimination from God's people (5). We should probably translate, 'Your plan against the poor will be confounded, for the Lord is his refuge' (6). David had brought the Ark to Zion (2 Sam. 6.17), and the cherubim above it symbolized God's throne (2 Sam. 6.2), so 'out of Zion' means from God's throne. There is no suggestion of captivity in v. 7—the RSV is correct as against the AV(KJV) and RV—so there are no grounds for questioning Davidic authorship.

This is a key psalm as shown by its being repeated as Psa. 53. It gives the explanation for the evil and suffering in the world. The

18

heathen, in any case, have rejected the testimony of nature. Among God's people there are those who are far more culpable, for they have rejected the special revelation given them. 'Who eat up My people as they eat bread': C. S. Lewis made Screwtape say, 'We want cattle who finally become food; He wants servants who can finally become sons. We want to suck in, He wants to give out.'

Psalm 15   The Reward of the Righteous

David, having considered various aspects of evil men and their evil ways, looks to the rewards of the righteous. The psalm takes the form of a consultation of the priestly or prophetic oracle (1) and the answer (2–5); the last line is probably, as RSV suggests, the psalmist's own comment.

We should ponder deeply on the answer. When we come to Psa. 24 we shall find it in a different setting, but here it is not intended to show man's inability to please God, but to stress the nature of the Divine requirements. 'Blamelessly . . . right' (2) refer to man's negative and positive conformity to God's will as judged by his fellowmen. My speaking 'truth' (2) shows that I fear God rather than man. 'Slander' (3) comes from my trying to receive honour from men, not by being honourable, but by robbing better men of their honour. 'Friend . . . neighbour' are here in parallelism and mean the same thing, viz., the person with whom I have normal contacts. He treats him according to Lev. 19.18. Then he accepts God's valuation of men around him (4). There is often much discussion as to the nature of worldliness, but in essentials it is the acceptance of this world's standards of value and judgement (Rom. 12.2).

For a Christian it may show deep lack of love to hold another to his promises, when unforeseen and unforeseeable circumstances have made the keeping of his word most onerous. But this will never justify a Christian's seeking release from a promise because it is unexpectedly difficult to fulfil. I have no right to pledge myself for the future, unless I am convinced it is God's will, and then I must trust Him to make it possible for me to keep my word. Most modern readers are startled by taking bribes for false evidence and interest on loans—the AV(KJV) 'usury' is misleading—being coupled together (5). Money played little part in David's society; most business was carried on by barter. To borrow normally meant that a man was in real need, and my lending was from my superfluity. If I took interest on the loan, it meant not merely that I was adding to my superfluity, but that I was increasing the very heavy load of repay-

19

ment. This principle still holds good, but very much borrowing by individuals, communities or the State today is purely a matter of convenience, and it is not unreasonable for them to pay me for their convenience.

Question: Is the world seeing these basic virtues in us?

Psalm 16
Fullness of Joy

This is one of a number of psalms which should be read on two levels. There are no grounds for doubting that this is a psalm of thanksgiving for preservation from premature death, which has created the hope of preservation also beyond death (11). It is a general thanksgiving (cf. the tense in v. 10), for David had passed through more than most men's experience of deadly danger. At the same time it is prophecy, using the king's deliverance as a foreshadowing of the far greater deliverance of the King of kings (Acts 13.35–37). In this and in all similar cases it is God's intention that we should read and apply the words on both levels.

The psalm is David's expression of gratitude. Past mercy induces present trust (1) and a preoccupation with God (2). God's character revealed to him draws him to those that reflect that character (3); 'saints' here has exactly the same use as in the New Testament, i.e. those who belong to God, but contrast note on Psa. 30.4. We are to infer that those described in v. 4 are the mighty in the land, but David turns from them to the humble godly.

He can afford to do so; God's care for him frees him from depending on men. In the ordinary small town or fortified village the land of the family-group, which was often conterminous with the total population, was largely held in common. Every year or period of years it would be divided by 'line' (6) into as many 'portions' (5) as there were families to work them, and these were then allocated by 'lot' (5). David compares himself to the Levites, whose portion and 'heritage' (6) was the Lord (Num. 18.20; Deut. 10.9; 18.1,2).

The language of vs. 7,8 really represents an ideal; in its fullness it has been satisfied only by Jesus. 'Heart' (7), ('reins', AV [KJV]) is kidneys, which are used in Hebrew to express the most hidden manifestations of the inner man. In v. 9 'heart' is the normal word; 'soul' ('glory', AV[KJV]) may very possibly be, literally, 'liver'. No one who has suffered the miseries of a bilious attack will doubt the suitability of the liver as the seat of the emotions. The closing verse shows how the experience of God's mercy has created a luminous certainty of mercies to come even beyond the grave.

Questions for further study and discussion on Psalms 9–16

1. How would you deal with (i) a Christian, (ii) a non-Christian obsessed with the feeling of his own insignificance?
2. What arguments could be deduced from common Christian experience for life beyond the grave?
3. Why does God expect His people to suffer?
4. How do you think that Psa. **15.**2–5 might be phrased in modern language?
5. What do you consider the reasons for there being so many more practical atheists today?
6. Is it possible to go through life without lying in any way?

Psalm 17   God's Side and the World's Side

One of the besetting sins of the Church has been its tendency at all times to equate its judgements with those of God. The latter are always absolute, the former inevitably relative. David was aware of this folly, but since he knew that his hearers would not think that he was claiming absolute Divine approval, he was not afraid of using apparently absolute language.

In the given historical position behind this psalm, probably when David was fleeing from Saul, he was right and the other side wrong; neither flaws in David's character nor individual merits among his enemies could alter this fact. It hardly needs saying that in its absolute sense this psalm is satisfied only by our Lord, but this is its secondary meaning.

The Old Testament saint could expect to experience his vindication (cf. Job **19.**23–27—'Vindicator' is better than 'Redeemer' in v. 25); the Christian may have to wait for it till the hereafter, but it is certain. He cannot claim to be sinless (1 John **1.**8), but he may and should be blameless (Jude 24). It cannot be that the heavenly Father could be indifferent to His children's honour, for His honour is involved in theirs. So His children must leave their vindication to Him (cf. 1 Sam. **24.**1–15; **26.**6–25). So vividly does David realize this that he can even pray (14, RSV) that they may have their transient satisfaction. The devil will cheat those that sell themselves to him, but God does not even deny earthly blessing to His enemies. Some take this verse as an imprecation, the heritage for their children being one of evil, but this is less likely.

David could be satisfied only by communion with God (15). We should probably translate, 'May I behold . . . may I be satisfied.' Day by day ('when I awake') he desired such fellowship that he could speak of seeing God. The AV(KJV) and RV 'likeness' is misleading since it suggests the transformation into Christ's likeness which awaits the Christian (1 John 3.2). We should think rather of Num. 12.6–8. As in Psa. 16.9–11 this inevitably leads to fellowship beyond death, though David may not have understood this.

Question: Can God offer you anything greater than Christlikeness?

Psalm 18 David's Vindication

This is really a counterpiece to Psa. 17, for it sings of David's vindication. It divides into two essentially parallel parts, viz., vs.1–30, 31–50; the former praises God for the help given the king, the latter for the grace given him as God's representative. The former describes a crisis in David's life, though the one event almost certainly stands for many; the latter describes how he triumphed.

The language of vs. 6–15 is taken from the theophany at the Exodus and Sinai, cf. Exod. 19.18 f.; Judg. 5.4 f.; Hab. 3.3–15. There is no evidence that David had any experience that would literally correspond to this, either when he was fleeing from Saul or during his wars as king. The implication is that, though his deliverance differed in form, it was as effective as that of the Exodus. The reality of God's salvation does not depend on the form it takes.

Some are unhappy about vs. 19–24, which they cannot reconcile with David's sin with Bathsheba. They overlook that, while a major sin may cause a Christian from then on to walk very carefully, justification by faith means that the sin is gone or reckoned as never having been there. It was not his own righteousness that David was claiming. Many sit in judgement on God, but do not realize that they are really judging themselves. It is as though God's awful purity reflected their impurity. This is the force of v. 26b, which is best translated, 'but with the perverted Thou dost deal perversely'.

Obviously the second section looks on to Christ (50), but it is true for every child of God. Whatever our calling we shall find that we are fully dowered with God's grace for that calling. David was no lover of war, and it is clear that his foreign campaigns were forced on him. So he is not glorifying war and his own prowess. He had been placed in a position where he had to lead the armies of God's people, so he gloried in the strength and skill God had given him. The psalm throughout is in the first person singular except in v. 31. It is David's recognition that the same grace had been given his officers and men. Let us not forget that there cannot be a leader without loyal followers, a king without loyal subjects.

Psalm 19 The Revelation of Nature and the Word

In Bible times the great danger was that man in his weakness should

22

deify the powers of nature, which he did not know how to control. Today it is rather that man, fancying he can control nature, should deify himself. One result of this change of attitude towards nature is that the modern hymn-book contains far more nature hymns than does the Psalter.

This psalm has nothing of the sentimentality of many modern nature hymns. It recognized in nature merely the power and wisdom of God, cf. Rom. 1.19,20. The AV(KJV) translation of v. 3 is possible, but the RV and RSV rendering is preferable; their very existence is adequate and speaks a universal language. Darkness for the ancient world was a picture of sin and chaos, so the sun served particularly to suggest God's victory. However, the sun is in no sense divine, but only one of God's creations for which He cares (4c).

Man cannot do without the sun, but he should find the law (*torah*) of God far more important. Nature speaks to man of his place as a creature, God's revelation of his standing as a son. *Torah* really means instruction, though being God's instruction it has the force of law. Hence the psalmist's parallels are not only commandment and ordinances but also testimony and precepts. God's instruction creates a necessary attitude of fear towards Him, but this fear is not a contradiction of love, for it leads to an ever-deepening desire to live a life according to God's will.

The character of God has not changed, and His moral demands on men remain the same today. Christ has borne the consequences of our falling short, but He has not taken away the obligation to do God's will, and so the Bible remains as a warning. Conscience is not enough, for it leaves us with blind spots which only God's revelation reveals. We may translate v. 13 equally 'presumptuous sins' and 'presumptuous men', and rightly so, for when we act presumptuously it is normally because we have been inspired by the example of presumptuous men. In v. 14b we have the same balance of truth as in the New Testament. The indwelling of the Word will make a man blameless, but not perfect; it will keep him from major sin, but will not eradicate sin from his nature.

Psalms 20 and 21   Prayer and Joy for the King

We have here two royal psalms, and it would be well to reread the introductory remarks on Psa. 2. Psa. 20 was written for a service of petition before the king marched to war, Psa. 21 for the service of thanksgiving afterwards. Obviously the latter is easier to apply to Christ, but both contain elements which do not really suit a

23

Messianic interpretation. Both could be used with reservations for Christian leaders today.

In Psa. 20 we hear the people, or a priest on behalf of the people, praying; the king speaks only in v. 6. He is so encouraged by the prayers of his people that he speaks out in faith. The psalm breathes the same quiet confidence as Rom. 8.37, but has not yet reached the heights of Rom. 8.35,36.

In Psa. 21 we hear the voice of the rejoicing people throughout. In v. 4, however hyperbolic the language, the reference is to preservation in battle; obviously in a literal sense it could be true only in the Messiah. Nowhere is the king praised. Throughout it is taken for granted that he gives glory solely to God, who is the sole author of his victory. It is recognized that the glory gained by his triumph has really been bestowed by God. It is not always right to reject the praise of man; where it is justified, we should accept it, with the firm qualification, 'It was all of God'.

The real thanksgiving of king and people lies not in praise for the past but in willingness for service in the future. The exhortation or prophecy addressed to the king in vs. 8–12 implies of necessity the co-operation of the people as well as the grace of God. Deliverance is so that we may be free to serve. Though the king is seen as taking the initiative in vs. 8–12, vs. 9b and 13 make it clear that he can do so only as he knows the will of God and does it. In v. 9a we have an incomplete simile. Its explanation can be found in Matt. 6.30 and Isa. 40.6–8. The enemies of the king, who are also the enemies of God, are likened to withering grass which is used as fuel for the baker's oven. The basic thought of this section may be compared with 2 Kings 13.14–19. We must be prepared to do God's work thoroughly.

Psalm 22   Why hast Thou Forsaken Me?

This psalm is used of our Lord in John 19.24 (in the best Greek manuscripts the connexion is not made in the other Gospels) and Heb. 2.12, and by inference in Matt. 27.39,43; Mark 15.29; Luke 23.35 and perhaps Heb. 5.7. It was used by Him in Matt. 27.46 and Mark 15.34. In these last two Jesus did not use the Hebrew, which almost all His hearers would have understood, but Aramaic. This should be a warning against assuming that He was either just reciting the psalm or indicating its fulfilment in Him. However wonderfully David's sufferings and his poetic expression of them foreshadowed the sufferings of the Messiah, it was a foreshadowing and not a direct prophecy, We should not try to force everything in the psalm to apply to Him.

'Why hast Thou forsaken me?' (1) is the obviously correct translation, but it could equally be rendered, 'Why didst Thou forsake me?' This is the natural translation of the Greek rendering in Matt. 27.46 and Mark 15.34 (cf. RV mg.). David cried out during his agony, Jesus when His agony of soul was past. Nowhere in Scripture is any attempt made to explain v. 1 in Jesus' mouth, and the psalm helps little, for its main stress is on the physical. Where a veil of reticence has been drawn by Scripture, we would do well to respect it. David and other Old Testament saints were permitted to foreshadow Christ's sufferings; we are allowed to share in them (Col. 1.24). But for all that the Sufferer of Golgotha towers above all lesser suffering in solitary grandeur. While we cannot but think primarily of Jesus as we read this psalm, we should not hesitate to see whether we can apply it in small measure to ourselves, though we are likely to conclude that He was forsaken so that we should never know forsaking.

One of the few places where the Hebrew choice of vowel points has probably been deliberately made to avoid the Christian interpretation is in v. 16b (see margin). On the other hand, in v. 21b the Hebrew 'Thou hast answered me' (margin) is probably correct. The voice of faith is heard even before deliverance has come.

In the application of the psalm to ourselves vs. 22–26 are of particular importance. Neither the Church nor the world is likely to listen to the proclamation of the gospel unless it comes from the lips of those who have personally experienced the love of God in affliction.

Psalm 23 The Shepherd Psalm

In Psa. 2 God's king was called to rule, but this he can do only because he knows what it is to be ruled. Whenever 'shepherd' is used metaphorically in the Bible, it means a king. This statement is not vitiated by the few passages where it includes high ministers of the crown, for their authority was derived solely from the king (cf. 1 Pet. 5.1–4). While some wish to see in this psalm the work of a shepherd lad, the depth of experience shown in it surely points to a composition by the mature king.

The most satisfactory interpretation of the psalm sees the shepherd metaphor throughout. In the drought and heat of a Palestinian summer 'green pastures' cannot be taken for granted. Their provision proves the shepherd's wide knowledge and great care. It is not enough to find water for the flock; it must be slow moving or the sheep cannot drink it. The Christian's way is sometimes very long

25

and tiring, but there is always refreshment and invigoration when it is needed (3). It does not matter much whether we render as in the text or margin, for God's ways are always 'right paths' (margin) and they lead to 'righteousness' (text); the leading is God's grace, not a sign of our merit.

Bunyan understood the valley of the shadow of death correctly. It is the place of extremest danger, the ravine through the hills which must be traversed to reach the green pastures, but in which the beasts of prey lurk waiting for the straggling sheep. In front of the flock goes the shepherd to meet whatever danger lies before; on his shoulders rest his club ('rod', cf. Psa. 2.9) and crook ('staff'). Any sheep looking up can see them and know there is protection and help. Behind the sheep are the shepherd's assistants or dogs, 'goodness and mercy' (6), lest any lose heart and straggle.

When the pasture is reached wild beasts may lurk around and lick their drooling lips, but the sheep can safely feed (5). For those torn by thorns and gashed by sharp stones there is oil for healing and the shepherd's bowl brimming over for the thirsty. The margin 'as long as I live' (6) is correct. God's goodness calls out the promise of continued worship so long as life lasts.

Question: What is our worship? See Rom. 12.1.

Psalms 24 and 25   God Comes to Dwell with Men

Psa. 24, which should be compared with Psa. 15, was doubtless originally written for the ceremony described in 2 Sam. 6.12–15, and it was probably used annually on its anniversary. God had no need to choose Zion (1,2), but once He had done it, it should have posed a major problem for its inhabitants. David had learnt that the vicinity of God was no light thing (2 Sam. 6.1–11). Ultimately there is only One to satisfy vs. 3–5, and He is also the King of glory. The choice of Psa. 24 as a proper psalm for Ascension Day shows true spiritual insight.

Psa. 25 is an acrostic psalm, but as in Pss. 9 and 10 scribal errors have to some extent hidden the fact—note the twenty-two verses. As so often in such psalms the development of thought is not obvious. The clue to David's thought is given by vs. 7, 11, 18. He did not, as we might have deduced from vs. 2 and 3, doubt God's ability or willingness to keep, but he questioned his own deserving of God's mercy. It seems likely that the psalm was composed before David's sin with Bathsheba, but yet in middle life, when he could see how the faults of youth were working themselves out.

David has no doubt that the past has been forgiven. Rather, the

26

mention of the past indicates the reality of his desire to press on to a fuller knowledge of God along with all God's people (3a, cf. Eph. 3.18). Doubtless v. 22 was a later addition to adapt the psalm to general worship, but its thought was inherent in it from the first. When we walk along a path beset by snares, prudence would suggest that we should keep our eyes fixed on the ground. David, however, saw safety in fixing his eyes on God, who would keep his feet for him (15). There is no conception here of automatic blessing. Not only does David walk humbly because of past sin, but he realizes that he must rely on God only to guide and teach (8,9); men must be willing to accept that guidance and teaching.

David was not praying for his preservation and the confusion of his enemies (16–21) for his own greater comfort and ease, but because he was God's king. We must learn when to say, 'Thy will be done', and when to claim deliverance as Christ's ambassadors.

Questions for further study and discussion on Psalms 17–25

1. How far do you consider Isa. 53 challenges the outlook of Psa. 17?
2. Do you consider that Psa. 19 justifies Wade Robinson's hymn,

   'Heaven above is softer blue, earth around is sweeter green;
   Something lives in every hue Christless eyes have never seen:
   Birds with gladder songs o'erflow, flowers with deeper beauties shine,
   Since I know, as now I know, I am His, and He is mine'?

3. How are we to explain the sense of being forsaken sometimes felt by believers?
4. How would you phrase Psa. 23, if you had to rewrite it for someone who knows only town life?
5. Would the realized presence of Christ make a difference in your home and church? In what ways?
6. How far can I really forget the sins of my youth?

Psalm 26   'Vindicate Me, O Lord'

The closing thoughts of Psa. 25 find clear expression here. 'Judge me' as in the AV(KJV) and RV misses the point. The only reason why David wanted to be judged was that he might be acquitted and so vindicated. In addition, the word for judge, *shophet*, really meant the one who would deliver the wronged, i.e. vindicate him. For many Christians the language of this psalm seems strangely unattractive. David's confidence seems to be based on self-reliance self-righteousness and good works.

Let us remember that God had chosen David in sheer grace to be His king, His 'son' (Psa. 2.7). That meant, making full allowance for the limitations of the Old Testament revelation, all that is contained in Rom. 8.28–30. It is no sign of humility for a Christian to deny the reality of Christ's work in His own people. Because of God's work in him David could utter truthfully vs. 3,4,5,8,11. On the other hand, he realized that his own estimate of himself was inadequate (2); only God could tell him whether it was correct, cf. 1 Cor. 4.4.

Some will still insist that they miss a true feeling of sinfulness. It is no honour for God, if, in answer to His declaration of justification, I keep on stressing that for all that I am a sinner, or if in reply to the assurance that Christ has borne all my sins and blotted them out, I retort that I do not *feel* that certain of them have been dealt with. David was certainly able to confess his sinfulness (cf. note to Psa. 6), but that was neither a parrot-like refrain nor an effort to please others, but when the Holy Spirit convicted him of sin.

Then we should consider that we can hardly expect people to listen to our proclamation of the power and love of God unless they clearly see them being worked out in us. How often we hear men say, sometimes longingly, 'But it does not work'. The gospel does work here, not merely in heaven, and there is no excuse for us if others cannot learn this from our lives.

Thought: 'I can do all things in Him who strengthens me' (Phil. 4.13).

Psalm 27 — Why Should I Fear?

There is general agreement that we have here two psalms, viz., vs. 1–6 and vs. 7–14, and it is widely held that they are by different hands. If Pss. 9 and 10, 42 and 43, should each have been divided into two, there is no reason why two unrelated psalms should not have become one. Personally I believe on technical grounds—God is spoken of in the third person in vs. 1–6 and is personally addressed in vs. 7–12—that the two sections are to be distinguished and probably separated in time, yet the whole is by one man. The second half shows how the joyful song of trust was a reality in the day of trouble, and so the two sections are linked by vs. 13 and 14, which commend God, who has been found true by experience, to others.

Repeated Christian experience has shown that where there is true trust in God, attacks and trials can be taken in one's stride (2). But then from time to time God permits the more drastic test which calls for the turning of our whole being to God. It was this that Christ meant, when He taught us to pray, 'Do not bring us to the test, but deliver us from the evil one' (NEB). In his book *1984*, Orwell pictured the final test that challenged a man's deepest fears and broke him down. This the Christian need not fear.

It is most unlikely that we are intended to take v. 10 literally. In Bible times the loyalty of the family was the supreme element in social stability, taking precedence even over the nation as a whole. There is an exceptionally strong metaphorical element running through this psalm. That is why the RSV emendation in v. 2b, 'uttering slanders against me', is completely unnecessary and in addition uncalled for by any difficulties in the Hebrew. Equally metaphorical is v. 4. David's supreme petition ('one thing') was obviously not that he should live in the sanctuary, but rather that he might know himself as God's guest and friend, which would result in protection and honour (5). This is underlined by v. 6, for obviously David could not enter the Tent (2 Sam. 6.17) to bring his sacrifice, nor would he have brought it into the Tent. In the pressure of extreme testing and persecution Divine protection may seem to vanish, but it is only a matter of time till we know it has been restored.

Psalm 28   A Cry in Time of Danger

There is no need to translate in v. 1 with the AV(KJV) and RV 'will I call'. The implication of the Hebrew tense, as brought out by the RSV, is that David found himself in pressing danger, which demanded *continuous* prayer. The language of the psalm is far too general for us to reconstruct its background. David was obviously in a position of extreme danger, where any delay in God's intervention—'if Thou be silent unto me'—might mean going down to Sheol. 'The Pit' does not bear some of its modern implications. Kirkpatrick is likely to be right in suggesting a time of plague. This is supported by 'take me not off' (3)—better, 'drag me not away'—which suggests the wicked being taken off to a premature death. It was not death David feared, but death before he had finished his life's work.

We should not regard vs. 4 and 5 as an example of Old Testament vindictiveness, out of keeping with the New Testament. Those called 'wicked' are those who have chosen evil with their eyes open, and try to subvert and destroy the good. Their destruction would

29

be the vindication of God's righteousness and sovereign rule.

Let us not speculate whether vs. 6–9 were the result of sudden inner realization that his prayers had been heard, or whether they were later added to the psalm in gratitude for preservation. The former is more probable. David does not suggest (7) that his was a partial trust, or that he had brought his emotions under control. The heart, i.e. the whole inner man, trusted and so the whole of him exulted.

Like king, like people (8). This is something that all called to leadership need to remember. Even if our position seems very humble, there are bound to be some who will look up to us as an example. It is remarkable how many are drawn to Christ not by what they hear from us but by what they see in us.

The psalm ends with the beautiful picture of God, the Divine Shepherd carrying His people—not as the AV(KJV), 'lift them up'. The people looked to David as their shepherd and expected him to carry them. He did so, but only because he was being carried. If God carries us, we can carry others, for the full weight rests on His arms.

Psalm 29   All Cry Glory

The Israelite view of nature was never sentimental, romantic or anthropomorphic. In its more normal forms it served as a reminder of man's divinely given responsibilities, the wonder of sky, sun, moon and stars demonstrating God's law and governmental power, e.g. Pss. 8, 19, 104. This psalm celebrates the glory of God as revealed by the unexpected and overwhelmingly uncontrollable.

The background is a freak thunderstorm accompanied by a hurricane. It started in the far north over the sea (3), swept in on the slopes of Lebanon (5) and stormed on southward through the length of Palestine, until it was lost in the wilderness of the wanderings, south beyond Kadesh (8). It is obvious that a storm that could break the cedars of Lebanon and make the age-old oaks whirl (9) must have caused a great deal of damage. Though it is not expressly stated, vs. 3 and 10 may well imply disastrous floods as well.

Under such circumstances we should probably attempt a theodicy, trying to justify the ways of God to man, unless, indeed, we foolishly attributed it all to Satan. Not so David. The momentary shaking of the foundations of the earth reminded him of Noah's flood—it is better to translate v. 10, 'The Lord sat enthroned over the Flood'. So he called on the angels (1)—what man could do it adequately?— to recognize God's strength and glory (*kabod*). In Hebrew glory

30

means literally weight, for it did not imply, as so often with us, pomp and circumstance, but the expression of true internal value. However attractive the rendering 'the beauty of holiness' (2), as in the AV(KJV) and RV text, it cannot be defended.

For David the storm spoke of human sin, hence the mention of the Flood, but it showed even more God's control over all the powers of nature. Hence the psalm can end quite naturally with a quiet prayer for strength and peace, i.e. prosperity. David was able to regard the storm in this way because, even without the cross, he could have complete trust in God. Though he obviously did not know Isa. 45.7, he would have found no difficulty in it, if he had lived in Isaiah's day. God's answer to all man's queries is the cross; all apparent contradictions in His character and actions find their solution there. So the man of God is able to accept God's working for good in all things, for he knows that God sits enthroned for ever.

Psalm 30 Salvation from Death

We have here a typical psalm of thanksgiving, in which the cause for thanksgiving is not stated very clearly, yet it can be adequately inferred from the general terms of vs. 1–3. It was for deliverance from danger or trouble that threatened David's life itself. The confession of deliverance turns to an appeal to his fellow-believers. Public confession of God's goodness to me has little purpose or place unless it magnifies God in their eyes, and causes them to trust, when they find themselves in similar distress (4,5). It is a pity that the RSV retained the rendering 'saints' in v. 4 and also in Psa. 31.23, for the Hebrew *hasidim* has no link in meaning with the New Testament *hagioi*, rendered 'saints'. It means 'loyal ones' or 'faithful' and has been so translated in Pss. 50.5 and 149.5. Where the loyal share their joy and sorrow, it will be easier for them to obey the injunction of Rom. 12.15.

David's trouble had come through his self-confidence (6,7). It was self-confidence based on past experience of God's goodness and the anticipation that God would continue it, but it was self-confidence for all that. He had forgotten that God's care was not based on his merit but on God's grace. There are three periods in the average life when this temptation is particularly prevalent and dangerous: in youth after the first thrill of conversion; in middle-age, when life settles down to an ordered routine; in early old age, when one is tempted to think as did Job (29.18–20).

Since the only remedy for David's trouble was to warn him and

31

remove his self-confidence (7b), as soon as he turned to God in prayer (8–10), he found the trouble vanishing (11,12). David had learnt one precious lesson through it. He had become a praiser, and the more we give thanks the less likely we are to be self-confident.

We do not know the history behind the heading, 'A song at the dedication of the Temple'. It hardly suits the dedication of Solomon's Temple, but would fit either that of the second Temple after the return from the Babylonian exile or the rededication by Judas Maccabaeus in 164 B.C., after it had been desecrated by Antiochus Epiphanes.

Question: What is the night to you (5): the end of a happy day or the promise of a bright tomorrow?

Psalm 31 — Trusting where there is no Hope

In the comments on Psa. 27 we considered the probability that it consisted of two psalms, both quite possibly by the same author. Here again we almost certainly have two psalms, viz., vs. 1–8 and vs. 9–24, but with the authors widely separated in time. The trouble in vs. 1–8 does not give the impression of being of the same nature as that in vs. 9–24. Note also that vs. 1–3 are the opening of Psa.71. There is no reason for questioning the Davidic authorship of the first part, for the second we might suggest Jeremiah, cf. v. 13 with Jer. 20.10,3.

In vs. 1–8 David is concerned with those who are trying to catch him out and put him to shame, so we may think of them being written while he was still at Saul's court. The RSV textual change in v. 6 has plenty of evidence in its favour and may be regarded as indubitably correct. At Saul's court there will not have been many idol-worshippers, but there were many who thought God was on their side in their machinations against David—a seriously false moral picture of God is regarded by the Bible as idolatry.

For Jeremiah the bitterness of 'terror on every side' was that the word of terrible warning to Pashur (Jer. 20.3) was turned by his enemies to a word of mockery (Jer. 20.10). Jeremiah had to go underground in the fifth year of Jehoiakim (Jer. 36.26) and we do not find any trace of him again until shortly before Jehoiakim's death (Jer. 35) some six years later. Some time in this period of hiding and retirement, rejected and forgotten by his people, would suit the language of vs. 9–24 very well, though this can never be more than a suggestion.

The feature of this section is the lack of consciousness of sin; there can be little doubt that the RSV is correct in reading 'misery'

32

with the Syriac and two Greek translations instead of 'iniquity', as do the AV(KJV) and RV in v. 10. Just as the light of the sun dispels the darkness of night, so the light of God's face dispels all spiritual gloom (16). Another link with Jeremiah is v. 21, cf. Jer. 1.18; 15.20. The writer longs for his vindication, because that will mean God's vindication as well. For 'saints' (23) see comment on Psa. 30.4.

A valuable study is to compare David's general attitude towards the wicked with that of the author of vs. 9–24. The clue to the difference is that the latter was a private individual, David is a king and so God's representative.

Psalm 32   The Joy of Sins Forgiven

This is the second Penitential Psalm and the last of the four psalms linked with David's adultery and murder (cf. comments on Psa. 6), and, as is shown in Rom. 4.7,8, is the song of the sinner's complete restoration to fellowship with God. It is complete restoration, for sin in all its aspects has been met. Rebellion (transgression) has been 'carried', the literal meaning of the word here used for forgiveness; failure (sin) has been covered; crookedness (iniquity) is not imputed. There is, however, a condition; the sinner must be honest with God (2b) and confess his sin without reserve (1 John 1.9).

The psalm divides into six sections:

(i) The happiness (cf. comment on Psa. 1.1) of forgiveness (1,2).

(ii) The misery of sin (3,4). The unbeliever considers that the sufferings that follow on sin are a sign of God's lack of love. David knew that they were His love-gifts to lead to repentance.

(iii) The road to forgiveness (5). In theory we no more need to confess our sins than we need to ask for our daily bread. But it is our asking that teaches us how indebted we are to God's giving, and our confession from which we learn how much we need God's mercy. Without confession, real confession, we are apt to become Pharisees spiritually, concentrating on our imaginary goodness.

(iv) The lesson of forgiveness (6,7). Though the RSV emendation is not necessarily the correct way of treating the very difficult Hebrew of v. 6, it makes good sense. David had been almost submerged by his sin; he had been within an ace of perishing. He could have been kept from it by prayer. Now he intended to be kept by prayer from the inrush of sin and trouble.

(v) The witness of the forgiven (8,9) (cf. Psa. 51.13). God is the restrainer of human evil, never allowing it to exceed certain limits. But how humiliating it is for man, created in the image and likeness of God, to be treated like an animal!

(vi) **The secret of blessing (10,11).** In the growing light of revelation men were to learn that the righteous, although surrounded by 'steadfast love', might have to suffer in God's service, but in that case it can be pure joy (cf. Jas. 1.2, where 'trials'—'temptation', AV[KJV]—means testings).

Thought: What a tragedy it is that some forgiven men do not know that they have been forgiven.

Questions for further study and discussion on Psalms 26–32

1. To what extent should a Christian be concerned either with his own vindication or that of another Christian?
2. Is it really possible for a Christian to know no fear?
3. Would you find difficulties in applying Psa. 29 to modern conditions? What do you find most reminds you of the glory of God?
4. What forms of self-confidence are prevalent in the Church, as you know it?
5. In your experience have you met those who believe that God will favour evil? Do you know of cases in the past?
6. In what way does lack of prayer favour the success of sin?

Psalm 33   God as Creator, Controller, Judge

This great anonymous psalm, to which no date can convincingly be attached, probably owes its present position to the way v. 1 takes up the thought of Psa. 32.11. Apart from this there is no connexion. Psa. 32 is deeply personal, Psa. 33 is as clearly congregational.

In Hebrew *dabar* means both 'word' and 'thing'. God's word, the expression of His will, is always effective, producing the result which He intends. We are apt to forget this aspect when we call the Bible God's Word. It is, but it is because the Holy Spirit uses it to achieve God's purpose in His revelation. Note that the psalmist places the morality of God's working (4,5) before His effective power (6,7). The RSV in rendering 'bottle' in v. 7 follows the ancient versions. There is no change involved in the Hebrew consonants.

The psalmist appeals to three things. (i) God's creatorial power (8,9). Presumably v. 9b refers especially to Gen. 1.9. (ii) God's control of history (10–12). Christ's statement that Satan is 'the prince of this world' must never be understood in a way that would contradict these verses. The Old Testament and especially the Psalter continually insists that God's will is sovereign and effective, even though man opposes himself to it. (iii) God's judicial activity (13–17). The stupidity and rebellion of man is seen most readily through his ways. For man, made in the image and likeness of God,

34

to place his trust in animals, or today, in the inanimate products of science, is to deny his high calling. The truly great generals of history have probably always been those who were more interested in their men than in their weapons, who placed morale before logistics. The man of the world would probably scoff at such an idea, for he is convinced that might is right, and he can see only that which lies under his nose. Yet human experience is full of the way in which God preserves His own (18,19). If He seldom lifts them to the seats of the mighty, it is because that is seldom His purpose, for they can normally serve Him better in their obscurity. The psalm ends in joyful trust with hope and grace meeting (20–22).

Question: If you had the fairy-tale three wishes, what would you ask for? Are you really satisfied with God's giving?

Psalm 34   There is no Position too Difficult for God

For the setting of this psalm see 1 Sam. **21**.10 -15 and the title of Psa. **56**. The latter indicates that the position was even more serious than the story might suggest. It is probable that David was never in a more dangerous position, even from Saul. It is possible, but improbable, that Abimelech is a scribal error for Achish; it is more likely to have been a royal title of the kings of Gath. This is an acrostic psalm, which suggests that David was so moved by his escape that he felt the need of such an artificial convention to discipline his feelings.

We are apt to think that our testimony to God's goodness and power has an influence on the unbeliever. David saw that his miraculous deliverance was rather an encouragement to the godly who were suffering (1–3). God has no favourites, so His grace to one of His children should be a guarantee of grace to others also. Radiance (5) comes not from the granting of our wishes, but from the disappearance of fear (4) and from fellowship with God. In reading v. 6 we should think of Matt. **5**.3.

The angel of the Lord (7) is God Himself localized in time and space; for the picture cf. Josh. **5**.13–15; 2 Kings **6**.15–17; Zech. **1**.8–13. To taste (8) is to make trial. Here 'saints' (9) is used in the New Testament sense, as also in Psa. **16**.3, not as in Pss. **30**.4 and **31**.23. The 'young lions' (10), whom we meet so often in the Old Testament, are in fact lions in their prime. While the statement is to be taken literally, it refers also to those who rely on their own strength and brute force.

In v. 9 David had called on his hearers to 'fear the Lord', so in vs. 11–14 he explains what it means. In the practical way of the

35

Old Testament he does not describe it, but what it does. We end with a description of God's care over those who fear Him. However high God exalted David, he never forgot he had been an ordinary man, nor his experiences when he was an ordinary man; this is one of the reasons for the universal appeal of his psalms. Our witness to the world is sometimes ineffective because we forget what it was like to be in the world.

Thought: If we were readier to bear affliction, we could be a greater help to those who bear it.

Psalm 35   Save Me from the Wicked

This is the first, though not the strongest, of the 'imprecatory psalms' we are to meet. Though vs. 4–6 are no more than a highly dramatic description of complete rout, the Christian hesitates to take such words on his lips. The usual explanation of such language is that it belongs to the Old not the New Testament, and must be so understood. Yet before this is regarded as adequate, attention should be paid to Rev. 18.1—19.2. The fact is that there is evil, so gratuitous, so unprovoked, so dastardly, that human language is not really adequate to describe it. If our Christianity cannot find place for words like Milton's,

> '*Avenge, O Lord! Thy slaughter'd saints, whose bones*
> *Lie scatter'd on the Alpine mountains cold*',

there is something wrong.

There are no grounds for doubting that Psa. 35 comes from the time of David's troubles with Saul. He recognized clearly that Saul was not entirely responsible for his actions (1 Sam. 26.19,20), but what are we to say of his enemies at court? Their actions are described in vs. 7,11–16, 19–21,25,26. It is hard to understand their motivation, for in no case could there be any question of their succeeding to the throne. Some will have resented that a young man from a poor family (1 Sam. 16.20) should have been promoted above them; others will have felt that their own inadequacies were shown up by David's excellencies; yet others were clever enough to see what direction Saul's madness was taking and they wanted to jump on 'the band-wagon' while they could. Some were probably just haters of good.

Note the translation in vs. 24 and 27. As in Psa. 7.8 it was not judgement that David wanted but vindication. It is really here that the difference in spirit between the two Testaments comes in. Very often my own vindication can be achieved only by the discrediting of another. If such is the case, cannot I wait till eternity vindicates me? Without the certain hope of the after-life David could be sure of his vindication only in the way suggested by vs. 4–6.

Question: Cannot you leave your honour in the care of your heavenly Father?

Psalm 36 God's Love and the Atheist

The English versions do not do justice to the spiritual horror of vs. 1 and 2, which should run, 'Rebellion speaks its oracle to the wicked deep in his heart—no dread of God is there before his eyes. It flatters him in his eyes, that his iniquity will not be found out and hated.' As in Pss. 14 and 53 it is the practical, not the theoretical, atheist who is being described. He is not merely a bad man; he has made evil his God, hence the word 'oracle' in v. 1.

The remainder of the psalm from v. 5 gives a picture of the God from whom the atheist has turned. The behaviour of men, however wicked, does not change the character of God. For David the height of the clouds or of the heavens could not be measured (5). 'The mountains of God' (*El*, not *Elohim*) may mean the mountains God has made, but more likely 'the strong mountains' (6). In comparing God's judicial decisions with the great deep or abyss, David implies that man cannot fathom the depths of wisdom involved in them. The change from Yahweh (Jehovah) to God in v. 7 implies that God's love is as wide as mankind and is not confined to the covenant people.

The metaphorical language of vs. 8 and 9 is pre-Israelite and finds its fulfilment in Jesus Christ, cf. John 4.14; 6. 27,35; Rev. 2.7,17; 22.1,2,17; 1 John 1.4–9, etc. Food and water are the natural expression of man's needs in the Near East; until modern artificial lighting was brought in, he was dependent on sun and moon, God's creations, for light.

David rounded off the psalm with a prayer that the plots of the atheist should fail (10–12). In faith we are given a final picture of them (12). They have been judged, and they lie there so heavily loaded with chains that they cannot move.

The title of the psalm calls for special notice. Literally it runs 'Of the servant of the Lord, of David'. David is looking away from his special position and has taken up that of anyone who is willing to be known as servant of the Lord. Servant is really slave, and is then used of the true worshipper because of the position he gladly takes up, cf. Rom. 12.1 and the title Paul constantly used (Rom. 1.1, etc.). It was from this standpoint that the evil of the atheist and the love of God became so clear.

Psalm 37   Commit your Ways to the Lord

After the vehement contrast of the evil of man and the love of God in Psa. 36 we are given here a reasoned apology for the ways of God with man. Once again it is an acrostic psalm. The picture of life we find in it is that offered by *Proverbs* and is true to very much Christian experience. But as Job has clearly shown, it is far from being invariably so. It is not that God changes, but His wisdom is too high for man to formulate a rule that will cover every case. So we should hesitate before quoting this psalm to those in serious trouble.

The believer is warned not to judge quickly by appearances (1,2), cf. Psa. 73.16–22. Trust in God is the answer to discontent (3,4). We should render 3b, 'Dwell in the land and follow after faithfulness', i.e. do not run about looking for a better place. In vs. 5 and 6 we have the reward of faith. The remedy for impatience is given in v. 7. In vs. 8 and 9 David takes up vs. 1 and 2 again and expands the thought in vs. 10 and 11; the latter is used in Matt 5.5.

We now pass over to the destiny of the wicked. His rage is seen to be impotent (12,13), and he hurts only himself by his violence (14,15). God's promise is not necessarily for more than daily bread (16,17), but when the need of the righteous is greatest, God's help is surest (18,19). The fate of the wicked is to vanish like the flowers, cf. Matt. 6.29,30, or smoke (20)— the AV(KJV) 'fat of lambs' is impossible.

From the destiny of the wicked we pass to the prosperity of the righteous. His growing wealth is seen in vs. 21 and 22. He is cared for and upheld by God (23,24). A long life confirmed these experiences (25,26). This Divine care calls for response (27,28ab). The acrostic demands that we follow the Septuagint in v. 28c and render, 'The unrighteous are destroyed for ever', so v. 28cd stands in contrast to v. 29. The righteous man's prosperity is based on his knowledge of God (30,31). The remainder of the psalm is a contrast between the righteous and the wicked.

Other aspects of the problem are found in psalms like **69,73,77, 88** and, of course, *Job.*

*Psalm 38   'My Iniquities Have Gone Over My Head'

This is the third of the penitential psalms and should in David's experience probably be read after Psa. 6. The illness there referred to has been intensified, so that David is now openly conscious of sins and willing to confess them, yet there is no indication that he is yet aware of his real sin. His memory has called back to him all manner of wrongdoings, which form a burden on his back which towers over his head and bends him double (4), yet there is no thought of Bathsheba and Uriah. David was not a bad man or a hypocrite. He had genuinely let himself be persuaded that he had done no more than was a king's right. Nathan's message (2 Sam. 12.1–15) was so effective, only because God had first 'softened up' David by illness. The most dangerous sin is always the unconscious one. 'I go about mourning' (6) means dressed as a mourner, which, if we may judge by later Jewish custom, was in the dress of one accused of serious crime. Yet, when the charge came, it took him completely aback!

The lament about friends and enemies (11,12) does not have the urgency and bitterness of some other passages, e.g. Psa. 41.5–10. At this time there was no real danger from them, but they were revealing their true attitude, which later made Absalom's rebellion possible. After all, it was David's nephew that struck the match that led to the explosion (2 Sam. 13.3). The language is too general and sometimes metaphorical for us to guess at David's disease. The metaphorical can be seen in v. 11, for 'plague' (*nega*) is normally used of leprosy, i.e. his friends treated him as though he were a leper.

David's real quality is seen in v. 16. He is not really concerned with his illness or even with his sins, but with the possibility that God's name should be blasphemed through him, but cf. 2 Sam. 12.9,14. Anyone who has this desire enthroned in his heart will find that suffering is only a God-given means by which we come to know His will and do it, even though it may involve a specific recognition of sins and a turning from them as we have in Psa. 51.

*Psalm 39   The Cry of a Sick Man

The motives for placing this psalm immediately after Psa. 38 are obvious enough, for here too a seriously ill man is speaking to God. For all that the atmosphere is quite different. There is little stress on sin, though it is not lacking (10,11), nor is there any thanksgiving for forgiveness, which we would expect, if it were in any sense a sequel to Psa. 38. Its links are far more with Pss. 77 and 73 than with Davidic psalms.

In vs. 1–3 we have the decision not to speak caused by the sight of the wicked and their prosperity. The psalmist felt he could not guarantee to control his words. It is hard to decide between the AV(KJV) 'even from good' and RSV 'to no avail' (2).

The silence was not fruitless, for when he could no longer keep his peace, his prayer was an entirely proper one (4–6). He was not foolish enough to ask to know how long he had to live. Such a thought is completely alien to the Bible. His illness had broken the pride of life, and he wanted to remain conscious of how short life is (4a); the measure by which his days would be meted was the handbreadth (4b,5). When all is said and done all life is a mere breath (5c, Psa. 90.9b). A handbreadth was four fingers wide (cf. Jer. 52.21 with 1 Kings 7.26). The message of this section is particularly needed today, when science and medicine seem to give life an illusory solidity.

In Isa. 40.6–8 the very transitoriness of man is proclaimed as a comfort (Isa. 40.1), for nothing less than that will really make man rest on God, for only in God's hand is a brief life worth while. So the psalmist turns to God in trust (7–11) and asks for forgiveness and vindication from the scorn of the atheist—'fool' is here *nabal*, the worst of the words so translated. The sadness of the closing section (12,13) must be interpreted in the light of the Old Testament. Even in the New Testament death is recognized as an enemy (1 Cor. 15.26); an exhausting illness late in life brings home as perhaps nothing else how much one would like to do for God and one's family, and how impossible it will be to do it.

There is an idea abroad that a Christian should not be ill. Much illness among Christians is probably unnecessary, but there can be no doubt that illness and bodily weakness are among God's potent methods for teaching us to see life in its true perspective.

Psalm 40   'I Delight to Do Thy Will, O My God'

Many readers will have used vs. 1–3, or have heard them used, as an expression of their spiritual experience. Yet vs. 6–8 as clearly speak of Christ (Heb. 10.5–9). The apparent contradiction is resolved when we recognize that this is one of David's psalms, springing from his own experience and yet looking forward to one who would fulfil it in a way he could not hope to. After all, we know that through the grace and predestinating choice of God vs. 6–8 are in measure true also of us.

In v. 2 the RSV by its emendation creates a unitary picture—AV(KJV) 'horrible pit' obscures the fact that the Hebrew suggests a dungeon—of one lost in the dark in a broken land of pits (Jer. 2.6) and quagmires (Mark 14.33,34), where the only thing possible was to wait for the light and rescue of God, till He put one on firm ground and in a sure way, where one can stride on singing. God's power shown in saving one makes others to trust.

In vs. 4 and 5 David turns from the particular to the general—with v. 5, cf. Psa. 139.17. We tend to dwell overmuch on our crises.

40

The ordinary walks of life will also give ample proof of God's love and faithfulness. The answer of him who realized this is the service of obedience (8). 'Ears Thou hast dug for me' (RSV mg.) is an anticipation of Jer. 31.33 and Ezek. 36.26. Heb. 10.5 uses the Septuagint rendering of the Hebrew. This is one of the cases where we can see the overruling of the Spirit in translation. The Hebrew points to obedience, the Greek to the perfect sacrifice. This section of the psalm ends with vs. 9 and 10, which recount the service, at least so far as David was concerned.

The mood changes so suddenly in vs. 11-17 that many think this is a different psalm. This conjecture is hardly necessary. It is repeatedly the experience of the godly that special deliverance and confession are followed by special persecution and renewed consciousness of sin. To apply v. 12 to Christ shows merely perverse ingenuity. 'Till I cannot see' (12) was explained in the notes on Psa. 38.4. What the wicked say (14,15) is intrinsically unimportant, but indirectly and quite consciously it is an attack on God through His servant. The Christian is never in greater peril than when he speaks as in Rev. 3.17. 'Blessed are the poor in spirit' (17; Matt. 5.3) remains his surest wealth.

Psalm 41   God's Preservation from Illness and Enemies
Here again the order is essentially artificial; the 'poor' of Psa. 40.17 is taken up here in v. 1. The psalm is popularly linked with Psa. 55 (but see comments there) and through it, with Absalom's rebellion and Ahithophel's part in it. In spite of the weakness of the link, it suits the time of the rebellion, and the illness described would go far in explaining David's lack of preliminary activity for which he is so readily blamed. Some, on the basis of 'I said' (4), put the psalm after his recovery, but it is easier to interpret the psalm as composed during his illness.

The psalm starts with a general truth (1-3), cf. notes on Pss. 73 and 77. 'The poor' is a different word to that in Psa. 40.17 and means essentially 'the weak'—the link between weakness and poverty is obvious. Particularly for a king, policy would commend his winning the affections of the powerful. The AV(KJV) of v. 3b has been a consolation for many, but there can be little doubt that the RSV has understood the Hebrew (see margin) correctly.

The general truth did not work out in David's case (4-6)—it is remarkable how often it does not; God works with individuals! He had not been healed and he was not being called blessed, at least by his enemies. We are introduced to the sick-visitors (7-10) comparing notes outside the palace and expecting the worst. Though the story in 2 *Samuel* does not hint at it, it seems probable that Absalom's rebellion was the reaction to David's recovery. It is reasonably certain that v. 9 refers to Ahithophel, but even when he is faced with treachery, David does not forget his friendship and so does not mention his name nor suggest the motives for his actions. In John 13.18 it is used by Christ of Judas, the author of even greater treachery. The voice of triumphant faith is heard in vs. 11 and 12. In all probability v. 12 looks back to earlier deliverances, which demonstrated God's attitude to him. It seems easier to understand v. 11 as a prophetic perfect, i.e. David is so convinced of coming aid, that he speaks of it as something actually present. If the background has been correctly drawn, it is clear that David did not realize the seriousness of the position. There is all the difference between an anxious waiting for dead men's shoes and a murderous rebellion, but the former can lead to the latter.

V. 13 is a benediction intended to mark the end of Book I.

Questions for further study and discussion on Psalms 33–41
1. How has your concept of the history of David been modified by Book I of the Psalter?
2. In what way are we to understand the title 'the prince of this world' given to Satan?
3. What should be the Christian attitude towards the deliberately wicked?
4. Discuss the role of illness in the life of the believer.
5. Compare and contrast Pss. 22 and 40 in their applicability both to David and Christ.
6. Can you find other characters in the Bible where general truths did not seem to work?

There can be little doubt that Books II and III originally formed a unity. All their special features are held in common. These include the ecclesiastical outlook of the psalms except the Davidic ones. Then, down to Psa. **84**, the name Yahweh (Jehovah) is almost entirely avoided, being replaced by God (*Elohim*), cf. Psa. **53** with **14**. The collection was evidently made at a time when the first steps were being made to avoid the use of Yahweh in worship.

The Sons of Korah are responsible for Pss. **42–49**; the remainder of their psalms are in Book III. 1 Chron. **6.33–38**; **25.4–6** show that some of them had responsibility for Temple music. There are no grounds for advocating a unity of authorship or date.

Psa. **50** is by Asaph; the Asaphite psalms are discussed in the introduction to Book III. David's name is attached to Pss. **51–65**, **68–70** and Solomon's to Psa. **72**. Pss. **66**, **67** and **71** are anonymous.

Psalms 42 and 43 Longings for God's House

Therecan benodoubtthatthesetwowere originally one psalm; hence there is no heading to Psa. **43**, cf. Psa. **10**. The psalm can be dated within narrow limits. The author lived near Dan (**6,7**)—his ancestors may have moved there with the tribe, cf. Josh. **21.5**—and he had been accustomed to lead the pilgrims to Jerusalem (**42.4**), while this was now clearly impossible. It must, therefore, have been written early in the reign of Jeroboam I, after the king had forbidden the North to go on pilgrimage to Jerusalem (1 Kings **12.28**), but before the psalmist decided to move to Judah (2 Chron. **11.13, 14**). The psalm falls into three sections, **42.1–5**; **42.6–11**; **43.1–5**, each ending with the same refrain.

Translate, 'As the hind brays over the aqueducts' (1). As the thirsty hind finds water but cannot drink it, so the psalmist knows where spiritual water is to be found, but cannot reach it. There was an old sanctuary at Dan (Judg. **18.30**; 1 Kings **12.29**); it was probably his unwillingness to recognize it that made him unpopular. The RSV is indubitably correct in transferring 'and my God' from v. 6 to the end of v. 5.

The region round Dan, lying in the shadow of Hermon, is undoubtedly the most beautiful in Palestine. In spring, when the pilgrims should have set out for Jerusalem, it resounded to the noise of waterfalls and running water (we cannot identify Mount Mizar). The wretched Levite felt that they were drowning him (7). Since he was looking back, the RSV is wrong in v. 8; render with past tenses. It would be better to translate 'a faithless people' in **43.1**, and we

43

should retain 'man' as in the AV(KJV) instead of 'men' (RSV); the priest of Dan may well be meant. 'Thy light and trustworthiness' (3), not 'truth', for which he asks, are probably intended to be his guides as he slips away from home with his family to cross over into Judah, a venture that would have met with heavy punishment, if he had been stopped by the frontier guards. The appearance of his psalm in the Psalter suggests he was successful. That we live with the knowledge that the worship of God is not restricted to Jerusalem or any other place (John 4.21) should not make us look down on the Levite, for whom Solomon's Temple was the breath of life. It was his love for God that mattered.

Psalm 44   'Why Sleepest Thou, O Lord?'

It is easy enough to show that this does not come from the time of the Maccabees, but it is impossible to assign any date to it with certainty. The strong affinities with Psa. 60 are insufficient to show it comes from the same time of crisis. The exceptional feature is the claim to national righteousness (17–22).

It begins with a glad confession that the conquest of Canaan was God's act. The armies of Israel were still inspired by the same trust as that shown by their fathers (4–8); the present tenses in the RSV (5) are better than the futures of the AV(KJV). It is not a question of hope for the future but of something happening until a very short time before.

Suddenly the whole position had changed (9–16). In Rom. 8.36 we find v. 22 (almost identical with v. 11) quoted. Paul then claims that in spite of this we are more than conquerors. If Christians find it hard to believe this, how much more the Levite psalmist. The spiritual man hates being shamed, because through him God's name is then derided. Yet there are times when God seems to ignore His honour and lets us be dishonoured too. Sometimes there is a rapid change that turns night to day, but there are other experiences we shall understand only at Christ's glorification at His return.

The psalmist declares that the calamity was unmerited (17–22). We should not adopt our most supercilious look and declare that there is no one without sin. What Job experienced as an individual, Israel in its defeat was now experiencing as a nation. If God gave His Son to apparently ignominious defeat on the cross, we must expect Him to treat His people in the same way occasionally. While we admire the faith shown in the appeal to God (23–26), we also recognize the partial knowledge and understanding of the Old Testament. The psalmist assumes that things must be wrong, that

44

God must be at fault. He does not stop to ask why this had happened. In our ignorance of the psalm's setting, we cannot say how the plea was answered. Rom. 8.28 is a far truer picture of the position which the man of faith should adopt.

Psalm 45   A Royal Wedding

Many readers will be familiar with an interpretation of this psalm that makes of it a direct vision or prophecy of Christ and His Church, and that with mystic fervour sweeps any contradictory element out of the way. Such an interpretation belongs to the devotional treasury of the Church, and in the right hands can be a source of much blessing. A closer study will suggest, however, that we are in the realm of the principles laid down in these notes under Psa. 2. No claim is made in v. 1, or elsewhere, that this is a prophecy, and the use of vs. 6 and 7 in Heb. 1.8,9 is equally compatible with a foreshadowing that could be true only in the Messiah.

While certain features of the psalm are compatible with its having been written about Solomon, this should not be taken for granted. The psalmist assumes that beauty of face and character must go together (2). This was true of David (1 Sam. 16.12). For v. 2b, cf. Prov. 22.11; Luke 4.22. Note the 'for ever'; it is a reminder of 2 Sam. 7.13,16. In vs. 3–5 we see how character and actions are matched.

'Thy throne, O God, is for ever and ever' (6): the rendering of the AV(KJV) and RV is that of all the old versions, the Septuagint being represented by Heb. 1.8. The RSV translation is probably impossible, though the margin, 'Your throne is a throne of God', is probably possible. As representative of God and foreshadower of the perfect Representative, the king is given a title only the latter can truly bear, cf. Isa. 9.6. In v. 8, the AV(KJV) is impossible; the ivory palace is one in which the rooms are inlaid with ivory, cf. 1 Kings 22.39. Unless v. 9 anticipates the marriage that follows, 'the queen' may be the queen-mother who occupied a position of special importance at court.

Both the RV and RSV are likely to be wrong in v. 13. The bride, however important, is taken to the marriage with all her finery shrouded; hence the AV(KJV) 'is all glorious within' is probably correct. In the interests of the allegorical interpretation, v. 16 is often taken as being addressed to the bride, but Hebrew grammar makes it clear that the king is being addressed. The psalm ends with a promise (17) more apt for the fulfiller than for the foreshadower.

If such can be the glory of an earthly marriage, what must the marriage feast of the Lamb be like?

45

Psalms 46 and 47   'The God of Jacob is Our Refuge'

It is fairly obvious that Pss. 46–48 belong together, and it is generally believed that they are from the time of Jerusalem's deliverance in the reign of Hezekiah. It seems likely that the Asaph psalms 75 and 76 belong to the same setting.

There is general agreement that we should insert the refrain of 46.7,11 after v. 3, for the absolute symmetry of the psalm demands it. It has either fallen out through scribal carelessness, or the Selah was considered indication enough that it should be read. So put a full-stop at the end of v. 2 and a comma after v. 3. The 'with us' of the refrain is a reminder of the promise of Isa. 7.14. We shall understand vs. 2 and 3 better if we remember that the mountains are a picture of all that is fixed and unchangeable, and the sea, of lawless chaos. In contrast we have the life-giving river (cf. Isa. 8.6). There is nothing that makes men feel weaker or more helpless than an earthquake—'the earth melts' (6). God's action in bringing peace is 'desolations' in man's estimate (8). 'Be still' (10), cf. Psa. 2.10, i.e. cease your activity.

Jesus Christ is not merely Lord of the Church but also King of the world, so Psa. 47 expands the thought of Psa. 46.10 as a further call to praise both by Israel and the nations. The singular 'people' in the AV(KJV) (1,3,9a) obscures this fact. It looks like national pride, when the peoples of the world are expected to show joy over the choice of Israel's heritage (4, cf. Psa. 67, etc.). But such a choice demonstrated that there is a world King, something heathenism could never affirm with certainty. Then for the Old Testament, the election of Israel never means the rejection of the world, but the affirmation of God's rule over it (Exod. 19.5). 'Clap your hands' (1), cf. 2 Kings 11.12; 'shout', cf. 1 Sam. 10.24. 'The pride of Jacob' (4), i.e. the land of Canaan. God's going up (5) implies His prior coming down to fight for Israel. The shout is that of the victor, cf. Num. 23.21. It is hard to justify the RSV in v. 9. We must either say, '... gather with the people of the God of Abraham', or 'gathered to be the people of the God of Abraham' (RV). In either case the prophetic promise shows the nations becoming God's through Israel. 'The shields of the earth', cf. Rom. 13.1,2.

Psalm 48   The City of God

In Psa. 46 the saving power of God was celebrated, here the safety of Jerusalem is proclaimed as the guarantee of God's saving power. First we have the beauty of Zion, here equivalent to Jerusalem. If we follow the AV(KJV) 'on the sides of the north' (2), it underlines the fact that Jerusalem's northern slopes are more beautiful, something that is almost invariably true in a Palestinian site. But it is doubtful whether this is a fair translation of the Hebrew, and the RSV is probably correct. For the ancient world of the Bible the abode of the gods lay in the far north, cf. the Greeks and Mt. Olympus. The psalmist proclaimed that this northern mountain is really Mt. Zion, where the one true God sits enthroned. 'The great King': the word for great is not the usual one for such contexts and is a deliberate challenge to the Assyrian king's claim to be 'the great king' (2 Kings 18.19,28). For Sennacherib's vassal kings (4), cf. Isa. 10.8.

Tarshish (7) is linked with the word for smelting metal. Places where metal ores were obtained were called Tarshish, and the ships of Tarshish which carried the ore were of necessity large. So the name came to be used generally of the largest ships, and stood for the pride of man in his manufacturing skill (Isa. 2.16).

The Sons of Korah had yet to learn that 'here we have no lasting city' (Heb. 13.14). The God-chosen picture of His rule among His people was the Tent, not the Temple (2 Sam. 7.6,7). In the moment the people of God become static they are in danger. Just about a century after the call to 'Walk about Zion' (12,13), Jeremiah had to denounce the people's false trust in the Temple (Jer. 7.4), and a few years later the walls were so reduced to rubble that one could not even go about them (Neh. 2.14). Perhaps that was one reason why Zechariah was to proclaim an unwalled city that could extend without limit (Zech. 2.1–5). Above all we must learn that the victory of today is the encouragement for tomorrow, not its rest. We are all apt to fall into the temptation that faced Joash (2 Kings 13.18,19).

Psalm 49   The Riddle of Life

Like Psa. 50 this psalm was almost certainly not written for the Temple worship, but it links, not with the prophets like Psa. 50, but with the wisdom literature, e.g. *Proverbs*. In the Psalter its closest link is with Psa. 73; its opening verses should be compared with those of Psa. 78. It is mainly concerned with the fate of the wicked and the reward of the righteous. Whenever it was composed, it was at a time when belief in life after death was still confined to a small minority. Probably, just because it· was not used in the Temple service, as it is not in that of the Synagogue, a number of textual corruptions have crept in, e.g. vs. 7,8,11,13,14.

The introduction (1–4) shows that the problem was not one peculiar to Israel. 'Proverb' (4) is correct; see comment on Psa. 78.2.

47

'Why should I fear?' (5): the substance of riches and the power they exert varies from period to period, but they are always real. There is one thing, however, they cannot do. They may buy medical attention one can never hope for from a national health service, but they cannot finally turn death away (7–9). The emendation of the RSV is surely correct, because the question is not what riches can do for another, but for their owner. All men inescapably face death (10–14). The AV(KJV) rendering in v. 11 contradicts experience. On the whole the wicked are not particularly concerned about posterity, that 'their houses shall continue for ever'; they are far more concerned about themselves, The RSV is supported by all the main versions. The great fault of the wicked is just that they are satisfied with what the world can give (13), the emendation in the RSV being probably correct. The translation of v. 14c is very doubtful, but the AV(KJV) can hardly be correct. That a day should come when the righteous then living should triumph over the wicked then living was, in spite of Kirkpatrick, hardly felt to be an answer to the problem of the prosperity of the wicked. The psalmist's hope was, like Asaph's (Psa. 73.24), that death would bring him closer to God (15) and so give meaning to his life. So with confident eyes he looked on life (16–20). Men might grow rich around him and impress others with their glory. Yet they would leave life with nothing, to go to nothingness, while the psalmist awaited God's greeting.

Psalm 50 True Worship

This is no psalm in the ordinary sense, but a prophecy in the manner of Isaiah. Evidently it was included in the Psalter because all the other writings linked with the name of Asaph were there, just as Habakkuk's psalm (Hab. 3), which was almost certainly once in the Psalter, was then appended to his book. The most fitting time for Psa. 50 would seem to be Hezekiah's reformation, though it could possibly be from the time of Josiah. It must be regarded as a prophetic address held in the Temple court at a high festival. It is addressed to those worshippers who overvalued the mere ceremonial, and to those who used it as a mask for their evil.

After a general introduction announcing coming judgement (1–6), there is the judgement on the formalist (7–15) and on the wicked hypocrite (16–21); the conclusion (22,23) is addressed to both groups. 'The Mighty One, God the Lord' (1) is literally *El, Elohim, Yahweh*, a combination found again only in Josh. 22.22; we might paraphrase, 'All Might, the Creator, the Covenant Maker'.

He is pictured as shining forth, i.e. appearing in a theophany, as once at Sinai (3; cf. Exod. 19.16–19), to judge those in the covenant. 'Faithful ones' (5), correct! It is the word wrongly translated 'saints' in Psa. 30.4. Clearly the formalists thought they were giving God something. Everything material in true religion has been given us by God for our good, not that we may give it Him. Thankfulness, sincerity and trust are all we can offer Him, cf. Psa. 51.17; Hos. 6.6; Jer. 7.21–23; Rom. 12.1.

We feel that the deliberate use of religious phrases and practices by the wicked is particularly abhorrent. For Asaph it was less their hypocrisy and more their actual deeds that were reprehensible (17–20). He knew that the full-blooded hypocrite is a rarity and that he is seldom a grievous offender against morality. These men had convinced themselves that God was an advocate of might is right, and that He helped those who helped themselves (21). Many of the great criminals of history have been religious, or superstitious. Naturally the formalists are very much to blame for this. They often live quite exemplary lives from the world's standpoint, but give the impression that their God is a ritualist and not the righteous Judge. The psalm ends with the double call. Note, both are said to forget God, the formalist as well as the wicked. From the former the true worship of thanksgiving is demanded, from the latter true reformation.

Questions for further study and discussion on Psalms 42–50

1. Have you noticed a general difference of attitude between the Davidic psalms of Book I and those of the Sons of Korah? How would you describe and explain it?
2. The Korahite love for the sanctuary has its parallels in Christianity; have you met it? Do you consider it justifiable?
3. In what ways could Pss. 46–48 be applied to the history of the Church?
4. Why does the thought of death seem to have less impact on the materialistic world of the West today? Is something lacking in the Church's teaching?
5. Re-phrase Psa. 50.7–15 to make it apply to your own church.
6. Why do we not pay more attention to what God has performed for our Christian ancestors? Are there any periods of Church history you feel you should know more about?

Psalm 51   A Broken and a Contrite Heart

This psalm has been separated from Pss. 38 and 32 mainly because it shows the effect on an individual of the Divine judgement proclaimed in Psa. **50**. It is the fourth of the penitential psalms, cf. note on Psa. **6**, and none has ever been prayed more fervently or more blessedly by those whose spirits have been weighed down by sin.

The Scriptural background of the psalm is the gracious revelation of God in Exod. **34.6,7**, so the three forms of sin are recited in vs. 1 and 2, cf. note on Psa. **32.1,2**. For 'cleanse me' (2), cf. the law of leprosy, Lev. **13.6,34**. There follows a radical and complete confession of sin, culminating in the nearest approach to the doctrine of original sin in the Old Testament (3–5). Many feel it inconceivable that David could have used the words of v. 4a. But will anyone truly conscious of *sin* think that he has sinned against any but God alone? The implications and effects on others of our sin are vast, and our responsibility is correspondingly great, yet whatever we do to our fellow man, there is always some possibility of excuse. When we face God there is none. The RSV suggests that the *consequence* of his confession is God's justification; the AV(KJV), more correctly, suggests that it is the *purpose* of his confession. If we read 2 Sam. **12.7–14**, we must marvel at the balance of mercy and justice displayed.

It was not 'truth' but 'trustworthiness' that God was looking for (6). 'Wisdom' is based on the fear of the Lord (Prov. **1.7**, etc.). While 'the bones' (8) refer primarily to David's illness (cf. Psa. **38**), yet true conviction of sin normally carries a physical as well as a spiritual effect. 'Hide Thy face' (9): even a Christian finds it hard to grasp that in Christ's justification there is nothing left for God to see. Though the Christian hair-splitter can show that v. 11 is not strictly Christian language, yet it is easy to demonstrate that what David feared can be suffered by the Christian also. The grieved Spirit, who is no longer heard, might almost as well have left the backslider. However much David may have deceived himself, his sins were deliberate, and for deliberate sins there was no sacrifice (Num. **15.30,31**). To have brought one would have implied that his sin was not so great. He had to become a new man (17). While David could have written vs. 18 and 19, he could not have done so then. They were supplied by him, or more likely by a director of Temple music, to adapt the psalm for congregational use.

Psalms 52 and 53   The Psalm of a Wicked Man

It may be difficult to think of Doeg (title, cf. 1 Sam. **21.7**) in the terms of this psalm. After all, though, he was chief herdsman, or keeper of Saul's mules (Septuagint). We should remember that earlier one of the chief persons at the English royal court, in fact and not only in name, was the Earl Marshal, i.e. the controller of the royal stables. That Doeg was able to carry out the massacre of 1 Sam. 22.18 shows the force at his disposal; he did not do it single-handed. His helpers were probably mostly his slaves.

We might reasonably ask whether Doeg really merited this denunciation (1–5). After all, he was carrying out his duty. Very often it is not what we do that matters, but when and how we do it. We may infer reasonably from 1 Sam. 22.6–19 that Saul was in one of his raving moods that day. Doeg knew very well that for him to make his disclosure then meant the maximum of mischief. David's reaction to the news (1 Sam. 22.22) shows that Doeg was acting according to his known character.

We know nothing of Doeg's fate, but we need not doubt that he disappeared in due course, execrated and unlamented. The 'fear' (6) is sheer awe at the operation of God's power. It is unlikely that we have the right to infer from v. 8 that trees grew in the Temple court. Here 'the house of God' is equivalent to 'the land of the living' (5) and refers to the land of Israel, cf. Hos. 9.15, where it must bear this meaning. 'The godly' (9); the RSV has preferred godly to faithful (Psa. 50.5) to suit the rendering of v. 1; see note on Psa. 30.4.

Psa. 53 is mainly a doublet of Psa. 14. God has been substituted for LORD. The main difference is v. 5, which suggests that the adaptation was made for some special occasion when the wicked received a manifest defeat. For the rest see notes on Psa. 14. The juxtaposition with Psa. 52 was in any case a very happy thought.

Question: What impression am I making on those that know me?

Psalms 54 and 55   Psalms of Treachery

David's experiences with the Ziphites (title, cf. 1 Sam. 23.19–29; 26.1–3, especially the latter) were among the most painful that he endured during the time he hid from Saul. They convinced him finally that he could never rely on the loyalty or even neutrality of his own tribesmen. The double deliverance from this treachery is reason enough for the language of vs. 6,7.

If we could place Psa. 55 within the period of Saul's persecution of David, its title would create no special difficulty. There is, however, little, if anything, that fits David the king; not even the circumstances of Absalom's rebellion. It is hard to see how David could have called Ahithophel 'my equal' (13). We shall do best not to look for its historical setting and to leave its authorship open.

51

Psa. 55 starts with a prayer for deliverance from the position of extreme tension in which the writer finds himself (1–3). He asks for nothing more than that he should be able to fly away and be at rest (4–8); contrast v. 6 with Psa. 11.1. Some are allowed to flee, others must stay at their post. He is troubled first of all by the general evil around him (9–11); while it may have been specially directed against the psalmist, it did not concern him alone. But there was one man in particular who had shown special treachery (12–14). One need not be among the great to feel the stab of disloyalty. The psalmist's broken heart breaks out in a cry for justice (15) and an expression of trust in God (16–19). The memory of his disloyal friend was so bitter that he suddenly brings him in again (20,21). Then with equal suddenness the storm stills and the writer is at peace (22,23), for he has cast his burden on God. The margin gives the real meaning of 'burden'. It is not something he has laid on himself, but something God has given him, and so he can allow God to carry it for him.

The psalm is not quoted in the New Testament, but the piety which interprets vs. 12–14, 20,21 of Judas Iscariot is obviously correct. The applicability of these verses to our Lord does not depend on our knowing who it was that so basely stabbed his friend in the back. It also has its application for the Christian, cf. Matt. 10.21,35,36.

Psalm 56 The Psalmist in the Midst of His Enemies

For the general setting of this psalm see the comments on Psa. 34. It consists of two prayers, each ending with a refrain, vs. 1–4 and 5–11; then there is a concluding thanksgiving (12,13). It seems clear that here David looks on his reception in Gath merely as the natural sequel of his treatment by Saul; the culmination of the experiences from which he had already suffered.

He was brought by it to an either-or experience. The death that was breathing down his neck in Gath was merely a more uncomfortable version of what he had been passing through ever since Saul had grown jealous of him. Now it had to be collapse or trust. He confessed his fear (3) for the one and only time in the Psalter— obviously the fear of the Lord is not included—and then put it behind him for ever. Twice over (4,11) he expressed his faith in words that re-echo in Heb. 13.6, though there it is actually a quotation from Psa. 118.6, which in turn was probably based on these verses of David's. In this second book of the Psalter God has been substituted for LORD, which only rarely occurs, so v. 10b is almost certainly the original of v. 10a, which has been inserted as well.

52

So the refrain becomes identical except for the substitution of 'man', i.e. mankind (11), for 'flesh' (4); each word in its own way stressed the frailty of his enemies, when they are faced by God. In vs. 1 and 2 the RSV follows the rendering of the ancient versions; the change in v. 7 involves the alteration of one letter. Glass tear-bottles are a commonplace from excavations of later sites, but the word used in v. 8 implies the ordinary skin water-bottle, so it is remembrance rather than treasuring up that is probably in David's mind. David had to perform his vows (12) because God had answered his prayer. To walk before God (13) means 'open to His scrutiny'.

Our enemies will always find support from the 'world'. If we renounce the weapons and aid of the world, we shall always find them stronger than us, but they are always weaker, so much weaker than God. The only reasonable thing for us to do is to trust in God and say good-bye to fear.

Psalm 57   God's Steadfast Love

There is every indication that this psalm comes from the same period as the previous one. There is no certain guide whether 'in the cave' (title) refers to the cave of Adullam (1 Sam. 22.1,2) or to the one at En-gedi (1 Sam. 24.3–8). An overall view of David's spiritual development may point to the latter.

It is incomprehensible why the RSV should have obscured the fact that Pss. 56 and 57 begin with the same words. The meaning becomes clearer, if we render in v. 1b 'my soul has taken refuge'; his experience of the past is his guide for the future. In his earlier psalms David does not directly mention his anointing by Samuel, which he is prepared to forget until the time is ripe, but he remains conscious that he has been chosen by God for His purpose. The Hebrew of v. 4 is difficult, but the RSV is probably not far from its meaning. Saul's troops were not the only dangers that beset David in his wilderness life. There was always the danger of marauders, looking for plunder, crossing his path. In addition, since there was a price on his head, there was always the possibility of treacherous men trying to gain the reward.

We should exalt God as the righteous King and Judge (5). The confusion of David's enemies (6) showed that He was this in very fact. These enemies were not the wild beasts of v. 4, but Saul's courtiers. They had been confounded both by David's being able to get away safely to the cave of Adullam, and even more by the failure of Saul's expedition at En-gedi (1 Sam. 24.8–22). Where God is concerned, what has been will be, so David could proclaim his coming vindication and triumph without hesitation. Since he was called to be king, his message would go out to the nations (9).

'My heart is steadfast' (7); this is a strong pointer to this psalm being later than Psa. 56, and to the cave being that at En-gedi. David is not afraid. The heart includes mind, will and emotions, and none of these could be swayed any longer by fear. There is a tendency for Christians to make excuses for their emotions, as though they did not matter. When we are overawed by the greatness of God, our emotions will join in bringing Him praise.

Psalm 58 Unjust Judges

The administration of justice in Israel was virtually entirely in the hands of the city elders, who are the people thought of in Deut. 16.18–20. Though we have an idyllic picture of them at work in Ruth 4, it is clear that very soon they began to favour their friends, and that the rich and powerful grew wealthier and stronger at the expense of the poor and weak. While a man of outstanding spiritual gifts might establish himself as a court of appeal (cf. Judg. 4.4; 1 Sam. 7.6,16), probably mainly in cases where the quarrel was between people of different communities or tribes, and the king was quickly looked on as a source of justice (2 Sam. 14.4; 15.2), yet there is no trace of professional judges before the time of Jehoshaphat (2 Chron. 19.5–11). The prophets do not give us grounds for thinking that his initiative worked for very long. Exod. 22.21–24 shows the importance God laid on the doing of justice for the poor and helpless, but it was just these who would find it hardest to appeal against injustice.

David, when he became king, was cognizant of the injustice around him—after all, he had suffered from it himself—but it was beyond his ability to track it down and root it out (cf. 2 Sam. 3.39). So in this psalm he placed a curse on those who were unjust in judgement. In v. 1a the AV(KJV) is impossible; we must choose between the RSV and RV, 'Do ye indeed in silence speak righteousness?', implying that they were silent, when they should have spoken for righteousness. The RSV 'you gods' bases itself on Psa. 82, but since it is a different word in Hebrew, the margin or 'you mighty ones' is better.

These unjust judges were not merely biased in judgement but positively evil themselves. Job 24.2–12 gives us some idea of what their rule could mean. However horrible the execration may sound, it is a prayer that their power, their 'teeth' (6), may vanish, and that they may rapidly disappear. 'Whether green or ablaze' (9) is a

54

doubtful translation, but the Hebrew is difficult. 'The righteous' (10) is essentially the man who has been wronged. He does not kill the wicked judges, but when they have met their death, he triumphantly rubs his feet in their blood. We should spend less time hating the picture and more contemplating the horrors of injustice that can bring men to behave like this.

Psalm 59   'Deliver Me from My Enemies'

In time this psalm is a little earlier than Pss. 56 and 57. Its position is probably governed by its giving a graphic picture of the type of person David cursed in Psa. 58. Later liturgical adaptations are visible in vs. 5b, 8b, and perhaps 11a, though David himself could have introduced 'my people' in a later version.

David's position at the time was one of peculiar difficulty both to himself and to his enemies. Had he let it be known that he had been anointed by Samuel, he could have quickly mounted a major conspiracy against Saul, which many, foreseeing his ultimate triumph, would have joined. To his enemies he was by his transparent honesty and lack of self-seeking a threat to their selfish plans. He both showed them up and virtually guaranteed that once Jonathan was king they would be swept from their place at court. Unless he became like them and allied himself to their plans, there was virtually nothing that David could do to defend himself. The type of slander he was exposed to is rather like a wall of fog bearing in on one from every side.

From the refrain in v. 17 we may infer that the RSV paragraph division is mistaken and that the main break should come after v. 9. In his prayer for deliverance (1–9) David compares his enemies to the pariah dogs of the eastern town. 'They come back' (6) refers purely to the dogs which gather in bands after a day's loafing in the sun. The choice of metaphor is based mainly on the cowardice of these dogs; they will slink away unless emboldened by numbers. The 'who' of v. 7c is, of course, primarily God. They were so confident of their hold over Saul that they would not have minded some man overhearing them. The second half (10–17) is concerned with the fate of his enemies. The apparent contradiction between 'slay them not' (11) and 'consume them' (13) should not be explained by justifiable poetic licence. Had they been swept away in a moment, accident might well have been claimed as the cause. When they melted away, slowly but surely as in Psa. 58.7,8, all would know that it must be God's judgement. Once again, as so often in the

Psalter, in vs. 16 and 17 the past is made the basis of future confidence.

Questions for further study and discussion on Psalms 51-59

1. What light does it throw on the Old Testament sacrificial system as a whole, that David was able to obtain forgiveness without sacrifice, but only by confession and contrition?
2. To what do you attribute the hatred and treachery that David met so often?
3. Why do we so often find it so difficult to follow David's example, to confess our fear and then forget it?
4. Our judges are normally a pattern of impartiality, but does the theme of Psa. 58 show itself elsewhere in our civilization?
5. To what extent, if any, would a Christian be justified in using language like that of Psa. 58.6-9 about others?
6. Why are so many Christians prone to slanderous gossip? What we can do about it?

Psalm 60   God the Giver of Victory

The story behind this psalm is found in 2 Sam. 10.6-19; 8.3-8,13,14 (1 Chron. 19.6-19; 18.3-8,12,13). The RSV rightly reads Edomites instead of Syrians in 2 Sam. 8.13. There is no contradiction in the victory being attributed to David in 2 Sam. 8.13, to Abishai in 1 Chron. 18.12, and to Joab here (title). It is never easy to divide the honour between the commander-in-chief, the general in the field, and the brigade commander. It would seem that Edom had taken advantage of David's preoccupations with the Syrians to attack him in the rear.

The 'Selah' should have kept the RSV from its mistaken paragraph division. There are three sections: vs. 1-4, 5-8, 9-12. In the first we have David's picture of staggering defeat. The Edomites had not merely attacked in the rear, they had obviously been able to inflict serious damage as well. The RSV has in part followed the main versions in v. 4, but has given them a twist, possibly owing to its mistaken paragraph division. We should render v. 4b, 'that they may betake themselves to flight from before the bow'. The great victories over the Syrians had been merely preparation for a greater defeat.

The prayer for an answer (5) is followed immediately by the divine oracle (6-8). Succoth is east of Jordan, so God is saying that the dividing of Palestine, east and west, is for Him to do, not Edom (6), and the defeated tribes are just those He will use for victory.

There is much to be said for Kirkpatrick's rendering in v. 8, 'Unto Edom will I cast My shoe', i.e. he is God's slave for menial tasks.

The 'who' of v. 9 is obviously God. No one else was good enough, so the whole result of the campaign depended on Him (the RV is indubitably wrong with its tense). Yet how was David to advance with confidence after the apparently unwarranted defeat he had suffered (10)? The psalm ends on a note of confident hope. It is worth pondering over the fact that David's sin with Bathsheba took place almost immediately after God had enabled him to smash Edom. Who knows? Had he not 'won a name for himself' (2 Sam. 8.13), he might not have acted like any other heathen tyrant.

Psalms 61 and 62   Silent Before God

Our interpretation of Psa. 61 will depend largely on how we understand vs. 6 and 7. The AV(KJV) and RV make of them a statement, presumably by the king himself, but RSV understands them as a prayer, presumably by the people; the Hebrew permits either interpretation impartially. If we adopt the latter we have a situation similar to that in Psa. 20. David is about to march to the frontier—render v. 2a, 'From the end of the land I will call to Thee'. He asks for the constant presence of God's rock (2) and for a safe return to God's sanctuary (4). The perfect tenses of v. 5 are probably to be regarded as futures expressed in the language of perfect confidence. The response of the people is not merely for the king but also for his dynasty and for the one in whom it is to culminate (see notes on Psa. 2). David ends the psalm with a promise of lifelong thanksgiving.

It would have been better had the RSV respected the deliberate structure of Psa. 62, which has *ak* standing at the beginning of vs. 1,2,4,5,6,9, and have translated it throughout by 'only' instead of fluctuating between 'alone', 'only' and 'but'. In some ways the psalm is a counterpart to Psa. 37.

No background is indicated, but we get the impression that David, while he has not been freed from his enemies, was in a position where he could survey the scene without immediate anxiety. Cf. vs. 1 and 2 with Psa. 18.2. David contrasts God's care with his enemies' hatred (3,4); the AV(KJV) has missed the meaning in v. 3. From his enemies he turns back to God (5–7) in words reminiscent of vs. 1 and 2 and encourages those who are with him (8). By rendering 'shaken' in v. 6 instead of 'moved', the RSV incomprehensibly hides the fact that we have an exact repetition of v. 2b, except for the word 'greatly'. The omission of 'greatly' in v. 6 may imply faith, or it may be due to an old scribal error, of insertion in v. 2 or omission in v. 6.

After a pause David has another look at men and things they value (9,10). Swift made fun of human pretentions by reducing men to dwarfs in Gulliver's journey to Lilliput. The differences between them became so small as to be ridiculous. Here it is the even more drastic comparison with God's standards, which reduces all men to a breath. So the psalm ends with the realization that only God's estimate is of value (11,12).

Psalms 63 and 64 Satisfied Thirst

The Wilderness of Judah is also called Jeshimon or Desolation, and there are few more desolate places in the world. Thirst and the longing to see something green must at times have become almost an obsession. That was how David longed for fellowship with God (1), not a mere transient gleam of glory divine, but the satisfying fullness he had once enjoyed in the sanctuary (2). At the same time it was no mystic union he longed for. God remained for him 'the other,' who always bestows His 'steadfast love' (3). On his rough couch or standing watch as sentry he could feast on God (5,6). It was what God had done that filled his heart with song (7,8), not because he desired the gifts, but because they revealed the character of the Giver. In God's light his enemies had become insignificant. They were bound to perish because they had set themselves against God (9,10). It is only reasonable to regard v. 11 as a liturgical addition or adaptation, perhaps as old as the time of David himself. What God was then in the time of outward desolation He remains in the days of human satisfaction.

Parallels to Psa. 64 can easily be found, some of the more important being Pss. 5,7,10,12,14,52,57. We gain the impression that David was in a position where his own troubles, though real, were not acute, and so he had time to lean back and look at things dispassionately. Apart from 'hear' the verbs in vs. 1 and 2 are futures, i.e. after the initial prayer David says what God will do, 'Thou wilt preserve . . . Thou wilt hide'. Here again we meet the type of man who was David's enemy at the court of Saul. They were not necessarily lawless and violent; their main weapon was slander, their chief aim the destruction of character. The 'who' of v. 5 refers in the first place to God, cf. Psa 59.7. The mention of God's arrow (7) is to stress the suddenness and unexpectedness of God's answer. Whether the emendation of the RSV in v. 8a is correct is doubtful, but it is neater and means substantially the same thing as the RV, 'They shall be made to stumble, their own tongue being against them'. For wagging the head in mocking triumph, cf. Psa. 22.7.

We do not recognize the judicial acts of God sufficiently. We have swung so far away from the horrid little moral tales for Victorian children, that we do not see the judgement of God at all.

Psalm 65 — God Has Visited His Land

In the second half of the psalm RSV has ignored the grammar of the Hebrew and has followed the AV(KJV). We should render (9), 'Thou hast visited the land and hast made it plentiful . . . (11) 'Thou hast crowned the year of Thy goodness. . . .' In other words, this is not a regular harvest festival psalm, but one written in a year when at the time of the Passover first-fruits (Lev. 23.10–14) the worshipper could look forward to a bumper harvest—the fields have not yet been reaped in v. 13. The same impression of a special occasion is made by vs. 5–8. If the psalm is by David, we cannot fix its background. Since there are none of the usual signs of Davidic authorship present, and there are strong similarities with Pss. 46 and 66, many think that the name of David was automatically written in by a scribe influenced by the preceding psalms, and that in fact we are in the reign of Hezekiah and in particular, in the fulfilment of Isa. 37.30.

There is a considerable difference of punctuation and hence of meaning in vs. 2 and 3 between the AV(KJV) and RSV. This is not caused by emendations but by a strict application of metrical principles in the latter. For rebellious man sin is that which drives him further from God. The psalmist maintains that this is exactly what should drive him to God! Though 'forgive' (3) will pass muster as a translation, 'Thou dost cover' or 'blot them out' would be preferable. The transgressions are pictured as on the point of overwhelming the sinner, but brought to naught by the sacrificial blood.

The RSV is correct in rendering 'Thou dost answer us', viz., our prayers (5), compared to the future tense of the AV(KJV) and RV. This is a recognition of a recent deliverance, which is typical of God's acts. We have largely lost the feel for the travail of the whole creation (Rom. 8.19–22), and so we are apt to overlook that it is the actual lands and seas (5)—not as in the AV(KJV)—that look to God, even as they sing to Him in v.13. 'The outgoings of the morning and the evening' (8) means from furthest east to furthest west. Presumably the picture in v. 11 is of God driving in His chariot to inspect His land, with resultant blessing; the fatness presumably refers to the olives. We should probably emend in v. 13a to 'The hills are clothed with flocks'; this is in any case what is meant. The flocks are on the hills, the grain in the valleys.

Psalm 66   God the All-Sovereign and Merciful

The only two periods which vs. 8–12 would seem to suit are the times of Hezekiah and the return from the Babylonian exile. Since the latter is not otherwise hinted at, we shall do best to assume the former, the more so as the speaker at the end seems to be the king. If this is so, the call to universal worship and thanksgiving is not merely for the revelation of God's power and care through Israel (cf. Psa. 67), but also because Assyria was a universally hated and feared nation. The psalmist recognizes that the awesome might of God is inadequate to win men's hearts. 'Cringe' (3) is an excellent translation, cf. Pss. 18.44; 81.15; Deut. 33.29 ('come fawning'), for there is no submission of heart involved.

Before mentioning the recent deliverance, the psalmist looked back to the Exodus with the crossing of the Red Sea and Jordan (6), for our thanksgiving needs to be put into perspective. Israel's recent sufferings were so severe that a number of metaphors are used which are not intended to be united into one picture (10–12). The meaning would have been clearer if v. 12a had been translated, 'Thou didst let men drive over our heads.' Egyptian and Assyrian inscriptions often show the conqueror's chariot being driven over his prostrate enemies. Whether or not the emendation in v. 12c is correct, it is the obvious meaning of the AV(KJV).

The singular in vs. 13–15 undoubtedly points to the king, probably Hezekiah, as speaker. There is no good reason for doubting that we hear him also in vs. 16–20. It is quite likely that he commissioned the psalm for the thanksgiving service. Even though RSV is correct in making vs. 18 and 19 refer to a particular person and incident, it does not mean that we are not entitled to make a general principle of them. There is such a thing as genuine unconscious sin, and this will never cause prayer to remain unanswered, though the answer may involve an unveiling of the sin. Where there is known sin, however, it is an insult to God to ignore it as one prays. No answer need be expected in such a case. Chronological difficulties make it questionable whether Hezekiah is referring in v. 16 to his cure (2 Kings 20.1–11).

Psalm 67   Harvest Home

In itself this psalm is just a happy hymn for harvest-home, and as such calls for little comment. It is, however, of utmost importance for the way in which it reveals how Israel thought of its election.

The worshippers pray that they may enter into the full realization of what the priestly blessing (Num. 6.22–26) involves (1). The unexpectedly early 'Selah' shows how important such a realization was for the psalmist. Then, when Israel is what Israel should be, God's way and salvation will become known to all peoples (2). God is called on to hasten the coming of that day (3). This knowledge and consequent worship of God will mean the end of human injustice and perplexities—justice and guidance are stressed (4). With the giving of an abundant harvest, it is clear that God's blessing is on Israel, and so the salvation of the world is seen to be nearer (7). Such is the understanding of the psalm by RSV; it is questionable, however, whether the psalm will bear this rendering.

We may translate in v. 6 and 7 either 'God is blessing us' or 'May God bless us'. In the light of v. 1 the latter seems preferable, for it is then a prayer that takes up the opening words. After all, the psalmist knew full well that an abundant harvest fell far short of the realization of the priestly blessing, and it would not automatically bring the peoples under God's rule. Particularly important is the realization that Exod. 19.5 does not imply that Israel's election was a rejection of the other nations. Israel was elected for the sake of the world, and Israel's blessing meant the blessing of the world (Rom. 11.12,15). All too often the Church has requited this belief by affirming in the teeth of Rom. 9–11 that the Church's election meant the rejection of Israel.

Psalm 68 God the Saving King

Doubtless David composed this magnificent hymn of praise and triumph for some special occasion, but the words rise so far above it that we can no longer identify its background, beyond accepting the possibility that it has to do with the bringing of the Ark to Jerusalem.

The opening quotation of Num. 10.35 has its first word significantly changed. Render, 'God arises; His enemies are being scattered, and they that hate Him flee before Him!' Equally in v. 2 and 3 we should have, 'the wicked perish . . . the righteous are joyful . . . they exult . . . they are jubilant.' In v. 4b translate, 'Cast up a highway for Him who rides through the deserts' (cf. margin and Isa. 57.14; 62.10). For God the desert is as fertile land.

The Exodus and Conquest were as much the norm for the praises of Israel as the cross and the empty tomb for the Christian. The Exodus figures in vs. 7–10. The psalter contains many details of it not found in the Pentateuch, cf. Pss. 77.16–18; 114.3–6. Very heavy rain is often an accompaniment of volcanic action and earthquakes; in v. 9 it is to be understood metaphorically as well. The Conquest is graphically sketched in vs. 11–14. There is no linguistic difficulty about v. 13, but there is no agreement on its meaning. The RSV makes the dove a description of the women dressed in the spoil—as good a way of understanding it as any. The same is true of v. 14; the Bible has apparently no other mention of this victory.

With vs. 15–18 we come to the transfer of the Ark to Mt. Zion. The contrast is drawn between the glorious peak of Hermon and the insignificant hill of Zion (cf. Psa. 125.2). We have a spiritually imaginative picture of God with all His hosts coming to His new dwelling-place, which is at the same time merely a taking-off place for heaven. The form of v. 18 which we find in Eph. 4.8 is probably based on the Jewish tradition we find in the Targum.

From the past David turns to the present (19–23), blessing and upholding for God's people, judgement on His enemies (21–23). 'Them' (22) are the enemies hiding there, cf. Amos 9.2–4. Then comes the future (24–27), and we glimpse the triumphal procession for God's final victory. But God's victory in and for Israel is that there may be blessing for the world (28–35). Egypt is referred to in v. 30a, cf. Isa. 30.7 (Rahab is a mythological monster); the bulls are the leaders of the peoples; the word rendered 'bronze' by the RSV (31) is of doubtful meaning. In Rev. 21.2 and 10 we have heaven and earth linked by the New Jerusalem, the bride of the Lamb; here heaven and earth are linked through Israel (34).

Psalm 69   The Cry of the Broken-hearted

Of all the psalms that bear David's name, this is the hardest to attribute to him. There is no difficulty about vs. 34–36, which are probably a liturgical adaptation like Psa. 51.18,19. But the whole attitude of the psalmist, though not unlike Psa. 55, cannot be reconciled with David's normal tones. Then it seems impossible to assign certain verses to any known incidents in David's life. Jeremiah could well have written the psalm, but that is mere supposition.

The psalm falls into two even portions, vs. 1–18 and 19–36. Each of these divides into three. In vs. 1–6 the psalmist calls to God for deliverance and this is balanced by vs. 19–21, where the inhumanity of his enemies is depicted. In vs. 7–12 he underlines that it is for God's sake that he is suffering, and from that standpoint he is justified in calling down vengeance on them (22–28). With more confidence he repeats the prayer for help (13–18), and similarly in vs. 29–36 the psalm closes with the confidence that his prayer has been heard.

The word repeatedly translated soul basically means throat; we seldom find this meaning, but it is in v. 1. While grammatically the RSV may be correct in making the end of v. 4 a question, it does not seem preferable to the statement in the AV(KJV) and RV. 'Folly' (5): the Hebrew word is found also in Psa. 38.5 and in *Proverbs*; here it is virtually a synonym for sin. In an age in which so much stress was laid on the rewards of the righteous, for a servant of God to suffer, however deservedly, would make others doubt (6).

The application of v. 9 to Christ in John 2.17 is no guide as to how we should understand 'Thy house' here; it can mean the Temple, or the land and people of Israel. An outstanding feature of the prophets is the way they and their message become identified. So mockery of the message is mockery of the prophet, and rejection of the message is rejection of the prophet (9). Once the message has been rejected there is nothing right the messenger can do (10,11). An indirect allusion to v. 21 seems to be made in Matt. 27.34, though there it is an act of mercy.

Some of the Old Testament saints were allowed to foreshadow the sufferings of their coming Lord by their own sufferings. Since they did not know they had this privilege, their own sufferings were the heavier. We know that we are allowed to share in His sufferings (Col. 1.24) and we should learn to rejoice in that fact, however grievous we may find the sufferings.

Psalms 70 and 71   A Thanksgiving

Psa. 70 is the same as Psa. 40.13–17, with the change of LORD to God, as is normal in Book II of the Psalter. It was evidently detached from Psa. 40 because of its suitability for certain occasions.

Psa. 71, like Psa. 86 and Jonah 2.2–9, is the work of one who, though not able to produce original work of his own, was so steeped in the compositions of earlier psalm-writers and prophets that he was able to weave their words together into a psalm of great beauty. To be able to use the inspired words of others can be as much a gift of the Spirit as the original inspiration. Any reference Bible will give the parallels.

The psalm begins with a prayer of faith in a time of trouble (1–3); the danger is specified (4) and the grounds of hope recited (5,6). From vs. 7–11 it appears that the psalmist's earlier life had been in some way a living sermon, 'a portent' (7). Now with increasing age it seemed as though he might be forsaken (8–13). At this point he begins his praise (14–19a), which leads to the hope of restoration (19b–21). Both the Hebrew and the versions show considerable variations in v. 20 between 'me' (so RSV throughout) and 'us'. It

63

would seem that the writer was in large measure speaking on behalf of his people. The verse hardly refers to the resurrection of the individual but to national resurrection (cf. Ezek. 37.11-14) in the return from the exile. We see this too in v. 21, where 'honour' is literally 'greatness', a word used elsewhere only of God, except in *Esther*. God's people represent Him and can therefore share in His greatness or honour.

'O Holy One of Israel' (22): that Israel was holy to, i.e. set apart for, God was self-evident. When God permitted Himself to be known through Isaiah as the Holy One of Israel, it meant that He had set Himself apart for Israel, namely, He made Himself known to the world only through Israel. In our worship of God we should always remember that we are members of God's people, so we should be prepared at times to be the mouthpiece of the Church as a whole.

Psalm 72   A Prayer for the King

The RSV is correct, compared with the AV(KJV), when it makes of the whole psalm a prayer. Solomon evidently composed a prayer for himself, presumably for use in the new Temple—we cannot justify the AV(KJV) rendering of the title. While there is nothing in the psalm that could not be prayed for Solomon, quite clearly he saw himself also as a forerunner of a much greater king.

The opening verses are a poetic expression of Solomon's earlier prayer (1 Kings 3.6-9). The concept is firmly anchored in the Old Testament that people and land belong together and that the welfare of the soil depends on the behaviour of the people, e.g. Psa. **107. 33-38**. So if justice were done, the mountain-land of Israel would flourish (3). The superlatives in vs. 5 and 7 are to be interpreted by 2 Sam. 7.11-16. Solomon knew that he was not the final link in the chain of promise, but for all that, he was a link in it.

It is clear that the geography of vs. 8-11 is primarily that of Solomon's kingdom, but it is deliberately expressed in language that could adapt itself to any increase in territory and geographical knowledge. In v. 9 the RSV follows the Septuagint, translating as 'May his foes'. The change is small and the parallelism of 'his enemies' suggests its correctness. This greatness was not asked for out of national or selfish motives, but because it would be the worthy attestation of the king's merits (12-14). The qualities Solomon singles out for special praise are those Isaiah attributes to the Messiah (**11.3-5**). Fundamentally too they are those Solomon asked for at the beginning of his reign (1 Kings 3.9), for absolute justice was the main quality he understood as characterizing true government. For the general picture, cf. Isa. 11.3–5. The psalm ends with three prayers: (i) for the king, for power and popularity (15); (ii) for the land, that it might be prosperous (16); (iii) for the royal house, that it might continue (17).

In vs. 18 and 19 we have a closing benediction for the second book of the Psalter as a whole, cf. Psa 41.13. The final footnote (20) is true for Books II and III of the Psalter (see note on Psa. 86 concerning its ascription to David). It does not apply to Books IV and V, but this is a later collection.

Question: Should the King's sons and daughters display today less righteousness than Solomon prayed for?

Questions for further study and discussion on Psalms 60–72

1. Why does the demand for justice figure so largely in the picture of the perfect king? What is the teaching in it for the Church?
2. What light is thrown on the New Testament doctrine of election by the election of Israel?
3. Discuss the possible value of silence before God.
4. Psa. 60 suggests no reason for David's disastrous moral defeat concerning Bathsheba. What reasons can you suggest for it? Do we have such experiences today?
5. Discuss Rom. 8.28 for the believer in the light of Psa. 69 and similar psalms.
6. How are we to know whether the disasters that overtake men are a Divine visitation and judgement, or merely inexplicable happenings?

The main features of this book are the same as those of Book II. Pss. 85–89 are probably an appendix to the collection, for LORD is once more used regularly in them. Pss. 73–83 are psalms of Asaph, and Pss. 84,85,87,88 are psalms of the Sons of Korah. Pss. 88,89 are attributed to Heman and Etham the Ezrahites, and Psa. 86 to David (but see note).

It is impossible to attribute all the Asaph psalms to one period or one author, but they are linked together for the most part by striking peculiarities of style and vocabulary, which at times makes them very difficult to translate with certainty.

Psalm 73   God My All in All

This is one of the greatest psalms in the Psalter. It is indubitably a sequel to Psa. 77, and those who do not lay special stress on reading straight through would do well to read Psa. 77 first.

As in Psa. 77 the author begins with a general truth, which most would agree with without discussion (1). The RSV is based on a different and a more probable division of the Hebrew consonants, thus rendering 'upright' instead of 'Israel' (AV). But, as Psa. 77 shows, it had not worked out that way with Asaph (2,3). It was a double contradiction. The wicked had things Asaph lacked, and he suffered things the wicked were spared.

The wicked are then described in vs. 4–12, at least as Asaph had observed them. The RSV rendering of v. 4a rests again on a different division of the consonants. Even bad men normally cloak their pride and violence; not so those known to Asaph (6). Today most of us in the privileged countries can afford to be fat, but in days of old obesity was often synonymous with extortion, unless it was due to glandular trouble. We can be certain that v. 10 is scribally corrupt; the RSV makes an intelligent guess at what may have stood originally. They were the type of men the psalmist had written about in Pss. 14; 10.4,11; 59.7; 64.5; 94.7.

How should we react to such facts? Asaph's impulse in his physical weakness was to deny God's care for him (13,14). He was wise enough, however, to realize that his experience could not be made to outweigh that of the majority of the godly (15). The solution to his agony had to wait until his turn came to serve in the Temple again (16,17), for such is the implication of the Hebrew. Asaph's problem, Job's problem, does not have an easy answer, and that given here (18–20) may not satisfy everyone, but it satisfied Asaph. The RSV is flabby in translating two different words by awake (20);

the second probably applies to God and means when He arises in judgement (cf. Pss. **7**. 6; **35**.23).

Asaph confesses his foolishness. He compares himself with an unthinking animal (21,22), but recognizes that God has been with him through it all (23). The end was that death would not interrupt his fellowship with God, but he would find himself in His glory (24). This brings him to the glad recognition that God was his all-in-all, who would support him even in death (25,26).

Psalm 74   The Destruction of the Temple

The author of this psalm was probably also responsible for Psa. **79**, the latter being the earlier. Both were caused by the destruction of the Temple by Nebuchadnezzar in 587 B.C. For a full understanding they should be read with *Lamentations*. Because of 'there is no longer any prophet' (9) some suggest it refers to the pollution of the Temple by Antiochus Epiphanes in 168 B.C. Clearly, however, time had elapsed since the destruction, and Jeremiah will already have been taken to Egypt. His presence there and Ezekiel's in Babylonia would be no consolation to those left in Judea.

The complaint of the psalm is not that God had given over His people and with them His Temple and honour to the enemy. They knew that the punishment was deserved. But once the survivors had repented, they thought that God would reverse the position at once. They ignored both God's word (Jer. **25**.11; **29**.10; **27**.7) and the possibility of a Divine purpose behind the delay. In fact, a long exile was a spiritual necessity for Judah at the time, just as times of weakness play their part in the Church's history.

Asaph has three arguments with which to move God. First he appeals to God's loyalty to His covenant (1–3,20,21); then he reminds God of His own honour (10,11,18,22,23); finally he expresses the confidence that God has the power to act (12–17). In these verses God's power and activity as Lord of creation and history are woven together. While vs. 16 and 17 refer to the creation only, vs. 13–15 deal equally with the Exodus and with the creation. The reference to the crossing of the Red Sea is obvious enough in vs. 14 and 13. Leviathan (cf. note on Psa. **68**.30) refers to the might of Egypt's army, which fed the desert dwellers, when their corpses were washed up on the shore. We should probably render v. 13b as, ' . . . the heads of the great dragon . . .'. Equally, however, it is a picture of God's creation of order from chaos, using the language of old mythology. Then v. 15 is equally applicable to the creation and to the granting of water in the wilderness and the crossing of the

Jordan. The implication is that if God controls both nature and history, there is nothing to keep Him from rescuing His people. But the fact that God can, does not always mean that He will. There are some textual difficulties in the psalm which do not affect the general meaning. It is a gain that the RSV eliminates the anachronistic 'synagogues' of the AV(KJV) in v. 8.

Psalm 75   Times are in God's Hands

This psalm, though very different in its original purpose, illustrates the spiritual principle the author of Psa. 74 missed. It starts in a service of thanksgiving, where the congregation is praising God for His mighty acts (1). Then a priest, or more probably a prophet, gives the Divine message to the people (2–8). In it God speaks of the principle behind His acts. There is a 'set time' of God's appointing (2), and so we have no right to pronounce judgement before the time (1 Cor. 4.5), but that is precisely what we do, when we tell Him it is high time for Him to act. God's toleration of the wicked does not mean that the moral pillars of the world are disintegrating (3).

The horn is one of the standing metaphors of the Old Testament and means strength. To lift up one's horn (4) means to display one's might boastfully. The Septuagint rendering 'Speak not insolently against the Rock' (5b) is probably correct. The 'but' with which v. 7 is made to commence obscures the meaning; 'for' would be better. 'Lifting up' is not to be linked with any group of men, or part of the world or society, for all lies in God's hands.

The picture of God's cup, of blessing as well as of condemnation, is a very common Biblical one. Here it is probably a cup of ordeal or revelation. Man's concepts of promotion, of getting on, are bound up largely with window-dressing, string-pulling and push. God's cup will reveal what is really in a man, and those shown up by it will not be spared one bitter drop. The psalm ends with thanksgiving, as it began (9,10). The singular implies that the king is speaking on behalf of the people.

Note: The picture of the world as a house with foundations and pillars is common in the Old Testament, cf. 1 Sam. 2.8; Job 9.6; 38.4–6. Hence the picture is also used metaphorically, cf. Pss. 11.3; 82.5 (for foundations). It is impossible to say whether the picture was still taken literally, but this should not be assumed.

Thought: That we are fellow-workers with God means that we are privileged, not that we are essential.

Psalm 76   God is Glorious and Majestic

The Septuagint adds 'With reference to the Assyrian', in the title. If this is not original, it shows an accurate judgement on the period and purpose of the psalm, which has a close affinity with Pss. 46 and 48. It serves too as a practical working out of Psa. 75, which may come from the same period. The psalm divides into four almost equal sections.

In vs. 1–3 the link between God and Zion is celebrated. However we explain the form of the name Salem (cf. Gen. 14.18), it is a deliberate linking with the Melchizedek story and so with Psa. 110. The deliverance from the Assyrians was merely one more demonstration of God's abiding presence and purpose until the final eschatological triumph. The principle holds good for us too, though we must not link God's presence with any special site or piece of ground, cf. Rev. 20.9.

The power of God is seen in the destruction of the enemy (4–6). While the picture (5,6) fits any scene of all-conquering death, it is peculiarly apposite for the story in 2 Kings 19.35, where the Assyrians die during the hours of sleep. There are textual difficulties in v. 4. The Targum, the old Jewish rendering into Aramaic, has 'Terrible' for glorious. RSV is not likely to be correct in following the Septuagint and translating 'the everlasting mountains'. This, especially in Palestine, where Hermon is the only outstanding mountain, makes an inept comparison; it was probably a guess because the translators into Greek could make nothing of 'the mountains of prey' (RSV mg.). If we must emend, 'than ravening lion' calls for little change in the Hebrew and fits the picture well.

The judgement of God (7–9) looks forward from what He has done to what He is to do. The judgement which saved 'oppressed' Israel will later save the oppressed within Israel.

God is all-sovereign (10–12). The statement of v. 10, seriously misunderstood by the AV(KJV), is one of the most important in the Psalter. It affirms that 'the wrath of men', i.e. their rebellion against God, is made by God to redound to His glory. He can even take the extreme overflowing of man's rebellion, 'the residue of wrath', and make of it a jewelled chain to ornament Himself with. We, placed as we are among our fellow-men, are almost deafened by the sounds of man's hatred against God. From God's exalted position it is seen working towards God's final triumph.

Psalm 77   The Pilgrimage of Faith

This psalm is the preparation for Psa. 73. As there, Asaph begins with a general statement of spiritual fact (1), but this is followed by an account of his grim experience, which seems to contradict it (2–4). In spite of the sincerity of Asaph's prayer, it apparently remained without answer (2). His remembrance of and meditation on God's revelation only left him worse off (3). His whole position was aggravated by his inability to sleep (4).

The second section (5–10) shows Asaph turning to his own past— in the light of vs. 11–15 we must so interpret v. 5—and failing to derive any peace of mind or consolation from God's past mercies to him. They only made his present position more inexplicable. There is a very real value in remembering God's past goodness and in bearing testimony to it, but in the crises of life it is inadequate. Asaph's judgement was, 'It is my weakness (rather than 'grief') that the right hand of the Most High has changed' (10), i.e. he acknowledges that his despair is his own fault, not God's. This does not bring him peace, but it is a major step on the way. When God is not what we expect, we should always blame ourselves.

In the third section (11–15) he goes back beyond his own experiences to the Exodus, which in the Old Testament plays the part of the cross and empty tomb in the Church's experience. The implication of 'Thy way . . . is holy' (13) is that God's acts are not to be measured by man's measuring rods. The special mention of Joseph (15) may point to God's grace in spite of Ephraim and Manasseh always being a troublesome element in Israel, especially the former.

Finally there passes before Asaph's inner eye the crossing of the Red Sea (16–20)—for the description, see comment on Psa. 68.7–10 —where no trace was left after all was over as to how the people had crossed; 'Thy footprints were not seen' (19). We may perhaps infer from v. 20 that Asaph turned to the shepherd picture of Psa. 23 for consolation. He was not yet at peace—for that we must turn to Psa. 73—but now his miseries, illness, sleeplessness, inability to pray and meditate, had grown small in the light of God's greatness, and dawn was not far off. It would be healthier if all Christians were as honest as Asaph instead of pretending that they always walk in the full light of Christ.

Psalm 78   Learning from History

This is the first and probably the earliest of a group of psalms which draw spiritual lessons from Israel's history, cf. Pss. 80,89,105,106. The long introduction points to the unusual nature of the psalm, when it was first written (1–8). The rendering 'parable' (2) is unfortunate; 'wise saying', 'instruction' or 'proverb' would be better, cf. Psa. 49.4. As much of the Spirit's illumination is needed for the understanding of salvation history as for understanding God's verbal revelation. Asaph wrote his psalm because parents had forgotten their duty to teach their children about God's mighty acts.

The story of Israel's disobedience and ingratitude (9–16) is headed by an outstanding example by Ephraim (9–11). Weiser suggests that it refers to the battle of Mt. Gilboa (1 Sam. 31), but there is no evidence of cowardice there. I suspect it may refer to the double defeat at Aphek (1 Sam. 4.1–3,10,11), which opened the way for the destruction of the temple at Shiloh. At v. 17 we go back to the sin of the generation of the Exodus. In vs. 24 and 25 we are dealing with pure poetry. Though the rabbis magnified the manna, they realized that it was essentially of this world order, even though it was miraculous, cf. Christ's words in John 6.30–33. The whole of vs. 21–41 refers to the wilderness period. The recitation of the plagues at this point instead of after v. 12 is for the sake of effect. In the plagues God had demonstrated His power, and so there was no excuse for doubt by the Israelites.

A link with later events is given by vs. 52–55, which carry God's mercies down to the conquest of Canaan. Then, in vs. 56–64, we have briefly the sufferings of the period of the Judges culminating with the destruction of the tent at Shiloh and the capture of the Ark—'His power . . . His glory' (61). The sudden 'awakening' of the Lord (65) can be dated from the rise of Samuel; it included the work of Saul, but Asaph really sees David and Solomon as the climax of the work initiated by Samuel. Since God is the Shepherd of His people, it was only fitting, and a proof of God's choice, that the king after His own heart should have been a shepherd too.

Asaph gives us a picture of consistent sin and apostasy, a dark picture of failure, relieved only by the light of God's grace and power. Neither Jew nor Christian likes to recognize that this summarizes the Old Testament story, but this is its message as a whole. Without the Spirit's illumination we cannot accept such an uncompromising picture of human failure.

*Psalm 79   'Where is Their God?'

This psalm is closely linked with Psa. 74, but it is earlier than it. In Psa. 74 the psalmist and his fellow-worshippers in the ruins of Jerusalem were impatiently awaiting the end of their sufferings and humiliation; here they are still crushed by the memory of the disaster, and their main hope is that their persecutors and taunters should be punished. While the verbal links with *Lamentations* are few, the whole outlook is the same.

Jeremiah was a prophet, Asaph was not (the Asaph of Psa. **50** lived earlier). Asaph mixed with the Temple set and the regular worshippers, Jeremiah's outreach was much wider. As a result Asaph saw true religion, where the prophet could not find even one man to do justice and seek truth (Jer. **5.**1). As a result Asaph could lament over the death of God's servants and loyal ones (wrongly translated 'saints'; cf. comment on Psa. **30.**4) and Jeremiah did not. If we compare the condemnation or contemptuous silence of Isaiah and Jeremiah, when faced with the reforms of Hezekiah and Josiah, with the cordial acceptance of *2 Kings* and the applause of *2 Chronicles*, we see that we are not dealing with an exceptional phenomenon. Many of our difficulties and misunderstandings come just from the fact that our frames of reference—the angles from which we view things—tend to be so different, so that our judgements on people and events vary greatly.

While we cannot exclude a literal understanding of v. 11, it is most likely a prayer for those in the 'prison' of deportation and exile, facing the probability that they would die there. Asaph had not grasped the teaching of Jeremiah and Ezekiel that those deported with Jehoiachin (2 Kings **24.**10–16) were precisely those who were experiencing the grace of God. For the prayer for God's vengeance on the nations, cf. the comments on Psa. **137.**

This psalm brings out the great educational principle that punishment is seldom more than superficially effective. Asaph was so sorry for himself and his people that he did not really realize the greatness of the sin that had made it necessary.

*Psalm 80   'How Long Wilt Thou Be Angry?'

Though this psalm has affinities with Pss. **74** and **79**, v. 2 suggests that it is earlier. Since we cannot trace any real connexion with the northern tribes during the Babylonian exile, we shall do best to date the psalm in the time of Hezekiah, when some in the North began to look to Judah (2 Chron. **30.**10,11), or possibly, as Weiser suggests, a little earlier, just before Samaria fell. There is nothing in the refrain (3,7,19) to suggest the exile, and the Septuagint adds a reference to the Assyrians in the title. Isaiah's vineyard song from the time of Jotham (Isa. **5.**1–7) seems to be the first extant comparison of Israel with a vine, so this may support the date suggested.

As in Psa. **79** there is no effort at self-vindication, but there is equally no real consciousness of sin. They suffer from estrangement

72

from God (4), from the scorn of their neighbours (6), from the vanishing of past glory (8–13), but there is no feeling that they are entirely to blame. One can sense a conviction that God has let them down a little, that conditions were not what might be expected in the covenant. Note the happy self-confidence of v. 18. This weakness is always with us in Church circles. It is very hard to accept that one has no merit at all.

The 'boar' (13) is Assyria. The omission in the RSV of v. 15b (see margin) is hazardous. True it improves the metre and v. 15b is almost identical with v. 17b, but this is not proof. If we retain it, 'son' equals 'branch', as translated by the AV(KJV). In v. 17 we have a prayer for the king. The RSV has unduly followed the AV(KJV) and so failed to make the sense clear; a better rendering would be 'the son of man whom Thou hast reared for Thyself'. There is clearly no Messianic implication. Probably Hezekiah is meant.

Some may suggest that if the explanation given is correct, there should not be a place in Scripture for the psalm. The Bible is not merely a revelation of God, but also of man. In the vast picture gallery of the Old Testament we see man from every conceivable angle. Until the perfect man came, one had to learn not merely from that which was done in the power of the Spirit, but also from what came through the promptings of the flesh, even religious flesh.

Questions for further study and discussion on Psalms 73–80

1. How has the coming of Christ changed our outlook on the problem of the suffering of the righteous and the prosperity of the wicked?
2. Do you find a tendency to try and hurry up God today? Do you consider it justified? For what reasons?
3. Do you find evidence in history that God does not let the moral pillars of society disintegrate beyond a certain point?
4. What do you understand by the term 'the prophetic outlook'? Where does it differ from the outlook of the normal Christian?
5. Do you believe that your denomination could disappear? Motivate your answer. (This does not take into consideration the possibility of a merger with another denomination.)
6. Can you honestly say, 'There is nothing upon earth that I desire besides Thee'? If not, why not?

Psalm 81   God Pleads With His People

Jewish tradition links this psalm with the Feast of Tabernacles and makes of it a New Year's psalm, i.e. a psalm for the Feast of Trumpets (Num. 29.1; Lev. 23.24), which, in spite of Exod. 12.2, was the New Year feast for much of the pre-exilic period and became the civil New Year after the exile. It has remained so ever since among the Jews. So 'the new moon' (3) is the Feast of Trumpets, and 'the full moon' the Feast of Tabernacles. RSV is probably mistaken in its omission of 'for a testimony' in v. 5a, cf. AV(KJV) and RV. The RSV margin is preferable in v. 5b.

Tabernacles was the festival of 'harvest-home' (Exod. 23.16; Lev. 23.39; Deut. 16.13), and it never lost this character. But it was also a commemoration of deliverance (Lev. 23.42,43), so much so that the hope of Messianic deliverance became increasingly linked with it, cf. comments on Psa. 118. This psalm was written at a time when there was tension between the natural impulse to rejoice (1–5) and the harsh political realities of the day.

In the middle of the half-hearted rejoicings Asaph stepped forward, moved by the Spirit. The 'voice I had not known' (5b) is God's. The redemptive aspect of the feast is reaffirmed, and the worshippers are reminded that the original redemption was followed by a period when it seemed of doubtful value. The incident at Meribah (Exod. 17.1–7) is in Psa. 95.8,9, as in Exod. 17.7, regarded as Israel's testing of God: here it is looked on as God's testing of Israel. It is sometimes necessary for God to withhold blessing for the time being to test what is really in those He has redeemed. Exod. 17.3 shows that they denied the reality of Divine action behind their deliverance.

The serious warnings in the Pentateuch, based on the same section of the Pentateuch, show how seriously we must take this psalm. So many factors intermingle in the make-up of a regenerate man, that we cannot take a smooth development of the Christian life for granted. There must be various provings, either by temporary withholding of blessing, or by other means, which will reveal what is really in a man. So often, however, instead of discerning God's hand (Heb. 12.5–12), we become despondent and doubt God's love. For 'cringe toward' (15) see comment on Psa. 66.3.

Psalm 82   A Psalm of Judgement

This is one of the most difficult of the psalms to interpret with certainty. It is a psalm of judgement; the question is, who is being judged? Some suggest the gods of the nations, especially Canaan, who are viewed as mere subordinates of Yahweh (Jehovah). Though this interpretation has been supported by influential voices, including

Weiser's, it must be rejected as running counter to the whole trend of the Old Testament. It is one thing to call the old gods demons (1 Cor. 10.20), another to call them gods and attribute to them functions in God's order. Another interpretation is that they are the great angelic rulers (cf. Dan. 10.13,20,21; 12.1). Yet another that they are those great men of Israel, who by reason of their judicial functions are representatives of God. Both have received influential support, but they seem to create too many problems of interpretation.

A more promising approach is to ask when this takes place. From v. 8 we gather that its effects are still future. So it is likely that we have a vision of God's judgement in the Day of the Lord. Then it is of no great importance how we identify those under judgement; they will include all, angels and men alike, who have been God's executive officers. Since the principles of God's judgement remain unaltered, the psalm is a solemn warning to all whom God has called to positions of authority (Rom. 13.1).

The criterion of judgement throughout the Bible is the way in which we behave to our fellow-men. Because the Old Testament is addressed mainly to the rich and powerful (ponder over Matt. 11.5, the last eight words) vs. 2–4 are apposite. Lord Acton was right when he said, 'All power corrupts, absolute power corrupts absolutely.' We have no right to opt out from the psalm because of our lack of power. Such men are a warning to us that 'But for the grace of God there go I'. Only the power of Christ can keep us. To reject Christ is to reject the first commandment (Mark 12.29,30), and with it goes the second quite automatically (Mark 12.31).

The psalm must not be interpreted as meaning that God ignores injustice for the time being. The prophets always insisted that the Day of the Lord was constantly breaking in. The end judgement on the unjust repeatedly finds its foreshadowing in judgement on some of the unjust.

Psalm 83   The Enemies of Israel

In the more ephemeral contemporary writings on prophecy this psalm is regarded as a prophetic preview of the present state of hostility between Israel and the Arab states. It is most likely that the writers are correct, but in a way that has not occurred to them. The psalm has a historic background earlier than the destruction of Assyria (612 B.C.), but more we cannot say. There is no evidence available to us of any attack on Israel involving precisely the nations mentioned in vs. 5–8, and there probably never was. It is not even said that they had attacked Israel, but merely that they had plotted to do so.

For mainly cultural reasons Israel today is a festering sore to the Arab states of the Near East. In Old Testament days the same was true with Israel and its neighbours, only the reason was mainly religious. So Israel knew that what we have learnt to call a cold war was there all the time.

The Church today is in exactly the same position, except that with it being world-wide, the attack is world-wide as well, with Communism the dark power in the background. We challenge the conceptions of those around us in every realm. We hold the absoluteness of revelation against the relativity of modern standards. We judge man's creations as the transitory things they really are, and human fame as something that withers overnight. Where we differ from Asaph is that we do not ask for physical victory over the world around us—unfortunately the Church has all too often made this mistake. We pray for the conquest of the world through the love of Christ, though we know that the full victory must await His coming.

Since Endor is geographically connected with the defeat of the Midianites—it lies on the northern slopes of the Hill of Moreh (Judg. 7.1)—but not with that of Sisera, there is much to be said for the emendation of vs. 9 and 10:

'Do to them as Thou didst to Sisera,
as to Jabin at the river Kishon,
and as to Midian, who were destroyed at Endor.'

It should not be forgotten that the original version of v. 12 was 'the pastures of Yahweh (Jehovah)'. The explanation of v. 13a (see RSV margin) is given by Thomson, *The Land and the Book*, p. 563, 'When ripe and dry in autumn, these branches become rigid and as light as a feather . . . and the wind carries these vegetable globes whithersoever it pleases . . . . Thousands of them come suddenly over the plain, rolling, leaping, bounding.'

Psalm 84   The Joy of God's House

Here, as in Pss. 42 and 43, we have the longing of the Levitical singer for the sanctuary on Zion, only that here there is no impediment in his way, except the restrictions of the rota of service (1 Chron. 25).

The RSV, in common with the earlier English versions, ignores the change of tense in Hebrew. Translate in v. 2, 'My soul longed, yea, fainted . . . now my heart and flesh sing for joy to the living

76

God.' He has arrived, and the despondency has vanished. Do not forget that the comparatively small sanctuary was the only part of the Temple complex reminiscent of the modern European place of worship. The remainder was open to the sky and to the birds. A distinction must be made between those heads of houses, priests and Levites who lived in Jerusalem and could attend the worship every day (4) and those who lived in the provinces and came to Jerusalem only for the great festivals and for a fortnight of duty in the year.

We would do better to translate v. 5, 'Blessed are those whose strength is in Thee, in whose hearts are the pilgrim roads.' The way to the Temple could be long and difficult, and the whole pilgrimage expensive and dangerous. But just as many have looked on a road leading to the distant hills until they could no longer resist its call, so he could not forget the Jerusalem road until he found himself being drawn towards Jerusalem once more. Baca (6) means balsam trees, not weeping. Balsam trees prefer dry soil, but on the most arid stretch of the way, spiritually, of course, the pilgrim brings blessing with him, and he grows less tired the nearer he draws to his goal. Jerusalem was not merely 'the city of the great King' but also of His earthly representative, and so a prayer is added for him (9). In addition to their other duties the descendants of Korah also acted as door-keepers, but this task was also done in rotation. Therefore v. 10b may be translated, 'I should rather be at the threshold of the house of God', meaning that even to take up the position of a suppliant before the outer gates of the Temple was preferable to ease where there was no thought of God. The traditional Jewish understanding for 'sun' (11), viz., 'a high wall' or 'battlement', is probably correct.

Psalm 85   The Day of God's Salvation

The singer looks into the future and sees the fullness of God's blessing (10–13), but it is clearly the days of the Messiah that pass before his inward eye. But under what circumstances does he have his vision?

The AV(KJV) and RV, by translating vs. 1–3 with perfects, imply that he has experienced a major change in Israel's fortunes, whether the return from the Babylonian exile, or the defeat of the Assyrians, or something else; in this case vs. 4–7 would suggest that there had been a disappointment to follow, as in fact there was after the return from Babylonia. The RSV and Weiser, on the other hand, have the past tense, implying that the psalmist was looking back to what once was, and this moved him to pray for the present.

There is, however, the distinct possibility that the verbs in vs. 1–3 are prophetic perfects, i.e. they state what will happen in such emphatic terms, that they are expressed as something already there. On the whole this is the most satisfactory interpretation. It makes the whole psalm an overflowing expression of the assurance that God will yet bring in Paradise upon earth once more.

Yet this Paradise is primarily a spiritual matter. God's steadfast love, His covenant love, meets for the first time faithfulness, man's unwavering response to God's revelation. God's righteousness had been compelled to cause suffering and want in reply to sin, but now it can kiss prosperity (peace, 10). God's standards, His righteousness, can reveal themselves from heaven even more fully than they did at Sinai and will be greeted by complete, unwavering response from man (11). Then and only then nature is transformed (12, cf. Psa. 67.6), and it becomes a throne for God's king (13).

That this vision found its fulfilment in Jesus the Messiah should be obvious. There can be no fulfilment of it, and never has been, apart from Him. The stress on spiritual qualities shows that these and not an earthly Paradise are what matter, even as in Isa. 11.1–9. God's king is the essential prerequisite for transformed nature. But this priority of the spiritual does not mean that we must therefore rob Rom. 8.19–22 of its apparently obvious meaning, or that the rule of the last Adam will not extend Eden over the whole material world. The trouble begins when the material predominates in our vision of the future.

Psalms 86 and 87　　　　　　　　　Citizens of God's City

Psa. 86, like Psa. 71, is a compilation from existing Scripture. Its ascription to David indicates how much the psalmist had derived from him, and how true to his thought he remained. Readers of Rutherford's letters sometimes find it hard to believe that the hymn, 'The sands of time are sinking,' is not by him, so carefully did Mrs. Cousin weave his language together. There is no justification for the rendering 'godly' (2), any more than there is for 'holy' in the AV(KJV). It means quite simply that he was 'loyal' to the covenant. Note the sevenfold use of Lord (*Adonai*); the psalmist felt himself in a special way the slave of his God. In v. 11c we have a unique expression, probably based on Jer. 32.39 and Ezek. 11.19. He wanted a heart that would not be divided between God and other things (cf. Psa. 73.25), and not torn between faith and doubt.

Psa. 87 is an enigmatic song of praise that yields up its secret to a little study. It is completely eschatological, looking forward joyfully to what will yet be. He sees not Melchizedek's and David's city, not the glories of Solomon's buildings, but the city which once Isaiah and Micah saw (Isa. 2.2-4; Mic. 4.1-4), the city of Heb. 11.10 and Rev. 21.2,10. Its citizens too are quite other than those rebuked by Isaiah and Jeremiah. Among them are some who once belonged to Egypt and Babylon—Rahab is a mocking name for Egypt (Isa. 30.7; Psa. 89.10), while Babylon (*Babel*) is itself a mockery (Gen. 11.9). The uncircumcised Philistine, some from Tyre, the harlot (Isa. 23.15-17), and distant Ethiopia also find a place. The grace of God will see to it that they are reckoned as home-born on exactly the same footing as those saved from Zion itself. Of all the passages in the Old Testament that foresee the bringing in of the nations into the people of God this comes nearest to the message of Eph. 2.11-22. There is no final judgement of nations as nations. God goes through the records of the nations, but picks out those that belong to His people. It is so in Matt. 25.32, where NEB rightly renders, 'He will separate men into two groups' (so also Phillips). Whether the Church has been right in frowning on dancing in this present evil world, so frequently an expression of sensuality and lust, let others judge, but in the day of God's glory every talent by which man can express praise and joy will be brought into play (7).

Psalm 88   The Dark Night of the Soul

The Bible covers the needs of all, and so we find those of the abnormal clearly recognized. Here we have the voice of the melancholic, of the man like William Cowper, where the rays of God's consolation seem incapable of dispersing the darkness around him. For Heman, unlike Cowper, the cause seems to have been physical rather than mental, but the two can never be entirely separated.

Apparently he had been ill from his youth (15), and his complaint was one regarded as a sign of God's anger (7,15,16). Certainly it was one that discouraged sick-visiting (8,18). In the hour of desperate need, 'My companions—darkness!' (18b). The broken-hearted cry of the psalmist was caused by the knowledge that his life had been as empty as a dead man's, and now he was drawing near the gates of Sheol (3-7). Though there is no positive indication of it, I feel convinced that he was a leper, excluded by virtue of his disease from the fellowship of his community and friends, and from the worship of God. In spite of this he had prayed and continued to pray. Without a gleam of light to cheer him, he could yet cry to Yahweh

(Jehovah) and call Him the God of his salvation (1, mg., and AV [KJV]). How movingly wonderful!

He has long ago found that in God's light he could see light, but let us learn from his cry. Firstly, should we be brought into touch with one in Heman's position, we may be able to bring him comfort through Heman's cry. More important is that it should enlarge our understanding and compassion. There are more than we think who live in darkness for mental and physical reasons. To try to bring light and comfort to them is an exacting task, but in them too we may find the voice of prayer which ascends, though there seems to be none to hear or answer. Let us beware that we do not try to persuade the afflicted that their suffering is the result of God's anger against them. Heman's life appeared to be in vain, yet God chose him to write this psalm for the hopeless. No life need be quite in vain, and reception in the future depends not on man's work.

Psalm 89   The Covenant in Peril

It is usually assumed that this psalm is exilic, but however drastic the language of vs. 38–51, there is nothing in them that speaks of the end of the monarchy, of exile, or of the destruction of Jerusalem. Since the Davidic king was God's representative, a relatively minor disaster, measured by man's measures, was spiritually a major one. Equally, no Christian has the right to regard defeat lightly. So the psalm could have been prompted by any one of a number of disasters that smote Judah.

The psalm begins with an announcement of the Davidic covenant (1–4). That this covenant was no vain human promise is shown by the proclamation of God's greatness (5–18). This is very similar to Psa. 74.12–17, though we have the impression that creation and not history predominates in vs. 9–12; yet Rahab is surely a side-glance at Egypt (cf. note on Psa. 87.4). More important even than God's power is the character of His rule ('throne', v. 14). Parallelism shows that 'our shield' refers to 'our king' (18).

The matter goes beyond the power and character of God, for it concerns His solemn promise, so vs. 19–37 give a poetic version of 2 Sam. 7.8–16. The RV is probably correct as against the AV(KJV) and RSV when it translates v. 19a 'to Thy saints', or even better would be 'to Thy faithful ones'. The emendation in v. 19b is unnecessary and improbable, so retain 'I have laid help' (AV). When we consider this promise, we must remind ourselves that the fulfilment of God's promises is always better than could have been anticipated, but this is normally in ways that could not have been foreseen. Our Lord's mission would have been virtually impossible, had there been a Davidic king on the throne at the time.

From the promise we pass to the grim reality (38–45). The 'Thou' in v. 38 is emphatic; there is no suggestion that God had failed. The language used in this section is largely conventional, so there is no point in trying to find the historical background; Amos 9.11 uses very similar terms. The reality drives not to hopelessness but to prayer (46–51). We may welcome the RSV emendation in v. 47a; an introduction of the psalmist's feelings is hardly in place. By its unnoted emendation in v. 50a, the RSV applies the scorning to the king, but the plural 'servants' (AV[KJV] and RV) is probably correct. By the time of Christ Ethan's words had become part of the national consciousness. No wonder they longed for a Messiah. Book III closes with the benediction of v. 52.

Questions for further study and discussion on Psalms 81–89

1. How seriously have you taken the warnings of the New Testament?
2. Have you ever found yourself in any position of authority? If so, did you really act justly in it?
3. What are some of the modern enemies of the Church that are waging a cold war, and perhaps violent hostility, against it today?
4. Try to put Psa. 84 into the language of today, when there is neither pilgrimage nor sanctuary.
5. Try to express in words your vision of what it will be like when Christ comes.
6. How can the Church best find a place for the mentally retarded, the chronically sick, the melancholic, and all others where a normal Christian life seems impossible?

Only Pss. 90 (Moses), 101 and 103 (David) bear the name of an author. The contents are predominantly hymns of praise. The authors' names are not indicated because there is no special link between them and the facts they commemorate.

Pss. 93–100 seem to form a group, which was probably used during the Feast of Tabernacles, when the sovereignty of God as evidenced in the existence of the Davidic monarchy seems to have been celebrated.

Psalm 90   The Brevity of Life

A true understanding of this psalm depends partly on recognizing the use of the Divine names. In vs. 1–12 only Lord (*Adonai*) and God are used. Not till v. 13 does the covenant name Yahweh (Jehovah) appear. The first section deals with the plight of man in general, the second brings out the difference made by the covenant.

The Septuagint and some Hebrew manuscripts are probably correct in reading 'refuge' in v. 1a. Man in his extremity has always been able to find refuge in God, the only uncreated and self-sufficient Being (2), who is the controller of the span of man's life, who calls him back to the dust, when the time is ripe. Could we live as long as Methuselah, almost a thousand years, it would be trifling in God's sight (4). As it is, we are merely ephemera, lasting but a day (5,6), for our sins (7,8) have shortened our lives until they are no more than a sigh, seventy or even eighty years long, and then the weaknesses of old age make a mock of man's boasted strength.

Bernard Shaw in *Back to Methuselah* saw clearly that the brevity of life is the supreme mockery of human effort. Just when we learn what to do and how to do it, failing strength and death end our efforts. Even Moses with superadded years and undiminished strength was unable to complete his work. But Shaw's solution is inadequate. The only answer is 'a heart of wisdom' (12). It will teach us to become God's servants (13), and as we come to know the covenant-making God, we are taken into His plans, so that our work becomes meaningful, and it is established (17), because it is now part of His purpose, and there will be others to continue it, when the time comes.

Modern life is so full; artificial light has lengthened our days; machinery has increased our output immensely; the aeroplane makes it possible for the tourist to cover 'the world of St. Paul' in one brief holiday. But when we give ourselves time to be still, our verdict on what we have done will be the same as Moses'. Only in Christ can we work for eternity.

There are some with so little feel for poetry that they make v. 4 and 2 Pet. 3.8 into a clock for Divine time. God does not let Himself be measured by any human measuring rod.

Psalm 91   The Security of the Saints

Before reading this psalm meditate on Rom. 8.28, noting the marginal variations, and, if possible, the rendering of the NEB. We have to face the apparent contradiction between what God calls good and that welcomed even by regenerate men. Psa. 91 is true, but it is true only to the eye of faith. The RSV emendations in vs. 2 and 9 make the psalm run more smoothly but do not affect its meaning.

The psalm is poetry of a high order, and there is nothing to be gained by attempting a literally exact interpretation at any point. The dangers described can, according to circumstances, be interpreted of purely natural dangers, of the wiles of evil men, and in some cases of demonic agency as well. Equally the terms describing Divine protection are not intended to be woven into a logical whole. Whatever the need there is God's care and shelter to be found.

There are two basic pictures. One is the man at home with God (1,9); not the one who asks God to protect his home, but the one who is where God has put him, and the difference is very great. The other is of the one who goes out on God's business (11). Again, this is not the one who asks God to protect his goings, but the one who walks the paths of God's choosing. The promise in vs. 14–16 shows that no guarantee of unrelieved prosperity, as man's concept goes, is involved. 'Deliver', 'trouble', 'rescue', indicate an outward appearance which seems to contradict the inner reality. The man who wrote Rom. 8.28 also wrote 2 Cor. 11.22—12.10 and Col. 1.24, but he was not conscious of contradiction. Man does not fear suffering, but apparently purposeless suffering. He does not shrink from early death, but from death that makes all his work void. It was summed up by an early Methodist preacher, 'I am immortal till my work is done.'

Some find parts of the psalm callous, e.g. vs. 7 and 8, but they are only a statement of fact. Repeatedly there is a flood from which to rescue Noah, a Sodom where there is a Lot to be saved. We must avoid two errors as we read the psalm. We may not claim its promises for our self-chosen position and activity. Again, we may not sit in judgement on our fellow-Christian who *apparently* has not experienced its truth.

Psalms 92 and 93   God is King

According to the Talmud Psa. 92 was sung during the drink offering of Num. 28.9,10. *Shabat*, the verbal root behind Sabbath, does not mean merely to rest—that is secondary—but to desist, to stop doing what has been done until then, cf. Heb. 4.9,10. We can do this, even mentally, only if what God has done is so great that it leaves no room for our trivial concerns. This psalm points to the varied workings of God that can fill our thoughts.

We have an introduction commending praise (1–4). The mention of steadfast love and faithfulness shows that God's covenant dealings are particularly under consideration, and so the first person singular must throughout be understood in terms of Israel, or today the Church. This makes the pointedness of v. 11 more understandable and also avoids the problem of the individual exception. It is the righteous and not the palm and cedar that are metaphorically planted in God's house (12,13). The praise is not merely for what God has done, but also for the hope it creates of the perfection of God's work in the Day of the Lord.

The opening words of Psa. 93 are variously translated, e.g. 'Jehovah hath proclaimed Himself King' (Kirkpatrick), or 'The Lord is become King' (Weiser). They probably mean 'Yahweh (Jehovah) and Yahweh only is King'. The robe is the outward manifestation, cf. Rom. 1.20. The great fear of Israel's heathen neighbours was a renewed inrush of chaos (Gen. 1.2), but the psalmist proclaims the impossibility of this. By the use of the perfect instead of the past in v. 3ab the English versions hide the fact that there is a reference both to the past and then to the present, i.e. 'the floods once rose up, O Lord'. In the beginning it seemed as though the waters, i.e. chaos, were lord (Gen. 1.2,9; Psa. 104.6–8); then at the Flood it looked like this again. The Lord ruled then, and He rules amidst the turmoil now. Christians reading Christ's reference to Satan as the prince of this world (John 12.31; 14.30), may tend to ascribe to him a power he certainly does not possess. He may, metaphorically, make the many waters thunder, but God's throne remains unmoved. Equally God's law stands firm (5). If God's house is so often the land of Israel, here it is probably the whole world (cf. Isa. 11.9), for this group of psalms has an eschatological outlook.

84

Psalm 94   The God of Justice

There are far too many Christians who have shut themselves into unwalled monasteries because they fear that their principles cannot otherwise be lived out. For the psalmist God's rule means that His principles are universally valid and their application universal. So the psalmist follows the psalm of God's unshakable throne with a call to God to reveal His moral nature.

The Hebrew in v. 1 is plural, 'Thou God of all vengeance'. This is really the prayer 'Thy will be done', not my will, for however much God's people suffer, those who oppress them are ultimately not their, but God's enemies. It is not clear whether vs. 3–7 refer to Israelites or foreigners; probably both are intended. Although we are God's 'people', God's 'heritage' (5), there is the temptation, now as well as then, to think that we must do something about our wrongs. So the psalmist rebukes those that think like that (8–11). He even implies in vs. 12–15 that for God's people these misdeeds become in God's hands His chastening or instruction. It does not make the acts right, but they become a blessing to those who suffer. So we can wait patiently until such time as God rights all wrongs.

The first person singular in vs. 16–23 shows that the king is now speaking. He has not been able to enforce justice, but he knows God is on his side (16). I should be indifferent to the wrongs done to me, but, so far as God enables me, I should seek justice for my neighbour. God is my preserver (17), my upholder (18) and my comforter (19). However powerful the opposition, it can never have God on its side (20); something we need to remember when totalitarianism of every kind threatens us.

A good German Christian said to me sadly with reference to the Nazi treatment of the Jews, 'But what could we have done?' He and his friends had bowed to the apparently overwhelming might of evil authority, which had framed 'mischief by statute'. These believers felt they could only bow to it. Authority in all lands is increasingly prepared to defy the law of God and to act as it sees best. In the face of apparently overwhelming power we must believe that the Lord is our defence and refuge.

Psalm 95   Today!

Here we meet the worshippers thronging to the great festival; in Jewish tradition it is a New Year's psalm. They are prepared to bring God the worship due to Him. He is both the great God and the universal Creator. The fixity of the dry land and the instability of the seas are alike His (5). What is more, His care continues over

His people (7)—'pasturing' is better than 'pasture'; God's active care is being stressed.

But as they come to the Temple gate they are stopped by a priest or prophet with the stern words, 'O that today you would hearken to His voice!' True prayer, true worship, are always a two-way process. Whenever we truly come to God, we may expect Him to speak to us. It would be well if we could be stopped at times at the entry of our place of worship with these words. So often our services consist of a flow of sound in which men speak to God or give their views about God in the sermon, but only the normally all too brief reading of Scripture gives God the opportunity of speaking to us.

Massah and Meribah come in Exod. **17.**1–7 and Num. **20.**2–13 and embrace the whole sweep of the wilderness period from the approach to Sinai to the start of the trek to the fields of Moab. They do not stand for their own intrinsic importance, but as the two landmarks showing the beginning and end of the unbelief that carried off the whole generation that came out of Egypt.

Hearkening to His voice (7) is not to be understood as some mystic hearing of an inner voice, though we may not exclude it. We must listen to the voice of God's acts and words recorded in Scripture and applied to us by the Holy Spirit. All too often we set barriers to God's speaking by demanding it should come within the framework of our tradition, theology or experience.

The use of this psalm in Heb. **3.**7—**4.**13 shows how important its implications are. It brings us to realize that our failure to hear is deliberate, springing from lack of faith (Heb. **3.**12). We put God to the test by demanding that He should do something before we trust and follow. Should He do it, we normally either find excuses for not taking His action too seriously or for asking for another sign shortly afterwards.

Psalms 96 and 97 A New Song

When the worshippers have listened to the urging of Psa. **95**, they are ready for Psa. **96**. They are to sing 'a new song' (1), partly because the psalm is full of the eschatological hope (13), partly because, when God's people listen to His voice, there are always fresh experiences of His grace; we are not meant to live on the experiences of our fathers.

Israel's experience of God is to show the nations that their gods are nothingnesses (the translation 'idols' misses the point; so also in **97.**7, where the rendering is 'worthless idols'). The mention of the heavens is not superfluous (5). In heathen mythologies the heavens are both the abode of most of the gods and also the limit of their movement and power. Yahweh (Jehovah) remains unlimited by His creation. This knowledge calls for proper acknowledgement (7–9). As in Pss. **29.**2 and **110.**3 we cannot justify the rendering 'the beauty of holiness' (9). The roaring of the sea is no longer the thundering of rebellious chaos, but the thanksgiving song of redeemed nature. When we speak of God's judgement, we are apt to equate it with condemnation; here it is equivalent to salvation (13), at least for those who welcome Him with joy. The same is true of **97.**8. Zion's joy is not because of the condemnation and punishment of the oppressors, but because of its deliverance and salvation.

Psa. **96** looked forward to the Day of the Lord; in Psa. **97** its coming is described. The language of vs. 2–5 is borrowed from the theophany at Sinai (Exod. **19.**18; **24.**17; Deut. **4.**11; Judg. **5.**4,5; Psa. **114.**4–7). Elijah had already learnt that God's presence was not bound up with these natural phenomena (1 Kings **19.**11,12), so the language of the psalm must be understood symbolically. The One who will rule openly is the One who rules now, though the fact may be hidden from all but the eyes of faith. So in vs. 10–12 the lives of God's loyal ones (10b; see note on Psa. **30.**4) are seen in the light of this confidence. What will be perfect happens now in part. There is no real recognition here of other gods (7,9). *Elohim* ('gods') means, basically, 'powerful ones'. Whatever powers there may be in earth and heaven they must bow to God.

Psalms 98 and 99   The Holy God

In Psa. **98** we are transported to the Day of the Lord, with His victory an accomplished fact. Very much of the language is identical with that of Psa. **96**. To speak of God's 'holy arm'—holy means separate— is to state that His strength alone sufficed for victory, i.e. salvation. His victory means 'vindication', literally righteousness, both for His age-long purposes and for His people. In v. 8 'Let the streams clap their hands' is a better translation.

Psa. **99** turns from the eschatological scene to the sovereign rule of God in world history, a rule that is expressed by the word 'holy' (3,5,9). It claims that there is a quality about His rule which marks Him out as distinct and separate from all man-made concepts. Probably we should render v. 1 as 'the peoples tremble . . . the earth quakes'. Human history, especially where it has come into contact with God's revelation, has always been singularly devoid of stability. Dan. **7** states a bitter fact, when it compares the great nations with wild beasts.

Much in the Law of Moses is comparable with the contents of the law codes of the ancient Near East, yet Moses' praise of it (Deut. 4.6–8) is literal fact. Could we know all the details, we should probably find that Israel, even at the height of prophetic denunciations, stood morally higher than its neighbours. God did not merely establish equity (4), but He was also in living contact with those who were His executive officers (6,7). It was not so much the Pharisaic concept of the Law that was at fault, but their belief that it was their *unaided* responsibility to apply it. All human systems of religion worshipped gods who were amoral and incalculable, and who could normally be wheedled or bribed into taking the part of their worshippers. Israel knew a God whose punishments started with His own people (8c, cf. Amos 3.1,2).

'Worship at His holy mountain' (9): for the nations the mountain of the gods was in the far north (cf. note on Psa. 48.2), but for Israel God was always in a sense Immanu-el. Already in the prophets we have the concept that Zion was only a prototype of something that would spread and increase, e. g. Isa. 2.2; 11.9; 57.15; 66.1,2. For the heathen the temples were places the gods might visit, for Israel the Temple was the guarantee of God's real presence, however little it could contain or constrain Him.

Questions for further study and discussion on Psalms 90–99

1. Discuss Paul's saying, 'The last enemy to be destroyed is death', in the light of Psa. 90.
2. Discuss Psa. 91 in the light of 1 Cor. 4.9–13 and 2 Cor. 4.7–12.
3. How do the pictures of the Day of the Lord and what follows fit in with New Testament teaching on the subject of the Second Advent?
4. How are we to explain the generally acknowledged weakness of our worship?
5. Contrast the heathen view of their gods with that of the Old Testament.
6. How do we reconcile 'Thou wast a forgiving God to them' with 'but an avenger of their wrongdoings' (Psa. 99.8)? Can you find similar contrasts in the New Testament?

Psalms 100 and 101   O Come into His Presence!

The joyful call to worship in Psa. 100 makes a suitable conclusion to the psalms of God's sovereignty. The call is to 'all the lands', literally 'the whole earth'. Israel knew that just as he had been chosen as a sign that the whole earth was God's, so his worship was a sign that one day all would worship Him. In v. 3 once again, a better rendering is 'pasturing' (cf. note on Psa. **95.**7). Yahweh (Jehovah) is the All-powerful, the Creator, the Elector, the Covenant-maker and the Preserver.

How do we bless God (4)? It is He that blesses us! The Hebrew word is linked with that for knees. The inferior kneels before the superior, as he gives of his best and so blesses. The recipient blesses the giver by humbly and thankfully accepting his gift. It is easy to call God 'good' (5), but what do we mean by it? In modern English there is a tendency to equate good with my wishes. If we read Gen. **1**, we shall come to the conclusion that there good means conforming with God's purpose. God is good in the sense that He never falls short of His revealed character.

The step from God as King to God's king is a small one. In Psa. **101** we have a picture of David's conception of what God's king should be like. Vs. 1–3 portray the king's character. It is likely that we should make the paragraph division at the end of v. 3, not in the middle, rendering the third line, 'I hate to do evil'. Then there follows a description of those who would be his ministers. It need hardly be said that the psalm gives us David's ideal, and that there were some at his court who fell very far short of it, e.g. Joab and Ahithophel. But even the ideal is sufficient to explain the deep hatred many felt for him, a hatred that showed itself in Absalom's rebellion and is mirrored in so many of the Davidic psalms. People do not like it, if your life puts them to shame; they like it even less, when you expect the same high standard of them. Obviously v. 8 could be spoken only by someone conscious of being God's representative, and that in a land which in theory accepted God's law.

Thought: Jesus did not condone sin; He forgave it and then lifted the sinner.

Psalm 102   A General Lament

This psalm would seem to stand in the same relation to an individual's lament in the Temple as Psa. **107** to an individual's thanksgiving, viz., it was there for anyone who could not compose his own lament and was too poor to have one composed for him. This explains the very general nature of the complaints, which makes it difficult to pinpoint the trouble. While much of the language of vs. 3–11 is entirely compatible with physical trouble, some of it suggests evil neighbours, and yet still more implies spiritual distress. In fact one would be hard put to it to find any form of deep distress that would not, at least partially, fit in.

89

Many deny this interpretation. Pointing to vs. 12–17 they claim it is the prayer of an exile in Babylonia (so Kirkpatrick). Let us not forget that, compared with the glories under Solomon, Jerusalem for the rest of the monarchy was a mere shadow of what it had been, just as the Church, in spite of its expansion, is only a shadow of what it once was. In addition, he who laments must always be reminded that he is a member of a body, and his lamentations must be fitted into the framework of the common good.

It is not sufficient, however, to set our troubles in the context of the Church. We shall see it in true perspective only as we place it against the background of God. The New Testament teaches us to judge earthly values by the way they last (1 John 2.17). We should use the same measure for our troubles (25–27). For the normal spiritual man it is easier to give up possible pleasures for Christ's sake than to bear suffering patiently and even to count it all joy (Jas. 1.2). Yet when we learn to see our troubles in the light of eternity, they shrink to the same measure as the pain we accept willingly at the hands of a doctor for our healing.

Many today maintain that the full acceptance of the Deity of Jesus Christ came only in the second century. The use of vs. 25–27 in Heb. 1.10–12 is one of the most striking indications of the falsity of this view. Quite clearly these verses refer to God, but equally clearly they are used in *Hebrews* of Christ without even a comment being deemed necessary.

Psalm 103   'Bless the Lord, O My Soul!'

It is worth pondering over the difference of title between Pss. 103 and 145. The reason is that the latter is pure, virtually impersonal, praise, while the former contains a subtle confession as well. David commences with a call to his whole inner being humbly to confess what he owes to God—for 'bless' see note on Psa. 100. There is a subtle, almost untranslatable, grammatical variation between vs. 3–5 and 6–14. In the former David confesses what God has done for him, and is therefore willing to do for anyone else in similar need, though 'you', 'your' refer throughout to his soul. In the latter he is appealing to the testimony of history, especially as it was seen in the Exodus. The juxtaposition of 'iniquity' and 'diseases' in parallelism (3) implies that the latter were caused by the former (cf. notes on Pss. 6 and 38). The eagle, more strictly the vulture (5), is mentioned merely because it never seems to grow tired.

In v. 6, as has already been indicated, we come to the Exodus in which Israel experienced vindication and justice. Since the two lines in v. 7 are in parallelism, we must take 'ways' and 'acts' as essentially synonyms. It does not suggest a higher relationship to Moses than to the Israelites. Exod. 34.6,7 is reproduced in a poetic version in vs. 8–10. The choice of east and west in v. 12, though an anticipation of modern knowledge, is to be explained by the fact that the traveller across the sea of sand or water was always conscious that there was more to come beyond the horizon.

The retention of AV(KJV) 'pities' in v. 13 is unfortunate. The word is from the root translated 'merciful' in v. 8. A better rendering would be 'compassionate' (8), and 'shows compassion' (13). It is linked with the word for womb and suggests the mother's intuitive understanding of her children.

Man can find meaning for his life and work only as he turns to the power and eternity of God (15–18, cf. Psa. 90); this is true also of the mighty spirits that act as His messengers and servants (20). The call to them is the same as the call to David's soul, i.e. 'bless'. The angel hosts are as dependent on God's grace and power as is ephemeral and sinful man.

Psalm 104   How Manifold are Thy Works!

Reread the notes on Psa. 19. In Psa. 104 the stress is not on nature in itself, but on nature as an expression of the wisdom and power of God. It is concerned entirely with this earth, for the heavens in vs. 1–4 are not the abode of God, but the surroundings of this world. In one way and another all the things mentioned were regarded as nature gods by the Canaanites, but here they merely glorify and serve Yahweh (Jehovah), viz., the sun, the vault of heaven, the rain clouds, the winds and the lightning-flash.

In vs. 5–9 we have God's control over chaos by His fixing the seas in their proper place, cf. Gen. 1.9,10; Job 38.10,11; Prov. 8.29. We can see the Palestinian in the description in vs. 10–13. His outstanding description of the landscape is hills and valleys, and the stress is on the water without which life becomes impossible. 'Wild asses' seem to have no purpose (Job 39.5–8), yet God cares for them equally with other parts of His creation. The world is made for man and his cattle (14,15), but it is no merely utilitarian world. Cedars, birds, the stork, the wild goat, the hydrax, which is virtually impossible to capture as long as it remains among the rocks (not coney as in the AV[KJV] or badger [RSV]), all show the wisdom of God, which makes of this world such a wonderful place. Even lion and man can play a kind of Box and Cox as they share night and day between them (20–23).

The sea awakened his wonder with its life and with man's ability to tame it with his ships (cf. Prov. 30.19). Even the sea-serpent, Leviathan, the symbol of chaos, has become a harmless and sportive thing (24–26).

The world is not merely God's creation; it is sustained by Him (27–30). The prayer for the extermination of the wicked (35) is not vindictive, but the expression of the confidence that when man is as he should be, the Edenic condition of the world will return.

This psalm is often compared with Akhenaten's *Hymn to Aten*. This may be found in many archaeological books, e.g. *Documents from Old Testament Times*, edited by D. Winton Thomas, pp. 145–148. To read it is to discover how infinitely superior the Hebrew psalm is. It would be a valuable exercise to decide what makes the difference.

Psalm 105 God's Faithfulness to Israel

Though there is a superficial resemblance between Pss. 105 and 78, they are fundamentally different. Psa. 78 sets out to explain God's working in Israel, whereas Psa. 105 is a straightforward hymn of praise. To understand it adequately we must remember that for the Old Testament the Exodus and Conquest play the same part as the Cross and the Resurrection in the New Testament.

The psalm begins with a call to praise (1–6). It is not merely the concern of Israel but also of 'the peoples' (1), for God's power in Israel is the incontrovertible evidence of His rule. Especially to be celebrated is God's covenant (7–11). The covenant implies both God's election and love and also His ability to make it effective, i.e. that He is sovereign. Then follows a reference to His care over the patriarchs (12–15). We realize readily enough that 'My anointed ones' is metaphorical, but may find their being called 'prophets' strange (15). The prophet is God's spokesman (Exod. 7.1,2), and he can be that by virtue of his life, of his very existence. Next the coming of Joseph and Jacob to Egypt is celebrated (16–25). The plagues have a special mention (26–36) because they demonstrated both God's power over nature and over the gods the Egyptians believed controlled nature.

In the account of the Exodus and wilderness wanderings (37–42) no mention is made of the people's murmurings (but see Psa. 106), because God would in any case have given the people all they needed. Far more striking is the omission of any reference to the covenant at Sinai. This shows that Paul's teaching in Gal. 3 and Rom. 4 is not something peculiar to him, as is often claimed. The psalmist, who doubtless valued the Sinaitic law and covenant very highly (45), realized that they had no bearing on the promise made to the Patriarchs. Paul expanded the idea, but it had already been clearly grasped by some circles in Israel. The reference to the Law-giving is in v. 45. The purpose of God's grace and faithfulness is that He should be glorified in the doing of His will. Paul also stresses that the sending of the Spirit was that 'the just requirement of the law might be fulfilled in us' (Rom. 8.4).

Psalm 106   A Lament over the Sins of Israel

Psa. 106 covers a good part of the ground treated in Psa. 105, but is entirely different in purpose. The former was a joyful hymn of thanksgiving, this is a lamentation. This is not belied by vs. 1–3. God remains good even when man sins; even when he is suffering from the results of sin man owes God praise. The psalmist probably finds himself in exile (47) and is praying for himself and for others of the righteous who are suffering for the sins of their people (4,5). This is denied by some, but the whole weight of thought looks in this direction. The leading conception is that it was not merely the generation of the exile but also that of the Exodus that had sinned (6). If the former had experienced the mercy and for-giveness of God, then the exiles might expect it too.

The thought of v. 8 is particularly common in *Ezekiel*. It is not easy to accept that the springs of grace are entirely on God's side. The order of incidents after the crossing of the Red Sea is not chronological and it is worth considering whether this has some spiritual significance. The language about Moses (32), 'on their account', agrees with Deut. 1.37 and 4.21.

Failure in the wilderness was matched by failure in and after the Conquest (34–39). Though vs. 37,38 read like a description of the darkest hour before Samuel, we should question this interpretation. Apart from the story of Jephthah we have no certain example of human sacrifice, and archaeology has shown that it was far rarer than was popularly supposed. If the psalm is exilic, the period of Ahaz and Manasseh, when human sacrifice was rife, is probably being looked on as the logical outworking of earlier corruption. In strict metaphor Israel's turning to other gods should have been called adultery, but this term is confined to normal breaches of the marriage bond. Where a woman was promiscuous as well as unfaithful she was called a harlot, and with such a woman Israel is being compared (39, cf. Jer. 2.33; 3.1,2). If the psalm is exilic, there are no reasons for confining vs. 40–46 to the time of the Judges;

they will cover the whole range of catastrophes down to the exile. As in the other books, v. 48 provides a closing benediction.

Questions for further study and discussion on Psalms 100–106

1. In what ways can the worship and prayer of the Church be regarded as representative?
2. Link Psa. 101 with the Parable of the Talents.
3. Make a comparison between Psa. 102 and the General Confession in the Anglican Prayer Book, or some similar prayer known to you.
4. Can you find New Testament parallels for the same events being looked at in such different ways as we have in Pss. 105 and 106?
5. Try to compose three or four extra verses for Psa. 103 to bring in the New Testament revelation as well.
6. Compare Psa. 104 with Job 38 and 39, and draw out the differences of approach. To what do you attribute them?

The majority of psalms in this book are anonymous, and are mostly hymns of praise of the same general type as in Book IV. There are, however, a number of Davidic psalms, 108–110, 138–145 and also 122, 124, 131 among the Songs of Ascents, which also include 127 by Solomon. Pss. 113–118 form the Hallel, which is used by the Synagogue, as earlier by the Temple, at the three pilgrim feasts and also the Feast of Dedication (*Hanukah*) and the New Moons. Pss. 120–134 are entitled 'A Song of Ascents'; there is general agreement today that this is a small collection of psalms for pilgrims going up to Jerusalem. They were originally written for other purposes but have acquired a special meaning through their setting.

Psalm 107   'O Give Thanks to The Lord!'

As pointed out in the notes to Psa. 102, this is a thanksgiving for all sorts and conditions of men. When someone brought a thank offering, it was normally accompanied by a suitable psalm. Where the number of such offerings made it difficult, or where poorer worshippers could not afford to have a psalm written for them, the various sections of this psalm covered the main types of thank offerings.

After a general introduction (1–3) the first section (4–9) deals mainly with pilgrims who have come for the great festivals at great personal danger. The RSV is correct in vs. 8,15,21,31, as against the AV(KJV) and RV; it is not a call to general thanksgiving but to those helped through the particular dangers.

It is unimportant whether we consider those mentioned in vs. 10–16 to be slaves in the possession of foreigners, exiles who could not return, or those imprisoned at home, or whether the section as a whole is metaphorical—it is the thanksgiving for men set free. The third section (17–22) covers every form of bodily illness. The fourth (23–32) deals with those who had braved the stormy waters of the sea. At any time of the year there was risk with the little galleys that plied the waters of the Mediterranean; it would have been specially so for pilgrims coming for Passover or Tabernacles, the former just too early, the latter just too late, to guarantee calms. We get the impression from vs. 26,27 that the psalmist had as little love for the sea as the pilgrims that felt compelled to travel on it.

The psalm ends with a hymn for the whole congregation (33–43). It praises God for His bounty and moral care of His people. It is a fundamental belief of the Old Testament that man and land are inescapably linked (Gen. 3.17, 18; Deut. 24.4; Jer. 3.1,9; Psa.

106.38). Modern man will not listen to such a teaching, for he considers he rules the soil through his modern techniques. Untimely frost, rain in harvest time, drought, tempest, blight and insect pests are all regarded as coincidences. But the psalm does not merely celebrate God's control of the soil (33–38), but also His moral control of society (39–41). Alas, it is rare for v. 42 to be true today.

Psalms 108 and 109 The Maligned Seeks Refuge in God

Psa. **108**.1–5 is Psa. **57**.7–11 and vs. 6–13 are Psa. **60**.5–12. There is nothing to tell us by whom and for what purpose these psalms were combined. We have here a justification, if we feel we need one, for linking different passages of Scripture together to serve a special purpose. Since the words are David's the title is fully justified, though he is not likely to have done the linking.

Psa. **109** is apparently an imprecatory psalm like Psa. **69**. Closer inspection makes this unlikely. Unless we place it very early in his life, it is difficult to attribute it to David; certainly it does not seem to fit any period after he fled from Saul's court. The interpretation given follows that by Weiser.

In vs. 1–5 the psalmist prays for defence against malicious and lying accusations. Then in v. 6 we hear the voice of his chief accuser. He demands that he be brought to trial and lists all the misfortunes that should overtake him (7–15). The accusation follows. He was without mercy to those in need (16, cf. Job **22**.6,7,9; **31**.16–22) and he had cursed others (17–19). Today cursing is normally no more than profane and thoughtless language; then it was regarded as the letting loose of powerful and malignant forces which could be best met by the launching of a still more powerful counter-curse (19)— another means was the neutralizing or overcoming of it by a blessing (28).

The psalmist feels crushed by the malignity and hatred he has aroused, but even more because he is ill (24), but this drives him to trust in God. His enemy had demanded that an accuser should stand at his right hand (6, margin); he prays that he may have God there as his defender (31). There are few things more crippling and crushing than the malicious and completely false accusation, where the single voice of the accused must stand against the unanimity of the perjurers.

That the above interpretation, making vs. 6–19 the malicious accusation, is correct, seems borne out by v. 29. This is so weak, compared with the previous imprecations, that it would be a strange anticlimax, if spoken by the same man. Acts **1**.20 can hardly be conceived of as contradicting it. Peter there quotes v. 8 as Scriptural evidence that an office may be taken from the evil man and given to another.

Psalm 110 A Priest For Ever

This psalm is obviously linked with David's installation as king of newly captured Jerusalem (2 Sam. 5.6–8). It will then have been used at subsequent coronations and their annual celebrations. The opening words should be translated, 'An oracle of Yahweh (Jehovah) to my lord.' Many modern scholars interpret this as an oracle to David confirming him in the office of priest-king held by Melchizedek and his successors. But that is to fly in the teeth of all the evidence. Apart from kings like Ahaz and Manasseh, Uzziah's tragic attempt to function as a priest (2 Chron. 26.16–21) stands unique in the record.

We must see in this psalm an oracle given direct to David by the Spirit in which it was given him to know that not he but the coming King would be God's perfect representative by being both Priest and King. The Hebrew text is very difficult, and the AV(KJV) is not always reliable.

With v. 2 cf. Psa. 2.9. The sending forth of the royal sceptre means the extension of his rule, and this will be God's action. In v. 3c it is difficult to choose between the text and margin. The mountains of Israel are God's and hence holy; the same is true of the army. In summer the dew comes silently and very heavily before dawn; similarly the youth of the land would appear unheralded and uncalled. Abram after his great victory over the four kings (Gen. 14.14–16) wished to give public thanks to God. The appearance of Melchizedek, king of Jerusalem and priest of El Elyon (God most High), gave him his opportunity, for the title of his God expressed Abram's own monotheism. So Melchizedek came into the Israelite Scriptures as the ideal picture of one who was both priest and king. The promise is then made (5a), 'The Lord protects you' (Weiser), expressing the meaning of being at his 'right hand'.

The tone of the psalm changes. We find ourselves in the Day of the Lord, for vs. 5b and 6 must refer to Yahweh (Jehovah), and this in itself is sufficient to show that the psalm was not understood to refer to David. We have the Messianic king in v. 7 as he co-operates with God in His triumph. It is clear that with the exile and the passing of the monarchy the meaning of the psalm was largely forgotten. This accounts for the scribal errors in the text.

Psalms 111 and 112 God's Blessings and the Blessed Man

There are two acrostic psalms here. Each line, except for the initial Hallelujah, begins with a different letter of the alphabet. The psalms form a pair, the former celebrating the goodness and greatness of God, the latter the prosperity and righteousness of His people.

As is normally the case with these acrostic psalms, there is no clear development of thought. Each statement is normally to be taken by itself. God's work automatically expresses His character (3a). He gave Israel the land of Canaan, formerly in the possession of so many nations (Gen. **15.**18–21), and so foreshadowed His placing the world under them for spiritual rule (6). It can only be regarded as regrettable that the AV(KJV) should have translated 'reverend' in v. 9. The word means 'to be feared' or 'terrible'. Weiser points out that 'holy' here is to be understood as 'unapproachable'.

In Psa. **112** the sentiments are, as might be expected, in the tradition of *Proverbs*, no mention being made of exceptions. Note the link made by v. 3b between the two psalms; since man's righteousness is derived from God, the same affirmation can be made of man's and God's. We should translate v. 4, 'To those who fear God he is like a light that shines in darkness; he is merciful, gracious and righteous' (Weiser); he shows the same type of attributes as does God. The RSV emendation is unfortunate, for we are dealing with the righteous man, not with God's actions. We must link v. 5 with v. 9 (cf. comments on Psa. **15.**5). The righteous is always prepared to lend, but when he meets the genuinely poor he gives. This is what is meant by saying he 'conducts his affairs with justice' (5b)—his standard is not human law, but the moral demands of God. As in Psa. **1** the wicked are introduced (10) to make the position of the godly stand out by comparison. Compare the two psalms and find how much Psa. **112** reflects Psa. **111.**

Psa. **112** is so far from much Christian, and also Jewish, experience that we may find it puzzling. It seems clear that for a considerable part of Israel's history God rewarded human attempts to please Him with length of years and prosperity. This must have grown steadily less as the monarchy slipped downhill.

Psalm 113 The God of the Poor and Needy

This is the first psalm of the *Hallel* (see Introduction to Book V). In the modern Passover service it and Psa. **114** are sung after the recitation of the Exodus story and before the meal; Pss. **115–118** are sung after the meal.

We should get the meaning better if we were to render, 'Praise,

O worshippers of the Lord' (1), the basis of worship being service (Rom. **12.**1). The name, i.e. character of God, is both to be 'praised' and 'blessed.' In other words, its expression in practice and its demands on the worshipper are to be gratefully and humbly accepted (cf. comment on Psa. **100.**4). It is one of the curiosities of life, that we meet those who are prepared to use the most extravagant language about God—not that it exaggerates His merits—and yet shrink from accepting His will for them. The praise of God should be unbroken (2) and universal—v. 3 means from east to west. God's glory, which is the expression of His character, is never static. Hence, to say that it is 'above the heavens' (4) implies that He is exerting His sovereignty. Nothing in the universe can shut Him in.

It would have been better if v. 5b had been translated, 'who sits enthroned on high'. In vs. 7 and 8 we have an almost verbatim reproduction of 1 Sam. **2.**8, while v. 9 gives the sense of v. 5cd in the Song of Hannah. Earthly kings faced an insoluble problem. They could not be in more than one place at a time. If David and Solomon opened their judgement hall to all and sundry, so that a fake widow (2 Sam. **14.**4) or a pair of quarrelling harlots (1 Kings **3.**16) could come in, it meant that they were not available for those that needed them in the provinces. Moreover, the more the kingdom and the population expanded, the harder it was to enforce justice. The very distance of God is a help! He can see all that is going on, and neither need nor distance can hinder Him from His righteous work. For us, justice has degenerated into dealing with infringements of law; for the Bible, justice is seeing that right is done. The poor and needy stand for all those who have been kept from what should be theirs, while the barren woman represents all who have not been able to bring their life to true fruition. The final Hallelujah belongs to Psa. 114.

Psalms 114 and 115   The Exodus

A particular demonstration of God's goodness was His creation of Israel as a people, and this is celebrated in Psa. **114.** It is outstanding metrically for the manner in which the parallelism is carefully balanced. God had started His people in the midst of strangers, and He brought them out to be His dominion and sanctuary. There is no contrast in v. 2, but rather the affirmation that Judah was the expression of all implied in the name Israel. God's purpose was that all Israel should be holy, set apart for Him (Exod. **19.**6; Lev. **19.**2), and His goal is that no sanctuary shall be needed apart from His people (Jer. **3.**17; Rev. **21.**22). At the Exodus nature saw that its

Creator walked amidst His people, and trembled. The reference in v. 8 is an encouragement. At Rephidim and Kadesh God had brought water out of the rock; similarly amid the hardships of a stony age He could bring refreshment to His people.

The song goes on in Psa. 115. The miracles had been done not for Israel's but for God's sake. He had gone on showing His steadfast love and faithfulness (1) in spite of the people's faithlessness, implied by the nations' mocking question, 'Where is their God?' Now the prayer is that He should act for His own honour's sake (1). God is a free agent (3) and He is not hindered by any of the 'gods' of the nations, who are man's creation. For the thought of idols and their makers see Isa. 44.9–20. The call to praise (9–11) suggests almost irresistibly that the psalm in its present form is post-exilic, for there is no mention of the royal house. It is not likely that any special classification is implied by 'You who fear the Lord' (11,13). Where there is trust there will surely be blessing too. We must think of vs. 14 and 15 being spoken by the priest in charge at the service.

In Rabbinic thought v. 16 plays a very important part. It has been taken to indicate that man should confine himself in his theological thinking and speculation to this world and that which happens in it. The knowledge of God and His activities which are confined to heaven lie beyond man's realm. It is doubtful whether the psalmist meant this, but if the Church had remembered the principle, it would have been spared much useless conflict.

Psalms 116 and 117 Public Thanksgiving

Psa. 116 is a simple psalm of thanksgiving for use in public (14,18) before the psalmist pays his vow (18) and brings his thank offering (17). Behind it lies an experience of being saved from death (3,8), but it is not clear, and in all probability it was not meant to be clear, what the danger was. The less clear-cut the language, the more all worshippers could use the psalm to express their experience also. Although the traditional interpretation is that it was illness, there are, however, passages that point to persecution being the experience from which he has been delivered.

It starts with an expression of deepest gratitude (1). There is much to be said for the emendation accepted by Weiser, 'because He inclined His ear to me, when I cried to Him' (2). The psalmist's prayer could be translated much more idiomatically, 'O Lord, I beseech Thee, save me' (4); he was thinking neither of soul (AV [KJV]) nor life. It is especially because the psalmist calls himself 'simple' (6) that it is likely his danger was from men, not bacteria.

100

The word suggests lack of experience. In *Proverbs* it is contrasted with the prudent and equated with fools. In other words, there is an element of blame in it, for all that he experienced the Lord's preservation. His walk would be in the land of the living because he had not died (9). That the danger was human is suggested also by v. 11. The 'cup of salvation' (13) may have been one at the thanksgiving meal, but the phrase is more likely to be metaphorical. The force of v. 15 is that the death of God's loyal ones (see comment on Psa. 30.4) is something He will not lightly permit.

Psa. 117, the shortest in the Psalter, is a call to the nations to praise Yahweh (Jehovah) because of His loyal love to Israel. For the thought, see Psa. 67 and 100. Paul was justified in using this psalm in Rom. 15.11 as a prophecy of the extension of God's mercy to the Gentiles in Christ. The choice of Israel was always for the ultimate blessing of the world as a whole. The final Hallelujah belongs to Psa. 118.

Psalm 118   A Royal Thanksgiving

Jewish tradition links this psalm with Tabernacles. It certainly was in the time of Christ and probably was from the first. From the same source we know it was used antiphonally, and it is easiest to understand if we think of it being chanted while the king moved from the Temple gate (19,20) to the altar (27).

It begins with an antiphonal call to praise (1–4). Then the king gives his thanksgiving (5–19,21); v. 20 is probably the answer of the door-keepers to the royal request (19). It may have a particular victory in mind, but we need not assume this. There are good reasons for believing that Yahweh's (Jehovah's) sovereignty as shown in the existence of the Davidic monarchy was celebrated during Tabernacles. As the procession enters the Temple court we hear the congregational praise and prayer (22–25) and the priestly greeting (26,27). The thanksgiving of the king (28) and people (29) ends the psalm.

That this psalm was early regarded as Messianic is shown by Mark 11.9,10; 'Hosanna'=*hoshia-na*, i.e. 'Save, we beseech Thee' (25). The use of the 'leafy branches' (Mark 11.8) and palm branches (John 12.13) was taken from Tabernacles; they were waved in the ritual. The answer of the gate-keepers (20) is a reference to Pss. 15 and 24. With 'the stone' (22) cf. Isa. 28.16, where 'testing stone' is the correct translation, and Zech. 3.9; 4.7. If we put these passages together, we reach the probability that we are dealing with the stone cut by the architect, which, when lowered into place as the last stone, will bond the whole building together and show whether the plans have been faithfully followed. In Matt. 21.44 (probably mistakenly relegated to margin by the RSV) the man who ignores it is the one who falls on it; the one who confidently awaits its being lowered into place is the one on whom it falls. The stone referred in the first place to David, whom the mighty in Israel neither wanted nor expected as king. By the first century A.D., if not earlier, Jewry knew that the Messiah would be equally unexpected.

There are translational difficulties in v. 27. The AV(KJV) by inversion obscures the force of v. 27a. The Hebrew is 'Yahweh (Jehovah) is el', i.e. might. The RSV is almost certainly correct in the second half. As the worshippers joined in a solemn dance around the altar of burnt offering and waved the branches they carried, it seemed as though they were bound together by them.

Questions for further study and discussion on Psalms 107-118

1. Are there further categories you would like to see included in Psa. 107 in the light of modern life? Compose a thanksgiving for them.
2. Consider Psa. 109 in the light of Matt. 5.11.
3. What does 'A High Priest for ever after the order of Melchizedek' mean to you in your Christian life and theology?
4. Can you draw any parallels between Psa. 114 and the history of the early church in Jerusalem?
5. Think of the idols of today. How would you mock them in the style of Psa. 115?
6. Make a fuller study of the thought of Christ as the Corner Stone.

*Psalm 119.1-32   The Praise of the Law

Psa. 119 is to Jewry what the marvellously written and illuminated manuscripts of the monks were for medieval Christianity. It is the attempt to glorify God by attention to the smallest detail. From v. 4 onwards every verse except v. 115 is an address or prayer to God, so it is a grievous error to suggest that the Law had taken the place of God for the author. Essentially the psalm rings the changes on various synonyms for Law, or more accurately (Divine) instruction. In the following list no attention has been paid as to whether the word is used in the singular or plural. We find: law (*torah*) 25 times; word (*dabar*) 23 times; sayings (*imrah*) 19 times; commandments (*mitzvot*) 22 times; statutes (*chuqqim*) 21 times; ordinances (in AV[KJV] normally judgements) (*mishpatim*) 23 times; precepts (in AV[KJV] also injunctions) (*piqqudim*) 21 times; testimony (*edut*) 23 times; way or path (*derek*) 12 times in a good sense, (*orach*) four times in a good sense. Only in vs. 90,122,132 do we fail to find one or more of these terms, and there, faithfulness, good and name are to be taken as equivalents.

For 'blessed' (1) see comment on Psa. 1.1. The prayer of v. 8 reads strangely until we remember that the psalmist was a member of a minority group. The difficulties through which Judea was passing at this period clearly suggested God's disfavour. A basic principle of the system introduced by Ezra was that the Law was intended to cover all the possibilities of life; hence man needed Divine wisdom to infer God's will for those eventualities not directly covered by it (12). He was not merely a learner but also a teacher (13). Though life after death is not mentioned in v. 19, or for that matter elsewhere in the psalm, at least a wistful hope is implied. Until the Pharisees were able to enforce their concept of the Law on the people in the period between A.D. 150 and 200, the main opposition came from the poorer people, who thought they had no time for study, and far more forcibly from the rich, who resented the constraint of the Law on them (23). The 'soul' (28) is the whole man; his sorrow at the godlessness of his neighbours will have affected his body as well, hence 'melts away'. His great fear was contravening the Law unintentionally. Lack of knowledge demanded a cautious walk. The greater the knowledge the greater the freedom on his path (32, cf. v. 45). The Christian equivalent is a prayer for the fullness of the Spirit.

*Psalm 119.33-72   Walking at Liberty

There can be very little doubt that this is one of the latest of the psalms. The author must have belonged to the school of Ezra, whose great work was to bring home to the Jews that the Law was the concern of all, not only of the priests and other privileged classes (Neh. 8). The work of Ezra was necessary, if the educational work of the Law was to be accomplished, both bringing home to men the meaning of sin and shutting them in to the coming Saviour. The process initiated by Ezra of necessity involved walking the edge of the cliff of Legalism, and very many in the course of time fell over, to merit Christ's condemnation on the Pharisees. Here, however, there is not the least trace of legalism, and so too we must say of some of the best lovers of the Law in New Testament times and also in later Judaism down to our time. That the danger existed is shown by the minimized feeling of sin in the psalm. The writer is more aware of what he has done of good than of what he has left undone, or even of active evil, but cf. v. 176.

The AV(KJV) is not likely to be right in v. 36, for we already see a preparation for the New Testament standpoint. Earlier Old Testament characters would have seen no contradiction between God's testimonies and 'gain'. The reproach (39) is probably that of hypocrisy; he says and does not do. For v. 45 cf. v. 32. We should probably understand willingness rather than experience in v. 46. We may link v. 54 with v. 19. For v. 62 see comments on v. 164. The name Pharisee means separated one. They kept themselves apart from many for fear of unconsciously breaking the Law, especially in matters of tithes and purity. The beginning of the movement is suggested by v. 63. Our Lord's willingness to have fellowship with the moral outcast would make Him as unwelcome today as He was then.

Psalm 119.73-112 'I Hope in Thy Word'

The psalm is the most perfect alphabetic acrostic in Hebrew and possibly in any language. Each of the twenty-two sections consists of eight verses, and each verse in a section begins with the same letter. Add to this extreme regularity of metre, something observable even in the English translations, and we understand why the psalm is a masterpiece of the miniaturist's art. For one without feeling for this the psalm can be poor stuff. 'This formal external character of the psalm stifles its subject-matter. The psalm is a many-coloured mosaic of thoughts which are often repeated in a wearisome fashion' (Weiser). For those with the necessary understanding it can be very precious. 'It conveys at first an impression of tautology. . . . It is infinitely varied in its expressions, yet incessantly one in its direction; its variations are so delicate as to be almost imperceptible, its unity so emphatic as to be inexorably stamped upon its every line' (Liddon). Readers of these notes will probably find themselves between these two extremes.

It is not spiritual pride we find in v. 74, but a recognition of the difficulties faced by the small group of the loyal ones who tried to keep the Law at all times. In v. 78 we have the only metrical irregularity in the psalm. The claim to be a leader (79) is found again in vs. 99 and 100; the AV(KJV) has a well-attested reading in v. 79, but the RSV is probably correct. We must understand v. 83 in the setting of its section. Smoke dries a wine-skin (not 'bottle' as in AV[KJV]!), and makes it useless. It would be left in the smoke only by oversight. He is suggesting that the deferring of God's

104

mercies is rendering him unfit for service. Basing itself very largely on v. 89, later Jewish thought maintained that the Law had been written in heaven before the creation of the world. In other words, like the Muslim view of the Quran, the Law in our hands is only a copy of a heavenly prototype. No such idea should be found here. The psalmist affirms that the Law, being the perfect expression of God's will, is immutable. It is outside the power of man who would like to change it. It is unlikely that we have a trace of spiritual pride in vs. 99 and 100. If we remember the representative nature of the psalm, we shall realize that it is a claim that true understanding must always be God's gift.

Psalm 119.113-144   'Thy Law Do I Love'

Beyond the probability that he lived about the time of Ezra, there is nothing we can affirm with any certainty about the author of Psa. 119. Conflicting conclusions have been drawn from the vague personal remarks. We should remember that a poem like this is not written in one glorious hour of inspiration, but represents revision on revision, polishing on polishing. So a considerable span of his life may lie behind his 'Golden Alphabet'. Another factor is that he was probably writing consciously as a member of a group devoting every spare hour to the common study of the Law. Therefore some of the apparently personal material may express group experience. The chief points enumerated are his trials (50,67,71, 75,107,153), contempt and ill-treatment (22,39,42,121,134). He met considerable opposition from leading men (23,51,61,87,95,110, 161). Though Ezra's presentation of the Law was joyfully received, we may be sure that there was growing opposition to his standpoint as soon as the implications were recognized. This is made clear enough by Neh. 13.

There is difficulty in v. 130 in all the English versions; the AV(KJV), though beautiful and true, is impossible as a translation. There is much to be said for Weiser's rendering, involving a minor textual emendation, 'The gate of Thy words shines'. Then the mention of the simple implies that he has only to pass through to obtain understanding. Link v. 131 with Psa. 42.1. We should take v. 136 seriously. One of the most endearing qualities of the better Pharisee was his willingness to teach those willing to listen.

Even if we allow for a great deal that is spiritually obvious in this praise of the Law, it is doubtful whether the psalmist would have said, 'Thy law is true' (142). As in the Old Testament generally, it means, 'Thy law is trustworthy'. It is not a denial of the possibility of fuller revelation, but the affirmation that the one that builds on it builds on rock. It is an amplification of the first half of the verse, which in essence affirms there is an absolute morality, something denied today by communists and humanists alike, as well as by some Christian groups. The commandments which give a testimony to God's nature (144) never give an inadequate picture. The mistake of the legalist is to give the obviously temporary commandment the same eternal validity as the others.

Psalm 119.145-176   'I Do Not Forget Thy Law'

The Law (*torah*) consists mainly of: (i) the historical section of the Pentateuch, which teaches us God's will from history; (ii) the ten commandments (Exod. 20.1-17; Deut. 5.1-21), which are clearly treated as the basis of the covenant and of all other law; (iii) three commentaries on the ten commandments, viz., Exod. 20.23—23.33; Lev. 17.1—26.46; Deut. 12.1—28.68; (iv) a long exhortation by Moses, Deut. 1.1—11.32 (excluding 5.1-21); (v) divers sacrificial and ritual laws, Exod. 25.1—31.18; Lev. 1.1—16.34, and many chapters in *Numbers*. The more (iii) and (v) are stressed, the easier the law seems to be to keep and the easier one lapses into legalism. The more (i), (ii) and (iv) are stressed the harder it is seen to be to do God's will. The former may lead to conviction of sins but hardly of sin. The psalmist gives the impression of being rather delicately poised between the two. He is not a legalist, but how easily he could have become one.

As was remarked earlier, cf. v. 144, under testimonies (152) he understands especially those laws which reveal God's character. These, by virtue of the fact, remain unchanged. We should do well to remember the truth of v. 160; no verse of Scripture will in itself give us the whole of truth. The psalmist was a 'Methodist'. In vs. 62,147,148 and now 164 we have information about his prayer habits. He mentions midnight (62), the beginning of the third watch (148) and dawn (147); the other four prayer hours would be the time of the morning sacrifice, midday, the time of the evening sacrifice and sundown. From this we may deduce he was not a manual worker—he may very well have been a Levite on the Temple staff. Unless we take the verse as does Kirkpatrick, 'Not merely morning, noon and night, but constantly and repeatedly', which is not his meaning, we must remember that the amount and regularity of set prayer depend on the position in which we have been set by God. The rabbis demanded no more than three times a day (cf. Dan. 6.10). The closing verse is better rendered with Weiser, 'I have gone astray; seek Thy servant like a lost sheep', or even better with Kirkpatrick, 'If I go astray, seek Thy servant like a lost sheep'. If he had been really conscious of having gone astray, he would hardly have left this picture to the end.

*Psalm 120   The Pilgrim's Call

This is the first of the group of psalms 120–134, all headed 'A Song of Ascents', or in the AV(KJV) 'A Song of Degrees'. This title has been explained in a wide variety of ways, some of them extravagant. Now there seems to be unanimity that it means 'a pilgrim song', and is actually so translated by Weiser—in the Bible one always goes up to Jerusalem, and this became a technical expression for going to a pilgrim feast. This special pilgrim collection has been made up mainly or entirely from psalms which had been written for other purposes. This shows us how we may legitimately use Scripture at times for purposes other than its original purpose. In practice this should be done with great care. The comments on these psalms will, where suitable, concentrate on the pilgrimage use the psalm has acquired.

The pilgrim to be, wherever he lives, on the Anatolian plateau of Asia Minor, Meshech (5), or on the steppe-land of Northern Arabia, Kedar, has grown weary of his heathen neighbours. He is not a missionary to them, but they find his life a standing rebuke and so bitterly calumniate him. It may well be that in the psalm's original setting Meshech and Kedar were used purely metaphorically, indicating that his fellow-Israelites were mere godless barbarians. He prays that they may be done by as they did. The sharp arrows and the glowing coals are excellent pictures of the malicious tongue, and he prays that they may reap what they have sown (3,4).

Whatever had taken this Jew to his outlandish home, for the great dispersion was often optional, he now concluded that his only hope of peace, even if it was only for the time being, was to leave home and seek the house of God. In the Middle Ages the concept of pilgrim was often defiled by not a little fraud and carnality. Today it tends to be dragged in the dust by being applied to tours designed to rush people around Palestine in comfort and at top speed. In Bible days a visit to Palestine was slow and hazardous, thanks both to nature and evil men. At Passover the journey to Jerusalem, especially by sea, was too early for safety; at Tabernacles the same applied to the return journey.

*Psalms 121 and 122

As the pious Jew made up his mind to be a pilgrim, he lifted up his inner eye to the far-distant hills of Judea and thought of the long way to go. He wondered where his help would come from, but answered his question himself (2). Then comes a friend's cheer (3–8). The rendering of the AV(KJV) and RV text, and also the RSV can be justified, but there is little doubt that the RV margin, Kirkpatrick and Weiser are correct with 'May He not suffer . . . may He not slumber', The friend then corrects himself (4); i.e. such a possibility must be excluded. With growing faith he applied what is true of the people of God as a whole to its individual member setting out at God's call (5). God is well able to guard at a distance, but here He is depicted as being so close that His shadow falls on him, and on his right hand at that. He will not even need to fight, for God will fight for him. Shade leads to the summing up of all possible enemies under the terms sun and moon. It is indifferent whether the light of the full moon can be a physical danger. So dwellers in the Near East have believed from time immemorial, and not a few Europeans who have lived there have come to believe it. The psalm ends with the confident assurance that from setting out to returning the pilgrim will be blest (8).

Psa. 122 lets us see Jerusalem in the longing pilgrim's heart. The RSV is probably correct in its rendering of v. 2, i.e. in dreams and longings the pilgrim has already been in Jerusalem. In vs. 3–5 we see the ideal Jerusalem, even as David, who wrote the psalm for some other purpose, longed that it should be. Note the stress on justice (5). Longing leads to prayer and activity (9).

We are pilgrims to the heavenly Jerusalem, where there is no cleavage between desires and reality. Today all too often it has remained a goal but ceased to be an aspiration; we no longer understand Phil. 1.23. We have also forgotten, all too often, that the Church, local or universal, is the foreshadowing of what is to be. We are most outspokenly conscious of the spots and wrinkles where Christ would see none of them.

Questions for further study and discussion on Psalms 119–122

1. Why is there nothing in prose or verse in the New Testament corresponding to Psa. 119? What takes its place?
2. Study the various phrases for Law (*torah*) used in Psa. 119. What light do they throw on the nature and purpose of the Law?
3. Would you be able (granted time and ability) to write a similar poem on the Bible? If not, why not?
4. How far are the difficulties of the writer of Psa. 119 yours?

5. Express in modern terms your understanding of the meaning of pilgrimage for the Christian.
6. What is your concept of heaven compared to the traditional one? What has made the difference, if any?

Psalms 123 and 124   'All Men shall Hate You'

The setting of Psa. 123 is the scorn with which the pilgrims are regarded (3,4). The psalmist knows only one way to rise above it, viz., by fixing his eyes on God. He uses a most striking picture, which he had doubtless experienced as guest in a very rich house. At the banquet, though the slaves lined the walls and could hardly see what the guests required, they were always ready to serve food and drinks as they were needed. The mystery was solved when he noted that the slaves were looking at the host, not the guests. He was watching his guests and with little signs with his hand was indicating what was needed. His wife told him afterwards that the same had been the case in the women's quarters. He had learnt to look to God like this, so there was neither eye nor ear for those that mocked and scorned. So often when we pray for guidance, we are not wanting to be dependent in this way on God, but we want to know the way that we may in measure be independent of Him.

Psa. 124 obviously comes from some crisis in David's reign, which we can no longer identify. Here it refers to the plots and traps through which the pilgrims had to pass. The picture in vs. 4 and 5 is taken from the dry *wadi* beds of Judea, which are very steep-sided. Though they contain water for only short periods after rain, there is often a little herbage in them nurtured by sub-soil water. If a shepherd has taken his sheep down into the *wadi*, and there is a thunderstorm in the mountains, a wall of water may rush down on him, giving him little chance to escape. That is one reason why Palestinian roads seldom follow the valley bottoms. The *wadis* are apparently as treacherous as his enemies but less dangerous (6,7). The psalmist puts his hope in the character and the power of God (8). We are apt to doubt either the willingness (cf. Mark 1.40) or the ability of God to help us and keep us from the enmity and malignity of men.

Psalms 125 and 126   The Lord Around His People

The development of new Jerusalem, i.e. the city outside the old walls, has today reached a point where it becomes an effort of imagination to understand the picture in Psa. 125.2. Formerly, apart from one or two special vantage-points, one could not see the city from a distance; one had to climb the ring of hills that encircled it. This was even truer of the pre-exilic city of the monarchy, which occupied the eastern ridge alone. The reason for the immovability of those who trust God is that they are not tested beyond what they can bear (1 Cor. 10.13); the power, 'sceptre', of wickedness will not be allowed to remain (this is the meaning of 'rest') in God's domain (3). The psalm was presumably composed during one of the many periods of foreign domination. The pilgrim is confident that the shadow towards which he is moving will be removed before long. Hence, while he prays for himself and those like him (4), he takes the doom of the wicked for granted (5).

The AV(KJV) by translating 'captivity' in Psa. 126.1 has seriously narrowed the scope of the psalm. The history of Israel is full of sudden reverses of fortune. The psalmist looks back to a recent one presumably within his own experience, perhaps the deliverance from Sennacherib, and remembers both the joy of the people and the impression made on their heathen neighbours. The clouds had gathered again, even if the position was not as bad as it had been, so the psalmist prays for even greater deliverance. The picture in v. 4 is that of Psa. 124.4 (see note), though now it is the blessing brought by the water that is under consideration, not its destructive power. No agriculture is possible until the former, i.e. the autumn, rains have begun. Then, especially if the rains have been delayed, the sower must go to his work regardless of wet and cold. His teeth may chatter and tears run down his cheeks (5,6), but they are a harbinger of blessing to come. For the pilgrim, the very fact that he was living outside the land showed that deliverance was needed. He longs that his weary way might foreshadow his permanent return to the land of his fathers. In the meantime he hopes that the hardships of the pilgrim way will bring a rich harvest.

Psalms 127 and 128   God's Care is over His People

In Psa. 127 the main thought is no longer linked with pilgrimage, but with the nature of the God of the pilgrim. This is expressed in the normal concrete Hebrew way by two examples. Worry is foolish, for human safety and prosperity depend on Divine care. The Hebrew of v. 2d is for us today ambiguous, and translations and commentaries have never agreed whether we should translate, 'He gives to His beloved sleep', or 'in sleep'. Seeing that the Psalter never suggests that the wicked are addicted to insomnia, the latter seems to be better and is adopted by Kirkpatrick and Weiser. Certainly the RSV cannot be excused for not mentioning it in the margin.

110

It is the Old Testament equivalent of Rom. 8.28 and Matt. 6.8,33.

Whatever might be the case with exceptional characters, ordinary people during the monarchy period had no hope of any purposeful life after death. It might seem, therefore, that life was regarded as vain, there being the same outcome for good and bad alike. Solomon speaks here of the large and healthy family given by God, which both justifies a man's life in future generations and guarantees his social position during his lifetime.

This outlook on life is continued in Psa. 128. It is one met frequently enough in the Psalter, e.g. Pss. 25,27,37,49. We associate it especially with *Deuteronomy* and *Proverbs*, also with Job's three friends. If we are to make sense of these parts of the Bible, we must assume that in its earlier periods God did in fact miraculously grant prosperity, health and long life to the godly, while the wicked normally experienced the opposite. Even then, as Job shows us, there were exceptions. With the decline of the monarchy these must have grown steadily more numerous. Although the New Testament clearly enough disassociates itself from this position, it still forms a foundation-stone for the thinking of many Christians. Major physical or financial calamity is often regarded as a sign of Divine punishment. The simple fact seems to be that while in some cultural and social settings the righteous are more likely to prosper, though with a due measure of persecution, and the wicked to perish; no such statement can be made of the Divine order. The Old Testament statements must be interpreted as a preparatory stage before the resurrection of Jesus Christ changed our whole perspective. Fundamentally, however, the protective power of God over His own remains unchanged.

Psalm 129   The Afflictions of Israel

This is by far the saddest of the pilgrim psalms. The sight of Jerusalem's walls was a reminder of all that Israel had suffered. We are apt to forget that in the 1,250 or so years from the Conquest to the Christian era there were first the afflictions under the Judges, and then from about 730 B.C. Jerusalem either had to pay tribute to or was under the heel of the Assyrian, Egyptian, Babylonian, Persian, Greek and Roman, with a brief break in the reign of Josiah and a somewhat longer one under the Hasmonaean priest-kings (132–63 B.C.). Not even Sennacherib's defeat freed Judah from the obligation of paying tribute. In spite of this, Israel was imbued with the defiant knowledge that it could not last. Even under Roman rule

111

they could say, 'We have never been in bondage to anyone' (John 8.33).

The striking picture in v. 3 is less a suggestion of complete barbarism, as in Amos 1.3, and more an identifying of Israel with its land. This had been used for the conquerors' pleasure, and its owners lashed like slaves. The Lord had freed them before (4), and so He would free them again. From v. 5 we may infer that the psalm is celebrating in v. 4 what had been, not what was when the psalm was written. Kirkpatrick is probably correct in seeing a statement of fact and not a prayer in v. 5.

A growing willingness on the part of Christians to give Caesar more than his due, combined with a contemptuous tolerance by society, mask the hostility of the State to what should be the absolutist demands by the Church for Christ. Therefore we do not sufficiently realize the instinctive revulsion of the world when faced by Israel's claim to election. In fact, in spite of the clarity of Rom. 11.29, the Church itself seldom takes it very seriously. For any who do, hatred of the Jew inescapably becomes hatred of God's will. So vs. 6–8 are not essentially vindictive, but a prayer for the vanquishing of God's enemies and the triumph of His will. In Palestine the earthen house-top becomes superficially soft during the rains, and grass seeds take root and sprout quickly, and wither just as quickly when the rains end, rather as in Matt. 13.5,6. The underlying picture differs little from the parable of the house built on the sand (Matt. 7.26,27).

Psalms 130 and 131   Satisfaction with the Lord

Psa. 130 is the sixth of the penitential psalms (cf. note on Psa. 6). The pilgrim's presence in the Temple has deepened his consciousness of sin. Already in the Old Testament the knowledge had begun that in spite of the fact that 'without the shedding of blood there is no forgiveness of sins' (Heb. 9.22), yet 'it is impossible that the blood of bulls and goats should take away sins' (Heb. 10.4). This was deepened by the dispersion far from the Temple, where perforce sacrifices could not be brought regularly. So, while he does not reject sacrifice, he casts himself on God's mercy (4). Yet he realizes that it is a kind of mercy which should cause fear of breaking God's will again. He compares his long, earnest waiting for the assurance of God's forgiveness with the sentry on the third watch (the Old Testament knows only three) straining his eyes for the first signs of dawn in the eastern sky, so that he can go off duty. The psalm ends with the confidence both of national salvation and even more of the individual from his sin. In fact it is the coming of the New Covenant he is longing for (Jer. 31.31–34).

In Psa. 131 we find the impression made on the pilgrim by the capital. He, the provincial, has now realized how little he really knows of high affairs in Church and State. But he accepts his ignorance and turns to God for full satisfaction. The RSV, faced with a sentiment which is hardly comprehensible in Western society unless the Hebrew is paraphrased, has so weakened the translation as to make it positively misleading. The AV(KJV) is essentially correct, but it is better to render v. 2bc, 'As a weaned child rests quietly at its mother's breast, so my soul is quieted within me'. Weaning was not carried out much before three years of age and sometimes was even later. So the child, deprived now of its mother's breast, but not of her love, rests contentedly. So also the psalmist knows that God's leading him in humble paths (1) is no denial of His love. Even so for Israel the true goal and riches are God, not the hopes of the world.

The interpretation of the psalm in the setting of David's life would probably place it in the years of waiting for God to accomplish His purposes with him. Then v. 3 is probably an addition (cf. Psa. 51.18,19) to adapt it for wider use.

Psalm 132   The Legacy of David

Before the pilgrims return home there must be a prayer for the royal line. The psalm was probably composed for the celebration of the Dedication of the Temple held during the great autumn festival (cf. vs. 8–10 with 2 Chron. 6.41,42). It is skilfully built up, every main section in the first half (1–10) being taken up in the second (11–18).

Neither the RSV 'hardships' nor the AV(KJV) 'afflictions' seems right in v.1; Kirkpatrick's 'trouble' is preferable. The story in 2 Sam. 6.1–19 suggests that the death of Uzzah is being hinted at. The completion of vs. 1–7 is given by vs. 11,12, cf. 2 Sam. 7.12,14–16. David's trouble was rewarded by God's care in establishing the dynasty.

The meaning of the rather enigmatic language in vs. 2–5 is given in vs. 6,7. 'It' is the Ark. Jaar (plural Jearim) means 'wood'. The Ark was near Kiriath (the town of) Jearim (1 Sam. 6.21—7.2)—the name Baale-judah (2 Sam. 6.2) comes from the town's other name, Kiriath-baal (Josh. 15.60). Ephrathah (6) elsewhere means Bethlehem, but here must be Kiriath-jearim. Ephrath, wife of Caleb, had a son Hur (1 Chron. 2.19), the 'father', i.e. founder, of Bethlehem (1 Chron. 4.4), while his son Shobal was 'father' of Kiriath-jearim (1 Chron. 2.50). Presumably both places received the name Ephrathah from Caleb's wife.

In vs. 8–10 we have a parallel to Psa. 24.7–10 and the poetic counterpart of 2 Sam. 6.13–15. The theme of v. 8 is taken up by vs. 13,14; vs. 15,16 correspond to v. 9, and vs. 17,18 to v. 10. Once again 'saints' (9,16) should be 'loyal ones', cf. note on Psa. 30.4. It is not chance that the Divine response includes the poor (15), whom the worshippers in their enthusiasm quite characteristically forgot. 'To sprout' (17) is from the same root as 'branch' (Isa. 4.2; Jer. 23.5; 33.15; Zech. 3.8; 6.12); in all these passages 'sprout' would have been a preferable translation. A 'horn' (17) generally stands for strength in the Old Testament, but in Dan. 7.7,8,24; 8.5 it is a symbol of a king, so it may very well be that we have a Messianic reference here. This is borne out by the puzzling closing words. The word translated 'crown' is also used of the high-priestly one (Exod. 29.6), while 'shed its lustre', or the AV(KJV) 'flourish', is cognate with the word used for the plate of gold on the high-priestly turban (Exod. 28.36). So there may be a veiled reference to the Messiah as priest for ever after the order of Melchizedek.

Psalms 133 and 134   Good-bye to Jerusalem

Now the journey back to Meshech or Kedar (Psa. 120.5) must begin. In the light of their slander and malice how united Jerusalem appeared! (Psa. 122.3). There is no room for complacency about the present state of disunity in the Church, but it is not really as bad as it is often painted. Compared with conditions in the world, the Church is remarkably united in spirit, though not in organization. The psalmist offers no prescription for the creating of this unity. The fact that they are 'brothers' (1) should be enough. The effects of this unity are compared with the perfume of Aaron's anointing oil, which spread from him to embrace all the worshippers as well. Another picture is of the dew, which so refreshes the parched land in the height of summer. The dew on the slopes of Mt. Hermon is exceptionally heavy (3); when it had been particularly heavy round Jerusalem, it could look almost like snow in the dawn light, reminding the writer of Hermon's snow cap. He could not have thought that it actually came from Hermon. True national life for Israel depended on the life in its religious centre (3). As long as that was sound the existence of the nation was assured.

The pilgrim collection ends with a greeting to those on duty in the Sanctuary. To 'stand' (1) is the attitude of service, cf. Psa. 135.2. In the time of Christ there were no night-time services in the Temple

114

(cf. v. 2), and 1 Chron. 9.33 is hardly adequate evidence that they were held earlier. With the steadily increasing complexity of ritual a well-established custom would hardly have been dropped without some trace of controversy surviving. During the great festivals the period in which the Temple courts were shut was reduced, but no extra services were held.

The greeting is probably addressed to those who had come to the Temple for duty the next day. They passed the night in the Temple precincts ready to commence even before dawn. They were expected to cut sleep to a minimum and to spend the rest of the time in devotional exercises. The greeting is really a call to the priest and Levites to do their duty faithfully, while the pilgrims faced their problems far away. The answer (3) was an assurance to them that the All-creator would bless them, wherever they might be.

Questions for further study and discussion on Psalms 123–134

1. The pilgrim collection is very rich in word pictures. Make a list of them and consider what modern equivalents could be suggested.
2. How do you explain the differing attitudes to prosperity in the Old and New Testaments?
3. Can you rewrite Psa. 127 in New Testament terms?
4. Make a comparison between Psa. 133 and John 17.20–26.
5. What are the main virtues inculcated by the pilgrim collection?
6. What do these psalms teach us about the role of patience in a Christian's life?

Psalm 135   The God of Creation and Election

There is a widespread opinion that this is a post-exilic psalm, but the sudden breaking in of the first person singular in v. 5 may suggest that it is the king who is speaking. The lack of reference to the royal house in vs. 19 and 20 would then be explained as a post-exilic deletion on grounds of prudence.

The reason for praise and the central theme of the psalm is God's choice of Israel (4) as His special 'possession'. This is the same word that is used in Exod. 19.5; it implies that Israel is altogether and solely at God's disposal. This is not a selfish reason for praise, for as we have seen earlier, e.g. Pss. 47,67,100, the election of Israel is for the good of the world. So far from Israel's God being a narrowly nationalistic one, as used to be so often alleged, the writer (5–14) stresses His control of all forces of nature everywhere for the good of all. This means that His destructions also are righteous judgements.

It follows that His carving out of a home for Israel (12) must have a wider purpose than merely the convenience of Israel. The most important part of this was the revelation of His name, Yahweh (Jehovah), which is His memorial, for it brings to mind all He is and does—the translation 'renown' (13, RSV) seems less suitable. Then in words quoted from Deut. 32.36 (14) he expresses his confidence that God's purposes with His people will be fulfilled.

Israel's God is not 'a God of the gaps', 'the God who always wins the last battle', the God who is appealing desperately for aid against the mighty. He is always presented as the Victor, who shows His righteousness by giving victory to His people. The psalmist looks round to see the enemies of his God and finds mere human handiwork (15–18, cf. Psa. 115.4–8). One of the great visions that runs through the Psalter is that Satan and his angels can work only through men, who are only flesh and blood, while the vaunted gods of the nations are nothingnesses, of no more power than the images by which they are represented. So all Israel is called on to bless, i.e. kneel trustingly and acceptingly before Yahweh (Jehovah) (19–21). Then through His people the blessing which is experienced in Zion will extend itself ever further outwards. Blessing for the world implies that the nations humbly accept God's giving, which involves a reversal of the original sin in Eden.

Psalm 136   His Steadfast Love Endures For Ever

This psalm is used in the Passover service after the completion of the *Hallel* (see Introduction to Book V and comment on Psa. 113). Judging by its contents, it may very well have been written for that purpose. By its very brevity the refrain, *ki le-olam hasdo*, is eminently suited to a family congregation. Down to the end of v. 18 the verses arrange themselves in threes; if we regard v. 26 as a closing verse, the same is true of vs. 23–25. The unevenness introduced by vs. 19–22 is probably designed to break the monotony of an unusually regular pattern.

The Passover service is marked by its loving attention to every detail of the deliverance from Egypt. But, as is the case in this psalm, it is done in an adequate framework. The Exodus, like Easter, is not just something that happened, but is the work of the one true God and Ruler (1–3). Nor can we separate God's work in creation (4–6) and His orderliness (7–9) from His work in salvation (10–12). True, salvation should have been unnecessary, but God created a universe which could find room for redemptive work.

The death of the first-born (10; Psa. 135.8) finds special mention,

116

for by its selectivity it rules out the possibility of pure chance. While it has been suggested that all the other plagues were intensifications of natural troubles that hit Egypt from time to time, the death of the first-born shows that the other calamities too had come at the direct command of God. It is clear that vs. 21 and 22 are a continuation of the thought of vs. 17 and 18. Sihon and Og are illustrations of the great and famous kings, who, however, included the kings of Canaan also. The word 'heritage' or inheritance (21,22; Psa. 135.12) is hardly a wise translation; it means one's possession, which in many cases may have come to one by inheritance. It is often used of an area conquered in war. Once again we find God's mercies to Israel (23,24) set within the context of His providential care to all (25). The Church has no right to clamour for anything that would mean loss and privation to others.

Psalm 137   By the Waters of Babylon

Assyria was one of the cruellest nations to which antiquity bears testimony, the chief evidence against them coming from their own records. Compared with them Babylonia, which together with Media destroyed the Assyrian empire, might seem relatively gentle. Yet there was a quality about her that made Habakkuk feel that she was too evil to act as God's executioner (Hab. 1.13), and in 2.6–17 he gives a series of short taunt-songs against her. We have the same feeling of repulsion in Isa. 14.4–21 and 47 and in parts of Jer. 50 and 51. Babylon had been from early days one of the greatest trading communities of the Fertile Crescent until the time came when its merchants cared little who ruled over them, provided they could continue to trade unhindered, It was not Babylon but the Chaldeans using it as a base and spring-board that destroyed Assyria.

If we may judge from *Ezekiel*, the Judean captives were officially treated with considerable liberality, and this seems confirmed by Jer. 29.4–7. The cruelty with which Zedekiah was handled (2 Kings 25.6,7) he brought on himself by breaking his solemn oath, and it was not typical. The clue to the bitter outburst of this psalm is given by 'the LORD's song' (4). To bid the broken-hearted make merry is cruel, but if in so doing he has to mock what he holds dearest and most sacred it is devilish. The Babylonians had become a people who judged a man's worth by the money he had or he could fetch. There was no sense of human dignity left for those in misfortune. They were prepared to discover the spot that would hurt him most and then twist a knife in the wound. The pursuit of money is one of the most dehumanizing influences in the world.

117

'Jerusalem' (5) was not necessarily the psalmist's home town, or the place of which he dreamt, but it was the place of Yahweh's (Jehovah's) Temple. He would rather have his tongue paralysed than with it mock his God and His abode (6). In his anguish he turned on two enemies (7,8); on Edom, who demanded the utter destruction of Jerusalem—recent archaeological discovery has shown how complete it was—and on Babylon, 'the devastator,' a reading supported by three of the old versions. They represented envy and soulless callousness. If anyone thinks this is Old Testament without meaning for him, let him ponder the triumph song of Rev. 19.1-5 over an even greater and more evil Babylon.

*Psalm 138   God Delivers and Will Deliver

There is no need to question the Davidic authorship of this psalm on the basis of v. 2. 'Thy holy temple', literally 'palace', could easily be a later adaptation of words suited for use before the Tent that housed the Ark in Jerusalem (but see note on Psa. 5.7). It is a psalm of thanksgiving in the sacred court, when the thank offering was brought for mercy shown elsewhere (3).

Weiser is probably correct in translating, 'I will sing Thy praise before God' (1c), i.e. in the sacred court. God has three main ways of answering prayer: He may intervene directly; He may give the one who prays added strength and ability; He may move others to do what is necessary. It is the second that is here being celebrated (3). Once again in vs. 4 and 5 we have the thought of Israel's worship influencing others. Here it is the king's bringing the kings of the earth to praise God. Our testimony to God's mercies and care is more likely to influence others than the mere proclamation of theology, however much this has its due place. It is not enough to be grateful for past mercies; one has to be prepared to trust God for the future as well (7,8).

*Psalm 139   The Electing Love of God

By any criterion this is one of the greatest psalms in the Psalter. Obviously it was not written for use in worship; it is too personal for that. It must be the product of David's old age, and in many ways it is a far higher psalm of praise than either 103 or 145, beautiful though they are. The fact that it was not written for public use probably explains its late position in the Psalter.

It begins with a confession of God's control and knowledge of his life. The language of v. 1 is not merely an affirmation of Divine omniscience, but implies also God's loving interest in His servant.

118

Rest and activity are alike to God (2), and thought is anticipated before it has become an actuality for David. 'From afar' must refer to the distance from David, not from God. Activity and rest are winnowed by God (3), i.e. it is not merely a knowledge of the facts but also their evaluation. In v. 4 the suggestion is that God knows David so well that He knows what he is going to say (RSV is correct as against AV[KJV]!). Nor does he confine himself to knowledge; David has experienced God's loving control, gently pressing him along the path of His choosing (5). All this experience awakens David's admiring wonder (6).

Could it have been otherwise? Is there anywhere where it would not have been true? David's answer is a decided No! (7–12). God rules in the skies—'heaven', v. 8—but also among the dead. If God is really present in Sheol, then it means that death has largely lost its sting. The picture in v. 9 is of his racing ahead of dawn at the speed of light ever westward to the wastes of ocean; but there, where chaos seems to rule, God is King. Finally, darkness is no shroud underneath which David could hide securely from the eye of God.

Far more important is that David's experience of God is no accident or the Divine response to his behaviour. In vs. 13–18 we have the clearest expression of personal election in the Old Testament. What David is, is the result of God's creating (13). Some such translation as that offered by RSV in v. 14 seems imperative; it is difficult to see how 'fearful', a word used almost only for God, could have been applied to David. We must use our poetic imagination in interpreting v. 15. His mother's womb was hidden secretly in the lowest part of her body. His choice of language was influenced also by the concept of 'Mother' Earth. In v. 16b his thoughts turn to the details of his life as foreseen by God. For reasons of poetic parallelism we must prefer Weiser's translation in v. 16a, 'Thy eyes beheld my days'. As David tries to sum up all in his life that he had to attribute to God, he pictures himself falling asleep and dreaming the night through of God's loving actions and yet not having exhausted them when he awoke (17,18).

The only answer David can find to all this is conformity with God's will (19–24). He desires a court conforming to God's will, but only God's acts of judgement can accomplish this (19). He regards God's enemies as he thinks God Himself must regard them. He knows, however, that he cannot trust himself, so he asks for a renewed investigation of his character, his thoughts and his life (23,24). It would have been better had RSV translated literally 'any way of grief'. David was not anticipating wicked acts, but he knew

119

that he might well grieve God. In the light of v. 8a it is probable that v. 24b contains a hope of continuing to walk with God after death.

Psalm 140 Wicked Men

We are back in the general atmosphere of Pss. 7,58,64, etc. It is a pity that the verse divisions hide the very even build-up of the material. There are six lines to each of the four sections (1–3; 4,5; 6–8; 9–11) with four in the epilogue (12,13). The absence of *Selah* after v. 11 and the change in metrical structure suggest that the epilogue was added for public worship.

The first two sections give us two different aspects, differentiated by the use of 'evil' (1) and 'wicked' (4), and held together by 'violent'. In the former we see the evil carried on mainly by words, in the latter by deeds. The only difference is normally one of opportunity. We should constantly bear this in mind, when we are tempted to sit in judgement on people. The thought life, which we cannot see, is normally the real clue to a man's acts, and only God has the knowledge to judge in that realm. Weiser's translation in v. 2b, 'and stir up quarrels continually', gives the psalmist's meaning. They were not of sufficient political stature to make wars.

The double description is followed by a double petition, vs. 6–8 dealing with vs. 4,5 and vs. 9–11 with vs. 1–3. In its setting 'Thou art my God' (6) means 'Thou art my Strong One'. Quite consistently Weiser translates, 'Thou hast protected my head in the day of strife' (7b). We must translate v. 9a, 'If those who surround me lift up their head'. David realizes that there is little that can be done, so long as evil is kept buried in the thoughts. So he prays that when those that think evil start doing evil ('lift up their heads'), God should act at once. For the 'burning coals' (10), cf. Psa. 120.4; the 'pits' are to be linked with v. 5. He looks on evil as a wild animal let loose by the wicked, but he knows that God is so perfectly in control that they may find the wild beast stalking them instead of the victim it was intended to catch (11).

The worshipper then bears his testimony to the loyalty of God to all who suffer from the evil of men. There may be an interval before the trial, but the verdict is certain. The psalm has stressed the crookedness of evil men and their methods, but when God's verdict is given, His own people will be seen to be upright.

Psalm 141   Alone among the Wicked

This psalm dates probably from the time when David was in the wilderness, or more likely in the Philistine land, for he is not able to attend the sacrificial worship of his people. The Old Testament knows a great deal of prayer in an emergency, but normally it was an accompaniment of the regular services in which sacrifice was the centre, and David misses the latter. It is a lopside Christianity which knows only private or only public prayer.

In Gath David realized how easily casual and unpremeditated words could be used to cast score on his God (3). In a generalized interpretation of the psalm 'dainties' (4) can naturally be explained as those extra luxuries that can be bought as a result of evil living. When we apply it to David, it probably refers to invitations to heathen meals and to food offered to idols that would be on the tables. It is not surprising that David took the first opportunity to ask for permission to leave Gath (1 Sam. 27.5). We often contrast our Lord's freedom in eating with notorious sinners with our fear of contact with the world. At least the sinners were Israelites, while David is concerned with raw heathen.

The Hebrew is very difficult in vs. 5-7, and Weiser does not even offer a translation of vs. 5c-7. In v. 5 Kirkpatrick's rendering is more attractive than that of the RSV,

'Let the righteous smite me, it shall be kindness:
And let him reprove me, it shall be as oil for the head;
Let not my head refuse it:
But still let my prayer be against their evil doings.'

The last line, however, does not seem to make sense in this setting. The RSV of vs. 6 and 7 contains so much emendation that one cannot really claim the good sense it makes as Scripture; the literal meaning of the Hebrew is given fairly closely by the AV(KJV).

From the final section (8-10) we may reasonably conclude that there were many in Gath who cherished deep grudges against David and his men for husbands and sons killed in earlier fighting, and that they were trying to find sons way to wreak their vengeance on them. When he had to walk a path that was heavily mined, to use a modern picture, David's one safety was to look to God, who would guide his feet aright.

Questions for further study and discussion on Psalms 135-141

1. Has Psa. 139 helped you towards a better understanding of your own election ?
2. Try writing a Christian version of Psa. 136.

121

3. Do you ever find money threatening to dehumanize you? Do you ever think of people in terms of cash value rather than God value?
4. To what do you ascribe our frequent hesitation to speak of what God has done for us, materially as well as spiritually? In what ways could the local church be encouraged to overcome it?
5. Why do we tend to be so unwilling to receive the smiting of the righteous?
6. Why is it that many who call themselves Christians do not mind if they are separated from public worship?

Psalm 142 Forsaken by Men

This is a simple little psalm of regular structure. As printed by the RSV its consists of four sections of five lines each, except for the third, which is one line short. It is possible that it dropped out through a scribal error. There seems to be no justification for the AV(KJV), which transfers the psalm into the past. The choice lies between the present (RV, RSV) and the future (Kirkpatrick). We may ascribe the psalm to those days of extreme desolation between David's first hiding in the cave of Adullam, after the fiasco of his first visit to Gath, and his being joined by a band of about four hundred (1 Sam. 22.1,2).

To cry with one's voice is to cry aloud (1). Even today in moments of extreme stress many of us feel the need to pray aloud. Nothing less can really relieve the inner tension. The traditional translation 'complaint' (2) is misleading, for it might suggest that David was complaining. It means no more than the matter that was filling his heart. 'Spirit' (3) is often used for the dominant influence in a person at a given time. After all his efforts to keep the peace with Saul, David's hopes and plans had suddenly collapsed, but God knew the path he would now have to follow. In v. 4 the RSV margin is probably correct. The force of the verse will become clearer if we remember 1 Sam. 18.5,7,16,30. The love and admiration of the people proved to be of very little worth in the moment of crisis, just as with our Lord.

The RSV is almost certainly wrong in v. 5. Translate, 'I cried . . . I said'. David is saying that he had prayed like this all along. Now in the time of his deepest need it was for God to help him (6). Unless we deny the Davidic authorship, we must take 'prison' (7) metaphorically; yet it was not entirely metaphorical. David doubtless had his vantage-points from which he could see the countryside, and he will have seen many a band of Saul's soldiers looking for him.

122

He could no longer move about freely. It seems almost as though David had a prophetic glimpse of what was to be, with those who had recognized God's ordering, the righteous (7), coming streaming to him. There is an interesting roll of honour in 1 Chron. 12.1–22 of men who joined him in increasing numbers, until it became clear, even before Saul's death, that he must become king.

Psalm 143   'Enter not into Judgement with Thy Servant'

This is the last of the seven penitential psalms; see comment on Psa. 6. God's 'faithfulness' is the unshakeableness and immutability of His character; His 'righteousness' His conformity to His self-revelation. How little there need be of the legal in God's righteousness is shown by the prayer that he should not be put on trial. The RSV is correct with 'is righteous' (2). The relationship of God to men is sometimes presented as though there were an abstract principle of justice which is higher than God and ties His hands. David knew that anyone wishing to deal with God on the ground of man's conformity to God's demands must inevitably be condemned, but for the one who came humbly, under the shelter of the cross that was to be, there was acceptance.

So great was the affliction the psalmist was passing through, he felt he must already be under the condemnation of God (3,4). There is no possibility of fixing the situation with greater clarity. The metaphorical picture is of a man in a dark dungeon with no possibility of emerging alive. Yet, as David thought of the past, probably Israel's rather than his own, he realized there was still hope for him (5,6). It seems clear enough from v. 6 that his trouble was mental and spiritual rather than physical. He longed for the morning of restored communion with God (8). There are two small changes in the RSV, probably both correct, in vs. 9 (indicated in the margin) and 10, where 'path' differs from 'land' (so AV [KJV]) by one letter.

'A level path': only one who has crossed rough moorland in the dark can fully realize the relief of reaching the metalled road. The fear of boghole and ditch, of sprained ankle and quagmire, are at last past. 'Cut off my enemies' (12): some of the psalmists write as pure individuals, but David, except where he is confessing his sins, is always the representative of the righteous among his people. If I wrong the individual Christian, God has many ways of removing him from the scope of my malice. When I seek to harm the people of God, it is bound to end sooner or later in my elimination (cf. Psa. 125.3). 'For I am Thy servant': David knew that the one who was fighting him was really fighting against God.

123

Psalm 144 King and People before God

With the exception of vs. 12–15a (but see below), the material of this psalm is also found elsewhere in the Psalter. It is likely, therefore, that as in the case of Psa. 86 (see comments) it is a compilation of Davidic material, and so fairly to be attributed to him. In that case we would translate in v. 10, 'Who didst rescue David Thy servant', which seems more probable, though it is an adaptation in any case of Psa. 18.50.

Basically the psalm belongs to the royal ritual. The king approaches God in gratitude for victories gained, with words derived mainly from his great ancestor (vs. 1,2 represent Psa. 18.2,34,39). This is followed by a confession of personal unworthiness based on Pss. 8.4; 39.5,6. This confession is spiritually necessary as a preparation for the prayer for Divine intervention (5–8). This is based on Pss. 18.9; 104.32; 2 Sam. 22.15; Psa. 18.16,48, where, however, we have description not prayer. We have the right to ask for very great things, but to do so is very dangerous, unless there is due humility first, as in vs. 3,4, so as to make right use of them. The promise of praise (9,10) is based on Pss. 33.2,3; 18.50.

The abruptness of vs. 12–15, having no visible connexion with what precedes, is to be explained by their being the response of the congregation to the king's trusting approach to God. This does not reduce the probability, urged by most modern commentators, that these verses too are based on earlier material, which, however, has not come down to us in its original form. Obviously, however, this theory does not affect the interpretation. 'Full grown' (12) is less likely than 'well grown'. It is not a prayer for precocious maturity, but for the attainment of a growth, where the accidents, etc., of childhood are no longer a threat. The exact meaning of 'corner pillars' is not clear. The frequently met suggestion that it is a reference to the Caryatides of Greek architecture is vitiated by archaeology's not having found any trace of such figures in Syria and Palestine. So the psalm is a happy combination of trust between ruler and ruled in the God who rules them both.

Psalm 145 David's Hymn of Praise

The Psalter ends with a group of six hymns of praise. Psa. 145 is an acrostic psalm. That it has only 21 verses is explained by one verse having fallen out in the Hebrew except in one manuscript; the missing verse is also found in the Septuagint and the Syriac. The RSV supplies it as the second half of v. 13. In spite of Kirkpatrick's reservation, there can be no reasonable doubt that the RSV is correct.

It is an instructive study to compare this psalm with Psa. **103**. As pointed out in the comments on it, Psa. **103** is essentially a personal thanksgiving, however much it generalizes David's experiences. Here in Psa. **145** David looks right away from himself to God. This is probably the reason for the acrostic; how else was he to keep himself within measure when dealing with such a boundless subject? The effect of it, however, as we have seen in other acrostic psalms, is to inhibit any clear development and order of thought.

The RSV has missed the meaning badly in v. 1. The Hebrew is '. . . my God, the King', i.e. 'Thou art the King' (Weiser), not merely David's, but the universal Ruler. God's revealed character, 'Thy name', calls for humble adoration ('bless') and public recognition ('praise'). The Septuagint rendering of v. 5a is preferable, 'They will speak of the glorious splendour of Thy majesty'. In v. 7 translate, 'They shall pour forth, like an ever-flowing river. . .'

In v. 8 we have a reproduction of Exod. **34.6**, cf. Pss. **86.15**; **103.8**. This is one of the great key-verses of the Old Testament and must never be forgotten as we form our conceptions of its theology. God's goodness (see note on Psa. **100**), as the parallelism in v. 9 shows, extends to all He has created. 'Thy saints' (10): 'Thy loyal ones', see note on Psa. **30.4**. 'Kingdom' (11) is parallel to 'power' and means sovereignty or royal rule; so also in vs. 12 and 13. In v. 13 'dominion' is similarly equivalent to 'rule'. We should compare vs. 15 and 16 with Psa. **104.27,28**.

The parallelism in v. 20 should make us think. The preservation of God's loving people is mainly by His presence. Though there are ample cases of the destruction of the wicked by God's direct action, normally His absence is in itself a sentence of destruction. The wicked reap what they have desired—absence from God!

Psalm 146 The One Foundation of Society

The last five psalms all begin and end with Hallelujah. They describe different aspects of the call to praise. Here God is celebrated as the one true foundation for human society, the only one who can ensure help and justice. The resemblance of vs. 1 and 2 to Psa. **104.1,33** is not fortuitous, for the psalm goes back to the fundamental relationship of God with man, even though they are enjoyed only by those in covenant with Him.

'Put not your trust in princes' (3) has become so familiar a rendering that one hesitates to point out that the meaning of words changes over the centuries. The word means a nobleman of any kind to whom men look up for reasons good or bad, but who is only a

125

common man ('son of man'), and as such is doomed to die like any other. The validity and power of the Covenant depend on the fact that Yahweh (Jehovah), the God of Jacob (5), is the Creator and Sustainer of all that is. If the great ones of this world cannot put through their plans, it follows that they are equally unable to ensure that their injustice (7) will succeed. The hungry in the Old Testament are likely to be those who have been unjustly robbed of their land. There is no reason why 'the blind' (8) should not be understood of the physically or spiritually blind. In the parallelism, however, it is likely to refer to the 'prisoners' (7), who have sat so long in the dark of the dungeon, that they scarce know whether their eyes can still function.

It is a striking commentary on Old Testament society that we increasingly find the poor, the humble, the bowed down and the righteous identified. It was this, even more than political causes, that created the intense longing for the coming of the Messiah in the time of Christ. Today, as social legislation and taxation have created some semblance of equality at home, it is the international disparity between nations that is filling men with a despair that only the Second Coming can dissipate.

In the Old Testament the alien ('sojourner'), the widow without influential relations and her orphan children, were the most helpless members of society (9). The Law of Moses stressed that they were peculiarly under God's care, cf. Exod. 22.21–24; 23.9; Lev. 19.33,34; Deut. 10.18,19; 24.17,18. These principles last as long as the Lord's reign, i.e. for ever.

Psalm 147 The Power and Care of God

Here the call is to praise God for His universal power and providential care for all.

We should seek a better balance in v. 1. Either render, 'Sing praises to our God, for He is good; for He is gracious . . .', or 'Sing praises . . . for it is good; for it is pleasant . . .'. The latter seems to be preferable. In vs. 2–4 we pass from the particular, through the general, to the universal; from Israel to the broken-hearted generally, and so to the control of the heavens. It is just because God's power is seen at every level that we can trust Him for our particular problem, be it great or small. The same principle is at work in vs. 5 and 6. To lift up the downtrodden and to cast down the wicked are an ideal. When the idealistic dictator attempts it, he meets so many complications that he soon wishes he had not meddled with such

126

matters. God has both the power and the understanding to do what man cannot accomplish.

Man's true position is to accept God's all-powerful wisdom (to fear Him) and to trust His loving purposes (to hope in His steadfast love). In so doing (11) he fits into God's providential care as the climax of His creation (8–11). While God's power is seen everywhere in nature (15–18)—since man, beast and plants in Palestine have seldom to face the rigours of icy cold, they feel it the more when it comes—its providential nature is realized only in Jerusalem (12), because only to Israel (19) has He given a full revelation of Himself. There is an over-readiness on the part of some to interpret everything as one of the signs of the times and to make rash prophecies about future events, yet Christians should be more ready than they normally are to declare the evidence of God's hand in things that happen. We should desire that prophetic vision which can from the march of history declare to men that God is on His throne and is ordering the affairs of men to glorify Himself. Above all, it is remarkable how often the self-confidence of man is dashed to the ground by natural factors beyond his control, but which are God's obedient servants.

Psalm 148   The Worship of Nature

We have here a glorious call to all nature to unite in praising God. The *Benedicite*, used in the Anglican Prayer Book as an alternative to the *Te Deum* in the regular Morning Service, is an expansion of this psalm taken from an apocryphal section of *Esther*. How many of those who enjoy singing it take it seriously?

The psalm proclaims the unity of all creation with man as its summit and purpose. It is one of the greatest tragedies of today that man having made himself autonomous, free of dependence on God as he thinks, has separated himself from Nature, and the more he knows, the greater the curse he can become to the Nature he was intended to rule. The psalm also proclaims that Nature as a whole has its lasting purpose. This song of praise is taken up again in Rev. 5.13, when the God-man takes the scroll of the future into His hand. There too in John's vision the four living creatures, the cherubim, the representatives of Nature, are next to the throne. In Rom. 8.19–22 we do not hear a song of praise, but a groan of long waiting which is yet to be satisfied. Any system of theology that does not find a place for this is deficient, however true it may otherwise be. It is a Christian task and duty to treat whatever part of the world God may place us in as part of God's creation to which we owe a duty.

127

The order of the psalm is a logical one. It commences with the heavens, both the higher and the lower, the abode of the angels and of the clouds alike (1–6). The RSV rendering in v. 6 seems indefensible. It has been influenced by passages like Psa. 104.9, which, however, speak of the lower, not the upper waters, i.e. of the seas. Weiser seems correct with 'a statute He ordained, which they do not transgress'. It refers to those laws of God's creating, which because of their certainty have made it possible for man to extend his knowledge into the depths of space. In vs. 7–10 we pass over to this world. Finally man himself is to join in (11,12). At the moment it may be heard only from His loyal ones in Israel or in the Church (see comment on Psa. 30.4), but as they truly sing His praises, the song will spread throughout the world.

*Psalm 149   A Song for God's Loyal Warriors

Here is a song for Israel to sing. It is in reality a song for the day when Israel is truly loyal to its God—for the rendering 'faithful' (5) or 'loyal ones' see comment on Psa. 30.4. It is a new song (cf. Pss. 33.3; 96.1; Rev. 14.3) because God is never static in His dealings with men. The two foci of revelation are the Exodus and the Cross, the Old Covenant and the New, but 'there is always fresh light to break forth from His Word', and fresh signs of the approaching triumphal day, when 'in the name of Jesus every knee shall bow'.

The order in v. 2 is carefully chosen. Jacob was made Israel by the action of God, even as the sons of Jacob were made Israel by God's hand at the Exodus. Zion then became the visible site of God's rule, even as the Church is the body of Christ, the colony of Heaven, where God's will is carried out. As was remarked on Psa. 87, in the present evil age it may not generally be advantageous to use the dance in Divine worship, but that is a testimony to the evil heart and ways of man and not to the wrongfulness of dancing. Puritanism has always been over-ready to abandon to Satan and the world that which rightly belongs to God.

It is a tremendous pity that the Jewish Zealot and the Church, reformed and unreformed, have been all too ready to interpret the two-edged sword (6) literally. Both in the Old and New Covenants those who took the sword perished by the sword. There was more excuse for the Zealot than for the zealous Christian, for the latter should have known that the two-edged sword is the Word (Heb. 4.12,13). What is more, we are apt to be so taken up with the low condition of the Church that we fail to realize the victories that Christ has won through it. We are so besotted by our own visions

128

of what should be that we fail to recognize God's working out of His will. Above all, we are so shocked (why?) when we hear of the furnace-breath of persecution playing on the Church in other lands, that we do not recognize the pure gold manifested where we thought there had been only dross. We also fail to realize that except under openly anti-God régimes, those now in authority feel themselves compelled to find excuses for doing what was virtually taken. for granted only a few centuries ago.

*Psalm 150   Hallelujah!

We have now four months' study of the Psalter behind us. What effect has it had on us and with what feelings do we finish? Virtually every hymn-book, apart from those arranged in alphabetical order, begins with hymns of praise and adoration. The Psalter, however, in its earlier parts is concerned mainly with the joys and sorrows of men, whether they are private individuals or in special relationship to God as His representatives among men. With few exceptions the note of unbroken praise comes to life later, not because it was written later, but because true praise is not abstract but issues from experience. If we have entered into the experiences of the psalmists, we should be in a position and mood to join whole-heartedly in the praise that closes the Psalter.

The final praise, which is also the closing benediction of Book V and of the Psalter, is a glorious climax of noise. Every instrument of the time is brought in to accompany the voices of those that sing, while the dance is there to express the emotions of those who cannot express them otherwise. The Temple courts must have witnessed scenes that would have shocked our staid Christianity.

There is no suggestion that it was a case of everyone for himself; it was everyone for the community and for God. It was not the din of a mob of individuals, but the harmony of individuals losing their inhibitions in the enthusiasm of the community. In fact, to use the language of the New Testament, it was every member contributing to the joy of the body. It is true as Francis Pott sang, 'Craftsman's art and music's measure for Thy pleasure all combine'. Beauty and dignity have their due place in Christian worship, but it becomes true worship only when every inhibition, not every discipline, disappears, and the Holy Spirit becomes Master of heart, mind, body and voice. So long as cultures and temperaments persist, no perfect form of worship will be found down here to embrace all God's children. It behoves us, however, to see that there are no limitations set on the Church's worship purely on the grounds of custom or decorum. In fact, were the worshipping community fully aware that Christ Jesus was standing in its midst, most of its problems and controversies would vanish like the mists.

Praise the Lord, O my soul; Amen and Amen!

Questions for further study and discussion on Psalms 142–150

1. Have the last six psalms of the psalter taught you anything about praise and worship? Have they suggested any ways in which the worship of your own community might perhaps be improved?
2. Can you write a Christian version of Psa. 145?
3. Can you think of cases where the Christian's turning to the sword, including the use of political power and pressure, has harmed the Church?
4. How are humility and boldness linked in prayer?
5. Find various passages where David speaks of deliverance from men's attacks. What is the common feature in them?
6. Summarize what you have learnt from your study of the Psalter.

Introduction to the Wisdom Books

From a very early period in Israel's history, there is evidence for a class of 'the wise'. Interestingly enough, the first references suggest that women occupied a large place in this group. Note, for instance, the 'wise woman' of Tekoa and her counterpart at Abel of Beth—maacah (2 Sam. **14.**2; **20.**15,22). Possibly, we may include such professional court-counsellors as Ahithophel and Hushai (2 Sam. **15.**12,32ff.; **16.**15–23). The 'riddle' of Samson (Judg. **14.**12–18) and Jotham's fable (Judg. **9.**8–15) are excellent examples of the techniques of 'the wise' in the ancient world. Solomon's right to a place amongst 'the wise' is undisputed (e.g. 1 Kings **4.**29ff.). Gradually, however, 'the wise' became a group associated specifically with the religious life of Israel, forming a third group alongside the priests and the prophets (e.g. Isa. **29.**14; Jer. **8.**8f.; **18.**18). Their main function was to provide a guide to everyday life and an answer to the life's problems, with the background of the Law.

It is this fact which distinguishes the Wisdom movement in Israel from similar groups in other ancient near-eastern countries. It has been of great value to study the biblical wisdom literature in comparison with other contemporary wisdom literature, but two points emerge from this investigation: firstly, Israelite wisdom literature is generally far superior to that of any other nation; secondly, in Israel there is an unmistakable religious foundation which can be no other than the Law, and which leads to a fundamental contrast between 'the righteous' and 'the ungodly', and not simply to one between 'the wise' and 'the fool'.

Two main types of wisdom literature may be distinguished:

1. The Proverbial. Each nation develops its own stock of proverbs which forms a kind of practical, everyday philosophy. The individual proverb observes connections or differences between things, and points lessons from these observations. The unit is usually the individual verse, although several proverbs with a similar theme may be grouped together. This means that any chapter in the book of Proverbs may deal with many aspects of life, whilst the whole book provides an adequate guide for the entire, everyday life. The religious life based on the Law is assumed and so the proverbs tend to be mainly ethical. The character which results from this instruction, being highly scrupulous, hard-working, prudent and neighbourly, is admirable. But there is a danger in an approach which concentrates attention on particular situations. Once the underlying assumption of a living faith and a covenantal relationship with God has been lost, this kind of approach could

131

lead to casuistry, with the aim of getting the most out of life in materialistic terms. The scribes of our Lord's generation are an example of this tendency, and the modern stress on 'situation ethics' does not escape it either.

2. That which deals with one major problem, or a series of interrelated problems. Here there is no set form; Ecclesiastes, for instance, uses a monologue approach which incorporates many proverbs whilst the book of Job is in dialogue form. One is virtually a lecture, whilst the other has the background of historical fact, living characters and complex, often diametrically opposed, emotions. In both books, however, there is a concentration on particular problems: Ecclesiastes deals with the apparent futility of life; Job, starting with the problem of the suffering of a righteous man, necessarily involves the question of justifying the ways of God with man, and also the possibility of man having a genuine, unbought religious faith.

The most influential, if not the most significant, phase of the wisdom movement was undoubtedly the post-exilic period, When the Law was firmly established, the prophetic voice increasingly lost its flaming passion and scribism became dominant. Ecclesiastes well illustrates the emptiness of this movement, with suggestions of spiritual bankruptcy and a lack of positive, passionate commitment to God, such as is found in the prophets. Yet this very emptiness pointed the way forward to the Saviour, One who could fill this spiritual vacuum and enable, as well as inspire, men to venture all for God.

Proverbs

INTRODUCTION

It is natural for man to crystallize his experience of life in short pithy sayings such as proverbs, and this form of literature has a history going back well beyond Solomon, that great collector and originator of proverbs (1 Kings 4.32). The book of *Proverbs* has an undoubted Solomonic foundation but it includes other material, notably 'the sayings of the wise' (24.23), a further selection of Solomonic proverbs incorporated by Hezekiah's scribes (715–687 B.C.) and contributions by Agur (30.1) and Lemuel (31.1). In its final form, therefore, it probably dates from the late seventh century B.C. The class of 'the wise' was an important one in Israel, to be set alongside the priests and prophets (Jer. 18.18). Taken by itself *Proverbs* may appear to be primarily concerned with material well-being, an early edition of 'How to win friends and influence people'. This is a false estimate for, as will appear, there is a spiritual 'backbone' in the book, moreover, it arose in a society where the Law was already accepted. In conjunction with the other books of the O.T. it provides a first-rate guide in the details of the daily life, with a stress upon character and behaviour which could not be presented so vividly in a formal set of rules. As the essence of a proverb is its simplicity and self-evident truth, an endeavour will be made to keep the comments in the same key. Moreover, since similar proverbs occur again and again, no attempt will be made to comment upon every proverb in any one section.

Proverbs 1.1-7

Prologue. Vs. 1–6 form one extended sentence in the Hebrew. It is a masterpiece of compressed thought and precision in language. The writer has not merely multiplied words, each has a nuance of its own, yet together they give an impression of the kind of teaching which is to follow. '*Wisdom*' (2) is the key word in *Proverbs*. It occurs thirty-seven times and indicates the skilful use of knowledge. '*Instruction*' (2) is closely associated with the discipline of spiritual education as in 3.11; 13.24. '*Insight*' (2) is the quality of discernment, the essential foundation of wise choice. '*Wise dealing*' (3) is the practical application of experience gained by personal experience or observation. It is used to describe Abigail, who saved the dangerous situation created by her churlish husband (1 Sam. **25.**3). *'Righteousness'* (3) is the first of three ethical qualities insisted on strongly by the prophets (e.g. Isa. **5.**7). It connects closely with conduct and is equivalent to 'good behaviour'. *'Justice'* (3), like insight (above), connects with the ability to choose, but has a more active sense, indicating the power to make, rather than to form, decisions. *'Equity'* (3) is a quality of character akin to moral uprightness. *'Prudence'* (4) derives from a root meaning craftiness and is applied to the serpent in the creation narrative (Gen. **3.**1). Here, however, it signifies the gift of being able to detect guile in others, in the sense of being 'wise as serpents and innocent as doves' (Matt. **10.**16). *'Knowledge'* (4) involves not just the amassing of facts but an acquiring of truth. *'Discretion'* (4) is the power to order one's life to the best advantage. It could be prostituted to selfish ends (cf. **12.**2), but used rightly, it leads to the kind of life which glorifies God. *'Learning'* (5) reminds us that true wisdom in life is something which we receive humbly, as pupils.

The *Septuagint* translation of the latter part of v. 5, 'that the man of understanding may gain a helmsman', is instructive. How we need a helmsman to guide us across uncharted seas, with rocks, shoals and quicksands in abundance!

Theme (7). This eleven-fold category of qualities might well prove daunting. The wise man, therefore, adds this foundational element, upon which all the other qualities rest. Fear is not a slavish terror which cringes, but a reverential awe, based on the fitness of things. God is God, sovereign, eternal and holy, and we are finite and sinful. But through His self-revelation in Christ, we may know Him, and believing and receiving His Son (John **1.**12), we gain ourselves a Helmsman.

Proverbs 1.8-33

Many of us recall, with gratitude, the advice given us by our parents in our formative years. Often it is the general impression, rather than the actual words, which remain in our memories. Sometimes, too, we are mindful of the pitfalls which we could have avoided had we taken their advice! Age, with its opportunities for increasing experience and knowledge of life in all its facets, is to be respected, and happy is the young person who has access to a helpful and kindly counsellor! Our reading today introduces the first of thirteen lessons on wise living, each one of which begins with, 'Hear, my son . . .' or something similar (**1.**8, cf. **2.**1; **3.**1,11,21; **4.**1,10,20; **5.**1; **6.**1,20; **7.**1, 24). The writer is inviting us, as disciples, into the

134

intimacy of the family circle, to sit beside him and receive the treasure of his ripe experience, a privilege which we should not regard lightly. Yet there is a sense in which our opportunity is even greater, for the whole Bible is the Word of God our Father who caused men to record these words (2 Pet. 1.21), and who speaks to us as we read them.

Watch the company you keep is the advice of vs. 8–19. Many a young person has been led astray by bad companions. Friends, like the books we read, have either an uplifting or a degrading effect; choose both carefully. The love of easy gain (13) is so strong a motive to lawless men that they are prepared to go to violent lengths to secure it (11 f.). But to be fore-warned is to be fore-armed (17). A clean break with such men is the only safe way (15).

The appeal of Wisdom (20–33) contrasts with the evil suggestion of violent men (11–14). Her voice reaches men in the open places of life, not in the recesses of some dark alley. In similar fashion the prophets proclaimed their oracles but the response from an insensitive nation was much the same; both the gentle appeal of Wisdom and the forthright 'Thus saith the Lord' of the prophets fell upon deaf ears and stony hearts. In both cases, the offer of mercy would be withdrawn and judgement would fall (24–32). If only men would learn that the way to true security lies in responding to God's voice (33)!

A Suggestion: In the light of the first paragraph, read Psa. 119.9, 97–105 (and the rest of the psalm if you have time!).

Proverbs 2

The quest for Wisdom (1–5). Notice carefully the verbs in this section, most of which are concerned with describing the desire and endeavour of the soul to gain its objects. There must be both the 'hunger and thirst for righteousness' of which our Lord spoke (Matt. 5.6) and the passionate quest of the psalmist—'As a hart longs for flowing streams, so longs my soul for Thee, O God' (Psa. 42.1). V. 4 refers more to the preciousness of the objects sought than to the arduous nature of the search, although both are necessarily involved.

The giver of Wisdom (6–8). In spite of the earnest striving of vs. 1–5 the paradox is that it is not we who ultimately gain wisdom. God graciously gives it to us. But human aspiration and divine bountifulness coincide, for God does not impart His gifts to those who treat them lightly. Only if we seek them diligently (4) will He give them (6). It is the same with the salvation which the N.T. reveals;

from the human point of view man repents (Acts 2.38; 3.19), opens his heart (Acts 16.14) and believes (Acts 16.31). Yet ultimately salvation is God's gift, not the result of man's striving (Eph. 2.8 f.).

The reward of Wisdom (9–22). The writer is at pains to make it clear that the quest for true wisdom pays rich dividends in both the material and spiritual realms. Two positive aspects are stressed: (i) There will be the understanding of the will of the Lord, bringing deep satisfaction (9 f.). (ii) The resultant life will be one of integrity and usefulness (20 f.). Between these sections we discover two negative aspects: (i) There will be deliverance from evil men (11–15, cf. 1.10–15), whose twisted characters are revealed in their distorted ways (notice the synonyms for 'crookedness' in this brief section). (ii) There will also be deliverance from the immoral woman (16–19), who is unmindful both of her husband ('the companion of her youth') and her God (17). The sacredness of the marriage bond in ancient Israel, reflected in the seventh commandment (Exod. 20.14), made the adulterer or adulteress a moral leper, excluded from the covenant. Vs. 18 f. vividly portray the permanent effect of such passing pleasures. Remember that the life of the godly still has its positive and negative aspects. There are things we cannot do (cf. Dan, 1.8,) but there are things which we must do (cf. Dan. 6.10).

Note: 'Saints' (8) is a word which implies loyalty and love in the covenant relationship with God.

Proverbs 3

Man's relationship to God is the subject of vs. 1–12. Notice:

(i) The inwardness of true religion (1–4). Obedience and loyalty to God must spring from the heart (3). In this realization the wise man shares with the prophet (Jer. 31.33; Ezek. 36.26 f.), the psalmist (Psa. 119.11), and the priest-scribe Ezra (Ezra 7.10). Observe our Lord's summary of the essence of true religion in Matt. 22.37–40.

(ii) Trust in the Lord (5–8). All of us desire our paths to be made straight (6), a verb which is used in Isa. 40.3 (cf. Matt. 3.3) and involves the removal of all obstructions. It conjures up a picture of a squad of labourers, under expert supervision, preparing the route for the royal progress of a great king. But the Lord cannot do this for us until we forsake our own insights and inclinations, and trust Him absolutely.

(iii) Honour the Lord (9 f). The O.T. teaches the wise general rule that if a man honours God, God, who holds in His hands the forces of nature, will honour him (1 Sam. 2.30, cf. Deut. 28). For the Jew there was always the temptation to misinterpret this rule, i.e.

to make it an automatic formula, 'If I am righteous, then I will prosper. I *want* to be prosperous, therefore I will be righteous'. The fundamental loyalty of vs. 1–4 operates here, however. We must love God for Himself, not for any reward we hope to gain, and our loyal obedience must be the reflection of this love in the details of the daily life.

(*iv*) Submit to the Lord (11 f.). As we will see, *Proverbs* has a great deal to say about chastisement in the father-son relationship, and, by analogy, the God-man relationship, a theme which is taken up in the N.T. (Heb. 12.5–11). Since God is all-wise and motivated by love, we can accept His correction with meekness, knowing that its end will be 'the peaceful fruit of righteousness' (Heb. 12.11).

In praise of Wisdom (13–20). There is a close relationship between the delineation of wisdom here and the N.T. teaching concerning Christ, indeed, as a devotional exercise we could substitute the name of our Lord (or the appropriate pronoun) for wisdom in this section. The N.T. teaches that Christ was the active agent in creation (John 1.3), the O.T. gives that honour to wisdom (19, cf. Job 28.20–28).

Wise rules for living (21–35). Here we meet more of the practical advice which abounds in *Proverbs*. Notice, however, the dependence upon the Lord, and the security this gives (23,26).

Proverbs 4

The father-son relationship is taken back a further generation (3). The writer of this series of lessons, a man deeply concerned for his son's welfare, testifies to the instruction which he himself received from his own father, the value of which he has proved in the intervening years. Happy is that family whose successive generations are knit together in the love of the Lord and in a desire to do His will (cf. 2 Tim. 1.5, where the example came through the mother and grandmother).

There is an emphasis upon perseverance in this chapter. The father was aware that a good brisk beginning is a good thing, but it needs to be followed by a steadfast continuance. This involves the will, and its qualities of patience and persistence. Notice such expressions as 'Do not forget, and do not turn away' (5), 'Do not forsake her' (6), 'Keep hold of instruction, Do not let go, guard her' (13). It has been said that we never graduate in the school of life, at least, not this side of death. The great prophet Isaiah regarded himself as one of God's pupils (Isa. 50.4), a confession matched by the greatest of all apostles (Phil. 3.12–16).

137

The way of the wicked is observed in vs. 14–17,19 and is summed up in the words 'deep darkness'. What a contrast is the path of the godly (18)! From the first glimmer of dawn there is a gradually increasing radiance, until the whole world is bathed in the light of the noon-day sun. Such a man, in Rupert Brooke's words, leaves behind him

'. . . a white
Unbroken glory, a gathered radiance,
A width, a shining peace, under the night.'

The apostle John works out the same contrast between the children of light and the dwellers in darkness (John 3.19 ff.; cf. John 8.12; 1 Thess. 5.4–8).

The various aspects of the righteous life are enumerated in vs. 20–27. It involves our hearing (20); our memories (21a); our hearts—the centre of our affections (21b, 23), rightly diagnosed as the mainspring of life (cf. our Lord's development of this passage in Mark 7. 14–23); our speech (24); our sight (25) and our wills (26 f.). Vs. 25 ff. supplement the teaching on perseverance noted above and have a ring similar to Paul's example of dedicated, Christ-directed effort (Phil. 3.7–14) and the picture of the Christian's marathon in Heb. 12.1 f.

A Thought: A race is run one step at a time. The Christian's race is run moment by moment. Let us make sure that, this day, as dedicated runners, we 'press toward the goal for the prize of the upward call of God in Christ Jesus.'

Proverbs 5—6.5

The frequency with which teaching occurs on the subject of the immoral woman shows how prevalent was the sin of sexual impurity in ancient Israel. In theory, harlotry was punishable by death (Deut. 22.20 f.) but it is clear that this extreme penalty was not enacted at this particular time. It is perhaps unnecessary to observe that, while it is the female seducer who is prominent in *Proverbs*, the male who pursues parallel practices as are here outlined (5.3–6) is guilty of an equally reprehensible crime. Wise advice is given to all who are confronted with this kind of temptation—keep as far away as possible (5.8). No shame attaches to a Joseph who puts the greatest possible distance, in the shortest possible time, between himself and the temptress (Gen. 39.12). Paul counselled his son in the faith, Timothy, to 'shun youthful passions' (2 Tim. 2.22), and his general advice to 'abstain from every form of evil' (1 Thess. 5.22) has its application here.

In blunt language the wise man gives the reasons for his counsel (5.9–14). The promiscuity which he condemns can end only in the waste and misuse of our resources, in conscience-smitten recrimination, and in social alienation. Sensible men and women will count the ghastly toll exacted by such transient 'pleasures' which leave the taste of ashes behind them. But the most pressing argument for personal purity is that life is to be lived in the light of the Lord's presence (5.21).

In contrast with this distasteful subject the rich satisfaction of the love-life in the marriage bond is stressed. The language, akin to that in the *Song of Solomon*, may be a little bold for our western tastes. But it is a salutary reminder that human love, in all its aspects, is blessed of God when it is employed aright. So precious and pure is this intimacy that it is used to describe the relationship between Christ and His Church (Eph. 5.31 f.).

Avoid rash pledges (6.1–5, cf. 11.15). A man who has boasted of his wealth will sometimes give assurances of financial support, which he is unable to honour, to a friend (1 f.). The sensible advice given here is to swallow one's pride and inform that friend of the true position. It will involve eating humble pie, but this will be preferable to involving a friend in ruin besides oneself, and possibly shattering a friendship. Our stewardship of that which God entrusts to us is to be realistic.

A Question: How much truth is there in the words of the poem, 'My strength is as the strength of ten, because my heart is pure'? (Alfred, Lord Tennyson).

Proverbs 6.6-35

A lesson from nature (6–11). The opening verse is one which most can quote, usually in application to others! The reference is to the harvester ant which labours diligently in the short period of harvest to ensure an annual supply of food. Without degenerating to the anxious care condemned by our Lord (Matt. 6.25–34) we are to take reasonable and sensible precautions for the future security of ourselves, our families, and as far as possible, the work of the Lord. In contrast to the ant is the sluggard. He doesn't *intend* to whittle his life away, but the 'only five minutes more' attitude leads to an ill-disciplined life. Poverty, and not simply of the material kind, will have scant mercy on such.

Avoid the mischief-maker (12–15). A. D. Power calls the character

139

here drawn so vividly 'The Perfect Bounder', a description which would be amusing were not the subject so serious. This is the tale-bearer, the scandal-monger, who insinuates with a gesture as readily as with words slanted to suit his purposes. This is the kind of person who can cause incalculable harm as he sows his evil seed of discord. How can we deal with a man so ripe for God's judgement? Refuse to listen to his allegations; or counter evil with truth, depending on the circumstances, and shun his company. The lack of an audience will soon put him out of a job.

Seven abominations (16–19). The 'six . . . seven' introduction (cf. the 'three . . . four' formula in 30.15,18,21,24,29; Amos 1.3,6,9,11,13; 2.1,4) indicates that the list is not meant to be regarded as complete. The spring of all these sins is the fourth (appropriately central in the list), i.e. a corrupt heart which generates evil in every other realm of life. Notice particularly how at least three of the abominations, the lying tongue (17a), the false witness and the sower of discord (19) connect with the worthless trouble-maker of vs. 12–15. A man who destroys his brother's character is as culpable in God's sight as a murderer (17b).

The adulteress (20–35). If the Bible student becomes weary with this kind of instruction he should remember that the reiteration underlies the deadly seriousness which God attaches to this type of sin. The wrath of the husband (34 f.) is serious enough, but it is secondary when compared with the searing, destructive effect (27 f., 32 f.) upon the offender himself. How important it is to have right attitudes and values in the heart itself (20–23)!

Questions for further study and discussion on Proverbs chs. 1–6

1. Consider the relationship of the book of Proverbs to the other books of the O.T.
2. With the background of 1.20–33, and other passages you can think of, account for man's slowness to listen to God's voice.
3. Using the comments on Prov. 2 as a basis, work out for yourself the positive and negative aspects of the Christian life.
4. In the light of all the teaching in this section concerning the heart, why is it vital for the believer to respond to God's demand 'My son, give Me your heart' (23.26)?

Proverbs 7.1—8.3

One of the great values of the Bible is that it provides actual illustrations as well as giving specific instruction. We see both the process and the effects of Lot's compromise (Gen. 13.10–13; 14.12; 19); the consequences of imperfect obedience by the Israelites in the Judges' period are sharply drawn (Judg. 2.1–5,11—3.8; 10.6–16, etc.), whilst the disastrous chain-effect of David's sin with Bath-sheba is faithfully traced (2 Sam. 11—19.4). Now, following upon multiplied warnings against sexual promiscuity the wise man gives an illustration of the way in which a young man is attracted by a harlot, ensnared and ultimately destroyed (6–23). The folly and futility of a night's 'pleasure' is forcefully presented and contrasted (23b) with the blighting and withering of a whole life. 'Is it worth it?' is the unvoiced question, to which the answer is an emphatic 'No!'

But how to avoid it? Our section contains two bulwarks against the immoral life.

Bulwark No. 1 (7.1–4) is to give the commandments of God the central place in our lives. 'How can a young man keep his way pure? By guarding it according to Thy word' (Psa. 119.9). This involves much more than a casual reading of Scripture. The Word of God must be reverently studied, and loved, so that it becomes part of us. Like Job, we must 'treasure in our bosoms the words of His mouth' (Job 23.12). The Jews of old sought to interpret such commands as 2b, 3a literally (as with Deut. 6.8,9), but their real application is spiritual; our sight and our actions are to be completely under God's control. There is to be no casual acquaintance, but a vital relationship with wisdom (4).

Bulwark No. 2 (8.1–3) is to give heed to wisdom. Here the appeal is to man's discriminating choice. To whose voice is he to respond? On the one hand there is the oily, seductive tones of the temptress, the destroyer of souls, operating under the cover of night (7.6–21). In sharp contrast is the frank, open appeal of wisdom, coming to men in the open places and the clear light of day (cf. 1.20 f.) and calling them to real satisfaction (8.4–36).

A Thought: Moses was willing to share ill-treatment with God's people rather than enjoy the fleeting pleasures of sin (Heb. 11.25). How much more then should we, rejecting the pleasures which destroy, be ready to choose all the positive blessings which God offers us?

Proverbs 8.4-36

The contrast between the immoral woman of the previous chapter and wisdom herself is maintained in vs. 4–9. There is no hint here of the devious ways and the deceptive language of the harlot, rather there is absolute rectitude, so that no one can possibly be led astray. But as the chapter proceeds, the comparison lapses; the vile woman disappears from the scene, and wisdom, in all her incomparable glory, holds the stage. Wisdom is shown to be indispensable in a triple setting: morality (12–14, 20a), wise government (15 f.), and true prosperity (17–21) are impossible without her. No wonder that she is so precious (10 f.)!

In vs. 22–31 the personification of wisdom reaches its highest point. The point is made that wisdom was indispensable to Yahweh Himself in His work of creation. The greatness of the universe is considered in detail, with its characteristic law and order, and the influence of wisdom is shown to extend to the tiniest detail. How can man live apart from this incomparable wisdom, when even God had such need of her! It is almost impossible for the Christian to read this section, however, without losing sight of the abstract conception of wisdom and substituting instead the name of Jesus Christ. For if this passage suggests that wisdom was the creative agent, the N.T. certainly gives that honour to Christ (John 1.1–3,10; Col. 1.15–17; Heb. 1.2; Rev. 3.14). In this personification of wisdom the thoughts expressed by the divinely inspired writer were so accurate that when the full revelation came through Jesus Christ, God's Son, the entire section could be lifted out and applied to Him, without emendation. Such is the mystery of Christ 'in all the Scriptures' (Luke 24.27), which includes the Wisdom Literature as well as the Law (e.g. Exod. 12.1–13), the Prophets (e.g. Isa. 53) and the Psalmists (e.g. Psa. 22).

Hebrew thought is essentially practical, however, and this sublime section, which lifts us up to the level of metaphysical truth, is no exception. The very greatness of wisdom has been extolled so powerfully to underline the necessity of taking careful heed to her voice (32 ff.). Even here the Saviour is not far away, compare v. 35 with John 3.14–16; 10.10; 14.6, and compare v. 36 with John 3.19 f.

Proverbs 9

The final chapter of this first section of *Proverbs* ends with another contrast between wisdom, viewed as a refined, hospitable lady, and folly, characterized by one of her main types, the harlot.

Wisdom, having made ample preparation for a sumptuous banquet, gives a gracious invitation to all, an invitation which is amplified by her maids (1–6). The 'seven pillars' of v. 1 have been regarded as an allusion to a particular type of heathen temple but more probably, in the parallelism of Hebrew poetry, they refer simply to the adequacy of the building to accommodate all the guests. Nothing has been left to chance. There is an obvious parallel in our Lord's parable of the great banquet (Luke 14.15–24) where the

142

invitation to the 'poor and maimed and blind and lame', as well as the riff-raff of 'the highways and hedges' matches wisdom's call to the simple (4). Both Testaments magnify the grace of God which excludes no one except the one who wilfully rejects it. The supply of bread and wine (5) is a reminder of Christ's provision for man's spiritual renewal and sustenance (Matt. **26.**26–29, cf. John **6.**48–58).

At the end of the chapter, providing a solemn conclusion to this series of lessons on wisdom, is the seductive call of the harlot (13–18). The grace, poise and industry of wisdom are replaced by clamour, shamelessness and slovenliness. The immediate pleasure may seem alluring (17), but the end product is the destruction of something vital, which makes a man's future little more than a living death. The seriousness of this kind of sin is thus further underlined (cf. **2.**18 f.; **5.**5; **7.**23,27).

Between these two well-defined sections (7–12) there is a selection of proverbs dealing with the wise and the foolish, with apparently little connection with the remainder of the chapter. But a connection there most certainly is, for it shows that the choice which men make, whether it be of wisdom or folly, depends on an attitude of mind which has been built up over a period. The scoffer does not thank anyone for offering him advice. Secure in his own conceit, he resents any attempt to change his pattern of life. But the wise man is always open to criticism, he welcomes it so that he might progress still further in wisdom. It is a paradox that, the more true wisdom a man possesses, the more he is conscious of the vastness of his ignorance. Notice too that the wise man has a sure foundation (10). V.12 bears on the subject of individual responsibility. It does not exclude the hereditary or environmental factors which shape us, but it enforces the solemn responsibility of using aright our God-given power of free will.

Proverbs 10

Up to this point we have been listening to a series of exhortations given by a father deeply concerned for his son's well-being, the last lesson being given by wisdom herself (**8.**1). Scholars are unsure as to whether the first section (**1.**2—**9.**18) is anonymous, with **1.**1 providing a general introduction to the book, or whether Solomon is the author, in which case **1.**1 would introduce that sublime section. No such uncertainty attaches to the second main section (**10.**1—**22.**16), which contains 374 proverbs, no doubt selected from the 3000 which Solomon himself collected (1 Kings **4.**32). The unit is the individual verse, with a contrast between the two lines of each verse, although the same themes recur, and there are actual repetitions (e.g. **14.12; 16.25**) which is only to be expected in a compilation. The main topics are the everyday issues of life, but the deeper matters of religion are by no means avoided (e.g. **10.27,29; 14.27; 15.16,33; 18.10**, etc.). In such a collection, there is a wide disparity, and not all reach the highest ethical level, but sound common-sense is evident throughout. It must be remembered that the structure for life erected here is based upon the foundation of true wisdom, with its major constituent, the fear of the Lord. Each verse naturally invites a brief pause for reflection. Many of them will suggest examples, either from Scripture, personal observation, or experience, and it would be a helpful exercise, when time permits, to note down some of these. We comment on but a few of the highlights.

V. 1: The solemn truth of personal responsibility (9.12) is complemented here by the effect of our attitude upon others (cf. 5). No man is an island, and the mutual impacts within the family circle are especially profound.

Two themes are touched upon several times in this chapter. (*i*) The contrast between the reward of the righteous and the fate of the ungodly (2,7,16,22,27–30). Derek Kidner (*Proverbs*, Tyndale O.T. Commentary) observes that such sayings are true at four levels; (*a*) logical—sin, seen as folly, sets up strains in the structure of life which can only end in breakdown; (*b*) providential—however much rope God gives us, He remains in control; (*c*) spiritual—whatever their worldly state, the righteous are the truly rich; (*d*) eternal—in the world to come, justice will be complete. (*ii*) There is an emphasis upon the effect of speech, both of the godly and the ungodly, which reveals the inward reality of the speaker (6,8,11,13,14,18–21,31,32). How we need to pray the prayer of Psa. **141.3** (cf. Prov. **13.3**)!

V. 15 has a limited application in this life only, a fact recognized in **11.4,28**.

Proverbs 11

Honesty in all our business transactions is commended (1). The kind of sharp-practice condemned here must have been prevalent in Israel (cf. Amos **3.5**). It was a breach of the covenant, since the same bond which linked the individual Israelite to Yahweh meant that he stood in a relationship of brotherhood to his fellows (Hos. **12.6**). No man who sins against his brother can have a clear conscience, or a close communion, with God.

Pride (2), the very antithesis of humility, is a peculiarly abhorrent

144

sin, since it puts man on a level of independence before God which
bears no relationship to the true situation. Such a man is heading
for a fall (cf. 16.18; 29.23).

The effect of righteousness (3–9), a theme which was prominent in
yesterday's portion, is to give a man security in life, even when
confronted with adversity or the slanderous attack of v. 9. The
meaning of v. 8 appears to be that the ungodly man, like Haman,
falls into his own trap whereas the righteous man, such as Mordecai,
is delivered (Esth. 5.14; 7.9 f.). It needs but a little experience of life
to make one aware that this is not always the case, the unrighteous
often appear to escape scot-free. There still remains, however, the
inescapable final reckoning (21, cf. Eccl. 12.14).

Vs. 10,11 and 14 are concerned with right government. It is no
new phenomenon that men who make no claim to personal holiness
themselves still expect complete integrity in those who govern them.
Stable government is impossible without this quality.

The subject of the slanderer (9a) is taken up again in vs. 12 f.
Three particular sins are dealt with: (i) slander itself, i.e. the statement of that which is untrue; (ii) the belittling of our neighbours,
i.e. the statement of that which is less than the truth; (iii) the tale-
bearer, who peddles second-hand gossip of a slanderous nature. The
right course is to refuse to pass on that which can only defile (13b)
and possibly to take the positive action advocated in Gal. 6.1.

Generosity and its reward, with a particular curse on the one who
exploits a time of scarcity to force up the price of grain, is dealt
with in vs. 24 ff. The principle holds good in the realm of nature
and economics, where there must first be a sowing or an investment
before there can be a return. But it is especially applicable to
Christian stewardship, not simply of money and charity generally,
but of our very selves (cf. 2 Cor. 8.1–5; 9.6–13; Phil. 4.10–19;
1 Thess. 2.8). Indeed, our monetary gifts are worthless unless
accompanied by the love of our hearts and the labours of our hands.

Proverbs 12

A sure foundation. The permanence of the righteous is noted twice
in this chapter (3,12). The analogy of a tree, with roots going into
the solid earth, giving security and nourishment, finds an echo in
Psa. 1.1 ff. and Jer. 17.7 f. The contrast is with the man-made
structure of v. 12a which does not stand the test of time.

Be realistic, is the plea of v. 9. A man who accepts his position,
works hard, and supports himself adequately has infinitely more
common-sense than the person who gives himself airs and graces

145

whilst going without the very necessities of life. Who does the latter think he is deceiving? He knows the real facts by the merciless pangs of hunger, his neighbours are not fools and God is not deceived. While not accepting the Victorian dogma that every man has his own unalterable station in life, given to him by a sometimes cruel fate, we must have our feet on the ground and not pretend that we are what we are not. V. 11 strikes a similar note.

A care for all God's creatures is another characteristic of the righteous (10). The book of *Deuteronomy* not only provides for the care of domestic animals (Deut. 22.1; 25.4) but even lays down humane laws governing bird-nesting (Deut. 22.6 f.)! God's care extends to the smallest of His creatures (Matt. 10.29). Archaeological evidence of spacious and well made stables suggests that Solomon himself gave considerable attention to his many chariot-horses (1 Kings 10.26). Perhaps he would have been a wiser king, and saved the kingdom for his son, had he treated his subjects with greater consideration (1 Kings 5.13 ff.; 12.4,14). Someone has suggested that it was better to be a horse than a human in Solomon's reign! A righteous man *has* regard for the life of his beast, but also for all those within his care, including servants, employees and family.

Words can hurt or heal (18). Some people pride themselves on calling a spade a spade, of meaning what they say and saying what they mean. This bluntness frequently causes unnecessary hurt. The frequent references in this chapter to sound, honest speech (6,13,14, 17,19,22) warn against dissembling or hypocrisy, and we must never gloss over a situation with glib words. This was Jeremiah's complaint against the false prophets of his day (Jer. 8.11; 23.17). But there is a 'speaking the truth in love' (Eph. 4.15) which does not trample upon the feelings of others. The effect of such a kindly, encouraging word is illustrated in v. 25 (cf. Isa. 50.4).

Proverbs 13

Four sources of wisdom:

(*i*) Wisdom may be derived from our parents (1). This, unfortunately, is not always so, and foolish, indulgent parents abound, perhaps especially in our present generation when so many do not assume their responsibilities towards their children. But the ideal remains, and is firmly enunciated in *Proverbs*, of a father concerned to pass on his wise, hard-earned experience to his son. A son who fails to profit from such an experience is well on the way to becoming the anti-social scoffer of the second half of the verse. Part of the instruction which we receive from our parents is in the form of discipline or chastisement. It is no kindness to leave wrongdoing

146

unpunished, indeed, such weakness leads to breakdown in our appreciation of right or wrong. (Cf. the N.T. commentary on this verse in Heb. 12.5–11.)

(ii) Wisdom may be gained from the Scriptures (13). The 'word' and the 'commandment' suggest the revelation given by God in the covenant relationship with His people. Obedience to this was the way of life (Deut. 30.15). This verse reminds us of the foundational element of Israelite life which is assumed in the book of *Proverbs*. We are fortunate to have God's fuller revelation of Himself and His purposes in both Old and New Testaments, a privilege which has an accompanying responsibility. We must be doers, not simply hearers (Matt. 7.24–27; Jas. 1.22–25).

(iii) Wisdom may be found in the accumulated heritage of the past (14, cf. the significant change in 14.27). The 'wise', as we have noted, were a special class in Israel, but we may apply the verse to the writings of all true saints, whether they be prophets, priests, psalmists, commentators, evangelists, mystics or missionaries, etc. They provide a fountain of rich spiritual experience from which we may be refreshed. Notice that the wise man was not afraid to mix his metaphors!

(iv) Wisdom comes by keeping good company (20). Solomon's son, Rehoboam, would have been wise to have taken this counsel to heart. Forsaking the sound advice of his older counsellors, who had followed the reign of his father from its bright beginnings to its tarnished end, he turned instead to the witless, power-hungry young men, completely incapable of the tact and restraint needed in wise government (1 Kings 12.6–16). The result was disaster.

A Thought for today: Have I closed my life to one or more of these sources of wisdom—parents, the Scriptures, Christian literature or Christian friends?

Questions for further study and discussion on Proverbs chs. 7–13

1. Starting from the comments on 7.1—8.3 make a list of the ways in which temptation may be overcome.
2. List the gifts which wisdom bestows in 8.4—9.6 and compare it with the gifts offered by Christ in the N.T.
3. How far is it legitimate to speak of 'Christ in all the Scriptures'? What examples can you add to those listed in the notes on 8.4–36?
4. Consider the place of the will (9.12), environment and heredity in determining character. What place is left for the operation of God's grace?
5. Work out the practical applications, spiritual as well as material, of the principles of stewardship enunciated in 11.24–28.

Proverbs 14

The Home Builder (1). Ch. 9.1–6,13–18 provide the background for this verse. The wise woman, by her foresight and industry, but above all by her relationship to God (cf. 26), exercises a wholesome, edifying influence in her home. Folly, on the other hand, by her indolence and corrupt character demolishes what little good remains. There is truth in the children's chorus, 'We are building day by day'—sensibly or shoddily (cf. 1 Cor. 3.10–15).

The depths of the human heart are observed in vs. 10,13. Each of us has an inwardness that we share with but a chosen few, and even then only infrequently. Joy and sorrow (cf. 2 Cor. 6.10), a sense of both achievement and failure, are inextricably bound together in this life, touched as it is by human sin. Friendship may be described as the mutual opening of hearts' doors. Prov. 18.24 hints at that Friend, above all friends, 'who sticks closer than a brother', who knows all the depths and desires of the human heart (Heb. 4.14 ff.).

Three proverbs in this chapter touch upon the subject of the poor. The first (20) is on the very worldly level of 'what can I get out of him?' The second (21), on a more humane plane, points out the sin involved in the previous verse and praises charity. Only the third (31) reaches the true estimate. All men are made in the image of God (Gen. 1.26 f.) and in God's sight are equal, irrespective of colour, wealth, or social standing. To treat any man as an inferior is a tacit denial of this fact and a dishonouring of our Maker.

'Godliness—fortress and fountain' is Derek Kidner's appropriate caption to vs. 26,27. In *Proverbs* the writer covers many aspects of wisdom but every so often he calls his readers back to the foundational element, the fear of the Lord (1.7; 9.10). Strength, sustenance and stability are the portion of the one who allows God His rightful place.

One of the present writer's enduring memories is of an old man, crossing Waterloo Bridge in wartime London, carrying a sandwich board on which was written v.34, a proverb with a history of almost three thousand years. The text should be written in large letters on the hearts of all who have a share in shaping national policies. The writers of Israel's history from *Joshua* to *2 Kings* were fully aware of this principle, and these records show clearly the moral, economic, political, social and spiritual deterioration which overtakes a nation that forsakes the ways of righteousness. The part of the Christian in this is to be like salt, adding flavour and staying corruption (Matt. 5.13).

Proverbs 15

Watch your words! The subject of speech crops up at least seven times in today's chapter (1,2,4,7,23,26,28), a reminder that so much of life's relationship depends upon what we say. If we want to be on cordial terms with our fellow men we must weigh our words as carefully as our actions. The apt answer (23) comes only from such a disciplined mind (28). The Christian's deeper motive is to glorify and reveal his Lord in every contact, hence the soft answer of the peacemaker (1), which dampens anger (cf. 16.32). It is instructive to develop the analogy of v. 4, contrasting it with the three images (rudder, fire, fountain) used by James (Jas. 3.1–12).

The Lord is watching! A powerful motive for guarding both words and actions is that the all-seeing eye of the Lord is upon us (3,11). Abaddon (lit. destruction or ruin) is synonymous with Sheol, the abode of all the departed. Hezekiah lamented that he would be cut off from the Lord in Sheol (Isa. 38.18) but Solomon, the prophet Amos (9.2) and the psalmist (139.8) each saw that there was no place outside the Lord's scrutiny and power. It is easy to quote verses assuring us of the Lord's presence (e.g. Matt. 28.20; Heb. 13.5); but we must also live, moment by moment, in this light.

A three-fold abomination (8,9,26). Evil actions (9) spring from a corrupt mind (26), so any cultic acts (8) performed by such a person are bound to be vitiated by hypocrisy. This condemnation is frequently echoed in the prophets (e.g. Isa. 1.11–15; Jer. 6.20; 7.21 f.; Hos. 6.6; Amos 5.21–24), for the outward forms of religion are completely unacceptable to God unless there is the inward reality. Do our prayers, devotions, hymn-singing, offerings and the other elements of our worship stand this kind of test?

True riches. What are the really valuable things in life? Solomon was quite sure that a right relationship with God (16) and with our families (17), even though accompanied by relative poverty, is greatly to be preferred to human riches (cf. 16.8). It is possible that Solomon learnt these lessons by bitter experience, for although he had immense wealth there is little evidence of domestic harmony in his family. Consider also the N.T. teaching on the subject of true wealth (cf. Matt. 6.19 ff.; 2 Cor. 4.18).

Be teachable, is the four-fold admonition of vs. 5,12,31,32. Such an attitude involves humility (33) but a false pride in this matter can be disastrous (32). Even Paul, the greatest of the apostles, considered himself a learner (Phil. 3.12–15).

Proverbs 16

'Thy way, not mine, O Lord'. It is an old saying that 'Man proposes; God disposes', and this is the message of vs. 1,9. Man, in spite of his undeniable ability, is fallible, and while he is able to make reasonable plans for the future he cannot control the multitudinous factors which could invalidate them. God, on the contrary, knows no such limitations. His knowledge of all events, past, present and future, is perfect and He is never caught napping. How wise of man, then, to take God into his planning right at the outset (3, cf. 3.5–8)! Such a course would save a man from many a frustration and make him far happier (20). V. 33 is within the same context of ascertaining the Lord's will. The reference is to Urim and Thummim, or its equivalent, which was probably a set of two, marked, flat stones, which the priest manipulated. An answer to an inquiry was made according to the combination which turned up, which is probably the background to 'the answer of the tongue' (1) and 'the word' (20). To the western mind it sounds an uncertain means of guidance, but it was firmly believed that the Lord overruled the process (33b). The disciples used the same method to find a replacement for Judas (Acts 1.26) but subsequently the descent of the Holy Spirit, and His indwelling of each believer, made possible a more direct and assured means of discovering God's will. The Lord's promise to His disciples was that 'He (the Holy Spirit) will guide you into all truth' (John 16.13).

The ideal king is portrayed in vs. 10,12–15. In many of the surrounding nations the king was regarded as divine and infallible, but not so in Israel, where the Lord was regarded as the true king of His people (Judg. 8.23) and the power of the king was limited (Deut. 17.14–20). These verses give a picture of an ideal king whose righteousness was such that his absolute power (14) could never be arbitrary. Such a high standard was never completely obtained in Israel, although Hezekiah and Josiah (2 Kings 18.5; 23.25) came close to it. But Israel's prophets never lost hope and foretold a Messiah, of David's line, who would achieve fully all that Israel's human kings failed to secure (Isa. 9.6 f.; 11.1–5). These promises have been fulfilled by Jesus Christ, the Son of David, the Son of God.

A thought: In the light of vs. 5,18,19 consider the aptness of the song of Bunyan's shepherd boy in the Valley of Humiliation:

> *He that is down needs fear no fall,*
> *He that is low no pride;*
> *He that is humble ever shall*
> *Have God to be his guide.*

150

Proverbs 17

Ability the true criterion (2). This is a proverb which does not always work out in experience. Commentators are quick to point out an apparent fulfilment in the case of Solomon's servant Jeroboam and his son Rehoboam (1 Kings 11.28–40). But Jeroboam misused his great gifts after becoming king of Israel (1 Kings 12.26–13.1) and earned for himself the prophet's condemnation and the unenviable epithet, 'who made Israel to sin'.

The refining process (3) involves great heat but it is carefully regulated. Its purpose is the elimination of all that is impure. The Lord's dealings with us, though sometimes painful, are equally as purposeful (cf. Jer. 6.27–30; Ezek. 22.17–22; Zech. 13.9).

Justice is the theme of four proverbs in this chapter. V. 8 is an observation, not a commendation of an all too common practice. It meant that the rich could always buy a decision in their favour and the poor, conversely, could never secure justice. But the judge who shows such partiality is roundly condemned (15,26) and the under-lying sin is as clearly exposed in v. 23. Israel's Law dealt with this aspect of the national life in the sharpest possible terms (Deut. 16. 18–20); 'Justice, and only justice—justice without intermittence— is to be thy constant aim in judgement' (so S. R. Driver brings out the force of Deut. 16.20). The thought here extends far beyond the law court itself, it involves straight and honest dealing with all our fellow men in every relationship.

Some brief points on other outstanding proverbs in this chapter:

A genuine forgiveness calls for the locking up in our heart and mind (it is not always possible to forget) of the matter which has been dealt with (9).

Don't start a quarrel, is the advice of v. 14. The picture is of a minor breach in a dam, but a trickle of water can increase the damage until an uncontrollable deluge is released.

There is good psychology in v. 22. The effect of feelings upon our general health, which is being stressed in modern medicine, was not unknown to the ancients. As Christians, we have so much to rejoice over, even when difficulties abound. Does our faith show in our faces?

The goal of the wise man (24) is well defined, and engages all his powers. The foolish man, conversely, either has an impossible objective, or allows his interests to be dispersed and dissipated (either meaning is allowable). Some people aim at nothing, and hit it every time!

A challenge: Is Paul's aim (Phil. 3.8–11) your aim?

151

Proverbs 18

An argument, a hurt or a slight, imagined or real, can lead to the irrational behaviour noted in v. 1, which Knox translates, 'None so quick to find pretexts, as he that would break with a friend. . . .' Husbands and wives, as well as friends, are not immune to this emotion, which can lead to a raking up of the past, or a scouring of the present, to find arguments, often worthless, in support of their position. To be forewarned concerning our very human frailty is to be forearmed! 17.14 has its application here.

It is apparent that Solomon did not suffer fools gladly! As well as the many references in the preceding chapters there are four more references in ch. 18 to the fool. His complete emptiness is expressed in v. 2. He just loves to hear the sound of his own voice, irrespective of what he has to say. A bracket of proverbs (6,7) underlines the pitfalls of such a position; such thoughtless utterances can so easily land him in trouble. V. 13 is in similar vein, for only a fool blurts out an answer before he has heard the question properly, or considered it thoroughly. Contrast the value of a wise man's speech (4,20) and notice again the power wielded by the tongue (21).

The sacredness of work is underlined in v. 9. The contrast may seem extreme to us but to the wise man the abuse of time or ability was as heinous a crime as the abuse of property. An honest day's work should be the aim of the Christian, and any time-wasting techniques, or a clock-watching attitude, should be avoided. Col. 3.17, 22 ff. gives similar sound advice. The ability to work is a gift of God; rightly used it brings great satisfaction.

Hear both sides before making a verdict! The setting of the proverb (17) is probably the law court, but it has a universal validity. There are always two sides to an argument, although both may not be of equal weight. So it is foolish to form an opinion on the strength of the arguments of one side alone, however speciously presented. Cross-examination and the testimony of the other party may lead to a different conclusion. Sometimes disputes can arise between Christians, and even more regrettable, they can persuade others to support them and thus widen the breach. The wise course is to get the parties together in the presence of a godly, impartial adjudicator, after the pattern of the 'umpire' of Job 9.33, who will listen carefully to both sides and bring about a reconciliation. (Cf. the example of Christ Himself, Eph. 2.12–18.)

Proverbs 19

The reader will have observed how frequently certain themes recur, some are found in almost every chapter. The topic of false witnesses, for example, is dealt with again three times in ch. 19 (5,9,28) and we may assume that this mirrors the contemporary scene, showing the prevalence of this offence. Another of the dominant subjects concerns the acquisition of wisdom or knowledge and its reward, and this may be found again in vs. 2,8,20,25. It will also have been noted that certain of the proverbs current in Solomon's time are still around today, perhaps in slightly modified forms, e.g. v. 2b and its modern variant, 'More haste, less speed'.

'Why does God allow this?' is often the outburst of the unbeliever who at no point has taken the Almighty into his plans (3). Most of us are familiar with this reaction when things go wrong, and the blame is immediately laid at God's door. But He cannot be held accountable for the effects of man's own wilfulness. The wisest course is so to walk with God that our lives are directed in accordance with His will (cf. 21).

The subject of 'fair-weather friends' is dealt with in vs. 4,6,7. The practical-minded James condemns the one who fawns upon the rich but treats the poor inconsiderately (Jas. 2.1–9). It is fatally easy to kowtow to a person of wealth or influence, but such a policy, besides being discriminatory, is injurious to our own characters. All men are entitled to our utmost consideration. V. 17 regards an unselfish, sacrificial consideration for the poor as a spiritual investment. The Lord, who knows our motives and is no man's debtor, allows no such loving action to pass unrecognized, but He seldom gives His rewards in cash, they are of a more enduring quality! Notice in the Gospels how often our Lord sought the company of those who could never repay Him, and observe His words on this subject (Luke 14.12 ff.).

Later on in the book the subject of the ideal wife is considered (31.10–31). Such a vital matter, in the nature of things, must·find a prominent place in the proverbial sayings of a nation. The preciousness of a good wife is noted in v. 14 (cf. 18.22) and contrasted with the contentious wife of v. 13b. A marriage 'in the Lord' is one of the greatest blessings that we can know in this life, indeed, it is a foretaste of what awaits the Church in its final relationship with Christ (cf. Eph. 5.21–33; Rev. 21.2,9 ff.).

Proverbs 20

The totalitarian note of v. 2 (cf. **19**.12) is qualified by vs. 8,26,28. A king's purpose in judgement is to separate the wheat from the chaff (the 'wheel' of v. 26 being the threshing wheel). His underlying spirit is clearly revealed in v. 28. Against this background the wrath of the earlier proverb (2) is the more fearful. The verses have their application to all who hold positions of authority, and they point away to One whose rule will be in perfect righteousness (Isa. **9**.6 f.; **11**.1–5), and whose ultimate wrath is to be dreaded (Rev. **6**.16 f.).

The lesson of diligence is frequently commended by Solomon and contrasted with the fate of the sluggard, sometimes in delightfully humorous terms (cf. **19**.24). There is, however, a serious side and this is well brought out in vs. 4,13 (cf. **19**.15). In ancient Israel the ground would be baked hard during the summer drought, and autumn ploughing was vital to enable early sowing, when the 'former rains' arrived. Otherwise, so short was the growing season, there could be no harvest and hunger would result. This lesson from the harvest field is reproduced in the spiritual realm, where there cannot be an ingathering of precious souls without sacrificial endeavour.

V. 9 strikes one of the most solemn notes of human experience, man's inability to effect his own self-cleansing from sin, and therefore his own salvation. It is not just a question of being as good as the next man, it involves our relationship with a holy God (cf. Job **4**.17). Paul's memorable passage on the universality of sin (Rom. **3**.9–20) sounds the death-knell of any vain hope of self-justification. It would be depressing indeed did it not lead on to the unfolding of the truth of justification by faith in the atoning work of Christ (Rom. **3**.21–26). Compare the meditation of the psalmist (Psa. **130**).

'The spirit of man' (27) appears to be a direct reference to his God-given conscience (cf. Zech. **12**.1; 1 Cor. **2**.11), which distinguishes man from the brute creation ('spirit' is lit. 'breath', the unique element in the creation of man, Gen. **2**.7). When sensitive to the Lord, conscience can probe and thus enable us to cleanse all the recesses of our lives. But conscience can be seared (1 Tim. **4**.2) or corrupted (Tit. **1**.15). The end of such a man will be moral and spiritual darkness (cf. v. 20).

A Thought for today: 'The fleeting pleasures of sin' (Heb. 11.25) invariably leave behind them the taste of gravel (Prov. 20.17) and the bitterness of a living death (9.17 f.).

Proverbs 21

The Lord is King. V. 1 pictures a farmer's accurate control, through irrigation channels, of the life-giving water which his crops require. No less absolute is the Lord's control over the policies and actions of kings, although they may be as little aware of the purpose behind their movements as the flowing water. Biblical illustrations of this may be seen in the cases of Pharaoh (Exod. 9.16), Nebuchadnezzar (Jer. 25.9; 27.6; 43.10), Cyrus (Isa. 45.1-6, cf. Ezra 1. 1-4) and Artaxerxes (Ezra 7.11-28). It is a comforting thought that the world rulers of our own generation exercise a strictly limited power under the same almighty control. V. 30 notes that nothing can prevail against the Lord. Since true wisdom, understanding and counsel have their genesis in Him, whatever lacks this origin is devoid of the very thing which makes it effective, and is therefore doomed to failure. Paul's commentary on this truth is worth pondering (1 Cor. 1.19-31). A complementary truth is found in v. 31, i.e. nothing can succeed without the Lord. The horse is used symbolically of all human preparation for combat (cf. Psa. 20.7) but the intervention of the Lord makes nonsense of human reckoning, either in victory (Lev. 26.8) or in defeat (Isa. 30.17). The host of Midian (Judg. 7.12) was no match for Gideon's three hundred men on this reckoning! There is a profound spiritual truth here, and Christians should be 'more than conquerors through Him who loved us' (Rom. 8.37, cf. 2 Cor. 2.14).

Sacrifice without morality is an abomination to the Lord (vs. 3,27). This is a warning which we have observed before (see note on 15.8). God is not to be bought off by our acts of worship, nor do we put Him in our debt by these. What the eighth century prophets knew of the character of God led them to denounce a shallow, hypocritical form of worship, devoid of ethical conduct. Samuel stressed the same truth to Saul at an even earlier period (1 Sam. 15. 22 f.). His words find an echo in v. 3 of our reading.

The way to riches, transient or lasting, is the subject of vs. 5,6,20. But treasure of another kind, which is infinitely more durable, is the reward of the man who is both godly and good (21, cf. 22.4).

A Question: What kind of treasure are you saving up? (cf. Matt. 6.19 ff.).

Questions for further study and discussion on Proverbs chs. 14-21

1. With the use of a concordance examine the importance, and the effects, of the 'fear of the Lord' (e.g. in 14.26 f.).
2. Collate the references to speech (the tongue and the lips) in the

155

Scriptures, using the note on ch. 15 as a basis. Why do you think so much is written on this subject?
3. Review the verses in *Proverbs* which deal with the place of the king (cf. the note on 16. 10,12–15). Are they applicable to modern governments? How far do they indicate the perfect rule of Christ?
4. Starting from Prov. 17.14; 18.1,17, what advice does the Bible give for dealing with quarrels?
5. Does God's omnipotence make Him responsible (or culpable) for the evil we bring upon ourselves (19.3)?

Proverbs 22.1-16

Riches or reward? Whether vs. 1,4, and the many other proverbs dealing with wealth, originated with Solomon, or more likely, were collected together by him, it is clear that they had their application to this fabulously rich king (cf. 1 Kings 10.14–23). Regrettably, Solomon did not always live by them, and his name was not cherished as it might have been in the next generation (e.g. 1 Kings 12.4). Most men set such great store upon wealth, possessions and the power they bring that the Christian must ever be on his guard to keep his standards in line with those of God. The degree of danger is highlighted by the attention given to this subject in *Proverbs* and elsewhere in Scripture.

Meeting Point (2). This proverb follows on v. 1, and shows that there is no basic difference between rich and poor, for the Lord is the Maker of all. Another inevitable meeting point for all men is in the fact of death (Job 3.17 ff.). But there is a spiritual death in which all men share because of their sin (Rom. 3.12) which brings them to a third universal meeting point—the place of human need and insufficiency before God. There is only one way of escape from this predicament (John 14.6), and again, there is no partiality or respect of persons with God. He (Christ) died for all (2 Cor. 5.14 f.).

The saying attributed to Ignatius Loyola, 'Give me your child till he is seven, and I care not who has charge of him afterwards.' is proverbial. The observation of the Jesuit was far from original, however, as v. 6 shows. The early years of a child are determinative. Most decisions for Jesus Christ are recorded before the school-leaving age. Hence the urgent need for parents and teachers to implant the highest standards in those entrusted to them. The subject of physical punishment is one of the discussion points of our age, and the advocates of 'free expression' are vocal in their opposition. The wise man had a more realistic attitude (15, cf. 23.13)!

Blessed are the pure in heart! The familiar beatitude (Matt. 5.8), which gives as its reward 'for they shall see God', has a most obvious connection with v. 11. Not all earthly kings have sought such company, preferring the base servility of the flatterer, but the King of kings seeks such, and calls them His friends (John 15.14 f.). Note the desirable combination of inward (purity of heart) and outward (gracious speech) qualities.

Proverbs 22.17—23.18

Today we begin the third sub-section of *Proverbs* (22.17—24.22). It deals with similar subjects as the second section and displays a remarkable similarity in outlook. The treatment, however, is different; the individual proverbs are generally longer and the thought, instead of being confined to one verse, often extends over several.

An interesting connection. Wisdom literature was not confined to Israel, and there are many parallels between Biblical texts, and even whole books (e.g. *Job*), and other literature of the Ancient Near East. But the closest connection is between Prov. 22.17—23.12 and an Egyptian text, dating from about 800 B.C., called 'The Teaching of Amen em-ope'. With about three or four exceptions, each verse in the Hebrew can be paralleled in the Egyptian, although the Egyptian variant is longer, being interspersed with verses that have no parallel in *Proverbs*. The evidence, though not decisive, suggests that the Egyptian author borrowed from a Hebrew original, which reflects on the latter's antiquity.

A profound difference. The difference in the 'theological platform' of the two variants is considerable. The Hebrew sage wrote for a people who trusted in Yahweh, and he believed that if his readers observed the wise sayings he culled, then their faith in Him would be strengthened (22.17 ff.). His purpose, therefore, was a specifically religious one, not simply a desire to impart knowledge. This concern is shown at the end of our portion (23.17,18). The wise man knew that, like the psalmist (Psa. 73), the godly are often tempted to ask 'What's the use of it all?' He set the future against the apparent inequality of the present, and that future, in God's hands, would bring the vindication of the righteous. Work out the parallels in the psalm quoted.

The ancient landmarks (22.28; 23.10). Arable land is too precious in Palestine to allow for a neutral strip between smallholdings. Even today, the visitor will note that the only visible sign of land boundaries are small piles of stones at the side of the road or track. Evidently it was common practice to move these a yard or so,

157

especially if the legal owner was unable to defend his rights (23.10). But the land was God's gift to His people, who held it in tenure for Him. As such it was inalienable, and the man who treated this lightly had God to contend with (23.11).

Proverbs 23.19—24.7

From Riches to Rags. Ch. 23.19–21,29–35 could be sub-titled 'The Descent to Insensibility'. It provides a graphic picture of the disastrous effects of intoxication, with a side-glance at gluttony, another form of over-indulgence. The initial attractiveness (31) is deceptive, for the end is destruction (cf. the parallel with the consequence of another form of folly in 7.21–23). The drunkard is literally not himself, for that part of him which makes him a man, in contradistinction to the animal creation, is the first to be affected by strong drink. Sense and speech become incoherent (33); there is loss of control and sensitivity (34 f.), and there is an appalling 'hangover' of misery (29), which is not confined to the drunkard himself. The end of this way is poverty (21). The degradation of such men is reflected in the senseless bravado of v. 35, which also reminds us that the desire for alcohol can become an addiction. Contrasting with this senseless course is the appeal to man's highest faculties—'direct your mind in the way' (19).

A personal appeal (23.22–28). Notice the appeal to the fifth commandment (Exod. 20.12) in vs. 22,25. The right kind of miserliness is stressed in v. 23; truth, wisdom, instruction and understanding are to be acquired, and used, but never sold. Appeal is made to the motive of satisfying our earthly parents (24), but a deeper motive is so to live that we gain the approval of our heavenly Father (Matt. 5.16). Over such the snares of the seductress (27 f.) have no power. But to those who succumb there is the danger of falling away from the faith (28b), for we cannot sin wilfully without affecting our spiritual life.

True strength and stability (24.1–7). In contrast with the violence of evil men (1,2) is the more durable strength of the wise (5). By his wisdom, understanding and knowledge he builds for life on a sure foundation, and furnishes his house with lasting treasures (3,4). The picture is one of patient, persistent, but very satisfying labour. Such a man is never at the mercy of his foes (6), and unlike the fool (7) he *has* something worthwhile to say 'in the gate', the place where vital matters of all kinds, political, judicial and social, were discussed. Perhaps there is also a hint that the fool will have nothing to say for himself in his own final judgement (cf. Matt. 22.11–14).

Proverbs 24.8-34

A fair-weather faith (10) is really no faith at all. Nothing reveals the genuineness or otherwise of faith as does adversity in one or another of its many guises. The endurance of such trials reveals 'the genuineness of . . . faith' (1 Pet. **1.7**). Our inspiration in this is to 'consider Him who endured. . . .' (Heb. **12.3**).

A fair-weather friend (11 f.) is similarly valueless. The reference is to a convicted man who is being led out to the place of execution. A witness who had something material to say which might have affected the verdict, could intervene publicly, in which case there would be a re-trial to consider the fresh evidence. Such intervention was often costly, but non-intervention was criminal, and cowardice and feigned ignorance were inexcusable. In a lesser realm we have a responsibility to speak out when the reputation of someone is being falsely and maliciously attacked. Note the fundamental motive advanced in v. 12—the Lord takes note. We *are* our 'brother's keeper' (Gen. **4.9**) and in the application of this responsibility we must not interpret 'brother' too narrowly. We have a peculiar responsibility to those who spiritually are as good as dead (cf. Eph. **2.1** ff.), pointing them to the Giver of life (John **10.10**).

The same appeal to the all-seeing eye of the Lord appears in vs. 17,18. The destruction of evil men is sure (15,16,19,20) but it is not to be received with vindictive delight by the righteous man. Jeremiah wept (e.g. Jer. **9.1**) at the thought of the destruction of the people who consistently rejected his message, and subjected him to all manner of indignities (e.g. Jer. **18.18**; **38.4** ff.). Our Saviour wept over the same city, and for the same reasons (Luke **19.41-44**). Notice, incidentally, the resilience of the righteous (16, cf. Mic. **7.8**), the result of his faith, as we have already observed (10).

Vs. 23–34 form an appendix to the third section of the book. V. 27, which could be sub-titled 'Don't spend your money before you've earned it', contrasts with the parable of the sluggard's garden (30–34) which is the longest proverb in the book. The lesson is that multiplied acts of indolence bring eventual ruination. Be diligent, in matters temporal and spiritual (Rom. **12.11**; Heb. **6.11** f.)!

A thought: The psalmist lamented 'no man cares for me' (Psa. 142.4). Could any of our friends be saying this today?

Proverbs 25

There were collections of Solomonic proverbs other than the main one incorporated in our book (**10.1—22.16**). The scribes of King

Hezekiah (715–687 B.C.) formed a selection of them into another anthology, forming the fourth main section of *Proverbs* (25.1– 29.27). There is evidence of an effort to group proverbs together, not only in subject matter, but even in sequence. Connections with other Solomonic material are evident and some proverbs are duplicated (e.g. 21.9, cf. 25.24).

The ways of God and the king (2–7). Scripture teaches that there is an inscrutability concerning the ways of God, for man who is finite cannot presume to comprehend One who is infinite (cf. Deut. 29.29; Isa. 40.13 f.; 55.8–11; Rom. 11.33–36). God does not explain fully the reasons behind His actions but we may rest assured that they are wise and beneficent. In contrast, the king has a public duty to 'get to the bottom of things' (2b), although, like God, he is not required to reveal his innermost thoughts. The teaching on the elimination of evil (4 f.) and the need for humility in the presence of one's superiors (6 f., cf. our Lord's development of this in Luke 14.7–11) apply equally in the spiritual kingdom. There can be no place for human pride in the presence of the King of kings, who was Himself 'gentle and lowly in heart' (Matt. 11.29, cf. Rev. 4.10 f.).

Rash words, and hasty litigation (8–10). The evidence of the eyes can be misleading, for it is subject to the superimposition of the mind, interpreting events in the light of our desires, etc. Hence, on a very human level, the need to corroborate our evidence. Our Lord stressed the need for reconciliation, not litigation, on the highest possible authority, that of God's forgiveness (Mark 11.25; Matt. 5.21–26; 18.21–35). Contrasted with this kind of speech is a series of similes commending the appropriate word (11), a word of admonition (12) and a faithful word (13). But there is no praise for the man who is 'all talk and no do' (14); rainfall is scarce in Palestine, so the simile portrays acute disappointment. Another allusion to the weather is in v. 23. As the north wind is invariably a dry wind in Palestine it is probable that this proverb originated elsewhere.

An often misunderstood proverb concerns the treatment of enemies (21 f.). We do not *set out* to revenge ourselves on our adversaries by being kind to them! The 'coals of fire' are not those of judgement, but of conscience, self-imposed by the offender. Matt. 5.43 ff. heads up the Biblical teaching on this point.

Proverbs 26

Three subjects are covered in this chapter:

(*i*) The fool (1–12). The fool of Proverbs is not necessarily one who is mentally weak or simple but one who is wilfully disobedient to the voice of divine wisdom. In this sense fool is synonymous with sinner. The apparent exception in v. 2 deals with a causeless curse, uttered by someone who believed (foolishly) that the mere uttering of a curse would bring harm to the object of his wrath. The apparent contradiction in vs. 4, 5 is paralleled by many contemporary proverbs, e.g. 'Out of sight, out of mind', cf. 'Absence makes the heart grow fonder'; or 'Too many cooks spoil the broth', cf. 'Many hands make light work'. In reality, each has its application, depending on the circumstances. There is a time when it is pointless to reason with a fool but there are also occasions when to remain silent would suggest to him that his own position was unassailable. For an excellent example of the latter, note Paul's words in 2 Cor. 11.1—12.11. Reliance of any kind upon a fool is to be avoided, but paradoxically, there is one who can 'out-fool the fool', i.e. 'a man who is wise in his own eyes' (12). Such can never come to the point where he admits his need.

(ii) The sluggard (13–16). We have met many of these proverbs before, e.g. v. 13 (cf. 22.13), v. 15 (cf. 19.24). The irony is excellent, but such is the sluggard's capacity for rationalizing his behaviour (16) that he would be untouched. Before we condemn him let us not forget the paltry excuses often advanced for not busying ourselves in the Lord's work (cf. Luke 9.57–62).

(iii) Trouble and trouble-makers (17–27). Most of us will have had bitter experience of the malicious character, who, when confronted with his neighbour's anger, attempts to evade responsibility for the havoc he has caused (18 f.). The whisperer, the hot-headed, the gossiper, the scheming hypocrite and the flatterer (20–28) are equally as reprehensible. V. 17 is a good general rule. Intervention from a third party usually makes things worse, because in a quarrel neither party is open to reason. But there is a time for intervention, if we are in a position to help, especially where physical danger or lasting damage (e.g. the break-up of a friendship or marriage) is threatened. The danger must then be faced and the role of a cowardly spectator eschewed. God's Son not only risked, but gave His life for our sakes, enduring 'from sinners such hostility against Himself' (Heb. 12.3) in the process.

Questions for further study and discussion on Proverbs chs. 22–26
1. Is the advice which is given in *Proverbs* concerning the training of children still relevant?
2. See 22.28; 23.10. Can you think of some 'ancient landmarks' (in the moral or religious sphere) which are being moved today? What should be our reaction?

3. In the light of **23.**19–21, 29–35, and other relevant sections (e.g. Gen. **9.**20–24), what should our attitude be to strong drink in our contemporary situation?
4. What attitude should a Christian take to the various kinds of trouble-maker enumerated in **26.**17–27?

Proverbs 27

The present and the future. V. 1 is capable of two interpretations. It could be a warning against procrastination, which shrugs off present responsibility with the words, 'There's always tomorrow.' More likely, however, it rebukes a false sense of security based on human planning of the kind which the N.T. condemns (e.g. Jas. **4.**13–17; Luke **12.**16–21). Equally to be avoided is that anxious care concerning the future which is the antithesis of true faith (Matt. **6.**25–34). The future, as the present, is in God's hands, so the Christian will plan wisely, but without presumption. Such planning is indicated in a delightful pastoral setting in vs. 23–27. If **31.**10–31 are concerned with the ideal wife, this shorter section may be entitled 'the ideal husband'! A job well done brings a sense of satisfaction more precious than material wealth (24).

Self-praise is no recommendation (2). Few things are more obnoxious than a man who is continually blowing his own trumpet. The verdict of others is more important, but even this is secondary to the praise of God (cf. John **12.**43). Notice in v. 21 that a man's character is revealed either by the things he praises (in himself or others) or by the way in which he reacts to the praise he receives.

The faithful friend is the subject of three proverbs. Vs. 5,6 belong together, for the 'hidden love' of v. 5 overlooks, or is afraid to expose, the faults of others. A true friend, seeing his companion going astray, must deal with him in a firm but kindly manner (cf. the attitude commended in Gal. **6.**1). This may cause a temporary wound, but it is the lasting effect which is determinative. The value of true friendship is often revealed in the day of adversity (10). Ties of blood, though precious, do tend to weaken over the years and it is a mistake to overlook a tried and trusted friend for the doubtful help given by a relative from whom one is far away, in more senses than one. This proverb, of course, does not deny the blessings which come from a united family, its concern is to highlight the value of a proven friend. The mutual benefit of such friendship finds expression in v. 17, where the 'sharpening' may be intellectual, moral or spiritual. Hence the importance of having the right kind of companion, who will sharpen, not blunt, our character.

162

Proverbs 28

The reward of a clear conscience is exemplified in vs. 1,13,14,17,18. 'Conscience doth make cowards of us all' is the theme of v. 1. How true this is in experience! Sin pays its wages (6.23) in spiritual (and possibly physical) death, and includes the gnawing fear of being found out for good measure. No one who is continually looking over his shoulder can enjoy life, he remains an uneasy fugitive (17), frightened of his own shadow. Far better, as v. 13 advises, to deal with the matter, both with those we have wronged, but above all, with the Lord, for He has provided a means of cleansing (1 John 1.9). It is vital, both for our peace of mind and our Christian testimony, that we keep short accounts with God. Three other positive steps towards a good conscience are recommended: to fear the Lord, to have a responsive heart (14), and to walk in integrity (18).

The subject of government, whether good or bad, is the dominating one in this chapter (e.g. vs. 2,4,5,7,9,12,15,16,28). The scribes of Hezekiah's time who copied out these proverbs could illustrate v. 2 from their own observation of the declining years of the northern kingdom of Israel. Six kings followed in quick succession during the period 746–732 B.C. Only one passed on the throne to his son, and most of them died violent deaths. The key word of 2 Kings 15, which tells of these events, is 'conspiracy' (10,15,25,30). A comparison of the years each king is said to have reigned shows that the land was, at times, divided up amongst various contenders for the throne. Such political anarchy was accompanied by the complete collapse of all moral, social and religious values, as shown in Hosea's prophecy. God's judgement finally fell, and Israel ceased to exist in 721 B.C. In contrast, these scribes rejoiced in the security of Judah, under the godly reformer, Hezekiah. Further examples could be drawn from the history books of Israel and Judah, the editors of which are careful to point out that the greatest benefit a king can bring to his people is to do 'what was right in the eyes of the Lord' (1 Kings 15.11, etc.). Hence the stress on attention and obedience to the law (4,7,9) as the inspiration and guide of the king (Deut. 17.18 ff.). What a world this would be if all men lived by God's standards, as revealed in His Word!

Proverbs 29

In this, the last chapter of regular-type proverbs, there is considerable duplication, an inevitable fact in such a collection. The place of reproof, and the dangers of a stubborn rejection, are shown in

163

vs. 1,15, to which may be added two proverbs which illustrate the 'wise son—glad parents' theme (3,17). Another kind of reproof is noted in v. 18 where 'prophecy' (RSV) is a more accurate translation than the 'vision' of AV (KJV), RV, although the latter rendering is equally true in experience. The word is the regular one used of prophetic revelation and the verse has a two-fold interest. First, it shows the function of the prophet as God's watchman, warning of the danger in rejecting God (cf. Isa. 21.8,11; Ezek. 3.17, etc.), or to change the metaphor, as the watchdog of society, guarding its conscience. Secondly, the parallelism of the verse shows that the basis of the prophetic appeal was the Law, i.e. the first five books of the Bible, the Pentateuch. The prophets' message was not the invention of their own hearts but an appeal to return to a revealed standard. In a world which has largely 'cast off restraint' the function of the Church is similar, viz. to call men back to God, to live and preach His standards and to warn of the consequences of neglecting these truths.

Wise government is dealt with yet again in vs. 2,4,12,14,16. Two other subjects which have recurred frequently are found once more; a comparison between evil and righteous men in vs. 6,10,27 and a comparison of the fool and the wise man in vs. 7,9 ff. Two difficult proverbs concern the treatment of servants: v. 19 applies only to servants of a particular mentality, as 17.2 makes clear; in v. 21 the meaning of the final word is obscure, 'heir' (RSV) is probably incorrect in a proverb which seems to be giving a warning against over-indulgent treatment. A more likely derivation (suggested by D. Winton Thomas and followed by Derek Kidner) connects with an Arabic root and gives the reading 'weakling', suggesting one who is flabby and lacking in moral fibre. This agrees with the stress in *Proverbs* on the function of discipline.

Notice the three-fold snare of this chapter. False flattery (5) can make a neighbour puffed up with pride, with the result noted in v. 23. Evil men are trapped by a web of their own spinning (6). Fear of what man will do, think, or say about us is another snare (25a). He who trusts in the Lord is safe (25b), and what a happy character he should be (6b)!

Proverbs 30.1-17

We know nothing about Agur apart from the information we glean from this chapter. Since Massa was the name of an Ishmaelite clan, he was almost certainly an Arab, a people traditionally renowned for their wisdom. Ithiel and Ucal may be two of his disciples. Agur was a keen student of life, and his method of instruction appears to have been to confront his listeners with several graphic examples of the point he was concerned to make, allowing them to make the application—a wise method of teaching since it enlists the co-operation of the student. The formula 'three . . . four' (15,18,21,29, cf. note on 6.16) indicates that the list was not meant to be regarded as complete.

The searching mind and the inquiring heart of Agur made him a humble man (1–4). It is often true that the more we know, the more we realize our ignorance, that we are but paddling in the shallows of a vast sea! His words (3 f.) are paralleled in the Lord's challenge to Job (Job 38,39) which made the latter aware of both his abysmal ignorance and his arrogant pride (Job 42. 1–6). The immensity and complexity of our universe points to the infinite greatness and wisdom of its Creator. How wonderful, then, is His humility in drawing near to mere men (cf. Psa. 113. 5–9)! The self-revelation of such a God, whatever form it may take, may be relied upon implicitly (5). V. 6 (cf. Rev. 22.6,18 f.) has its application to the Scriptures.

The dangers of prosperity and adversity are noted in vs. 7 ff. The point of v. 10 is that unfounded slander could bring a harsh punishment upon a servant in an age when a master had absolute control over his dependants. The servant's curse would then be well-founded, and in the ancient world would be conceived to have effective power (cf. 2 Sam. 3.28 f.). Ungrateful impiety, self-righteousness, pride and slanderous, malicious speech are condemned in vs. 11–14. V. 11 has its sequel in v. 17, with its picture of an unburied corpse suggesting a dishonourable end. Whilst the meaning of the word translated 'leech' (15) is uncertain, no ambiguity attaches to the section. It condemns the insatiable craving for worldly pleasures or possessions. How important it is to have the right kind of desires (e.g. Matt. 6.33; Col. 3.1 f.)!

Proverbs 30.18-33

Four wonderful things (18 f.). The connecting link between these has been seen in a movement which leaves no trace behind, although the serpent hardly fits into this pattern. Rather, it is the movement itself which is in mind, with the associated thought of mastery within a particular element. The 'way of a man with a maid' has a much broader connotation than the sexual act, it refers to the movement of love from its first tentative beginnings until there is a complete unity (Gen. 2.24; Eph. 5.31). A shattering climax, so surprising that it is not included in the pattern, concerns the adulteress, to whom her act of sin is of no more consequence than a meal (20).

Four obnoxious things (21 ff.). All these refer to the unbearable conduct of an upstart, intoxicated by unexpected success. The fool (22b) of the second example is properly a churl (as in the proper name, Nabal, 1 Sam. 25), who might make an effort to be pleasant for the sake of food, but not when he was well fed. The third, concerning the unmarried woman, may appear uncharitable, but it refers to taunting, vindictive conduct such as Peninnah showed to Hannah (1 Sam. 1.6 f.).

Four small but sensible things (24–28). The purpose of the wise man was practical and this is not an exhortation to appreciate even insignificant creatures, but a call to imitate their qualities. The ant (25) has already been used as an object lesson of prudent foresight in 6.6–11. The badgers or marmots (Moffatt) display wisdom in using natural features to provide a refuge which more than compensates for their own vulnerability. Discipline and orderliness, albeit of a frightening kind, are characteristic of the locusts (27), and the lizard (28, 'spider' AV [KJV], is erroneous) is commended for its audacity or enterprise. In each case the first line introduces some limitation. The qualities of prudent planning and discipline are equally desirable in Christians, who have found in Christ a secure refuge from danger (cf. Isa. 32.1 f.; Rom. 8.1). Moreover, we may dwell with the King (Eph. 2.6)!

Four stately things (29 ff.). Each example illustrates stateliness of movement. No obvious moral is drawn, or even hinted at, unless it be that each possesses a certain confidence which leads to poise. If this be so, it is another example for the Christian whose confidence, born of Christ's victory, should lead to an air of assurance (John 16.33).

P.S. Be humble, avoid evil, or suffer the inevitably painful consequences (32 f.)!

Proverbs 31

A mother's advice is frankly but lovingly offered in vs. 1–9. The RSV is probably correct in connecting Lemuel, like Agur (30.1), with Massa. He was the king of his people. His name means 'belonging to God', which reflects both the vow and the desire of his mother (2b). The sound counsel which she offers reveals an attitude far removed from an empty piety or wishful thinking. She was amongst those sensibly spiritual people who accept their responsibilities in connection with the fulfilment of their prayers. So she

166

warns her son to avoid sexual promiscuity or drunkenness but to gain instead a reputation as the champion of the oppressed.

The ideal wife (10–31). The twenty-two verses of this section form an acrostic poem, with each verse beginning with one of the letters of the Hebrew alphabet. It is probably anonymous, although it has been attributed to Lemuel's mother. It presents an attractive picture of the function of a wife in an upper class home. Her affluent position is indicated by her many maid-servants (15), her ample resources (16), the quality of her materials (21 f.) and her husband's prominent position in the community (23). But her dependability (11), industry (13–19,24,27), generosity (20), foresight (21,25), sagacity and kindness (26) may be emulated by those in less fortunate circumstances. Small wonder that she earns the loving, respectful admiration of her family (28 f.)! The source of her beautiful character, not beauty of the skin-deep variety, springs from her relationship to God (30). This can never be purchased by wealth, it is open to all. Hence this poem is much more than a valuable witness to the place and functions of a wife in Israelite society. In a book which has a great deal to say, by way of warning, against the ways of the immoral woman, it is refreshing to note, in contrast, the gracious, bountiful and upright wife of our section (cf. 9.1–6). The language of this lovely poem calls to mind the interdependence between Christ and His bride, the Church (Eph. 5.23–32). The latter acknowledges His lordship and works this out in loving, diligent service, whilst the former delights in her, rejoices in her faithfulness and regards her as infinitely precious (cf. Eph. 1.18).

Questions for further study and discussion on Proverbs chs. 27–31
1. What lessons can we learn from *Proverbs* on the subject of true friendship? (cf. the notes on ch. 27, and use a concordance).
2. Draw out the basic principles of wise government in chs. 28,29.
3. Starting from the note on ch. 29, can you work out the contribution to the total revelation of each of the major parts of the O.T., viz. the *Law, Historical Books, Prophets, Psalms* and the *Wisdom Literature?*
4. What has ch. 30.2 ff. in common with Job 38,39; Isa. 40.12–26; Rom. 11.33–36?
5. With ch. 31.10–31 as a model, can you compose a short poem (5–10 verses) on (*a*) the good husband and (*b*) the ideal child?

Ecclesiastes

INTRODUCTION

The title in the English versions comes from the *Septuagint* (Greek), whilst the sub-title, 'The Preacher', derives from the Hebrew '*Qoheleth*', indicating one who addresses an assembly. Presumably the writer was a leader in one of the assemblies of 'the wise' in Jerusalem. Conservative scholarship is unanimous in holding that Solomon was not the author, and sets a date varying from *c.* 425 (E. J. Young) to *c.* 200 B.C. (J. Stafford Wright). The Preacher condemns the ruling power in 3.16; 4.1, witnesses to a period of poverty and anarchy (4.13-16), and implies that many generations had preceded him in Jerusalem (1.16: 2.9), which could hardly apply to Solomon. Classical Hebrew tradition dated the book from Hezekiah's reign (*c.* 700 B.C.). The apparent scepticism and pessimism of the book has perplexed many, but the author was a realist, who refused to be satisfied with the glib, slick answers which traditionalists gave to life's problems. The book may be described as his quest for truth, which led him up many a dark alley and cul de sac. His faith in the existence of God, which is never in doubt, eventually led him to the only logical solution. We live in an age when doubt has become fashionable, and the message of this book is appropriate, although it does not rise to the sublime heights of some other O.T. books.

Ecclesiastes 1.1-11
Prologue

The author describes himself in v. 1 (cf. 12) as the 'son of David, king in Jerusalem' but nowhere does he actually call himself Solomon, nor does he make more than a pretence to be Solomon. The use of the name draws attention to the fact that the greatest king of Israel, renowned for his wisdom and possessing great wealth, failed to secure enduring satisfaction in life. What hope was there then for lesser mortals!

Vanity! The word occurs about forty times in all and may be regarded as the author's verdict on life apart from God. The repetition in 'vanity of vanities', itself twice repeated (2, cf. 12.8) is the Hebrew way of expressing the superlative—here is an emptiness indeed! Man's quest for ultimate and enduring truth appears to him to be completely deceptive. Generations come and go, each with their ambitions and fears, and there seems to be no appreciable impact upon the world. The same cycle is apparent in nature. The sun, which appears to be moving majestically and purposefully through the heavens, dips beneath the western horizon only to emerge at its starting point on the next day. The circuit of the wind seems even more monotonous, as suggested by the four verbs used in v. 6, each of which derives from the same root. The Preacher's third illustration concerns the constant outpouring of innumerable streams into an ocean which never becomes appreciably deeper since, in some mysterious way (probably because the streams themselves were believed to be fed from the same Great Deep), the waters returned to their source again. It is perhaps strange that what we view as the evidence of the harmonious and intricate balance of nature should be so construed by the wise man. Nature, he laments, never advances. But his deeper complaint is that past generations are forgotten (11) and that the same fate will ultimately overtake the present generation.

Two things help to relieve the gloom of this prologue: (i) The author himself does not advocate opting out of life's responsibilities, rather, he commends active involvement (11.1–6). (ii)God's estimate, not that of finite man, is the ultimately important fact (3.17; 12.14). Man makes mistakes in actions and judgements, He never does.

Ecclesiastes 1.12—2.26   A Fruitless Quest

From 1.12—2.11 the writer is clearly claiming to be Solomon but every so often his disguise slips, and while he does not tell us who he is, we can discern who he is not! For instance, the expression 'all who were over Jerusalem before me' (1.16; cf. 2.7,9) could refer to David, or one of the later kings of Judah, but it could not conceivably be used by Solomon. In this section he explores the achievements which the wealth and wisdom of Solomon made possible. He does not deny that life has its transient pleasures (note the frank admission of 2.24), but he cannot find the ultimate goal of life in any of these. His was a whole-hearted quest, for he entered the labyrinth of madness and folly (1.17). It was also a rational, clear-minded quest which eschewed the escape from reality by 'drowning one's sorrows in drink' (2.3). Pleasures and possessions of all kinds (2.1–10), such as only a Solomon could afford, architectural achievements such as Solomon himself effected (2.4 ff., cf. 1 Kings 6.1—7.51) with the aid of slave labour (2.7a, cf. 1 Kings 5.13–16; 9.15–22); all these were pursued, not without a certain satisfaction (2.10). But even Solomon had not discovered the true secret of life, so in 2.12b the mask of pretending to be the king of Israel's golden age is laid aside—no one can do any more than *he* did in this life,

169

therefore life's ultimate goal cannot lie in the pursuit of pleasure.

The superiority of wisdom over folly is self-evident (2.13), but the author questions whether it has any ultimate superiority (14–23). Death comes alike to both (14 ff.) and the honest industry of the wise man, involving wearisome toil and sleepless nights of planning (23) seems pointless, everything has to be left behind. Then one who has expended no effort reaps the reward. The darkness of much of the O.T. teaching concerning this aspect of death is illumined in the N.T. There is the possibility of being 'rich toward God' (Luke 12.21), of laying up 'treasures in heaven' (Matt. 6.20), of an interest and investment 'in the things that are above, where Christ is' (Col. 3.1). This is true wealth which does not disappoint. The writer of *Ecclesiastes*, by his honest scepticism, has served succeeding generations well by pointing out the emptiness of materialism and thus preparing the way for Christianity. And while his final note in our section (2.26b) is one of pessimism, yet his faith is such that he advocates full involvement in this life (24) and sees at least some recompense in God's ordering of the universe (26).

Ecclesiastes 3   Eternity in Man's Mind

There is the chill of despair in this chapter which is most keenly felt in vs. 20 f. The author is struck by the fate which overtakes both men and beasts (18–21), the breath leaves their bodies, which are then reduced to the elements. It is surprising to discover that in the Israelite cultus, *Ecclesiastes* was associated with the most joyous festival, that of Tabernacles, which celebrated the harvest of grapes, figs and olives (*Ecclesiastes*, together with *Song of Songs*, *Ruth*, *Lamentations* and *Esther*, formed the Five Rolls, or *Megilloth*, each of which was read at a particular feast). Unquestionably this was deliberate, possibly with the intention of reminding those who shared in the joyous festivities that there was a more serious aspect to life.

In fairness to the Preacher, it must be pointed out that he identifies human beings and the brute creation only in the fact that death overtakes both, he does not deny that man's life is on a higher plane. Doubtless he would accept the orthodox Jewish belief that man was made in the image of God as the crowning point of His creation, and given dominion over all lesser creatures (Gen. 1.26 f.; Psa. 8.3–8). This is movingly reflected in v. 11 'He has put eternity into man's mind'. Cattle do not ponder over the great problems of life, or wrestle with the question of the ultimate relationship of the created to the Creator. But man does, and his agonized quest for an answer shows his awareness of a meaning and a destiny to life.

He cannot accept that death ends all. The tensions of *Ecclesiastes* find their focal point in this dilemma, that man's consciousness promises so much but apparently ends so ignominiously. Man is made for God and is incomplete without Him, hence the frustrations and tensions in man as man alone. This 'God-shaped blank' in every man's mind, at which the Preacher hints, is also witnessed in St. Augustine's memorable words, 'Thou hast created us for Thyself, and our heart cannot be quieted till it may find repose in Thee.'

Not until the final chapter of his book does the Preacher discover the 'Ariadne's thread' which leads him out of the labyrinth of speculation although he approaches a solution in v. 17. Here he simply notes God's sovereignty (10–15) and restates his earlier advice (2.24) that life on this earth is to be enjoyed, not endured (12 f., 22).

Notes: Vs. 2–9 form a beautiful poem which observes the antitheses which abound in man's life from the cradle to the grave. V. 15b, when taken out of its context, is suggestive of the questing heart of God (cf. Luke 15). But in context it affirms the divine control of the repetitive cycle of nature and comes close to making Him the slave of His own creation.

Ecclesiastes 4   Inhuman and Futile Behaviour

Robert Burns lamented that 'Man's inhumanity to man makes countless thousands mourn'. Our author observes this (1 ff.) and in the extremity of depression he considers it better to be dead or unborn than alive in a world where such evils abound. That this is but a passing mood is shown by 9.4 ff., but it is an emotion shared by many in this century, when the brutal oppression of Police States has taken toll of tens of millions of lives. Escape from the contemporary scene is the coward's way, however. The right course, albeit the costliest, is to defend the basic rights of men whenever and however they are denied.

The pressures which come from the rivalry of 'keeping up with the Jones' ' are illustrated in vs. 4–6. Competition sharpens a man's natural ability, but when it becomes cut-throat it has dangerous side effects. The point of v. 6 is that it is preferable to have one portion with peace of heart than two portions and a heart-attack! 'A striving after wind' is a favourite phrase of the writer which indicates something completely unsatisfying, like a meal of thin air. But sandwiched in this good advice is a condemnation of the equally foolish policy of a self-destructive indolence (5). Keep the balance!

171

The parable of the rich fool, in its O.T. version, is told in vs. 7 f. (cf. Luke 12.13–21). It remains true that 'you can't take it with you' and if there is no loved one to labour for such miserly and completely selfish conduct is doubly pointless.

'United we stand, divided we fall', sums up the thought of vs. 9–12. Two heads are better than one, where support, satisfaction and security are concerned. Various ingenious explanations of v. 12b have been advanced, such as the father, mother, child relationship, or the doctrine of the Trinity. But whilst the strength of these unities is undeniable, our verse simply means that mutual security is further increased when there are three, rather than two.

Vs. 13–16, like 1–3, cannot have been written by Solomon. The perils of the monarchy and the fickleness of the crowd appear to be the main themes of a difficult section. Three principal characters may be detected—'an old and foolish king'; his son, 'that youth, who was to stand in his place'; and 'a poor and wise youth', possibly a usurper. Any connection with an historical situation, within or without Israel, is conjectural. Probably the writer is concerned to do no more than illustrate that even a king can topple from the pedestal of popular acclaim, i.e. there is no permanence in any social relationship.

Ecclesiastes 5.1—6.9

Realism regarding Religion and Riches

Religion (5.1–7). In our final estimate of the meaning of *Ecclesiastes* and our assessment of the faith of its author, this is an important section. The scepticism which abounds elsewhere is completely absent; the writer shows his adherence to the traditional forms of religion in a down-to-earth way which compares with the attitude of the prophets. 'To draw near' (1) is a semi-technical expression for the worshipful approach to the Lord (cf. Zeph. 3.2; Heb. 10.22). This was normally accompanied by a sacrifice, but if the latter were offered on its own, without a corresponding inwardness (cf. Psa. 51.17) it was an insult to God (see the notes on Prov. 15.8; 21.3,27). Far better to approach God empty-handed but with a deep desire 'to listen', which in Hebrew thought betokens not simply the hearing of words but obedience to them. This reality in worship rests upon the relationship between an Almighty God and finite, creaturely man. Any presumption is out of keeping and unpardonable, hence the admonition to 'Guard your steps when you go to the house of God.'

The sanctity of vows uttered before God is the second of the two

172

religious topics (2–7, cf. Deut. 23.21; Prov. 20.25). Vows were to be meaningful, with every word weighed carefully, in contrast to the inconsequential meanderings of dreams and the empty prating of fools (3,7). The 'messenger' (6) probably refers to the Temple official whose duty it was to collect the revenue from vows. Any attempt to evade the responsibilities assumed would cause more than the anger of an official however, it would bring the wrath of God, with its effective power (6b). This seems to be the point of v. 2b; God's infinite greatness is not compatible with wordy but empty promises. Deut. 23.22, however, makes it plain that man is not compelled to make vows, but a vow undertaken must be held seriously.

Riches (5.8—6.9). These, like power, can corrupt and human government can degenerate into a bureaucracy tainted at its every level (8). They can never satisfy (10 f.); they engender envy in the poor (12); they are transient, and an unsuccessful business venture can cause them to vanish overnight (13–17). Nor is it much better to amass possessions for our successors if we fail both to enjoy life, and to discover its real meaning before death brings all down to the same level (6.1–9). Life is brief and riches are passing, but the Preacher nevertheless recognizes that they are a gift from God, to be enjoyed (5.18–20).

A challenge: In the light of the opening paragraph, how did I approach God's house last Sunday? How should I approach God in worship next Sunday?

Ecclesiastes 6.10—7.29   Man's Frailty

The Preacher returns to the theme of man's creatureliness (6.10 ff.), which makes him so helpless in the presence of God. One is reminded of Job, who was full of complaints against God when in dialogue with Eliphaz, Bildad and Zophar, and longed for the opportunity to present his case before the Almighty (e.g. Job 13.3,18–24; 23.3–7; 31.35–37). But when confronted with the Almighty he was speechless (40.3–5). This concept of a God-man confrontation is common in the Scriptures and its inevitable result is to demonstrate man's utter impotence (Isa. 41.1; 43.8 f.; 45.9 ff.; Rom. 9.19–26). The transitoriness of life, and the limitations of human knowledge, grieved our author deeply and left him feeling crushed. But this was not the effect produced by the Lord's appearance to Job. Silenced, conscious of sin, yes! especially the sin of having questioned the integrity of God. But as a result of the revelation of chs. 38–41 Job found a new source of trust in the wisdom and

173

omnipotence of the Almighty. He could make no mistakes. The N.T. unfolding of God's character and purpose speaks also of His abounding love for all His creatures (Rom. 5.8; 2 Pet. 3.9). Man is finite, but God in Christ has reached down in salvation that we might share His deity (1 John 3.1 f.).

In ch. 7.1–12 the Preacher culls from contemporary proverbs to illustrate his general theme, that life is coloured and qualified by the shadow of death (1,2). Nevertheless, the pursuit of wisdom, especially if one has the resources to implement it (11 f.), and such moral qualities as justice (7), patience and persistence (8), self-control (9) and an acceptance of the present (10), all have a certain value in this life.

A direct attack then follows on the popular view, challenged also by Job (Job 21), that there is a direct equation between righteousness and prosperity on the one hand, and sin and adversity on the other. This, bluntly states the Preacher, just doesn't square with the facts (15, cf. 8.14). With considerable courage he relates both adversity and prosperity to the inscrutable dealings of God with men (14). We may not agree with the conclusion he draws from this (16 f.), that man should steer a middle course, avoiding extreme positions, but this was characteristic of the widespread Hellenistic thought. Our Saviour certainly calls us to be 'out and out' in discipleship (e.g. Matt. 10.37 ff.; 16.24–27).

More emptiness in life's pursuits is shown in vs. 19–29. Human estimates must always be qualified, for wisdom (19 f.) is never absolute and judgements are never impartial (21 f.). Ultimate reality and satisfaction continued to elude his desperate search, and he concludes by noting the crookedness of man which appears to have defeated the creative purpose of God (29).

Ecclesiastes 8   Compromise and Frustration

The way of compromise (1–9). What is the right course of action when commanded by the king to do something which is wrong, or which goes against the grain? The Preacher looks at this problem sceptically, because it illustrates how little real freedom man has. The kings of his day could be arbitrary and despotically harsh (3 f., 9), and the situation was complicated by the oath of loyalty to the monarch (2). But the wise man knows the way out of a difficult situation (such is the force of the second line of v. 1). Since the king's authority was unquestionable, an appearance of implicit obedience was to be conveyed (2–5a). The wise man was not without freedom however, for the timing and execution of the command

174

was still within his control (5b). A sensitive conscience retained a certain elasticity of action. The Preacher cannot get away from his main theme however, the complete uncertainty concerning the future, described as 'man's trouble' (6b). He has no power to prolong life or to avert death, whilst war relentlessly claimed its victims (8). A deeper insight, in the moral realm, concerns the same tenacious power of evil over its victims; sin enslaves, and man by himself cannot effect his freedom (cf. Rom. 6.16–23).

The Preacher's advice (5) is hardly heroic, and must not be regarded as the standard for the Christian, who must never compromise his testimony (cf. Matt. 10.16–33).

Frustrating inequalities (10–17). History seems to show no moral purpose whatever (10 f., 14). The sinner 'gets away with it' (11) and so others are encouraged to evil. No clear pattern of rewards or punishment emerges in this life. In sharp contrast with this philosophy of despair is the affirmation of vs. 12 f. Indeed, many scholars regard this as a gloss to correct the heretical tendencies of this section. More likely it illustrates the tension between the observations of the eye and the postulates of faith. So much that the Preacher saw could lead him to doubt what he accepted by faith. He is not alone in this. The way of faith is never easy, but a real faith can stand the test of apparent inconsistencies. Faith rests, not in circumstances, but in the very character of the One in whom we believe. But the Preacher's faith at this point knew no such stability; his longing centred in man's mastery of life's problems (17); his advice rises no higher than 'make the most of things' (15).

Note: 'under the sun' (17), as elsewhere in the book, means 'in this life'.

Ecclesiastes 9   The Hand of God

The apparent pessimism of vs. 1–6,11 f. is qualified by the conviction, expressed in v. 1, that whether good or evil befall the righteous man, his fate is securely in the hands of God. The Preacher has never really doubted this fact, he does not bring in the idea of God at the end to account for life's inequalities. But he does lament that there seems so much of chance in this world. Death, the great leveller, ultimately claims all men (3). Those who deserve to be successful (11) do not always reap their due reward. He does not understand how men can live such evil and purposeless lives (3). All the same, it is better to live than to die, for the living have consciousness, even though it be but an awareness of the inevitability of death (5). The absence of a future hope in this period is shown by the grim description of existence (it could hardly be called life) in Sheol, 'no work or thought or knowledge or wisdom' (10b). The tragedy of successive forgotten generations weighed heavily upon him (6).

Once more the practical concerns of the Preacher are apparent (7–10). He advocates no passive, stoical acceptance of a distasteful situation, but a living of life to its fullness. Observe also his conviction of God's sovereignty within this life (9b).

Wisdom v. power (13–18). Victory does not always go to the side which has numerical superiority or superior equipment. Wisdom, expressed in strategy and tactics, can make up for deficiencies in these realms. But the Preacher is equally quick to observe another evidence of injustice, that credit is not always given to the one who deserves it, especially if he be a relative 'nobody'. So the writer adds another point to his impressive catalogue. Man, he declares, is an ungrateful creature. But there is a God who takes a careful and accurate account of man's actions and motives (2 Chron. 16.9; Prov. 5.21).

A thought: Compare the motive of v. 10 with the higher motive which is to govern our actions (Col. 3.17,24) and then apply the latter to this day's activities.

Ecclesiastes 10.1—11.8   Make the Most of This Life

In ch. 10 the Preacher gives further advice, selected from the proverbial literature of his age. The contrast between the foolish and the wise, which figures prominently in the book of *Proverbs*, appears in vs. 1–3, 10, 12–15. 'Right' and 'left' in v. 2 are synonyms for good and evil respectively. The point of v. 3 is that foolishness shows in the most ordinary aspects of life. Vs. 10,15 illustrate the folly of misapplied strength, the latter verse speaking of one who is so weary that he doesn't know *how* to drag himself home. Wisdom, therefore, is of value in this life. The way in which the Preacher speaks of the powers that be discloses his bitter experience of capricious and irresponsible rule (e.g. 5 ff., 16 f.). The wise man, therefore, has need of self-control (4, cf. 8.1–9) and caution (20). In vs. 8 f. he shows that every occupation has its hazards, and there are side glances at laziness (18) and money as the universal provider (19).

A call to action (11.1–8). This is an important section in which the author begins to crystallize his thought. His quest for ultimate truth and for the supreme purpose in life, has led him to criss-cross restlessly the tracks of human experience. He has not, at this point, found what he sought, but he has learnt a great deal about life itself. Many interpretations have been given to v. 1, the one which suits

176

the context is that it advocates liberality, even in a situation which appears to have little prospect of reward. Hymn writers have adopted this interpretation (cf. v. 6) in connection with the proclamation of the gospel. V. 2 suggests a wise distribution of business interests, the antithesis of 'putting all your eggs in one basket'. It is not likely that all will fail simultaneously. So in v. 1 there is the acceptance of risk, but in v. 2 there is a precaution to avoid total failure. Another, more extended contrast follows. Nature's laws cannot be broken (3) but since man does not control these, nor understand them, he must act resolutely and independently, not waiting for the perfect time which may never come. God alone is in control (4–6). His general verdict is that life is sweet (7) and therefore to be accepted joyfully (8a). But a shadow falls upon it, 'night comes' (8b, cf. John 9.4). Life is to be lived under this realization, so that man can extract the maximum amount of enjoyment and usefulness from it. The Saviour, in John 9, speaks of the coming of night as bringing an end to the 'works of Him who sent Me'. For His twentieth-century disciples too, there is an end to the opportunities of service in this life. But for the Preacher the end was 'vanity' (8b); for the believer in Christ and the fellow-labourer with Him it is 'Well done, good and faithful servant . . . enter into the joy of your master' (Matt. 25.21).

Ecclesiastes 11.9—12.14   The End of the Quest

A word to young people (11.9—12.1). The Preacher again commends a full-hearted enjoyable participation in life, whilst recognizing that youth is transitory. But never does he commend the search for happiness as an end in itself, or advocate unbridled licence. The happy youth is the one who takes God into account and who lives in the light of His judgement (9b). A relationship with God is essential to making the most of this life.

The inevitability of death (12.2–8). In a deeply moving passage old age is pictured as the winter of life, when all warmth and light have departed (2). In the succeeding verses the various members and faculties of the body are viewed as a household which has known the ravages of time. Notice the allusions to the arms, legs, teeth and eyes in v. 3; to increasing deafness in which the normal sounds of life become a confused blur and musical appreciation vanishes (4); to the fear of heights, the difficulty of getting about and the failure of desire, even if it be springtime (5). Various picturesque metaphors for death itself follow (6), after which man returns to the elements (7), his cycle of life completed. 'Vanity of vanities' (8, cf.

177

1.2) indicates the Preacher's judgement on human existence, by itself, as utterly pointless.

Appreciation (9–12). These verses do not fit easily into the context, and it has been suggested that they are a tribute to the Preacher, added by his disciples. More likely is the view that they show, in spite of the apparent despair of v. 8, that the wise man followed his own advice to make the most of things. In a characteristic manner he contrasts two aspects of the teaching of the wise. The first is in appreciation (11), speaking of the stimulus ('goads') and the coherence ('nails', which secure things together) which wisdom provides. The second gives a warning, which many a student has echoed, that there can be too much of a good thing (12)!

Finally, he draws the strands of his philosophy together (13 f.). Within life man has a solemn responsibility to honour God and keep His commandments. But this life, so apparently pointless, is not the end. Man does not promise so much or long for so much to end in dust. There *is* a hereafter, in which all the apparent injustice of this life will be rectified. The judgement, touched upon in 3.17; 11.9, comes into sharp focus as the solution to man's eternal questionings. What appears so perplexing to man will find its perfect answer at God's judgement seat. Thus, while the Preacher does not rise to a full doctrine of the resurrection, he does show the moral necessity of a future judgement, and it was only a question of time before the complementary truth was appreciated, that man himself must *see* this final judgement.

Questions for further study and discussion on Ecclesiastes

1. What corrective would you apply to the pessimistic view of the lack of influence of successive generations in 1.1–11 (cf. Prov. 10.7)?
2. If riches and possessions cannot give full satisfaction in this life (see note on 1.12—2.26) to what effective use can they be put?
3. How would you answer anyone who advocates the policy of withdrawal noted in 4.1–3?
4. What spiritual application concerning the blessings of fellowship can be drawn from 4.9–12?
5. Do you consider that there *is* a relationship between righteousness and material prosperity? (See note on 6.10—7.29.)
6. Work out the advice of 11.1–6 in terms of Christian service.
7. What validity have the solutions which the Preacher advances to solve the problems of life?

The Song of Solomon

INTRODUCTION

There is no impossibility in the Solomonic authorship of this book which tradition uniformly ascribes to him. The name of Solomon occurs several times but there is no difficulty about an author writing in the third person about himself. Solomon had a reputation both as a lover and a poet, and the references to Jerusalem, Carmel, Sharon, Lebanon and Hermon as within the same kingdom suggest a date before the division of the kingdom after his death. The book has been interpreted in a number of ways, e.g. (i) A six-act drama telling of the developing love between Solomon and the maiden. (ii) A five-act drama with three principal characters: Solomon, the Shulammite maiden (6.13) whom he attempted to win, and the shepherd-lover to whom she remained faithful. (iii) A drama enacted in the harem at Jerusalem, Solomon, the Shulammite and the ladies of the harem being the participants. (iv) A collection of love poems, by one author, with no connecting theme other than love itself.

The view which we adopt, without dogmatism, is the second of these alternatives. The evidence of a 'chorus', formed by the women of the harem (2.7; 3.5; 5.8; 8.4, etc.) suggests a continuity, but it is not a drama in the normally accepted sense, for it combines imaginary and real episodes. Goethe described it as 'a medley'. The book, on this interpretation, forms a deeply-moving unity. The love described is suggestive of the greater love between God and Israel, or between Christ and the Church, but its primary value is to extol the preciousness of human love.

The Song of Solomon 1   The Crisis of Love

This book, which is the delight of some Bible students, is an enigma to others. The Jewish scholars who finalized the canon of O.T. Scripture had reservations concerning the Song. It was one of the last books to be regarded as canonical, and then principally on the basis that it was an allegory, revealing God's love to Israel. Similarly, when the canon of Christian Scripture was being finalized, an allegorical interpretation of the Song in terms of Christ and the Church was a determining factor in its acceptance. The Christian sees the divine overshadowing in this, and allows the Song its full place in the Scriptures. Here is a book which, whatever interpretation is accepted, has a great deal to say about human love, and which nowhere mentions the name of God (except descriptively in the Hebrew of **8.6**). At the outset it may be observed that this highly important aspect of human life is not outside the interest of God.

'The Song of Songs' (**1**) is another illustration of the Hebrew superlative by repetition (cf. Eccl. **1.2**; **12.8**), meaning 'the best of songs'. Love is ever the inspiration of song, both in the natural and spiritual realms. Human love is the theme of the greater portion of that ephemeral music which passes monotonously through the gradings of the 'hit parade', as well as those more enduring melodies which abound in folk-songs. Divine love is the theme of an equally great number of Christian hymns. Indeed, Christianity has been called the 'singing faith', and it is God's love that prompts this outburst of praise.

The scene in this first chapter appears to be the king's palace in Jerusalem. A country maiden, her features darkened by exposure to the sun, has been brought to the harem, where she faces the scrutiny of the other wives and concubines (**3–6**). But her heart is not in the palace but with her far-away shepherd-lover. In her mind she traces the track that will lead her to him (**7** f.). Her reverie is abruptly interrupted by the king, who tries to win her over by conventional flattery and promises of rich ornamentation (**9** f.). But she is not to be so cheaply enticed, and while the king is banqueting (**12**) she fortifies herself by imagining that she is back with her true lover in some forest glade, with a carpet of green grass beneath and the over-reaching boughs of cedar and pine above (**17**). A recollection of true love, whether it be of husband or wife, sweetheart or child, friend or Saviour, will serve to keep us in the hour of temptation.

Note: The comparison of v. **9** is a very flattering one in the East, where horses are greatly prized and, like women, highly ornamented.

The Song of Solomon 2

Absence Makes the Heart Grow Fonder

The maiden's soliloquy continues. Her place is not in the ornate splendour of the court, she is a country flower (**1**) best seen in its native habitat. Possibly the metaphor recalls a simile used by her shepherd-lover, who, with that singleness of devotion which excluded all rivals, regarded her as a lily amongst worthless brambles (cf. the derogatory remarks of Jotham in Judg. **9.7–15**). In a natural transition of thought she considers what her lover is to her, strong, sturdy and fruitful as an apple tree (**3**). Solomon's banqueting hall seems very tawdry in comparison with this setting for such a feast of love (**4**). Perhaps the words of vs. **5** f. came out in the form of an ejaculation, which was overheard and misunderstood by the women of the harem. They imagined that she was pining for Solomon, and crying out for love apples which were widely believed to stimulate sexual love and fertility (cf. the mandrakes of 7.13, cf. Gen. 30.14 ff.). The Shulammite wanted none of this. Her great longing was to be reunited with her sweetheart. She imagined him, young, lithe, and supple, coming to her to rescue her from virtual imprisonment in the harem (8–15). Such a deliverance would indeed be comparable to the transition from winter to springtime (11 ff.). Springtime in Palestine is incomparably the loveliest of the seasons. In the summer and early autumn the land is gradually scorched by the sun and seared by drought, whilst winter is the rainy season. But in the springtime the warm sun and the soft 'latter rains' combine to deck the earth with beauty. But there was more than this to attract her away from Jerusalem, there was the security in the presence of her lover—doves, in Palestine, nest in the cliff-faces (14). V. 15 seems to be a snatch from a rustic song. Here the maiden may be singing it in answer to the request of v. 14, the familiar song, sung in a special way, telling him where she was.

The daydream ends abruptly with an affirmation of love (16). There is also the deep yearning that at the close of day her lover might come home to her (17). Clearly she is sick at heart, and desperately unhappy. But by fortifying herself with her love she is erecting a fortress which will withstand all the well-practised blandishments of Solomon. So this chapter speaks its direct word to the hearts of all those who have known true human affection. Beyond this, it echoes the longing for the return of the One whom the hymn writer described as the 'Lover of my soul'. 'He . . . says, "Surely I am coming soon." Amen. Come, Lord Jesus!' (Rev. 22.20).

The Song of Solomon 3.1—4.6

The Battle for the Heart

The day-dreams of the previous chapter here become nightmares (3.1–4). 'By night' is plural, suggesting that this kind of dream was repeated nightly. During the daytime the intensity of the Shulammite's love brought hope, but in the night subconscious fears rose to the surface, and in her dreams she scoured the streets of Jerusalem looking for the object of her affections. The quest, fruitless at first, is at last rewarded and the lovers are reunited. The adjuration of v. 5 (cf. 2.7) is possibly caused by the continued fear that the other women would, by their concoctions and wiles, stimulate a physical response which she is unwilling to make herself.

181

A picture of ostentation, power and luxury is conveyed in 3.6–11. The maiden is brought to a vantage point where she may be impressed with the sheer magnificence of her suitor-king. The royal progress of Solomon is accompanied by columns (another plural form) of smoke, possibly referring to the clouds of dust such a procession would raise as well as the clouds of the most expensive incense. The king's palanquin (9 f.) is the 'Rolls Royce' of the tenth century B.C. But the bodyguard of sixty picked warriors is an ominous reminder of the insecurity and basic fears of the king— 'uneasy lies the head that wears the crown'. The RSV (and AV [KJV]) is almost certainly wrong in v. 10, where 'it was lovingly wrought within', in the light of the cognate Arabic, should read, more prosaically, 'its interior was furnished with leather'. The absence of true love on the part of his wives and his subjects was, in fact, one of the tragedies of Solomon's reign. Nor would the Shulammite, if she was the pure maiden we believe her to be, be greatly impressed with the invitation of v. 11, for Solomon's mother was Bath-sheba, who was as blameworthy as David in the sin which destroyed her first husband, Uriah, and subsequently wrought untold havoc in David's family (2 Sam. 11–19).

Solomon appears to be the speaker in 4.1–6. The language of love here is pompous and artificial, a string of formal compliments. Some of the allusions have clearly lost something in translation, e.g. in v. 2, sheep are washed before shearing, not afterwards, and in any case, there are few things *less* comely than a sheep which has just been shorn! The inference of v. 6 is clear, however, and must have sounded ominously in the maiden's ears—Solomon would return to her at nightfall.

The Song of Solomon 4.7—5.16

The Call of True Love

In contrast with the fulsome praise of Solomon (4.1–6) the language of love of the shepherd (4.7–15) is characterized by frankness and simplicity. It has been observed that the references in v. 8 would be impossible for any bride! Amana is the mountain range of which Hermon (known by the Amorites as Senir, Deut. 3.9) is the chief peak. But there is no need to take this literally, the speech is purely imaginary, constructed in the girl's mind. Her need was, first, for her true lover; secondly, to raise up a bulwark against the insinuations of Solomon. When the mind is completely occupied and satisfied with a deep affection there is small danger of surrender to another competitor. This fact has its application in the Christian

182

life, where Satan would seek to win our souls, blinding our minds with the dazzling prospects which he, posing as an angel of light, dangles before us (Luke 22.31; 2 Cor. 4.4; 11.14). But where the whole life is given over in love to Christ such allurements are shown up for what they are, empty baubles, tinsel and glitter. Only Christ can really satisfy. There is another intensely practical lesson to learn from this book, concerning the essential purity of human love and the need for singleness of heart towards the legitimate object of our affections. Where there is this conscious giving of oneself in love there is deliverance both from the wandering glance and the enticement of any tempter. Notice here the allusion to the purity of the maiden in 4.12. But she is not in the least ashamed to anticipate the delights of her wedding day (4.16), when her ardour will be matched by the passion of her beloved (5.1).

Again (cf. 3.1–4), the intensity of love and desire, and the enforced separation from its object, lead to a disturbed night and a dream which, this time, has no happy ending (5.2–7). Compare the teasing, playful reaction of v. 3 with the actual state of her heart (4). Her urgent but fruitless search (6,7), reflects the agonizing tension in which she was placed. The answer to her question to the ladies of the harem (8 f.) probably underlines still further her predicament, for its inference is that she was not the first to be taken away by the king's officer from home and lover. When the king's wandering eye fell upon a beautiful maiden it was so easy for him to arrange for a new acquisition for his harem, which eventually totalled over a thousand (1 Kings 11.1–4). The Shulammite, vehemently extolling the virtues of her lover (5.10–16) must have been aware that in spite of the outward opulence, she was in an atmosphere not unlike that of a prison, in which so much true love and cherished hopes had been crushed. What prospect had she of breaking free when so many had failed?

The Song of Solomon 6.1—7.9

The Conflict Renewed

There is heavy sarcasm in the question of the Shulammite's companions (6.1). It rubs in the fact that her lover is absent and that, humanly speaking, there is no possibility of joining him. Brought back thus to reality, the maiden admits that he is indeed away on his farm in the north (2). However, separation, both in distance and circumstances is no barrier to love and the two remain united (3). It is in this realm that the proverb, 'Absence makes the heart grow fonder', has its application. Again we find a suggestive reminder of the relationship between Christ and the believer, who knows that no power, in life or death, in this world or any other world, 'will be able to separate us from the love of God in Christ Jesus our Lord' (Rom. 8.39). And again the wonder of enduring human love, and its preciousness, come into focus.

Solomon makes a further bid to gain the affection of his newest concubine in vs. 4–10. Yet clearly he is ill at ease (cf. 4 f., 10). This maiden was unlike those who, flattered by the attention of one so great, fell easy victims to his polished, professional approach. Whether it was the look of reproach, or scorn, or determination which the king saw, he was unable to meet her eyes (5). Solomon was not completely profligate, and the integrity of this simple maiden touched his conscience. Upright character and conduct always have their influence upon others, no matter how depraved they be. The man of God is like salt which both flavours and preserves from corruption. More often than not this influence is unconscious, as in the case of the Shulammite, Moses (Exod. 34.29 f.), and Paul and Silas (Acts 16.25). In this instance the desire of the king was actually increased for this maiden who was on such a different plane from his other wives, concubines and etceteras (8 f.). To him she was 'on her own'.

The only response from the maiden is the implied regret that she had ever been spirited away from that springtime setting which was so indelibly imprinted on her memory (11 f. cf. 2.10–15). The cry of the bystanders at this time (13a) is echoed by her determination not to gratify the passing whim of the king, as if she were a cheap, professional entertainer (13b). Once again Solomon resorted to the flattery of which he was master, seeking to make her amenable to his approach, but all in vain. Between the king and his subject there was a great gulf fixed, the barrier of her pure undivided loyalty to her shepherd-lover. Neither Solomon's wiles nor even the fiery darts of the devil could prevail against that.

Note: Tirzah (6.4) was an important town, about seven miles north-east of Shechem. It was the capital of Israel in the early ninth century B.C.

The Song of Solomon 7.10—8.14

Love Triumphant

The Shulammite is alone again. Solomon has gone and there is no suggestion that he has been able to overcome her spirit. The decisive battle has been won, though as yet she is unaware of it. Now, the strain of conflict momentarily passes, she finds refuge again in her daydreams of love (7.10—8.3). There is a simplicity of scene and detail which is refreshing after the stifling atmosphere of the court. Notice the maidenly reticence, not without a certain sauciness, in 8.1! There is a final plea to the women of the harem not to attempt to break down her resistance (4).

From this point onwards, the scene changes. Neither Solomon nor the court ladies appear directly and the maiden appears free from the virtual imprisonment of the harem. The inference is that Solomon, worsted in the conflict for her affections, has had the good sense to admit his defeat and the grace not to take revenge. She is free to return to her shepherd-lover, leaving perhaps a wiser, if a sadder, Solomon. V. 5 pictures the triumphant homeward return, followed by a passionate outburst in praise of love, which has survived the jealousy of the women of the harem (6b,7a) and the allurements of the wealthiest king of Israel (7b). Love was indeed triumphant and since these days has often shown itself to be 'strong as death'. The N.T. has brought its revelation of a love which is *stronger* than death, even the outpoured love of Christ in death. The love which this has inspired, together with faith and hope, will endure when 'death is swallowed up in victory' (1 Cor. 15.54, cf. 13.8–13).

The meaning of vs. 8 ff. has been disputed, but possibly they reflect the conscience of the Shulammite's brothers, who promise to protect their younger sister more adequately. The site of Baal-hamon is unknown, but it may have been a particularly productive vineyard in the area where the Shulammite lived. Solomon, avers the maiden, is welcome to it, she now has for herself the vineyard which she once feared lost for ever (1.6), i.e. her lover. So again her voice lifts, inviting him to come to her (13 f.). Now there is nothing to hinder the fulfilment of her longing.

Our interpretation raises again the question of authorship. Did Solomon write this story against himself? Or should 1.1 read 'which is about Solomon' (a possible interpretation)? Our view is the former, largely because no one else in Israel would dare write about Solomon in this way. If we are correct, then he was a wise king indeed and we are greatly in his debt for this story which, although embarassingly bold at times in its language, speaks to the heart of the sublimity of human love, and hints at something greater still, the love of God in Christ.

185

Questions for further study and discussion on the Song of Solomon

1. Do you agree with the interpretation adopted in these notes? If not, work out in detail your own.
2. What lessons may we learn from this book about human love?
3. In what ways do these chapters hint at Christ's love for us?
4. Why was this book included in the canon of sacred Scripture?
5. May we discover anything in this book about the ways in which the evil one works to overthrow our love for Christ?

Introduction to Prophecy and the Prophetic Books

Whilst Abraham is called a prophet (Gen. **20.**7) and Moses is the ideal, proto-type prophet (Deut. **18.**15 ff.), the great age of prophecy began in the declining years of the Judges' period. The prophets occupied a unique place and made an invaluable contribution to the national life, although frequently their influence was greatest long after they themselves had died. They were largely associated with periods of crisis: Samuel was influential in bringing Israel out of the moral and spiritual darkness of the Judges' period; Elijah and Elisha emerged during the sharp crisis caused by Jezebel's importation of Baal-worship; Amos and Hosea in Israel, and Micah and Isaiah in Judah, were the great eighth-century prophets who thundered against the declining standards of their age; Jeremiah, Zephaniah, Ezekiel and Obadiah were involved in the final judgements on Judah, whilst Haggai, Zechariah, Malachi and possibly Joel were connected with the re-establishment of a purified temple-cult in Judah.

The greatness of these men is enhanced by the gross darkness that surrounded them. They were the 'angry young men' of their generation, but they differed from their twentieth-century counterparts in that their condemnation was based on what they knew of God and His revealed will; they were not innovators but traditionalists in the best sense. To describe them as the 'great ethical prophets' is true, but misleading, for their ethical insistence was itself based on a fundamental, personal experience of God. Knowing God, they spoke, and became the moral, religious and political counsellors of their generation. Two main themes dominate in their oracles: *(a) Privilege*—Israel was chosen by God to enter into a unique covenantal relationship with Him (e.g. Hos. **11.**1–4; Amos **2.**9–11; **3.**1f.); *(b) Responsibility*—Israel was accountable to God and owed Him humble, loving allegiance (e.g. Hos. **6.**6; Mic. **6.**8). Failure in this responsibility involved forfeiting the responsibility.

The six words used to describe them are important; they include 'man of God' (1 Sam. **2.**27), watchman (Jer. **6.**17) and the Lord's messenger (Hag. **1.**13). Two Hebrew words are translated 'seer', one derived from the verb to see (in a unique sense the prophet was the man who saw what was going on) and another from a verb denoting prophetic vision (1 Sam. **9.**9; 2 Sam. **24.**11). But the normal word translated 'prophet' (Heb. *nabi*) is by far the most important. Its meaning in Israel is indicated by the terminology of Exod. **4.**16; **7.**1. Just as Aaron was a 'mouth' for Moses, the prophet was God's mouthpiece, i.e. His spokesman or announcer, broadcasting His will to their contemporaries in terms of divine concern and divine participation in history. There is a sense in which the Christian has precisely this function to fulfil today.

A distinction may be made between the great natural prophets, such as Samuel, Elijah and Elisha, whose utterances have survived in only fragmentary form, and the writing prophets, whose oracles are recorded in the prophetic books. But this distinction must not be over-pressed, for men like Amos, Hosea and Isaiah stood in the same spiritual tradition as their predecessors. Moreover, to describe the later prophets as 'writing prophets' overlooks the fact that in some cases at any rate the prophecies were written down by the *disciples* of the prophets themselves, possibly posthumously.

A distinction may be generally made between the canonical prophets and the cult-prophets. The latter were attached to the various shrines, and as the quality of religious life declined, so these false prophets became more time-servers, concerned with popular, nationalistic hopes and showing an easy-going, flabby attitude towards national and individual sin. It is no wonder, therefore, that they came under such heavy attack from the true prophets (e.g. Mic. 3.5–7; Jer. 14.14 f.; 23.9–32) and that a prophet like Amos even repudiated the description of 'prophet', so debased had it become (Amos 7.14).

Post-exilic prophets such as Haggai, Zechariah, Malachi and Joel have frequently been criticised for their apparent lack of stress on specifically moral issues. But this overlooks two vital facts: firstly, the blatant moral and religious sins of *pre-exilic* Israel, judged so severely by God, were no longer so prominent; secondly, it was absolutely vital, if Judaism was to survive, that it had a focal point in a Temple where a pure worship could be established. Even bricks and mortar acquired a spiritual significance in this period, but moral and religious issues were by no means overlooked.

Finally, no more misleading term has ever been applied than the adjective in the 'Minor Prophets'. Many have understood this to mean 'unimportant' and have neglected these books, to their own incalculable loss. Minor these prophets may be, but in brevity only, since all twelve fitted conveniently into one scroll, whereas the prophecies of Isaiah, Jeremiah and Ezekiel required a scroll apiece. But in all other respects the prophets stand together as the men who mediated the will of God to their generations.

The Prophets of Israel and Judah

	ISRAEL		JUDAH	
EIGHTH CENTURY	c.770 c.760 c.750–725 722/721 The Fall of Samaria	JONAH AMOS HOSEA	742–c.687 c.736–710	ISAIAH MICAH
SEVENTH CENTURY			c.627–582 c.625 c.625 c.605	JEREMIAH ZEPHANIAH NAHUM HABAKKUK
SIXTH CENTURY			592–c.570 c.587 587–538 520–515 520–515	EZEKIEL OBADIAH THE EXILE HAGGAI ZECHARIAH
FIFTH CENTURY			c.460 c.410 (A minority of scholars would date Joel c.836)	MALACHI JOEL

Isaiah

INTRODUCTION

Isaiah of Jerusalem was one of the four great, eighth-century prophets. Amos and Hosea prophesied a generation before him in the northern kingdom of Israel. Micah was his contemporary in the southern kingdom of Judah. Both Israel and Judah had enjoyed political and economic prosperity during the mid-eighth century but this was accompanied by grave abuses in every realm of life. Isaiah prophesied from 742 B.C. (6.1). The latest date which can be assigned to his ministry is 701 B.C., the year of Sennacherib's invasion, but it is virtually certain that he continued to minister after this event. A Jewish tradition that he was sawn asunder (cf. Heb. 11.37) during the early years of the apostate king Manasseh (687–642 B.C.) may well be correct. His prophecies are not in strict chronological order and there is an evident tendency to group together oracles of a particular type (e.g. the prophecies concerning foreign nations in chs. 13–23).

Isaiah had a deep sense of the holiness and almightiness of God, realizing that this related to 'the whole earth' (6.3) not simply to Judah. This fact transformed his personal experience (see note on ch. 6) and profoundly influenced his outlook on every other subject. Such a God must be taken seriously. It was deep disloyalty to rely on foreign allies rather than in His promise of protection; it was hypocrisy to go through the motions of a religion that was divorced from social and moral uprightness. God was not dead in the eighth century B.C. (or in our present generation!) and He would act.

Following the historical interlude (chs. 36–39) the remainder of the scroll of the prophet Isaiah divides up naturally into two. Chapters 40–55 have their setting towards the end of the Babylonian captivity (c.540 B.C.), when the return from exile was imminent. The prophet's mission was to encourage a faint-hearted people to step out (literally as well as metaphorically!) upon the promises of God. Nowhere else in Old Testament is the absoluteness of Yahweh, central in Israel's monotheistic faith, so clearly revealed. The other great feature of these chapters is the concept of the Servant of the Lord. In chs. 56–66 the scene appears to change to Judah and Jerusalem. The Temple is in ruins but about to be rebuilt (63.18; 64.11; 66.1). The twin dangers of this period are depicted as formality in religion and the adoption of heathen practices. The most likely setting, therefore, is the period between 538 B.C., when the Jews returned home, and 515 B.C. when the second Temple was completed (Ezra 6.15).

This immediately raises the problem of authorship, since the complete scroll of Isaiah covers a period from 742–515 B.C. On the surface, it seems unlikely that the Jews would include three sets of oracles on the one scroll, leaving the second and third anonymous, when in the 'Book of the Twelve' (minor prophets) the identity of each is carefully preserved. But it would be unusual for Isaiah to cover two crisis periods in future centuries, as well as that of his own time; usually God has His man available in an hour of crisis. Moreover, the prophecy actually *looks back* upon events such as the Fall of Jerusalem, so that the standpoint of the latter chapters appears genuinely exilic or post exilic. Neither of these difficulties is insuperable, however. The element of predictive prophecy, often in considerable detail, in the Old Testament, is undoubted, and frequently the prophets used the so-called 'prophetic perfect', foreseeing future events as already complete. The reader will detect many similarities of style, language, thought-forms and theology between the three sections of Isaiah, and when the fact of divine inspiration is taken into account, there is nothing impossible in a unity of authorship.

Further reference to authorship will be found in the standard Introductions. R. K. Harrsion's 'Introduction to the Old Testament' (Tyndale Press) is particularly commended.

Isaiah 1.1-15 The Great Accusation

This blistering attack on Judah's hypocritical religion has been described as Isaiah's most representative prophecy. It must have seared the very ears, as well as the consciences, of his hearers, smugly confident as they were that their conventional religion was acceptable to God. Blow by blow Isaiah demolishes such false security.

Sin, he declares, is basically rebellion against the Lord (2–4). The heavens and the earth are invited to witness so abnormal a crime, as though the whole universe was a court-room presided over by the Almighty (cf. Deut. 4.26; 32.1). Even the ox and the ass, the two most common domesticated animals, were capable of showing some gratitude and sense of ownership, but Israel was quite heedless and ungrateful. The tender, paternal care of the Lord contrasted sharply with the shabby indifference and wilful rebellion of His people. For this reason His rod of correction had fallen upon the nation (5 f.). The picture is of a slave who has been punished so frequently for his misdeeds that there was no area of his body which was unaffected. But there was not the slightest sign of repentance, which would have allowed the master to drop the rod and seek to heal the wounds. In vs. 7–9 this imagery is abandoned and the cold, hard facts of history substituted. In Isaiah's own lifetime Judah was subjected to attacks from Israel (the northern kingdom, which lost its identity in 721 B.C.), Syria, Edom, Philistia and the mighty Assyria. All of these were 'the rod of My (i.e. God's) anger' (10.5), and Judah was brought very low; a booth or lodge (8) was a frail structure of branches designed to give shelter from the sun at harvest-time. Only a few faithful survivors prevented a parallel with the total destruction of the notorious cities of the plain (Gen. 13.13).

One can imagine how the rulers and citizens of Jerusalem would cringe with horror when they were likened to Sodom and Gomorrah (10)! In this one sentence Isaiah sweeps away all their false complacency as the covenant-people. Their disobedience placed them outside the covenant and made them fit only for the judgement. Sacrifices (11 f.), religious festivals (12 ff.) and prayers (15) were so much humbug when their hands were blood-stained. God would have none of them.

Note: Isaiah's teaching on the remnant was of great importance in later theology. Trace his distinctive views in 6.13; 7.3; 8.16–18; 10.20–22; 11.11,16.

A thought: What would be God's verdict on our religious acts when set against the background of our lives?

Isaiah 1.16-31   Repent or Perish!

The prophets were not opposed to the sacrificial system as such, but they make it quite clear that without a genuine repentance, accompanied by a life which is pleasing to God, all man's cultic acts are useless (16 f., cf. Hos. 6.6; Amos 5.21–24; Mic. 6.6 ff.). Isaiah and his fellow-prophets insisted strongly on social righteousness because of what they knew of the character of God. He was a holy, righteous God, and since individual Israelites were linked with Him in the covenant, they were linked with each other also, a relationship

192

which was to show itself in brotherly love. The same is true of the Church today.

One of the great evangelical appeals of the O.T. sounds out in vs. 18–20. But notice how God, even when He desires our good, never forces His will upon us. The onus of choice rested squarely upon the people, who held their destinies in their hands. But salvation was not something they deserved, or could earn, it was purely of God's grace, given to those who would respond to Him in obedience.

The appeal to come to the Lord for cleansing is underlined dramatically by a further unfolding of the desperate plight of Jerusalem and its rulers (21 ff.). Notice the three suggestive metaphors which Isaiah employs: the harlot (21), a common symbol of the nation's infidelity and uncleanness, especially in *Hosea* and *Jeremiah*; adulteration, in which there is an abnormal reversal of the refining process; and wine which has been watered down (22). In each case something which was originally good has been spoilt. Two illustrations of this, as applied to Judah, are given. (*i*) The complete corruption of the ruling classes and the courts is exposed (23). (*ii*) The fertility cults, imported from neighbouring heathen countries, are indicated in vs. 29 ff. The debased sexual element in these made a strong appeal to man's sensuous nature, but weakened his moral and spiritual fibre and made him fit only for judgement.

God cannot tolerate such iniquity, whether it be in the eighth century B.C. or the twentieth century A.D. (24–28). He who is 'the Holy One of Israel' (4) is also 'the Mighty One of Israel' (24), and He would act decisively against those who had made themselves His enemies. The analogy used, that of the refining process (cf. Job 23.10; Ezek. 22.17–22; Mal. 3.2 f.), shows that this judgement is strictly controlled and for a definite purpose. The evil alone will be eliminated, so that Zion might again be characterized by righteousness. Even in His wrath the Lord remains merciful (Hab. 3.2).

Isaiah 2 — Future Blessing and Judgement

The title (1) probably refers to the collection of prophecies in chs. 2–4. In today's portion we have two oracles, both of which concern the future, although markedly dissimilar in their contents. The ethical appeal of v. 5 links the two sections together. It expresses what ought to have been Judah's response in the light of the promises of vs. 2 ff., and contrasts strongly with the actual conduct of the nation (6–22).

The golden age is foretold by Isaiah in vs. 2 ff. Jerusalem will become the centre of worship for the entire world, and universal peace will result from the Lord's rule. The same prophecy, in a slightly longer form, is found in Mic. 4.1-7 and a part of it is reproduced in Joel 3.10, showing that this message of hope was common to many, if not all, of God's prophets. Jerusalem was to be the teacher of the world, the focal point of divine instruction and enrichment. The missionary movement of the O.T. invariably has this theme of the nations converging upon the city of Zion (e.g. Isa. **49**.6,7; **60**.3; **66**.23; Jer. **3**.17; Zech. **2**.11; **8**.20 ff.; **14**.16). But a marked change is apparent in the N.T. The death of Christ and the gift of the Holy Spirit have made for a new dynamic in evangelism, in which Jerusalem is the starting point, and the end of the earth the ultimate goal (Acts **1**.8). In this missionary programme every believer has a vital part to play (Matt. **28**.18-20).

The day of reckoning (6-22) is deliberately set alongside this conception, as though to indicate that mercy and judgement are complementary. The frequent references to 'the day' (11,12,17,20) recall the attack of Amos on his contemporaries a generation or two before Isaiah (Amos **5**.18-20). They looked upon the Day of the Lord as the time when God would intervene on their behalf to slaughter all their enemies, but Amos corrected their false sense of privilege and insisted that judgement would begin with them. Isaiah has an identical emphasis, and in the terrible judgement of that day all the false supports of Judah, including their reliance upon heathen superstitions (6a), foreign alliances (6b), riches (7), weapons and fortifications (7,15), idols (8,20) and their own self-sufficiency (11,17), would be swept away. Men would be left stripped and helpless, only the Lord would be glorified in that day (11,17). Compare this O.T. judgement on the sins of God's people with the N.T. picture of the testing of the works of the Christian on 'the day' (1 Cor. **3**.10-15).

Isaiah 3.1—4.1 A Sick Society

A situation bordering on anarchy is described in 3.1-15. Everyone capable of giving leadership would be removed. The all-inclusive nature of this operation is revealed in the expression 'stay and staff' (both of which come from the same root), equivalent to our 'bag and baggage'. Military and civil rulers are included, as well as those who had led the nation astray by false prophecy and heathen religious practices. The government would be in the hands of the immature and incapable (4) and all the normal values of life would be inverted. The intimidatory tactics of the militant Red Guard in modern China's 'cultural revolution' have produced the same kind of tragic situation as we find in vs. 4,5. So desperate would the situation be that men would seek to press-gang leaders on the flimsiest pretexts, only to be curtly rebuffed—no one would be anxious to take over in such chaotic times (6,7). Only one class is exempted from the general judgement—the righteous (10, cf. 2 Pet. 2.9). The reference in v. 12 is probably to Ahaz, king of Judah from 735–715 B.C., whose rule was weak and incompetent. In the absence of adequate leadership the Lord Himself would intervene as both Advocate and Judge (13 ff.). Notice the uncompromising language in which He condemns the constituted authorities for their avaricious cruelty—a reminder that all who wield authority have a sacred responsibility to those under them.

3.16—4.1 are concerned with the women of Jerusalem. The opening verses depict a contemporary fashion parade! The prophet intended his hearers to observe the sharp contrast between the intolerable condition of the poor (14,15) and the pointless ornamentation of the Jerusalem matrons, matched by their suggestive gestures. The 'tinkling with their feet' (16) was caused by ornamental ankle chains which must have made walking quite an effort! One writer, reassuringly, points out that not *all* the items in vs. 18–23 were necessarily worn at the same time! So Isaiah satirizes those who, at enormous expense and considerable inconvenience, tried to keep up with fashion, always a harsh mistress. It is, of course, foolish to suggest that the Christian should be drab or careless in dress, but of far greater importance to God is the adorning of 'the hidden person of the heart with the imperishable jewel of a gentle and quiet spirit' (1 Pet. 3.3,4).

Judgement would fall upon these women, cruelly indifferent as they were to the needs of the oppressed. It would include the reproach of childlessness (4.1) which G. T. Manley calls 'the awful curse of the East'.

Isaiah 4.2—5.7   Fruitfulness and Fruitlessness

A connection with yesterday's portion is indicated by 4.4. The intervention of the Lord is like a coin with judgement on one side and blessing on the other. In many of the prophets the blessings of the golden age follow swiftly upon the most sombre denunciations, a reminder of God's original plan which cannot ultimately be thwarted even by man's sin and waywardness. Some have given the oracle in 4.2–6 a Messianic setting, but since 'the branch of the

Lord' is parallel to 'the fruit of the land' (2) a more general application is probable. The righteous remnant who survived would enjoy perfect fellowship with their God, whose presence would be manifested amongst them as it was in the wilderness period (5, cf. Exod. 13.21,22). He would overshadow them with His protection like a canopy. This oracle was only partially fulfilled historically, and like many other prophecies, it points forward to a consummation at the end of the age.

The Song of the Vineyard (5.1-7) is a lyrical parable of judgement, which is the more impressive because it is in the form of a love-song addressed to Isaiah's contemporaries (1). Loving, lavish care had been bestowed upon this vineyard, nothing had been left to chance, nor was there any lack of expectancy—a wine vat had been prepared in anticipation of a bumper harvest (2). But the result was cruelly disappointing and the only recourse, humanly speaking, was to abandon the whole project and make a new beginning. Thank God that, in actual fact, He did not allow the infidelity of His people to turn Him aside from His redemptive purposes, but out of seeming disaster He made a new beginning. This prophecy was fulfilled in 587 B.C., when the Babylonians ravaged the countryside and battered Jerusalem to the ground, but God began to build up immediately through a godly remnant, under Ezekiel's leadership, in exile. He can do the same with our barren, fruitless lives, if we will allow Him. Read carefully the second part of v. 7. What does the Lord look for in our lives? What does He find?

Isaiah 5.8-30   A Six-fold Woe!

(i) Woe to land-speculators (8 ff., cf. Mic. 2.2). The promised land was a God-given inheritance, held in sacred trust by the individual Israelite, hence the importance of a continuity of possession (cf. 1 Kings 21.3). In both Israel and Judah the rich landowners used the plight of the poor as a means of enlarging their own estates, the wretched peasants being forced to sell cheaply to pay their debts. The Lord makes it clear that the punishment upon these unscrupulous men would match the crime, they would gain no advantage from their exactions. A 'bath' (10) was a liquid measure equal to about eight gallons; a 'homer' was the equivalent dry measure, but instead of an increase at harvest there would actually be a decrease, for an 'ephah' was a tenth of a 'homer'.

(ii) Woe to the drunkard (11-17). The considerable number of references to drunkenness in *Isaiah* attests its prevalence (5.22; 19.14; 24.20; 28.1,7). Drunkenness in the morning was considered to be particularly reprehensible (cf. Acts 2.15). Strong drink has brought ruin to many individuals and the dissolute character which it produces has brought nations low. Death and exile (national death) are foretold as the consequence of the misgovernment by these undisciplined leaders.

(*iii*) Woe to the blasphemous (18 f.) who were enthusiastically pulling sin on like men drawing a heavily laden cart, meanwhile mocking God and taunting Him to act, if He could.

(*iv*) Woe to the morally-perverted (20). Sin inevitably warps our judgement and affects our sense of values. It also makes a man insensitive towards God (12b).

(*v*) Woe to the self-conceited (21). Such 'know-alls' have no conscious need of God, but their confidence is completely illusory (cf. Prov. 16.18).

(*vi*) A further woe is directed against the drunkard, but the context limits it to the judges of Judah (22 f.). These men ought to have been the champions of the oppressed. Instead, they were mighty only in their drinking bouts.

Such a catalogue of sins merited a sudden and devastating punishment. This Isaiah foretells (24 f.). Even the mighty Assyria responds to the bidding of the Lord (26–30).

Isaiah 6   Encounter with God

A knowledge of this chapter, with its account of Isaiah's inaugural vision and call to the prophetic office, is of vital importance in understanding the teaching of this great prophet. It may well be that the death of good king Uzziah (742 B.C.), whose rule had resulted in the stability of the nation for almost half a century, had brought the young Isaiah to the Temple, the more so as the international situation was becoming increasingly dominated by an Assyria obviously bent on conquest. Four elements in this chapter deserve careful attention:

(*i*) Isaiah was made aware of the majesty and holiness of God when he saw part of His glory ('train', 1, indicates the skirts of His garments) and heard the chant of the seraphim (1–4). This vision henceforth determined his conception of Judah's God. He was the One Sovereign God, and no power, whether it be a heathen emperor or a heathen deity, could stand before Him.

(*ii*) Confronted with an absolutely holy God, Isaiah became acutely conscious of his own and the nation's sin (5). Our sense of sin is always relative, and it is the man who lives close to the Eternal

Light who is most sensitive to sin. Many contemporary theologians have a weak view of sin, not so Isaiah.

(*iii*) God took the initiative and provided the means of cleansing from sin (6 f.). This is the evangelical note which is characteristic of the Scriptures. He is ever the One who draws near to effect the salvation which man is utterly unable to gain.

(*iv*) The cleansed Isaiah promptly aligned himself with the Lord, as His messenger. This was a natural and spontaneous response, paralleled by that of Paul (Acts 22.10, cf. 9.6 AV [KJV], RV). He was made to understand the difficult nature of his ministry, with many heartaches, disappointments and the inevitability of final judgement in spite of his warnings. But there was a ray of hope, for v. 13 speaks of a remnant which would survive the destruction and the holocaust.

There is a sense in which this experience of Isaiah's must have its parallel in our lives. We too are confronted with a holy, almighty God, whose very purity reveals the depth of our sin. But God, through His grace, has provided a way of forgiveness (2 Cor. 5.21; 1 Pet. 2.24). Surely our logical response is to volunteer, 'Here am I! Send me' (cf. Rom. 12.1)!

Questions for further study and discussion on Isaiah chs. 1–6

1. Make a catalogue of the sins which were prevalent in Isaiah's age. What, in your estimation, was Judah's cardinal sin?
2. Consider the bearing of sacrifice, etc. upon the Hebrew's relationship with God. Take Jer. 7.21–25; Hos. 6.6; Amos 5.21–24 and Mic. 6.6–8 into account. What relevance has this to our own situation?
3. What may we learn from these chapters about the fact of purpose in history?
4. What do these chapters teach us of the relationship between God and Judah?
5. Compare the call of Isaiah with other 'calls' in both O.T. and N.T. Can you detect a basic pattern? What is the importance of a 'call' in connection with the exercise of a Christian ministry of any kind?

Isaiah 7   Trust in the Lord Alone

The historical background of this chapter may be found in 2 Kings 16.5–18 and 2 Chron. 28.5–21. Israel and Syria had rebelled against their overlord, Assyria, and were attempting to force Judah into their alliance. As well as this threat from the north there were attacks upon Judah from Philistia in the south-west and Edom in the south-east. It was a major political crisis, with king Ahaz seemingly trapped. But Isaiah the prophet discerned something more important still, a major religious crisis, for Ahaz was about to appeal to Assyria to intervene and save him. Isaiah's message to Ahaz was to trust in the Lord alone. There is a play on words in v. 9 which may be rendered, 'If you will not be *sure*, you cannot be *secure*'. Foreign alliances, Isaiah saw, were disloyalty to Yahweh, a virtual denial of His ability to save. Hence the urgency with which Isaiah invited Ahaz to request any sign as a confirmation of His power. Ahaz was a weak king, however, and his seemingly pious words in v. 12 covered a decision which he had already taken. The shock-troops of Assyria seemed to him a more tangible asset than reliance upon the invisible Yahweh. It was a mistake which has been repeated many times since. Isaiah was right, of course. Politically, it was an error to call in Assyria, it only made Judah more subservient. Assyria was bound to crush this rebellion anyway. More fundamental was the fact that the Lord God can be relied upon.

The Immanuel oracle (14–25) was given in spite of the refusal of Ahaz. There must have been an historical fulfilment, for before the child about to be born was capable of choice the threat from Israel and Syria would be eliminated, but Judah itself would have suffered severely, as the rest of the chapter indicates. It remains true, however, that the world was saved by 'Immanuel', God with us, and Matthew was perfectly correct in seeing this prophecy as a germinal concept fulfilled in Christ.

Notes: (*i*) If vs. 15,16 refer to a choice between pleasant and unpleasant food the time indicated would be about three years; if they refer to moral discrimination, about fourteen years is required.

(*ii*) Curds and honey (15,22) are the staple diet of a nomadic community, not an agricultural, and these references (cf. the general tone of vs. 17–25) indicate that Judah would be reduced to a nomadic state.

Isaiah 8   'God is with Us'

The chapter introduces us to another of the sons of Isaiah. When the prophet confronted Ahaz (ch. 7) he took Shear-jashub, whose name, meaning 'a remnant shall return', was itself a symbol of judgement. This fact would be realized by the king and indicates that Isaiah had connections with the court. The name of the second son, Maher-shalal-hash-baz, literally 'speeds booty, hastens spoil', was a further prophecy that Judah's enemies in this particular crisis, Israel and Syria, symbolized by their capitals (4), would be destroyed.

The waters of Shiloah (5–8) have usually been taken as an allusion to the invisible presence and supply of the Lord (cf. Psa. 46.4,5). The reference may be to the brook which flowed from the Gihon spring, which was connected by a conduit (the precursor of Hezekiah's tunnel, 2 Kings 20.20) to Jerusalem's water supply within the city. The symbol would then be of a city temporarily beseiged but under Yahweh's protection. This, Judah was not prepared to accept. Therefore the might of Assyria, suggested in the reference to the River (Euphrates, 7), would sweep upon them like a rushing, engulfing torrent. There is a further appeal by the prophet (9–15) to rely on the Lord alone, forsaking the way of worldly wisdom and political machinations (10).

Following the rejection by Ahaz of his advice in the national crisis Isaiah appears to have gone into partial retirement—no oracle of his can be accurately dated for at least ten years after 735 B.C. He took practical steps (16–18) to gather about him a circle of disciples who would form a nucleus of the remnant, which he foresaw would survive the impending judgement. There was little hope for a people who had forsaken the living God and His Law, and were resorting to the dubious practices of necromancy and spiritism (19,20). Such a course could only issue in darkness. We may marvel at the clarity with which Isaiah saw the issues at stake and the way in which he was prepared to rely implicitly on the Lord. But then, is not the Lord Sovereign in all things, the Almighty? Isaiah did not fear and nor need we.

Isaiah 9.1-7 The Prince of Peace

This Messianic oracle climaxes the thought of the preceding chapter. The people of Judah, led by their apostate king, Ahaz, were like blind men passing through a desolate land, a situation of unrelieved gloom (8.21,22). Here the prophet's thought soars into the future. Zebulun and Naphtali felt the full weight of the reprisal raid made on Israel by the Assyrian king, Tiglath Pileser III, who deported many of the inhabitants of this area. But in this same region the Messiah Himself, the Great Deliverer of His people, would arise. God would not leave the land in perpetual darkness; in the area where the misery was most acute, Galilee of the nations, the Light of the whole world would arise. In that glorious day the Davidic dynasty would be permanently established and the Messianic kingdom would be ushered in, leading to peace, prosperity, justice and righteousness (7). The triumph over the oppressor would be as convincing as the sweeping victory won by Gideon over the Midianites (4, cf. Judg. 7.19—8.12).

There is a natural connection of thought between the son of v. 6 and the Immanuel prophecy of 7.14, but here the ultimate fulfilment in Christ is uppermost. The name of the Messiah (6) is composed of four components which, taken together, reveal Him in all the perfection of His being:

(*i*) Wonderful Counsellor. He will be a ruler of unparalleled wisdom. Here there may be an oblique comparison with the indecisive, childish government of Ahaz.

(*ii*) Mighty God, or Hero God. Supernatural wisdom would be accompanied by the superlative strength needed to implement His counsels.

(*iii*) Everlasting Father. The very attribute of God the Father Himself, revealed in a loving, solicitous care for His people, would characterize Messiah.

(*iv*) Prince of Peace. King Ahaz had failed abysmally in the first requirement of a good king, i.e. to secure peace and to rule in peace. As we contemplate these regal and divine qualities we remember that this promised Messiah is our Lord and Saviour Jesus Christ. He is our divine King, who secured peace by the outpouring of His own life and love (cf. Eph. 2.13–18), and He will not fail in any aspect of His rule.

Isaiah 9.8—10.4   What Makes God Angry?

This section forms an epilogue to the attempt by Syria and Israel to force Judah into their anti-Assyrian alliance. It concentrates on the northern kingdom of Israel and it is apparent that the wrath of Assyria has already fallen upon it. At this point we may pause to note that Isa. 1.1—10.4 may have been the 'first edition' of Isaiah's prophecy, written on the occasion of the partial retirement from public life which we observed in connection with 8.16 f. This would include his early prophecies against Judah (chs. 1–5); the account of his call to the prophetic office (ch. 6), and the historical detail of the events leading up to, and following, the rejection of Isaiah's advice to Ahaz (chs. 7–10.4).

This section is divided into four parts by the grim chorus of the last parts of 9.12,17,21; 10.4. It occurs also in 5.25, but in this case it is Judah, not Israel, which is under review.

(*i*) 9.8–12. The knowledge of v. 9 would not come through the word of Isaiah but by bitter experience which would destroy Israel's

201

arrogant pride. Self-confidence (dressed stone instead of brick, cedar instead of sycamore, 10) is often a commendable virtue but in this case it was sheer presumption.

(*ii*) **9.13–17.** The disaster which would overtake Israel would remove all their leaders. So serious would the situation be that the Lord could no longer commend mercy to the fatherless and widows (17).

(*iii*) **9.18–21** presents a graphic picture of a forest or scrub-fire, an all too frequent occurrence in Palestine, especially in the heat of summer, when the land becomes like a giant tinder-box. The complete failure of the harvest would make men cast off all moral restraint, acting like animals fighting for what food remained.

(*iv*) **10.1–4** brings a woe against Israel's corrupt judges which is reminiscent of Amos, the champion of social righteousness. In the day of judgement these evil men will have no shelter, certainly not in their ill-gotten gains. Death or a shameful captivity would be the only alternatives. There is a reminder here of that ultimate judgement day in which the only ones able to stand before a holy God are those clothed in the righteousness of Christ (cf. Matt. 25.31–46; 2 Cor. 5.1–5; Rev. 3.5).

A Question: Are there elements in our national life which rouse God's anger?

Isaiah 10.5-34 How Big is Your God?

The immensity of Isaiah's faith is shown clearly in vs. 5–19. The insignificant kingdom of Judah, smaller than an average-sized county in England, worshipped Yahweh. The great world-power was mighty Assyria, renowned for its cruelty and reliance upon massive force, whose armies had crushed all opposition. Its military achievements were matched by arrogant boastfulness (12–14). Whether the victim was Jerusalem or any other of the cities which had fallen (9–11), all were considered puny in the face of such irresistible might. It was as easy as robbing a bird's nest (14)! But Isaiah saw history in its correct perspective. Yahweh was not simply a national god, one of many whose power was confined to their own frontiers. He was the Lord of Hosts and His sway was universal. It was His will which was being worked out, and He used Assyria to this purpose just as a workman manipulates his tools. When that purpose was realized He would discard the implement, punishing it for its sins of cruelty and pride. The world-power of Assyria has long since vanished from the international scene, and the weapons of her twentieth-century successors are not the sword, spear and sling.

But the truths of this chapter remain valid. All power is subject to the will of God, and He is still on the throne of His universe. What an encouragement to the godly, especially to those who are suffering under the cruel yoke of our modern tyrants!

The key to vs. 20–34 may be found in v. 22, 'Destruction is decreed, overflowing with righteousness'. However, a righteous remnant would survive this judgement against an apostate Judah, and for these there is a word of encouragement, assuring them of a divine limitation to the forces of Assyria. Vs. 28–32 convey a graphic picture of a massive army advancing swiftly upon Jerusalem. All the places named are within a three-hour march of Judah's capital, suggesting the imminence of danger. Nob (32) was the hill immediately to the north of the city. But just as a proud cedar comes crashing to the earth under the woodsman's axe, so Assyria will be suddenly smitten (cf. Ezek. 31.3–14).

Isaiah 11 The Rule of Christ

After the prophecy of Assyria's fall we are given another glimpse into the Messianic kingdom. There is no hint of exultation over the defeat of the tyrant. Peace reigns completely. The Prince of Peace (9.6) rules and wars have ceased. Another contrast is between the proud cedar (Assyria) which is felled, and the 'shoot from the stump of Jesse' which springs to vigorous life. Attention is focused first of all on the Messiah (1–5) and then on His kingdom (6–9). The character and spiritual endowments of the ruler would ensure the quality of His rule. Like the judges of ancient Israel, He would be One anointed with the Spirit of the Lord (2), but the effect of this would be more than a temporary deliverance and respite for His people. Six aspects of the Spirit's outworkings are given, in three pairs:

(*i*) 'The spirit of wisdom and understanding.' Such intellectual gifts are essential for a ruler.

(*ii*) 'The spirit of counsel and might.' *Counsel* is the ability to apply wisdom and understanding in particular cases, whilst *might* is the means of implementing them.

(*iii*) 'The spirit of knowledge and the fear of the Lord.' The Messianic King would have a perfect knowledge of God (cf. Jer. 9.24) and a deep reverence for Him.

Unlike so many earthly rulers His management of the affairs of His people would be characterized by absolute integrity (3–5). Such rule would reverse the effect of man's original fall so that the whole of nature would be transformed (6–9, cf. Rom. 8.19–22). This

203

aspect of Isaiah's prophecy still awaits its fulfilment, and the N.T. teaches that this will be realized at Christ's return. The remainder of the oracle (11–16) had a definite, if partial, historical fulfilment in the return from Exile (c. 538 B.C.) which is compared with the Exodus from Egypt (16). Note that Isaiah's thought embraces Israel, whose capital, Samaria (after a rebellion subsequent to the one we noted in ch. 7) was destroyed in 721 B.C., its inhabitants being deported. There was no trace of bitterness towards Israel concerning its earlier unbrotherly conduct.

Note: 'The shoulder of the Philistines' (14) refers to the Shephelah, the low range of foothills between Philistia and the mountains of Judah. Philistia, together with Judah's traditional enemies, Edom, Moab and Ammon, would be subjugated.

Isaiah 12   Something to Sing About!

So certain was Isaiah that God would bring back His faithful remnant from captivity that he composed this psalm of praise in anticipation of the event! The chastisement of the exile is viewed as in the past (1) and has given way to the enjoyment of God's salvation. V. 3 may be an allusion to God's provision for the Israelites in the wilderness period. In any case, the return from Exile is viewed as a second Exodus, a decisive turning-point in the history of the nation, and a remarkable evidence of God's intervention. So just as Moses and his contemporaries celebrated the deliverance at the Red Sea in a rapturous hymn of praise (Exod. 15.1–21) those delivered from bondage in Mesopotamia would praise the Lord. Two centuries were to pass before this event, which Isaiah foresaw with such clarity, came to pass. In 538 B.C. the Persian king, Cyrus, issued his edict allowing the Jews to return to their homeland (Ezra 1.2–4) and 42,360 (Ezra 2.64) brave souls, under the leadership of Zerubbabel, began the long trek back to Zion. Soon after their arrival the foundation of the Temple was laid, and at this ceremony the saving acts of the Lord were sung as Isaiah had foretold:

'For He is good,
for His steadfast love endures for ever toward Israel.'
(Ezra 3.11, cf. Jer. 33.10 f.).

Notice the call to gratitude, testimony and praise in vs. 4 ff. especially because of the presence in their midst of 'the Holy One of Israel' (one of Isaiah's distinctive names for God, the other being 'the Lord of hosts'). Such a salvation, and such a Companion, were far too wonderful to keep to oneself! The sin of ingratitude is all too prevalent today, and we easily forget the extent of the blessings which God has given us. He has provided a salvation, through the death of His Son, which makes the miracles of the Exodus and the return from Exile pale into insignificance. Let us express our gratitude in praise and in testimony to others concerning His great work for us!

Questions for further study and discussion on Isaiah chs. 7–12

1. What are the permanent values of Isaiah's conception of a God who is active and powerful in history?
2. Consider the relationship between prophecies which have been fulfilled historically and those which appear to be related to the end of the present age.
3. How would you go about convincing an unbeliever that the prophecies in 9.2–7 and 11.1–5 relate to Jesus Christ?
4. What part do gratitude and praise play in the religious life?

Isaiah 13 God and the Nations

This chapter commences a section (chs. 13–23) dealing principally with foreign nations who at one time or another had persecuted Judah. There is one oracle against Jerusalem itself (22.1–14). One lesson which we may draw from these chapters concerns the universal sovereignty of God and His interest in the actions of all men. The religion of much of the ancient world was 'territorial henotheism', that is, the exclusive worship of one god amongst many, each deity being regarded as intimately connected with a particular nation (e.g. Chemosh the god of the Moabites, Milcom the god of the Ammonites, etc.). The power of these gods was considered to reach no further than the national frontiers, and when a man passed that boundary, he passed beyond the god's protection. The God of Judah (and Israel) was not on this plane. He controlled the universe and all world-powers were answerable to Him.

Isa. 13 is a magnificent poem depicting the fall of Babylon. Humanly speaking it was the Medes who sacked the arrogant city, but they are not even mentioned until v. 17. Instead, it is Yahweh who is pictured as a great General, calling up His battalions and preparing them for action (3 ff.) to punish Babylon for its cruelty and sinful pride (11). It was not so much the day of a Median triumph as the Day of the Lord (6,9), a precursor of His final triumph over all the powers of evil.

The literal fulfilment of vs. 19–22 has often been noted. The 'Arab' (20) originally referred to a desert-wanderer. These were normally glad to utilize the shelter of a ruined city, with its water-supply. But the fate overtaking Babylon would be so devastating that it would become an omen of ill-fortune, and so would be shunned by the nomadic peoples.

Note: The Medes (17) were an Iranian race who became associated with the Babylonians in the overthrow of Assyria in the late seventh century B.C. About the middle of the next century they linked up with the Persians to overthrow their former ally. Vs. 17 f. refer to an implacable hostility to Babylon which would not be diverted by bribery.

Isaiah 14.1-27   Pride Comes Before a Fall

The fall of Babylon will be followed by the return from Exile and a complete reversal of the situation (1–4a). This section forms a connecting link between two prophecies concerning Babylon.

There follows a remarkable 'taunt-song' against an unnamed king of Babylonia, Nebuchadnezzar being an obvious suggestion. Some scholars have suggested that since Assyria was the enemy in Isaiah's day the song originally referred to an Assyrian king, possibly Sargon or Sennacherib. This is not necessary, since Isaiah foresaw the rise of Babylonia and the captivity of Israel (39.5–8). The kings of these great world-empires were invariably proud men, indeed, many of them were regarded as the personification of the pagan deities. In graphic terms the fate of this particular monarch is depicted. Death, the great leveller, brings him down to Sheol, the shadowy abode of all the departed, irrespective of wealth or rank. There is even a hint that he was assigned to the deepest level of Sheol, possibly because of a dishonourable burial (11,15,18–20), causing the other inhabitants to marvel (10–20). The reference in vs. 12 ff. is to an ancient Canaanite myth where Helal, the Morning Star, son of Shahar (Dawn), attempted to rise above all the other luminaries, but was cast down by the Sun. Our Lord's similar description of Satan's fall (Luke 10. 18) has caused the name of Lucifer (12, AV, [KJV]) to be regarded as synonymous with Satan. The passage is a solemn warning against human pride and a reminder that one day we must all give an account of ourselves before God (Rom. 14.10 ff.; 2 Cor. 5.10). Notice how vague is the view of the after-life at this period. Soon after, a more definite doctrine concerning life after death (cf. the note on 26.14,19) began to develop. Certain facts aided this, such as (*a*) the strength of fellowship with the Lord which, the righteous reasoned, could not be broken even by death (e.g. Psa. 16.10; 73.24); (*b*) the problem of suffering (e.g. Job 14.13,14; 19.25 ff.); and (*c*) the stress on the individual encouraged by the prophets.

Jeremiah and Ezekiel fostered this, but no full doctrine of the after-life was possible before Christ's resurrection (2 Tim. 1.10).

Vs. 22 f. form a prose conclusion dealing with the fate of Babylon itself (cf. 13.19–22).

Vs. 24–27 form a separate oracle, but since it tells of a similar destruction of Assyria, there is an affinity of subject. For the historical fulfilment of the prophetic word see 37.21–38. Note how sure Isaiah was of this fact (27), and consider the bearing of this upon those prophecies in God's Word which still await fulfilment.

Isaiah 14.28—15.9   Condemnation with Compassion

Since Ahaz died in 715 B.C. the first oracle (14.28–32) may be accurately dated. Isaiah foretells that the easing of Judah's control of Philistia will be followed by a more serious oppression from the north, undoubtedly a reference to Assyria (31). Judah must withstand any involvement with Philistia against Assyria; her trust must be in the Lord alone (32).

The attention of the prophet now turns to Moab, Judah's eastern neighbour (15.1–9). There was a relationship between the two countries, since Moab was the son of an incestuous union between Lot, the nephew of Abraham, and his elder daughter (Gen. 19.36 f.). But there was little brotherliness between them. Moab refused to allow the Israelites to pass through her territory at the time of the Exodus, as a result of which Moabites were excluded from the congregation of Israel (Judg. 11.17, cf. Deut. 23.3–6). Henceforth, apart from occasional friendly contacts (e.g. Ruth 1; 1 Sam. 22.3 f.), there was general hostility between these two related nations.

Isaiah, who foresaw the judgement that was to descend upon his own nation, realized that other nations would also be involved. In Moab's case the aggressor is not named, but as the general move-ment of the campaign is from north to south, with the refugees streaming southwards into Edom (5), it may be assumed that Assyria was God's agent (cf. 10.5) in this case also. The attack would be a swift one: Ar was situated beside the Arnon; Kir was twenty-five miles to the south, but both would fall in the one night. The whole nation would be in deep mourning over this catastrophe (2–8).

One remarkable feature is the absence of any vindictiveness on the part of Isaiah. Many of his compatriots would have rejoiced in the downfall of their traditional enemy, but Isaiah was moved with compassion (5), especially as he foresaw still further bloodshed (9). All war brings untold misery and suffering, and should call forth our sympathy, whatever our own political alignment. There must be also the understanding that through the events of history the Lord works His own will and purposes of judgement.

Isaiah 16 Moab's Plea Rejected

In their predicament the Moabites sent ambassadors from Sela (i.e Petra, a famous and wellnigh impregnable natural fortress) to Judah, appealing for help (1–5). Their gift of lambs would be appropriate, since Moab is a pastoral country. The main purpose of the delegation was to secure entry into Judah for the considerable number of refugees displaced by the foreign invasion (3 f.). The appeal was backed up by a promise, couched in language which would appeal to the authorities in Jerusalem, that such a generous action would facilitate the establishment of the Davidic dynasty (5).

On humanitarian grounds the plight and plea of the Moabites may have had a considerable effect upon the Jews. But it was rejected (6–12). Almost certainly the reference to the traditional arrogance and boastfulness of Moab (6) shows that the authorities of Jerusalem detected a ring of insincerity in the specious language of the ambassadors. Moab had to face its own problems alone (7), without any official intervention from Judah, although the prophet himself was greatly moved (9,11).

We find an interesting sidelight upon the prophetic methods in vs. 13 f. Isaiah acknowledges that his prophecy concerning Moab, including probably 15.1—16.12, was not original. Suggestions concerning its original setting include: (*i*) the invasion of the Israelite king, Omri, which resulted in the annual tribute noted in 2 Kings 3.4; (*ii*) an invasion by a later king of Israel, Jeroboam II (cf. 2 Kings 14.25), when Uzziah was king of Judah. If either of these was the occasion then the name of the original prophet has been lost. But Isaiah may be referring to an earlier prophecy of his own, possibly connected with a known campaign of Sargon II of Assyria against the nomadic tribes of north-west Arabia in 715 B.C. If this be so, then the prophecy of a further campaign (14) would refer to either a second campaign by Sargon in 711 B.C. or to Sennacherib's invasion of the area in 701 B.C.

Isaiah 17.1—18.7 False Religion and Foreign Alliances

Two oracles are to be found in today's portion:

The first (17.1–14), which links together Syria (indicated by its capital, Damascus, 1,3) and Israel (Ephraim/Jacob, 3,4), clearly indicates the Syro-Ephraimitic alliance already referred to (7.1–9.21).

The failure of this alliance and the downfall of its participants are noted in language with which we are already familiar (1–6). The main interest of the chapter concerns the references to the heathen cults practised so widely in Israel which, standing at the cross-roads of world-trade, absorbed much that was alien to its native faith. The elements of Canaanite religion are noted in v. 8. The indiscriminate erection of altars was forbidden in Exod. 20.24–26; they were only to be built 'in every place where I cause My name to be remembered', i.e. the place of a theophany (a divine manifestation). The Asherim were probably wooden pillars, the formal substitute for sacred trees and a symbol of the female sexual element in the debased Canaanite religion. In vs. 10b, 11 the reference may be to Adonis-gardens. These had little depth of earth, thus encouraging brief but rapid growth, symbolizing the death and resurrection element in the heathen cults. One wonders how this kind of religion could ever have been substituted for a faith in the living God who had saved them (7,10). The Assyrian flood would sweep away such an apostate people (12–14).

The second oracle (18.1–7) was directed against the Ethiopian ambassadors. An Ethiopian dynasty, established in Egypt about 714 B.C., pursued a consistently anti-Assyrian policy which would match that of Hezekiah. The point of the prophecy, therefore, was to deter Hezekiah from involving his country in any alliance with Ethiopia. He, and indeed all peoples (3), were to look to the Lord who controlled the destinies of all nations. He would cut off the oppressor at the appropriate time (5 f.). Nevertheless, there would be contact with the Ethiopians ('a people tall and smooth', 7), but this would be religious, not political, brought about by Yahweh's decisive defeat of the Assyrians.

Note: The 'land of whirring wings' (1) may allude to the insect-infested Nile delta or to the abundance of sailing boats in Egypt.

Isaiah 19.1-15 Our God is Able

A glance at a map shows the importance of Palestine, that narrow corridor between the Mediterranean Sea and the Arabian desert. It was the land-bridge between Egypt and the successive empires of Assyria, Babylonia, Persia and Greece. Egyptian foreign policy, therefore, was vitally concerned with the small kingdoms which occupied this area, particularly Judah, Israel and Philistia. When Egypt was strong she sought to extend her influence more directly in this region, but at times of weakness she endeavoured to use these small States as a buffer against aggression by the major powers to the north-east. It was always a great temptation to Judah to link herself with Egypt, hoping thereby to guarantee immunity from attack by an aggressor. But Egypt was a notoriously unstable ally, making specious promises of help but offering remarkably little actual assistance, as Judah discovered to her cost on more than one occasion. Isaiah was acutely aware of the dangers of alliance with such an unreliable power, but he was equally alive to the spiritual peril of ceasing to trust in Yahweh, whose power was sufficient to deliver them from any foe.

In these verses Isaiah anticipates a period of great distress for Egypt. First of all, they would experience the horrors of civil war (2,3). Since Egypt was a federation of lesser states there was an underlying jealousy, and a predisposition towards disunity. The subsequent weakness would make her an easy prey for a harsh tyrant (4), which may allude to the Assyrian conquest of 670 B.C. or to the native tyrant, Psammetichus I (663–609 B.C.). There would be a natural calamity also, with the waters of the Nile failing, which would lead to the collapse of Egypt's main industries, farming (7b), fishing (8) and textiles (9). The wise men of Egypt (11–13), who were internationally famous, would be as helpless to avert disaster as the exponents of idolatrous and magical practices (3). What a comfort it must have been to the godly remnant grouped around Isaiah to realize that their God WAS able (1,4,14)!

Isaiah 19.16—20.6   God Controls History

Our first section (19.16–25) is a unity, subdivided into five by the introduction 'In that day' (16,18,19,23,24). The context requires a time when Egypt would be in considerable fear of Judah (16 f.), which may indicate the period immediately after the decimation of the Assyrian host and the miraculous deliverance of Jerusalem (37.36 f.). The prediction of v. 18 anticipates the day when there will be Jewish colonies in Egypt. There is no documentation of such an event until the sixth century B.C., but it is conceivable that there were earlier settlements. The remaining three oracles are surprising, for they foretell a time when there will be a witness to the Lord in Egypt, and a day when His mighty acts would be wrought for Egypt as He had repeatedly delivered Israel in the period of the Judges (20). Moreover, both Egypt and Assyria, who had been thorns in Israel's flesh for so long, would become with Israel the means of universal blessing (23,24). Such universalism, in a national context of suspicion of Egypt and fear of Assyria, is truly remarkable, and witnesses to God's care for all nations.

Our second section (20.1–6) is history rather than pure prophecy, but it has been included here because it connects with Isaiah's denouncement of alliances with Egypt. We regard visual aids as a modern innovation, but in fact such devices were regularly employed by the prophets, especially in times of crisis, when they endeavoured to enforce their messages by 'eye-gate' as well as by 'ear-gate'. Sargon, the Assyrian king (722–705 B.C.), is nowhere else mentioned in Scripture, but Assyrian records note the capture of Ashdod, a Philistinian city, in 711 B.C. Isaiah was commanded to dress and act like a prisoner of war (2 f.) for a three-year period, witnessing to the defeat of Egypt and the deportation of its inhabitants. Their route would lead along the narrow coastal plain, and the procession would be watched, in consternation, by the Philistines and the men of Judah. If this was the fate of those to whom they were running for help, what chance would they themselves have! The answer, unspoken by the people, had been voiced time and time again by Isaiah; there was One who was more than sufficient in this crisis, Yahweh, the 'God of your salvation', and, 'the Rock of your refuge' (17.10). Those who trusted Him completely would find Him wholly true.

Isaiah 21 God of the Nations

In this chapter we find three apparently unrelated oracles:

(i) The fall of Babylon (1–10). The prophet's thought is projected into the sixth century B.C. when Elam and Media (2) were associated in the onslaught which brought proud Babylon, itself the successor to the Assyrian power, to its knees. In vs. 1–5 the prophet appears to be an eyewitness of the overthrow of the city, and at the sight of the horrors attending such an event his own heart recoils in deep emotion (3 f.). In spite of the untold misery Babylon had caused, no one could exult in such circumstances. The picture of the festivities of the nobles (5), when they ought to have been preparing for action, calls to mind the licentious orgy of Belshazzar's feast on the night of his death (Dan. 5). In vs. 6–10 the prophet is no longer present at the scene of destruction, but rather waits for the messenger bringing the tidings of the final overthrow of Babylon. Such an end is certain, not because Isaiah has spoken, but because the Lord of hosts has spoken through him (10). The word of God cannot fail to be fulfilled.

(ii) There follows a short, enigmatic oracle concerning Edom, often referred to as Seir, or Mt. Seir (11 f.). Since no known site of Dumah has been identified in Edom some scholars have preferred a plausible emendation of the first line, which then reads, 'A voice is lifted up from Edom'. If this be accepted, a link with the former oracle is probable. From Edom, languishing in the night of oppression (presumably from Babylon), a voice comes to the watchman of v. 8 to inquire how long the darkness of affliction is to last. The reply seems to suggest that the relief (morning) will be temporary; it will be succeeded by further suffering (night). But further inquiry is invited.

(*iii*) This prophecy relates to Arabia (13–17). The Dedanites were members of an Arabian tribe who are pictured as seeking refuge from an unnamed oppressor. Driven from their normal haunts they fall back upon Tema, an oasis in the desert of Arabia. Another powerful Arabian tribe, Kedar (16 f.), appears to be involved in the same catastrophe. Again, it is worth noting that Isaiah saw clearly that the Lord controlled the destinies of all nations, from the powerful Babylon down to and including the inhabitants of the desert.

Isaiah 22 Unseemly Conduct

Commentators are divided as to whether the siege of Jerusalem depicted in vs. 1–14 is in the past, or the future. Most likely, as vs. 12–14 seem to suggest, it was actually in progress. The reference in v. 3 is probably to those who fell away to the enemy; an Assyrian inscription relating to the events of 701 B.C. (Taylor's Prism) speaks of mercenaries who deserted Jerusalem in this crisis. The day of the Lord which so many desired was one that began in judgement upon Jerusalem itself (5, cf. Amos 5.18 ff.). Certain precautions had been taken by the rulers to ensure an adequate water supply and to strengthen the defences (8–11, cf. 2 Chron. 32.2–8,30). But at this point of the siege, at any rate, there was no living faith in the Lord, no seeking His face in humility and penitence. Rather, there was a brazen 'devil-may-care' attitude akin to that of Belshazzar, who, when Daniel foretold the end of himself and his kingdom, applauded and honoured Daniel instead of humbling himself before Daniel's God (13, cf. Dan. 5.22–30). Such insensitivity to the challenge of the hour, such an obsession with eating and drinking, were criminal in God's sight. If, as we have suggested, the events here do relate to 701 B.C., it must be noted that God, in fact, spared Jerusalem largely through the humility, piety and faith of its king Hezekiah and the Lord's prophet Isaiah. Such men were, and still are, the salt of the earth.

The oracle against Shebna (15–25) is remarkable inasmuch as it is the only case in *Isaiah* of a prophecy against a named individual.

The position of 'steward' (15) was an important one, its parallel, 'over the household', indicates the position next to the king himself. Since no genealogy is given for Shebna it is surmised that he was a foreigner. This finds some support in the Aramaic form of his name —possibly he was a Syrian. Isaiah attacks him for his pretensions in hewing out a rock tomb, normally reserved for those of noble birth, and also for his ostentatious use of ornate chariots (16,18). The prophet shows that he will never use the tomb himself for he will be taken away violently and die in captivity. By the time of Isa. 36 Shebna had been demoted somewhat, being replaced by Eliakim, as Isaiah foretold (20–24) but the complete fulfilment of Isaiah's words is not actually recorded.

A thought: Note God's concern about unseemly conduct, both of a city and an individual. What about my country—and myself?

Isaiah 23   The Glory of the World Passes

The city of Tyre was one of the most famous in the ancient world. Its mariners were the explorers and merchants of the period. Their deeds are extolled in classical and Biblical literature, e.g. Phoenician seamen in both the Red Sea and the Mediterranean helped in the prosperity of Solomon's empire (1 Kings 10.11,22). Phoenician craftsmen were renowned throughout the region (1 Kings 5.6,18) and one of them, Hiram, was the chief architect of Solomon's magnificent Temple (1 Kings 7.13–45). The city of Tyre was virtually impregnable, surviving successive sieges by the Assyrian kings, Esar-haddon (671 B.C.) and Ashurbanipal (664 B.C.) and the Babylonian Nebuchadnezzar (585–572 B.C.), when other great cities fell.

But the judgement of the Lord was to fall on Tyre also. The references to Sidon (2,4,12), to the inhabitants of the coast (2) and to Canaan (11), show that the whole of Phoenicia was included in this divine punishment. The prophet imagines sailors from Tyre hearing of the desolation of their mother-city when they arrive at, or return from Cyprus (1). The startling news is pictured as spreading rapidly throughout the surrounding countries, causing consternation everywhere, but especially in Egypt (5), whose trade-links with Tyre were so strong. In particular, Tyre was dependent on the grain supply of the fertile Nile valley (3). The reason for this destruction was the overbearing pride of Tyre, and the corruption which so often accompanies power (9,12).

V. 13 is a very obscure verse which seems to suggest that it was the Chaldeans (i.e. Babylonians), not the Assyrians, who fulfilled this oracle, but this is not certain. The apparent fulfilment of the prophetic word was the destruction of Tyre, after a long and skilfully executed campaign, by Alexander the Great in 332 B.C. The promise of a partial restoration after seventy years (15–18) would then take place in the period of the Seleucid (Syrian) kings, whose kingdom, centred on Antioch, included all the small States of Palestine. No full revival of Tyrian power is envisaged, however, and the language is caustic rather than consoling. Tyre, like a harlot (17), will prostitute her gifts and resources, but these will finally be dedicated to the Lord (18). Tyre is a picture of all the glory of this world, which eventually passes away. Materialism has the appearance of permanence, but in fact, it is the unseen things of the Spirit which endure (2 Cor. 4.18).

Questions for further study and discussion on Isaiah chs. 13–23

1. What principles of judgement may we discern in these chapters?
2. Consider the action and influence of God upon the nations of Isaiah's day. What lessons may we draw and apply in the contemporary international situation?
3. With the use of a concordance and/or Bible dictionary, examine the part played by Babylon in history and in prophecy.
4. Notice how frequently the pride of nations, cities and individuals is condemned by the Lord. Why is this 'sin of the spirit' so grievous in His sight?
5. Starting from ch. 20, make a list of other occasions where prophets used 'visual aids' to press home their message. Note the degree of success in each case.

Isaiah 24   The End of the World

Chs. 24–27 form another separate section in *Isaiah*, often referred to as 'The Apocalypse of Isaiah'. Here the focus of attention changes from the present and the immediate future, to events at the end of the present world-age. Apocalyptic literature and thought became very popular in the inter-testamental period, e.g. the covenanters at Qumran, as the Dead Sea Scrolls indicate, were obsessed with an apocalyptic approach which foresaw the 'end' in their own period. Apocalyptic literature developed certain characteristics, especially in the non-biblical books, where the elements are often grotesque. Biblical apocalyptic thought, found principally in the books of *Isaiah, Daniel, Zechariah* and *Revelation*, is restrained and focuses on the sovereignty of God. There is a natural fitness in the presence of this kind of approach within the prophecies of Isaiah, for it deals

214

with God's final victory at the end of the age. Who was better fitted to speak of this than the prophet who was so profoundly aware of the inevitability of God's judgement upon a sinful world! His perception that God used Assyria as the rod of His anger (10.5) would lead on naturally to the view of God as the great World-ruler acting in final judgement against sin. Those who deny the insights of these chapters to Isaiah should bear in mind that he was not bound by the spirit and attitudes of his age. In touch with God, he was a spiritual giant, and it took the nation several centuries to catch up with him, if indeed it ever did!

The desolation which will overtake the whole earth is vividly depicted in vs. 1–13. The 'everlasting covenant' (5) connects more naturally with the universal covenant of Gen. 9.16 than with the Sinaitic covenant with Israel. In vs. 14–16a the recital of destruction is interrupted by a song of praise from the Lord's people as they see the vindication of their faith, and the majesty of their Lord. The prophet, foreseeing further catastrophies (17–23), finds it impossible to join in such a song at such a time (16b).

Note 'the host of heaven' (21) may refer to rebellious angels, in league with the world powers in their onslaught upon the people of God, pointing to a final conflict in heaven as well as on earth (cf. the imagery of Dan. 10.20 f.). Or it could refer to the heavenly bodies (cf. 23), in which case the reference would be to idolatry, since these were all objects of false worship.

Isaiah 25   The Day of Triumph

The prophet composes a hymn of praise in anticipation of the Lord's great victory (1–5). The city (2, cf. 24.10,12) is probably used representatively of the oppressor rather than one particular city. Even the great world powers (3) would be forced to acknowledge the immeasurably greater power of Israel's God, exercised on behalf of His chosen people (4 f.). The Lord is mighty to deliver His people, as Daniel's friends discovered (Dan. 3.17), a fact confirmed in the experience of God's people throughout the centuries. The N.T. reveals that this final day of vindication for the righteous will be heralded by Christ's appearance in glory, when the promise of Phil. 2.10 f., experienced already in the lives of believers, will be fully realized.

There is also the anticipation of a triumphant feast in honour of the victory (6–9, cf. Rev. 19.9,17). All signs of mourning will be removed (8), for God's people will rejoice in the completion of their redemption (9). V. 8 is quoted in Rev. 21.4 (cf. 1 Cor. 15.54) in a moving passage which springs from the assurance of final triumph through Christ's death, resurrection and coming again. In a situation of prosperity and security it is not always easy to realize the comfort this conception must be to multitudes who, because of their faith, are languishing in prison or facing daily persecution and privation. Let us pray that our persecuted brethren may endure through the strengthening presence of the One who will vindicate His own at His coming.

Notes: V. 6, 'wine on the lees well refined' is wine where the sediment has been allowed to remain, thus improving the quality, but calling for great care in straining off before use. V. 7, 'the covering' and 'the veil' (which are parallel) probably allude to the removal of every sign of mourning. There may be an associated thought that the spiritual blindness of all nations will be banished at this revelation of God's omnipotence.

Finally, there is a return to the earlier note of exultation at the overthrow of the aggressor (10 ff.). The specific mention of Moab in such a general context is surprising. There may be an allusion to some otherwise unknown historical incident, or Moab may be used to represent all Judah's enemies. Since the words for Moab and enemy are very similar, other scholars favour a slight emendation.

A thought for today: 'Let us be glad and rejoice in His salvation' (9).

Isaiah 26 Thy Dead shall Live!

The prophet breaks out into yet another psalm of thanksgiving (1–6). Those who are conscious of God's delivering power cannot too often celebrate His saving acts. Vs. 3 f. come very close to expressing the essence of Isaiah's faith. Israel's God was a God of power who could be relied upon. This had been proved in many a political crisis, e.g. the occasion when Jerusalem was threatened by Syria, Israel, Philistia and Edom (Isa. 7). Whereas weak King Ahaz feared to put God to the test, and turned in desperation to cruel Assyria, Isaiah knew the peace of an absolute trust. It was the same in 701 B.C. when Sennacherib's host seemed certain to overwhelm the beleaguered city (37.21–35). It is the same today, whether our crisis be political, economic, emotional or physical—there can be perfect peace where there is perfect trust.

A prayer of faith (7–19), uttered during the crisis, is met by the assurance of vs. 20 f. Notice the sincerity, loyalty to Yahweh and heart-hunger for Him expressed in vs. 8 f., 12–15, even in a time of great distress (16 ff.). There is an awareness that the Lord is already at work, but the plea is for the full manifestation of His glory, that their adversaries may be made aware of their folly in resisting the Lord God.

One of the remarkable features of this chapter concerns the doctrine of resurrection. The fate of the ungodly is depicted with grim finality in v. 14. In stark contrast to this is the promise to the faithful who have perished in the persecution. These, humanly speaking, would be deemed certain to miss the joyous moment of God's final victory. But, Isaiah avers, they would not be excluded from the thrilling experience of ultimate salvation, for God Himself would work a miracle in raising .them from the dead. It appears unrealistic to limit this to a national resurrection in the return from Exile (the undoubted meaning of Ezek. 37.1–14). It is equally carping to deny that this can be Isaianic because a doctrine of individual resurrection was late in emerging. This *is* the first clear reference in Scripture to an individual resurrection and it comes most naturally from this God-filled, divinely inspired prophet. But a full doctrine of resurrection was not possible until Christ was raised from the dead (1 Cor. 15.12–26).

Isaiah 27 God's Victory

The Ancient Near East had a rich mythology, in which the land of Canaan shared, as evidenced by the archaeological discoveries at Ras Shamra (the site of ancient Ugarit, whose final destruction coincided approximately with the time of Moses). In particular, at the Autumn New Year Festival, there was the celebration of the gods' victory over the forces of chaos, based upon the Creation-epic. The story is known to have been diffused over a wide area, including Mesopotamia, where creation was conceived to be the result of a victory over the chaos-monster, Tiamat. It is evident that the O.T. writers were familiar with this theme, and they employed it frequently to illustrate the almighty power of the Lord, and His victory over all His enemies. It goes without saying that the tale was not conceived to have any substance or historicity; in using it Isaiah and others had completely 'de-mythologized' it. In much the same way we may refer to Hercules or Atlas without accepting that these characters ever existed. Other instances of this imagery in the O.T. include references to Leviathan (Psa. 74.13,14) and Rahab (Job 26.12). Some have seen in our reference (27.1) an allusion to Judah's principal enemies: 'Leviathan the fleeing serpent' may indicate the swift-flowing Tigris and, together with 'Leviathan the twisting serpent' (possibly the meandering Euphrates), point to the great Mesopotamian powers of Assyria and Babylon; 'the dragon

217

that is in the sea' may similarly indicate the Nile, the symbol of Egypt. Isaiah's contemporaries would understand this reference to a victory as decisive in its effects as the transformation effected by God's creative acts.

But first there must be a process of judgement, in which Israel itself would be disciplined, as indicated in the picture of a beating rod being used to separate the precious grain from the chaff (12). It would include the devastation of Jerusalem (10 f.). No real blessing could come to a nation so void of spiritual discernment (11) that it forsook the living God for an empty idolatry (9). After this judgement would come the final blessing in the ingathering of Israel (13) which would then become a source of fruitfulness for the whole world (6). Whilst the world has been enriched immeasurably by the Jewish people throughout the ages the complete fulfilment of these promises may still lie in the future.

Isaiah 28   The Wise Farmer

The pride and drunkenness of the northern kingdom of Israel (called Ephraim after its chief tribe) are condemned (1–6). The oracle, therefore, must be before 721 B.C., the year of the final defeat of Israel at the hands of the Assyrians. But even in this catastrophe the Lord will preserve a remnant (5 f.).

Isaiah is also concerned with the rulers in Judah who are guilty of the same sins that caused the fall of Israel. There is a sickening picture of drunken debauchery, the more horrifying since it involved the religious leaders, making them incapable of exercising effective leadership (7,8). Isaiah records the indignant expostulation of these men at this point (9 f.). They regarded themselves as adults, not children, to be lectured in this way. Possibly there is mimicry in their words (10) as they mockingly refer to his persistent condemnation of their deeds. Isaiah indicates that the Lord has other ways of speaking than by the lips of His servants the prophets. When these are rejected (which includes the rejection of the Lord Himself, the only source of rest and security, 12), He will employ another weapon, an alien army (11), doubtless the Assyrians, to effect His will.

With an even greater clarity, this catalogue of the sins of Judah's rulers continues (14–22). They brazenly reject Yahweh's covenant and form their own plans to meet the emergency. The 'covenant with death' and the 'agreement with Sheol' (15,18) may indicate a dependence upon the dubious forces of necromancy and spiritism. Or it may be an ironic allusion to an alliance with Egypt which is pre-doomed to failure. She would be unable to hold back the flood of Assyria (15,18). The reference in v. 21 is to David's convincing double-defeat of the Philistines (2 Sam. 5.17-25). Since the nation had rejected its sure foundation of a quiet, unruffled faith in the Lord (16) the 'strange work' of chastisement would fall upon them (21).

Reassurance is given that God's employment of the Assyrian is not purposeless (23-29). Using a series of agricultural analogies Isaiah shows that the diverse actions of the farmer are all suited to particular crops. If one can commend the wisdom of a farmer, how much more can one depend on the greater wisdom of God directed towards His gracious purposes of ultimate blessing!

A thought: 'Why should I start at the plough of my Lord, that make the deep furrows in my soul? I know He is no unwise husbandman, He purposeth a crop'. (Samuel Rutherford.)

Isaiah 29   'God . . . Exists' (Heb. 11.6)

Once more Isaiah takes up the solemn theme of judgement against Jerusalem (1-11). The modern reader may become weary at such repetition, but he must bear two facts in mind: (*i*) There is a judgement upon the sin of individuals and communities. This stems from a sovereign, holy God who controls all the forces of nature and nations. The Bible takes the fact of sin seriously, and so must we, if we are to retain any relationship to its revealed truth. (*ii*) The very repetition of these oracles, warning of impending judgement, speaks of God's patient forbearance. He does not act precipitantly, but allows full opportunity for repentance and reformation. But let no man mistake this for weakness, or imagine that God will not act in final judgement.

'Ariel' (1 f.) obviously indicates Jerusalem, it could mean 'lion of God' but this hardly suits the context, unless it be used ironically. More likely is the suggestion that it means 'altar-hearth', and that the whole city is viewed as a place of sacrifice, the offering being the citizens themselves. The details of the siege, worked out in the following verses, are like a ghastly nightmare to the besieged (8). They were morally and spiritually blind, as were the false prophets in whom they trusted, so that they were quite incapable of understanding the principles behind the Lord's drastic dealings (9-12).

Hypocrisy in religion (13) is surely one of the most abhorrent sins. To go through a form of prayer, mouthing insincere words which mean nothing, may win the approbation of men. But they will not please a living God, who merits our full attention, our choicest gifts and our outpoured adoration. Let us be on our guard against insulting God by going through a pretence of honouring Him. Positively, 'let us draw near with a true heart in full assurance of faith' (Heb. 10.22). In politics also (15 f.) Isaiah's contemporaries were acting as though God, their Creator, did not exist. They would find out their mistake, to their great cost, but after the judgement God would reveal His ultimate purpose of blessing, security and prosperity, accompanied by true worship (17–24).

Note: V. 17 symbolizes the renewed prosperity. The forest would come under cultivation, and the growth on arable land would be so prolific that it would look like a forest (cf. 32.15).

Isaiah 30.1-17 Trust in God Alone

Bad politics are often associated with false religion. Isaiah had consistently stressed that the nation's security lay in its faith in God, who was mighty enough to protect them from all adversaries. His compatriots in general, and their rulers in particular, had no such faith, and as a substitute for reliance upon the Lord they sought alliances with Egypt. The utter folly of this was apparent to the prophet, whose faith gave him a true perspective, but it was not obvious to the rulers, frantic as they were for some kind of security. At a period of internal unrest and external weakness in Egypt the ambassadors of Judah flocked to her for help against a wellnigh invincible Assyria! The incongruity of it was apparent; Egyptian alliances could bring only shame and disgrace (5). In caustic tones Isaiah refers to Egypt as 'Rahab who sits still', an apparent contradiction, since Rahab was the turbulent chaos-monster of mythology. Isaiah saw that her deeds would not correspond with her boastful assurances of massive help against Judah's enemy. In vain would the richly laden caravans carry the price of this alliance across the desert sands (6).

Instead of listening to this merciless exposure of their folly, the men of Judah sought to silence the prophets (10) and even to eliminate from their consciousness any recollection of 'the Holy One of Israel' (11). They were not the first, nor the last, of those who have sought to stifle the voice of truth. It was the expedient of Amaziah the priest of Bethel (Amos 7.12); of the princes of Jerusalem in Jeremiah's time (Jer. 38.4); of the men of Nazareth (Luke 4.29) and the murderers of Stephen (Acts 7.57 f.). It was especially characteristic of Jerusalem (Matt. 23.37). The Lord shows the result of such folly: their alliance would be like a jerry-built wall, which would collapse and crush them (13 f.); the promise of Lev. 26.8 would be reversed, and instead of victory over superior forces they would be routed by insignificant numbers (17). What unutterable folly to forsake the One who could save (15)! The same danger confronts us today, to rely upon 'the arm of flesh', be it wealth, power, organization, technique or ingenuity. Nothing can substitute for a humble, complete trust in the Lord 'who alone does wondrous things' (Psa. 72.18).

Isaiah 30.18—31.9   Five Pictures of God

(i) The Lord as Teacher (30.20). The affliction which had fallen upon Jerusalem was motivated by God's gracious purposes (18) and by His desire for their spiritual healing (26). But when a teacher's instruction is ignored, as Israel so wilfully ignored the counsel of God given through the Law and the prophets, the rod of correction has to be applied. This is not a pleasant process but it becomes bearable when it is realized that the chastisement is in love, designed to produce 'the peaceful fruit of righteousness' (Heb. 12.5–11).

(ii) The Lord as Judge. His sovereignty extends over all nations (30.28), and Assyria, in particular, will feel the full force of His rod (30.31). The 'burning place' (30.33), as the RSV margin suggests, may be a place name, Topheth, a site in the valley of Hinnom where children were sacrificed to Molech. The grim promise is that the Assyrians will provide such a sacrifice. But God was concerned with the judgement of His own people as well as their enemies and His control of the international situation was directed towards that end (31.9b).

(iii) The Lord as Wise (31.2). Human wisdom prompted Judah to turn to Egypt for help. Isaiah ironically reminds his hearers of a higher wisdom and a greater strength (31.1 ff., cf. 1 Cor. 1.20–25). Flesh and blood are not to be compared with Almighty God (3) and at His direction both helper (Egypt) and helped (Judah) would come tumbling down.

(iv) The Lord as Shepherd (31.4). The natural interpretation of this verse is that Assyria is the lion, savaging his prey, Jerusalem. Such a powerful beast is not to be frightened away by a group of shepherds, representing Egypt and Judah's other puny allies, who can make a lot of noise but display no real power. But when the Lord intervenes, such intervention is decisive, and the victim is delivered.

(v) The Lord as a mother-bird (31.5) hovering over her young to protect it from attack by a bird of prey, brings a final picture of His tender dealings with His own. Our Saviour Himself used similar

221

imagery when describing His own attitude to the Jerusalem of His day. But His offer of protection was rudely rebuffed (Luke 13.34).

Isaiah 32 The Lord our Refuge

Scholars are divided as to whether vs. 1–5 refer to the Messiah. Strictly speaking, the section is not Messianic in the same sense as 7.14; 9.2–7; 11.1–9. The mention of princes in conjunction with a king appears decisive. Isaiah is probably contrasting things as they were—an incompetent king (Ahaz) and corrupt officials, with things as they ought to be—both king and rulers standing as bulwarks against vice and oppression. But since this ideal was never to be realized in the reign of any subsequent monarch, Jewish or Gentile, and since such idealism can never be achieved before the Messiah reigns, we may be forgiven for including these verses with the other Messianic sections. Certain it is that no one but Jesus Christ fulfils the requirements of v. 2. Notice again the stress on justice in dealing with one's fellows, with one's vision and judgement uninfluenced by bribes.

Isaiah then departs from his earlier line of thought, being led from the ideal to the actual observation of the surrounding evil (6–8). Once more there follows the familiar threat of judgement upon such an inversion of true values (9–14, to which v. 19, out of place in its present context, should probably be added). But judgement is never the prophets' last word. They were vividly aware that God's will could not be made of non-effect by man's disobedience; He would bring about His kingdom of peace, prosperity and happiness when His punishment, meted out in absolute equity, was completed. So Isaiah anticipates the age when God's Spirit would be poured out upon men. In this post-Pentecost age (Acts 2.1–4) we see these promises worked out in spiritual, not material terms. The righteousness so sadly lacking in ancient Israel is now made possible and each child of God is called to display the nine-fold fruit of the Spirit (Gal. 5.22f.). The same indwelling Spirit gives us power to witness to Jesus Christ, the source and secret of the transformed life (Acts 1.8).

Look again at v. 2, thinking of the imagery of each line. Is the Lord all this to you?

Questions for further study and discussion on Isaiah chs. 24–32

1. Consider the relationship between prophecy which connects with the prophet's contemporary situation and that which relates to the end of the age.

2. What reasons underlie the teaching of a final judgement?
3. Make a list of the prophecies in this section which still await fulfilment.
4. Discuss the use which the prophet and other Biblical writers make of heathen mythology.
5. Why was Isaiah so strongly opposed to alliances with Egypt?

Isaiah 33
A Hymn of Victory

The whole chapter, with such apparent diversity in its sections, is probably a psalm composed to celebrate the amazing deliverance from the Assyrian army in 701 B.C. It may be compared with Psa. 46 which, in all likelihood, was composed at the same time and for the same purpose. Notice the dramatic movement of thought; the cruelty of the besieging power (1); the plea of the besieged (2); and their assurance, based on past mercies, of the Lord's intervention (3-6); the disorder in the land, brought about by the invasion (7-9); the intervention of the Lord (10-13); the reaction of the ungodly (14) and the answer to this of the Lord's people (15,16); and finally, the reiteration of a complete victory over the Assyrians (19) and the security and prosperity of Jerusalem (17-24). The significance of v. 17 is that the king will be able to assume his rightful position. No longer will he be cooped up in his capital, the ancient frontiers of the realm will be regained. It is one of the great tragedies of Jewish history that this singular deliverance of Jerusalem became the central theme of a false theology which, over a century later, led to the downfall of the capital at the hands of the Babylonians. Jerusalem had been spared in Isaiah's time, subsequently its inhabitants believed that it would *never* fall, that the Lord of Hosts was *bound* to deliver it, irrespective of the character of its inhabitants. This was the fatal dogma of Jerusalem's inviolability. No doubt the Jerusalemites of Jeremiah's age quoted Isa. 33.20 (cf. 31.5; 32.18; 37.35) in support of the orthodoxy of their doctrine. But Jeremiah hit hard at this popular heresy and prophesied that a moral God would destroy an immoral city, however favoured it may have been in past history, just as He destroyed the sanctuary at Shiloh (Jer. 7.8–15; 26.1–6). It is a solemn thought that there can be a dead, barren orthodoxy, apparently supported by Scripture (or by an appeal to eminent church leaders and saints of earlier ages) which merits only the judgement of God.

Finally, look at the contrast between vs. 2 and 14. Isaiah knew what it was like to experience the burning holiness of God (ch. 6). We too may draw near to such a God on the basis of Christ's atonement, and in this relationship the prayer of v. 2 may be our experience as we face each new day.

Isaiah 34   'Our God is a Consuming Fire' (Heb. 12.29)

It is generally agreed that chs. 34 and 35 form a unit, the one fore-telling a decisive judgement on the Lord's enemies, the other speaking of the return of His people to their own land. Much of ch. 34 concerns Edom, which had a long-standing enmity against Israel. It began (Gen. 25.23; 27.40,41) during the lifetime of Jacob (the progenitor of Israel) and Esau (the founder of Edom), and continued subsequently, reaching a new peak in the time of Isaiah (2 Kings 16.6). Long after Isaiah's death this bitter animosity flared up again in the crisis of 587 B.C., when Edom, like a jackal slinking after the Babylonian lion, helped in the final humiliation of Jerusalem, an intervention which called forth a bitter protest from the prophets and psalmists (Obad. 10–16; Lam. 4.21,22; Ezek. 25.12–14; 35.5,10–15; Psa. 137.7). In this gruesome oracle Isaiah speaks of Edom's final judgement, resulting in the complete desolation of her land. The 'book of the Lord' (16) refers not to any collection of Isaiah's oracles or any other portion of the O.T. but to what might be called 'the book of fate', decreed by the Lord. Edom's fate is irrevocable, and all the creatures named in vs. 13 ff. will occupy her territory, now denuded of its human inhabitants.

There is evidence, however, that Edom is here used symbolically of all the heathen nations who are opposed to the Lord. In v. 1 all the nations are summoned together to hear God pronounce the sentence of doom (2) upon them and the present world order. As we noted in an earlier section, this will include the astral bodies themselves (4, cf. 24.21,23). This theme of a final judgement, of a hell as well as a heaven, of a God who will call men to account, is not a popular one in this twentieth century and is rarely heard from our pulpits. But if preaching and teaching are to retain any relationship to Biblical truth, they must take this well-documented fact into account. There is going to be a great white throne (Rev. 20.11), with a final division of all men (Matt. 25.31–46). It is well to ponder on the significance of that awesome phrase, 'the wrath of the Lamb' (Rev. 6.16), and to recall that 'It is a fearful thing to fall into the hands of the living God' (Heb. 10.31). This realization will keep us from complacency in our Christian service, for the fate of the lost cannot be a matter of indifference to the redeemed who understand these things.

It is fitting that the last oracle of the first section of *Isaiah* should be one which rejoices in God's salvation. In the preceding chapters we have frequently noted the certainty of judgement, which included the deportation of many of the survivors to Mesopotamia, the seat of the great world-powers of Assyria and Babylon. Such was the vision of Isaiah that he looked beyond the period of chastisement to the time when God would fulfil His gracious purposes to His people, in their own land. This inevitably involved the return from captivity, and it is this which is depicted so movingly in ch. 35. This future event would be as great a miracle as the Exodus from Egypt in the time of Moses, when God led, protected and supplied the needs of those whom He had redeemed. The route from the Tigris-Euphrates basin involved traversing some desolate, arid areas, but these would be transformed and the journey of the returned exiles would be a march of triumph. Those who were weak and crippled in spirit or tongue-tied because of despair would be encouraged and liberated as the Lord opened up His way before them (3–9). Once more there was the prospect of worshipping the Lord in Jerusalem in an atmosphere of radiant joy which banished for ever the shadows of the past (10).

The writer was 'introduced' to this lovely psalm by a fellow officer on H.M.S. *Indefatigable* during the war years of 1944/45. A Christian, with a glowing testimony to a living Christ, he revelled in this passage. Our 'desert' was not one of sand but a waste of sea, at action stations, with danger and privation in close attendance and so many of the normal amenities of life removed. But God, we realized, was able to transform the most desolate situation, and the small Christian group on board enjoyed 'waters in the wilderness' and 'streams in the desert' (6). Situations vary from year to year and from individual to individual, but God never changes. He remains the God of the impossible, there is nothing too hard for Him. The 'desert' through which you are passing today, or may be called to pass through in the future, can 'rejoice and blossom abundantly' (2) and you too may see His glory and majesty in His work of deliverance (2,4).

Isaiah 36.1-20   An Impossible Situation

Chapters 36–39 form an historical interlude between the two sections of the book. So often during these notes we have mentioned the events of 701 B.C.; today's portion narrates the gripping events of that momentous year. This is history at its best, no dull recital of statistics and dates but an account which enables us to sense the haughty arrogance of the Assyrian and the chilling clutch of despair at the hearts of the Israelites. The enemy was not only a massive military power, there was clearly an excellent intelligence service and a first-rate propaganda machine. Indeed, so efficient was the latter that the Jerusalem authorities wished to conduct the negotiations in another tongue (36.11). There was an element of truth in the eight-pronged argument of the Rabshakeh (a civilian post equivalent to 'chief steward' or 'envoy'): (i) Mere words seemed a futile defence against the legions of Assyria (5). (ii) Egypt was a completely unreliable ally (6)—Isaiah had been telling his compatriots this for a generation! (iii) Hezekiah, in his reformation, had closed down all the sanctuaries tainted by the Baal cults and had partially centralized worship in Jerusalem (7). The unenlightened Assyrian interpreted this as an insult to Yahweh who had been falsely worshipped at these outlying shrines (cf. 2 Chron. 31.1). (iv) The men of Jerusalem, unskilled in cavalry or chariot warfare, were confronted with an army which could easily *spare* two thousand horses (8,9); (v) Their presence at the walls of Jerusalem, the Rabshakeh suggested, was at the behest of Yahweh Himself (10). (vi) There was a personal attack on Hezekiah, designed to weaken his leadership (14,15,18). (vii) Observe also the appeal to self-interest. If they surrendered they would not only save their lives but would be taken to a much better land (16,17). (viii) Finally, there was the appeal to hard facts. No other great city had withstood the Assyrian steamroller and so their gods had been thoroughly discredited (18 ff.). The mention of Samaria, the capital of Israel (destroyed in 721 B.C.), would bring the lesson perilously close to home. Already Lachish, twenty-five miles to the south-west, had fallen (2), together with most of the other cities of Judah (1). But the Assyrians were unaware that Judah's God was not to be put on the same level as impotent idols of wood, stone and silver, and the protestation of faith in Him was not 'mere words'.

Isaiah 36.21—37.13

'Our Eyes are upon Thee' (2 Chron. 20.12)

Hezekiah's men, whatever may have been their inward reaction to the challenge of the Assyrian envoy, remained outwardly loyal to their king (36.21). His chief officers, including Shebna, whose ostentatious pride we observed in 22.15–19, even showed signs of humility and repentance (or was it despair?) in this crisis (36.22;

226

37.2). Hezekiah was equally aware of the obvious danger which confronted him, his capital and his people. Jerusalem was held in a vice-like grip, with no prospect of breaking free.

The king's reactions are instructive. He was one of the better kings of Israel, indeed he had already gained quite a reputation for his major religious reformation (2 Kings 18.3–7). This championing of Judah's native faith would itself be regarded by Assyria as a rebellious act, for all subject peoples were required to pay deference to the Assyrian gods. Hezekiah's great mistake was in seeking to hasten this process by enlisting Egyptian help. This policy, as we have observed, alienated Isaiah, who saw that an unqualified reliance upon God was a sufficient guarantee of protection. Now Hezekiah found himself at the end of his tether. Assyrian troops, having shattered his country, were poised for the final assault against Jerusalem, whilst his ally, Egypt, had failed him. It is not surprising that he went to God's house in this time of need, for he was no stranger to its courts (37.1). But it was an admission of the error of his policies, a public eating of humble-pie, when he turned to Isaiah for help (37.2). The prophet's response was immediate and a model of graciousness, without the slightest suggestion of an 'I told you so' attitude (5 ff.). The siege was finally ended in precisely the way indicated here, unrest in Babylonia forcing Sennacherib to return home in haste, leaving the remnant of his army to follow at a later date.

Before this deliverance, however, the threat from Assyria increased in intensity (8–13). Jerusalem was granted a temporary respite by a brief appearance of the Egyptian army which compelled the Assyrians to withdraw. To crush any spirit of rejoicing in Jerusalem a threatening and insulting letter was sent to Hezekiah by the Assyrian king himself, reminding him of the impossibility of deliverance. The pall of gloom over Jerusalem must have seemed even more intense. It was a time for God to act.

Isaiah 37.14-38

'Nothing is too hard for Thee . . .' (Jer. 32.17)

Hezekiah's response was the same as on the occasion of the earlier threat (14, cf. 37.1). What a wise king to take to the Lord the burden of the peril which confronted Judah, for He too was included in the Assyrian insult! The safest thing to do with all things which hurt or imperil us is to share them with God in prayer. 'Cast your burden on the Lord,' said the psalmist, 'and He will sustain you' (Psa. 55.22). Hezekiah's prayer (15–20) was a model of brevity as well as of

227

beauty. It contained a worshipful reminder of God's greatness (16) and it reached to the very heart of the situation—Sennacherib's blatant insult to the living God (17). It recognized the point which the blasphemous Assyrian had failed to perceive, that there was an essential difference between the heathen gods of the nations and the Lord God of Hosts. It is upon this one, true God that Hezekiah rolled his burden (20). It is an instructive study to compare Hezekiah's prayer with those of other men of God who were 'up against it' (cf. Jehoshaphat, 2 Chron. 20.5–12; Jeremiah, Jer. 32.17–25; the disciples, Acts 4.24–30).

The 'virgin daughter' defies Assyria (21–29). Hezekiah did not need to send messengers to Isaiah on this second occasion, for the two were now in close contact. The prophet's oracle connects with his earlier prediction of God's use of Assyria (10.5–19). Arrogant in her consciousness of the merciless power of her troops, Assyria was ignorant of the fact that God was manipulating her to execute His own carefully designed plans (26 f.), after which He would compel her to return homewards like a brute beast (29).

Promise and fulfilment (30–38). There was an unconditional promise that Jerusalem would be spared (33 ff.), and that, within three years, ravaged Judah would be restored to normal (30 ff.). The army of Sennacherib was smitten, probably with a particularly virulent plague. Herodotus, the Greek historian, records that the Assyrian camp was infested with mice (or possibly rats) which could have been the carriers. Twenty years elapsed before the Assyrian king was murdered by his sons, but the historian who noted this fact (38) had not forgotten the prophecy concerning this event (7).

A thought: The God who humbled proud Assyria is still the 'God of the impossible', able to deliver His people.

Isaiah 38 {style="display:inline"} The Lord of Life—and Death

A king's life extended (1–8,21 f.). There is no suggestion that Hezekiah's illness was a punishment from the Lord. Generally speaking, he had been a good king, indeed, he and Josiah, of all Judah's kings, are given exceptional praise (2 Kings 18.5; 23.25). In part, his grief may have been caused by the plight of the nation, under threat from Assyria (6), or by uncertainty concerning the succession, for since his life was extended by fifteen years (5), Manasseh, who followed him, was not yet born (2 Kings 21.1). Manasseh's long reign was one of apostasy, corruption and bloodshed, and it has been suggested that Hezekiah's request for an extension of life was a mistake, leading to a period out of the divine

228

will. There is not the slightest hint of this in our chapter, although it remains a wise general counsel to leave the ordering of our lives in God's hands. Vs. 21 f. probably came before v. 7 originally, and should be read in this sequence. The 'dial of Ahaz' (8) is literally the 'steps of Ahaz', not a sundial as we know it, although it would serve the same purpose, but a westward facing flight of stairs. Normally the declining sun (a fitting picture of the approach of death) would cause the shadow to move slowly up the steps—now, at Isaiah's word, the movement was reversed a full ten steps. We are not told the mechanics of this miracle.

Hezekiah's psalm (9–20). It was the custom in ancient Israel, following any experience of answered prayer, to come to the Temple with an appropriate sacrifice which was frequently accompanied by a psalm of gratitude. The underlying principle is as desirable today, although the temple of the human heart may be substituted for a material building (1 Cor. 3.16; 6.19). The grace of gratitude to God is something which merits cultivation. The chief interest in Hezekiah's psalm is the evidence it provides of his conception of the after-life in Sheol, a dim and dismal region in which the bitterest element was the severance of all conscious fellowship with God (11,18 f.). Even a godly king did not share the insight of Isaiah, who saw that God was able to break the dread power of the grave (26.19). Our Lord's death and resurrection have brought such light and liberty that abject fear of death (such as Hezekiah's) has been abolished (1 Cor. 15.54–57). Is this not a sufficient reason to lift our hearts in a psalm of praise to God throughout this day?

Isaiah 39 Ulterior Motives

A kindly, courteous, 'get-well-quick' delegation from Babylon. That is how this chapter reads at first sight, but was it quite as innocent and well-meaning? Two facts make it clear that there was much more in it than a purely social occasion; first, the stress on the fact that Hezekiah showed the Babylonian envoys all his treasure and resources (2,4); secondly, the violent reaction of Isaiah, the prophet who was so opposed to involvement in foreign alliances.

Two more facts help us to form a clear picture of the pattern of events. First, a close examination of the dating of chs. 36 and 37, compared with chs. 38 and 39, reveals that Hezekiah's sickness and recovery (38 and 39) came *before* the Assyrian invasion of Judah of 701 B.C. ('the fourteenth year of Hezekiah', 36.1). Accepting the fifteen-year extension to Hezekiah's life (38.5) and working back from the date of his death, his near-fatal sickness must have occurred about 703–702 B.C. Further proof may be found in 38.6, where the deliverance from Assyria, already narrated, is still in the future. Secondly, we know that Merodach-baladan of Babylon was the principal agent behind the widespread revolt against Assyria, following Sennacherib's accession in 705 B.C. The motive behind the embassy to the newly-recovered Hezekiah was to link him in with this general revolt against Assyria. Hezekiah showed his willingness to comply by revealing all his resources, which would be essential to the success of any revolt. It was this involvement with Assyria's chief opponent which brought upon Judah the devastating attack of Sennacherib's army. No wonder Isaiah was so deeply concerned! His prophecy of the rise of Babylon was fulfilled less than a century later, when Assyria was finally crushed, and in 597 B.C. a descendant of Hezekiah, Jehoiachin, was taken captive to Babylon (cf. 7), where the royal line of Judah continued until the return from exile in 538 B.C.

The reason for the inversion of chapters in this section (chs. 36–39) is clear. Assyria is the world-power which dominates the scene in Isaiah's early prophecies (1–35), so chs. 36,37, telling of God's victory over the Assyrian host, are appropriately placed. In the second half of Isaiah's book the overthrow of Babylon and the return from exile is the dominant theme, so that chs. 38,39, which foretell the captivity (39.6 f.), are a fitting prologue. Spiritual connection was of greater importance than chronological exactitude to the Hebrew historian.

A point to ponder: The devil, like Merodach-baladan, often conceals his evil motives by a flattering, conciliatory approach. We need to be on our guard against his wiles: (2 Cor. 11.13 ff.; 1 Pet. 5.8 f.).

Questions for further study and discussion on Isaiah chs. 33–39

1. The Lord promised deliverance for Jerusalem in Isaiah's age (31.5; 32.18; 33.20; 37.35). What factors could cause Him to permit the later destruction of 587 B.C.?
2. With the background of oppression and deliverance in ch. 33 trace the parallels from your own experience of salvation.
3. Why are such passages as Isa. 35 applicable to God's people in every age? What comfort have you derived from it?
4. What were the essential weaknesses in the Rabshakeh's attempt to undermine the morale of the Jerusalemites (36.4–10,12–20)?
5. What is the significance of the 'historical interlude' (chs. 36–39) in Isaiah?

230

An historian might have stressed the fact that the crumbling Babylonian Empire was about to give way to the more virile power of the Persians and their allies, the Medes. But the prophet saw an event of greater importance than the emergence of Persia, an enlightened world-power which dominated the scene for more than two centuries. God was about to act in a new and decisive way in bringing back His people from exile in Babylonia. Here was an example of His grace and power in salvation which would compare with the Exodus from Egypt! A new day was breaking for the Jews, and the prophet, seeing the first faint gleam of light against the eastern sky, lifted up his voice to exhort and to encourage his people to return.

But why should they need encouraging? Surely, once they realized that the full period of their captivity, foretold by the prophet Jeremiah (Jer. 25.11 f.; 29.10), was completed there would be no holding them back! It is apparent, however, that the exiles shrank from venturing on what must have seemed a foolhardy adventure. It involved leaving behind the comfort and relatively high standard of living which many had attained in the Exile for a dubious future in a ruined city and a desolate land. Hence the prophet's ministry of encouragement. First (1 f.), there was the assurance of God's complete forgiveness. His hand of chastisement, laid upon the nation for its multiplied sins, was regulated by mercy. Here was assurance for the Jew, conscious of the nation's sin, and perhaps feeling that the Lord had irrevocably cast off His people (cf. Psa. 77.7–10)! Then follows (3 ff.) an assurance that the Lord would go before them, opening up a way through the wilderness. Nine hundred miles, and a journey of some four months (cf. Ezra 7.8 f.) lay between Babylon and Jerusalem, but the Lord, like a multitude of labourers preparing the way for a royal procession, would smooth their path. Best of all was the comfort which derived from the character of God Himself (6–11). The beauties of nature, and man himself, were transient, but God was eternal and His word unchanging. He was almighty, but His immeasurable power was balanced by His incomparable gentleness (John 10.1–18). What He promised, though still future, was certain, so that the herald could proclaim over battered Jerusalem, 'The hour of deliverance has come' (9 f.).

A prayer: O Lord, show me this day Thy tender comfort, and make Thy way smooth before me.

The key to this magnificent section is the lament of Israel in v. 27. The nation was 'down and out', its optimism sapped by the long years of exile. It was passing through a phase when God seemed far away and even, perhaps, unconcerned for His people. The Lord is the speaker here, and His words have the same relevancy and power as when they were first uttered to encourage a wilting Israel. Four pictures emerge in vs. 12–26:

God is the almighty Creator (12 ff.). The whole universe is on a Lilliputian scale when compared with Him! The oceans fit into the palm of His hand and the outstretched heavens are no more than a span, the distance between the thumb and the little finger of an outstretched hand! Creation, in all its complexity, is His work alone (cf. Job 28.20–28; Prov. 8.22–31; Rom. 11.33–36).

God is sovereign over the nations (15 ff.). We live today in a man-centred universe, but God, in a few verses, cuts not only man, but the great world-powers, down to size. The 'drop from a bucket' (15) is that which drips from the outside of the bucket when it is drawn up from the well! Equally 'not worth bothering about' is 'the dust on the scales' which a buyer would never dream of demanding from a vendor! How ridiculous to compare such a God to impotent idols, themselves created by puny man (18 ff.)!

God is the Lord of history (22 ff.). Every period of history has its proud, strutting dictators; lording it over their fellow men; regarding themselves, and being regarded, as all-powerful. 'Grasshoppers', is the divine estimate of such (22). Changing the metaphor, He speaks of their transience (24).

God is the controller of the heavens (25 f.). The giant telescopes of our generation were undreamed-of in the prophet's generation, but there was the awareness of a vast but ordered complexity in the movement of the astral bodies (cf. Psa. 8; Job 38.31 ff.).

The prophet concludes this hymn of praise with a glorious climax (28–31). Failure, of any kind, is inconceivable to such a God. But more thrilling than this, almost breath-taking in its audacity, is the promise that frail man may, by the waiting of trust, worship and prayer, share in the divine omnipotence! The reverse climax of v. 31 is intentional. Not only is there grace given for the exceptional task, there is also that spirit of brave, persistent endurance for those many days which can only be described as ordinary, when we seem to be plodding along.

Monotheism, the view that there is only one God, was not a new concept in Israel. It was implicit in the Mosaic period, when Israel's God was shown to be so irresistibly great that the gods of other nations were driven completely out of reckoning. Similarly, in Amos 1.1–2.3, the prophet, in his survey of neighbouring nations, shows that God is not only concerned with their misdeeds but is able to punish them. But Isaiah, in these chapters, reaches the fullest expression of a monotheistic faith. Not only does he demonstrate the supremacy of Yahweh, the God of Israel, but with withering satire he shows the utter stupidity of idol worship, concluding that no gods exist apart from the Lord (24,29).

One of the essential attributes of God is His ability both to foretell and to control future events. This He challenges the idols to do, but they are completely incompetent (21–24). Not so Yahweh! Summoning the nations as to a great tribunal (1) He declares what He is about to do. The oracles supposed to come from the false deities were so vague and elastic that, no matter what happened, their devotees could claim that they had foretold it. But God speaks in clear, precise detail (2 ff., 25–29). In 44.28 and 45.1 He names this conqueror who was to effect Israel's deliverance. Cyrus, before his conquest of Babylon in 539 B.C., had extended his kingdom from the east of Babylon in a great arc as far as the Aegean Sea, so he is fittingly described as 'one from the east' (2), and 'one from the north' (25).

There are two other sets of contrasts in this chapter. In vs. 5–13 the false trust of idolatrous worship is compared with the secure foundation which Israel has in relationship to the Lord. V. 8 introduces the 'Servant' concept which is so important in these chapters. This is a fluid conception; at times (as here) the whole nation of Israel is the servant; at times it is the remnant, a spiritual Israel; but at certain points, and especially in 52.13–53.12, the Servant is an individual who can be no other than Jesus Christ. A servant in Israel, was a slave, but since Israel was linked with its Master in the covenant, the servant was in a position of privilege, based on God's saving acts, which was accompanied by solemn responsibilities. The second set of contrasts, in vs. 14 ff., is between what Israel felt itself to be, i.e. a worm, and what God would make it. A 'threshing sledge' (15) was made of heavy timbers, studded on its underside with iron or basalt teeth. Notice also the renewal of the theme of a triumphant progress across the desert, in which the Lord makes tender and gracious provision for every need of His children (17–20, cf. 35; 40.3 ff.). He is just the same today.

In vs. 1–4 we find the first of four passages which are generally called the 'Servant Songs'. The other three are 49.1–6; 50.4–9; 52.13–53.12. Since there are other allusions to the 'Servant' in these chapters a unity of authorship is generally accepted. But as these four passages have a distinctive view of the Servant some scholars believe that they were once a separate collection which the prophet incorporated into his work. Our view is that they are an original and integral part of the text. It is important to realize that, whether the Servant be Cyrus, Israel, the remnant in exile, the prophet himself or the Messiah, he is viewed as the one who fulfils the Master's will. In our chapter we find three distinct interpretations of the Servant:

The Servant as Messiah (1–4). At our Lord's baptism He was commended in words (Mark 1.11) which combine phrases from Psa. 2.7, generally recognized as a Messianic Psalm, and Isa. 42.1. Thus, at the outset of His ministry, He was aware of the fact that He was both the Davidic Messiah and 'the Servant' of Isaiah's prophecy. The meekness and fortitude of the Servant, His gentle but faithful ministry of encouragement which realizes the hopes of the nations, were perfectly fulfilled in Jesus Christ. 'Justice' (1,3,4) is here equivalent to 'true religion', in the sense of conforming to all the ordinances and requirements of God.

The Servant as Cyrus (5–9). A minority of scholars regard this as a continuation of the first section, i.e. as still referring to the Messiah. But a comparison with other sections (e.g. 44.28–45.7), and the reference to a great deliverance near at hand (9, cf. 41.1–4, 21–27) show conclusively that Cyrus, the Persian king, is in mind. So there follows naturally a psalm of praise (10–17) in which the Lord is viewed as a mighty warrior, exerting Himself to effect His people's deliverance (13), and as a travailing woman (14), a picture which indicates how imminent His deliverance is.

The Servant as Israel (18–25). There is a tragic irony in these words. Israel was commissioned to an exalted task, which serves to underline the ignominy of her failure. Because of this, judgement had fallen, not simply as a result of military or political weakness, nor because of the invincibility of their foes, but because of the Lord's righteous anger, resulting in His chastisement of Israel. Israel the Servant failed, but Jesus Christ, the Servant *par excellence*, knew no such failure.

To appreciate the full significance of vs. 1–9 it is necessary to scan through the final verses of the previous chapter (42.18–25). Here is a miracle of grace indeed! In spite of Israel's infidelity and waywardness He continued to love her still, and she remained precious in His sight (4, cf. Hos. **11**.1–9). The constancy of God's love can never cease to be a source of amazement, not only to ancient Israel but also to the twentieth-century Christian. How little we merit the divine favour! How often the confession of the psalmist rises from our hearts, 'He does not deal with us according to our sins, nor requite us according to our iniquities' (Psa. **103**.10). But in both Testaments a work of redemption is necessary, and of this the Lord speaks (1,11–14).

Notice the tender promises of help and protection given to those who venture forth at the word of their Redeemer-God (2). But since Israel was held captive in alien Babylonia there was, of necessity, the overthrow of the oppressor (14). Redemption, although it was included in the Lord's overall dealings with the nations, was costly. In the N.T. the purpose of redemption is spiritual and the cost was borne, not by the blood of an enemy, but by the offering up of the sinless life of God's only-begotten Son.

God's redemption, then, could not be merited, but nor could it be gained by punctilious devotion to cultic acts (22 ff.). The reference appears to be to an elaboration of the sacrificial offerings, devoid of any inward, spiritual content, an attitude strongly deplored by the prophets (cf. **1**.11–15; Amos **5**.21–24). Sin could never be dealt with by such superficial ceremonies (24). But now God, of His own volition and grace, would blot out their sins and, paradoxical as it may appear, an omniscient God would forget (25)!

There was, however, a pertinent corollary to the Lord's redemptive activity. Israel, the servant, was to be God's witness (10,12). Those redeemed by such spectacular activity were not to be slow in speaking of these things (cf. Psa. **107**.2), they must also live in the light of them. The same principle holds good today.

Note: V. 27: 'your mediators' includes both prophets and priests. Even such a great leader as Moses was not exempted from this condemnation (e.g. Num. **20**.10–13, cf. Deut. **4**.21 f.).

Isaiah 44   God and the Desolate

Sometimes even Christians can be extremely critical of those who are dejected and depressed, or unable to face a new and challenging situation, possibly because of an awareness of their own past failures. It is instructive to observe how patiently and gently our Shepherd-God (40.11) dealt with Israel. His was indeed a ministry of comfort and encouragement (40.1), as chapter after chapter reveals. We too may experience that same understanding sympathy which never condones sin but puts new heart and assurance into us (Heb. 4.14 ff.).

So it was in our portion. Israel, chosen of God, is termed 'Jacob' (1,2,21), a reminder of that weak and very human ancestor who was at last brought to the point of full trust (Gen. 32.24–30). The intimacy of the Father-son relationship is shown in the use of the poetic Jeshurun (2), a term of endearment meaning 'upright' (cf. Deut. 32.15; 33.5,26). There is a reminder of His elective-choice of Israel before its birth as a nation (2,21), a mystery in which both a prophet and an apostle shared (Jer. 1.5; Gal. 1.15). In each case this was an election to service, in the Master-servant relationship (1,2,21). A promise of His outpoured blessing upon future generations (3b,4) was important to a nation like Israel, with its rich sense of a corporate life which embraced successive generations. Even the Gentiles, seeing the evidence of God's hand upon His own people, would join them as proselytes (5), an indication of the missionary heart of the prophet. Once more this incomparable God reveals His authority in His ability to foretell the future (6 ff.), using the most powerful king of that generation, Cyrus, as His instrument (26 ff.). Assurance after assurance follows in comforting succession, each so certain of fulfilment that all nature is invited to form a choir to celebrate in advance His redemptive work (23)!

We must not overlook the devastating attack upon idolatry in vs. 9–20 (cf. Jer. 10.1–16). Nowhere in the O.T. is the utter incongruity and stupidity of idol worship revealed so clearly. In the light of our relationship with our Saviour-God, modern-day idolatry, whether it be of wealth, possessions, a pop-group or a sportsman, or anything else, is equally as absurd.

> 'The dearest idol I have known, whate'er that idol be,
> Help me to tear it from Thy throne, and worship only Thee.'

Isaiah 45.1-19   Cyrus and Yahweh

The terms used to describe Cyrus are startling. In 44.28 he is called 'My shepherd' but here he is actually styled 'His anointed', or, in the more familiar transliteration of the Hebrew, 'His Messiah'! Israelite kings, and even priests, were anointed (e.g. 1 Sam. 24.6; 2 Sam. 19.21; Psa. 2.2; Lev. 4.3) but this reference to a heathen king is unique in the O.T. Roland de Vaux observes that, in the ancient world, the great kings of Egypt and the Hittite empire, etc., were not themselves anointed, but their vassal kings were. From this he infers that the king of Israel was anointed because he was conceived to be the vassal of Yahweh, the true King (cf. Judg. 8.23). Such a usage would fit admirably into this present section, where Cyrus is viewed as the Lord's subordinate (cf. 44.28).

Was Cyrus himself a believer in the Lord? His decree in Ezra 1.1–4, which allowed the Jews to return to their homeland, suggests that he was, but this was drawn up to suit the religion of the people he was addressing. Archaeological discoveries come to our aid at this point, for in the Cyrus Cylinder he ascribes his victories to Marduk, the Babylonian deity, whilst in another text discovered at Ur he gives the credit to Sin, the moon-god. Decisive use must be made of v. 5, where it is categorically stated, 'You do not know Me'. Such was the power of the God of Israel that He could take up a heathen king who had no desire to serve Him, and use him to work out His divine purposes. There are interesting parallels with 10.5, where the mighty Assyria is called 'the rod of My anger', and with Jer. 25.9; 27.6; 43.10 where Nebuchadnezzar, the Babylonian king, is designated 'My servant'. Dictators and tyrants, great and small, still strut across the stage of world-history and it is comforting to realize that they, too, are as much subject to the Lord's overruling as were these ancient world-powers.

This raised a problem in the minds of many of the prophet's contemporaries, and it is only fair to observe that this doubt was shared by the prophet Habakkuk, in connection with God's similar use of the Babylonians, viz. 'How could a pure and holy God employ such an impure instrument?' (Hab. 1.13). Habakkuk saw that his course was to remain faithful to his ministry, even though he did not fully understand the ways of God with men. Isaiah (9–13) relates the objection to the sovereign will of God, about which there must always be an inscrutable element. Man may not be able to comprehend the ways of God, but he can trust Him.

Questions for further study and discussion on Isaiah chs. 40.1—45.19

1. List, and consider, the ways in which 40.1 is worked out in this section.
2. How may 40.3–5 be applied to Christian service and witness (cf. Matt. 3.1 ff.)?
3. Consider the ways in which monotheistic religion is revealed in these chapters.
4. In what ways does Cyrus, 'His anointed' (45.1), anticipate the Messiah, our Lord Jesus? Can you detect the profound dissimilarities?

5. What encouragement have you been able to derive from these chapters?

Isaiah 45.20—46.13   Who Carries Who?

There are indications that the prophet's message did not find a ready acceptance amongst certain classes. Some 'were incensed against Him' (i.e. Yahweh, **45.**24); others are described as 'transgressors' (**46.**8) and 'stubborn of heart' (**46.**12). It is a mark of our human fallibility to blame our misfortunes upon God and to close our hearts and minds to His offer of salvation. Notice the effect upon Isaiah's contemporaries in **46.**12; God was about to do a great work (**46.**13), but they would miss it completely if they continued in such an intransigent attitude. The invitation of **45.**22 still heralds forth, but it is no longer limited to a deliverance from Babylon, it relates to freedom from the bondage of sin, on the basis of Christ's atoning work on Calvary. Paul refers the promise of **45.**23b to the Saviour in Phil. **2.**9 ff.

There is another telling contrast between the effective power of Yahweh and the impotence of idols. The heathen gods of the nations needed to be carried, and **45.**20 speaks of them as being borne along by their devotees in a religious procession. There is a procession of an entirely different kind in **46.**1 f., however. The picture is of a fallen city, with a pitiful stream of refugees in flight. The few household possessions and personal treasures salvaged from the disaster are heaped high on the backs of their overladen beasts. Amongst these are their idols, useless encumbrances, strapped to the backs of their donkeys and preventing them from carrying a more profitable load, the very epitome of ineffectiveness! Israel's God is completely other (3 f.). He created Israel, dealt tenderly with her in her infancy and would not forget or forsake her in her advancing years. Notice the emphasis on His ability to carry His people. Sir George Adam Smith comments on this passage, 'The truth is this: it makes all the difference to a man how he conceives his religion—whether as something that he has to carry, or as something that will carry him.' The latter is the faith of the Bible and it is the only faith worth having.

Note: **46.**1: Bel and Nebo were two of the most important Babylonian deities. Bel, which corresponds with the Canaanite Baal, was one of the titles of Marduk. The name of Nebo (or Nabu) is compounded in the names of three Babylonian kings, Nabopolassar, Nebuchadnezzar and Nabonidus.

From the earliest chapters of the Bible (Gen. 11.1–9), until the final chapters of the book of *Revelation* (14.8; 17.5; 18.1–24), Babylon is the symbol of an organized humanity proud in spirit and rebellious against God. It is the theme of the prophets (Isa. 13; Jer. 50; 51) and of the psalmist (137.8). Of necessity, the return of the Jews to Zion involved the overthrow of Babylon, who had deported them and innumerable other peoples, and held them, against their wills, in an alien land. The prophet now concentrates on this element, showing the complete humiliation of the oppressing city, but demonstrating also that this is a moral judgement.

The first charge is of the overweening pride which made her exalted, in her own consciousness, as the 'mistress of kingdoms' (5,7). Her self-commendation, 'I am, and there is no one besides me' (8,10), was an arrogation of the very place of God Himself. Here was a nation which regarded itself as the Supreme Power! Such an attitude, which casts off God, discards also the responsibility of care and compassion for others, and this forms the second charge (6). The people of Judah had been committed to Babylonia for chastisement but she had treated them with abominable cruelty. Historically, this is attested in the small number of those who escaped the destruction of 588–587 B.C. and went into exile (Jer. 52.28 ff. notes a total of only 4,600 in three deportations), whilst archaeology reveals that an equally pathetic number, no more than 20,000, remained in a desolated land. Four out of every five Jews perished at this time. Charge number three concerned Babylon's reliance upon sorcery and divination (9,12–15); such rank superstition was an insult to the intelligence of those created in the image of God. There could be no sure word, and certainly no salvation, from such, and the prophet's withering condemnation, they wander about each in his own direction' (15), applies equally to the multiplicity of false cults which abound today.

Babylon has long since been in ruins, but the attitudes which it personified remain today. False pride which pretends to find security apart from God; false religion which makes a fair show outwardly but cannot satisfy man's basic needs, and the spirit which abuses or oppresses others, these are all anti-God and are destined to be dealt with in God's righteous judgement.

Isaiah 48   Israel in the Classroom

There is a marked change of tone in this chapter and the notes of consolation and encouragement are not so evident. They are there none the less. God, the all-wise Heavenly Father, is pressing home the lessons which Israel ought to have learned by experience. The key to the understanding of this chapter is in v. 17, where God reveals Himself as the Teacher and Guide.

Israel is reminded firmly of the sin which brought upon her the judgement of God (1–11). Theirs had been a false trust (1 f.) which honoured Him in words only. From its birth (8b), presumably a reference to the period of the Exodus and the covenant at Sinai, Israel had been rebellious, stubborn (4) and idolatrous (5b). On account of this the prophets, for centuries, had denounced the people, foretelling in detail the downfall of the nation (3). These prophecies, as well as the history books of the O.T., show us how impervious Israel was to these warning voices. Indeed, not until the Exile, and then largely because of the ministries of Jeremiah and Ezekiel, was there any awareness of the apostasy which had been judged so summarily. One of the puzzling facts of human experience is the incurable slowness of individuals and nations to learn and retain the lessons which experience teaches. But the Lord was a very patient Teacher and never gave up (9), continuing the refining process until all the dross was burnt away (10). Now a new chapter of events was about to be inaugurated and He again demonstrates His superior power in foretelling them (6 ff., 12–16).

The Lord's lament over His people is comparable with the anguish of our Saviour over rebellious Jerusalem (18 f., cf. Matt. 23.37 f.). The one condition attached to the covenant which the Lord had graciously made with them was that they should be loyal, loving and completely obedient (e.g. Deut. 30.20). This they had withheld, and so they forfeited peace, which can never be the portion of the ungodly (18,22). The promises made to Abraham of a numerous seed also remained unfulfilled (19, cf. Gen. 12.2; 13.16; 22.17). Now they were being given a second chance in a new Exodus (20 f.) and the prophet urges them to seize it without hesitation. A similar urgency attaches to the decision which we are called upon to make when we are confronted with the challenge of Christ (Luke 9.23–26,57–62; Acts 26.28 f.; 2 Cor. 6.1 f.).

Isaiah 49   God Still Cares

Reading this chapter, one is prompted to ask the question of the Ethiopian eunuch to Philip on the Gaza road, 'About whom, pray, does the prophet say this, about himself or about some one else?' The context of Acts 8.26–40 makes it clear that the eunuch was reading Isa. 53, but the problem of the identity of the Servant is also relevant to our chapter (vs. 3,5,6,7). At times the Servant appears to be the prophet himself (e.g. v. 2), and v. 3 gives an identification with all Israel, but this is further qualified in v. 5, with its picture of a ministry *to* Israel. There is an anticipatory hint of the Messiah in v. 7 (cf. 53.3). As so often in Scripture, an intelligent observation of the context is decisive. This shows that these oracles, or sermons, were addressed to the godly remnant of the Jews in Babylonia. Notice the prophet's eight-fold appeal:

1. He points out that God had called and prepared the true, spiritual Israel for a unique purpose (1 ff.). 2. He assures them that God, far from rejecting them completely because of their failure, was vindicating and restoring them (4 f.). 3. He foretells that, exceeding this ministry to Israel, there would be a witness and a ministry to the whole world (6). 4. Instead of being the underdogs, the rulers of the nations would do them homage (7,22 f.). 5. He predicts the restoration of the exiles to their homeland, an event which is so certain of fulfilment that he composes a hymn of praise in advance (8-13, cf. 2 Chron. 20.21)! 6. In a passage which reveals the faithful and compassionate heart of God there is the assurance that they were not forgotten by Him (14 ff.). 7. This is followed by the promise of a glorious home-coming to a restored and re-populated Jerusalem (17-21). 8. Finally, God reveals Himself as the God of the impossible, the Champion and Redeemer of His people (24 ff.). So this chapter takes its place in the overall ministry of comfort and encouragement to the insignificant company of Jews in mighty Babylon.

The revelation of a saving-ministry to the nations (6b) is one of the outstanding conceptions of the O.T. Israel was a highly privileged nation, but the divine choice involved considerable responsibilities, e.g. Exod. 19.6, which envisages a priestly ministry of mediation to all the world. So often privilege passed over into presumption, accompanied by an attitude of superiority to the Gentiles, as revealed in the unlovely Pharisaic Judaism of our Lord's time. The new Spiritual Israel (Rom. 9.6 ff.; Gal. 3.29; 6.16) has greater privileges than ancient Israel, but the temptation of spiritual pride must be strongly resisted. Rather, a humble, compassionate and sacrificial ministry to all men is to characterize its members.

Isaiah 50   Faith in the Darkness

Who is to blame (1-3)? We often display a special ingenuity when it comes to shifting the blame for our own misdeeds! Instead of accepting our own responsibility, we so often lay the blame on circumstances, on hereditary factors, on others, on fate or on God. This is just what the exiles were doing. Instead of accepting captivity as God's chastisement for sin (2) they attributed their fate to His rejection of them (1). God points out that when He spoke to them, doubtless through the prophet himself, their lack of attention or response was tantamount to a rejection of Him (2a)! The reference of the allusion to God's power in nature (2b,3) is not clear; it could be to the crossing of the Red Sea (Exod. 14) or to some natural phenomenon in Babylonia itself, possibly a severe drought accompanied by sand-storms. But the lesson drawn is plain enough; God has effective power to deliver His people.

Patient endurance in God's service (4–9). This is the third of the Servant Songs (see note on Isa. 42), in which the prophet seems to be referring to his own experience. His was a ministry of encouragement to his dispirited compatriots (4a), but he speaks to the hearts and consciences of all those engaged in pastoral work when he alludes to the source of his message, and indeed, of his own strength (4b). To strengthen others demands far more than our human resources, we need to wait on the Lord regularly morning by morning, letting His Word, and the sense of His presence, flood our waking thoughts. We know that the prophet faced opposition (cf. **45.9** ff.; **46.**12), and the physical violence which he suffered (5–8) may have come from his fellow-countrymen, unwilling to accept his exhortations to return to Jerusalem. On the other hand, such opposition may have come from Babylonians who were incensed at his forecast of their overthrow and the triumph of Cyrus, their enemy (e.g. **45.**1 ff.; **46.**1 f.; **47**). There is more than a hint of a connection with Jesus Christ, the Suffering Servant, in the meek acceptance of humiliation and suffering (6 f., cf. Matt. **26.**67; **27.**28–31,39–44, etc.).

Trust in the darkness (10 f.). A faith that cannot venture out into the unknown, that fears to hazard itself upon the word of God, is no faith at all. So the prophet gives his challenging invitation to others to venture all upon God (10). But the self-reliant, who try to illumine the darkness by their own feeble efforts, know no such assurance (11).

Isaiah 51   Numbers are Not Everything

The major part of this chapter (1–16) is addressed to those who responded to the prophet's appeal (**50.**10) and prepared to embark on an adventure of faith, leaving the known and venturing out into the unknown. Were they appalled at the smallness of their numbers? There is evidence to suggest that they were, and that their relative insignificance appeared to magnify the obstacles to be overcome, viz. a proud and still-mighty Babylon; a long, hazardous journey; and a devastated Judah. The prophet invites his hearers to look back to the very source of their national history. God had brought into being a nation through a single couple, an old man and a woman well beyond the age of child-bearing (2, cf. Gen. 16.2; 17.17; 18.11–14; Heb. 11.11 f.). What the Lord had done before He was surely able to do again! What a comfort it is to realize that God is not, 'always on the side of the big battalions', as Voltaire's contemporaries said! He defeated the Midianite host with 300 men who did not strike a blow until the enemy was in full retreat (Judg. 7). He brought the giant Goliath crashing to the ground through the sling of a shepherd-boy (1 Sam. 17). With a handful of dedicated men He turned the world of the first century A.D. upside down (or was it 'right way up'?!—Acts 17.6). The Lord is never bound by numbers, and we must eschew this feeling of crushed impotence brought about by the fact that few today seem wholly dedicated to Him.

So the prophet again lifts up his voice, heralding forth the words of God, to assure His people. The imminent deliverance was more certain than the continuance of the universe itself (4 ff.). They need not fear, for their opponents would descend into oblivion (7 f., notice the similar promise given to the prophet himself, 50.7 ff.). Further confidence is engendered by the timely reminder of the Lord's power revealed at the Exodus (9 f., where Rahab, the chaos monster of mythology, symbolizes Egypt, as in Isa. 30.7), and this leads on to the 'Psalm of the Returned Exiles' (11, cf. 35.10) and yet more assurances of divine comfort and help (12–16).

Finally, the prophet's imagination wings over hundreds of miles of inhospitable territory to a battered Jerusalem, nestling in the brown hills of Judah (17–23). He pictures her as she was after Babylon's savage attack, but now the Lord's cup of chastisement was passing to her persecutors. Her darkness and humiliation were about to end, the dawn was at hand and it was time for her to bestir herself (17).

A point to ponder: 'Nothing can hinder the Lord from saving by many or by few' (Jonathan, in 1 Sam. 14.6).

Isaiah 52.1-12   Good News!

The opening verses (1 f.) follow naturally from the picture of Jerusalem's humiliation in 51.17–23. The prophet's mind leaps to the final impression (1), returning secondarily to the necessary first step (2). This is the first clear reference to a new and purified Jerusalem, which doubtless encouraged the religious separatism characteristic of post-exilic Judaism. This conception of a New

Jerusalem was taken up by the Christian Church, projected into the future, and associated with the complete renewal at the end of the age, when Christ returns in power and glory (Rev. 21.1–22.5). The structure of vs. 3–6 is so difficult that the RSV does not attempt to render it in poetry, but there is no ambiguity about its meaning. The mention of a release from the degradation of slavery (2) might suggest the necessity for the payment of a ransom. Yahweh makes it clear that this is not so. The punishment of the nation for her sins was solely due to Him, and there was no obligation whatever to Babylonia; both the enslavement and the deliverance derive from His sovereign will. Two other oppressing powers in Israel's history, Egypt and Assyria, are cited in support. The family of Jacob had gone down to Egypt of their own volition, only to be enslaved subsequently. The Assyrians, although acting as the Lord's instrument (Isa. 10.5 f., 15–19), were motivated by entirely selfish desires (Isa. 10.7–11,13 f.). The Jewish rulers, generally, looked upon the Exile as an indication of Yahweh's inferiority, and some even despised Him for what they imagined to be His weakness (5). They would soon learn otherwise (6).

Three stanzas concerning the great deliverance climax this section. In the first (7 f.) the steps of the herald bringing the good news to Jerusalem are traced, and the watchmen of the city are seen looking expectantly for the first signs of his appearing. A few years later, 42,360 (Ezra 2.64) returned exiles marched into the ruined city. It might seem incongruous to speak of this as 'the return of the Lord to Zion', but the prophet, in faith, saw that this would be the small beginning of a new and decisive phase in the Lord's redemptive purposes. In the second stanza (9 f.), the city itself is invited to celebrate the divine comfort (cf. 40.1; 49.13; 51.3,12) and redemption (cf. 43.1; 44.22 f.). Finally (11 f.), the scene switches to Babylon, and the captives are urged to make their departure in terms which suggest a second Exodus. One remarkable feature is the anticipation that Cyrus would allow the Temple vessels to be returned to Jerusalem (Ezra 1.7–11). Normally, a victorious nation placed the gods of the defeated in its own temple as a sign of the superiority of its own gods. But since Israel's faith was imageless (Exod. 20.4 ff.) the Temple vessels had been taken instead. Miraculously preserved in this remarkable way, they were now to be restored to their rightful place.

Questions for further study and discussion on Isaiah chs. 45.20—52.12

1. In what way does the prophet demonstrate the greatness of Israel's God?

2. For what sins is Babylon condemned in ch. **47**?
3. Follow the history of Babylon, both actual and symbolical, in the Bible.
4. What may the Christian learn from the teaching on 'the Servant' in this section?

Isaiah 52.13—53.12   The Suffering Servant

Amongst all the treasures of devotion and prophecy in the O.T. this passage is surely one of the most significant. Possibly only Jeremiah's conception of the New Covenant (Jer. **31.**31–34) equals its tremendous insights into the final outworking of God's redemptive purposes. In the preceding chapters we have seen how the interpretation of the Servant passages flows between the nation Israel, the godly remnant in Exile and the prophet himself, with more than a hint of the Redeemer. But here, whilst there are still echoes of the suffering endured by the nation and the persecution heaped upon the prophet, there is a projection into the future which centres upon a unique Person, different from even the greatest of the prophets. His majesty and victory appear both at the beginning and the end (52.13,15; **53.**12), which connects with the other O.T. prophecies concerning the triumph and kingly rule of the Davidic Messiah (e.g. Isa. **9.**2–7; **11.**1–9).

But in between there is the revelation of unique suffering and humiliation, borne humbly yet vicariously for all men. Mirrored here we have a summary of all those dreadful events in the last day of our Lord's life upon earth: His silence before His accusers; the rejection and hatred of the religious leaders; the faithlessness of the disciples; the cruel lacerations of the scourge, the crown of thorns and the gaping wounds caused by the rough, iron nails which held Him to the cross; His death between two thieves and His burial in the tomb of a rich man, Joseph of Arimathea (Luke **23.**50–53). It has been observed by C. R. North that prophets like Jeremiah suffered in the course of their ministry, but in the case of the Servant, suffering was not merely an incidental but the means whereby His ministry was brought to a triumphant conclusion. In this He can be no other than our Lord Jesus Christ. Yet Israel, to whom this prophecy came, with incredible blindness of heart refuses to recognize Him! Such passages as Mark **10.**45; Luke **4.**16–21; **9.**22; **18.**31 ff., etc., show clearly that our Lord conceived His ministry after the pattern of the Servant of the Lord, and the light from this fourth Song, especially, irradiated the stony pathway which led to Calvary.

Here we stand very close to the loving heart of God, who suffers to redeem. But we must not overlook the triumph which is revealed. The Servant, buried after His vicarious suffering, is supernaturally vindicated and sees the fruit of His travail (10 ff.). Nothing less than a resurrection is involved, which, at a time when the view of the after-life in Israel was so vague, makes this prophecy yet more remarkable. Christ is still alive!

Isaiah 54   Trust God—Prove God

The prophet, using three striking illustrations, speaks of the restoration of Judah and Jerusalem:

Barrenness (1–3) was a mark of shame in ancient Israel (cf. Peninnah's taunt, 1 Sam. 1.6), but more than this, it meant that one was cut off from sharing, through one's children, in the future of the nation. The promise to the exiles was that there would be a new fertility after their return to Zion, with the nation again becoming numerous. During the exile, Edom from the south, and Samaria from the north, had encroached upon Judah's territory, but this would all be regained (3). A change of picture in v. 2 uses the illustration of a bedouin tent. The enlargement of one's home was a relatively simple matter, simply the incorporation of extra skins into the tent, allowing for extra-long cords because of the reduced pitch of the tent, and more substantial stakes to bear the increased weight. The Jews were being challenged to an act of faith, depending solely upon the Lord's promises. As such, it provided the text and the inspiration of William Carey's memorable sermon at Nottingham on 31st May, 1792, with its complementary themes:

'EXPECT GREAT THINGS FROM GOD
ATTEMPT GREAT THINGS FOR GOD'

History records the effect of this sermon in the birth of the Baptist Missionary Society and the genesis of the modern missionary movement. And to modern Christians, as well as to exiled Judah and eighteenth-century Baptists, there comes the continuing challenge to 'make longer cords and stronger stakes'.

In vs. 4–10 Judah, in exile, is viewed as a wife judicially separated from her Husband, Yahweh, because of her sin. The prophet's bold conception of such an intimate relationship between God and His people is paralleled in Hosea, whose heart-breaking relationship with his faithless wife taught him so much of the Lord's travail for wayward Israel (Hos. 1–3; cf. Jer. 2,3). Not for one moment did He cease to love Judah (8,10), and the joy consequent upon reconciliation would make the long, frustrating years of exile seem but a fleeting moment (4,7,8). The constancy of the divine love,

246

even in the face of provocation, is one of the many wonders of Biblical revelation and human experience.

The New Jerusalem (11–17). We have already noted the antecedents of this conception in 52.1 f., but the parallels with the Christian view in Rev. 21.18–21 are even more apparent here. Note carefully that material well-being is to be coupled with that spiritual and ethical prosperity (13 f.) which was so lacking in pre-exilic Jerusalem.

Isaiah 55   True Satisfaction

The Jews in Babylon, after the first shock of exile, settled down in their new sphere, encouraged by the letter which Jeremiah wrote to them (Jer. 29.4–7). As the years passed, and many of them prospered, their sense of vision dimmed. God had called Israel into covenant with Himself, they were His people, a kingdom of priests, with a priestly ministry of mediation for the whole world (Exod. 19.6). Apart from Him they could find no true satisfaction. Now, as the hour of liberation approached, many of them were unwilling to respond. They were in danger of becoming a nation of tradesmen (note the bustling energy of v. 2a) instead of a nation of priests. To these the prophet gives his invitations to 'solid joys and lasting treasure' which 'none but Zion's children know', all free through the covenant-grace of God (1–3a). He promises them the stability of a covenant-relationship as enduring as that with the Davidic house (2 Sam. 7.12–16; a number of scholars suggest a connection with the promise of the Davidic Messiah in Jer. 30.9; Ezek. 34.23 f.; 37.24 f., in which case the reference would be to the establishment of the Messianic kingdom). What David was (4), Israel would be (5), in this glorious future.

Nowhere in the O.T., however, is there any suggestion that Israel's position was divorced from responsibility. Obedience, the offering of love and loyalty, were the requisites of the Mosaic Covenant (Exod. 24.7), and this is again required (2b,3a, where 'hearken', etc., involves obedience). There was also the imperative to forsake sin and to seek the Lord earnestly and repentantly (6 f.), in a call to salvation which is as richly significant today, through Jesus Christ, as it was when it was first uttered (cf. Acts 2.21,38; 3.26; 13.38 f., etc.).

The remainder of the chapter (8–13) contains three stanzas of encouragement to the Jews to return. The first (8 f.) gives the assurance that what God has prepared for them far surpasses their power to conceive (cf. 1 Cor. 2.9 f.). The second (10 f.), speaking of the certainty of fulfilment of the divine promise, is amplified in the third (12 f.), where the familiar themes recur of a

247

triumphant departure from Babylon and the renewal of nature itself as they journey homewards. It reinforces the prophet's invitation to the things that really satisfy, away from the bustling city to the glorious universe and the wonderfully ordered world of nature, created by the One who leads them home (12a).

Isaiah 56   Too Small a Circle

Large-hearted religion is the theme of vs. 1–8. It is usually agreed by scholars that chs. 56–66 of *Isaiah* relate to the period after the return from Exile in 538 B.C. There are a number of connections with the condition of Judah in the eighth century B.C., but on the other hand, the judgement of the Exile appears to be in the past (e.g. 56.8; 57.16 f.). In any case, the setting is Judah and Jerusalem, not Babylon, as in chs. 40–45. The reference to the Temple (5,7) suggests a date for this oracle after 515 B.C., when the Second Temple was completed.

The Lord's people, in both O.T. and N.T. periods, have always been confronted with problems of membership. How is older legislation governing those eligible to belong to the group to be interpreted in the light of new situations? On the one hand there were prophecies that, on the return from Exile and the re-establishment of worship at Jerusalem, the Gentiles would respond and would share with the Jews (e.g. 45.22 f.; 49.6, cf. 2.1–4). Obviously, this prophecy was being fulfilled, for Gentiles were being attracted to the worship of the Jerusalem community (3,6). But this was not without opposition from those who, concerned with the purity of the group, wanted to exclude all non-Jews. A complicating factor was the presence of a number of eunuchs, which was probably a legacy of court-service in Babylonia and Persia. According to the provisions of Deut. 23.1 these unfortunates were specifically excluded from the Temple-worship. Isaiah, declaring the mind of the Lord, not simply his own opinion (1,4,8), advocates a generous attitude and rejects exclusivism. The outreaching mercy of God (8) condemns the attitude of those who draw so narrow a circle. The real standard is not birth, but obedience to God in both religion and morality (2). Note the stanzas below.

The rebuke of the final verses (9–12) is directed at the nation's leaders. Elsewhere 'watchmen' (10) is a synonym for 'prophets' (Jer. 6.17; Ezek. 33.7). It is tragic when the spiritual guides of a nation are so self-indulgent that the flock entrusted to them is completely unprotected (cf. Jer. 23.1–4; Ezek. 34). The Lord makes clear the severe condemnation which attaches to those who abuse their responsibilities in this way (Ezek. 3.16–21; 33.1–17).

248

> 'For the love of God is broader
>   Than the measures of man's
>   [mind;
> And the heart of the Eternal
>   Is most wonderfully kind.

> But we make His love too narrow
>   By false limits of our own;
> And we magnify His strictness
>   With a zeal He will not own.'

(F. W. Faber.)

Isaiah 57 God Does Care

Two classes are to be distinguished in this chapter, the 'righteous'
(1) and the 'wicked' (21). The former group were probably those
who had recently returned from Exile, the latter were those who,
remaining behind in Palestine, had become virtually semi-heathen
through inter-marriage. Between these two there was an ever-
increasing gap.

The opening verses (1 f.) state the problem, which is a recurring
one in the O.T., that misfortune and even death make no distinction
between the righteous and the ungodly (Eccl. 9.1–6; 12.1–8).
What is the use then of being righteous? The psalmist faced this
problem (Psa. 73), and here the righteous endured the taunts of
evildoers on the same issue (4). In reality, however, they were
mocking Yahweh, who therefore summons them to judgement (3).
First of all, He condemns them for their evil and idolatrous practices
(3–10), using the analogy of spiritual adultery employed by other
prophets (e.g. Hos. 1–3; Jer. 2,3; Ezek. 16). The references show
that this was a continuation of the Canaanite nature worship,
which included ritual prostitution and child-sacrifices. Probably,
as Jer. 44.15–23 indicates, this kind of worship, characteristic of
the worst periods of the monarchy (2 Kings 16.3 f.; 21.1–9), had
continued in Palestine whilst the exiles were in Babylonia. The
'symbol' (8) is an allusion to the mezuzah, the leather receptacle
containing portions of the Law of Moses which was attached to
the doorpost of every Jewish home (Deut. 6.9), signifying a life
lived in obedience to God's commands. The sign which characterized
the ungodly was their fornication. They interpreted the silence of the
Exile, when no prophetic voice was heard, as an indication of God's
impotence (11), but they would find out, to their cost, the inability
of their idols to deliver them (12 f.).

In sharp contrast to the fate of such evil men, the promise concerning the righteous (13b) leads on to a passage of encouragement
(14–19). The people who had returned to Jerusalem with such high
hopes were crushed in spirit (15) by adversity, which suggested the
continuing anger of God (16). God seemed to be hiding His face

249

(17). The result of this was that despairing Israel continued to backslide (17b). God promises that all these barriers would be broken down (14), and that there would be a living communion (15) and peace (19) with Him. Human weakness and unworthiness are very evident in this passage, and it is the God of grace who alone can revive (15 f.), heal and comfort (18), and give peace (19). In this final state of blessedness the wicked can have no share (20 f., cf. 48.22).

Isaiah 58   Religion on the Cheap?

Isaiah, in 56.10, had condemned the religious leaders as blind watchmen and dumb dogs, unable to give any warning bark. Such men were prophets in name only, for the essential function of a prophet is to herald forth, in unmistakably clear tones (1), the divine proclamation, whether it be one of condemnation (as here) or blessing. Amos spoke of his ministry as the roaring of a lion (1.2; 3.8). There is a superficial view that the prophets were concerned only with the future, but in actual fact, the bulk of their oracles were concerned with the present—they were the critics of contemporary life. The withering exposure of a purely formal religion which we find here should be set alongside 1.10–17 and our Saviour's trenchant words in Matt. 23.13–36. No doubt the message which the prophet brought would be highly unpopular, since it stabbed hard at the consciences of men who resented having their smug complacency disturbed. In our own generation the man who would speak out for God in condemnation of contemporary ethical standards or practices must expect the snarls of a generation which has largely cast off restraint and abandoned traditional standards. But the man of God knows that real happiness, satisfaction and true prosperity can only come as God is honoured and His standards accepted (8–14).

In this chapter the prophet attacks two practices: fasting (2–7), and Sabbath observance (13). There is no suggestion that these were wrong in themselves, but the way in which they were observed made them simply the hollow shells of a hypocritical religion, empty of any real content. They fasted as an outward form (5) that they might be in credit with God (3), but their actions were the very reverse of the humility symbolized in the outward forms (3b, 4a). The true purpose of fasting (4b) was that prayer might be reinforced, but such communion with God must, inevitably, result in compassion to one's fellow men (6 f, 10, cf. Jas. 1.27). This is not to be expressed in that token-involvement with the world's need which masquerades under the description of 'charity'; it necessitates 'pouring oneself out for the hungry' (10). Such costliness is, however, compensated abundantly by the blessings which are promised here.

Isaiah 59   Conditions of God's Intervention

Condemnation (1–8). Isaiah's scathing denunciation of hypocrisy in religion (ch. 58) is followed by an equally blistering attack upon the corruption and violence prevalent in the law courts (3–8). The people were complaining of God's inability to deliver them in much the same way that the exiles in Babylon had lamented His lack of power to release them from captivity (1, cf. 50.2). The prophetic diagnosis is that the separation between God and His people was the direct consequence of their sin (2). Sin separates between man and his Maker. Here the emphasis is upon the initiative of God, but in Gen. 3 it was Adam and Eve who, conscious of their sin, hid themselves from the presence of God (Gen. 3.8). Sinful man cannot abide the presence and scrutiny of a holy God, hence the desire to avoid the light which John notes (John 3.19 ff.). The bloodletting which vs. 3,7 imply was probably due to the misuse of the death penalty by lies, bribes and dishonest witnesses. Only as the way was made straight could the glory of the Lord be revealed (40.3 ff.), but the lives of these men were twisted and distorted (8).

Confession (9–15a). Here the people confess the sin of their rulers and judges which has involved them in such a predicament. There is a connection (9) with Amos 5.18,20, where the prophet, attacking the false notion of the day of the Lord as a time of national vindication, declares that judgement will begin with God's sinful people (cf. 1 Pet. 4.17). 'This fate', Isaiah's contemporaries declared, 'has now overtaken us.' They also accepted for themselves the verdict on the nation as God's blind servant (10, cf. 42.18 ff.). There is hope for an individual or a nation which is aware of its true condition before God!

Divine Intervention (15b–21). When sin is confessed and forsaken the Lord can intervene in salvation, proving that His arm has effectual power (16, cf. 1). Vs. 18 f. speak of the physical vindication of Israel before her adversaries, but the parallelism of v. 20 indicates that His redemptive work also operates on a higher, spiritual plane, concerning itself with Jacob's (i.e. Israel's) sin. The final verse (21) reveals the complete certainty of His promises.

A thought: Compare the armour of God (17) with the armour of the Christian in Eph. 6.10–18 and 1 Thess. 5.8.

Questions for further study and discussion on Isaiah 52.13—59.21

1. In what ways does 52.13–53.12 remind us of Jesus Christ?

251

2. What application has 54.2 f. (and its context) to the condition of the Christian Church?
3. Do we ever get 'something for nothing' (55.1)?
4. What are the sins which caused the withholding of God's deliverance (chs. 56–59)? Is there any abiding principle here?

Isaiah 60   Glory

The glory of the Lord is one of the distinctive themes of the O.T. It was revealed at Mount Sinai when God entered into a covenant with His people (Exod. 24.15 ff.; Deut. 5.24); at Kadesh-barnea its manifestation prevented the slaughter of Moses, Aaron, Caleb and Joshua by a disillusioned Israel (Num. 14.10); at the dedication of Solomon's Temple its appearance was the climax of the ceremony (1 Kings 8.11); the psalmist saw it revealed in the thunderstorm (Psa. 29.9); its association with the inaugural vision of Ezekiel strengthened him for his difficult ministry to the Jews in Exile (Ezek. 1.1–28), whilst his contemporary, Habakkuk, looked forward to the golden age when the whole earth would be filled with God's glory (Hab. 2.14).

Here the prophet foretells the imminence of another spectacular manifestation of divine intervention. Jerusalem is called to awaken (1, cf. 52.1) to meet what the prophet envisages to be the establishment of the Messianic age (2, cf. 9.1–7). No longer would the Lord's glory be revealed only on rare and fleeting occasions, it would shine continually in its full splendour, making the sun and moon quite superfluous (19 f.). A magnificent pageant is depicted, in which scene follows scene in vigorous, breath-taking succession, Jerusalem itself being the principal setting for the action. First, Zion is likened to a once-desolate mother, made radiant with joy at the restoration of her children (4 f., cf. 54.1–10). Next, an immense camel caravan approaches from the south, reminiscent of the celebrated visit of the Queen of Sheba to Solomon (1 Kings 10.1–10). There follows a remarkable scene as multitudes of sheep converge on the holy place and offer themselves as sacrifices (7). Scene number four focuses attention westward to the Mediterranean, where the white-sailed ships skim the ocean bringing their precious human cargo (8 f.). In the remainder of the chapter attention is on Jerusalem itself. A foreign army had battered down its walls in 587 B.C.; now these would be rebuilt with non-Israelite labour (10), yet, paradoxically, they would be completely unnecessary in an age of peace (11,18)! The Temple would be rebuilt in greater splendour than the Solomonic original (13,17, cf. 1 Kings 5.8–10), and the people, no longer forsaken (15), would enjoy universal homage (16),

252

security (21) and prosperity (22). All this is assured because of the name and character of Israel's God, as the climaxes at the end of vs. 9,16,22 make clear. A portion of it was fulfilled historically, but perhaps the greater part awaits fulfilment in the New Jerusalem (Rev. 21.22–27).

Isaiah 61 The Difference God Makes!

Commentators are divided as to the relationship between 61.1–4 and the four 'Servant' passages in 42.1–4; 49.1–6; 50.4–9; 52.13–53. 12. It is true that the name of the 'Servant' does not appear in it, as in the other Songs, but it is full of the spirit of the Servant of the Lord. We have frequently observed the fluidity of the Servant-conception. Referring to one who is in a peculiar relationship of privilege to God which issues in faithful ministry, it includes Israel the nation, the righteous remnant in Exile, the prophet himself and the Messiah. Here the primary reference is to the ministry of the prophet himself, the herald of good news to his distressed compatriots, for, if v. 10 refers to the same person as vs. 1–4, the speaker is not the bestower but the recipient of salvation, and so not Messiah Himself. But our Lord Jesus Christ, who, as we have seen in the note on 52.13–53.12, assumed for Himself the role of the Suffering Servant, made the opening verses of this chapter the first public utterance of His ministry in Galilee. In the synagogue at Nazareth He deliberately selected this portion and claimed that it found fulfilment in Him (Luke 4.16–21). There is no hint in this section of a salvation won through suffering, but then, no single prophecy, or type, gives an all-inclusive picture of Christ. Rather it highlights the joyous aspects of our Lord's life, as He brought light, liberty, healing and comfort to men. For our prophet, the historical context involved the prosperity of Jerusalem (4–9) and vengeance upon her enemies (2, line b). It is significant that our Lord, in reading from this chapter, stopped short of 'and the day of vengeance of our God'. Christ, in His incarnation, did not come to condemn the world (John 3.17), but to bring deliverance from sin's bondage, and yet, such was man's reaction to His presence, that he condemned himself by rejecting the Light (John 3.19).

Notice how, in this chapter, there is a combination of external and internal events. God was moving on a massive scale on the political scene, re-establishing His afflicted people in their war-ravaged land. But His concern also included the afflicted, the broken-hearted, those in bondage (of what kind is not specified), those who mourned and those who were faint-hearted. The Sovereign

Lord of the Universe still exercises this tender ministry in the lives of needy men.

Isaiah 62

The emphasis of this chapter is upon intercession. In the previous two chapters the prophet has spoken of the imminence of the Lord's work of deliverance, both material and spiritual, for Israel. Now he declares (1) his resolution to 'pray constantly' (1 Thess. 5.17, cf. Acts 12.5; Rom. 1.9, etc.) until he sees the fulfilment of his prophecies. It is of the utmost importance to observe that, in this call to prayer, he is as much the Lord's spokesman as when he was delivering the Lord's oracles. In this prayer he associates others with him (6 f., where 'watchmen' is best understood as 'prophets', as in 21.8–12; 56.10; Ezek. 3.17), urging them to give the Lord no rest, an injunction which is suggestive of our Lord's parable of the importunate widow (Luke 18.1–8).

The function of prayer in the God-man relationship is one which is perplexing to some who question whether God answers prayer, or wonder why He doesn't answer a particular request first time. The answer, surely, lies in the Father-child relationship. No human father always answers, 'Yes'; sometimes the answer is in the negative; sometimes delay, or some moderation of the request, is advisable. A child whose every whim was satisfied immediately would undoubtedly be spoilt, precocious and unappreciative. But the relationship with the parent, regarded as a kind of 'universal provider', would suffer most. God is our Heavenly Father, aware of our real needs (Matt. 6.25–33), and all His dealings with us are to encourage us in our love and trust. The enriching of our characters is of far greater importance to Him than the satisfying of our clamour for material prosperity. God could provide for every need. of His children, without delay, but He limits Himself, in His wisdom, so as to allow us, in the prayer of loving trust, to co-operate with Him.

Not all are able to give this kind of response. Their God is too small, merely the genie who answers when they rub the magic lamp. It is certain that many Israelites were unable to share the prophet's vision. But to those who were, there came the assurance of a new relationship (2–5); a new prosperity (8 f.); a new Jerusalem (10–12) upon which pilgrims would converge. No longer would Zion be forsaken like a divorced bride (4, cf. 49.14–18; 50.1), or desolate like a barren wife (cf. 54.1–8; 49.19 ff.). Isaiah's view of God as the bridegroom of His people finds its fulfilment in the relationship between Christ and the Church (2 Cor. 11.2; Eph. 5.21–33; Rev. 21.2).

Isaiah 63

If God is sovereign and righteous then He must act against sin, whether it be personal or national. A God who tolerated evil, and stood idly by, would not be God in any ultimate sense. But the sombre scene of His judgement is always qualified by the realization that, in His gracious but righteous love, He has provided the means whereby the pernicious effects of sin may be dealt with. In vs. 1–6 the theme of judgement is dominant. The heart trembles at the imagery used, depicting the total overthrow of an oppressor, but the mind lays hold on the fact that there is no human caprice or revengeful spirit here, God's dealings with men are in perfect equity. There is good reason to believe that Edom and its capital, Bozrah (cf. Jer. 49.13; Amos 1.12), are here used representatively of all the Lord's enemies. Certainly there is justification for this attitude, for a long history of bitter animosity between Israel and Edom culminated in events shortly after the overthrow of Jerusalem in 587 B.C. It was the Babylonian lion which laid Judah low, but it was the Edomite jackal which fell upon her as she lay helpless. Obadiah's brief prophecy is a bitter protest against such un-brotherliness, and Jeremiah, Ezekiel and the psalmist joined in the lament (Lam. 4.21 f.; Ezek. 25.12 ff.; 35; Psa. 137.7). For this reason Edom became the epitome of the enemies of the Lord's people.

The remainder of the chapter, and the whole of the next, contains the prophet's prayer for the deliverance of his distressed people. Like Samuel, faced with the Philistine onslaught, he first raised his 'Ebenezer' (lit. 'stone of help', 1 Sam. 7.12), reminding himself of all God's mercies in the past, particularly at the Exodus, and thereby strengthening his faith (7–14). What God had accomplished in the past He could do again! It is one of the remarkable features of Jewish piety that they believed that the whole power of God, revealed in the significant events of their history, could be brought to bear upon their own personal problems (e.g. Psa. 22, especially vs. 4 f.). God does not dole out His aid in minute rations.

From this there springs the plea for present help (15–19). The events of destruction and exile might seem to belie their ancestry, but God was still their Father, He had not cast them off (16). In the O.T. period the concept of God as Father was rarely used possibly because it suggested a physical connection, as in the Canaanite fertility cults. Jeremiah (3.19), Hosea (11.1,3) and our prophet employed it, however, and so prepared the way for its richly significant use in the N.T. period, when a new dimension was added by the incarnation.

Isaiah 64 — Man Waits—God Works!

The humanistic thought and theology of the past generations have left the legacy of a man-centred universe. *Man* achieves this and explores that; man's mind becomes the arbiter and touchstone of all things; even in religion the emphasis is upon what man believes and does, sometimes in such a way as to rule out any possible intervention by God and, indeed, to make His very existence superfluous! The emphasis of Isaiah in this chapter brings the man who thus deifies himself down to earth with a bump; salvation is God's work, not man's. He continues his prayer with an impassioned plea to God to act decisively, to reveal His awesome glory as He did at Sinai, and by the River Kishon (Exod. 19.16–20; Judg. 5.4 f.). Israel's part was to wait for the divine Worker (4), to yield to His touch, as inanimate clay is moulded by a skilful potter (8).

There is a lesson here which both humbles and inspires. God still works for the one who waits for Him. But this verse must not be wrenched from its context and made to support a doctrine of passivity. The *kind* of person for whom God works in this wonderful way is specified. 1. He is a man of prayer, pleading with passion even as the prophet did. 2. He is a man of faith, mindful of God's past mercies and certain that He can renew them. 3. His life reveals the moral standards of God, not with a chill, formal correctness but with the joyous warmth of heart obedience (5). God *meets* such. He is not remote and untouchable, willing to be found by man but unwilling to find; His is a questing love which seeks and surprises the believer at every point (cf. Psa. 59.10; 79.8). 4. He is a man humble and realistic enough to face up to his sin and shortcomings (5b–7). 5. He is a man deeply concerned for the honour of God (2b, 9–12). Observe how v. 11 and 63.18 show conclusively a setting after the destruction of the Temple. 6. Finally, the promise of v. 4b must be set within the wider context of the prophetic activity. Isaiah and his fellow-prophets were not men given to inactivity, dwelling at ease in Zion (Amos 6.1) as immobile spectators of God's exploits. But in all their strenuous endeavours there was that quiet spirit of waiting upon God. Such waiting has a trustful yet thrilling expectancy about it, for its object is the covenant-keeping, almighty God, whom we too may address as 'our Father' (8, cf. Matt. 6.8 f.).

256

The two final chapters of *Isaiah* contain God's answer to the prayer of His prophet (63.7–64.12). The Jews were asking, 'Where is He...?' (63.11,15), to which God replies, 'Here am I...' (65.1). All the while His hands had been outstretched in a loving, welcoming invitation (2) but the nation has not responded. Several centuries later the descendants of these Jews rejected God's Son in much the same way (Luke 13.34). There are still those who hear the gracious invitation of Christ (e.g. Matt. 11.28 f., or Rev. 3.20), but keep the door of their lives fast closed in His face.

The prophet, in his intercession for his people, had linked himself with the nation in its apostasy (64.9 f.), not standing apart in critical condemnation. In this attitude of identification he was in good company (e.g. Ezra 9.6–15; Neh. 9.16–37; Dan. 9.4–20), and an example to all would-be intercessors. But God quickly makes it clear that there are two sharply differentiated classes: on the one hand, those who, like the prophet, were waiting upon Him in humility and faith, as we observed in yesterday's portion; on the other hand, those who worshipped Him in name only, whilst indulging in the practices of false religious cults (3 ff., 11). He illustrates the distinction by quoting from what was probably an ancient song of the vintage harvest (8), when the clusters of grapes were being sorted according to their quality. This decision as to the ultimate destiny of the two groups within the nation was not an arbitrary one. Grapes have no control over their condition, but people have, and these faithless Israelites had rejected God's advances over a lengthy period (1 f., 12). Destruction, therefore, would come upon them (6 f., 11–15), but the godly would enjoy all the blessings of the Messianic age (9 f., 17–25), in which their former calamities would be forgotten.

Notes: The false worship of vs. 3–5,7,11 seems to combine elements from ancient Semitic heathenism and the Mesopotamian practices of spiritism and necromancy. The nature cults are indicated in 'sacrificing in gardens' (3, cf. 1.29 f.; 57.5 f., 66.17). V. 4a suggests consultation of the dead and possibly dream-oracles. 'Swine's flesh', prohibited in the Torah (Lev. 11.7), was connected with certain extreme celebrations in the worship of the Babylonian god, Ninurta. V. 11: 'Fortune' and 'Destiny', best rendered as the proper names of gods, Gad and Meni, known in Syria, Palestine and Egypt. They were probably astral deities of fate.

For an understanding of this chapter it is essential to bear in mind the two groups which we distinguished yesterday, the righteous remnant, and the mass of the people whose religion was depraved. The Temple was apparently not yet rebuilt (1, cf. 63.18; 64.11) but already many were regarding it in formal and material terms, as though it was God's house, to which He would be confined. It was a superstitious faith akin to that of the Israelites of Samuel's time, who took the ark into battle against the Philistines, thinking that thereby they would compel God to come and fight for them (1 Sam. 4.3–11). The prophet was not against the Temple worship (cf. 23), but like Solomon at the dedication of his magnificent sanctuary, he recognized that an almighty, universal God could not be confined within four walls (1 Kings 8.27). Amos, attacking the formal religion of his day, went so far as to declare that God was not to be found at any of the major sanctuaries, but the individual Israelite could still seek Him (Amos 5.5 f., cf. 4.4). So it has been in every age; the dwelling which the Lord, the Creator of all things, most desires is the humble and contrite heart (2, cf. 57.15).

The same dead formalism obtained in the acts of worship of these apostates. V. 3 sets four idolatrous acts alongside four authorized elements in the Israelite cultus. The meaning could be that the empty fulfilment of 'orthodox' religion is as unacceptable to Yahweh as rank heathenism, but more likely these idolatrous elements were superimposed upon the legitimate cultus. The Jews were completely indifferent to the God they professed to worship (4) and maltreated and mocked His true worshippers (5). But the vindication of the godly and the overthrow of idolators would begin at the very spot where God's name was profaned (6). All the judgement about which the remainder of the chapter speaks concerns the opponents of the righteous remnant, but the Gentile nations, responding to the declaration of God's glory (19), would come to worship Him (23). This prophecy received a greater fulfilment when the Jews, perpetuating the same tragic policy of reliance upon the outward forms of religion, rejected Christ, whereupon the door of salvation was opened to the Gentiles (Acts 13.46 f.).

So our prophecy ends on the solemn note of judgement, never a pleasant or a popular subject, especially to a generation with easy standards. But the picture of a God who finally judges must not be misrepresented. In His patience and longsuffering He waits with outstretched arms (65.2). This element of divine grace is one of the distinctive elements in the O.T., as in the N.T. Equally so, judgement is an essential theme of the N.T., and at the end of this present age, Christ, whose gracious invitation to men is 'Come' (Matt. 11.28), will say to those who, in their wilfulness never really knew Him, 'Depart' (Matt. 7.23).

Questions for further study and discussion on Isaiah chs. 60–66

1. What do you understand by the 'glory of the Lord' (60.1)? With the help of a concordance trace its manifestation in Scripture.
2. In what ways is 61.1–4 representative of: (*a*) the prophet himself; (*b*) Jesus Christ; (*c*) the modern-day Christian?
3. What is the relationship between prayer and the sovereign will of God?
4. Using a concordance and a good Bible Dictionary (e.g. the New Bible Dictionary, IVF) trace the relationship between Israel and Edom (see note on ch. 63).
5. Beginning from the plea of 64.1, make a list of the times when God intervened decisively in the lives of individuals and nations. What lessons may we draw from this?

Jeremiah

INTRODUCTION

The prophet Jeremiah is surely one of the most misunderstood men of all time. His very name has become a synonym for one who is always complaining. In reality he was an exceedingly courageous man. Called to an extremely difficult task, that of proclaiming God's judgement upon an unresponsive, apostate Judah, he stuck to his task for forty years in spite of popular resentment, which sometimes took violent forms. A lesser man would have given in long before this. Jeremiah had an especial heartache, for he was every inch a patriot; he loved his people and it grieved him to see them inching towards the disaster which he foresaw so clearly, but to which they were so blind. He was obviously familiar with both the message and spirit of the prophet Hosea, who prophesied in Israel a century before Jeremiah's ministry to Judah. Both men viewed their people's sin as unfaithfulness towards God. There

259

is little chronological order in the chapters of Jeremiah, which makes it confusing for the Bible student. The following table lists the various reigns and the chapters which may be reasonably ascribed to each:

Josiah (640–609 B.C.)	chs. 1–6
Jehoahaz (3 month reign in 609 B.C.)	nothing (but see 22.11 f.)
Jehoiakim (609–597 B.C.)	7–20 (except 13.18 f.); 22.1–23; 23; 26; 35; 36; 45
Jehoiachin (3 month reign in 597 B.C.)	13.18; 22.24–30; see also 52. 31–34
Zedekiah (597–587 B.C.)	Warnings: 24; 27–29; 51.59,60 Promises: 30–33 The last siege: 21; 34; 37–39
After the fall of Jerusalem	40–44
Prophecies against the nations	46–51
Historical finale	52.1–30

Jeremiah 1.1-8   God's Man in a Dark Day

The seventh century B.C. was a disastrous one for Judah. It began brightly enough, with the closing years of the reformer-king, Hezekiah (715–687 B.C.). But Manasseh, his son, was the worst king of Judah, and during his long reign (687–642 B.C.) the land was filled with corruption and violence, true religion almost ceased and the Temple fell into disrepair (cf. 2 Kings 21.1–18; 22.3–7). He was succeeded by Amon, a king of equally evil repute, whose reign was cut short by an uprising (2 Kings 21.19–26). Josiah, an eight-year-old king, commenced his reign with two colossal disadvantages: from the point of view of heredity he had as father and grandfather the two worst kings of Judah; from the point of view of environment he lived in the dark ages of the nation. But God is never bound by these factors and He worked in the tender heart of the young king. The chronicler notes three stages in the work of reformation. When Josiah was sixteen there was a personal experience of God which must have been closely akin to conversion (2 Chron. 34.3). True reformation must always begin in the human heart, but it can never stop there, and four years afterwards, as the same verse indicates, he began a sweeping purge of idolatrous practices in Judah, even extending his reform measures into the old northern kingdom of Israel. A decline in the power of Assyria, Judah's overlord for more than a century, enabled Josiah to push ahead with his pro-

260

gramme without opposition; indeed, Judah was virtually independent at this time. The date when this second stage commenced was 628 B.C. (stage three, 2 Chron. 34.8, cannot be considered here).

Just one year after, in 627 B.C., God called Jeremiah. Josiah's reform may have helped to develop the consciousness of the young man, but God knew that the valiant efforts of the king would not suffice to hold back the floods of ungodliness in Judah. Already He was raising up a prophet who was to speak the final word of judgement. The word 'youth' (6) in Jeremiah's protestation indicates a person without full rights in the community. We may assume that, in this context, it refers to someone between seventeen and twenty years of age. Was Jeremiah half-expecting this call? Certainly his only protest was on the score of his youthfulness. God wanted a man with a very gentle and tender heart for this unrewarding ministry of condemnation. Jeremiah's subsequent career shows that he had this quality in full measure.

Jeremiah 1.9-19   A Tough Assignment

Two further points from yesterday's portion merit attention. First, Jeremiah was a member of a priestly family at Anathoth (1), a small town a few miles north-east of Jerusalem. He may have been descended from Abiathar, David's priest and friend, who was banished to Anathoth during the early years of Solomon's reign (1 Kings 2.26 f.). There is no evidence that Jeremiah ever practised as a priest, unlike Ezekiel, his younger contemporary, whose prophetic ministry was permeated with priestly symbolism and interests. Secondly, there is a note of inscrutable finality concerning God's call to Jeremiah. Like John the Baptist (Luke 1.15) and Paul (Gal. 1.15) he was marked out by God before he was born (5). On the human side it appears that *we* choose, respond and offer ourselves, but the ultimate truth is that 'You did not choose Me but I chose you . . .' (John 15.16).

Jeremiah's call was confirmed, and the future course of his ministry indicated, by two visions. Whether these were true trance visions, or whether Jeremiah saw them with his physical eyes before their spiritual significance was revealed, is immaterial. The first, the rod of almond (11 f.), depends for its meaning on word-play, so beloved by the Hebrews. There is an assonance between 'almond' (Heb. 'shaqed') and 'watching' (Heb. 'shoqed'). The almond blossom, one of the first to bloom each springtime, would remind Jeremiah of the One who was not asleep, but wakeful and watching. The boiling pot (13) indicated a judgement coming out from the north. Earlier commentators referred this to an invasion of Scythians

261

c. 626 B.C., but, historically, it is doubtful whether there was such an invasion, and a reference to the Babylonians, who finally destroyed Jerusalem, seems preferable. In any case, such was the geographical position of Judah, hemmed in on the east by the desert and on the west by the Mediterranean Sea, that, unless Egypt were the aggressor, any attack by a major power must come from the north.

The proportions of Jeremiah's ministry, two-thirds of judgement and one-third of upbuilding (10, cf. 31.28); the exhortations not to fear (8,17) and the promise of superhuman strength in an incredibly difficult situation (18 f.) meant that he was under no illusions concerning the nature of his task. Forty years of unremitting opposition faced him, yet God kept him steadfast, and, even more miraculous, kept him unsoured in disposition and gentle in heart.

Jeremiah 2.1-22 What Went Wrong?

Chapters 3 and 4 date from the earliest years of Jeremiah's ministry, when Josiah's reformation was in full swing and the prophet was doing all in his power to promote an inward and spiritual reponse, not simply an outward show in which merely the externals of heathenism were removed. Jeremiah looked back upon the wilderness period with a certain nostalgia (2,3a), in marked contrast to the viewpoint of the Psalmist (e.g. Psa. 95.8–11), Ezekiel (20.13) and even Hosea (9.10; 11.1), although Hosea does seem to regard the earliest part as a time of purity (e.g. 2.15). Probably the reference of Jeremiah is relative; compared with the situation in his day the wilderness period seemed like the golden age, for at least there was repentance then. 'Was the fault in Me?' God asks (5), but then shows that it was, in fact, base ingratitude which led the nation to go astray, forgetting all His mighty acts (5–7). The leaders, both civic and religious, seemed involved in a deliberate conspiracy against Him (8).

Because of this God charges His people with an unnatural crime, unparalleled amongst the heathen, of changing their gods. Cyprus (10) was the western-most point in Judah's geography, whilst Kedar was a desert tribe in the east, so the appeal is from west to east, i.e. anywhere. A 'fountain of living waters' (13) was an extremely rare luxury in Palestine, whose water supply was dependent upon the seasonal rains, but Judah had forsaken the provision of divine grace and instead, with prodigious energy, was seeking an inferior substitute, a quest that was quite illusive (13). There are still those who cannot accept that salvation is a free gift of God, to be accepted by faith (cf. Eph. 2.4–9), and, like the Galatians, seek to add a religion of their own making (Gal. 3.1–5; 4.8 ff.). Not only was

Judah disappointed, she had become impoverished by attacks from surrounding nations (14 ff.), and even here, instead of seeking the Lord, she was attempting to remedy the situation by a policy of alliances with Egypt and Assyria (18). She was a servant turned rebel (20a), a harlot (20b), and a degenerate vine (21, cf. the development of this analogy in Isa. 5.1–7). The guilt expressed in these metaphors was more than skin-deep, it could not be washed away by soap and human energy. Only a true repentance matched with the grace of God could restore the relationship shattered by Judah's sin (cf. Joel 2.12 ff.).

Question: What 'broken cisterns' (13) are men hewing out for themselves today?

Jeremiah 2.23—3.5   Dare to be a Daniel!

How insidious are the effects of compromise! Israel, under the leadership of Moses, approached the Promised Land with a strong faith in Yahweh, who had delivered them from Egypt and entered into a covenant with them. Warning after warning was given concerning the dangers which they would face in Canaan. Specific instructions were given to deal uncompromisingly with the debased nature-cults of the Canaanites (e.g. Deut. 12.1–3). But little by little, through mixed marriages (cf. Judg. 3.6), and probably because it was deemed wise to show deference to the Baal-gods who were supposed to control fertility in nature, the high standards of the Mosaic religion were eroded away. The end product was a situation in which Yahweh was worshipped in name only, the form of worship being identical to that of the surrounding heathen. Yet Jeremiah's contemporaries were totally unaware of this, and protested vehemently that they had not forsaken the Lord (2.23,35)! The prophet, in unequivocal tones, makes clear the nature of their offence. The many references to abnormal sexual gratification underline one of the prominent features of the Canaanite religion, where male and female cult-prostitutes were connected with the sanctuaries (2.23–27, 33; 3.1–3). Another allusion to this aspect is found in v. 27 (cf. 3.9). At each Canaanite shrine there was an asherah, probably a wooden pillar which was a formal substitute for a sacred tree, representing the female sexual element, and a mazzebah, or stone pillar, indicating the male element. Jeremiah, ironically, inverts the genders. Added to this rank idolatry (28) were their sins of rebellion (29 ff.) and forgetfulness of God (32), their cruel treatment of the poor (34), and their frantic quest for alliances with their more powerful neighbours, always regarded by the prophets as an act of disloyalty to God. But the Lord had more power than the foreign powers in whom they trusted (37), and He effectively controlled nature, not the Baal-gods (3.3). Judah was to find out this to her cost.

The way of compromise is inevitably the way to disaster, as the life of Lot makes clear. It is a great privilege to be linked in a covenant-relationship with God, but it involves being absolutely true to Him, and unyielding to the subtle pressures of temptation.

Jeremiah 3.6-25   'Return, O Faithless Children!'

A warning (6-11). Jeremiah was familiar, not only with the historical events connected with the end of the northern kingdom of Israel in 721 B.C., but the significance of this act of judgement, prophesied by Hosea. Hosea was like Jeremiah in that both men knew much loneliness and heartache in their ministries and both viewed the apostasy of their peoples as spiritual adultery. But Jeremiah points out that Judah was the more blameworthy, for to her sin was added a brazen defiance of the stark warning provided by the fate of Israel a century before. In v. 10 (and possibly in 3.5) there is an allusion to the superficial response of the nation to Josiah's reformation, a subject to which we shall return tomorrow.

A promise (12-20). Notice the numerous occasions on which the word 'faithless' occurs in this chapter. Yet in spite of this, God was willing to forgive and restore His people on one condition only, that they acknowledge and repent of their guilt (13). The gracious, merciful love of the Father (19) shines out the more against the dark, sombre background of such national apostasy. Here Jeremiah speaks of a return to the land which would include even the exiled Israelites, although v. 14b indicates only a limited response. Wise. leadership; absence of reliance upon outward forms; an effective ministry to the nations, and a new unity, were to be the features of the Messianic kingdom (15-18).

A confession (21, 24 f.). If only . . . How often we use these words in vain self-incrimination. But here they have real substance. If only Judah had hearkened to the prophet who strove to prick her conscience into making such a frank confession! Jerusalem, with its Temple, would not have been destroyed; Judah would not have been devastated and there would have been no Exile. How dearly she paid for her continued rebellion! Sin is never slack in paying its wages, spoiling, scarring and destroying (cf. Rom. 6.21 ff.).

A prayer (22 f.). Like the confession, this is the prayer which the nation ought to have prayed in response to the gracious invitation of God. But it was never prayed. Nor was Hosea's similar appeal to his people heeded (Hos. 14.1 f.). There is no hope for

264

FOREIGN DEITIES

Ishtar

Canaanite fertility goddess

Canaanite baal

Storm-god, Hadad

Baal as storm-god

any nation, or individual, which, confronted with its sin, and given an opportunity to repent, prefers to go blindly on its pathway of self-destruction.

Jeremiah 4.1-18 Skin-deep Religion

This section marks one of the turning-points in Jeremiah's prophecy. Up to this point he has concentrated on exposing the nature of Judah's sin, and appealing to her to repent and to return to the Lord. His evangelical appeals to repentance continue throughout the remainder of his ministry (e.g. 4.14; 18.11), but a new and sterner note of impending judgement now enters in. We have noted a plausible connection between chs. 2 and 3 and the opening phases of Josiah's reformation, with at least two hints that, for the majority of the people, the reform movement was a matter of words only (3.5,8). Now Jeremiah (1–4) comes out in a direct frontal attack upon Josiah's massive reform as something which was purely superficial. They were not really returning to the Lord if they retained their abominations (a cumulative reference to all their idolatrous practices), and were religious simply in fits and starts (1). It is obvious, too, that their protestations were not matched by truth, justice and uprightness (2). But the real diagnosis comes in vs. 3 f. The reformation was purely on the surface; it was like sowing seed on land which had not been ploughed, or which was choked by a rank growth of weeds (3, cf. Hos. 10.12 f.). There must be deep ploughing, and the eradication of that which hinders growth, both in the realm of the spirit and in nature, before there can be a bountiful harvest. Our Lord's parable of the Sower has its application here (Matt. 13.3–9, 18–23). Changing the analogy, Jeremiah shows that the outward, covenant-sign of circumcision was inefficacious unless there was a corresponding inward separation to the Lord (4). As Paul pointed out six centuries later, 'real circumcision is a matter of the heart' (Rom. 2.29, cf. Col. 2.11). Any form of religion, even if, like circumcision or sacrifice, it has scriptural endorsement, which is just an outward show is unacceptable to the Lord. He abominates the 'whitewashed tombs' type of religion (Matt. 23.27).

On account of this the prophet sees the approaching judgement (5–9, 11–18). The description is the more vivid because he uses the prophetic present, which sees the judgement as already in progress, so certain is its fulfilment. At this stage Jeremiah allowed the false prophets the same degree of sincerity which he himself knew, attributing their easy, complacent message to the same Lord who had inspired him (10). Later on he was to find out the truth (14.13–16; 23).

Jeremiah 4.19—5.6 A Fruitless Quest

The theme of impending doom continues throughout this section. The imagery changes: first, it is viewed as a searing wind blasting in from the desert (4.11 f.); next, as an invasion by a foreign army (4.13,15–18,29); then by a shattering earthquake, followed by a ghastly silence in which even the song of the birds is stilled (4.23–26), and finally, as an encroachment by the predatory beasts of the wilderness (5.6). Four points, however, are made clear: 1. This bitter calamity is the result of the nation's sin (4.18). 2. No matter how stern may be the oracles of doom, no matter how close the twelfth hour, there is always a way of escape if there be genuine repentance (4.14). 3. The Lord, and His prophet, find no vindictive delight in the misfortunes of their people (19–22). It is as well to remember this, for many people view God as a Shylock who grimly anticipates exacting His pound of flesh, whereas God's judgements always come from a heart of love. The agony of spirit reflected here echoes the tender picture of the relationship between God and Israel in Hos. 11.1–9. Jeremiah himself suffered so much from his people that, humanly speaking, he might have been excused for gloating over their miseries when his prophecies came to pass. But Jeremiah was not that kind of man; he had God's love in his heart. 4. The coming catastrophe was punitive, but purposeful, God would not completely blot out His people (27).

In 5.1–5 Jeremiah was sent on a search for one righteous man in Jerusalem. As the Lord would have spared Sodom for the sake of ten righteous men (Gen. 18.32), so He would do for Zion if one such man could be found. But there was not one. Large-hearted Jeremiah was prepared to make excuses for the poor (4), but rebellion against God was not confined to this class, even the leaders of the nation, who were conversant with the divine requirements, had completely cast off restraint (5). The same desperate situation was noted later on by Ezekiel (Ezek. 22.30). Clearly, this was no time for half-measures.

A challenge. God still needs men and women who will 'stand in the breach' for Him.

Questions for further study and discussion on Jeremiah chs. 1.1–5.6

1. Compare the 'call' of Jeremiah with those of other Biblical characters. What is the significance of this experience?

267

2. What qualities would God require in a man called to such a difficult task as was Jeremiah?
3. Using such passages as Jer. 2.21; Deut. 32.32 f; Psa. 80.8–16; Isa. 5.1–7; Ezek. 15.1–6; 19.10–14, etc., consider the significance of the analogy of the vineyard in Scripture.
4. Following through the line of thought suggested in the notes on 2.23–3.5, compare the compromising Lot with the resolute Daniel.
5. Why did Josiah's reformation fail? What are the prerequisites of true revival? See note on 4.1–18.

Jeremiah 5.7-31   A Rebellious Nation

Two pictures, one depicting the depravity of man, the other the greatness of God, are contrasted in this passage. National and individual sins were certainly written large, including: the casting off of all restraint and a wild abandonment to sexual orgies (7 f.); a brazen heart of unbelief, which denied the effective power of God (11 ff., 22 f.). These lead to moral and spiritual insensitivity (21); idolatry (19), and corruption and violence amongst those who ought to have been giving wise leadership (26–29). Jeremiah, in his diagnosis, puts the principal blame squarely upon the shoulders of the religious leaders (30 f.). The essential quality of a prophet was that he acted as God's spokesman, mediating the divine will to the people (cf. the instructive analogy of Exod. 4.15 f; 7.1 f.). When this was ignored, and prophecy became simply the voice of a crowd-pleasing expediency, every standard of life, moral, social and religious, was bound to suffer. The common people, given easy assurances by those in authority (12), could hardly be blamed for living as though God did not exist. In our own age church leaders of every denomination have the same weighty responsibility as the watch-dogs over every aspect of the national life.

But the grace and greatness of God is shown with equal clarity. In the opening question of v. 7 there is an indication of a loving, merciful heart which yearns to pardon. He is no weak, tolerant deity, however, but One whose very essence is righteousness, which demands that such sin be punished. Hence the 'chorus' of vs. 9 and 29. His sovereignty means that He has effective power to fulfil His purposes so that the great world-powers move at His bidding (15 ff., notice the direct quotation from Deut. 28.49, which envisaged such a situation as this). The last word, however, is not of judgement. God would not obliterate all traces of His people (10,18), although exile awaited the surviving remnant (19). Jeremiah also depicts God as the great Creator (22) and as the 'Author and

Giver of all good things' (24). How foolish it was, and is, to turn from Him! Seeking satisfaction apart from Him can lead only to impoverishment (25), although this may be in the more enduring realm of the character, or the spirit, rather than in material things.

Jeremiah 6

This is the last chapter which may be dated in the reign of the reforming king, Josiah. In these opening chapters we have seen how Jeremiah did his utmost (chs. 2,3) to foster a true spirit of repentance, only to discover (ch. 4) that the reformation was in outward form only. The first hints of an inevitable judgement appear in ch. 4, becoming more intense in ch. 5, as the absence of even a small group of godly men becomes apparent. Now, in ch. 6, the note of doom sounds louder and more insistent as the prophet realizes just how corrupt and rebellious the nation was. Indeed, in the vividness of his imagination he sees the invasion as already in process (1–5), noting the harsh shouts of the attackers as they made their plans, answered by the agonized cries of the defenders (4 f.). Jeremiah calls upon his own tribe, Benjamin, to flee before the invader (1) and for the people south of doomed Jerusalem to be warned. Tekoa was about 12 miles south of Jerusalem, whilst Beth-haccherem was a hill between Bethlehem and Tekoa (1). The real tragedy of the situation is laid bare in vs. 6 f., where the Lord appears as the general commanding the siege forces. There was no hope for this evil city, which had enjoyed such immense privileges over a period of four centuries. And yet, paradoxically, there was hope. The end was near, but it had not yet come, so the Lord made a further appeal (8), warning the nation yet again of the precipice over which they were poised. Yet another exhortation follows in v. 16, so that no Jew could complain that the Lord had acted precipitantly.

But Jerusalem had gone beyond the point of repentance, as the remainder of the chapter makes clear. They would not hear (10); they were completely unashamed (15), and their answer to every advance was, 'We will not . . .' (16 f.). Their sacrificial system, elaborated as it was by costly unspecified innovations, was sheer mockery in the light of this (20). So heinous was Judah's sin that the Lord, who insists so strongly throughout Scripture upon the care of infants and the aged, is unable to advocate any mercy even for these (11 f.). Using the picture of a refiner of precious metals (27–30), He shows that the normal processes had been completely inefficacious, the dross still remained, contaminating the whole mass of metal. It was, therefore, fit only for the scrap-heap.

269

A comparison with ch. 26 shows that both chapters relate to the same event, in the opening months of Jehoiakim's reign, i.e. 609/8 B.C. In ch. 7 attention is focused upon the sermon itself, whereas in ch. 26, following a brief summary of Jeremiah's message, the main interest is upon its sequel. This was Jeremiah's great challenge, which took the form of a scathing attack upon the superstitious faith of his contemporaries. It won few converts but made him many enemies, especially amongst the priests and the prophets, and probably resulted in his excommunication from the Temple (cf. 36.5). But no one was left in any doubt about the views of a true prophet concerning the contemporary worship.

The miraculous deliverance of Jerusalem from Sennacherib's army (2 Kings 18.13–19.37) almost a century before had become legendary, and issued in the dogma that the city itself was inviolable, since it contained the Temple, God's dwelling-place. Since only Jerusalem had been delivered, whilst the rest of the land was devastated, the view became current that God was not really interested in His people, but only in His house, therefore, if anyone was in the proximity of the Temple, he was safe. This reduced God to the level of the heathen deities. No doubt the adherents of such a view, clearly revealed in vs. 4,8,10, could quote such passages as Isa. 31.5; 32.18; 33.20; 37.35 in support of their 'orthodoxy'. But a barren orthodoxy, or a cold formalism devoid of true spirituality, is never acceptable to God, especially when accompanied by the misconduct noted in v. 6 and the bare-faced idolatry of vs. 17 f. The 'queen of heaven' was the Babylonian Ishtar, identified with the planet Venus, whose worship, similar to the cults of the Canaanite goddesses, Asherah, Ashtaroth and Anath, was probably introduced into Judah by the apostate king, Manasseh (2 Kings 21.3 ff.). Barely suppressed in Josiah's reformation, it re-established itself after his death. With a strange human perversity, the survivors of God's judgement against the nation for its idolatry blamed that catastrophe upon their neglect of the cult of the queen of heaven (Jer. 44.15–19)! Yet Jeremiah made it clear that a judgement, similar to that which befell the ancient sanctuary of Shiloh, and the former kingdom of Israel, was about to fall on them (12–15). Shiloh, the central sanctuary of the Judges' period, was almost certainly destroyed after the double defeat of Israel by the Philistines at Aphek, where the Israelites had been guilty of a superstitious faith in the ark which paralleled that of Jeremiah's compatriots (1 Sam. 4). The immensity of Judah's sin, and peril, is indicated in the fact that it was beyond the power of prayer (cf. **11.14; 15.**1). Nevertheless Jeremiah continued to pray, and to plead with his people to the very end.

Jeremiah 7.21—8.3   'The Lord has Rejected'

Judah's elaborate sacrificial system, with its five principal types (burnt offerings, peace offerings, gift offerings, sin and trespass offerings) was time-honoured, stemming as it did from the Mosaic period. The Temple-sermon (3–15), with its shattering attack on the Jews' attitude to the Temple, was now followed by an equally devastating verbal onslaught on the sacrificial system. Verses 22 f. are not a denial of the Mosaic origin of sacrifice but a statement of priorities. God's first word to Israel, newly-emerged from Egypt, was not about sacrifices, as though He needed to be fed. As a matter of historical fact, legislation for the cultus was secondary to the demand for loyal and unquestioning obedience. Without this, the whole sacrificial system became null and void. There is a fearful irony in v. 21. The essential feature of the whole burnt offering was that it was entirely consumed by fire (Lev. **1.**9,13), unlike the other offerings, where at least a portion was shared by the priest or the worshippers. God here is virtually saying, 'What does it matter to Me; eat the lot!' Disobedience of the most wilful and stubborn kind, disobedience that shrugged off the Lord's chastisement, was characteristic of the nation up to and including the prophet's day: v. 28 could well be the epitaph of Judah.

Two further examples of the utter degradation of religion are cited. It is easy to pass over v. 30, but let the significance of 2 Kings **23.**4–7 sink in; in the Temple planned by David and constructed by Solomon, were all the trappings of the immoral Canaanite fertility-cult! It is a fearful warning of the consequences of compromise which had its roots in the Judges' period (e.g. Judg. **2.**1–3, 11–15,19; **3.**6 f., etc.). Child-sacrifice (31), so repugnant to the modern reader, was relatively rare in the ancient world, being reserved for occasions requiring desperate measures (e.g. Judg. **11.**30 f.; 2 Kings **3.**27). Judah, in the depth of its apostasy, was outdoing the heathen! Topheth probably derives from the Hebrew word for 'fire-place' (cf. Isa. **30.**33). The 'valley of the son of Hinnom' was south-west of Jerusalem.

The desecration of a corpse (33,**8.**1–3) was considered an awful fate in the ancient world (cf. Amos **2.**1). There is a gruesome congruity about the bones of the devotees of the heavenly host being openly strewn before their impotent objects of worship.

271

Yesterday we noted that Judah refused to accept the correcting rod of discipline (7.28); today's portion opens with an indication of her chronic inability to profit from her mistakes (8.4–7). In contrast with the migratory birds, who had evolved a consistent pattern of life which made for survival, she was utterly inconsistent, and would have to learn the hard way. We note a smugly complacent sense of security in their possession of the sacred Scriptures (8). But when these were distorted in interpretation they afforded no more than a refuge of lies. The multiplicity of cults, all quoting Scripture suitably doctored, or wrenched from its context, is a striking, modern-day example of this. The 'wise men' (9) formed the third main group in Israel, together with the prophets and priests. Their chief function was to relate the principles enunciated in the Law to the details of the everyday life. Their successors were the scribes so familiar to us in the N.T. The fundamental error of each group was the light way in which they glossed over the nation's sin (11 ff.). Drastic surgery, not sticking-plaster, was required.

Jeremiah himself was under no illusion. He foresaw the drastic measures which the Lord would use, and, with his sensitive spirit, he lived through the agony which was to burst upon Judah (8.14–9.3). Anticipation of the misery of the refugees (14 f.) at the approach of a ravaging army (16 f.) caused him acute physical and spiritual revulsion. Two metaphors show the seriousness of the situation. 'Harvest' (20) refers to the main cereal harvest, whilst 'summer' refers to the vintage harvest (grapes, etc.) in early autumn. If one harvest failed, it was possible that the other would see the people through the winter, but if both failed, starvation confronted them. Hence v. 20 became proverbial for a desperate situation. The second analogy, drawn from the medical world (8.22), likens Judah to a desperately ill patient. Yet there was medicine available (balm from Gilead, little more than a day's journey away) and a physician, Dr. Jeremiah, to apply it. For the nation to refuse its medicine was wanton suicide. All the prophet could do was to lament the certain death of the patient (9.1).

Jeremiah 9.4-26   Something to Weep Over

One of the vital concepts of the O.T. is that of the covenant. God, in His grace, had bound Israel to Him. This meant that all Israelites were bound to one another, and whilst they were to show loyalty and obedience to God (e.g. Deut. 30.20), they were equally required to display brotherly love to one another. Such sins as those noted in vs. 4–8, which repudiated the covenantal obligation, were virtually a denial of the covenant-relationship. The same principle applies in the N.T. dispensation; hence the frequent exhortations to show love within the fellowship (e.g. John 13.34 f.; Gal. 6.10; 1 Thess. 4.9 f.), and the condemnation of the one who claims to love God but hates his brother (1 John 4.20 f.). Jeremiah, foreseeing the consequence of such unbrotherliness (9), calls for a funeral dirge to be chanted over all Judah. Only the scavengers would be left to haunt the desolate ruins (10f.).

But if vs. 4–8 show the outward signs of a morally sick society, vs. 12 ff. reveal the root cause of Judah's malaise. Their attitude to one another was wrong because their relationship to God was wrong. In stubborn wilfulness they had rejected the revelation of truth and were following the sensual Baal cults. Again (cf. 10 f.), there is a forthright condemnation of such sin and a warning of inevitable judgement (15 f.). The symmetry is also preserved in the calling in of the professional mourners (cf. 2 Chron. 35.25; Mark 5.38 ff.) to lament over the stricken nation (17 ff.). Notice the grim personification of Death as the Reaper (21 f.).

Judah had plenty of false confidence: in the Temple (7.4,10,14); in the Scriptures (8.8); here we find an equally false trust in wisdom, might and riches (23), shared, one suspects, by men of all races in the twentieth century. Probably there was a trust in circumcision also (25 f., see note on 4.4). None of these is a sufficient foundation for life, the only real basis is a personal knowledge of God (cf. Matt. 11.27), accompanied by a display of the ethical qualities noted in v. 24.

Note: V. 26: 'that cut the corners of their hair' (cf. 25.23; 49.32). This practice, in honour of the gods of the heathen, is condemned in Lev. 19.27.

Jeremiah 10   'The True God'

The first sixteen verses declare the greatness of God and the impotence and insignificance of idols, and should be considered in conjunction with other great monotheistic passages (e.g. Deut. 4.32–40; Psa. 115.3–8; 135.15–18; Isa. 40.19–26; 44.9–20; 46.1–9). There is a threefold contrast here: 1. Contemporary heathen worship attached great importance to the sun, moon and stars (e.g. 2, cf. 8.2; 2 Kings 21.5; 23.5; Zeph. 1.5), but the Lord Himself made the heavens (12). 2. Idols were constructed by men, and were unable to speak or walk (5), they had to be secured to prevent them from falling (4)! But God was the King of the nations (7), with

such sovereign power that all peoples trembled before Him (10).
3. One of the great attributes of a deity is effective power to help,
but here idols were completely valueless—no helpful advice could
be expected from wood (8)! But Yahweh was true, living and eternal
(10), the Creator (12) and Controller of the forces of nature (13).
For skilled craftsmen to misuse their talents in such a way was to
prostitute their God-given abilities (14). Man, fashioned in the image
of God (Gen. 1.26 f.; Psa. 8.5) still demeans himself when he worships
anything, or anyone, less than God.

The prophet speaks in v. 17. The warning could relate to an
historical occurrence, such as the three-month siege of 597 B.C.
which issued in the first deportation, but more likely, it is Jeremiah's
vivid imagination which, foreseeing the certainty of such an event,
views it as already accomplished. Jerusalem is personified as a tent-
dwelling mother, bereft of her children, in vs. 19–21 (cf. the reversal
of this analogy in Isa. 54.1–3).

Prayer, for Jeremiah, was converse with God, as vs. 23 f. illustrate. It is a confession of human frailty and a humble acceptance
of divine chastisement which claims the mercy of God, lest our sins,
receiving their due desert, bring us to destruction. There is a paradox
in the second line of v. 23. Man seems to control his own progress,
but the fact is that man, vitiated by sin, is incapable of achieving
his own true destiny. He desperately needs God, as the wise man
realized (Prov. 20.24, cf. Psa. 37.23).

Questions for further study and discussion on Jeremiah chs. 5.7–10.25

1. Are the sins noted in 5.7–31 as prevalent in our own generation?
2. Why was Jeremiah so certain that judgement was coming upon
   his people? Make ch. 6 your starting point.
3. What do you think a twentieth-century 'Jeremiah' would say
   if he preached a 'Temple Sermon' (7.1–15) in one of our leading
   churches? What effect would it be likely to have?
4. Beginning with the note on 7.21–8.3, trace the history and effect
   of Israel's compromise after the settlement in the Promised Land.
5. How does Jeremiah attempt to show (in ch. 10) that Yahweh
   was the one true God? If you have time, link in other supporting
   evidence.

Jeremiah 11   Back to the Fundamentals

2 Kings 23.3 speaks of a covenant made between King Josiah, the
people and the Lord, following the discovery of the lost 'book of
the covenant' in 621 B.C. Some scholars have viewed Jer. 11.1–13
as a powerful sermon preached in support of this covenant, usually

known as the 'Josianic Covenant'. A powerful sermon it certainly is, but this setting is unlikely. There is evidence of open, uninhibited idolatry in vs. 12 f. which would be impossible in Josiah's reign once the reform was in operation. As 2 Kings 23 shows, heathenism was eradicated by force, not words. The setting appears rather to be the reign of the godless Jehoiakim (609–597 B.C.) when every vestige of Josiah's reform had disappeared. Jeremiah, in fact, is calling the nation back to a more fundamental covenant than Josiah's. 'This covenant' (2,3,6,8) is the Sinaitic Covenant, as vs. 4,5,7,8 show. The nation had shifted from its basic foundation and the prophet saw that it had to get back to the first relationship of loyal obedience. It was a question of returning to their first love (cf. Rev. 2.4 f.). Jeremiah (9), like Isaiah (Isa. 1.2), views Judah's sin as revolt or rebellion, a crime the more vile because it was against a God who continued to love the nation (15). Formal acts of religion were sheer hypocrisy in such circumstances. So the nation, intended to be like a fruitful olive tree, but now producing no fruit, would be destroyed (16, cf. John 15.1–17).

There are certain passages in our prophecy, often called the Confessions of Jeremiah, which may be studied apart from their context to allow us to see the intensity of Jeremiah's spiritual struggle when he was alone with God. They are 11.18–20; 12.1–6; 15.10–12, 15–21; 17.14–18; 18.19–23; 20.7–18. The first of these (18–20) follows a plot on the prophet's life by his own townsfolk of Anathoth. Possibly they resented the fact that one of their number had spoken out so strongly against the Temple (7.1–15). It remains true, as our Lord Himself observed, that 'A prophet is not without honour, except in his own country, and among his own kin, and in his own house' (Mark 6.4). He, like Jeremiah, faced an attempt on His life by the people of His own city (Luke 4.29). But unlike Jeremiah, who prayed that he might see God's vengeance upon his enemies (20), Jesus Christ prayed for the very men who caused His death (Luke 23.34, cf. Isa. 53.7; 1 Pet. 2.23; Matt. 5.44).

Jeremiah 12   The Whole Plan of God

The problem of an apparent injustice on God's part, which allowed the righteous to suffer misfortune whilst the ungodly appeared to flourish (1 f.), was not confined to Jeremiah. The psalmist, filled with envious misgivings, questioned the worthwhileness of the morally upright life until, within the sanctuary, he saw things in a fresh perspective (Psa. 73). The whole book of Job deals with the same problem. Job was convinced of his complete integrity; his companions, Eliphaz, Zophar and Bildad, were equally convinced that such unique misfortune indicated God's judgement upon his sin. Not one of the four, of course, was aware of the behind-the-scenes dialogue between God and the accuser (Job 1.6–12; 2.1–6) which showed that Job's suffering was for a purpose, to prove that man was capable of trusting God apart from what he could get out of it (cf. the sneering accusation of 1.9). The *whole book* of Jeremiah shows that there is a moral law operating in the world, but the prophet, smarting at this time under the attack on his life (11.21), impatiently clamoured for God to hasten up His processes of judgement (3 f.). He did not allow God that divine patience and forbearance which characterizes all His dealings with men. God's answer to this petulant outburst was hardly encouraging, there was worse to come! One day the hand of every man would seem to be against him (e.g. 36.26; 38.4 ff.). The 'jungle of the Jordan' (5) was that narrow strip of dense vegetation which bordered the river. The unfailing supply of water and the fierce heat of the rift-valley combined to cause a jungle-like growth which was infested with lions (49.19; 50.44; Zech. 11.3). Jeremiah had need of the strength that was promised him at the time of his call (1.8, 18 f.).

Nevertheless, judgement *was* in process (7–13). The historical background of this passage is probably 2 Kings 24.1–4, when Judah, after Jehoiakim's rebellion against Babylonia in 602 B.C., was subjected to sporadic attacks by her neighbours, instigated by Babylon, until Jerusalem itself fell in 597 B.C. But notice the personal terms used to describe Judah (7–10), indicating that this was a chastisement regulated by love. In such a context of persecution by neighbouring states it is remarkable to observe that these 'evil neighbours' (14) are promised a share in a glorious future, following a chastisement similar to that inflicted upon His covenant-people, providing they accept the testimony of Judah to her Saviour-God (14–17, cf. 46.26; 48.47; 49.6,39).

Jeremiah 13   'Good for Nothing'

Two parables graphically illustrate the condition of Judah and the fate about to overtake her. In the first (1–11) Jeremiah was commanded to take a loin-cloth, signifying that God's people ought to have clung to Him in loyalty, love and trust (11, cf. Deut. 10.20; 11.22, etc.). Each return trip to the Euphrates would involve a distance of 1,600 miles (Ezra and his company took four months to complete a one-way journey, Ezra 7.9) and because of this it has been suggested that Jeremiah made only a token journey to some suitable riverside location. There is no hint of this in the narrative,

276

however. The inference is that Mesopotamian influence in religion, introduced during the reign of the wicked Manasseh (2 Kings 21), had corrupted the nation to the point of worthlessness. Possibly also there is an allusion to the Babylonian captivity. Jeremiah's starting point for his second parable (12 ff.) was a conventional platitude expressing the hope of future prosperity, to which the people smugly replied that this was what they were expecting (12). Then followed the devastating revelation that the whole nation would be filled with drunkenness and then destroyed (cf. the similar imagery in 25.15–28; 51.7). Jeremiah took no delight in this disclosure, he could only weep bitterly at a nation which was like a man stumbling over treacherous, mountainous terrain in pitch-blackness (15 ff.).

The king of vs. 18 f. is Jehoiachin, the son of Jehoiakim, who reigned for three months in 597 B.C., whilst Jerusalem was besieged by the Babylonians (2 Kings 24.8–12). As he was only eighteen years old the queen mother, Nehushta, would have considerable influence upon him. Jehoiachin submitted to the Babylonians and he and his mother were taken into captivity (cf. 22.26; 29.2; 52. 31–34). The 'Negeb' (19) was the southern region of Judah. The deportation which followed this Babylonian campaign included the rulers, leading citizens and craftsmen (2 Kings 24.14 ff.).

The remainder of the chapter (20–27) probably dates from the time when Judah first passed under Babylonian control, in 605 B.C. It reveals a nation far from God, with its sin so deeply ingrained that change was virtually impossible (23). Multiplied acts form character, and when those actions are evil then the resultant character becomes a chain which the grace of God alone can break. Only He could make Jerusalem clean, but this involved drastic measures.

Jeremiah 14   The Great Drought

Palestine was especially dependent upon the seasonal rainfall. It had few perennial rivers and its hilly and undulating terrain made complex irrigation systems like those of the Nile and Tigris–Euphrates basins impossible. There were relatively few springs and wells. If the rains were withheld the consequences were serious. According to ancient Jewish traditions, if the 'former rains' had not arrived before the ninth month, Chislev (November–December), then an extraordinary three-day fast was held. Such a fast is indicated in 36.9 and it is possible that our chapter is connected with the same situation, when the whole land was suffering incredible hardship (1–6). Jeremiah's acquaintance with country-life is shown in the aptness of his illustrations: the hind (5) is a creature renowned for the care of her young; the wild asses (6) are amongst the hardiest of animals, well able to endure drought.

The prayer of vs. 7 ff., 19–22 is best regarded as the prayer which Jeremiah himself prayed. There is deep humility, a frank confession of sin (7,20), the recognition of past mercies (8a) and the pleading of the covenant-relationship (9b,21). If only the nation had taken up this cry from the heart, and made it its own, then God could have shown forgiveness. But supplication cannot 'come before the Lord' whilst there is unconfessed sin in the life (cf. 36.3,7). Their trust was not in Him, but in the Baal fertility-gods who were as impotent in rain-making as in all other realms (22, cf. 3.1 ff.). Even the prayer of the godly was quite unable to avert the divine judgement (11), whilst fasting (12) was sheer hypocrisy in such circumstances. Judah, with unrestrained feet, had wandered away from God into the paths of false cults and abominable practices (10).

God's revelation to Jeremiah highlighted the disparity between such a message and the easy assurances preached by the false prophets (13). Earlier on (4.10) Jeremiah had accused God of responsibility for these diametrically opposed messages, but now he discovers the true situation (14 ff.). The authority of the prophets rose from a source no higher than themselves. Popular they might be, numerous they certainly were, but these advantages were deceitful; only the real word of God will stand the test of time and experience. In ch. 23 we shall see Jeremiah's final exposure of these 'blind leaders of the blind'.

Jeremiah 15   A Prophet in Despair

A nation which is beyond the power of prayer is in a bad way indeed (1). The reputation of Moses and Samuel as intercessors was built upon such incidents as those noted in Exod. 32.11–14, 30–34; Num. 14.13–19; 1 Sam. 7.5–9; 12.19,23, cf. Psa. 99.6. The command here (cf. also 7.16; 14.11) must be regarded as conditional rather than absolute. Jeremiah continued to plead with his people and to pray for them, but whilst they remained adamant (cf. 17.1) and unrepentant there could be no forgiveness. Compare the types of destruction in vs. 2 f. with those pictorially represented by Ezekiel (Ezek. 5.1–4). The reference to Manasseh (4), in whose reign the whole nation was led astray (2 Kings 21), must not be taken in isolation, as Jeremiah's contemporaries did. They excused themselves from moral responsibility by attributing the disasters which overtook them to the sins of their forefathers, but Jeremiah, whilst not overlooking this factor, made clear that the judgement of God was upon them, personally, for their sins (16.10–13; 31.29 f., cf.

278

Ezek. **18.**1–4). Such a visitation, indicated in vs. 5–9, was probably the Babylonian raid of 598/7 B.C., which was in reprisal for the rebellion of Judah in 602 B.C. (2 Kings **24.**1,10 ff.).

The remainder of the chapter (10–21) is of immense importance in our understanding of the relationship between God and His prophets. Two fallacies are here exploded: 1. the view that the prophets were superhuman, men who never faltered in their ministries, no matter how acute the opposition they encountered; 2. the view that when God spoke through a man He took such full possession that all traits of human personality were by-passed, the prophet becoming an automaton rather than an ambassador. Jeremiah here lapses into acute self-pity and launches a bitter attack upon God that reached perilously close to blasphemy. His message of condemnation alienated him from all men (17) and earned him their bitter reproach (10). It was an impossible task (12). So the prophet who had accused his people of self-deception in hewing out cisterns that could hold no water (**2.**13) now lays a similar charge (18b) against God. How gracious was God to His overwrought servant in the face of this querulous outburst! He did not write Jeremiah off as a failure, but showing him the worthlessness of such unfounded accusations, He indicated the way of restoration through repentance (19) and divine strength (20, cf. **1.**8,18). Compare His gentle dealings with Elijah (1 Kings **19.**3–18).

Jeremiah 16   The Cost of Discipleship

Jeremiah was called upon to pay a heavy price because of his ministry as the Lord's spokesman to a rebellious people. We have noted his isolation from his fellows, 'all of them curse me' (**15.**10), and loneliness, 'I sat alone' (**15.**17). Today we see a progressive withdrawal from the various spheres of social life. First of all, Jeremiah was forbidden to marry (2); then he was commanded to take no part in any funeral rite (5), and finally, he was debarred from participating in any joyous occasion (8). What this meant to a heart as exquisitely tender as Jeremiah's can only be imagined. In the tightly-knit community of Judah it was tantamount to a self-imposed excommunication. When it is realized that these acts of sacrifice involved the whole of his ministry, then some conception of the spiritual agony that Jeremiah endured can be gained. Was this the kind of increased difficulty that the Lord foresaw in **12.**5? A. S. Peake's comment on **15.**19 has its application to these apparently onerous demands: 'Unshrinking obedience, rendered without hesitation or complaint, that is the condition imposed by God upon those who aspire to the high dignity of His service. And the reward of

279

service faithfully rendered is, as in the Parable of the Pounds, more service.' But in the final analysis, the Lord's service is one of immeasurable enrichment, not loss, as J. G. Whittier penetratingly observes:

'Who calls Thy glorious service hard?
Who deems it not its own reward?
Who, for its trials, counts it less
A cause of praise and thankfulness?'

Jeremiah's apparently anti-social conduct was to be a witness to the devastation that was about to descend upon Judah, when all normal activities of a community would cease. The parable of his withdrawn, celibate life was to be supported by plain explanation (10–13). The thoroughness of the impending calamity is shown in v. 16: the 'fishers' would first net the big haul, presumably a reference to deportation, to be followed by the 'hunters', who would ferret out the individual survivors. But the dark night was illumined by the promise of a miracle, greater than the Exodus, in the return from captivity (14 f., cf. 23.7 f.). This, together with the divine strength noted in v. 19a, must have sustained our lonely prophet during his long, lone vigil.

Jeremiah 17 The War Within

Today's chapter contains a series of oracles with little apparent connection. The first (1–4) follows closely upon the thought of the preceding chapter. A 'pen of iron' was used for cutting inscriptions in rock or stone. The point of the metaphors is not the hardness of the materials used but the indelible nature of what is written. Two realms are specified: 'their heart' (1), which covers their personal life; 'their altars', which comprehends their worship. The first part of the 'Parable of the Two Trees' (5–8) may arise from this description of those who had turned away from the Lord (5). The 'shrub' of v. 6 could be the dwarf juniper, stunted and barely alive in an area of low rainfall and poor soil. The man whose trust is in the Lord, in contrast (7 f.), is in touch with an unfailing supply of nourishment which ensures abundant growth, luxuriant foliage and continuing fruitfulness (cf. Psa. 1.1–4; John 15.1–17). Sterility or fruitfulness in life is still determined by our relationship to our Lord.

The personal confession of sin found in v. 9 probably resulted from a sudden discovery which Jeremiah made of the secret, turbulent depths of his own heart. This may well have been revealed by the bitter, vindictive outburst of v. 18. If so, then vs. 14–17 come into perspective. Jeremiah, appalled at what he finds within himself, and conscious that this is not hidden from the Lord's all-seeing eye (10), seeks deliverance from the only One who can cleanse and heal (14). The provocation which he endured daily is noted (15) and the Lord is called upon to witness that his better self doesn't exult over the prospect of disaster upon his adversaries (16). Jeremiah's attitude when Jerusalem fell (see note on ch. 40) shows the triumph of this higher nature. The conflicting emotions which warred within Jeremiah's heart may be compared with Paul's inward struggle (Rom. 7). Notice where both found their victory (Jer. 17.17, cf. Rom. 7.25).

Compare Jeremiah's teaching on the Sabbath (21–27) with Amos 8.4 ff; Neh. 10.31; 13.15–22. The Jews were using the Sabbath to bring in their crops, or their wares, in preparation for the domestic or business life of the next week.

Questions for further study and discussion on Jeremiah chs. 11—17

1. Make a list of the various covenants found in the Bible, showing the significance of each.
2. What answer would you give to the question of 12.1?
3. What does ch. 14 teach us concerning the place and content of prayer?
4. What may we learn from chs. 15,16 about the relationship between God and the true prophet?
5. Sin: (i) its effect on the life; (ii) its relationship to the will; (iii) how it may be dealt with. Consider ch. 17 under these headings.

Jeremiah 18.1-17   Let Him Mould Thee

The imagery of the potter's wheel is probably the most familiar of Jeremiah's object-lessons. Just as the potter, seeing that his creation is not working out as he planned it, can reduce the clay to a shapeless mass and begin again, so God, in His absolute sovereignty, can change His plan for a nation and also, of course, for an individual. The concept is capable of gross misunderstanding, and God could be viewed as irresponsible or capricious. Or He could be regarded as 'magnified man' who 'changes His mind'. Or it could be objected that man is *not* inanimate like clay; he has a mind, feeling and a will; and that, therefore, the analogy is inapplicable. None of these objections is legitimate, and the application here is carefully safeguarded. God deals graciously and patiently with men, in accordance with moral and spiritual laws which He Himself has integrated into this world. We can yield ourselves to Him in complete confidence. Man is never at the mercy of an unfeeling deity; it is in his power to repent (8,11) and align himself with God's beneficent purposes. The analogy teaches that God's dealings with mankind are creative and purposeful and that He works in accordance with that law which is the expression of His being. He is Sovereign both in His graciousness and His judgements, but man's response determines which set of eternal rules shall apply, and even here, God's long-suffering allows man every chance. Judah's stubbornness (12–17) in forsaking the Lord and following other gods was something unparalleled in the ancient world (cf. 2.9–13). Small wonder, then, that the nation had lost its way (15)! 'So it was of old; so it is now. When the heart is estranged from God, and devoted to some meaner pursuit than the advancement of His glory, it soon deserts the straight road of virtue, the highway of honour, and falls into the crooked and uneven paths of fraud and hypocrisy, of oppression and vice' (C. J. Bell: *The Expositor's Bible*).

Note carefully the cardinal rule of prophecy which is enunciated here, that both the promises and threats of God are not absolute but conditional. Judah so often presumed on the divine promises, viewing them from the point of view of privilege and not of responsibility, in spite of prophetic warnings of the disaster that would overtake such an attitude. The apparently unconditional promises concerning the Davidic line (e.g. 2 Sam. 7.12–16; Psa. 89.3 f.) were qualified by such expressions as in 1 Kings 2.4; 3.14; 6.12; 9.4–9. Conversely, there was forgiveness for even repentant Nineveh (Jon. 4.11). Consider carefully the conditional element in Matt. 6.12, 14 f.; 18.35.

Jeremiah 18.18—19.15   Speak the Truth in Love

The men of Judah, having rejected Jeremiah's message (18.12), now set about silencing the messenger himself (18.18,20,23). They resented the claim, implicit in his prophecies, to have greater discernment than the three traditional groups of spiritual counsellors: priests, prophets and the wise (18). Official religion was united in opposition to Jeremiah. The outburst of vs. 21 ff. is capable of two explanations. It is just possible, since the nation had refused his message and spurned the divine call to repentance (18.12), that Jeremiah is here judicially delivering up the nation to the inevitable consequences of its chosen course (18.15), without any vindictiveness on his part. But v. 23 does not tally with such a view. More preferable, then, is the view that this is another passionate outburst rising from the wounded spirit of the prophet. Perhaps at this point we may detect the poignancy of his mental agony. He loved his people:

he interceded for them (18.20); in his better moments there was no pleasurable anticipation of revenge (17.16); he wept over the fate which awaited them (9.1; 13.17). But their relentless opposition and wilful misunderstanding of his motives drew from him these demands for harsh vengeance, in sharp antagonism to his true self. One feels a deep sympathy with him, but this unveiling of the bitter conflict within his heart underlines the weakness of the human spirit, even that of a great prophet. Only in the love of Christ can we overcome evil with good (Rom. 12.14–21, cf. Matt. 5.43–46).

In ch. 19 we have another acted parable concerning the shattering judgement about to come. The valley of the son of Hinnom (2), probably the present Wadi al-Rababi, was connected with the worship of Molech, which included the offering of child sacrifices (4 f., cf. 2 Kings 16.3; 21.6). 'Topheth' (6,11,13, cf. Isa. 30.33) derives from a word meaning 'fire-place'. The name 'Potsherd Gate' (2, RSV), probably to be identified with the Dung Gate (Neh. 2.13, etc.), may indicate that the valley was being used as a rubbish-tip (cf. 2 Kings 23.10). As well as references to the Canaanite fertility cults (4 f.) there are allusions to the astral worship emanating from Mesopotamia (13). Following the main prophecy in the valley itself (1–13) there was a postscript in the precincts of the Temple (14 f.). A 'potter's earthen flask' (1) was very expensive, hinting at Judah's preciousness in the estimate of God.

Jeremiah 20   Songs at Midnight

Jeremiah's postscript in the Temple courts (19.14 f.) was cut short unceremoniously by the intervention of Pashhur, the officer responsible for law and order in the Temple (cf. Luke 22.52; Acts 4.1; 5.24). The beating involved forty lashes across the soles of his feet, and the stocks, which secured feet, hands and neck (cf. 29.26), would bend his body almost double. Such a cramped position, which was maintained all night, may have been the customary punishment inflicted upon false prophets (cf. 2 Chron. 16.7–10). Any man held up to such public ridicule and outrage would be wary about speaking out of turn after such treatment. But Jeremiah was not cowed by the superior rank, and ability to inflict even harsher punishment, of his persecutor (3–6).

The structure of vs. 7–18, in which a short hymn of praise (13) is sandwiched between two sections of acute depression, has led many to assume that vs. 14–18 should stand *before* vs. 7–12. Certainly this makes good sense, and allows this, the last passage which reveals Jeremiah's private agony of heart before God, to end in praise and victory. It has often been observed that Jeremiah's

283

doubts were never expressed in public. Outwardly he was the firm, unyielding prophet of the Lord, conveying faithfully the divine will to his people. But when alone with God, the tensions of his position were revealed. We cannot but be grateful for this revelation, for we too may suffer misunderstanding, resentment, ostracism and persecution from those to whom we speak in the Lord's name.

Following the reconstruction suggested above, Jeremiah, after his day and night of discomfort and shame, felt that he had been an utter failure, and that it would have been better had he never been born (14–18, cf. 1 Kings 19.4). He accused God of involving him in such general resentment, for whenever he spoke it was about judgement—an unpopular theme to a complacent people (7 f.). But silence, the natural expedient in such a situation, was impossible, for he was so convinced that his message was of the Lord that it could not be contained (9), no matter how bitter the antagonism he encountered (10). A new serenity appears in vs. 11 f., silencing his indignant outburst, strengthening him against all opposition and enabling him to triumph over physical persecution. The powerful Lord, the discerner of the thoughts and intents of every heart (12), was with him and so victory was assured—hence the final psalm of praise (13). Compare Jeremiah's experience with that of Paul and Silas, which ended in a midnight prayer and praise session in a Philippian jail (Acts 16.25).

Jeremiah 21 A False Optimism

This chapter takes us forward, out of chronological sequence (see Introduction) into the last years of the reign of Zedekiah, when Jerusalem was besieged by the Babylonians (588–587 B.C.). Zedekiah was a weak, indecisive king, completely dominated by his nobles, who advocated a pro-Egyptian, anti-Babylonian policy. His authority was undermined by the fact that the Jews still regarded Jehoiachin, who had been taken captive in 597 B.C., as their rightful king, and looked forward to his speedy return from captivity to resume his reign (e.g. 28.4).

The king was really looking for a miracle to help him out of his predicament (2). God had worked wonders before, was there any chance that there might be a repeat performance? The truth was that neither Zedekiah, nor the nation, had any right to expect such an intervention. Jeremiah made it plain that the wrath of God was coming upon them for their social, moral and religious corruption (12, cf. 22.1–9). His forecast concerning Jerusalem's future was uncompromisingly pessimistic (3–7), for not only Nebuchadnezzar, but God Himself, was fighting against them. The only hope was to flee the doomed city before it fell and desert to the Babylonians (7–10). We can understand how Jeremiah's contemporaries would regard him as a traitor and a fifth-columnist (cf. **38.4**). But he was not pro-Babylonian, he was pro-Yahweh, and he saw clearly that Jerusalem's only recourse was to submit to God's righteous chastisement. This the favoured city would not do. Arrogantly secure in her own estimation, because of the great deliverance of 701 B.C., when Sennacherib's host was turned away (13, see note on **7.1–20**), she was unaware that her conduct made it impossible for the Lord to deliver her on this occasion (14). Samson 'did not know that the Lord had left him' (Judg. **16.20**); Jerusalem was equally unaware of this tragic fact (cf. Paul's deep concern in 1 Cor. **9.27**).

Notes: V. 1: Pashhur (cf. **38.1**), not the same as Pashhur the priest (**20.1**). V. 12: 'Execute justice in the morning'. This could be simply an allusion to time, since the cooler morning hours were usually the time when cases were heard. On the other hand, and better suited to the context, this could be a plea to Zedekiah to make justice his first, most pressing, concern.

Jeremiah 22   Even Kings are Subject to God's Judgement

This chapter contains a series of oracles, most of which directly concern the kings of Judah.

The first (1–8) is directed against the Davidic dynasty itself. We have already observed (see note on **18.5–11**) the conditional nature of the promises about the permanence of the royal line. Jeremiah was convinced, because of the sins of the ruling kings of his time, that the royal house was about to fall (5,30). The reference to the shedding of innocent blood (3) suggests that this prophecy was delivered in the reign of Jehoiakim (cf. 17; 2 Kings **24.4**).

The second (10 ff.) may be dated in the early months of Jehoiakim's reign (609–597 B.C.). Josiah, killed in a battle with the Egyptians at Megiddo in 609 B.C. (2 Kings **23.29**), was 'him who is dead'. His son, Shallum, whose throne name was Jehoahaz, was the popular choice as his successor, but he was deposed by the Egyptians and taken captive after a three-month reign (2 Kings **23.30–33**). Thus he was 'him who goes away'.

The third (13–19) concerns Jehoiakim, another son of Josiah, whom the Egyptians placed on the throne in place of his brother Shallum. Faced with a crippling tax imposed by the Egyptians, he extracted this from his subjects by heavy taxation (2 Kings **23.33** ff.) and then embarked on a lavish palace-building scheme, forcing his subjects to work for nothing. This Jeremiah vigorously condemned (13 ff.). The reference to Josiah (15 f.) shows Jeremiah's great respect for this godly, reforming king. The oracle concerning Jehoiakim's fate (18 f., cf. 36.29 ff.) is the most outspoken against any ruling king. Was it literally fulfilled? 2 Kings 24.6 gives no hint of this, but Jehoiakim's death occurred whilst Jerusalem was besieged by the Babylonians because of his rebellion. There is plausible support for the view that there was a palace revolt, when the king was assassinated and his body cast over the wall, indicating to the Babylonians that Jerusalem dissociated itself from his rebellious policy. Certain it is that Jerusalem escaped relatively lightly when it eventually surrendered.

The fourth (20–23) personifies Jerusalem at this time of distress (597 B.C.).

The fifth (24–30) deals with Coniah, the shortened form of Jehoiachin, the son of Jehoiakim, who submitted to the Babylonians after a three-month reign. He was taken into captivity (2 Kings 24.12–15), never to return, in spite of popular prophecy to the contrary (Jer. 28.4, cf. 52.31–34). Although his grandson, Zerubbabel, became the governor of post-exilic Jerusalem (Ezra 3.2,8; 4.2; 5.2), no descendant of Jehoiachin actually succeeded to the throne.

Jeremiah 23.1-15   False Shepherds

Prophetic guilds were a feature of other nations long before they were introduced into Israel. Their first mention in the Bible is in connection with Samuel, who appears as their leader (1 Sam. 10.5; 19.20). Later on, the great prophets Elijah and Elisha, in the northern kingdom of Israel, had strong links with them (2 Kings 2; 4.1,38–44; 6.1–7; 9.1). No doubt the members of these guilds, schooled under such godly leaders, acted as an extension of their ministry, broadcasting the true teaching concerning God and His moral and spiritual demands.

But with the passing of the years the prophetic guilds had degenerated. Possibly under the influence of surrounding nations, they had attached themselves to the royal court, and their prophecies became allied to political factors (e.g. 1 Kings 22.5 f.). By the time of Jeremiah they were no more than time-servers (cf. Mic. 3.5), giving the kind of messages they felt that the king and people wanted. Yet Jeremiah, initially, regarded them as sincere, and attributed the difference between his message and theirs to the deception of the Lord (4.10). Later on (14.13–16) he realized his enormous mistake and discovered the true nature of this false prophecy. In our portion today (and tomorrow) he launches a full-scale assault on the false prophets, who were misleading the people and who were thus partially responsible for the calamities which awaited Judah. In vs. 1–4 other classes, including the priests, princes and probably the king himself, are included, but from v. 9 the main attack falls upon the prophets. The prophets of Samaria (i.e. Israel, 13) were bad enough, but their counterparts in Judah had exceeded them in their immorality (9–15). Their lives were a complete travesty of the prophetic office.

Jeremiah obviously felt a deep sympathy for the ordinary people of the land. Like the Saviour, 'he had compassion for them, because they were harassed and helpless, like sheep without a shepherd' (Matt. 9.36). In faith he anticipated the day when the Lord would raise up true shepherds over His flock (3 f.). The return from Exile is clearly discernible in vs. 7 f., but vs. 5 f. go far beyond any application to a post-exilic leader. Zerubbabel was hailed in such language (e.g. Hag. 2.20–23; Zech. 3.8; 4.6–10; 6.12 f.), but the final fulfilment is in Christ, who is both the Good Shepherd (John 10.14) and the embodiment of the Messianic ideal (Isa. 9.6 f.; 11.1–9, etc.).

Jeremiah 23.16-40   Marks of a False Prophet

The prophet continues his scathing indictment of the popular cult-prophets. Added to the immorality of their lives (10–15) we may note the following characteristics:

1. A light view of sin (16 f., cf. 6.14). Instead of taking the people to task for their sin they proclaimed a glib message which condoned sin, thus giving a feeling of easy assurance (cf. 14).

2. Their message arose from a source no higher than their own hearts (16,26). They had never been face to face with the Lord, receiving His word in personal encounter (18,22), nor had they ever received His divine commission (21,32). They showed a complete lack of originality, mouthing platitudes borrowed from others (30), or deriving their prophecies from their dreams (25–27).

By implication, the true prophet was a man whose character matched his calling and his words. A man commissioned, he has spent time in secret with the Lord that he might discern His will. His ministry, which will treat sin seriously, is directed to the end of turning men away from their ungodliness. The words of such, reinforced by the power of the Spirit of God, will be like a burning fire or a hammer-blow (29). These qualities are as vital in the Christian era as they were in the O.T. world. False prophets still abound, but they are as unlike the true as straw is to wheat (28). The Septuagint correctly renders v. 23 as a statement, not a question,

'I am a God at hand . . .' The false prophets could not hide from His penetrating gaze (24).

The final section (33–40) contains a long and involved play on the word 'burden'. This was normally a synonym for the prophetic oracle (e.g. Nah. 1.1; Hab. 1.1) as a weighty, divine pronouncement. Jeremiah had much to say of a serious nature, so much so that this expression had come to be a term of mocking contempt on the lips of those who greeted him with, 'What's the *heavy word* from the Lord today?' The prophetic oracles, God declares, would cease, and the people themselves, now become burdensome to the Lord, would be flung away from Him. A man dare not mock God.

Questions for further study and discussion on Jeremiah chs 18—23

1. Is there such a thing as unfulfilled prophecy (see note on 18.1–17)?
2. What use does the Bible make of the analogy of the potter's craft? Take note of such passages as Rom. 9.19–24; 2 Tim. 2.20 f.
3. Why was official religion, in its various departments, so united in opposition to Jeremiah?
4. What factors made Jeremiah's ministry so distressing to him personally?
5. What may we learn from Jeremiah's exposure of false prophecy (23)?

Jeremiah 24   Good and Bad Fruit

The opening verse enables us to date this incident soon after 597 B.C., when Jehoiachin and the leading citizens, the 'cream of the land', were deported. An understanding of this helps in the solving of one of the minor problems of the book of *Jeremiah*, viz. the princes, in ch. 26, which may be dated c. 608 B.C., treat Jeremiah fairly, whereas in ch. 23, which dates c. 587 B.C., the princes appear most vindictive towards him. The answer is that they are a completely different set of men, those remaining in the land after the deportation of 597 B.C., being markedly inferior, as this chapter suggests.

It may be that those who had escaped deportation were priding themselves on this fact, and perhaps ascribing it to their superior virtue. If so, God's word through Jeremiah quickly demolished their pretensions. The vision of Jeremiah may be compared with that of Amos (8.1–3) but the significance in the latter depends on word play (see RSV margin), whereas here the symbolism is visual and obvious. First-ripe figs, available about the end of June, were a much-prized delicacy. But fruit deteriorates very rapidly in the hot summer of Palestine, unless it is dried properly. The clear statement is that the hope for the future lay with the group who had gone into captivity. History shows the truth of this insight. The captives, augmented by further deportations in 587 and 582 B.C. (52.29 f.), turned to the Lord in repentance, and under Ezekiel's leadership, a new kind of faith, loyal to the covenant-relationship with God, was forged. Those who remained in the land became largely semi-heathen and a source of trouble to those who returned with Zerubbabel in 538 B.C.

Note: V. 8: 'those who dwell in the land of Egypt'. This may refer to those deported together with Jehoahaz (2 Kings 23.31 ff.) but more likely, it refers to those who had fled to Egypt to escape the Babylonians.

A question: What factors made for the remarkable difference in quality between these two groups?

Jeremiah 25.1-14   A Rejected Testimony

From 628 B.C. (the 'thirteenth year of Josiah', 3, cf. 1.2) until 605/4 B.C. (the 'fourth year of Jehoiakim', 1) Jeremiah had kept hammering away at his fellow-countrymen. His message was a consistent one: forsake idolatry; repent of sin; worship the Lord in purity and keep His commandments from the heart. Otherwise judgement would surely fall. He was to continue this warning, exhortatory ministry for a further eighteen years. But the people, with seared consciences and hardened hearts, paid as little attention to him as they had to the prophets who preceded him (4). God's long-suffering, which allowed Judah ample time for repentance, was about to give way to direct chastisement. Just a few months before this prophecy Egypt and Babylonia had clashed at Carchemish, a major ford at the River Euphrates, with Babylonia emerging as a decisive victor. Shortly after this Nebuchadnezzar succeeded to the throne. Jeremiah now hails this new world-power as the means by which God would chastise His people (8–11), with Nebuchadnezzar, the mightiest man on earth, fulfilling the subordinate role of 'My servant' (cf. 27.6; 43.10). Historically, this prophecy was fulfilled when the Babylonians marched south and Judah passed under their control. According to Dan. 1.1–4 the temple treasures were seized and hostages were taken (the slight difference in date is caused by a different mode of reckoning).

Jeremiah set a limit of seventy years upon this period of Babylonian supremacy (11 f.; 29.10). If this be taken from the time of this prophecy (605 B.C.) then it was reasonably accurate, since the Babylonian yoke was broken in 539 B.C. Others suggest the period between 587 B.C., when the Temple was destroyed, to 515 B.C.,

289

when the second Temple was dedicated (Ezra 6.15 f.). The chronicler views these seventy years as sabbath years (2 Chron. 36.21), in lieu of a period of 490 years in which the Mosaic laws concerning sabbatical years had not been kept (Lev. 25.2–7; Deut. 15.1 ff.). Babylonia, however, was no pure agent of justice; she was a cruel, avaricious heathen-power, subject herself to the judgement of God (12, cf. Isa. 10.12–19).

Note: V. 10: 'the grinding of the millstones', a characteristic sound in the East, indicating the daily chore of replenishing the supply of meal. Every home, however poor, would have its lamp. Jeremiah graphically highlights the unnatural silence and the frightening darkness of a desolated Judah.

Jeremiah 25.15-38   God and the Nations

When God called Jeremiah He appointed him 'a prophet to the nations' (1.5). Some have objected to this title, believing that Jeremiah was simply God's messenger to his own nation, but such an objection seems quite unwarranted. Clearly, Jeremiah was principally concerned with Judah, but Judah was caught up in the vortex of international events. The prophet lived through the period when Assyrian power declined, a period of Egyptian occupation and a period of Babylonian supremacy, including three separate occupations of Jerusalem. During the latter period (605–587 B.C.) there were constant anti-Babylonian intrigues and alliances between the small nations. Jeremiah discerned the chastening hand of God in this complex pattern of events: Nebuchadnezzar was God's servant (25.9, etc.) and the minor kingdoms of Edom, Moab, Ammon, Tyre, Sidon and Judah were warned not to rebel against him (27.1–15). The limits set to Babylonian power, and the moral judgement upon her (25.12, etc.) strengthen the picture which Jeremiah presents of a Sovereign God of universal power. In the closing chapters of his book (46–51) are grouped his oracles against foreign nations, including one significant section (48.11 ff.) where God's treatment of Moab compares with His fatherly concern for Judah. Notice also Jeremiah's advice to the exiles in Babylon to pray for their oppressors (29.7). God was concerned for all nations.

The Septuagint places chs. 46–51 between vs. 13 and 15 of our chapter, omitting v. 14, but this interrupts a continuity of theme between the two halves of the chapter. The first half notes a judgement on the nations at the hand of Babylon, followed by the judgement of Babylon herself (9–12), a pattern repeated in the second half where Babylon (26, Sheshach, AV [KJV] is a Hebrew cipher for Babylon) is the last to drink the cup of the Lord's wrath. The imagery must not be pressed, and any suggestion that Jeremiah actually went to these nations and cities, or forced their representatives to drink, is unnecessary. Apart from this, the chapter is self-explanatory. It is never pleasant to read of destruction, but this is the corollary of the Lord's righteousness. It must also be remembered that it was anticipatory, and thus allowed the nations concerned time to repent. God is never arbitrary in His judgements nor hasty in His decisions.

Jeremiah 26   Courage—in Full Supply

Since 7.1–20 deals with the same events as this chapter, it would be helpful to reread it and the corresponding note. Here the emphasis is upon the *sequel* to Jeremiah's Temple Sermon, with only a brief summary of the message itself (2–6). The religious leaders, including both priests and prophets, were foremost in the opposition to Jeremiah's outspoken criticism, with the people, easily aroused, following their lead (cf. Matt. 27.20, and note the hypocrisy of the priestly accusation in Luke 23.5). The princes, on the contrary, gave Jeremiah a fair hearing (10–19), and it is significant to note the sobering effect this had upon the populace, who no longer sided with the religious leaders (16). But no prejudice is as blind as that which springs from religion. Note the admirable courage and quiet dignity of Jeremiah (12–15). There was no modification of his message to create a less-prejudicial atmosphere, for he was convinced of the divine source of his message (cf. Luke 12.11 f.).

Support for a verdict of 'not guilty' was drawn from the precedent of Micah (18) over a century before. From the legal point of view, such a use of precedent in reaching a decision is of great interest. From the point of view of Scripture it shows how the words of the great prophets were treasured, and so remembered that they could be readily quoted. From the historical point of view the importance of this incident is equally as great. The prophecy concerned, which comes from Mic. 3.12, is shown to have had a decisive effect upon King Hezekiah, possibly even being the starting point of his reform (2 Kings 18.3–6). Not all the prophetic oracles fell upon deaf ears!

The case of Uriah (20–23) illustrates the danger in which Jeremiah lived throughout the reign of the vindictive Jehoiakim (cf. 36.26). It also underlines the courage of Jeremiah, who did *not* run away. How many more prophets were frightened into silence we do not know. Apparently there were rights of extradition between Egypt and Judah at this time (22 f.). The final verse (24) shows that Jeremiah was still in danger even after his acquittal.

His protector, Ahikam, who had been associated with Josiah in his reform (2 Kings 22.12), was the father of Gedaliah, the governor appointed by the Babylonians after the fall of Jerusalem (40.5). Jeremiah was not absolutely friendless (cf. 38.7–13).

Jeremiah 27 Submit to the Yoke

The message to foreign ambassadors (1–11). The first verse should read Zedekiah (as RV margin, RSV), not Jehoiakim (AV [KJV]), as the remainder of the chapter makes clear (e.g. 3,12,20). The date, 594/3 B.C., is indicated more precisely in 28.1. It is clear that the envoys of the nations had assembled in Jerusalem to hatch a scheme for rebellion against Babylon. In 51.59 we discover that Zedekiah was summoned to Babylon in this same year, probably to give an account of his part in this plot which came to nothing. Jeremiah saw that the Babylonian supremacy was allowed by a Sovereign God (5–7) and that failure to submit to this yoke was unutterable folly—man can resist man but man cannot fight against the will of God (8–11). We see also something of the divine concern for other nations. So sure was Jeremiah of the truth of his God-given message that he was prepared to set himself against the complete array of prophets, diviners, dreamers, soothsayers and sorcerers (9 f.). Only a man who is sure of God can do this.

The message to the king (12–15). What did Zedekiah think when Jeremiah appeared before him complete with 'thongs and yoke-bars' (2)?! Judging by the frequency with which he consulted this prophet he did not consider him merely an eccentric, but on the other hand he did not follow his advice, so intimidated was he by his advisers. Jeremiah gave the same solemn warning to the king; security lay in submission to the Babylonian yoke, not in hearkening to the false prophets, who sought to fan the flames of a misguided patriotism.

The message to the priests and people (16–22). Once more the realistic Jeremiah sought to quench the prevailing false optimism. Normally a conqueror would take the idols of the countries he defeated and place them in the sanctuary of his own god, but as Judah's faith was imageless the Temple vessels had been taken in lieu (2 Kings 24.13 suggests that some had been melted down). The remaining vessels had acquired a great significance in the light of this, and their return was a point of honour. How chilling Jeremiah's words must have seemed, when he foretold that the vessels which had been left by Nebuchadnezzar in the Temple would also join the Babylonian hoard (19–22)! But God was not indifferent to this situation and He would vindicate His honour

292

in His own time and way (22b). See Ezra 1.7–11 for the thrilling way in which God moved the heart of a heathen emperor to fulfil this prophecy.

A point to ponder. In a time of crisis, intercession, not false optimism, is called for (18).

Jeremiah 28 Confrontation

We do not know how long Jeremiah, with his 'visual aid' of a wooden yoke about his neck, had been walking the streets of Jerusalem. But the presence of the priests and all the people (1) suggests that this was a contrived occasion, designed to challenge Jeremiah's exhortations to bow to Babylonian supremacy, and, if possible, to discredit him. Hananiah, a time-serving prophet, was the one chosen to make the challenge. Notice how he could honour God with his lips in the standard introductory formula to his oracle (2). This was a crowd-pleasing statement typical of false prophecy, the kind of thing the people wanted, to bolster up their sagging morale. Hananiah gave it to them in full measure; not only would the Temple treasures be returned (cf. 27.16) but Jehoiachin and all the exiles would return from a shattered Babylonia (3 f.).

Jeremiah's 'Amen' represents the deepest longing of his heart. Humanly speaking, there was nothing he yearned for more than the prosperity of his people, but he knew that this could never be, and that events would demonstrate this (5–9). The appeal is to the directions of Deut. 18.20–22 (cf. Deut. 13.1–5, which teaches that any prophet who caused the people to apostasize, whether his oracles were fulfilled or not, was to be put to death).

The quiet dignity of Jeremiah's utterance goaded Hananiah into the use of physical violence; often the resort of those whose arguments are weak (10 f.). Jeremiah accepted this meekly, and offered no immediate retaliation (cf. 1 Pet. 2.23). The people probably thought Hananiah's action most expressive and voted him the victor. But the last word was not from Hananiah, nor even from a publicly humiliated Jeremiah, anxious to hit back, but from the Lord (12–16). A symbolic wooden yoke *could* be broken, but the Babylonian overlordship was certain. The inference is that the people, having rejected the wooden yoke of submission laid upon them for their sins, would find the indestructible iron yoke of servitude infinitely more uncomfortable. But Hananiah would not live to see the falsity of his predictions, for God views this kind of sin, which leads a whole nation astray, with peculiar abhorrence. Hananiah, in fact, survived only two months (17, cf. 1).

Jeremiah's first letter to the exiles in Babylonia was probably sent early in the reign of Zedekiah, c. 596 B.C. The fact that it was sent with Zedekiah's own envoys (3) suggests that it had his approval. Perhaps he wished to douse the anti-Babylonian sentiments that plainly were as apparent in Babylonia as in Jerusalem, since they were associated with the return and re-enthronement of his predecessor, Jehoiachin (e.g. **28**.4). The occasion may have been the annual payment of tribute. Jeremiah first gave good advice to the exiles (4–7), urging them to settle down and live a normal life. Most likely, in expectation of a brief sojourn in captivity, they were wary of acquiring houses, land, and even children, since these would be encumbrances in the event of a return journey to Jerusalem. Most remarkable is Jeremiah's exhortation to pray for their captors, and seek their well-being (7). False prophecy was also flourishing in Babylon, like a rank weed (8 f., 15,21 ff.). Its theme was the same, sanguine one as in the homeland, viz. a swift return. The abysmal moral depths of the men who proclaimed it paralleled those of the false prophets of Jerusalem (23, cf. **23**.10 f., 14). As in the case of Hananiah, God would make a signal example of His displeasure (21 f.).

Verses 16–19 seem to interrupt the sequence (cf. 15,20), and their anti-monarchical sentiments are unlikely in correspondence taken by the king's own envoys. Probably they are part of a second letter in which Jeremiah made clear the principles underlying the divine judgement, thus destroying any delusions which the captives may have cherished concerning Jerusalem's inviolability. Before there can be a true building-up there must be a clearing away of the shoddy erections of godless jerry-builders. Soon after this, in 592 B.C., God raised up a prophet in Exile, Ezekiel (Ezek. 1.2 f.), who heralded forth the same notes as Jeremiah.

There was a certain section in Babylon who objected to Jeremiah's 'interference' in their affairs. They regarded his letter as the ramblings of a maniac and attempted to engineer official reprisals against him (24–28). What a pity that, in their narrowness of outlook, they overlooked the beautiful promises in his letter (10–14)! Fortunately for Jeremiah, they chose the wrong man, Zephaniah, described in **52**.24 (cf. 2 Kings **25**.18) as 'the second priest' (i.e. deputy to the high priest, Seraiah), who twice acted as link-man between Zedekiah and Jeremiah (**21**.1; **37**.3). Instead of acting on Shemaiah's suggestion he allowed Jeremiah to read the letter. The prophet's third letter to Babylon, in which he exposed Shemaiah's hypocrisy, was addressed to all the exiles (31 f.), suggesting that Shemaiah may have been the spokesman for a considerable group.

Questions for further study and discussion on Jeremiah chs. 24—29

1. Consider the validity of the title 'a prophet to the nations' (cf. note on 25.15–38) as applied to Jeremiah.
2. Compare and contrast the trial of Jeremiah (26) with that of our Lord.
3. What were the reasons for the strong hold which false prophecy had on the Jews (chs. 27–29)?
4. What personal qualities, and other factors, helped to sustain Jeremiah during his difficult prophetic career? What may we learn from this?

Jeremiah 30 Beyond the Judgement

The book of v. 2 probably includes chs. 30–32, all of which deal with the future restoration of Israel and Judah (cf. 3). It is of crucial importance to realize *when* the prophecies were uttered and grouped in this permanent form to witness to future generations. The historical context is clearly indicated in 32.1 f. (cf. 33.1). Jerusalem was in the final stages of the eighteen-month siege which ended with its destruction by the Babylonians. The other cities of Judah had already fallen to the invaders, who had wrought a systematic devastation in retribution for the rebellion. In all probability, the temporary relief which came when the Egyptian army made its one gesture of intervention (37.4 f.) had ended in disillusionment and the realization that Jerusalem was completely on her own. The situation, humanly speaking, could not have been darker, but at this very point God commands Jeremiah to speak out concerning the future. Never is He taken by surprise; nor is He just one move ahead; rather, He sees the end from the beginning and all His dealings are purposeful. The bitter chastisement of the downfall of the nation, its capital, its Temple and its ruling house were all regulated by His love, matched perfectly by His righteousness (11, cf. Heb. 12.5–11; Rev. 3.19). So, in the darkest hour of Judah's national life, these prophecies pierced the gloom and threw a glorious light on the future beyond the immediate chastisement. The themes of punishment for sin and future blessing are often found in juxtaposition in the prophets, especially in *Isaiah* (e.g. Isa. 1.24–2.4).

Notice the absence of a narrow nationalism in Jeremiah, for the northern kingdom of Israel is included in his oracles of restoration (3 f., cf. Ezek. 37.15–23). Sin is shown to be the fundamental cause of the catastrophe (14b,15b), which could not be averted by her 'lovers' (14a); probably an allusion to abortive foreign alliances, principally with Egypt, by which Judah had sought security. There is a sixfold restoration: of health (17); of the exiles to the homeland (3,10); of Jerusalem (18b); of the Davidic line (9,21); of prosperity (18 ff.); of true worship and fellowship (22). Before this could be achieved, however, there must be the Lord's righteous judgement. Nebuchadnezzar's armies might be battering at the walls of Jerusalem, but the real Agent is graphically revealed in vs. 23 f.

Jeremiah 31.1-26   Beauty for Ashes

The assurances of mercy and consolation continue in this section, which contains two interesting connections with other great prophets. As Jeremiah surveys the past, there are unmistakable connections with Hosea. 'From afar' (or, 'of old', 3, AV [KJV]) probably relates to the revelation at Sinai, when God entered into a covenant with His people and gave them His law. Verses 3 and 20 echo the tender sentiments of Hos. 11.1–9; 14.4. Israel is viewed as a virgin (4), once more linked with her Lord in a relationship as fresh as on the day when He brought her out of Egypt (cf. 2.2 f.; Hos. 2.14–23). Both prophets insisted strongly on the need for repentance, and that not of a superficial kind, before there could be any reconciliation or restoration (18 f., cf. Hos. 14.1 ff.). The references to 'the mountains of Samaria' (5), 'the hill country of Ephraim' (6, cf. 9,18,20) and the centralizing of worship in Jerusalem (6,12) show that Jeremiah envisages the unity that existed before the disastrous rupture between North and South (1 Kings 12).

But as Jeremiah contemplated the future there are equally clear links with Isaiah. Rachel, the mother of Joseph and Benjamin, is pictured as weeping in despair over the exiled tribes (15). To her comes the comforting assurance that her children will be miraculously returned to her (16 f., cf. Isa. 49.14,18–26; 54.1–10). The prophecy of a joyous, triumphant return to Jerusalem, with a complete transformation of nature, and a new prosperity (7–9,11–14), is echoed in Isa. 35.5 ff.; 41.18 f.; 42.16; 43.19 ff., etc. Notice, too, the exhortation to the exiles to return (21 f.), another characteristic feature of Isaiah's prophecy (e.g. 48.20; 52.1 f.).

There are two problem verses which merit consideration. The reference in v. 22, where, in this new situation, 'a woman protects (Heb. 'compass', as in AV [KJV]) a man', is best interpreted as signifying the absolute security Israel will enjoy. The menfolk will be able to go about their work, for the risk of attack will be so minimal that security can safely be left to the 'weaker sex'!

The second (26) has been held to indicate that Jeremiah received these oracles in a dream. But since he seems unrelentingly opposed to this form of revelation (e.g. 23.25–28), it is best interpreted in the spirit of Psa. 126.1. Such a miracle was almost unbelievable, too good to be true! But it WAS to come true, thanks to the grace of God.

Jeremiah 31.27-40 The New Covenant

Two great concepts emerge from our portion today. The first (27–30) concerns individual responsibility. The Jews were absolving themselves of responsibility for their misfortunes by blaming them entirely on the sins of their fathers (cf. the proverb of v. 29). This led to an apathy which crippled a moral response in repentance and reformation. Jeremiah (cf. Ezek. 18) hit hard at this fallacy and insisted that the present generation was itself personally responsible (30). Hereditary and environmental factors cannot be overlooked, but nor must the place of the human will or, above all, the grace of God.

The second great conception concerns the New Covenant (31–34). As we observed in our comments upon Isa. 52.13–53.12, this is one of the most significant of all the tremendous insights which the O.T. provides. It is Jeremiah's ultimate word, not only to his own people but to the whole world. It sprang from all the disappointments of his own forty-year ministry. Religion, he had long foreseen, involved a personal knowledge of God (9.24; 24.7), but his own teaching of this truth to others (cf. 34) had resulted only in a frustrating fruitlessness. Wherein lay the weakness? God was still God, gracious and faithful, and the people had His righteous law and were bound to Him by covenant. There was no fault in God, (observe the tender reference to Him as 'their husband', 32, cf. Hos. 2.16), but there was a fundamental weakness in man, who lacked the inward dynamic to make faith effective. The New Covenant, Jeremiah realized, must be inward, not external and it must provide adequate power to fulfil all that was latent, but rarely realized, in the Old Covenant. In this new relationship sin would be dealt with so completely that even an all-knowing God would remember it no more (34b)! Jeremiah had observed not only his own failure to move the people but also the impotence of Josiah's massive reformation. His vision of the miracle which was necessary (cf. Ezek. 36.26 f.) was not to be fulfilled until the N.T. period. Our Lord accepted and sealed this New Covenant by the shedding of His own blood (Matt. 26.28) and His followers worked out the details of His ministry against the background of Jeremiah's prophecy (Heb. 8.7–13). We live in an age when the promises of

God, so certain of fulfilment (35–40), have been realized in Christ. Then let us enjoy, and live by, our privileges!

Jeremiah 32.1-15 A Personal Venture of Faith

The siege of Jerusalem was well advanced by this time and future prospects were bleak (see note on ch. 30). Jeremiah's imprisonment is attributed to the princes in 38.4–6, but as noted in 38.13, even after Ebed-melech's compassionate act the old prophet was still retained in custody. This was probably due to the king's express command, as noted in v. 3. No doubt the king shared the resentment of the princes at what was considered to be Jeremiah's subversive prophecies, especially as they involved him personally (3 ff., cf. 38.1–4).

At this point Hanamel came to Jeremiah. Why did he come with this particular request (8)? It has been suggested that Hanamel was short of money due to the siege and that this sale was an obvious solution to this need. But the land itself, at Anathoth, was utterly worthless, since it was already in the hands of the Babylonians, and Jerusalem's days were numbered. Only a fool would buy, or expect another to buy, in such circumstances! The decisive clue is our knowledge of the antagonism which Jeremiah endured from his own family (11.21 ff.). Doubtless they knew of his prophecies of a glorious future, and Hanamel's action was a challenge to match optimistic utterances with corresponding actions. Had Jeremiah refused, then he would have been discredited. It seemed foolish to buy land in such a situation, but the transaction was a visible expression of confidence in God, in the prophetic word, and in the future (15). So Jeremiah was able to discern God's hand in this (6 f., 8b), even though Hanamel's motives were suspect. The form of the transaction is interesting (cf. Lev. 25.25–28), particularly the storage of the deeds of purchase in earthenware jars to ensure their preservation, a feature vividly illustrated in the preservation of the Dead Sea scrolls in similar containers for over 2,000 years. This is the first mention of Baruch, who figures prominently from this point onwards in the book of *Jeremiah* (12 f.). He was the brother of Seraiah, a very important official (12, cf. 51.59).

A thought for today. Faith must always be expressed in actions.

Jeremiah 32.16-44 Faith Vindicated

Were Hanamel's eyebrows arched in incredulity at his kinsman's gullibility? Was there a ring of mocking laughter from the bystanders at this 'take-down' of an unpopular prophet? Did Jeremiah have a twinge of doubt after he had parted with his seventeen shekels of silver (9) for a field that was absolutely valueless in the circumstances? If he did, and he was but human, it is instructive to observe how he rolled the burden of responsibility upon the Lord (Psa. 55.22), and fortified his own faith in prayer. In his recollection that God was the great Creator, and that nothing was too hard for Him (17), he links with others who were confronted with impossible situations (e.g. 2 Chron. 20.6 f.; Isa. 37.16; Acts 4.24). Then he pleads the character of God, especially His faithfulness within the covenant-relationship with His people (18 f.). Next he remembers God's gracious deeds in the past, in particular His grand work of redemption in the deliverance from Egypt (20 ff.). This is followed by a frank confession of Israel's unworthiness and the rightness of God's judgements (23 f.). It is not difficult to see how these things relate to our own prayer-life and attitude to God. He is still sovereign and gracious and we are bound to Him in a covenant based upon the redemptive act of His Son, Jesus Christ. There is nothing too hard for Him!

God's answer to Jeremiah's prayer began at this very point (27). There is an amplification of the sin of Judah which had caused His displeasure, and an assertion of the inevitability of judgement (28–35). The accusation of v. 34 indicates that the cult symbols and worship of the gods of Canaan and Mesopotamia, expelled from the Temple in Josiah's reform (2 Kings 23.4,6), had been allowed to return in the two decades of apostasy which followed his death. The national religious life had been thoroughly corrupted. But God looked beyond the immediate judgement to the time when a righteous remnant would return from Exile to a new security in which everyday life would be resumed (37,41–44). Most wonderful of all, in terms which parallel those of the New Covenant (31.31–34), there would be a new unity between the people and their God, matched by a new righteousness in daily life (38 ff.).

Jeremiah 33   The Haven Beyond the Storm

This is the final chapter of promises. In the remainder of the book the prophet tells us of historical events concerning Jerusalem during the final siege and subsequently, and adds the oracles against other nations. Before we begin to consider the final overthrow of the rebellious city, it is as well to ponder carefully these promises which look beyond that desolation. The invitation in vs. 2 f. is akin to Malachi's 'put Me to the test' (Mal. 3.10). It links with the comforting assurance of the previous chapter (32.17,27). Notice the five great promises:

1. The restoration of the people and Jerusalem (4–9). The desolation about to descend is viewed as divine surgery which would ultimately bring health to a chronically ill society (6). Israel and Judah would return, and Jerusalem, from which He had hidden His face (5), would become so glorious that the nations would tremble (9).

2. The restoration of the land (10–13). V. 10 anticipates the tragic state of Jerusalem as though it were already accomplished. But then the normal round of life and worship would be resumed. There is an idyllic pastoral scene in vs. 11 ff., where the shepherds tend their flocks, or count them into the sheep-fold at night—a wonderful picture of security.

3. The restoration of the line of David, and

4. The restoration of the Levitical priesthood (14–22). In a limited sense these oracles had fulfilment in the return from Exile, in Zerubbabel and Shesh-bazzar, both of the royal house of David (Ezra 1.8 f.; 2.2, etc.). At the same time a special appeal was made for the Levites to return (Ezra 2.40 ff., cf. 8.15–20). In time, however, both Levitical and kingly offices disappeared, but the hopes of the prophet and the nation were realized in Christ, the Substance of every type in the O.T. He was great David's greater Son and our great High Priest!

5. The restoration of confidence (23–26). In answer to the lament of the people that they had been forsaken God replies that this is as unlikely as a change in the ordinances of day and night or the constitution of the universe itself. When God says, 'I will' (26b), He means it!

After Jeremiah's oracles concerning the city were proved to be true, the chastened remnant took up these prophecies of restoration and treasured them. A later generation rejoiced in their fulfilment (cf. v. 11 with Ezra 3.11).

Jeremiah 34 God is Not Mocked

Archaeology has provided us with a graphic commentary on v. 7. At Lachish, twenty-one ostraca (i.e. broken pieces of pottery used for writing lists, letters, etc.) have been discovered dating from the time of the Babylonian invasion. One of them (Ostracon iv) reads, '. . . we are watching for the signals of Lachish, according to all the indications which my lord hath given, for we cannot see Azekah.' This is usually taken as an allusion that Azekah had just fallen to the Babylonians, and that the smoke-signal or beacon, indicating that the city was still holding out, was no longer made. Only Jerusalem and Lachish were uncaptured, so the Babylonian

300

campaign was marginally further advanced than in our chapter. The key to the understanding of ch. 34 is v. 22. The Babylonians had temporarily lifted the siege (ch. 37 provides greater detail). Jeremiah's personal oracle to Zedekiah (2–5) was probably designed to quench any optimism that this respite may have raised, the doom of the city was certain, although Zedekiah's life would be spared.

The remainder of the chapter uncovers an acute moral situation. Possibly as a result of the kind of exhortation in 21.12, some attempt had been made at reform in the beleaguered city. The king himself had taken the lead and a solemn covenant had been ratified in the Lord's name in the Temple (8–15). The particular point at issue concerned Jewish slaves who were by law to be granted their freedom in the Year of Jubilee (Exod. 21.2–11; Lev. 25.39–46; Deut. 15. 12–18). It is impossible to imagine anything more binding than this form of covenant. But it had been broken (16), doubtless when the threat of Jerusalem's fall seemed to have been averted. A vow made in the hour of crisis had been hypocritically repudiated. It was a double-dealing expediency which dishonoured the Lord's name (16). The adoption of a religious attitude to get one out of a dilemma is repugnant to the Lord, and only judgement can fall upon such (17–22). The Bible teaches that vows made to the Lord are to be treated seriously (Deut. 23.21 ff.; Eccl. 5.2,4–6). 'Do not be deceived; God is not mocked . . .' (Gal. 6.7).

Questions for further study and discussion on Jeremiah chs. 30—34

1. List the promises which are found in chs. 30–33. To what extent were they fulfilled?
2. How were the provisions of the New Covenant (31.31–34) fulfilled in the N.T.?
3. What practical lessons may we learn from Jeremiah's prayer (32.16–25)?
4. What reasons for the inevitability of the fall of Jerusalem may be discerned in chs. 30–34? Have they an application to our modern situation?
5. Why does Scripture insist so strongly on the sanctity of vows? Are there any exceptions?

Jeremiah 35   Obedience and Disobedience

The Rechabites were an extremist sect originating with Jonadab, the son of Rechab, in Israel about 842 B.C. (2 Kings 10.15–23). At that time Baal-worship was very widespread, and the Rechabites were a Puritan protest-group against the excesses of the Canaanite civilization. They advocated a return to the nomadic way of life, exemplified by living in tents, which was characteristic of Israel in the pre-Canaanite period. Houses, agriculture and the cultivation of vineyards, which required sedentary occupation, were banned. Possibly the group transferred itself to the more conservative Judah either before or after the fall of Samaria in 721 B.C. Most likely they were a voluntary sect rather than the literal descendants of Jonadab, and 'our father' (8) is to be understood in this way. The present emergency (reference to a Babylonian invasion in Jehoiakim's reign, v. 11, suggests a date c. 598 B.C.) had driven them into the unusual environment of a city.

Jeremiah was commanded to offer them wine publicly, which they refused, whereupon their loyalty became the basis of an oracle. There is no suggestion that God was commending the *content* of their vows; such passages as Deut. 6.10 ff.; 7.12 f.; 8.7–10 make it quite clear that the land was His gift to Israel and that the nation was to settle down and enjoy it to the full. But such loyalty, even if it was to something occasioned by circumstances rather than directly required by God, was praiseworthy, especially when compared with Judah's disobedience to a revelation fully supported by God's divinely commissioned prophets (13–16). Judah's disloyalty merited punishment therefore (17), but the Rechabites would be rewarded (18 f.). 'To stand before' (19) is a technical expression which includes a sense of privilege in the very act of serving. It is used of prophets (e.g. 1 Kings 17.1), of priests (Num. 16.9; Deut. 10.8, etc.), and kings (1 Kings 10.8). The Christian, in his enjoyment of the divine presence and favour whilst he serves, realizes this privilege in its fullest measure.

Jeremiah 36.1-10 The Word of God

This is the only description we have of the actual way in which a prophetic book came into being. It is hardly necessary to point out that every single word contained in Scripture has come to us through human instrumentality. The pen would be made from a split reed, kept sharp by a pen-knife (cf. 23); the ink was probably made from soot mixed with a watery gum; the scroll could be of leather, vellum or papyrus, but again, the context is determinative. A scroll of papyrus was formed by pasting individual sheets together and this is clearly the kind of roll which Jehoiakim destroyed (23), besides, the burning of the other materials, leather or vellum, on an open fire would cause a most offensive smell! Jeremiah did not write the scroll himself, but employed a scribe, Baruch (4). But behind the men and the materials there was the inspiration of God Himself

302

(2,4,6). The essential feature of Scripture is that 'men moved by the Holy Spirit spoke from God' (2 Pet. 1.21).

It appears that Jeremiah was excommunicated from the Temple because of his outspoken comment in his Temple Sermon (5, cf. chs. 7,26). The word 'debarred' ('shut up', AV [KJV]) could indicate ritual defilement, but this was usually for a limited period and there seems to have been no immediate urgency to read the scroll (6). The extraordinary fast of v. 9 (cf. note on ch. 14) was probably in connection with a severe drought. Alternatively, it could have been concerned with the approach of the Babylonian army following its victory over the Egyptians at Carchemish the previous year, 605 B.C. ('the fourth year of Jehoiakim', 1, cf. 46.2). Possibly, there was a combination of reasons, but the contents of this chapter show that there was no genuine desire to meet with God. Supplication does not 'come before the Lord' (7) unless the heart is right.

The purpose of the whole Word of God is revealed in this chapter. The wrath of God against the sin of His people (7b) and the certainty of divine judgement (3a,29b) are shown. In spite of this, there comes the call to true repentance in the twice-repeated 'that every one may turn from his evil way' (3,7), and there is also the assurance of a merciful God when there is such repentance (3b). The truths that God is 'a devouring fire' (Deut. 4.24; Heb. 12.29) and yet One who 'delights in steadfast love' (Mic. 7.18) are held in perfect balance in the Scriptures.

Jeremiah 36.11-32   Jehoiakim Versus God's Word

Jeremiah's scroll was read three times. The first time, on a great public occasion, was probably from a room overlooking the Temple court, thus making an effective pulpit (10). There is no indication of any response. The second (11-19) was to the princes, whose response reflected creditably upon them. They were obviously concerned with the contents of the scroll, which foretold the divine judgement, and they knew enough of Jehoiakim to anticipate that his reactions would be violently unfavourable. Yet such was their sense of honour and obligation that they felt compelled to report the matter to him (16). There was an equal concern, in which their goodwill is apparent, towards Jeremiah and Baruch, and precautionary measures were taken for their safety (19). The wisdom of this is shown in v. 26. Three of these princes were courageous enough to protest against the king's burning of the scroll (25).

The third reading, before Jehoiakim himself, provoked a completely different response (20-26). The king seems deliberately to have repudiated the reformation of his father Josiah. His actions were not the result of a passing fit of anger but a calculated act of contempt for the prophet and his prophecies of judgement. This was the second time in Jeremiah's lifetime that a portion of God's Word had been read to a reigning king, but how different was Josiah's reaction (2 Kings 22.11–20)! Having destroyed the scroll, the vindictive Jehoiakim sought to silence those responsible for it, but in vain (26).

Here was a king who set himself in opposition to the Lord. But the words of God which he thought he had destroyed are preserved for us today (27 f., 32). Doubtless this scroll, which included Jeremiah's prophecies up to this date, formed the nucleus of our present book. Some scholars believe that ch. 25 (note the date in 25.1) was the final chapter in this original draft. This was not the last attack on the Word of God. Kings and governments have set themselves against it; sceptics and liberal scholars have sought to discredit or dismember it; but it remains indestructible. The man who acts as Jehoiakim did will be judged (29 ff., see note on 22.18 f.), but 'the word of the Lord abides for ever' (1 Pet. 1.25).

Jeremiah 37 False Hopes Dashed

The RSV makes it clear that it was Zedekiah, not Coniah or Jehoiakim, whom Nebuchadnezzar appointed as king (1). We have already noted (ch. 34) the shameful episode which followed the temporary lifting of the siege of Jerusalem narrated in vs. 1–15. Pharaoh Hophra had undoubtedly prompted Zedekiah to rebel against Babylon, and when, following the appearance of the Egyptian army, the Babylonians were forced to withdraw, it seemed a vindication of this policy. Zedekiah evidently thought that even Jeremiah might have to revise his forecast as a result of these encouraging events. Hence he sent to him a second time (3,7, cf. 21.1–7), Zephaniah again acting as one of the messengers. Jeremiah's message must have had the effect of a bucket of water on the fire of hope that had been kindled in the king's heart! Optimism was unwarranted, for the Babylonians would return; indeed, so certain was their victory that, even if their army were destroyed, the surviving wounded would still be sufficient to overcome Jerusalem (7–10).

It is obvious that many who heard Jeremiah followed his advice to desert to the Babylonians (38.2, cf. 38.19; 39.9; 52.15), which would hardly increase his popularity with the military authorities. It was natural, then, that Irijah should suspect Jeremiah himself of desertion (11–15), although a certain vindictiveness is also apparent. The prophet could now be maltreated with impunity since his prophecies, with the withdrawal of the Babylonians, seemed to be proven false. The purpose of Jeremiah's visit to Anathoth (12) is obscure, but possibly it was connected with the early stages of the transaction noted in 32.1–15.

After Jeremiah had languished for a considerable period (v. 19 indicates that the siege had been resumed) in a temporary prison in Jonathan's house (15) he was brought before the king, who enquired of him a third time (16–20). He may have imagined that Jeremiah, broken in spirit by brutal treatment, would be more likely to give a favourable oracle. But a prophet who had faithfully proclaimed the word of God, in the face of intense antagonism, for forty years, was not likely to crack under this kind of pressure. His message was as uncompromising as before (17). He also took the opportunity to point out that the false prophets had already been discredited (19), and to plead for better conditions for himself (20).

Jeremiah 38   Courage and Compassion

The chapter is remarkable for the courage shown by Ebed-melech, and the monumental indecision of Zedekiah the king. Hope of effective Egyptian intervention was now non-existent, for the Babylonians were again firmly entrenched about the city. There was hope for individuals if they deserted (2), and the city could escape complete devastation if it surrendered (17). No hope of reprieve remained for the pro-Egyptian princes who completely dominated Zedekiah, and they were prepared to fight to the last (cf. 39.6b). Jeremiah was cruelly accused of fifth-columnist activities and indifference to the welfare of the people (4). The weakness of the king is revealed in his compliance with the request of v. 4. The princes, stopping short of making a violent end to Jeremiah, threw him unceremoniously into a disused water-cistern, with the obvious intention of causing his death either by exposure or starvation. Anyone who spoke out for Jeremiah would face their anger.

No protest at this brutal treatment came from any prince, priest or prophet, or indeed any Jew. The lone voice raised was that of an Ethiopian palace slave, we cannot even be sure that Ebed-melech ('servant of the king') was his proper name. The fact that he risked his life by interceding for Jeremiah (cf. 39.17) prompted the king into taking the only vigorous action recorded of him, apart from his final flight (39.4). The 'three men' (10, RSV) would be sufficient to lift an emaciated prophet from the cistern, but the 'thirty men' of the AV (KJV) may be preferable, indicating a considerable bodyguard to discourage any intervention on the part of the princes.

It is instructive that Ebed-melech went about his work of deliverance in a thoughtful, compassionate way, knowing how the naked ropes would cut into the limbs of a half-starved Jeremiah (11–13). Would that all the 'servants of the King' in our generation went about their ministry in the same considerate manner! Note the sequel to this incident (39.15–18).

For the fourth time Zedekiah sought Jeremiah's counsel (14–28). One gains the impression that he wanted to follow the prophet's advice, but his own personal fears (19) and the intimidation of the princes seem to have paralysed his will. He was a king with a wish-bone instead of a back-bone. It is not enough to *know* the will of God, one must also *do* it (cf. Matt. 7.24–27; Jas. 1.22–25). Jeremiah's unpopular advice, if followed, would have saved Jerusalem from the fearful fate which overtook it.

Jeremiah 39 Nemesis

The city of Jerusalem has a long and blood-stained history, but possibly only the Roman destruction of A.D. 70 can have been more gruesome than this one in 587 B.C. The narrative, a condensaticn of ch. 52, tells its own grisly story of the capture of the city after an eighteen-month siege. According to 52.29 only 832 survivors of the stricken city were taken into captivity, although this figure may relate to men only, or be reduced because of the high mortality rate during the long trek to Babylonia. Zedekiah's attempt to escape was thwarted by the vigilance of the Babylonians (4 f.) and a peculiarly terrible fate befell him. His eyes were put out, but he lived on, with the slaughter of his sons remaining as the last image of his sight (6 f.). Special attention was given to the anti-Babylonian nobles (6b). Nergal-sharezer (or Neriglissar, 3), the son-in-law of Nebuchadnezzar, was to succeed to the throne in 560–556 B.C. The Rabsaris was the 'chief court official', the Rabmag was another high official whose precise function is unknown. Humanly speaking, it seemed the end of the road for Judah, for its land was devastated and occupied, its Temple and capital were destroyed, and its royal line was taken into captivity. But this catastrophe, caused by Judah's apostasy and intransigence, was strictly controlled by God, who purposed not the end but a new beginning.

The reputation of Jeremiah, known to the Babylonians through the deserters, may have convinced them that he was on their side. Certainly, after an initial period at Ramah, north of Jerusalem (40.1), they treated him favourably (11–14). Since Nebuchadnezzar was at Riblah (6) at the time it is likely that the case of Jeremiah was referred to him for special consideration.

The oracle concerning Ebed-melech, out of place chronologically, is included here to indicate its fulfilment. Probably it was originally between vs. 13 and 14 of ch. 38. Events were happening on an international scale, but the God who controls nations also cares for individuals, and Ebed-melech's courageous action (38.7–13) had not escaped His notice. Notice also that one man, besides Jeremiah, had his confidence in the right place (18b). Was he one of the despised prophet's few 'converts'?

Jeremiah 40   The Aftermath

One of the greatest things about Jeremiah was his continued love for his people. Few men have been so maligned, mistreated and misunderstood as was this lonely prophet during the forty years of his vigil. Now his prophecy of utter destruction had come to pass and he, personally, was vindicated. Not many could have relinquished the opportunity to press home the bitter truth with such words as, 'I told you so', or, 'You've made your bed, now you can lie on it'. But Jeremiah was not a vindictive man, nor did he feel the slightest elation at the downfall of his adversaries. They were his people, he loved them and he wept bitterly for them, as the book of *Lamentations* shows. In this he reminds us of Christ. After the Babylonian victory Jeremiah was one of the few completely free men left in the land (1–6). Given the opportunity of an honourable and comfortable retirement in Babylon, where he was regarded as a friend (4), he chose instead to remain with the poor despised remnant in Judah (6). His true greatness of character and largeness of heart are movingly revealed in this choice.

The Babylonian choice of Gedaliah, the son of an old friend and protector of Jeremiah (cf. 26.24), was a wise one. He immediately set about re-ordering the life of the community (7–12). Under his encouragement the leaders of the guerrilla forces and their followers settled down, and the refugees returned from the surrounding kingdoms (11 f.). A limited security and prosperity seemed assured (12). But then Gedaliah received warning of an assassination attempt (13–16). Ishmael (14) was probably prompted by jealousy, since he was a member of the royal line. He may also have represented a minority who objected to Gedaliah's policy of co-operation with Babylon. But Baalis, possibly playing on these motives, was using him as a tool for his own ends (14); a weak Judah would allow him to extend his own territory. Gedaliah, who appears as an honourable man, had the defect of being too trusting, which caused him to overlook sensible precautions which might have prevented the second tragic chapter which was about to come.

Questions for further study and discussion on Jeremiah chs. 35—40

1. What useful functions were served by such groups as the Rechabites and Nazirites? Have they any equivalent today?
2. In what ways is ch. 36 representative of the whole history of the Bible?
3. What does the Bible teach us about the perils of indecision? As well as the case of Zedekiah, consider also Josh. 24.15; 1 Kings 18.21; Luke 9.57–62; Acts 24.25, etc.
4. What lessons may we learn about our Christian service from the incident concerning Ebed-melech (38.7–13)?

Jeremiah 41   A Vicious Assassin

Jerusalem fell on the ninth day of the fourth month (39.2; 52.6) and just one month afterwards, on the tenth day of the fifth month (52.12), Nebuzaradan arrived to superintend operations. Since the events of ch. 40, especially v. 12, indicate a considerable lapse of time before Gedaliah's assassination, it is likely that the seventh month (41.1) does not relate to the same year. Another deportation in 582 B.C. (52.30) was almost certainly in reprisal for the death of Gedaliah and the Babylonian troops (41.3), so the events of our chapter may be dated 583/2 B.C. Ishmael was one of those men who are able to destroy but not to build up. Since the sharing of a meal was regarded as a covenant of brotherhood (cf. Psa. 41.9; John 13.18,26–30) the treachery of his act would be the more reprehensible (1b). It is subsequently made clear (10) that only the immediate entourage of Gedaliah was slain (3).

We considered yesterday the possible motives for Ishmael's action, but there can be no justification for the senseless murder of a group of pilgrims. Two points are of particular historical interest: First, the cities named (5), all from the old northern kingdom of Israel, suggest the effects of the reforms of Hezekiah and Josiah in this area (2 Kings 23.15–20; 2 Chron. 30.1–12). Secondly, it is obvious that the devastated Jerusalem still continued to act as the focal point of worship, although Mizpah was now the administrative centre. Ishmael showed himself to be hypocritical (6), brutal (7) and avaricious (8). Moreover, since the water supply is so precious in Palestine, the fouling of a cistern was a peculiarly irresponsible act of vandalism (7,9). No wonder that the people whom he carried away as hostages or prisoners were glad to be rescued from him (10–13)! Johanan, whose good advice had been disregarded by Gedaliah (40.13–16), was thoroughly competent to deal with a situation involving military skill, but his only thought

308

subsequently was to escape to Egypt from what he imagined to be the inevitable Babylonian reprisals (17 f.). In this policy he was to clash with Jeremiah.

Jeremiah 42   Thy Will, Not Mine!

We do not know what Jeremiah was doing at the time of Gedaliah's murder, or whether he and Baruch were amongst those taken captive by Ishmael. But in this crisis, with the threat of savage Babylonian revenge hanging over them, the whole populace (1) came to secure an oracle from him; something which had never happened in the forty years before Jerusalem fell. Did their reference to 'the Lord *your* God' (2) indicate that they no longer felt in living touch with God themselves? If so, then Jeremiah's use of 'the Lord your God' (4) in his reply may have encouraged *them* to use the more personal form in v. 6.

Were they sincere in their request or had they already made up their minds? A firm intention to seek refuge in Egypt is certainly evident in 41.17 f., and Jeremiah's words (14) are probably quoted from the apparently excellent reasons generally advanced in support of such a policy. Probably they were sincere, but they were absolutely sure in their own minds concerning the right course, and they could not imagine that the prophet's advice would so flatly contradict the conclusions of their own sound reasoning. What they were really looking for was confirmation of a pre-determined course. It is as easy today to deceive ourselves in prayer, to seek a rubber-stamp from the Lord for the policies we devise, saying, if not in so many words, 'Lord, show me Your will, but make it *this* way!'

The ten days which Jeremiah took before he felt able to pronounce the divine oracle (7) must have seemed interminable to the Jews, living as they were in such apparent danger. Surely time was the essence of the contract! But Jeremiah refused to be hustled, for he was anxious not to confuse the will of the Lord with what either he or the people wanted to do. Taking time to ascertain the Lord's will is not wasting time. The reply, when it came, was not welcome, for it advocated remaining in the land and put strong sanctions against flight to Egypt. The people heard Jeremiah out (43.1) but before he had finished he was made aware of their hostility, and he knew that he, as a prophet, was being rejected once more (20 ff.).

Jeremiah 43   Men of Little Faith

Fear can blind the mind and distort the judgement. It was fear of the Babylonians which caused Azariah, Johanan and company to see only one course of action, namely, to seek sanctuary in Egypt. Jeremiah's advice was so unacceptable to them that they refused to recognize its divine origin and instead accused him of lying to them. This bare statement was modified by the assertion that he was unduly influenced by Baruch, who had been his close companion for at least twenty years (32.9–16; 36.4–8,26–32; 45). Just what Baruch stood to gain by exerting such influence is not clear. To have remained and faced Babylonian anger called for an unusual degree of reliance upon the power of the Lord to preserve them, and they were incapable of such trust. It could have been argued that they stood a good chance of placating their overlords, since they themselves had dealt so speedily and convincingly with the assassins of Gedaliah (41.11–16). And, moreover, the Lord was trustworthy. But the arm of flesh (Egypt) seemed a greater guarantee of safety than the arm of the Lord. So a large company came to Tahpanhes, in the eastern part of the delta, just inside the Egyptian border (7). Presumably Jeremiah and Baruch, who had advocated remaining in Judah, were taken there against their will (6).

Once more Jeremiah found himself in opposition to contemporary thought, and once more he displayed conspicuous courage in his forthright opposition. The significance of v. 9 is obscured by considerable divergences in the principal texts, but the structure erected by Jeremiah was probably a kind of pedestal or platform upon which the throne of Nebuchadnezzar could be placed (10). The inference of the oracle (10–13) is that the Jews in Egypt would not be safe from the Babylonians, but we have little historical data concerning its actual fulfilment. Nebuchadnezzar did invade Egypt in 568 B.C., when Amasis was Pharaoh. No record is preserved of the extent of his success, but Egypt remained independent throughout the Babylonian period. One thing is sure, the future of Judaism did not lie with the Jewish community in Egypt, which had rejected the Lord a second time.

Jeremiah 44 Which Assessment is Right?

Here we have the last recorded oracles of Jeremiah. The place names mentioned in v. 1 indicate a wide dispersement of the Jews in Egypt: Migdol was on the north-eastern frontier; Memphis (Noph, AV [KJV]) was a few miles south of modern Cairo; 'the land of Pathros' refers to Upper Egypt. This dispersion must have taken some years and a date c. 580 B.C. is not improbable. Jeremiah, by this time, must have been in his mid-sixties; he had been a prophet for about forty-seven years (see note on 1.1–8), during which period he had faced unrelenting opposition and endured severe hardship. He had seen his nation decline from a relatively strong independent state to the point of near extinction, and little fruit seemed to have been borne by his ministry. Yet, in these final words, his utter faith in an omnipotent God, and his perception of fundamental truths, are as clear as ever. The first fourteen verses are a repetition, on a smaller scale, of his condemnation of Jerusalem. The sin of the nation, its rejection of God and His prophets was reproduced in Egypt, so the calamity which befell Judah would have its parallel amongst the Jewish refugees there. Only a handful would survive to tell the tale (14,28).

Jeremiah's assessment of the situation was flatly contradicted by his hearers, many of whom had lived through the same events. They blamed their misfortune on Josiah's reformation, which had eliminated the worship of Ishtar, the queen of heaven (15–19, cf. note on 7. 1–20)! Since that day, they complained, nothing had gone right. Jeremiah countered this by pointing out that it was this idolatrous attitude which had precipitated God's desolating judgement (20–23), and that the same pattern would be reproduced in Egypt (24–28). No doubt the Jews remained unconvinced, but history underlines the fact that Jeremiah's appraisal of the fate of his people was correct. The future of Judaism lay with the small group of exiles in Babylon who accepted the national catastrophe as God's judgement, and who sought a new future in conformity with His requirements.

Pharaoh Hophra of Egypt was displaced as sole ruler by one of his officials, Amasis. For a period the two men ruled together, but eventually, as friction between them mounted, Amasis had Hophra put to death and became undisputed king in 569 B.C. It is unlikely that Jeremiah survived to this time, but the fulfilment of his words concerning Hophra (29 f.) would sound the death-knell of any hopes still cherished by the Jews in Egypt.

Jeremiah 45 Sorry for Yourself?

The table in the Introduction will help to solve the chronological difficulties in the book of Jeremiah. This chapter takes us back to 605 B.C. and connects with the events of ch. 36. It will be remembered that Jeremiah and Baruch were in great danger due to the vicious antagonism of King Jehoiakim. Baruch obviously did not take kindly to the universal opposition, spearheaded by the king himself, which seemed to be his lot as Jeremiah's scribe and companion. Notice the self-centredness of his attitude indicated by the five personal pronouns in v. 3 (cf. the same number in the Pharisee's self-congratulatory prayer, Luke 18.11 f.). Baruch was positively wallowing in self-pity! We have noted frequently (e.g. 15.15–21) that Jeremiah was faced with the same problem. Baruch, like his master, doubtless loved his people and found the role of being in unyielding opposition to the popular opinions and standards an extremely distasteful one. Jeremiah had a sharp lesson to learn (15.19) and so had Baruch, if he were to continue in the Lord's service.

The first lesson was that the heartache of Baruch was nothing when compared with the spiritual agony in the heart of God Himself (cf. Hos. 11.1–9). His judgement upon the nation involved the shattering of that which had been built and planted, laboriously and lovingly, over centuries (4). Such demolition, inevitable because of Judah's sin, was none the less painful to Him; indeed, Baruch's suffering was infinitesimal in comparison.

The second lesson was that if Baruch were to be a true servant of the Lord, then self must be resolutely thrust into the background (5). Did he perhaps wish that he and Jeremiah could join the ranks of the professional prophets, whose crowd-pleasing oracles ensured for them the popular acclaim? To do this would mean the forfeiting of any right to represent God. He requires the surrender of self, so that His will becomes our delight (cf. Psa. 40.8). Christ Himself is the supreme example of such selflessness. For Baruch the way ahead would be rough. Like Jeremiah he would be misrepresented (e.g. 43.3), persecuted (36.26) and eventually taken into Egypt against his will (43.6). Are we prepared to share likewise, in some small measure, in the suffering and rejection of our Master (cf. Luke 9.23–25; Phil. 3.10; 1 Pet. 2.19–23)?

Jeremiah 46.1-26   Against Egypt

Jeremiah was contemporary with four of the kings of Egypt, Psammetichus I (663–609 B.C.), Neco II (609–593 B.C.), Psammetichus II (593–588 B.C.) and Hophra (588–569 B.C.), all of whom belonged to the XXVI Dynasty. When Assyrian power declined, about the time of Jeremiah's call, Egypt was encouraged to contemplate a revival of her power over the neighbouring small kingdoms, including Judah. It was to combat these plans that Josiah led his people against the Egyptians at Megiddo in 609 B.C., a battle in which he lost his life (2 Kings 23.29 f.). Thereafter, for four years, Judah passed under direct Egyptian control. But the rising world-power was Babylonia, not Egypt, which was frequently torn by internal dissensions, and lacked sufficient power to maintain an empire. The battle at Carchemish (2) in 605 B.C. was decisive in

312

transferring the balance of power to Babylonia. Jeremiah ironically depicts the well-equipped (3 f.) and boastful, highly-skilled (7–9) forces of Egypt and contrasts this with the sequel of an overwhelming defeat and a shameful flight (5 f., 10 ff.). This episode, historically, was typical of Egypt, who promised so much and realized so little. So often she encouraged the smaller nations to rebel against their overlord, whether it was Assyria, or later on Babylonia, promising them help which was rarely forthcoming and never adequate. Instead of a staff which her allies could lean upon she proved to be no more than a broken reed (2 Kings 18.21; Ezek. 29.6 f.). Israel's prophets were discerning enough to observe this, and with their own assurance that the Lord Himself was able to preserve His own people, they roundly condemned alliances with Egypt (e.g. Hos. 7.11; 12.1; Isa. 30.1–5; 31.1 ff.).

The connection of vs. 13–26, which foretell an invasion of Egypt by Nebuchadnezzar, is uncertain. If it is to be connected with the earlier part of the chapter, then it prophesies that the Babylonians would follow up their victory at Carchemish by occupying Egypt. The degree of penetration is indicated by the reference to Amon of Thebes (25), which was about 330 miles upstream from modern Cairo. But no such occupation took place at this time. Alternatively, the prophecy could be linked with the events of ch. 43, which we have dated about 582 B.C., in which case the reference would be to the Babylonian attack on Egypt in 568 B.C. One thing is clear, Jeremiah envisaged the decline of Egypt as an international power, and this was certainly fulfilled.

Jeremiah 46.27—47.7   The Sword of Judgement

The first brief oracle (46.27 f.) is identical with 30.10 f. It was probably included again at this point to contrast the future salvation of Israel with the impending overthrow of Egypt (46.1–26).

Chapter 47 depicts the overthrow of Philistia, but two distinct phases are discernible. In v. 1 the reference is to Pharaoh Neco's campaign of 609 B.C., which had a twofold purpose: to prop up a tottering Assyria against a powerful Babylonia, thus maintaining the balance of power; to extend his own empire in a time of international chaos. This movement threatened the sovereignty of the small states like Judah and Philistia, and we observed yesterday that Josiah died in attempting to impede Neco's advance. The Greek historian Herodotus records a tradition that after the battle at Megiddo, Neco overthrew Kadytis, which is usually identified with the Philistine city of Gaza.

The reference to 'waters are rising out of the north' (2) shows

313

that the remainder of the chapter is concerned with the Babylonian invasion, the inference being that the Egyptian campaign would shrink into insignificance in comparison. Tyre and Sidon (4) were Phoenician, not Philistine, cities, but they were probably in a desperate alliance with the Philistines against the overwhelming might of Babylonia. Compare Jeremiah's description of the Babylonian flood (2) with Isaiah's prophecy of the Assyrian torrent (Isa. 8.7 f.). The shaving of the hair of the head and self-mutilation (5, cf. 48.37) were signs of mourning which were forbidden in Israel (Deut. 14.1). The fate of the 'remnant of the Anakim' (5, RSV) is of peculiar interest, since this aboriginal race of giant-like people was exterminated in Israel and survived only in a few Philistine cities, as noted in Josh. 11.21 f. (cf. Num. 13.22,28,32 f.). Jeremiah's anguished protest of 'How long . . .?' (6), which reflects his humanitarian outlook, is answered in v. 7. Judgement is never a pleasant thing, either to experience or to witness. But neither is the sin which causes the sword of judgement to fall. We may rest assured that God's judgement is in perfect equity.

Questions for further study and discussion on Jeremiah chs. 41—47

1. Why did the Jews reject Jeremiah's advice and go down to Egypt? What was their fundamental error?
2. Consider the danger of making up our own minds about what we are going to do *before* we have sought God's guidance.
3. Notice the two assessments of the situation in ch. 44. Is there any sure way in which we can distinguish between two divergent alternatives?
4. What practical lessons may we learn from the oracle to Baruch (ch. 45)?
5. Now that we have completed the section dealing with Jeremiah himself, make a list of his admirable qualities, and his weaknesses. What can we learn from him?

Jeremiah 48   Against Moab

Moab, which was related ethnically to Israel (cf. Gen. 19.37), settled in the area south-east of the Dead Sea shortly before Israel's conquest of Canaan. The alternation between friendship and enmity which existed from the earliest times is illustrated in Jeremiah's own lifetime: bands of Moabites, attacking under Babylonian orders, ravaged Judah soon after 602 B.C. (2 Kings 24.2) but by 594 B.C. Moab was implicated with Judah in an anti-Babylonian alliance (27.3). Geographically, Moab was more isolated than Israel and Judah, which were on the main trade-routes and were also surrounded by other kingdoms. Moab's isolation enabled her to escape many of the international upheavals which weakened her neighbours (11), and she was often able to strengthen herself at their expense. Some of the large number of cities mentioned in this prophecy were originally in the tribal portion of Reuben.

Notice the three-fold trust of the Moabites in v. 7; in their fortresses, their riches, and their god Chemosh. To this must be added a confidence in their own fighting qualities (14). All this encouraged an arrogant pride which became characteristic of Moab (26,29 f., 42, cf. Isa. 16.6; Zeph. 2.8-11). The picture which this chapter conveys is the shattering of such complacent self-sufficiency in a massive invasion, with its brutal accompaniments: looting, slaughter, captivity, untold misery and bitter lamentation. Jeremiah, like Isaiah, shows a genuine sympathy with Moab's predicament (17,36, cf. Isa. 15.5; 16.9,11). V. 11 suggests that the Lord's dealings with her are moral and remedial, as with Judah, which will lead to future restoration (47). V. 10, described by A. S. Peake as 'This bloodthirsty verse' and regarded by him as an interpolation, is not to be interpreted literally, but as a hyperbolic statement of the completeness of the judgement about to fall. Such an event inevitably involves bloodshed, but the Lord takes no delight in the death of the most rebellious sinner (cf. 2 Pet. 3.9).

Jeremiah 49.1-22   Against Ammon and Edom

The prophecy against Ammon (1-6) is a reproduction in miniature of the one against Moab in the preceding chapter. Ammon, like Moab, was related to Israel (Gen. 19.38; Deut. 2.19), and settled between the Arnon and Jabbok rivers at about the same time. The encroachment on the territory of Gad (1) is probably to be connected with the campaign of Tiglath Pileser III in 733 B.C. (2 Kings 15.29), when there was a wholesale deportation of Israelites from this area. Ammon, like Moab, was involved in raids on Judah about 602 B.C. (2 Kings 24.2), and in the anti-Babylonian alliance less than a decade later (Jer. 27.3). Her national deity was Milcom (the RSV rendering, supported by the Septuagint and other versions, is preferable to the Malcam of the Hebrew text). Ammon's trust was in her riches and in the extremely fertile valleys which were the main feature of her territory (4). Jeremiah prophesied her destruction, which would enable Israel to regain its rightful territory (2), but with an eventual restoration (6).

No such hope of restoration attaches to the prophecy against Edom (7-22), another of the small kingdoms which, like Moab, was settled about fifty years before Israel's occupation of the

Promised Land. Edom, traditionally regarded as descended from Esau, had even closer links with Israel than Moab and Ammon (e.g. Deut. 23.7 f.) but her attitude during the Babylonian invasion of Judah, when she actively assisted the aggressor, was the cause of bitter reproach from subsequent Jewish prophets (e.g. Lam. 4.21 f.; Psa. 137.7; Ezek. 25.12 ff.; 35; Obad; Joel 3.19; Mal. 1.2 ff.). Notice the extremely close connection between vs. 14 ff. and Obad. 1–4 and between vs. 9,10a and Obad. 5 f. Probably Obadiah was quoting from Jeremiah, or both may have used a common original. Edom was renowned for her wisdom (7); her cruelty (16a); and the strength of her natural fortresses (10a,16). Sela, her capital, was one of the most impregnable cities of the ancient world. But nothing could shield Edom from the complete desolation about to descend, for she, above all the nations, merited judgement (12).

Jeremiah 49.23-39   Against Damascus, Kedar and Elam

The prophecy against Damascus (23–27), probably representative of all Syria, is surprising in this context. Syria had been the dominant power in the entire region during the ninth century, and Israel, in particular, had suffered at her hands (e.g. 2 Kings 10.32 f.; 13.3 f., 7,22), but crippling defeats by Assyria c. 805–803 B.C. had made her a second-rate power. All three of the towns mentioned in v. 23 fell to the boastful Sennacherib a century later (2 Kings 18.34; 19.13; Isa. 10.9). The main point of the prophecy is the fear engendered by the Babylonian advance (23 f.). Jeremiah borrowed v. 27 from Amos 1.4, whilst v. 26 is repeated in 50.30.

Jeremiah next turns his attention to the inhabitants of the desert (28–33) whose security lay in their power to strike quickly and then melt away into the inaccessible reaches of the desert. Such mobility enabled them to capitalize on the misfortunes of their sedentary neighbours during the international upheavals of the period. The Babylonians took firm steps to control these predatory tribes. Josephus makes a passing reference to a conquest of Arabia by Nebuchadnezzar (28,30), and a later Babylonian king, Nabonidus. Kedar (28) was the name of an Arabian tribe inhabiting the desert east of Palestine. The location of Hazor (28,30,33) is not known. It is probably a collective name for the tent-villages of the semi-nomadic Arabs.

Elam (34–39), a powerful kingdom more than 200 miles *east* of Babylonia, was the most distant nation referred to by Jeremiah. Some Elamites had been deported to Samaria by the Assyrians (Ezra 4.9 f.). The Elamites were renowned as warriors (Ezek. 32.24) and archers (35, cf. Isa. 22.6). Clearly, Judah was hoping that the

Babylonians would be diverted from their westward campaigns by a preoccupation with mighty Elam, their eastern neighbour. Jeremiah shattered this false hope; Elam would prove no lasting barrier to the rising power of Babylonia. The reference to a restoration (39) was fulfilled in that Elam, with her capital, Susa, later became the centre of the Persian Empire (Dan. 8.2; Neh. 1.1).

Jeremiah 50.1-20   Against Babylon

Chapters 50 and 51 are concerned with the overthrow of Babylon. The only direct clue as to the date is given in 51.59 f., the fourth year of Zedekiah, i.e. 594/3 B.C. Objections have been made to the dating of all these oracles at this particular time, but none of them is really valid. It is true that Jeremiah appears to refer to the destruction of the Temple (50.28; 51.11), which took place in 587 B.C., but in fact Jeremiah had been foretelling this since 608 B.C. (26.1,6). Similarly, there is a reference to the Exile in 50.4, 33 f., but again, Jeremiah had warned his people of this calamity, unless they repented, as early as 608 B.C. (7.15). Indeed, some of his countrymen had *already* been taken away in the deportation of 597 B.C. (24.1). It is equally unrealistic to assert that Jeremiah was pro-Babylonia, because of his prophecies of the certainty of their victory (e.g. 34.2), and that therefore these anti-Babylonian oracles must come after Jerusalem fell, when Jeremiah was disillusioned by Babylonian cruelty. Jeremiah was no more pro-Babylon than he was anti-Judah; he simply saw with stark clarity that Judah must be punished for her transgression and that Babylonia was the Lord's chosen instrument to effect this. A precedent for Jeremiah's oracles against Babylon is to be found in Isaiah, who envisaged both the Lord's use and overthrow of Assyria (Isa. 10.5–19). Jeremiah, in our passage, actually links these two events (17 f.). There is no reason, therefore, to deny these prophecies to him, or to give them a date after the events which they describe.

The concept of the Shepherd of Israel is prominent (6,19) but there is nothing weakly sentimental about this, there must be a genuine repentance (4 f.) and the elimination of sin (20) before the nation could be restored. Babylon's overthrow was to come through an enemy from the north (3,9), a probable allusion to Media (cf. 51.11,28). For Bel (2) see note on Isa. 46.1.

Jeremiah 50.21-46   A Strong Redeemer

The theme of Babylon's downfall continues in this section. There is a subtle word-play in v. 21. Merathaim, which means 'double rebellion' or 'double bitterness', is a modification of 'The Land of

317

the Bitter River', the name of a district in southern Babylonia. Pekod, meaning 'visitation', or 'punishment', derives from the name of an eastern Babylonian tribe, the *Puqudu*. These two names sum up the essence of Jeremiah's prophecy; Babylon had been guilty of rebellion against the Lord (24,29), therefore the Lord would punish her (27,31). The elements in this moral visitation include: the cruelty of Babylonia (29); her heartless attitude towards her captives (33), and her idolatry (38). Throughout the chapter the complete destruction of Babylon, resulting from a massive invasion, is envisaged. Those critical scholars who reject the possibility of such a foretelling of the future, and who would put these chapters after Babylon's fall in 539 B.C., face an insurmountable problem. If these words were written after the event, they would surely correspond more accurately with the events themselves. But while Babylonia did fall to the invincible power of the Medes and the Persians, so complete was its decline, moral and spiritual as well as political, that, following a pitched battle outside the city, Babylon itself fell almost without a struggle and was quietly taken over by its conquerors with a minimum of destruction. Such prophecies as vs. 39 f. were fulfilled much later. Vs. 44 ff. are almost identical, apart from the names, with 49.19–21.

God as the Redeemer of His people (33 f.) is a favourite concept of the second portion of *Isaiah*, where it occurs no fewer than fifteen times (e.g. Isa. 41.14; 43.14; 44.6, etc.). The redeemer-kinsman in Israel was responsible for redeeming alienated property (e.g. Ruth 4.1–6, cf. Lev. 25.25) or relatives (Lev. 25.47 ff.), and for the avenging of blood (e.g. Deut. 19.4–6). From this there followed the thought that the Lord, the Kinsman of His covenant-people, had effective power to act on their behalf and carry through His purposes. They could have confidence in Him.

Jeremiah 51.1-26   A Power Greater than Babylon

We continue our study of this extended oracle against Babylon, the great world-power of Jeremiah's age. Alternating with passages depicting the helplessness of her inhabitants and the certainty of her overthrow there are sections which reveal the Lord as He exercises His sovereign control of the nations. This included His own people, who seemed as significant in these international conflicts as a pawn in a game of chess. They were reminded that these events did not mean that the Lord had forsaken them (5a). The emendation of 'their land' (5b, AV [KJV]) to 'the land of the Chaldeans' (RSV) is unnecessary. Israel and Judah are in mind, apparently forsaken because of their sin. But the overthrow of

318

Babylon would coincide with the moment of their release and vindication (10). The imagery of the cup (7) recalls Jeremiah's parable of **25.**15–29, but in the latter it was a cup of judgement, whereas in the former it is the cup of evil example and influence (cf. the remarkable parallel in Rev. **17.**4). In the other oracles against the foreign nations we have noted the things in which they boasted; the strongholds and treasures of the Moabites (**48.**7); the fertile valleys and wealth of Ammon (**49.**4); the impregnability of Edom (**49.**16); the isolation of the nomadic tribes (**49.**31). Part of Babylon's security lay in the fact that it was surrounded by waterways, including the Euphrates, and an elaborate system of canals; hence such references as v. 13; 50.38. But these would prove ineffective (51.32).

Vs. 15–19 repeat, with minor modifications, the oracle of **10.**12–16. They paint a word-picture of a God who is sovereign in His might and magnificent in all His conceptions. Babylon, and every other world-power, would perish, but He knows no such fallibility.

To whom do vs. 20–23 refer? Since **50.**23 describes Babylon as 'the hammer of the whole earth' it seems best to refer this section to her also. But because of her sin, especially against the Lord's people (24), she would incur His implacable judgement (25 f.). Compare Isa. **10.**5–19; Ezek. **31.**1–14. 'For dominion belongs to the Lord, and He rules over the nations' (Psa. **22.**28).

Jeremiah 51.27-64   The End of Babylon

The destruction and desolation of Babylon dominates vs. 27–58. The nations are marshalled against her (27 f.), including the three groups noted (27), who had been brought by conquest into the Medo-Babylonian alliance. The death-throes of the land; the collapse of the soldiers' morale; and the frantic scurrying of messengers bearing the evil news, are graphically depicted (29–32). Babylon, described in v. 26 as a desolate waste, is now represented as in the final stages of harvest (33). The imagery varies in the remaining oracles in the section but the death-knell of Babylon sounds in them all. For instance, in vs. 38 ff., its inhabitants, likened to lions' whelps growling for their food, are to be given a meal, but not of the kind they desired. It will transform the savagery of lions into the docility of domesticated animals.

But within this major theme there persists the minor theme of the vindication of Judah and Jerusalem in this act of judgement upon the aggressor (34–37,49–57). Nebuchadnezzar, who initiated this period of Babylonian dominance over Judah, becomes its symbol (34), but when the Lord, the Champion of His people, steps into the arena of history then proud Babylon is vanquished (36 f., 54–58). The lament of v. 51 arises from the fact that the desecration of the Temple appeared to involve Yahweh's inferiority, but the desolation of Babylon would reveal the utter impotence of her idols (52, cf. 47).

The historical note which concludes the chapter (59–64) allows us to date all the prophecies against Babylon (cf. comment on 50.1–20). In the note on ch. 27 we suggested that this visit of Zedekiah was the aftermath of an abortive attempt at rebellion by an alliance of states, including Judah, to which Jeremiah was diametrically opposed. It is significant that at the very time when he was counselling submission to Babylon he could also foretell, in such uncompromising terms, her ultimate overthrow. But the timing, Jeremiah saw, as well as the means, was in God's control. Man must not seek to wrest the initiative from Him.

Jeremiah 52   A Chapter Closes

There are only slight variations between this chapter and 2 Kings 24.18–25.30. The account of Gedaliah's governorship and assassination, and the subsequent flight to Egypt, already dealt with in 40.5–43.7, are omitted (cf. 2 Kings 25.22–26). Far greater detail concerning the Temple treasures is given in Jer. 52.17–23 (cf. 2 Kings 25.13–17), perhaps to emphasize that, instead of the return of the vessels taken by Nebuchadnezzar in 597 B.C. (as predicted by the false prophets, e.g. 27.16; 28.3), they had lost those that remained (cf. 27.18–22). There is nothing in 2 Kings which corresponds with Jeremiah's list of the three deportations (28 ff.). Much of the historical detail given here is to be found in 39.1–10.

Three minor points call for comment. 1. The apparent contradiction between vs. 12 and 29 is readily explained; in the former the accession year of Nebuchadnezzar has been included, in the latter it has not. 2. The attention given to the priests—three orders are noted—in the official reprisals of v. 24 may suggest the prominent part they played in the anti-Babylonian revolt. 3. For the historical background of v. 30 see the note on ch. 41.

The inclusion of a section from the official records is certainly appropriate. In a precise, factual manner the end of a chapter in the national life of God's people is told. This was the result of their rejection of true religion, in spite of repeated warnings by true prophets like Jeremiah. The official history, contained in the books of *Samuel* and *Kings*, was formed from earlier sources by men of the next generation, who had suffered themselves as a result of the nation's disobedience. They had taken heed to the neglected prophets of earlier generations, as the editorial comment of v. 3 shows. It was too late to avert the national disaster, but in the Lord's mercy it was to prove the beginning of a new chapter in which a remnant, chastened in spirit, sought Him in contrition. Moreover, dark as the days seemed to be, there came the remembrance of other prophecies which looked beyond the judgement to a glorious future, so there was an undying hope in their hearts. The elevation of Jehoiachin in 561 B.C., noted in the appendix of vs. 31–34, might encourage a nationalistic hope, but the real future lay in such a spiritual community.

Jeremiah may have failed in his strenuous efforts to turn his people back to the Lord, but in his conception of true religion as a vital, inward relationship with a living God (e.g. 9.24) he was to set the necessary standard, not only for the immediate future, but for all time.

Questions for further study and discussion on Jeremiah chs. 48—52

1. Make a list of the things in which the heathen nations trusted. What real security do such things give?
2. What moral principles did Jeremiah discern in God's use of the Babylonians and His ultimate overthrow of them?
3. What may we learn from chs. 50,51 concerning the restoration of the Jews?
4. Does 52.31–34 indicate the continuation of the false nationalistic hopes revealed in 28.2 ff., 11, etc.? What are the weaknesses of such a position?

Lamentations

The ascription of this Book to Jeremiah is not found in the Hebrew manuscripts, but first occurs in the Greek Septuagint translation after 200 B.C. Probably the collection of poems comes from more than one author, and Jeremiah could have been one of them. The acrostic style of writing strikes the average westerner as artificial, but this would not apply to the contemporary oriental mind and, in any case, form is no deterrent to reality, as with some of George Herbert's poems. The acrostic style here means that each verse, or group of verses, begins with a fresh letter of the alphabet, and works in order through all twenty-two letters. Psa. 119 similarly has an acrostic with eight verses to each letter. The metre, with a longer line balanced by a shorter to complete the sense, is known as the *qinah* metre, and it is used for funeral laments.

A lament of this kind is difficult to divide into sections, but roughly we may note: (*i*) The description of Jerusalem's present state and how it came about (1–7). Her allies have turned against her (2), her festivals have ceased (4), and she has no leaders (6). A further description of how her enemies treated her (7) is found in Obad. 10–14.

(*ii*) The reason is ultimately the sins of the people (8–16). We note that Jerusalem's cry to God not only appeals to His pity (9,11,16), but confesses her sins (14), and admits that her sufferings have come through the anger of the Lord (12). It is common to find v. 12 applied to Christ's sufferings on the cross, and the verse is certainly true of these, when Christ took our sins upon Himself; but in the context the reference is to Jerusalem bearing her own sins.

(*iii*) Submission to God's hand (17–22). Again there is the confession which admits that God is in the right (18). This is often a hard admission to make. One can feel the agony of heart that is wrung out even while the people make confession. Thus the verses combine the cry to God with further descriptions of the tragic state of the city and its people. The last two verses are a tentative prayer that God will vindicate His righteousness among the other nations. If Judah has needed to experience judgement to lead her to repentance, then others need the experience of judgement also.

As we read these laments, we may be enjoying all the comforts of home, and these descriptions seem rather remote. But some of our fellow Christians are suffering as Jerusalem suffered. We ourselves may also suffer various kinds of deprivation. Such suffering is always a call to heart-searching, but not all suffering is due to personal sin (e.g. 1 Pet. 5.6–11).

Compare this chapter with the parable of the prodigal son (Luke 15.11–32).

Lamentations 2   The Lord's Doing

This lament is largely a vivid description of what the writer sees and has seen. There are phrases that suggest that Jeremiah might well have written this section before he was taken to Egypt. Note what is said about the false prophets (14, cf. Jer. 23.16,25), the law and the prophets, (9, cf. Jer. 18.18), and the phrase about terrors on every side (22), a favourite phrase of Jeremiah's (Jer. 6.25; 20.3,10; 49.29).

Moreover it would be like Jeremiah to declare repeatedly that it is the Lord who has brought all these tragedies upon Jerusalem (1–8), for he had frequently prophesied that the Lord would bring destruction on the city (e.g. Jer. 19.7–9). God has even destroyed that which, as it were, formed the base of His throne on earth, His footstool (1), which is either the ark with the mercy-seat upon it (1 Chron. 28.2), or the whole Temple (Ezek. 43.7; Pss. 99.5; 132.7). The author uses various pictures, including that of the booth of leaves and branches which sheltered the watchman when the fruit was ripening, and which was left to fall to pieces after the harvest (6, cf. Isa. 1.8).

Next comes a description of people (9–17). Leaders have gone (9), old and young are helpless (10), and infants are starving (11,12). If only the prophets had spoken clearly about sin, as Jeremiah had done (14). Now the enemy imagine that they have scored over God in destroying the city (15,16), but they were only instruments in God's hands (17, cf. Isa. 9.8–17).

The lament closes with a call to prayer (18–22). Nothing is said directly about repentance, but the whole tone of the chapter, which has admitted the hand of God, takes such repentance for granted. Surely the little children, on whom so much of the future depends, may look to God, when even their mothers cannot feed them (19), but actually murder them for food (20, cf. Jer. 19.9).

A horrible description; but there are times when we must understand what suffering is.

Lamentations 3.1-33 — Personal Tragedy

In this lament each letter of the alphabet occurs three times as the initial letter of a line, i.e. the Hebrew A is the first letter in vs. 1,2,3; B is the first letter in vs. 4,5,6, etc. The tone is personal, and the lament might easily be included among the *Psalms*, without a specific reference to the destruction of Jerusalem. Either the author speaks for himself, or he is the representative of the remains of the nation in their approach to God.

It is interesting to see that several often-quoted texts come in this chapter, especially in vs. 19–27, and 33. The language also reminds us of some of Job's words (e.g. Job 16.6–17; 30.16–23). There is also a superficial likeness to Job in that at first there is no confession of sin, although one assumes that the writer has passed through the experiences of chs. 1 and 2, which clearly confess that the sins of the people have brought the heavy hand of God upon them. Probably a number of years have passed, and the author looks now for the fulfilment of the promises of restoration and renewal that were also given by Jeremiah and Ezekiel (e.g. Jer. 33; Ezek. 36). He is clearly a godly man, concerned to live to the glory of God. He prays that he may experience the mercy and compassion that are found in God.

With vivid pictures he describes the tragedy of his present existence (1–18). Then he turns his eyes from self to God (19–33). We note the great covenant word which the RSV regularly translates as 'steadfast love' (22). The covenant is a powerful plea, as in the claiming of the Davidic covenant in Psa. 89, which in vs. 38–45 again reminds us of this lament. The covenant can never be presumed upon, but the author here truly casts himself on God as his only 'portion' ('allotted share', Moffatt), is prepared to wait for Him, and to work out lessons of disciplined patience that he has learned while he was young (24–30). He knows that God does not torment mankind for the joy of seeing them suffer (33).

We often need patience, cf. Heb. 10.35–38: Jas. 5.11.

Lamentations 3.34-66   Prayer in the Dark

We noticed that at first there was no confession of sins. Now the speaker remembers all the oppression of which the prophets had spoken (34–36), and declares that this is one reason why the Lord came down in judgement (38). *Good* and *evil* here mean God's hand in history in blessing and calamity (cf. Zeph. 1.12). There are other sins also, and we must examine ourselves in the sight of God, and not only examine, but repent and turn back to God (39–42). Sin has put a dark cloud between God and man, and now we seem to be praying still in the dark (43–45).

The writer becomes freshly aware of his enemies, who were glad to see Judah and its peoples, including the writer, brought low (46–51). Vs. 52–57 clearly speak of persecution, but it seems as though we have picture language rather than a literal description. One is reminded of Jeremiah in the dungeon pit, but vs. 53 and 54 were not literally true of his experience (Jer. 38.6–13). Similar picture language occurs in Psa. 40.1–3.

In vs. 58–66 the writer sees by faith that God is intervening to vindicate His servant, or servants. This leads him to take the position which Jeremiah took in several of his prayers, when he saw that his enemies were God's enemies, since he was being attacked because he was true to the message that God gave him (e.g. Jer. 11.18–20; 17.14–18). The author of this lament does not go as far as Jeremiah, since he was not being persecuted for his faith, but the enemy, in their treatment of Judah, were going far beyond what God would have had them do as His instruments (cf. Zech. 1.15). So, while he does not pray for their destruction, he asserts that God will hold them guilty for what they are doing while they hold the land in occupation (64–66).

Peoples without God's revelation through His written Word are responsible to Him for acts of atrocity that shock the human conscience (cf. Amos 1).

Lamentations 4

In this lament an eye-witness has given one of the most vivid pictures that we have of a conquered city. He presents themes that we have already seen, especially in ch. 2, but in an even more moving way. There is no reason why Jeremiah should not be the author, although in v. 20 he seems to commend king Zedekiah instead of condemning him as he did in his prophecies. But in v. 20 he describes the king as the people hopefully saw him at his coronation.

Try to soak in the pictures of Zion, comparing them with ruined or bombed buildings that you know, and visualizing the state of the people in the light of horror pictures of suffering peoples today. Read of the debris blocking the streets (1); of people as they were before the disaster and as they are now (2,5,8); of mothers unable to feed their starving children (3,4); of the horrors of cannibalism, when suffering has killed the finer feelings (10); of good-looking men whose faces are pinched and unrecognizable (7,8), and who are thankful to find a home in a rubbish dump (5); of crops pillaged by the invaders (9).

Sometimes we can see no reason at all for a nation's sufferings, but the people of this nation know that their wrongdoing had brought a seemingly impregnable city to the ground (11,12). The religious leaders had backed the cruelties that meant persecution, conviction, and death for the innocent, who had land or property that could be seized (13, e.g. Isa. 1.15; Jer. 2.34). But when Jerusalem was captured, those prophets and priests that escaped were so battered and wounded that no nation would receive them, recognizing them as being far from holy men (14,15), which indeed is how God Himself regarded them (16).

Now we are taken back to memories of the fall of the city. There was a vain and persistent hope that the Egyptians would come to the rescue (17; Jer. 37.5–10; Ezek. 29.6,7). The tall Babylonian siege towers made it dangerous for anyone to walk in the streets within range of arrows or stones (18). Then came the fall of the city, and the break-out (19; Jer. 39.4,5), with the capture of Zedekiah as he tried to cross the Jordan to safety (20). There is little doubt that the Edomites, who knew the routes and crossings, helped the Babylonians here, and this is why vs. 21,22 turn against Edom. Obad. 14 clearly shows what they did. So, when Zion is restored, Edom will still be kept low, and Mal. 1.2–5 records that this was fulfilled. Ultimately Edom was subdued and absorbed into Israel (see notes on Ezek. 35).

Pray for those who are being driven to believe that they were better dead (9).

Lamentations 5

Although this lament has twenty-two verses, it is not an acrostic. It is, however, an equally vivid eye-witness picture to what we had in ch. 4. So again we have scope to let the picture sink in, and remember that these horrors still haunt the world in one part or another.

We cannot tell how long these conditions lasted, but the probability is that the land in general was occupied by Edomites and others, who took steps to see that Jerusalem was not rebuilt, and that the Jews themselves, who had not been taken to Babylon, should be exploited to the utmost (Ezek. 36.1–7).

The reference to Assyria in v. 6 is difficult, since she had long ceased to be an empire, although Egypt was a place to which refugees had gone (Jer. 43). Perhaps the verse is a condensed allusion to former alliances with Assyria and Egypt that the prophets had denounced (2 Kings 16.7–9; Isa.7.1–9; 30.1–7), i.e. once our fathers looked to them for grand military help; now we should be thankful if they would give us enough employment to supply the bare necessities of life.

The result of the sins of the fathers is truly stated (7), but it is not the whole truth if (as Ezekiel shows in 18.1 ff) it becomes an excuse for sitting down passively. The description continues, with former slaves ingratiating themselves with the occupying nations (8), and with crops seized in sudden raids (9). Good native leaders are dealt with by arrest and torture (12). Press gangs take the young away (13) and the old have no heart for free speech in meetings at the city gates (14), and there is no more music and dancing (14,15). We are like dethroned kings (16).

We cannot only blame our fathers, but we ourselves are involved in guilt, and are morally, spiritually, and physically sick (16,17, cf. Isa. 1.5,6; Jer. 8.22; 17.9). As the writer looks at the ruins of Zion (18), he lifts his eyes to the eternal God (19, cf. Heb. 1.8). Restoration cannot be only from rubble to reconstruction, but must be from a self-directed life to God Himself at the centre (21).

Which prayer must ultimately take priority: 'Restore me to my ...' *(we can fill in the blank); or, 'Restore me to Thyself'? (cf. 2 Cor. 12.8–10).*

Questions for further study and discussion on Lamentations

1. Is there any value in taking a straight look at our sufferings?
2. How far does *Lamentations* keep a balance between looking at ourselves and looking to God?

3. Is all suffering deserved? Can we pass judgement on individual cases?
4. At what point can a Christian pass from confession to claiming the promises of God?
5. If you are interested in questions of authorship, consider whether Jeremiah may reasonably be suggested as the author of any or all of these laments. Note that the ascription to Jeremiah is only traditional, but tradition generally contains some truth.

Ezekiel

INTRODUCTION

Ezekiel was a Jewish exile in Babylonia. He was taken captive with the young king, Jehoiachin, in 597 B.C., and there is no indication that he ever returned to live in Judah. He was called to be a prophet about 593 B.C. Jerusalem was still intact, since the next siege and destruction of the city was in 588–7 B.C. There were so-called prophets in Jerusalem and Babylonia who were declaring that the Jehoiachin captives would soon return (Jer. 28.1–4; 29. 15–28). Jeremiah in Jerusalem and Ezekiel in Babylonia both announced the doom of Jerusalem and a further captivity unless the people really repented. Yet both prophets were shown that there would eventually be a return and Jerusalem would be rebuilt, but this would be accompanied by repentance and renewal.

Roughly speaking the *Book of Ezekiel* may be divided into three sections according to subject matter:

1–24 The doom of the rebellious nation.
25–32 God's verdict on some other nations.
33–48 The restoration and renewal of Judah and Israel.

Ezekiel 1.1-14   Visions in Exile

The setting is Babylonia in a Jewish settlement by the large canal, Kabaru, which formed an eastern loop in the Euphrates from above Babylon to Uruk (Erech) via Nippur (1). Ezekiel was living there as one of the exiles taken with King Jehoiachin in 597 B.C. (2; 2 Kings 24.8–16). He was a priest, but we have no

328

other record of his father, Buzi (2). If the reference in v. 1 is to his age, this would coincide with the time that he would probably have entered on his full service of priesthood at the age of 30 had he remained in Jerusalem. (N.B. Levites in Num. 4.3, and Jesus Christ in Luke 3.23).

Although he could not act as priest, God called him as prophet. Ezekiel here and elsewhere describes the experience of inspiration as being seized by the hand of God (3; 3.14,22; 8.1, etc., cf. 1 Kings 18.46; Isa. 8.11; Jer. 1.9). The result here is an amazing vision of God. In reading it we realize that Ezekiel is struggling to convey the indescribable. Notice his use of such phrases as 'the likeness of', 'something that looked like', 'the appearance of'.

The visionary appearance of God comes in a storm cloud, (Job 37.22–38.1) from the north, the direction in which one would normally go to Jerusalem from Babylon via the Fertile Crescent. The cloud flashes fire (Exod. 19.16), and unfolds to disclose its source in a centre like dazzling reflecting metal (4). From the cloud come four living creatures. Later Ezekiel refers to them as cherubim (ch. 10), and John also sees them around the throne of God in Rev. 4.6,7. Some have found a symbolic meaning in their four faces as representing aspects of created life (10), but they may well be angelic attendants of the throne of God, depicted as Ezekiel and John saw them, just as Isaiah describes them as seraphim (Isa. 6.2).

Their four faces look in four directions with each human face looking outwards (10). Their legs and hands are of human type (7,8), though instead of human feet they apparently have something like a rounded hoof (7). Today Ezekiel might have described them as castors, the point being that they could move instantly in any direction (9,12). They each have four wings; one pair covers their bodies, the other pair extends straight from their shoulders so as to touch the tip of their neighbour's wings (11). They thus form a square, living and instantly mobile (14), and later we find that they are supporting the visionary throne of God. Meanwhile Ezekiel sees fire at the centre of the square, probably now as an altar fire from which torches are kindled (13, cf. Isa. 6.6).

God's servants are able to go where His Spirit wishes them to be (12; Rom. 8.14).

Ezekiel 1.15-28 Visions of God

As the vision unfolds it is seen that the four cherubim form part of a chariot. Although this has four wheels, one under each cherub, and thus centralized, each wheel is composed of two wheels apparently at right angles to each other. This is impossible in reality, but in the vision it enables the chariot to run instantly in any direction without turning (16,17). The wheels shine like yellow quartz (16), but they are not dead metal; their livingness is shown by their eyes with which they can see the way (18, cf. Rev. 4.8), and by their life-link with the living creatures above them (20,21).

The significance of the vision unfolds further: it is not simply an interesting glimpse of angelic beings. Now Ezekiel sees a gleaming crystal platform over their heads (22). Next he notices the wings extended in motion and lowered when at rest. In the speed of movement their wings roar in the air like a waterfall or thunder (23,24). Then comes a sudden silence as their wings are lowered and the chariot stops, and Ezekiel hears a voice from above (25).

This leads to the culmination of the vision, the gloriously bright figure of God, in appearance like a man, enthroned on the crystal platform. The description suggests that Ezekiel did not see a face and body that he could have drawn, but rather a fiery brightness that had a human shape and that he knew to be living and personal. Note his careful use of words, 'the appearance of the likeness of the glory of the LORD' (28). No one in O.T. times saw God in His full Being (John 1.18. N.B. John was well aware of O.T. appearances of God). But from time to time God revealed Himself in a selected form. Many believe that such visions were pre-incarnation appearances of Jesus Christ, as John 12.41 suggests in the context which refers to Isa. 6. Such appearances could illuminate, but could not redeem: for redemption full Incarnation was necessary, and not simply an appearance as a Man.

God above the cherubim is not confined in the Temple (Exod. 25.22; 2 Kings 19.15), nor anywhere else (Psa. 18.10; John 4.21-24).

Ezekiel 2.1—3.3   Message Received

The title 'Son of man' (1) occurs some 90 times in this book. It is a Hebraism which is an emphatic form of 'man'. It probably reminds Ezekiel, that in comparison with the majesty of God, he is merely mortal man. We still need this reminder, which is not inconsistent with the love of God. Ezekiel's attitude and God's call to him to rise should be compared with Dan. 10.9,10 and Acts 26.14–16.

There are a number of references to the Spirit in *Ezekiel*; these should be noted as they occur, and might well now be scanned in a concordance. We have already had a specialized reference in 1.12,20,21. Now the Spirit is the inspirer of the prophetic word, who enters into Ezekiel (2).

Note how Isaiah (6.9–12), Jeremiah (1.17–19) and Ezekiel, here (3–7), were all given a depressing call. They were needed in a desperate situation, and had to be prepared for a large measure of rejection and even threats on their life. There is always a mystery about preaching and speaking the Word of God. It may be law, love, or threat—all three are the Word of God—but experience shows that many who hear will reject.

We must, however, be convinced that the message is truly God's. A prophet was always confident that God had given him His true Word. Thus Jeremiah had God's words put into his mouth (1.9), and Ezekiel here is given a written scroll to digest. It is the objective Word of God which becomes part of himself. That is why we study the Bible and do not merely skim through it. The words that Ezekiel was to utter at this stage in his ministry were of gloomy tragedy (10), but in so far as they were God's words for him they were as sweet as honey (3.3). When John was given a similar scroll in Rev. 10.8–11 it also was sweet to the taste, but was bitter to his digestion. How enthusiastic we are when we suddenly see the glory of the gospel that God has given us to pass on! How bitter we find it when we are faced with the rejection of what means so much to us! (Jer. 15.16–18).

If even Christ's preaching 'failed' (Luke 13.34), what hope is there for our witness (1 Cor. 9.22)?

Ezekiel 3.4-15   People Next Door

Ezekiel had the hardest commission of all—to witness to his next-door neighbours. People with prophetic or pseudo-prophetic gifts were regarded with awe in countries beyond their own, e.g. Elisha (2 Kings 5 and 8.7–9), Jeremiah (39.11–14) and Jonah (3.6–10). Ezekiel might have traded on this, and had a more encouraging life (5,6). We must take this into account in weighing up a possible missionary call.

Verse 7 is one of the most dangerous verses in Scripture, though the Bible does not hesitate to include it, and indeed, there is a similar sentiment in the N.T. (Luke 10.16). It is a call to intense humility, for fear that we comfort ourselves concerning our off-putting presentation of the truth by calling our rejection the rejection of Christ. Off-putting presentation can lie in our own character as well as in inept words out of season. Yet v. 7 must at times bring comfort to the true Christian who burns to see others won.

This may demand a certain toughness (8,9). Again, these verses can be dangerous if they are taken out of the context of the whole

Bible. We must seek the power of the Spirit to make us less persor ally sensitive, while remaining lovingly sensitive to the needs aroun us. Distinguish Christ's toughness towards the hard religiou leaders from His tenderness towards the outcasts of society.

One cure for a wrong attitude is the preliminary application of th Word of God to ourselves (10). Let what we hear with our ears g(deeply into our hearts (Matt. 13.23). Then go out with God' message.

When Ezekiel was inspired as a prophet, he had strange experiences Like the Lord Jesus he felt himself driven by the Spirit (Mark 1.12) Already the honeysweet Word had become bitter (14) as he strode down the banks of the canal to the exile settlement at Telabib. He knew the general drift of the Lord's will, but for seven days he waited until the actual word for the moment was given to him.

Consider Luke 4.24.

Ezekiel 3.16-21   Watchman's Warning

A prophet knew the difference between his own thinking and the Word of the Lord that laid hold of him. Here v. 16 may be compared with Jer. 42.7. Ezekiel has to see himself as a watchman on sentry-duty to warn the people of the city (17, cf. Jer. 6.17; Hab. 2.1). The trouble is that the people may be too sleepy or too busy to take the warning when it comes (Luke 21.34).

This is one of the passages in Scripture that links sin and death. It is not always easy to know whether the reference is to the death of the body or to the eternal death. Physical death for human beings comes because of sin (Rom. 5.12), but it also signifies death on a further level, the death of the personality separated from the life of God. So the Christian passes from death to life through living faith in Christ, having his sins taken away through the work of Christ (John 5.24). But unless he lives until the second coming of Christ, his body will die, since death, having entered in, still operates in the material world (1 Cor. 15.26). But this death of the body will be reversed at the Second Coming and the resurrection. With renewed bodies, after the pattern of Christ's risen body, we shall be complete men and women through all eternity.

The warning in vs. 18-21 is to repent and turn from our wicked ways, since these are ways of death. The verses have their fullest meaning when applied to eternal death, though violent death sometimes comes as a sequel to an evil life. This could be the thought of v. 20. The stumbling-block may be a disaster which God brings. We are not concerned here with the N.T. teaching of eternal salvation in Christ, but we see that even a good man, with a wealth of good actions behind him, may sink to the lower levels of world-behaviour. The N.T. shows that sometimes God allows premature death for such a person so as to cut him off from further wrongdoing (1 Cor. 5.5). If only he (and we) had responded to the watchman's warning!

Meanwhile we have responsibilities both as Christian watchmen and as citizens who need to hear the watchman's voice.

Study: Contrast this passage with Isa. 56.10–12.

Ezekiel 3.22-27   Kept Back

We have been a long time over preliminaries. Ezekiel is still waiting for the moment when the Word of God will come to him for the people. Probably he still needed personal preparation, so that he would see his calling more clearly. It was not sufficient to be a mechanical talking computer. His inner life must be true to the God-given message, and he must know the greatness of his responsibility.

First he has a renewed vision of the glory of the Lord (22,23). Already, perhaps, he had begun to turn in on himself under the strain that he could foresee was coming. A wise man once said something to the effect that we should take ten looks at Christ to one at ourselves.

Surely the time has now come to speak! Yet surprisingly Ezekiel is ordered to shut himself in his own house. The probable meaning of v. 25 is that God will restrain him as though he were tied with ropes (cf. 4.8), though some interpret the verse to mean that his opponents will tie him up to prevent him from prophesying. The former meaning links well with v. 26, which again describes an act of God. Not only would Ezekiel be restrained from leaving home, but he would be totally unable to speak at all until the moment arrived to give the Lord's message.

The situation is puzzling at first sight. In the previous portion we saw the urgency to speak as a watchman because the people were rebellious. Now Ezekiel has to be silent because they are rebellious. The answer probably can be seen from the varied responses of people to the presence and talk of Christians. There is a place for talking about Christ and a place for quiet assurance that refuses to argue. No doubt a rumour had gone around that Ezekiel had been called to be a prophet. People came along out of curiosity (33.30–33), but found Ezekiel unmoving and silent in his house. This exasperated them and roused their curiosity for the message when it came. Yet in his silence Ezekiel was seeing his people with fresh eyes. He was ready for the Word to fall.

Consider occasions of silence in Pss. 4.4; 62.1; Matt. 26.63; John 8.6; 19.9.

Ezekiel 4.1-8 Serious Play

To act the siege of a city with the aid of a picture and imitation 'guns' sounds like a children's game. But prophets were often told to drive home their message by strange acted parables (e.g. Isa. 20.2,3; Jer. 13.1-7). The Jews were thinking of restoration rather than the destruction of Jerusalem, and certainly they did not suppose that, if a new attack came, God (as represented here by His prophet) would cut Himself off by an iron wall (3).

While he conducts the siege Ezekiel has to lie on his left side for 390 days and on his right for 40 days. There are three problems here:

(*i*) Did he lie for the whole period without moving? On physical grounds this is unlikely. Probably he lay like this during the hours when he was acting as prophet, and at other times behaved normally. There was no point in acting a parable with no one present to learn from it.

(*ii*) The period between Ezekiel's call (1.1,2) and his next dated utterance in 8.1 is one year and one month. We are not certain what calendar Ezekiel follows, but the period would be near enough to 390 days. To add another 40 would be too much. Probably for 40 out of the 390 days Ezekiel would turn over after completing the left side sign. The Greek Septuagint has 190 days, in which case the periods could be consecutive.

(*iii*) Commentators differ over the application of the numbers. Ezekiel could be reckoning from 922 B.C. when the northern kingdom of Israel split off in rebellion after the death of Solomon and made the golden calves (1 Kings 12). The round figure of 390 (a day for a year) brings us to 532 B.C. Babylon fell in 539 B.C., and the exiles were free to return in 538 B.C. If the Septuagint is correct, the date begins with the fall of Samaria and exile of the northern kingdom (722 B.C.) and takes us to 532 B.C., as before.

The 40 years for Judah date from the coming fall of Jerusalem in 587 B.C. Here again we must regard 40 as a round number, which has a symbolic significance as being the time of wandering in the wilderness before the first entry into Palestine. Yet by 547 B.C. Cyrus was already threatening the power of Babylon.

Consider the place of symbols in conveying truth, e.g. Sacraments.

Ezekiel 4.9-17

By his signs Ezekiel was told to drive home the horrors of the coming siege of Jerusalem. In a sense he is called to identify himself with the sufferers. His food is to be coarse and scanty; plain bread and vegetables weighing about half a pound a day. Be realistic. If you cannot visualize this, weigh some bread on the kitchen scales. Ezekiel ate one meal a day, a famine meal every time. Some Christians wish to identify themselves with their brothers in need in the same sort of way as Ezekiel, and at the same time send them the cost that they save. Ezekiel was allowed two pints of water daily, but this had to be exactly measured out as though it were rationed (11,16).

Then came the order to use human excrement as fuel for cooking. Ezekiel took the lesson, but refused the action. As a priest he had always kept the Mosaic laws of cleanness and uncleanness. Although in v. 14 he refers to the general laws of uncleanness (e.g. Exod. 22.31), he must have had Deut. 23.13 also in mind. Most of the laws of hygiene in the Pentateuch make obviously good sense, and even those which are obscure undoubtedly have some reason that was valid under more primitive conditions.

God shocked Ezekiel into feeling the horror of exile in lands that were unclean (13). They were unclean because their religion and morals contained so much that attracted and yet contaminated. It is true that in the Holy Land the people of God had admitted any number of unholy Canaanite ways, but at least it was their land and they could reject them. As a minority in a foreign land they would have to bow to the will of the majority, and put up with things that horrified them if they cared for the true God at all.

Dried animal dung was used as fuel in the east, and still is, and it was not regarded as ritually unclean. However, in the siege all cattle would be killed for food, so only human excrement would be available for fuel.

Note how ancient is the expression of bread as the staff of life (16; Lev. 26.26; Psa. 105.16; Isa. 3.1; Ezek. 14.13).

To learn sympathy we must learn to share (1 Pet. 5.9).

Ezekiel 5
God the Enemy

This chapter is the completion of the signs in ch. 4, as is shown by v. 2. Shaving the head and beard was a sign of mourning (Isa. 22.12; Jer. 41.5). Ezekiel's first action shows that mourning would come through the sword of invasion. Afterwards, the hair itself represents the people, one part destroyed in the city, one part in battle, and one part blown into exile. Even some of the last group must be thrown into the fire, and the meaning of v. 4 may be that the wind blows them away burning. Thus the exiles already in Babylon would have an influx of fresh exiles still ablaze with their wickedness (cf. 14.22,23).

Jerusalem, the chosen city, was the spiritual centre of the earth (5) and, indeed, of the universe, since Jesus Christ died there (Col. 1.20). Yet her people had adopted lower moral standards than the unenlightened pagans (6; Rom. 2.13–16) while substituting what was obviously wrong in paganism for the revealed standards of God (7, cf. 1 Cor. 3.3; Gal. 5.19–21).

From v. 8 onwards note the number of times when God says what 'I will' do. Here was the tragedy. They had turned God into their enemy. The destruction of Jerusalem is never regarded in the Bible as a chance event. Whether or not we choose to refer to the hand of God, history shows that moral degradation in various forms has resulted in the collapse of kingdoms and empires.

Note the accusation of defiling God's sanctuary (11). We shall read more of this in ch. 8. Meanwhile we can read 1 Cor. 3.16,17; 6.19,20, and take Ezekiel's lesson.

The strong language of v. 13 sounds shocking, but forms part of the whole picture. The Lord has told Ezekiel to act out a siege in which God Himself is the King who marches against a rebel city. Only when the city is subdued or destroyed is the King satisfied. The next siege of Jerusalem will be like that. The evil is so great that God cannot stop half-way. Otherwise what opinion would other nations form of His standards? We shall see the reverse picture in 36.19–21.

Study: It is worth comparing what God says here with what He said through Moses in Lev. 26. There are some similar phrases.

Questions for further study and discussion on Ezekiel chs. 1—5

1. Compare the calls of Ezekiel, Isaiah (ch. 6), Jeremiah (ch. 1), Moses (Exod. 3).
2. Compare Ezekiel's opening vision with Rev. 4 and 5.
3. What passages indicate that Ezekiel was more than God's typewriter?
4. Why should God be concerned about the behaviour of Jerusalem?

Ezekiel 6   Glamorous Religion

In reading the O.T. we must all the time be alive to metaphors and allusions, or we shall not make sense of the words. Thus God is not angry with the mountains (2) any more than with the cedars and oaks in Isa. 2.13,14. Probably in any part of Palestine at this time you would have found some mountain or hill crowned with an altar, one or two standing stones, a wooden pillar, and a clump of evergreen trees (Jer. 3.6–9). They were flourishing centres of the old Canaanite religion which should have been destroyed (Deut. 7.5). It is likely that some of the Jews and Israelites deceived themselves into thinking that they were worshipping Jehovah there: the local god went by the name of Baal, and this could mean 'lord' or 'master'; so why not apply it to Jehovah (cf. Hos. 2.16)? Others made no pretence about it. Jehovah was the God for special occasions at Jerusalem, but one had better keep on good terms with the local gods and goddesses as well, especially as the form of worship was sensual and exciting. This problem confronts Christians in some of the newer churches overseas. In civilized countries there are other substitutes.

There must have been some similar worship in the ravines and valleys (3; Isa. 57.5,6; Jer. 2.23; 7.31), perhaps sometimes cave worship of an earth-mother, or, as Isaiah and Jeremiah suggest, child sacrifice.

Now Ezekiel declares the helplessness of these nature gods and goddesses. Their worshippers run to their altars for sanctuary, and are killed and left to rot in the ruins (4,5). In a sense, they themselves become sacrifices. Certainly this is what Jeremiah was saying to the people in Jerusalem (Jer. 7.31–8.2).

The tragedy was that less than 30 years earlier King Josiah had been through the land destroying the centres of degraded worship (2 Kings 23.4–20), but this is the sad history that has been repeated again and again—enthusiasm, reform, coolness, relapse. Yet relapse may be followed by repentance, and this is the theme of vs. 8–10. The immediate prospect is terrifying, with the land devastated from south to north (11–14).

Read one of the Letters to the Seven Churches, e.g. Rev. 2.19–29.

Ezekiel 7.1-13   Doomsday

Here is a final cry of doom. Note the repetition of 'has come', applied to 'the end' (2,6), 'doom' (7,10), 'the time' (7,12), 'the day' (10,12). One really needs to read this aloud to get the full horror as Ezekiel's audience must have heard it. There are turning-points in history where we see a people brought to judgement. Because we are all so closely bound together, the innocent suffer with the guilty, but the innocent may see the rottenness of the whole body and make their protest for as long as they possibly can.

Ezekiel sees the movement of God against Judah's 'ways' and 'abominations' (3,4,8,9). The religious abominations were mentioned in 6.1–7 and will appear again in ch. 8. In estimating God's verdict we must remember that Israel was intended to mirror God's Person to the nations. When the mirror reflected the most superstitious and degraded religious practices in existence, it had to be broken, mended, and redirected.

The 'ways' were ways of antisocial behaviour, much as the prophets continually castigated (10,11). There had been far too much violence and injustice from the time of Solomon onwards (e.g. Isa. 5). Countries rising to independence, and to the opportunities of money and power, have to fight the same problems. In England we have the phrase 'I'm all right, Jack', meaning that I must look after myself irrespective of other people's needs and feelings. The business world offers severe temptations to ruthlessness. 'The day' can wreck the Stock Market as well as impoverish a country.

On Ezekiel's lips vs. 12 and 13 presumably mean that the devastation of the land will rob buyer and seller of their property, but the exact interpretation is difficult. Perhaps we may paraphrase: The purchaser must not rejoice at getting a bargain, nor must the seller regret having to part with his property, since he will not be there to watch another man occupying it: purchaser, seller, and indeed the whole nation, will be broken up in exile or death.

Consider permanent values, e.g. Matt. 6.19–21; 1 Cor. 3.11–15. (Note 'The Day'.)

Ezekiel 7.14-27   Unreliable Standards

The situation foretold in this section is reflected later in *Lamentations*. Meanwhile the picture unfolds as the gradual breakdown of all the 'securities' of life. This is the sort of thing that under the providence of God may pave the way for a genuine conversion today. Or it may lead to a sense of frustration and hollowness.

The challenge comes, but we have deteriorated too much to be free to meet it (14; John 8.34). The outlook is hopeless wherever we turn (15). We begin to be aware not only of our helplessness, but of our sin (16,17; Rom. 7.24,25). We repent in shame (18; 2 Cor. 7.10). We realize that our values are worthless under test. There are permanent things that money cannot buy, and we cannot eat money (or houses or television sets) when what we need is food to keep us from starvation (19; Psa. 49.6,7).

For many people in Judah money had been a stumbling-block of iniquity, that is, they had tripped over it and gone headlong into the bog, or into the animal pit (19). We have often joined in prayers for the needs of the poor. If the Bible is correct, the very rich need our prayers just as much as the very poor (Matt. **19**.22–24; 1 Tim. **6**.17–19).

The particular stumbling-block here is the use of silver and gold to make idols (20), and idols are substitutes for the true God. For us a God-substitute may be expensive or fairly cheap. In equating covetousness with idolatry (Col. **3**.5), the N.T. shows how wide an application this word has. In history a rich church has suffered at the hands of a greedy or needy world (21–23).

At another level unchecked violence breeds more violence, and trigger-happy aggressive nations, companies, or individuals, must not be surprised if they are one day cornered themselves (23–25).

There was a time when God's people could have enjoyed the Word of God, and the sane advice of wise men (26), and had a good and stable government (27). But the professional prophets and priests lost touch with the Word, and the ruling classes drifted into standards that made for destruction rather than stability (Jer. **5**.27–31).

Thought: 'I'm terribly sorry for Mr. . . . ; he has such a lot of money.'

Ezekiel 8.1-6
Image or Glory

Ezekiel is transported from Babylon to Jerusalem. He describes the sensation in v. 3. We are naturally curious to know 'how it was done', but the only clue is that it was an extension of a simple vision, and that its originator was the Spirit of God. It is unlikely that his body vanished from the sight of the elders (1). We can find a partial parallel in well-authenticated telepathic experiences, in which someone has 'seen' an event happening at a distance. The pictures that Ezekiel sees are partly real and partly symbolic.

This was not natural telepathy, but a special divine communication, introduced by the appearance of the Lord whom he had seen in his opening vision (2, cf. **1**.26,27). When the Lord touched him, the Spirit enlightened him (cf. the association of the prophet and the Spirit in Rev. **1**.10–16; **4**.1,2).

Ezekiel became, as it were, God's television screen, so that the exiles might see for themselves the utter degradation of Jerusalem, and thus understand why it had to be judged so drastically.

The Temple and the open-air altar of burnt offering were surrounded by a rectangular court. There was a gate in the north wall of the court opposite the altar. Ezekiel was set down by this gateway, probably just outside it. He faces north, away from the

Temple court, and looks across the next court to another gateway in which stood 'the image of jealousy' (3).

The word 'image' is *semel*, which occurs elsewhere only in Deut. 4.16 (where it is translated 'figure') and in 2 Chron. 33.7,15, of a special 'idol' set up by King Manasseh in the Temple. Although this idol was later removed, Ezekiel's use of the word may mean that a replica, if not the original, was put back. The word also occurs in Phoenician writings.

Some think that only the stand of the image was there, because of the reference to 'seat' in v. 3, but v. 5 refers to the image itself. Perhaps the image was taken off its stand and carried in procession, and then replaced.

This image moved God to jealousy (3). Note the way in which jealousy is ascribed to God in connection with alternative gods (Exod. 20.5; 34.14; Deut. 4.24). There is nothing derogatory in it. God is jealous for our total devotion, not only for His own sake but for ours.

Consider the contrast between v. 3 and v. 4.

Ezekiel 8.7-18 — Deviant Religions

Many Christians reading this chapter today find it rather remote from their experience unless they have had encounters with Satanism and witchcraft. But Celtic missionaries to Britain encountered this sort of syncretistic worship as they formed Christian communities, and many younger churches all over the world have members who are tempted to add the spirits of the old religion to their Christian religion. Ezekiel sees three forms of worship.

(*i*) *A secret society for the élite* (7–13). Christianity has always been open to all. By contrast there are pseudo-Christian and non-Christian movements that offer secrets to people who like to feel that they have something exclusive. Paul deals with such people in Col. 2. Ezekiel sees 70 men, superior elders, worshipping animal spirits in a secret room. The room was perhaps too small to accommodate idols, so the best artists had depicted Egyptian, Mesopotamian, and Canaanite animal deities in pictures on the walls. Outstanding among the worshippers was the son of Shaphan. Shaphan had been King Josiah's right-hand man at the time of the Reformation (2 Kings 22.3 ff.). They justified their new religion on the ground that God had deserted the land (cf. Isa. 28.14,15; Zeph. 1.12).

(*ii*) *A religion for women* (14,15). Nature religions commonly contain a ritual for the god of vegetation and life, who dies in the autumn and comes to life in the spring. Tammuz, Adonis,

Osiris, Baldur, are all variants of beautiful young gods who are mourned by devoted women when they die each year. By contrast Jehovah is the living God (Deut. 5.26; Psa. 42.2). Yet even He became Man in order to die once, and only once, for the sins of the world (Heb. 9.26).

(*iii*) *Worship of the sun* (16–18). These worshippers showed their contempt for God by standing in such a way that they had their backs to the Temple while they reverenced the sun (cf. 2 Kings 23.5,11), worshipping the creature rather than the Creator (Rom. 1.25). The branch held to the nose may have been in imitation of the Egyptian *ankh*, a symbol of life, which is shown in carvings as held to the nose, or it may have been connected with plants sacred to Tammuz or some other god. The word 'branch' here is the same as 'slips' in Isa. 17.10.

If I enjoy all that is mine in Christ, there is no need to look further (Col. 2.3).

Ezekiel 9   The Great Division

Within the city, rotten to the heart, God knows His own people. Ezekiel has already been shown that God accepts responsibility for the destruction of the city and consequent exile (ch. 5). So now he sees, not the Babylonians, but angelic messengers of destruction. They march in past the image of jealousy and the mourners for Tammuz, and take their stand near the sun-worshippers, invisible to all except Ezekiel.

Before they start their mission of death, one of their number, in appearance like a scribe, is sent to mark the foreheads of all who truly care about the declension from God. There is a prophetic significance in the Hebrew word for the mark (4). It is the Hebrew letter T (Tau), which at that time was written as a cross. Without being superstitious we can rejoice in this anticipation of salvation through the death of Christ on the cross.

The Cross separates the living from the dead (6). One of the most awful sentences in Scripture is 'Begin at My sanctuary' (6). It is possible to be involved in religion up to the hilt, and yet to be away from God and under His judgement (Rev. 3.1–6).

Ezekiel sees all this happen symbolically. When the reality came, there were enough faithful men, women, and children who were saved to join the nucleus of the repentant and restored nation later. Yet it was true that God did not pity the nation as it was (10), in the sense of relenting, to allow them to continue as before.

The last word of the chapter lies with the scribe (11). Whatever may be the fate of the rebels, he has found all God's true servants, and none of them is lost.

Compare this marking with Rev. 7.3, 4; 13.16; 14.9; 20.4; 22.4.

Ezekiel 10. 1-8   The Glory Prepares to Go

The glorious presence of the Lord prepares to leave the Temple. Ezekiel sees a vision of God and the cherubim that is virtually the same as that which he had seen in Babylonia. God is not limited by distance. Ezekiel now records faithfully what he heard and saw.

A voice tells the scribe, who had set the mark on God's true people, to take coals of fire from within the living creatures and the wheels and scatter them over the city, presumably as a symbol of destruction (2). One of the living creatures helps him, and draws out the fiery coals (7).

The interpretation of God's movement in vs. 3 and 4 is not certain. When Ezekiel describes his vision in ch. 1, he does not speak of the living creatures as cherubim. In this chapter he recognizes that this is what they were (20), and probably connects them with the cherubim over the mercy seat in the Holy of Holies. This is where God manifested Himself (Exod. 25.22; Num. 7.89; 2 Kings 19.15). The probability is, therefore, that in 9.3 and 10.4 the cherubim from which the glory of the Lord went up are the two golden cherubim in the Holy of Holies. The significance is that the glorious presence of God is leaving the Temple. The other cherubim, bearing the chariot firmament, come and stand ready to receive the glory of God (3). Note that in v. 1 the throne on the firmament is empty, in contrast to 1.26–28, so v. 4 can hardly mean that the Lord leaves the throne. The distinction between the two sorts of cherubim was obvious to Ezekiel, and is obvious to us when it is pointed out.

The sad thing was that Ezekiel was evidently the only person who saw the glory of God. The rest had eyes only for images, pictures, and the lesser glory of the sun.

Ezekiel also hears the roaring of the wings of the cherubim (5). The noise is like the voice of God Almighty. Perhaps the reference is metaphorically to the thunder, as in Psa. 29.3–9. (cf. 1.24; John 12.28,29).

'God is still on the throne.' Which throne?

Ezekiel 10.9-22   Reluctant Withdrawal

There is no need to make much of minor differences between this vision and that of ch. 1, e.g. the different order in which things are mentioned. The one puzzling difference is the faces in v. 14, where here Ezekiel speaks of cherub, man, lion, eagle, instead of man (in front), lion (right), ox (left), eagle (back) in **1.10.** If we remember that Ezekiel is wrestling to convey the strange sequence of a vision, we may explain the difference by the position from which Ezekiel saw the creatures. In ch. **1** they were moving towards Ezekiel with the man's face in front. Now they are south of Ezekiel and move east, with presumably the man's face still in front but no longer facing Ezekiel. Thus the ox face of each of the four would be looking towards Ezekiel, and he calls this the first face, the face which had now become the standard cherub face from his viewpoint. The very obscurity, which has to be interpreted somewhat like this, is a mark of authenticity; it would have been so easy to tidy it up by substituting *ox*.

In v. 18 the glory of the presence of the Lord, which first left the Holy of Holies for the threshold of the Temple, now settles on the chariot throne. Then the Lord on the throne moves to the East Gate of the Temple court and pauses again. It almost seems as though at each stage of withdrawal the Lord waits to see if He is to be recalled. But the men who faced east worshipping the sun (**8.16**) must have looked through the vision at the gate: their eyes were so dazzled by the created ball of light that they could not see the True Light.

Note that when the Lord does finally return, He is seen coming back through the East Gate (**43.4**). This was presumably the gate by which Jesus Christ entered the Temple courts when He came from the Mount of Olives, and, being rejected, He left by the same gate (Matt. **21.12–17**). He also is the Glory of God (John **1.14**).

Note the phrases which describe the easy movement of the cherubim in immediate response to God's will. Is there a lesson here?

Ezekiel 11 No Room for God

This is the end of the Jerusalem visions. Ezekiel has had two indications of the coming destruction by violence (**9.7**) and by fire (**10.2,7**), but he has not seen them carried out. Now he is told to denounce a group of plotters, and suddenly he sees one of the leaders drop dead (**13**) The other leader, Jaazaniah, may be the brother of Jeremiah's opponent Hananiah, who is also the son of Azzur (Jer. **28.1**).

Commentaries differ widely over the interpretation of their words (**3**), and we can note three main possibilities.

(*i*) 'It is not yet wise to rebuild the houses outside Jerusalem that were destroyed in 597 B.C. We must trust to the city walls to protect us, as the cauldron keeps the flesh inside it from the flames'.

(*ii*) 'We cannot rebuild the houses, but, if we stay as we are, we shall be cooked..So let us make a pact with Egypt against Babylon' (cf. Jer. 37.5–10).

(*iii*) Follow margin, 'Is not the time near . . . ?' or Greek Septuagint, 'Are not the houses recently built?' The thought then could be, 'The bones and rubbish have gone into exile; we are left as the tasty meat'.

These plotters had also been guilty of oppression and violence (6,12). Now they will suffer in their turn (7–12). The visionary (?) death of Pelatiah is a foretaste (13).

The section vs. 14–21 favours interpretation (*iii*) above. The Jews in Jerusalem despised those like Ezekiel who had already gone into exile. Now we can see the link with the vision in ch. 1. The presence of God is not tied to Jerusalem: indeed God is now leaving the Temple. Yet those who are in exile still enjoy God as their sanctuary (16), and Ezekiel's vision in ch. 1 demonstrated His presence in Babylonia: there was the same glorious God as had been in the Temple.

Now for the first time Ezekiel speaks in miniature of the future return. He develops this theme later. The return involves both repentance and renewal (17–20).

Finally, God is seen leaving the city by way of the Mount of Olives (23). It is no coincidence that some 600 years later Christ ascended from the same mountain close to Bethany which is on the south-east slopes (Luke 24.50; Acts 1.12).

Are there such things as holy places? If so, what makes them holy?

Questions for further study and discussion on Ezekiel chs. 6–11

1. How far does God here regard the nation as a whole, and how far is He concerned with a faithful nucleus?
2. What picture do these chapters give of social evils in Judah?
3. What is wrong with idolatry?
4. Draw a tentative diagram of the cherubim, the wheels, and the chariot-throne.
5. What other passages in Scripture show that God is a sanctuary for His people wherever they are (11.16)?

Ezekiel 12 — No Empty Signs

This chapter falls into three sections. Although uttered in Babylon, it reveals the impending doom of Jerusalem.

(*i*) *Sign of exile* (1–16). Ezekiel packs a rucksack with bare necessities, and walks out of the house with it in broad daylight. When night is falling, he repeats the sign, only now he digs a hole in the wall of his house and crawls out like an escaping prisoner with his face covered to obscure his sight. Next day he gives the meaning. Many in Jerusalem will pack their bags for exile with whatever they can salvage. In particular King Zedekiah will creep out of the city walls by night (12; 2 Kings 25.4), but the Lord plans for him to be caught and brought to Babylon. He will, however, come as a blind man (13; 2 Kings 25.7). Others will be scattered through different countries (15). We know that many went to Egypt (Jer. 43.7).

(ii) *Sign of terror* (17-20). Ezekiel eats his meals with his hands trembling, and glancing around all the time as though he expects an enemy to spring on him. The picture is of exiles being rounded up; all possible refuges have been demolished, and at any moment their guards may decide to beat them up (Jer. 40.1).

(iii) *Scorn of prophecy* (21-28). Ezekiel and Jeremiah had clearly been speaking of the coming destruction for some months. Yet nothing had happened, and people were growing sceptical (22). Rival prophets were foretelling a speedy return to a flourishing Jerusalem (24; 13.16; Jer. 28.1-4; 29.8,9,15,21). God warns the people that the doom is certain. It will not be delayed much longer (25).

The concluding verses say much the same, but from a slightly different angle. Whereas some were saying there would be no destruction of Jerusalem, others did not deny this, but thought it would not come for centuries (27). We are reminded of modern attitudes, such as the idea that we cannot see the hand of God in history: that we can accept the piling up of national and international evils without reference to the judgement of God: that we need not think of the possibility of the Lord's return in our lifetime, since science cannot admit supernatural interventions (2 Pet. 3.4).

Look up other passages which make light of God's apparent inaction, e.g. Isa. 5.19; Zeph. 1.12; Mal. 2.17; Matt. 24. 48-51.

Ezekiel 13
Bogus Prophecy and Magic

The people were puzzled by prophets who spoke in the Name of the Lord, but who turned out to be false (1-16, cf. Jer. 23). They appeared to have the visions, voices, and ecstatic experiences of the true prophets, but their messages came from the depths of their own mind—many today would call it their Unconscious (2; Jer. 23.16). They never spoke of repentance, but guaranteed that the blessings of God were just around the corner. We are reminded of the so-called Cargo Cults in Melanesia, where the people wait passively for the predicted arrival of a Messianic figure in a great ship or plane, bringing a cargo of all the luxuries which the white man has kept for himself.

These prophets did not strengthen the moral defences of the nation (5), but painted the shoddy façades to make them look good (10, cf. Jer. 6.14). This temptation faces us today with rotten books and pictures. Many justify them, but our national resistance crumbles under the storms (11–13).

Another ancient and modern perversion is magic and superstition (17–23). Occult forces can be mobilized against other people through suggestion and, probably, directly. In Babylonia Jewish women were selling charms and spells. They were ready to do anything for even a small reward, putting a curse on the innocent, and promising a long and safe life for wrongdoers (19).

It is not easy to know the form of their spells. They certainly used armbands and veils, and it seems that these were first placed on their clients (18), and then on the witch (20,21). The order and the context suggest that the veils were worn to preserve life and probably bring luck. The armbands were destructive. Perhaps something belonging to one's enemy was taken to the witch, who folded it in a handkerchief, and tied it to the wrist of the client with some recital of spells. She then transferred it to her own arm, and projected a curse into it while she continued to wear it.

Note. RSV disguises the fact that 'souls' in vs. 18 and 20 and 'persons' in v. 19 represent the same Hebrew word *nephesh*. A consistent translation of either 'souls' or 'persons' would be better.

For other occasions of testing (11–14) note Isa. 28.16–18; Matt. 7.24–27; 1 Cor. 3.11–15.

Ezekiel 14.1-11 Deception

This is an important passage concerning finding out the will of God and doing it. It arises when some leaders of the nation come to Ezekiel to hear a message from God. Yet they are idolaters, either literally (as in Isa. 48.5 which refers to the exile, even though written before the exile), or morally and spiritually (as in Matt. 6.24). It would seem as though they wanted to hear God's will, and then decide whether they would do it: would it fit their pattern of life, or would it cause too much upheaval (cf. Jer. 42.5,6; 43.1–4)?

This is making mockery of God. So far from giving a reassuring message through the prophet, God will take the questioner at his face value. He has chosen to be on the side of God's enemies, so God will treat him as an enemy, with the hope that the suffering will bring about true repentance of heart (4–6).

Yet suppose a prophet does give a spurious answer in the Name of the Lord? God accepts responsibility for deceiving him (9). This is an important principle of God's working. If we have some great gift and are being used in the service of God, and then try to use it in our own interests, or divorce it from the requirements of Christian living, God may turn the gift against us. A theologian, who abandons revealed truth for clever ideas of his own, first deceives himself, and then, by divine rule, becomes blind to the truth. A Christian worker, who deceives himself by unwise relationships, may, by divine rule, become so blind that he brings moral chaos on himself and his family. The Hebrew mind, looking to the way in which God has ordered cause and effect in physical, moral, and spiritual spheres, might say that, if a man threw himself over a cliff, God had destroyed him; we would introduce God's 'law' of gravitation as an intermediate link in the chain.

Note some other places in Scriptures where the working of God-given laws is referred to as God's action, e.g. Isa. 6.9, 10: Matt. 13.14, 15; Exod. 4.21; 7.22; 8.15; Rom. 1.24, 25.

Ezekiel 14.12—15.8   Who will be Saved?

One of Ezekiel's central messages is *individual responsibility*. Here is one aspect of it. It is not divorced from *corporate responsibility*, and the Bible is concerned with both group and individual. In ch. 18 Ezekiel, under God, will discuss whether the individual can break the chain of evil that has come from the past. Here he makes the point that a nation cannot shelter under the goodness of a few individuals. Some thirty years previously this is what had happened with King Josiah. He had carried through a great reformation (2 Kings 22,23), but the contemporary and subsequent words of Jeremiah show that the people did not go with him in their hearts.

Ezekiel contemplates greater characters than Josiah, three outstandingly good men, Noah, Daniel, and Job. Even their presence would not save the country in its hour of crisis, unless the people listened to them and followed their example (cf. Jer. 15.1).

It is not easy to draw the frontier line in the O.T. between physical life and the new eternal life of God. Since so little is revealed about eternal life until after the coming of Jesus Christ, the O.T. has to speak on a physical level and we may need to transmute it on to the higher level. Not all the good men in Jerusalem survived the destruction of the city (14,16,18,20) but all were preserved in life.

The remainder of ch. 14, in fact, speaks of survivors who are far from righteous. This, of course, does not exclude righteous survivors (9.4–6), but tells the exiles that when they find these fresh exiles flooding into Babylonia, they will see that Ezekiel has not been exaggerating the black picture he has drawn of them.

Chapter 15 is a brief parable about the wood, not this time the fruit, of the vine. God, the Divine Carpenter, has not been able to make anything out of the vine nation. Now that it has been partly charred by the fires of judgement, it is even more useless, and it must be burnt up (with v. 4, cf. John 15.6). We must take the parable, like other parables, as it is, and not look for points that it is not intended to illustrate. From another angle Isaiah drew a similar lesson from the illustration of the fruit (5.1–7).

Note on 14.14: Daniel may be the Daniel who was becoming known at the court of Nebuchadnezzar. Or his link with Noah and Job may equate him with an ancient righteous king of whom we read in Canaanite literature—a sort of King Arthur.

Consider how far we are relying on other people's righteous activity in church life.

Ezekiel 16.1–34   The Unfaithful Wife

The Bible sees human marriage as a symbol of the relationship between God and His people, just as our parental relationship symbolizes the relationship between God and ourselves (Eph. 5.25–33; 3.14,15). So here, and in ch. 23, Ezekiel graphically works out the picture of Israel as the unfaithful wife, a picture found also in Hos. 1–3; Jer. 2; Isa. 1.21; 50.1.

Ezekiel begins with the city of Jerusalem, which was an old Canaanite foundation (3; Gen. 14.18). Amorites and Hittites both held Palestine during the second millennium B.C.

Note the birth customs (4) and the willingness to throw out girl babies at birth (5), a custom which lingered until well after the time of Christ.

Ezekiel passes from the city to the people of Israel who came to occupy it. It is difficult to apply a fixed stage in history for each picture, but we perhaps have the move from the wandering Abraham and his descendants (6, 7; Gen. 15), through the Sinai covenant (8; Exod. 6.6–8), to the time when David captured Jerusalem, and he and Solomon beautified it (9–14).

The phrase in v. 8 describes the symbolic act whereby the husband took his wife under his protection (Ruth 3.9). In v. 10 the Hebrew word for 'leather' is the same as is used for the covering of the Tabernacle (Exod. 25.5, where RSV has 'goatskins'). There is no need to suppose that this leather was from one sort of animal only. 'Silk' is just possible as a translation of the material in v. 13, although there are no records of its import from China until after the time of Ezekiel. The nose ring (12) was a regular ornament (Gen. 24.47; Isa. 3.21).

There are two charges of unfaithfulness and promiscuity:

(i) *With idols* (15–22). Some were crude male deities (17). Others were deities like Moloch to whom children were offered in sacrifice to be burnt in the fire (20,21). For the theme of v. 17, cf. Hos. 2.5–8. For the sacrifice of children, cf. Jer. 7.30–32; 19.4,5; 32.35.

(ii) *With foreign countries* (23–34). This also is compared to adultery in Hos. 8.9. There was always the desire to form alliances with Egypt or Assyria as a way of escape, instead of sincerely turning to God. Ezekiel contemptuously declares that Israel got nothing out of these other nations (33,34). With vs. 24,25, cf. Isa. 57.7–9.

Compare with this section, Eph. 5.25–33.

Ezekiel 16.35-63 Worse than her Sisters

The glamour fades from the spurious lovers and they become destroyers (35–41). This is how the Bible always views sin; it may be fascinating for the moment, but its wages are death (Rom. 6.23; Heb. 11.25). Note how God also accepts responsibility for the destruction (42,43). When we cycle with the wind, it is our friend; when we cycle against it, it is our enemy. Remember that the Bible often gives one aspect of God's character and dealings at a time. Here we are shown a city and nation that is thoroughly rotten and godless. In other places we are shown groups within the nation who hear and turn to God.

In v. 44 the picture changes slightly. Judah is grouped with other peoples who had low morals and low religion. She is a true daughter of Canaan, who ignored the true God and sacrificed her children (45). She is a sister of Samaria and her dependent towns ('daughters'), and of Sodom and her dependants and associates, but her standards are even lower (47,51). The sins of Sodom here include what we know of from Gen. 18.20–19.11, but go wider into the luxuries and sins of civilized prosperity (49,50; Gen. 13.10).

The section 53–55 presents a difficulty. History shows that Samaria was restored, and the Samaritans became a flourishing community. Sodom, however, is still buried. Ezekiel probably has two groups in mind. Samaria represents those who in the past were a breakaway from Judah. Sodom represents the dregs of Canaanite society, and would be those who had not had any allegiance to Jehovah (cf. Matt. 10.15; 11.23,24). Note that in each case 'her daughters' takes the picture further than the individual city mentioned.

Thus God says here that Samaria and Canaanite cities will be released one day from the dominion of Babylon and rebuilt. After the return from exile, all the land had a measure of relief, and many ultimately turned to the true God, before and after the time of Christ (Mark 7.26).

What then would happen to Judah? Would she be excluded from the restoration? This is the theme of vs. 60–63. The covenant will be renewed (cf. Jer. 31.31–34), and the people will be ashamed of their old ways. As a fact of history the Jews absorbed the nations of Palestine, and by the time of Christ there was a measure of unity in the land (61).

Consider vs. 49, 50 as applicable to nations today.

Ezekiel 17　　Allegories of Transplanting

Among other things this chapter contains a criticism of King Zedekiah. He had made a pact, binding him by oath to Babylon, but he broke it in the hope of help from Egypt. Both Jeremiah and Ezekiel accused him of disloyalty, and urged submission to Babylon again (Jer. 37.6–10; 38.17–23).

The general theme of the allegories is clear in the light of the comments in vs. 11–21.

(*i*) The Babylonian eagle takes King Jehoiachin from Judah to Babylon in 597 B.C. (3,4; 2 Kings 24.8–16; 25.27–30).

(*ii*) The Babylonian eagle makes Zedekiah king in Judah. Note the meaning of 'low spreading' given in 13,14 (5,6; 2 Kings 24.17).

(*iii*) The Egyptian eagle attracts Zedekiah and his people (7). The exact meaning of the final words of v. 7 and the following verse is far from clear in the RSV. The Egyptian eagle did not transplant anyone to Egypt at this time, although he had taken Jehoahaz in 609 B.C. (2 Kings 23.31–35). Since the margin shows that the Hebrew text has 'it was transplanted', it is preferable to retain this, as the AV and RV do, whether or not we run the two verses together. Then the reference is back to v. 5. Zedekiah had been taken up from the royal family and replanted as king by Babylon, without his needing to turn to Egypt.

(*iv*) Zedekiah and his people will be uprooted. There is a further problem of 'he' in v. 9, but it could be the king of Babylon. While the switch from Egypt to Babylon would be too violent with 'he' in v. 8, it would be less abrupt here. But v. 20 perhaps indicates that 'he' here could be God Himself.

(*v*) Ultimately God will bring His Messiah, presumably from the line of the king already in Babylon (22–24). The word 'sprig' links on to the Messianic title of 'branch' in Isa. 11.1; Jer. 23.5; 33.15; Zech. 3.8; 6.12. Three Hebrew words are used. Ezekiel's word is the feathery top of a tree; the other words describe the shoot coming from the stump of the line of David. The nations find shelter under the Messiah (23, cf. Matt. 13.31,32). The 'mountain height of Israel' is a term that looks beyond the literal Jerusalem (cf. Isa. 2.2,3; Heb. 12.22–24). What a fine ending to a gloomy chapter!

Consider the importance of keeping one's word (e.g. Psa. 15.4). Breaking the covenant with Babylon is breaking the covenant with God (19).

Ezekiel 18   The Past and the Present

There was a proverb circulating in Jerusalem (Jer. 31.29) and Babylon in which the present generation blamed their sufferings on the sins of their fathers. To a certain extent this was true, but Jeremiah and Ezekiel challenge the false conclusion that they could now do nothing about it. The second commandment (Exod. 20.5,6) had spoken of the cumulative disaster that mounts up when generation after generation refuses to repent. This is also the teaching of Jesus Christ (Matt. 23.35,36). Ezekiel asserts that each generation is responsible for breaking the evil tradition or for maintaining the good one. We must learn from our parents by way of example and warning.

The sins in vs. 5–8 are both religious and moral, and all are found in the Law, after the references to special forms of idol worship in v. 6 (cf. 6.1–7), e.g. (in order) Exod. 20.14; Lev. 18.19; Exod. 22.26–27; Exod. 20.15; Deut. 15.7–11; Exod. 22.25; Exod. 23.6–9.

Note that the Bible does not condemn all lending of money at interest as wrong in itself, e.g. Deut. 23.20; Luke 19.23. But it envisages interest-free loans to God's people who are in real need.

Note the sequences in this chapter; good father—bad son—good son. Commentators differ over the extent of the term 'die' in this chapter. Sheer fact, of which Ezekiel was as fully aware as we are, makes it impossible to limit it to physical death, but physical death in Scripture is linked with eternal death. It would, however, be wrong to emphasize 'soul' in v. 4 as though it were intended as a contrast to 'body'. The latter word does not occur here, and the Hebrew *nephesh* often means no more than 'person' (e.g. Exod. 1.5).

Although v. 24 raises difficulties in the N.T. context of the final perseverance of the saints, such warnings must stand in Scripture.

No person—believer or unbeliever—ever has the right to say, 'Because I was righteous once, it does not matter whether I am plunging into sin now.'

The chapter ends (25–32) with an appeal to turn to God in repentance from their twisted ideas about Him. Thus they will 'get' a new heart, which is, of course, the gift of God (11.19; 36.26). *Consider the importance of vs. 23 and 32.*

Ezekiel 19   Lion Hunt

The RSV carefully sets this chapter out as poetry, printing the lines according to the balance of the rhythm. This is known as the *qīnāh* or 'lamentation metre', which we have already noticed in the *Book of Lamentations*. It is worth reading aloud.

The lament is for three kings of Judah. There is no doubt about the first being Jehoahaz who was taken prisoner to Egypt in 609 B.C. (3,4; 2 Kings 23.31–33). Commentators usually identify the second with Jehoiachin, who was taken to Babylon in 597 B.C. (5–9), and the third with Zedekiah, who was king at the destruction of Jerusalem in 587 B.C. (10–14). The puzzling thing is the omission of Jehoiakim, who succeeded Jehoahaz and reigned 609–598 B.C. Possible explanations are:

(*i*) Jehoahaz and Jehoiachin are selected because they both shared the fate of exile. Since they reigned for no more than about three months each, the language of vs. 3,4,6,7 must represent their potentialities as their mother saw them.

(*ii*) The second is Jehoiakim, who was taken to Babylon for a short period (2 Chron. 36.6; Dan. 1.2), although he actually died during the siege of Jerusalem (2 Kings 24.1–6). The third king is then Jehoiachin (10–12), and the contemporary king Zedekiah is only part of the ruin, without the strength a ruler needs (13,14).

Notes: The symbol of the lioness as the mother of the kings of Judah links up with Gen. 49.9, cf. Rev. 5.5 of Christ.

In vs. 4 and 9 the hooks are appropriate to wild beasts, but they were also used for prisoners. The Assyrian king, Ashurbanipal, kept a king on exhibition in a cage at Nineveh (9).

In v. 14 note that the destructive fire comes from the stem of the vine itself. Thus Jerusalem and the royal house are the cause of their own destruction. Note how Ezekiel follows through the picture of this verse to a glorious end in 21.25–27.

The closing note by the final compiler of the book probably indicates that this lamentation had passed into regular use as a dirge.

Consider when we should lament for leaders.

1. Sir Robert Anderson wrote a book called 'The Silence of God'. Consider this as a title for these chapters.
2. How far are magic and superstition attempts to have the super-natural without the moral and spiritual claims of God?
3. How does the N.T. keep the balance between individual and corporate responsibility?
4. Why is the breaking of a promise or covenant regarded as such a serious crime in the Bible, and why is it so lightly regarded today?
5. How far does a nation share responsibility when its leaders are bad?

Ezekiel 20.1-22   Verdict of History

It is easy to come, as the elders did, to get a message from God's minister. It is less easy to listen to a diagnosis of blind rebellion—blind because we have not seen that we are perpetuating the self-centredness of our forefathers. Thus Ezekiel expounds history in the light of God's honour and the nation's disregard of Him. Note the repetition here and elsewhere in *Ezekiel* of 'for the sake of My name'. This does not mean that God refuses to act out of love for people, but is concerned only with His own reputation. God's people are intended to be the reflection of God's own character (Exod. 19.6; Lev. 11.44,45). Their poor behaviour gives the outsider a poor view of God's character.

In this chapter God reviews the different periods of Israel's history.

Egypt (5-9). This is the only place where God says that He told Israel to avoid idolatry in Egypt. The probability is that the strong action of Jacob in Gen. 35.1-4, in making all his household put away pagan gods, was the word of God for his descendants in Egypt. The fact that they turned so easily to fresh idols like the golden calf, indicates that many, as Ezekiel says, must have been attracted also by Egyptian religious practices.

The Wilderness (10-22). The first major thing that God did was to give His people rules for living (11), i.e. the Law, and an inner and outward mark of devotion to Himself, i.e. the weekly Sabbath (12). During the next few readings note Ezekiel's emphasis on the Sabbath. His contemporary, Jeremiah, also emphasized its obser-vance as a mark of spiritual vitality (Jer. 17.21-27). There are two examples of profaning the Sabbath during this time (Exod. 16.27; Num. 15.32), but the accusation here must include the general attitude towards the worship of God (note v. 16). Underground hankering after idols made Sabbath worship a pure formality (cf. Isa. 1.13). The significance of v. 22 is that, if God had not ultimately brought the people into the promised land, the Egyptians and others would have thought He was unable to do so (Exod. 32.12).

Psalm 106 may profitably be read alongside of this chapter.

Ezekiel 20.23-49   Man's Choice—and God's

This section (23-31) continues the earlier history of rebellion. In the wilderness the people were warned of the consequences of diobedience and idolatry when they came into the land (23, Lev. 26; Deut. 28). Yet they disobeyed, and consequently God gave them up to the degradation of Canaanite worship (26, 27), which accompanied the glamour of the high place ceremonies (28,29). If we link the thoughts of vs. 25 and 26 with Rom. 1.24-32, we can see that there is no contradiction between this passage and Jer. 7.31, which says that God did not command these things. God abandoned them to the customs and consequences of the religion they had chosen. *Bamah* is the regular word for 'high place', and v. 29 is a punning connection with *mah* ('what') and *bo* ('go'). Whatever its original derivation, the Hebrews took it from the Canaanites. God asks them to consider what is this place of worship that they unthinkingly patronize.

Next (32-39) God speaks of the sifting out of the idolaters. He will not allow them to continue their syncretistic religion (32), but will deal with them in exile. The wilderness (35,36) is clearly not literal, but a wilderness of experience. Before the Shepherd admits the flock to His land, He will separate the sheep from the goats (37,38).

The restored community will be a holy and devoted group (40-44). The tragedy was that those who returned with such enthusiasm, as we read in *Ezra* and *Nehemiah*, gradually slipped back again, though not into the crudities of high place worship and human sacrifice. The history between the Old and New Testaments is often a sad one, but with a strong nucleus of firm believers.

In vs. 45-49 there is a fresh type of prophecy, which perhaps is to be linked with the next chapter. One might have supposed that, if Nebuchadnezzar were invading from the north, the south would escape. But this is not to be, and the picture of the blazing trees moves to the blaze which will burn the whole nation. Thus

Ezekiel speaks an allegory for those who have ears to hear (cf. Isa. 2.13,14).
Compare this chapter with Jer. 3.6 and 7.30–34.

Ezekiel 21   The Sword of the Lord

The jerkiness of vs. 1–17 is probably due to something that Ezekiel is doing. Since he and other prophets often reinforced their messages with dramatic signs, he has perhaps drawn a sword and is whirling it round, making it flash in the sun, and shouting his words in disjointed sentences. Yet these sentences are linked by a vital theme: The Lord had used a stick of wood to chastise His people, but they had treated it as of no account (10,13). Now He has drawn the cutting sword of invasion, siege and capture, and in such an event both good and bad die or are taken into exile (4). The sword that Ezekiel displays is not just a threat, but continues where the rod leaves off (13), i.e. the day of warning is over. The N.T. treats the Second Coming in similar terms. One may ignore the warnings of history, but the final Day of the Lord cannot be ignored (cf. v. 7 with Luke 21.26).

In vs. 18–23 Babylon is invading. Nebuchadnezzar tosses up to see whether to besiege Jerusalem or Rabbah. Where we might toss a coin, Nebuchadnezzar's diviners judged by the fall of arrows, shaken and thrown down; by some consultation of images; and by signs in the liver of a sacrifice (21). Jerusalem is chosen. All the same, the people of Jerusalem do not believe that the decision will be effective (23). The remainder of v. 23 is difficult, but perhaps means that Zedekiah is guilty of breaking his oath of allegiance to Nebuchadnezzar (2 Kings 24.20).

This, however, does not exhaust the meaning, since the following verses show that both people and king are rotten at heart. Yet v. 27 is one of the great Messianic promises of the O.T., although it is often overlooked. It is similar to the promise of Gen. 49.10, (RSV). After the exile there were no more kings of David's line. Zerubbabel, who was leader soon after the return, was of David's line, but was never king.

Finally God speaks to Ammon (28–32), who had escaped the Babylonian attack, and who in fact turned against Judah and exploited her defeat (25.3). Ammon's turn will come for the sword, and her name will be forgotten (32).

'Whose right it is' (27). 'The highest place that heaven affords is His, is His, by right.' Why 'by right'? (See Phil. 2.5–11; Rev. 5.9–14.)

355

Ezekiel 22
National Decay

It is only too easy to read these accusations simply as descriptions of the state of Jerusalem immediately before the exile. The fact is that most great nations have taken the same road. The words could have been written of Assyria, Babylon, Greece, and Rome, in their days of decadent domination. We do well to watch the contemporary situation. While there is considerable desire to help the underprivileged and the sufferer today, governments and power blocks continue to create fresh areas of misery, sometimes violently. The claims of God give way to the worship of man's inventions. Family life is disrupted, and abnormal sexual behaviour is advertised by films and books. Even our responsibility towards our neighbour goes by the board if through its abuse or abandonment we can make a little extra for ourselves. All these wrongs are found in vs. 1–12.

Israel and Judah were more fortunate than other nations which disintegrated when their morality exploded (Mal. 3.6). God took His people into exile, but used the exile to clean and renew them (13–16), even though, at first, their life gave the outsider a poor impression of God (16).

Meanwhile the siege approaches, and the country people crowd into Jerusalem for protection (19). They will be like metal and dross in a cauldron, with the fire blazing underneath. The point of the comparison here is not that the dross rises to the surface so that it can be skimmed off, but that the solid metal is melted into a fluid mass. All are subjected to judgement. The picture of refining is used also in Psa. 12.6; Prov. 17.3; Isa. 1.25; 48.10; Jer. 6.28–30; Mal. 3.2,3; 1 Pet. 1.7. Although the RSV makes v. 18 match v. 20 (see margin), the order of the Hebrew text makes reasonable sense, i.e. 'all of them are brass . . . in the midst of the furnace; they are the dross of silver' (RV).

The final charge is against the men in power who misused their position (25,27. What is power today?), religious leaders who abandoned what God had revealed (26), and prophetic preachers, who spoke easy platitudes (28). Small wonder that the ordinary masses had slipped morally (29). If only there had been God's men to speak and to act! (30, cf. Isa. 59.16; Jer. 5.1).

Consider v. 14. Habits of wrong living (13) sap our courage and strength when the hour of trial comes

Ezekiel 23.1-21
Broken Relationship

For the second time (ch. 16) Ezekiel takes up the picture of Judah as the unfaithful wife, but now he gives prominence to unfaithful Israel also, as does Jeremiah in 3.6–10.

356

'Oholah' means either 'tent' or 'possessing tents'. The reference could be to the original wilderness state before the people were settled in towns (cf. Jer. 2.2), or, if the picture of the tent is that of a dwelling, God dwelt among the Northern Kingdom and had His true followers there (e.g. 1 Kings 19.18). The word used of the Tabernacle is basically the same. 'Oholibah' means 'my tent is in her', probably with reference to God's special dwelling in the Temple in Jerusalem.

The chapter does not make pleasant reading. Perhaps our danger has been in looking at the sins of God's people too academically. We disapprove of them at an intellectual level. But the crude descriptions here stir our deepest emotions. Persistent sin is not just something for which God gives us a bad mark. It is a horror of broken relationship that, if we could see it with God's eyes, would shake us as much as does the story of these two sluts.

The danger of commenting like this is that those readers who are too introspective may be driven into themselves beyond what is right. Notice, therefore, how the two wives are pictured in self-centred indulgence, which they welcome and do not resist. They are not to be compared to those Christians who know both victory and defeat with sins that attack them, and who keep looking to the Lord.

We are more likely to be overlooking sins of unfaithfulness, while we build up patterns of behaviour which fit the standards of the world rather than the way of God. Mammon comes in various disguises (Matt. 6.24), as well as in the disguise of Assyria and Babylon, and our energies may go into self-advancement (for which Assyria and Babylon offered enticing prospects) rather than into devotion to God.

For examples of appeals to foreign nations, see such passages as 2 Kings 16.7; Isa. 7.17–25; Hos. 7.11. There is no direct reference elsewhere to overtures to Babylon (16, also v. 40), but foreign alliances produced foreign standards of life and religion (e.g. 2 Kings 16.10 f.; Isa. 2.6; Jer. 7.18).

Rev. 17.1, 2; 18.1–10 are somewhat of a parallel to this chapter.

Ezekiel 23.22-49   The End of it All

The orgies end in death. The lovers, with no ties of marriage, terminate the affair when they wish. All the rag, tag, and bobtail join in the humiliation of Oholibah. Pekod (23) is a tribe east of the Tigris (Jer. 50.21), and Shoa and Koa have been identified with other tribes in the same area. Even the Assyrians, conquered and absorbed by the Babylonians (Chaldeans), are in the Babylonian

357

attack on Jerusalem. Cruelties like those described in v. 25 were actually practised, and physical brutalities on prisoners of war and political detainees are unfortunately not unknown today.

There is a profound psychological truth in vs. 28, 29 (cf. 17). Sex without love only too often ends in frustration and hatred (2 Sam. 13.15). Quite apart from sex without marriage, a marriage that is grounded simply on physical attraction is likely to collapse, because there is no union of mind and spirit.

In vs. 32–34 Ezekiel uses a new metaphor, that of a cup of wine which makes the drinker dead drunk. To us this is a strange picture of God's judgement, but it occurs elsewhere in Scripture, e.g. Psa. 75.8; Jer. 25.15 f.; Lam. 4.21; Rev. 14.10; 16.19. The symbolism is that of the drunkard who collapses helplessly, and who is then a victim for his enemies as well as an ultimate misery to himself. The contents of God's cup have a similar effect. We have seemed to ourselves to be so strong that we could defy God's standards and even God Himself; suddenly in the crisis we are helpless. Today our fresh knowledge of the plight of the alcoholic can vary Ezekiel's illustration. The alcoholic is not, of course, more wicked than others, but he cannot achieve contented sobriety so long as he goes his own way and believes that next time the crisis comes he will be strong enough to conquer. Only when he comes to the end of himself and casts himself upon God can he stop destroying himself.

The closing verses (36–49) are a summary of all that has gone before.

The formation of habit-responses is part of our God-given personality. It is vital to see that our habits are constructive and not destructive (Phil. 3.19; 4.11–13).

Ezekiel 24.1-14 The Rusty Pot

Like most preachers Ezekiel uses an illustration more than once, varying the application according to the point of his message. He has used the picture of the cauldron in 11.3–12. Now he takes it up again. Jerusalem is the cooking pot, and its people are the meat that is to be cooked. But the pot is rusty and filthy as well. When the meat is cooked up and emptied out, the pot is set on the fire again and heated until it melts, thus destroying itself with the rust and filth. Thus God declares that Jerusalem cannot be saved; it can only be destroyed.

The chapter is dated in the ninth year of Jehoiachin's captivity, which was also Ezekiel's captivity. This makes the date January, 588 B.C. Although Ezekiel is in Babylon, he is prophetically told by God that on this very day Nebuchadnezzar has begun the siege of Jerusalem. The date agrees with 2 Kings 25.1. As an additional witness Ezekiel writes down the date, so that it can be checked later (2).

It is possible that the Hebrew of v. 6 (see margin) implies that at Jehoiachin's captivity captives were selected by lot. Now all will be taken indiscriminately.

The blood in v. 7 is that of murder, wrongful conviction, and human sacrifice. Blood unjustly shed cries for vengeance (Gen. 4.10; Job 16.18). The people who committed the crimes did not even trouble to conceal them (7). So God takes them at their word, and does not cover up their sins in forgiveness (8). Yet God had been willing to forgive them provided that they would let Him make them clean (12,13). The Bible looks at cleansing from both the divine and the human point of view. God Himself makes us clean (e.g. 36.25; 1 John 1.7) and yet we must make ourselves clean (e.g. Isa. 1.16; 2 Cor. 7.1). There is no practical contradiction here. We may start by saying 'No: I will go my own way'. We may then repent and begin to make the effort to reform. Then we see our own inability and call to God to do what we cannot do.

Compare what is said here about blood and cleansing with Heb. 12.24, 25.

Ezekiel 24.15-27   Deep Sorrow

It is significant that the squalor of free love in ch. 23, with the further allusions in 24.13, should be followed by the picture of the close of a happy marriage. A happy marriage is one of God's greatest gifts to mankind, as Ezekiel had found. In many respects Ezekiel was a hard man, if we are to judge by the content of his sermons, but he had to steel himself to resist the rot in the nation. Now in this sidelight we see him as a man devoted to his wife, 'the delight of his eyes'. Suddenly he loses her, and he is forbidden to mourn openly for her. We need not press v. 16 to mean that God acted in an arbitrary way, but the phrase reminds us that God's hand is to be seen even in what we call the normal processes of life. We do not know whether Ezekiel's wife was already ill.

At this moment of acute distress, God uses the tragedy as yet another prophetic sign. The meaning of this sign is not obvious to us at first sight, but the exiles in Babylon, to whom Ezekiel is speaking, must face the loss of the Temple and city, which are dear to them. When the appalling news reached them, they would be shocked into genuine mourning, far beyond what might be expressed by the traditional signs (21–24).

Ezekiel is further told that one day the news will come through a refugee. God will warn him of this previously, and he will be dumb with horror, just as he was dumb at his wife's death (17). But when the refugee arrives, he will be ready to talk freely with him (25–27, cf. 33.21,22).

For the signs of mourning mentioned here (17,22) see 2 Sam. 15.30; Isa. 20.2; Jer. 16.7; Hos. 9.4; Mic. 3.7.

It is worth noticing how marriage was used as a prophetic sign with two other prophets. Jeremiah was forbidden to marry because so many children would die in the coming siege (16.2–4). Hosea learnt from the unfaithfulness of his wife how God felt about the unfaithfulness of His people (Hos. 1–3).

God does not forbid deep emotion provided that it is real (17; Matt. 5.4; Acts 20.37, 38).

Questions for further study and discussion on Ezekiel chs. 20—24

1. In what way do these chapters show that God is the God of history?
2. Check the nations and places mentioned here, using a good map. Which were the closest neighbours of Israel and Judah?
3. Why do we assume that God is not limited by time? What indications are there in these chapters that Ezekiel was given supernatural knowledge of present and future events?
4. Does the strong language of ch. 22 justify the production of pornographic literature today?
5. In the light of 24.17, how far should a Christian normally observe the social customs of the country in which he is living at the moment?

Ezekiel 25   Ancient and Modern

As we begin this new section of the Book, we may perhaps wonder why God takes up space with nations that have long since vanished. It is significant that they have vanished. Everyone has heard of Jerusalem: few could place Rabbah, the capital of Ammon (5), or the important cities of Moab to the north-east and east of the Dead Sea (9), or Teman and Dedan in the north and south of Edom (13). Although the Philistines (15) gave their name to Palestine, they also vanished as a nation. We can speak of ourselves as members of Jerusalem and of Israel (Gal. 4.26; 6.16; Rev. 21.10,12,14), but not of Rabbah and Ammon. The gods of these nations are now no more than mythological curiosities. The God of Israel is the God of our Lord Jesus Christ, and is our God today.

Secondly, we must remember that these nations and their

360

threats were as real to Israel and Judah as are the great nations of our day to us. So long as nation competes with nation, these chapters are topical. The same old methods of international competition are still present, and the same old attitudes of groups of people; surely they still come under the judgement of God.

Ammon evidently took advantage of Babylon's victory and grabbed whatever land and property that they could. This is implied in v. 3 and is confirmed by Jer. 49.1. Here is the temporarily strong nation taking advantage of the weaker neighbour. There were, of course, Jews who eluded the Babylonians and remained in the land, as members of the Northern Kingdom did after the Assyrian invasion.

Moab probably also took the opportunity of gaining extra territory, but Ezekiel singles out her sceptical attitude, which denied that there was any special relationship between Israel and the true God (8). Moab and Ammon were, in fact, soon overrun by invading Nabateans.

Edom was terribly treacherous at the fall of Jerusalem (Psa. 137.7; Obad. 10–14). Edom also was overrun, and, eventually, in 109 B.C. it was finally subjugated by the Jewish leader, John Hyrcanus (14).

The Philistines are denounced as always looking for an occasion for war (15). The name Cherethites is probably connected with Crete, which is one of the places from which the Philistines came (Zeph. 2.5). David had a group of Cherethite mercenaries as well as others from Gath (2 Sam. 15.18).

Groups and nations, as well as individuals, have their own character.

Ezekiel 26   Sea Traders

It is surprising to find three whole chapters devoted to Tyre, since there is hardly any mention of her, and her fellow-city of Sidon, in the history of Israel. As these chapters indicate, the Phoenicians, who lived in the coastal strip which contained these two cities, were more concerned with sea trading than with extending their territory. At the same time they were ready to move in when the Jews and Israelites moved out (2).

Earlier Tyre had treacherously broken a pact (Amos 1.9), and she is selected as an example of proud self-sufficiency by Isaiah (Isa. 23) as well as by Ezekiel. One way of reading these chapters is after the pattern of Rev. 18, where indeed some of the phraseology there applied to Babylon is applied to Tyre in *Ezekiel*, as the RSV margin here shows. Babylon and Tyre represent the attitude of civilization without the standards of God, the attitude which has come to be characterized as 'I'm all right, Jack', i.e. 'Never mind about others, so long as I have what I want—not just what I need'. This attitude rouses others to want what we have, and Babylon and Tyre become the target of other nations.

Ezekiel is given this message shortly after the fall of Jerusalem. Nebuchadnezzar now turned his attention to Tyre, which held out on its island for thirteen years. It is now known from inscriptions that Nebuchadnezzar eventually forced its submission and put a puppet king on the throne. Ezek. 29.18 records that he did not obtain enough spoil from the city to pay for all the efforts he had made.

In fact, he did not destroy Tyre, but Alexander the Great exactly fulfilled vs. 8–14 in 332 B.C. Certain prophecies are conditional, as God says in Jer. 18.7–11, and as Jonah found when he said by the word of God that Nineveh would be destroyed within forty days. Nineveh humbled itself and was spared for the time being, though ultimately it reached a peak of wickedness and was destroyed. Perhaps Tyre was humbled in the same way, and its doom was averted until later.

What will people connect with us when we go (17)?

*Ezekiel 27.1-24 · An Affluent Society

Whereas a commentary on ch. 26 can be in general terms, this section must obviously be largely notes on the peoples and countries with whom Tyre has been trading, so far as these can be identified. We follow the RSV which sometimes renders the names differently from the AV and RV.

In vs. 3–9 Tyre is pictured as a great ship made from the finest materials. This section is in verse, as the RSV indicates, but there is no reason to regard the prose that follows (10–25) as by a different author. Like Isa. 3.18–23 it is very much of a catalogue, which is hard to put into verse.

Wood for the ship comes from the north of Palestine (5,6). Senir (5) is the Canaanite name for Hermon (Deut. 3.9; other references can be found under Senir and Shenir in an AV concordance). Elishah (7) is thought by some to be Enkomi on the east coast of Cyprus (also Gen. 10.4). Sidon, the island city of Arvad, Zemer, and Gebal (known by the Greeks as Biblos), are all Phoenician coastal cities (8,9).

To defend herself Tyre had mercenaries from Persia, Lydia (Lud), and Put (10). The last named is likely to be Libya, but may be the Egyptian Punt on the African coast. Other troops come from Arvad (already mentioned), and Helech, which is probably Cilicia, and from the unidentified Gamad (11).

The ships of Tyre traded all over the known world. Tarshish is Tartessus in Spain (12). Javan is the name for the Greek Ionians, and Tubal and Meshech are probably peoples to the south of the Black Sea (see also 38.2,3). Inscriptions refer to Tegarama (14) as between Carchemish and Haran on an important trade route through Armenia. Rhodes, Edom, Judah and Damascus (15–18) are well known. Helbon (18) is north-east of Damascus, while Uzal (19) is likely to be Izalla in north-east Syria, which is mentioned as supplying Nebuchadnezzar with wine.

Then the description moves to Arabia, where are the peoples mentioned in 20–22. Finally, Mesopotamian peoples and towns are listed (23). Of these, Eden is the Assyrian province of Bit-Adini between Haran and the Euphrates (cf. 2 Kings 19.12), but Canneh and Chilmad are unidentified.

Tyre was an affluent society—for some (13, cf. Rev. 18.12, 13). So Luke 12.15 is relevant.

*Ezekiel 27.25-36   All are Involved

We began the chapter with the finest ship in the world. This was Tyre. Then came the catalogue of her greatness. Now we return to the first picture, but what a difference! The ship is shattered by the storm, and is lost with all her crew, and all her rich cargo. The poem slips easily into its application. The world is astounded at the ruin of the great trading power from whom they gained all the necessities and luxuries of life.

The collapse of a great power inevitably brings fear to others (35), for no one knows whose turn it will be next. If Nebuchadnezzar spares others now, there will soon be some other conqueror.

In v. 36 the merchants *hiss* at the fallen city. The word occurs in other passages also in connection with destruction, and is coupled with 'astonishment' (1 Kings 9.8), 'curse' (Jer. 25.18), 'reproach' (Jer. 29.18), 'horror' (Jer. 51.37), 'clapping hands, wagging the head, and gnashing teeth' (Lam. 2.15,16). In spite of this we do not know its exact significance. It could be an expression of disapproval and rejection, as when an audience hisses bad performers. It could be the equivalent of spitting to avert the evil eye, or curse. Or it could be a whistle of amazement at what has happened, as one might say 'Phew!'

Whatever the significance the reactions of those who are not sharing Tyre's doom remind us of how we are nationally bound together. One group cannot perish or rise to power without affecting all.

'It can't happen to us.'

Ezekiel 28.1-10   Pride Before a Fall

This is a remarkable chapter which has been treated differently by various commentators. The main problem comes in the next portion, where one has to decide whether or not there is a description of Satan. For today's reading we can all agree that Ezekiel is describing Ithobaal II, the king of Tyre. He is here given the title of 'prince' or 'ruler' (2), which does not exclude kingship, but is commonly used of others than kings. The use of the lesser word is a suitable introduction to a chapter on pride.

The theme of the humbling of the proud has formed the subject of many stories and plays, and our own generation has seen it happen more than once. God has no room for the proud (Psa. 119.21; Luke 1.51), because pride is a denial of man's place as the servant of God, and the essence of the fall was a desire to become self-controlled, fixing one's own standards of good and evil, instead of being God-centred.

Here God strips off the disguise. The king of Tyre regards himself as the Lord of the world. He has the deep knowledge to manipulate people and markets for his own ends (4,5).

The reference to Daniel is interesting (3). There is no reason why this should not be to the Daniel at the court of Nebuchadnezzar, though he must have been still quite a young man and not very well known. Otherwise the reference is to the great and righteous Daniel of Canaanite literature which would be appropriate in addressing a Canaanite king (see note at end of ch. 14).

When the great ship of Tyre sinks, the king will perish. A ruler tends to act as though he will live for ever, like an immortal god, but each has to prove by death that he is no more than mortal (9). Before we condemn the king of Tyre, we may remember that sin in Eden was the desire to be as God (Gen. 3.5), and this desire still haunts us all. In some department of life I am almost certainly saying 'I am a god'.

By way of contrast, Phil. 2.5–11 is an excellent commentary on this. Our Lord Jesus Christ came down from the glory of Godhead, and chose to die for us as man.

Ezekiel 28.11-26   Fallen Rebel

In v. 12 the king is addressed by the regular title for king, and many Christian commentators have interpreted what follows of Satan, as king behind the rulers of this world. A similar interpretation is given to Isa. 14. Others believe that the king is here addressed as the primeval man in terms of a Phoenician version of the Eden story.

These notes will assume that the king is addressed in terms of his master, Satan. The character of Satan, here described, comes out in him. Thus this chapter and Isa. 14 throw light on the fall of Satan, and indicate that he was a created being who fell through pride.

The link with the Eden story is given near the beginning (13) to call attention to the identification with the tempter who was there; but the description of his magnificent glory belongs to his original creation and his place on the mountain of God, i.e. heaven. This description is too extravagant for Adam, though, on the interpretation it might be true of some Canaanite primeval man.

The Hebrew of v. 14 is difficult. The RV addresses him as 'Thou wast the anointed cherub that covereth'. The cherubim in the holy of holies covered the mercy seat and the ark (Exod. 25.20; 1 Kings 8.7), and symbolically guarded the approaches to God. Hence, Satan may have been once the chief guardian of the throne of God. The RSV emendation could mean that Satan had a cherub as his escort.

Neither Satan nor man was created evil (15), but both had free will, and were more than puppets or animals controlled by instinct. Both chose to be as god (Isa. 14.13,14), but the special thing that moved Satan was a desire to have yet more splendour (17). The reference to trade in v. 16 shows that there is a blend of the king of Tyre and his master. The king traded for his own power. Satan sold his glory for violent rebellion, and was cast out from the mountain of God. Again the RSV has emended the reference to the guardian cherub in v. 16, while the RV retains, 'I have destroyed thee, O covering cherub, from the midst of the stones of fire.' With the RSV, the same cherub who barred the way to Eden (Gen. 3.24) may have driven Satan from heaven.

In vs. 17–19 the earthly king comes to the fore again, but, like Satan's, his doom is inevitable. V. 18 shows that he has been concerned with fostering evil, materialistic values, and false religion, all of which carry the fire of their own destruction within them.

The remainder of the chapter concerns Tyre's neighbour, Sidon, who will not escape (20–23), and gives a brief promise of Israel's restoration (24–26). Note the allusion in v. 24 to Num. 33.55; Josh. 23.13. In ch. 34 onwards we shall be reading much more of Israel's restoration to blessing.

Satan is a rebel, not an eternal god of absolute evil. What follows from this?

Ezekiel 29.1-16 King Crocodile

The next four chapters concern Egypt. The date of this section

(1) is 587 B.C., shortly before the fall of Jerusalem. The Pharaoh addressed is Hophra, also called Apries, who had recently come to the throne. Each Pharaoh was regarded as divine, and presumably some made more of this than others. Hophra boasts that he is the maker and lord of the Nile. This is a claim that one finds in Egyptian writings, e.g. 'The Nile is at his service, and he opens its cavern to give life to Egypt.'

God addresses him as the great crocodile lying in the Nile. The word translated 'dragon' (3) denotes any monster, and the context here obviously means the crocodile. So far from owning the river, he is dragged from it and flung out on the land (4,5, cf. 32.4,5). This may have been fulfilled literally, since Hophra was deposed by a rival (cf. Jer. 44.30), and his body may well have been flung out in contempt (cf. Jer. 22.18,19).

In addition to his sin of pride, Pharaoh is charged with being a broken reed (6, cf. Isa. 36.6). The reference is to Hophra's campaign into Palestine, which temporarily caused the Babylonians to retire from the siege of Jerusalem (Jer. 37.5). But Hophra was not strong enough to carry the campaign through. He promised Judah more than he could perform, and once again his pride was humbled.

The reference to the desolation of Egypt (9–12) is probably symbolical of the subjugation of the country. From this time onwards it lost political power, after the defeat of Hophra's successor, Amasis, by Nebuchadnezzar. We do not know whether the land itself suffered disasters and famine from Migdol in the north to Syene (Assouan) in the south (10), but the symbolism could be used as the symbolism of the crocodile is used earlier. The forty years could be the symbolic equivalent of Israel's forty years of discipline in the wilderness.

The restoration of Egypt came under Greek rule, and Alexandria especially became an important centre of Judaism and Christianity, thus probably fulfilling Isa. 19.19–25. Present-day Israel would certainly appreciate v. 16.

> '*I am the master of my fate,*
> *I am the captain of my soul.*'
> True or false? (See Josh. 24.15; Luke 12.16–21.)

Ezekiel 29.17—30.19   Pattern of the Last Day

We noted in ch. 26 that Nebuchadnezzar eventually forced Tyre to submit, but he was unable to plunder it as he had hoped. It was easy for Tyre to remove its treasures by sea before finally submitting. Probably v. 18 refers to the Babylonian troops who were forced

366

to carry great stones to try to build a causeway from the mainland to the island city, as Alexander the Great did later.

A Babylonian inscription says that in 568 B.C. Nebuchadnezzar fought against the army of Amasis, who had succeeded Hophra on the throne of Egypt. Josephus also records that he invaded Egypt (cf. Jer. 43.8–13). Doubtless he obtained sufficient plunder and tribute to compensate for what he had hoped to obtain from Tyre (19).

The horn of v. 21 may be the Messiah (Psa. 132.17), although it might here be simply a symbol of strength (Jer. 48.25). The following sentence could be an indication that in subsequent prophecies Ezekiel would be inspired to say more about this horn, as indeed he was in chs. 36 and 37.

In ch. 30 we have the setting of the doom of Egypt against the ultimate picture of the Day of the Lord (cf. Joel 1.15, of the locust invasion, and Isa. 13.6,9, of Babylon). The fact is that from time to time a nation reaches a climax of oppression and moral decay from which God humbles and often destroys it. The final Day is yet to come when God will put down all sin wherever it is found. Thus previous Days of the Lord become patterns of the final Day.

In 30.1–9 Egypt and all her helpers are beaten, including Ethiopia, Put (Punt on the west coast of the Red Sea), and Lydian mercenaries.

For Nebuchadnezzar's invasion (10,11), see yesterday's notes. Finally, there is a general picture of doom (12–19) falling on the many gods and goddesses of Egypt (13) and on the self-confident cities. Of the cities mentioned here, Zoan, Pelusium, Pibeseth, and Tehaphnehes (Tahpanhes), are in the Nile delta. Memphis and On (Heliopolis) are just south of the delta. Pathros is the general name for the southern part of Egypt (Upper Egypt), and Thebes is one of its cities.

What are the things mentioned here that will come under judgement on the Day of the Lord?

Ezekiel 30.20—31.18   The Withered Tree

The first prophecy here is dated about three months before the fall of Jerusalem. We have no independent evidence of what happened when Nebuchadnezzar invaded Egypt, though Josephus records that he took back a number of Jews as captives. He would undoubtedly have taken many leading Egyptians also (23,26), as was his custom when he conquered a country.

Chapter 31 is dated approximately one month before the fall of

Jerusalem (1). Now Ezekiel uses a picture of Egypt similar to that which he had used of Judah in ch. 17. Egypt is the towering cedar, with its roots going down to the underground streams. It shelters bird and beast, and is the envy even of the trees of the garden of Eden. This is the picture that Egypt presents to itself and the world.

But in v. 10 we detect once more the Satanic impulse to pride (28.17), and so Egypt in her turn has to be brought low. We have already seen in ch. 29 that history records the gradual deterioration of Egypt. Although Nebuchadnezzar did not occupy it, in 525 B.C. Cambyses, king of Persia, became king of Egypt also. Two centuries later it passed into the control of Greece, and in 30 B.C. it became part of the Roman empire.

The end of Egypt is also pictured as a descent to Sheol, the place of the dead (15–18, cf. Isa. 14.15–20). Its supply of living waters is cut off (15) and, consequently, the lesser trees that are associated with it die also. Their miserable consolation is that they have perished in what they would consider to be good company (16, cf. Isa. 14.10,11). The reference in vs. 16, 18 to the trees of Eden cannot mean that the actual trees in the garden of Eden are cut down, but that Eden-like trees perish. Similarly, the expression 'ships of Tarshish' came to mean any big ships resembling the large ocean-going vessels that sailed to Tarshish (Isa. 2.16).

The final reference to the uncircumcised (18) is to those who are outside of the covenant (28.10; 32.21). The term is understandable, though the Bible in other places makes it clear that God is concerned with circumcision of the heart and not simply with physical circumcision, important though this was as the covenant sign (Deut. 10.16; Jer. 4.4; Rom. 2.25–29).

Note other tree pictures in Psa. 1; Jer. 17.6–8.

Ezekiel 32   Death without Glory

Jerusalem has fallen and Ezekiel still continues his prophecies against Egypt (1,17). Naturally, he spoke of many other things during this whole period, but the editor of the Book, whether or not he was Ezekiel himself, has placed this collection in a single group.

Most speakers use illustrations more than once, and in vs. 2–8 there is a repetition of the thought of 29.3–5. (See notes.) The opening words differ, since here we have Pharaoh's regard for himself as a lion, whereas he is no more than a crocodile stirring up mud and filth. So God will haul him out and throw him on land to be eaten by birds and beasts. The symbolism of the great Day of the Lord comes again (7,8, cf. 30.3).

Then comes the repetition of the reaction of other countries at

Egypt's fall (9,10, cf. **31**.16), and the mention of Babylon and other great powers as God's agents (11). The symbolism of desolation, an uninhabited and neglected country, indicates the ruin of the empire (13–15). The theme of lamentation for past glory will be taken up by the mourning women (16, cf. **19**.14).

Now follows a dramatic lamentation such as might well be chanted by the mourners (18–32). Note the magnificent repetitions and refrains. Although the passage is printed as prose, it has the effect of poetry.

The lamentation accompanies the funeral (18). Mighty Egypt has gone the way of all flesh (19–21). Each empire, with its ruler, imagines that it has found the secret of immortality, but one follows another to death. Assyria has gone with all her violence (22,23). Elam, once a great power, was absorbed by Persia (24,25). Meshech and Tubal (**27**.13; **38**.2,3), powers to the north, perish in their turn. The Greek Septuagint and the Syriac version omit 'not' in v. 27. But if it is retained, the reference could be to the picture in **39**.11–16 where the hosts of Gog, who was the chief prince of Mesech and Tubal, lie unburied for a long time, whereas other warriors killed in battle were normally buried quickly. Edom (29) and the Phoenician cities (30) perish also. This is the only consolation Pharaoh can find (31, cf. **31**.16). He is in the company of every kind of fallen greatness.

Togetherness may be deadly. We have read here about nations. As individuals we may ponder Psa. 49.10–20.

Questions for further study and discussion on Ezekiel chs. 25–32

1. What can modern business learn from these chapters?
2. What can politicians learn from them?
3. What passages of fear and threat move you most here? Can you get the feeling of something real that is happening?
4. Why is pride especially obnoxious to God and to man? What does the N.T. say about it?
5. Jesus Christ used pictures from nature and experience in Matt. **13**. Which of the objects from which He drew His illustrations are also used in these chapters?
6. Consider how far predictions in these chapters may fairly be regarded as literal, and how far as expressing truth in illustrative terms.

Ezekiel 33 The Present Moment

There are repetitions of two earlier prophecies in vs. 1–20. Ezekiel is once again reminded of his call to be a watchman (1–9, cf. 3.16–21).

Jeremiah also needed a second commissioning in terms very similar to those used at his call (Jer. **15**.19–21, cf. **1**.17–19). We are enthusiastic when the Lord first becomes real to us, but it is not too difficult to lose the vision.

This section rounds off Ezekiel's ministry during the period before the fall of Jerusalem (21,22), and is a reminder that his work is not yet over. Now the fresh exiles and those who were left in Judah, as well as those who had been taken at the same time as Ezekiel, needed further warning.

So Ezekiel first warns his fellow exiles as he had done previously (10–20 cf. ch. **18**). The common opinion was that they had become so involved in their own and their forefathers' sins that they could do nothing to help themselves. So God reminds them that He is concerned with the present moment, and they must be, too. They must not presume on a past good life if they are now drifting into evil. Yet neither must they sink into despair over the past if now they are ready to turn to God in repentance. But would they take the point, or merely look upon Ezekiel as providing a little entertainment for a drab existence (30–33)?

There is a message for those who had eluded the Babylonians (23–29). They were saying that, if Abraham, a single individual, was given the land, how much more would they have it now for themselves. The answer is that they would not escape suffering for the wrongs that characterized them in common with the rest of the nation. The *Book of Lamentations* shows their sufferings.

Now at last comes the news that Jerusalem has fallen (21,22). Ezekiel had experienced one of those periods of dumbness that sometimes preceded a striking message or event (3.26,27, cf. 24.25–27). Next morning he and his fellow exiles heard the news.

The date in v. 21 is superficially difficult. Jerusalem was captured in the 11th year of Zedekiah's reign and of Jehoiachin's captivity (e.g. Jer. **39**.2; 2 Kings **25**.2), and it is unlikely that the news took nearly 18 months to reach Babylon. It may be that at this point there is a difference between the Palestinian and Babylonian reckoning of the date when the new year began, whether in spring or in autumn. The Greek Septuagint, however, reads 'the eleventh year', which removes the difficulty.

How important is our past?

Ezekiel 34   Shepherds and the Shepherd

Although, as we have seen in ch. **33**, Ezekiel still has the responsibility to warn, he is now set free to talk to his people of what God will do with them and for them after they have learned the lessons of the exile. We must be prepared for a blend of near and distant future, such as we often find in prophecy (1 Pet. 1.10–12). Thus this chapter begins with contemporary bad rulers and ends with the Messiah.

This seems puzzling, but it makes sense. There are certain laws of God that run through history, and yet find their full meaning in the two comings of Jesus Christ. We saw in 30.1–4 that this is true of the judgement of the Day of the Lord; there are lesser days of God's intervention on the way to the Second Coming. Similarly every ruler is intended to be a true shepherd, and every king should be a true David, just as every human being should be truly in the image of God. When we fail, we do not thwart the final purpose of God, however much, from the human standpoint, we appear to have delayed it. God's perfect Man and perfect David has come and will come. Thus a passage about the rulers of God's people inevitably ends with Christ, however many good and bad rulers there may be beforehand.

The comparison of rulers and shepherds comes several times in the prophets (e.g. Isa. 56.11; Jer. 25.34; 50.6; Zech. 10.2,3) and naturally reminds us of Jesus Christ (e.g. Isa. 40.11; Zech. 13.7; John 10.1–7; 1 Pet. 5.3,4). A passage which closely resembles this chapter of *Ezekiel* is Jer. 23.1–6. Note also how, by comparing vs. 15 and 23, we have an underlying hint of the deity of our Lord Jesus Christ.

An additional picture is used in vs. 17–24, comparable to Christ's parable of the sheep and the goats. It is not only the leaders who are at fault, but within the flock there are those who are concerned only with their own interests, and not content with this, are deliberately spoiling life for others. Today one thinks of those who foul literature, stage, screen and television.

The chapter ends with the good rule of the Messiah. The days of the Messiah began with Christ's first coming, and although the Jews did enjoy God's blessing on their return from exile, the language here carries us into the sort of metaphors that the N.T. uses to describe the New Covenant that Jews and Gentiles enjoy in Christ (e.g. John 7.37,38; 15.1–7; Rom. 11.17–24; Gal. 5.22,23).

Consider the Shepherd work of Jesus Christ.

Ezekiel 35 The Opportunist

Ezekiel has already included Edom briefly with other nations that come under the censure of God (25.12–14). Now he is given a longer message. The strong words should be compared with other Edom passages, especially Psa. **137**.7; Obad. **8–14**; Isa. **34**; Jer. **49**.7–22; Mal. **1**.2–5.

It is strange how the rivalry between Jacob and Esau was perpetuated in their descendants. Isaac was shown by God that there would be this struggle (Gen. **27**.39,40), and history records it from time to time (e.g. Num. **20**.14–21; 2 Sam. **8**.13,14; 2 Kings **8**.20–22). Edom thought that eventually Israel would be obliterated, and she joined with the Babylonians in rounding up the refugees and taking what she could by way of spoil. For this she is condemned in vs. 1–9.

The further condemnation (10–15) is for land-grabbing. Now that so many of the people had gone into exile, it might seem that the Lord had left the land completely, and had retired defeated. From one aspect it was true that the Lord had left His Temple and city (**11**.23), but He had not abandoned His people altogether, and still owned the land (10). The land was not for Edom to take, especially since she supposed that she had defeated or abolished God in taking it (12,13). God was not just an idol attached to a tribe, one who perished when his worshippers perished.

Mount Seir (2) is the name for the northern mountains of Edom, south of the Dead Sea. At some time between this prophecy and Mal. **1**.3, Edom's territory was overrun by the Nabataeans. Eventually Edom was conquered and absorbed by the Jews, although ironically the Herods were Idumeans (Edomites). Herod the Great knew the Lord (15) sufficiently to rebuild the Temple from 20 B.C. onwards, although he and his descendants turned their hostility against Christ and the Christians, and once again showed themselves enemies of the people of God.

When did I last take advantage of someone else's misfortunes?

Ezekiel 36.1-21 God's Reputation

This chapter introduces an important principle, for which some have criticised Ezekiel (see also ch. 20), in that God is concerned for His Holy Name (21) rather than with love for His people. It is wrong to set the one against the other. God loves all mankind, but His purpose in choosing Israel was that they might make Him known to the world. Unfortunately they interpreted this choice solely in terms of power, and not of moral and spiritual values. So long as they had the land, the city, and the Temple, and their kings conquered the surrounding nations, they felt that all was well (e.g. Jer. **7**.4).

As a result of their behaviour (17) they conveyed the impression that their God was no different from the gods of the nations round about, for whom the word *holy* had no moral significance. The

372

messages of all the prophets were directed towards what it meant to be the people of God, a meaning already contained in the ten commandments. But every prophet was rejected by the nation as a whole, although always there were some who listened.

Thus God had to demonstrate that it mattered more what His people were in themselves than where they lived, and, for the sake of His Name (i.e. His character and reputation), He took them into exile.

Now the situation was different. Many of the exiles were learning the lesson. Yet the pagan peoples were interpreting God's character as though He were powerless to defend and restore Israel (6). So again God acts for His Name's sake.

This section follows on from ch. 35 with the key word 'mountains', although it is obvious from what is said that all the land is included. The word prepares us for a certain amount of symbolism, just as when the Temple is called the mountain of the Lord (Isa. 2.2,3). 'Mountain' in the O.T. sometimes has a mystical sense. Hence we shall see that these promises of return to the land go beyond mere literalism, just as the return from exile in Isa. 40–55 gets its full meaning from the return from the exile of sin which comes through the work of Christ.

Meanwhile the words had a literal fulfilment. The Jews did possess the land again, and it became fruitful.

Check some of the symbolic references to mountains, e.g. Psa. 125. 1,2; Isa. 65.25; Jer. 51.25; Zech. 6.1; Gal. 4.24,25; Heb. 12.22; Rev. 21.10.

Ezekiel 36.22-38   The Gospel Promise

The opening verses clearly bring out the point that God's Name, or reputation, was suffering. It was profaned by the low standards of behaviour, but also by the apparent powerlessness of God to restore His people if they turned to Him in repentance. These verses promise more than a bare return. The people certainly enjoyed the land again, although the Books of *Haggai, Zechariah,* and *Malachi* show that they still often fell back, just as the Christian Church has done since Calvary and Pentecost. But certainly the exile implanted in the people as a whole a disgust for idolatry (25).

Verses 26,27 point to the New Covenant and the work of the Holy Spirit based on the finished work of Jesus Christ on the cross. The Old Covenant specifically begins to anticipate the New (e.g. Jer. 31.31–34; Joel 2.28,29). In the New there is the approach from within, where the Spirit comes to take up the transforming control. He could not do this, as He does now, until the redemptive work of

Christ was complete (John 7.39), even though from time to time in the O.T. He inspired individuals for special tasks (e.g. Exod. 31.3; Judg. 6.34; 2 Sam. 23.2; Ezek. 3.12).

The terms of the promise in vs. 25–27 show that we are not wrong in looking for symbolic interpretations in these chapters. No one supposes that the reference in v. 25 is to literal water, but Ezekiel speaks of the reality, underlying the ritual sprinklings of the Law, e.g. Num. 19.17–19; Heb. 9.10; 10.22.

It is likely that Christ was calling the attention of Nicodemus to this passage when He spoke in John 3.5 of the new birth through water and the Spirit; the Ezekiel promise was about to be fulfilled. Paul also speaks of the stone and the heart of flesh in 2 Cor. 3.3. Note also the inwardness of Jer. 31.33,34. As Christians we know this new life, and agree with the verdict of v. 32; how could we be saved on the ground of our own achievements and non-achievements?

Meanwhile the returning Jews knew God's power to cleanse (33; Zech. 3.1–5) even though they had not yet come into the era of the Spirit; and they repeopled the land (34–38).

Study the negative and positive aspects of vs. 24–27—the cleansing and the renewing.

Ezekiel 37.1-14 Life from the Dead

The promises of ch. 36 might well sound incredible to prisoners immersed in the mighty Babylonian power. Once they had been a living and vital organism. Now they were scattered like bones lying stark and dry under the desert sun.

This is how they appear to Ezekiel in his vision. Can they live again? To man it seems impossible, but God knows the answer (3). The answer lies in the word of the Lord (4); that declaration which effects what it promises (Isa. 55.11).

The resurrection that follows does not refer directly to individual resurrection from death. It is symbolic of the recreation and revitalizing of the nation as a whole, as the interpretation shows (11–14).

Bringing the bones together is only a beginning. Clothing them with muscles and skin is still only a step on the way. The body is still dead, since it lacks the vital breath of life. In what follows it is impossible to be consistent in our translation of the word *ruach*. It is the word that appears in vs. 9 and 14 as 'breath', 'wind', and 'Spirit'. Thus in the Hebrew there is a link that we may miss in English. Nicodemus also was reminded of this in John 3.8, where

374

the margin points out that in Greek also the word *pneuma* has the double meaning.

This helps us to understand the nature of the new birth. The body needs breath if it is to live. Man has dropped from the life of God through the fall and through personal sin, and the Bible describes our state as death, even though we still have biological life (John 5.24; Rom. 5.15; Col. 2.13). The new birth involves both the removal of sin through the work of Christ, and also the reception of the breath of the Spirit to vitalize and renew us (John 3.5, 14-18). Thus we see the analogy between the natural and the spiritual; what is true at one level is true at the other also.

The picture is applicable both to individual and to Church life. Humanism has to stop with v. 8. So do many schemes for unity within the visible Church. Naturally we want the visible 'body' to be as tidy as possible, without any limbs missing, but we may forget the prime importance of the Holy Spirit. The Bible does not teach that the Holy Spirit is in every man, but that He comes in to make alive.

Consider some analogies between the Holy Spirit and breath.

Ezekiel 37.15-28 Nations United

We must decide what is the proper interpretation of the uniting of the two kingdoms. The Northern Kingdom of Israel was taken captive to northern Mesopotamia in 721 B.C. The Southern Kingdom of Judah was taken to southern Mesopotamia in 586 B.C. There was no mass return of Israel comparable to the return of Judah, and the so-called 'lost tribes' have by some been identified with peoples who moved across Europe into Britain, and Biblical promises to Israel are applied to them.

Ezekiel takes two sticks, with the name of Judah and associated tribes on one, and the name of Ephraim, the son of Joseph, and the largest of the northern tribes, with its associated tribes, on the other. He then puts the sticks end to end and folds his hand over the join, so that they appear as one. The meaning is drawn out as union in the land, with 'David' ruling over both, with a special covenant, and with the presence of God in His sanctuary among them.

We must remember that very many Israelites remained in Palestine. Some have calculated that only 1 in 20 were taken away. Both Hezekiah and Josiah, after the Northern captivity, summoned those who remained to come to the Passover (2 Chron. 30; 34.9; 35.17,18). After the return of the Jews, distinction was made between semi-pagan Israelites who had been mixed with the imported colonists (Ezra 4.1-3), and those who made a clean break with paganism (Ezra 6.21). Thus, the two peoples were united, and it would also be most improbable if some Israelite exiles from Mesopotamia did not join in the return of their Jewish kinsmen, although their longer period in exile had attached them more closely to their new homes. Later the two divided again into Jews and Samaritans.

However, the promise here, as in Jer. 33.14–26, is linked to the days of the Messiah. This is the N.T. truth that Jews and Samaritans are all one in Christ (Acts 8.4–17), and also that Gentiles are equally one with them (Gal. 3.28,29). We note also Christ's words to the Samaritan woman about the unity of worship (John 4.19–26). Even the actual land (25) becomes unimportant. Jerusalem on earth was sacramental of Jerusalem above, of which Jews, Israelites, and Gentiles are citizens in Christ (Gal. 4.26; Heb. 12.22). And we, too, enjoy the everlasting covenant (26; Matt. 26.28).

Compare what is said here about reunion in the Messiah with Jer. 31 (note v. 31) and Hos. 3.4,5, and note the marginal references in v. 27.

Questions for further study and discussion on Ezekiel chs. 33–37

1. Is it every Christian's duty to be a watchman?
2. Must the Christian watchman warn *everyone?* If not, how does he know whom to warn?
3. In the light of 33.32, should a preacher aim at being a good speaker?
4. What light do these chapters throw on the Messiah?
5. What do these chapters say about salvation from sin?

Ezekiel 38.1-13   The Last Battle

This is the first of a series of chapters on which most commentators would admit that they cannot speak with any certainty. In this chapter we have to ask: When does the attack take place? Who are the people concerned? How much is literal and how much symbolic?

The N.T. has a reference to this passage, where, in Rev. 20.7–9, at the end of the Millennium Satan gathers 'the nations which are at the four corners of the earth, that is, Gog and Magog' and attacks 'the camp of the saints and the beloved city.' The present commentator believes in a literal reign of Christ on earth with His people (not only Jews), and so is inclined to place the *Ezekiel* passage at the end of this period, during which there will be universal peace and dropping of armaments (11).

Others regard the Millennium of Rev. 20 as picturing the present rule of Christ during the gospel age, with the power of Satan potentially broken. At the end of this era there will be a heading up of evil and a final attack on all the people of God. There is much in Scripture to indicate that there will be such an outburst before the Lord returns (e.g. 2 Thes. 2.3,4; Rev. 16.12–16), and even those who believe in an earthly Millennium commonly accept this, and may think of another Gog and Magog attack at this time.

Others who believe in a great national future for the Jews take this chapter as an attack on the land of Israel, either at the end of a period of tribulation before the Lord returns, or at the end of the Millennium.

In any case we must somehow link this chapter with Joel 3 and Zech. 14, which also describe a great attack on Jerusalem, during which the Lord appears to overthrow the enemy.

Of the peoples named here, several occur in ch. 27 (see notes). Those in v. 2 are in the north, Persia (5) is east, and Cush and Put are south. Gomer (6) is the name for the Cimmerians in Cappadocia, and so are to the west. Thus the enemy comes from all quarters (Rev. 20.8).

The name Gog is otherwise unknown, but he comes from the land of Magog (2), who is linked with some of these other names in Gen. 10.2.

God threatens the attackers with defeat (3,4), but foretells that their attack will not come until the distant future (7). God's people will be dwelling quietly (11) at the centre of the earth (12). Traders from Arabia and distant Tarshish come to make a profit out of the war (13), as already happens today.

The LAST battle. What a wonderful adjective!

Ezekiel 38.14-23   Challenge to Antichrist

Gog is the leader, and swoops down from the north (15), although we have seen that his allies come from all points of the compass. It is striking that God says He will bring the invader (16). On other occasions when God brings the invader, it is to punish His people (e.g. ch. 21), but this is for the final overthrow of evil, and the consequent vindication of God's good Name. If this is Satan's last attempt to rally the world against God (Rev. 20.7–10), his defeat is the day for which all creation has waited since the Fall.

There is a strange challenge in v. 17. God asserts in a rhetorical question that Gog is the heading up of all that the prophets have spoken concerning 'antichrists'. In the O.T. there were proud defiers of God (e.g. Isa. 10.7–19; 14.12–20) even when they were for a time God's instruments of punishment. Since the address to

377

Gog was far in the future when Ezekiel spoke, we may include the prophecies of Dan. **11**, Christ's words in Matt. **24**.15, and Paul's words in 2 Thess. **2**.3,4.

The invaders are destroyed by earthquake (19,20, cf. Zech. **14**.4,5), by violent distrust of one another (21, cf. Zech. **14**.13), by pestilence (22, cf. Zech. **14**.12), and by torrential rain and fire from heaven (22, cf. Rev. **20**.9). The end result is the vindication of God and the recognition by everyone of His sole Godhead (23).

This is, after all, the ultimate purpose of creation, the sole glory of God. It is wrought through history, through the incarnation and the work of Jesus Christ, and rounded off by the second coming and all that goes with it (Phil. **2**.5–11). It would be a happy thing if all could be achieved through love alone, but experience and Scripture show that love has been abused and resisted. We do not like to think of the judgements of God, but ultimately the great Surgeon cuts away the cancer that clamours for its right to dominate the body.

Surely God must one day vindicate and be vindicated. Mal. 3.13–4.3.

Ezekiel 39.1-16   Armaments and Bones

It seems likely that this chapter is a second sermon on the invasion, and thus vs. 1–6 form a brief recapitulation of ch. **38**. God brings the host of invaders, renders them powerless, and destroys them. The result is the full vindication of God, the final summing up of the purpose of creation, the day towards which all prophecy points (8).

The emphasis now is not on destruction, but rather on the removal of every trace of rebellion and sin. If the invasion is literal, and centred on the land of Israel, then all that is said about the removal of its traces must be literal, too. Thus the weapons of war are completely burnt up (9,10), and the bones of the rebellious dead are taken across the Jordan and buried in a valley east of the Dead Sea, so that the Holy Land is no longer contaminated by them either in fact or in reminder.

The valley may be in the Mountains of Abarim (11, margin), which are east of the northern end of the Dead Sea. The bones buried there will be so many that they block the way through the valley (11), or perhaps the block is a moral ban on going through such a polluted place.

The removal of the bones is comparatively easy at first, and everyone takes part (13). After seven months all obvious traces will have been removed, so a group of investigators is appointed to finish the work (14). Ordinary people still help by calling attention to to any bones that they find (15). There is no known city of Hamonah (16), but if a valley is to be called Hamon-gog, there could also be a near-by city with a somewhat similar name.

A literal interpretation, which puts these events at the end of the Millennium (Rev. 20.7–10), would indicate that there is still a period of life on earth before the ushering in of eternity.

Meanwhile the spiritual trend of this section is towards the abolition of armaments. The abandoned weapons are not to be used again, but must be totally burned. They do not form part of the spoil that may be kept (9,10; Isa. 9.5). Also all traces of the rebellion must go. Today our towns and cities are full of contaminating bones that reek of moral decay, and ordinary people and experts are unable to clear them out of the land.

Can we bury a bone today? Gal. 5.19–21.

Ezekiel 39. 17-29   Death and Discipline

The previous section spoke of burying bones. Certainly it would not be easy to remove so many corpses to a valley beyond the Dead Sea. Now it appears that birds and beasts first flock to the battlefield to feed on the bodies of the slain. The reference in v. 18 does not mean that large numbers of animals will be killed with the invaders, but, as v. 19 indicates, the picture is that of a great sacrifice, where the bodies of Gog's host are the equivalent of sheep and bulls (cf. Rev. 19.17,18).

This metaphor of the Lord's sacrifice is both strange and repugnant to our ways of thinking, but it occurs also in Isa. 34.5–7; Jer. 46.10; Zeph. 1.7–9. There is no suggestion in these passages that people are sacrificed to appease the Lord, though there is the implication that the Lord cannot rest until all sin is removed. Rather, the metaphor is drawn from what all Israelites could picture. Very few of us in England have ever seen an abattoir, or slaughter-house, or watched the ritual slaughter of animals, so it would be useless to use them as an illustration of blood pouring everywhere. But every Israelite had watched the blood flowing at the sacrifices. This was not pointless slaughter, since most sacrifices were eaten by the worshippers after they had been offered. They provided the fairly infrequent occasions when the average man had a meat meal. But here the quantities of blood that flowed at the sacrifices are used pictorially of the death of those who have campaigned against God.

The vindication of God is seen as much more than the destruction of His enemies. It is seen in the history of His discipline of His people (21–29). This is of vital importance to us who read these chapters. We can stand at a distance and thank God that we are not in Gog's army. But God is even more concerned about His Israel. History shows that not only the Jews were sent into exile to emerge in greater purity, but churches also, who have grown prosperous and forgetful of God and His real claims, have gone down before their enemies. In their captivity a nucleus of faithful believers has risen again.

At the end of time we shall understand and approve God's dealings with all His people. Rev. 15.3,4.

Ezekiel 40.1-16 The Way In

The closing chapters describe a temple in great detail. It does not correspond to the one that was built after the return, nor to Herod's Temple. Some therefore hold that it has yet to be built, and that it will be a centre of worship for the Israeli nation.

This commentary is based on the belief that the visionary temple is intended to be symbolic. It seems unlikely that God will re-introduce animal sacrifices (**43**.18–27) after all that is said in *Hebrews* about their abolition through the sacrifice of Jesus Christ. It seems unlikely that the miraculous river flowing from the temple (**47**) is literal. Moreover the section is introduced as a vision on a high mountain with 'a structure like a city' near by (**40**.2). The words suggest a three-dimensional picture. Therefore, just as Heb. 9 finds a permanent message in the structure of the Tabernacle, so we must look for the significant elements in this vision of the city and temple, noting how it portrays the character of God, the manner of approach to Him, and our way of life as the people of God.

The date is 572 B.C. Ezekiel, like Jesus Christ in His temptation, is taken to the top of a very high mountain (2; Matt. 4.8). Jesus was shown the glory of the world. Ezekiel is shown the community of God. He is given a shining heavenly guide, who carries a measuring rod of about 10 feet 4 inches. (The so-called 'long cubit' of v. 5 was 20.679 inches, as opposed to the ordinary cubit of about 17.5 inches.)

The guide measures the temple area, just as in Rev. **21**.15–17 John's guide measures the heavenly city. It is not easy to follow the description without a plan, but the essentials are as follows. The outer court is square, with a central gate in the wall on each side at the top of a flight of steps (5,6). The gate is like a college gate at some universities, with side rooms for the guards, and a further porch with side posts (jambs) leading into the court (7–11). The side rooms had something built up in front of their entrances (12), possibly for the guards to stand on. The doors of the side rooms were at the back, opening into the court. Light was admitted through a series of windows, like the slits in old castles but widening outwards instead of inwards (16).

We cannot find a spiritual significance in every measurement, but we note the symmetry of the temple and its precincts (cf. Rev. 21.16).

The approach to God is through a narrow gateway (Matt. 7.13; John 10.1.).

Ezekiel 40.17-49 Approach to the Temple

Ezekiel passes through the eastern gateway into the outer court (17). A raised pavement, level with the inside of the gate, runs round the inside of the walls, with thirty rooms opening on to it (17,18). These rooms would be for the use of the Levites and others who serve in the outer court. If we picture the inner court as a square in the centre of the outer court, the distance between the outer and the inner gates is 100 cubits (19).

There are also similar gates in the north wall of the outer court (19-23) and in the south (24-27). There is no similar gate on the west, since the inner court, in the exact centre of the outer court, opened westwards into the temple, and this led on to the west wall.

Next Ezekiel goes up by eight steps to the south gate of the inner court (28-30). Its dimensions are the same as the outer gates, and as the inner gates on the east (32-34) and north (35-37). The north gate had a special room for the preparation of the offerings (38-43).

There were two extra rooms just inside the inner court by the north and south gates, the former for the priests who had a general ministry in the temple, and the other for the priests of the family of Zadok, who had special responsibilities for the sacrifices at the altar (44-46). The inner court was 100 cubits square, the same measurement as the distance across from the outer to the inner gates.

At last Ezekiel comes to the actual temple (48,49). He had ascended steps into the outer (**40.6**) and inner (**40.31**) courts, and now he ascends ten more into the vestibule. On either side were two pillars, either to support the structure, or corresponding to the two pillars in Solomon's Temple. The meaning of these is uncertain, but their names Jachin and Boaz (1 Kings 7.21) may well have been the first words of two texts inscribed on them, e.g. '*He will establish* thy throne' and '*In the strength* of the Lord I will

EZEKIEL'S TEMPLE

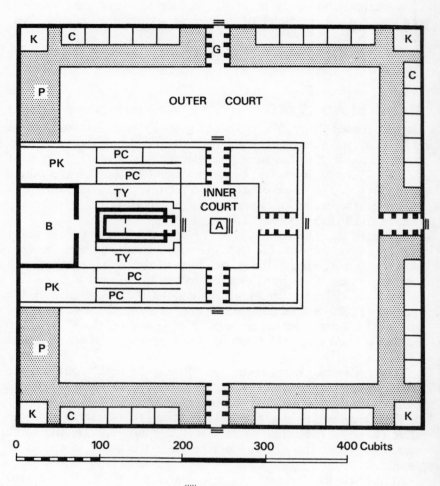

A	Altar	
B	Building	
C	Chamber	
G	Gateway	
K	Kitchen	

P	Pavement
PC	Priests' chambers
PK	Priests' kitchen
TY	Temple yard

rejoice'. The words would be a special reminder to the king, and perhaps he stood by them at his coronation (2 Kings 11.14).
We cannot go further than the outer court—without Christ.

*Ezekiel 41.1-11   The Heart of the Temple

Ezekiel passes through the porch into the temple itself. The RSV uses the word *nave* of the larger room within the temple. The measurements of v. 1 are those of the entrance through the wall from the porch to the temple; the wall is six cubits thick. The width of the entrance is ten cubits, and, once one passes through, there are five cubits of wall on each side, thus making a total breadth of twenty cubits (2).

Both courts are exact squares, but the temple is rectangular (2), directing the attention towards the end, where was the inner room, or holy of holies. Ezekiel as a priest could go into the nave, but only the high priest could enter the inner room. Thus he records that the angel alone went in and announced the dimensions (3,4). The inner room is exactly square (4). Its height is not given, but it may have been a cube, as in Solomon's Temple (1 Kings 6.20).

The description of the side rooms (5–11) is difficult to follow. They were probably used to store gifts and tithes and various temple vessels (cf. Neh. 13.5,9,12). They were built on a raised strip on the north and south of the temple, i.e. along the length of it (8). The temple wall narrowed at each storey to form a shelf, or offset, on which each higher room could be supported. This made the rooms a little wider as they rose. There were thirty rooms on each of three floors, and they were reached by a stairway.

They could not be entered from inside the temple, but they opened on to the platform. The implication of v. 11 is that there was only one door in the centre of each side, and the stairway must have started from there.

'The chambers of the court' (10) are those described in ch. **42**. There is a space between them and the edge of the temple platform. They are on the north and south (the long sides) of the temple.
Psalm 84.4,10.

*Ezekiel 41.12-26   Inner Beauty

The west side of the temple was different from the others, in that across the pavement there was another building, which ran up to the western wall of the outer court (12). It was set broadways on to the end of the temple. No indication of its use is given, but presumably it was for storage. The distance from the west end of the temple to the west wall, taking in this other building, was equal to the length

383

of the temple itself, i.e. about 174 feet (13). The measurement across the front of the temple (14) is the total width of the inner court (40.47), on to which the temple opened. Similarly, behind the temple, the extra building, with wall space on either side, occupied the same length as the inner court (15). Thus the inner court, the temple, and the extra building, with the rooms and walls attached to them, formed a rectangle running up to the western wall of the outer court.

Like Solomon's Temple, this one was panelled throughout (15,16). Nothing is said about the roof, but obviously this temple had one, since windows were needed for light and air. It is not clear how the windows were covered (16), but perhaps they had shutters to keep out storms. Ezekiel could see that the panelling ran as far as the outside of the entrance to the holy of holies (17), but he was not allowed to see whether it ran into the inner room.

The walls were covered with wood carvings of cherubim and palm trees (17–20). Solomon's Temple also had these, together with flower motifs (1 Kings 6.29). These cherubim, being carved against the flat wood, had only two of their faces depicted, whereas in his opening vision Ezekiel had seen four (1.10).

Ezekiel had already seen the altar of burnt-offering in the inner court (40.47). Now he is shown a table standing in front of the entrance to the holy of holies (21,22). This is for the showbread (Exod. 25.23–30).

There were double doors at the entrance to the temple and to the holy of holies (23,24), and the former had the same carvings as on the walls (25).

Cherubim reminded the priests of attendance in the service of God. Palm trees reminded of strength and nourishment (dates) for man (Psalm 92.12–14).

Ezekiel 42

Opposite to the long sides of the temple, and level with the walls of the inner court, there were rooms for the priests. They were in three storeys, built against the outer court (3). A long corridor divided them into two blocks, and the doors of the southern block opened into this corridor (4). If the other doors also opened north (4), there must have been room for a way between the rooms and the outer court in addition to the inner corridor. Each set of rooms was narrower than the one below, so as to leave a gallery, on to which presumably the rooms on the first and second floors opened (5,6).

The block that faced the temple took up twice the length of the block facing the outer court (8), and the extra space was made up by a wall (7). There was an entrance at the east on the corner that touched the outer court (9,10,14).

Separation is an important theme in these chapters which emphasise the majesty and holiness of God. In pre-exilic times Canaanite influence had degraded the true character of God, as we saw in chs. 8 and 9 and there was little sense of man's sin as he came before God (Isa. 1.4,11–17).

In these rooms the priests are to eat their portions of the sacrifices that have been dedicated to God (13, cf. 44.28–31). What has been given to God is separated to be used as He shows; we cannot take it back again as we wish. Moreover the priests must wear special clothes when they are functioning as priests in the temple (14). God and man are separate, and until the time of Christ only a privileged class could serve in the temple. The clothes spoke of separation to God from the dirt and dust of ordinary life.

The whole temple area forms a square, measuring nearly 300 yards on each side (15–19). Once again a wall marks off the sacred from the secular (20).

What significance is there in symmetry? Cf. Rev. 21.15,16.

Questions for further study and discussion on Ezekiel chs. 38—42
1. What other passages of Scripture indicate special attacks on the people of God in the last days?
2. Is it relevant to these passages that the Israelis have now returned to the Holy Land?
3. Draw a sketch map of the Temple.
4. Think of some buildings, rooms, or open spaces of approximately the areas mentioned in these temple chapters. One cubit is 20.67 inches, three about five feet, 100 about 60 yards.

Ezekiel 43 First Things First

The temple is useless without the presence of God. It is like a man, made in the image of God, without the Holy Spirit. In an earlier vision (11.22,23) Ezekiel had seen the glory of God departing. Now the Lord returns into the temple, while the prophet remains in the inner court (4,5).

God's voice from the temple describes this as His throne, the centre where His presence is focused, as we can focus the sun on one spot with a magnifying glass without making it leave 'heaven'. If His presence is to remain, the old separating evils must go. God mentions the immoralities of ch. 22, but adds the evils that had come from the royal palace being virtually within the temple

385

area (7,8). The reference to the dead bodies (7) may be to burials or to monuments (margin) in proximity to the temple. In Manasseh's reign certainly all sorts of desecration had occurred (2 Kings 21.1–9).

Just as God first declared His law to the Israelites before He made the covenant (Exod. 24.3), so now He first describes the way of separateness and approachability (10–12). It is not surprising that He starts with the altar of burnt-offering in the centre of the inner court (13, cf. 40.47). We too can approach God only through the blood shed on the altar of the cross.

The altar has a square base one cubit deep, with a rim on top. The words in brackets (13) mean that this is the long cubit (40.5). On this base rests a smaller square two cubits high. Another smaller square rests on this and supports the actual hearth, which, like the square, is four cubits deep. There are horns on each of the four corners.

Each square, being smaller than the one below, has a step one cubit wide all round. The total height of the altar, including the horns, is twelve cubits, or some 20½ feet. Although steps ran all round, they were too deep for the robed priests to use, so on the east side they were filled in with steps of normal size, so that the priests faced the temple when they sacrificed (13–17). The blood was smeared on the horns (20), and people seeking sanctuary could seize them (e.g. 1 Kings 1.50).

Even our holiest efforts are mixed with impurities, and the work of our hands, even an altar built for God, needs to be 'decontaminated' (26). All sacrifices in the O.T. anticipate the final sacrifice of Christ, so the three chief sacrificial animals are offered here (18–27).

Heb. 9.22–24.

Ezekiel 44.1-16   Faithful and Unfaithful

Ezekiel is brought to the east gate of the outer court (1), through which he has seen the glory of God streaming in (43.1–4). Now it remains for ever shut (1,2). This reminds us that none can go the same atoning way by which Christ went into the heavenly temple (Heb. 9.11–14). The prince, who in some points also typifies the Messiah, does not go through the gate again, but enjoys the oneness of fellowship with God there (3).

Instead of returning to the inner court by the obvious way, Ezekiel is taken by way of the north gate. The reason appears in 46.1, i.e. the east gate was opened only on the sabbath.

God has spoken of the holiness of the temple things; now He speaks of the holiness of the people who use them. It is clear from

Ezekiel's Altar

vs. 5–8 that in the last days of Solomon's Temple the priests had allowed anyone, even uncovenanted pagans, to act as priests and temple servants. Either they had been lazy or busy with their own affairs, and had hired others to do their work; or they had taken bribes from pagans who wanted to serve in the Temple, perhaps for the offerings that they were able to take home and resell.

To understand vs. 10–14, we note that the family of Levi had different functions. Most were temple servants, but those who were descended from Aaron were priests in the temple (e.g. Num. 8.20–26). These verses deal with the latter group (13). They had previously countenanced idolatry, and now they are to be degraded to the level of the other Levites.

The new priesthood is confined to the line of Zadok, who was a descendant of Eleazar, the third son of Aaron. Representatives of this line had evidently stood firm (15,16). Even though this visionary temple was not built after the return, the line of Zadok continued to hold the high priesthood until 171 B.C.

God has not given my work for others to do.

*Ezekiel 44.17-31   Good Servants of God

At first sight these regulations for the priests seem strange, but by analysing them we shall find that some are practical, and others have a general application to us as Christians, since we are all priests (Rev. 1.6).

Linen clothes were worn because the priests could easily become too hot through the fire on the altar. The smell of perspiration can be unpleasant, and this suggests a lesson in personal hygiene (17,18). The idea of communicating holiness (19) is that any close experience of God set a person or thing apart. Anyone who treated him or it lightly, violated this set-apartness, which was communicated to them in a wrong way.

Their hair style must not follow extreme fashions to conform to current religious or social customs (20). They must be in full control of their faculties so as to offer intelligent worship to God, not using drink (or drugs?) to release their inhibitions (21, cf. Prov. 31.4,5). They must have a good wife. She must not have been divorced, or even a widow who had become used to a very different form of life than that which she would have as the wife of a priest (22).

The laws of clean and unclean are mostly commonsense. They show that in food (e.g. Deut. 14.3–21) and in hygiene (e.g. Lev. 13.9–17; Deut. 23.12–14) God is concerned for the well-being of the whole person.

The priests are to have the wisdom to act as judges, but they must be very different from the sort of judges that the prophets denounce (e.g. Isa. 1.23). They themselves must be under the judgement of God in their observance of the worship (24).

Some of the Mosaiç laws were designed to cover risks which would not always be present. Thus anyone who had contact with a dead body had to be isolated as unclean for fear of infection, and then be formally, as well as practically, cleansed with water and with a sin offering (Num. 19.11–22). We conclude that the offering was a reminder that death came into the human race because of sin. The priests may have contact with close relatives who have died; God does not discourage reasonable mourning (25–27, cf. 24.17).

The priests earn their living by doing the special work that God has given them, and their income comes from the offerings (28–30). God still calls some to what we call wholetime service, and in giving for their support we are giving to God, as were the people who brought their offerings to the Temple (1 Cor. 9.13,14).

Finally, the priests must not risk infection from eating tainted meat (31).

How do these rules apply to us?

Ezekiel 45   Just and Righteous

Ezekiel has described the temple and the laws for the priests, using the third person. Now he directly addresses various sections of the community. Even though this temple and city are visionary, the restored Israelites must learn the principles that must govern what they actually do.

The princes (8,9) are to mark out the land in a way that safe-guards the separateness of God. There is to be a reserved area of something like eight miles (east to west) by seven (1). In the centre there is the temple area, already measured in 42.15–20, of some 300 yards square, with an unoccupied strip of about thirty yards around it (2).

Next a rectangle is measured off, running the full length from east to west, and containing the temple area (3). Thus this strip is approximately eight miles by three and a half, and is for the priests' homes. A similar strip for the Levites adjoins it on the north (5). On the south a strip half the width is for the city, containing houses and.park land (6, cf. 48.15); this, added to the sacred rectangular portion, forms a square.

Just as priest and sacrifice represent Christ and His offering, and yet need reapplication to Christ Himself, so also does the prince as the completely righteous Messianic ruler. His person and actions are relevant for us if they are reapplied. Thus, in vs. 7,8 his possessions run right across the land, including both sacred and secular areas.

Other princes rule with him (cf. Rev. **1.**6; Eph. **2.**6), and are to be like him in their love of righteousness (8,9). For example, they are to ensure proper standards of honesty. Traders must give full measure, with the bath of 5¾ gallons for liquids, and with the ephah which was the equivalent dry measure. The homer is ten times the capacity. The shekel is about 11.39 grams or 0.402 oz. (10–12). See also Lev. **19.**35,36 and Amos **8.**5 for examples of short measure for purchases and heavy weights to weigh the buyer's silver.

The offerings of each person are proportionate to his earnings, and are one-sixtieth of cereals, one hundredth of oil, and one-two hundredth of sheep. These offerings are accepted as atoning for sin (13–15). Cereal and vegetable offerings commonly accompanied the animal sacrifices, which were atoning because of the shed blood (**46.**5; Num. **15.**1–10). The prince is responsible for collecting the offerings (16,17). He would have the authority that the priests might lack (e.g. Neh. **13.**10–13).

Even the temple needs to be 'cleansed' once a year (18,19, cf. Heb. **9.**23) because its ministers are human and sinful, and even though they have kept from deliberate sin, there is much that contaminates (20, cf. Psa. **19.**12). All leads to the great Passover festival of redemption (21–24), and to the Feast of Tabernacles six months later (25), when the harvest has been gathered in (Lev. **23.**39–42).

Separation, sin, atonement, righteousness; what is the relation between them?

Ezekiel 46   Festivals and Offerings

The sabbath and the first day of each month are marked by the opening of the east gate of the inner court (1). The prince passes through the porch, and from there watches the priests offering the sacrifices on the altar in the centre of the inner court (2). Neither he nor the people actually enters this court. To ensure reverence, there are two lines of worshippers coming to the entrances to watch the offerings, each moving in one direction only (9,10).

The burnt offering (4) was entirely consumed by fire on the altar, picturing the entire offering of Christ on the cross. The offerer identified himself with the animal, which then died in his place (Lev. **1.**4). From the accompanying cereal offering (5) a handful was burned to signify its acceptance by the Lord, while the remainder was given to the priests (Lev. **2.**1–3). The good things that God gives are to be enjoyed in the context of redemption.

Although the turn of each week and each month is marked for cleansing and dedication, the prince is encouraged to come on other occasions with freewill and peace offerings (12), and, while for some of the offerings he and his people have a minimum of accompaniments prescribed, they are told sometimes to search their hearts and make their decision about how much to give (11, cf. 1 Cor. 16.2).

Whether or not the prince attends, he provides the daily burnt offering, thus putting every day, as well as every week and month, under the cross (13–15).

His gifts are not only to God, but may be to his sons and to his servants as a reward for faithfulness (16–18). His land stretches across Palestine, so he has plenty to spare. People with great possessions are not always generous, and in the old days kings and rulers had sometimes dispossessed their subjects to reward themselves or their favourites (18, cf. Mic. 2.2). Members of the royal family may keep the land and hand it on; others may hold it only until the year of liberty, which came every fifty years (Lev. 25.10).

If Ezekiel has not moved since he stood in front of the temple in 44.4, he now goes into the outer court, and round to the entrance to the priests' rooms (19, cf. 42.9). Here the priests ate most of the guilt offering and sin offering (20; Lev. 6.24–7.7). The people ate most of each peace offering (Lev. 7.11–18,28–36), and these must be what were cooked in the enclosures at each corner of the outer court (21–24). We cannot participate in the atoning aspect of the death of Christ, but we must be personally linked with Him in His death (Rom. 6).

How far may a sacrifice be a substitute?

*Ezekiel 47.1-12   Living Waters

The pictures in the vision have been built up gradually. Ezekiel had not been shown the river when previously he had stood at the door of the temple, but now he is shown how the presence of God at the centre means life for the barren land. The stream begins as a trickle, coming out from the south-east of the temple, flowing past the south side of the altar of burnt-offering, and out under the south wall. Ezekiel goes out of the north gate, and past the closed east gate, until he comes to the stream, which soon turns towards the Dead Sea (1–3).

He is told to step into these living waters. After just over one-third of a mile the water is up to his ankles. Another third, and it reaches his knees. After about a mile it rises to his waist. Then, only a mile and a third from its source, the waters form a deep river

(3–5). Ezekiel walks back (6), and is struck by the number of trees on the banks (7). The river flows into the Arabah depression, in which lies the Dead Sea (8). Wherever it goes, it freshens the salt and stagnant waters, so that fishermen can make a living along the west shore of the Dead Sea (9,10).

Yet its course is selective, and the valuable chemical salts are unaffected (11). The trees on the bank share the everlasting life which has its source in the temple, and they bear fresh fruit continually, and supply healing medicines in their leaves (12).

This is almost certainly the Scripture that Christ had in mind in John 7.38. His words must be understood in the light of the truth that our bodies become temples of the Holy Spirit (John 7.39; 1 Cor. 6.19). The Spirit in the depth of the temple of our being flows out into a dead world.

From another aspect the picture in this chapter is taken up in the view of the New Jerusalem in Rev. 22.1,2, and it also rounds off the picture of the living waters which flowed from Eden (Gen. 2.10). In between we have reminders that flowing streams are parables of the flowing life of God (e.g. Psa. 42.1; Jer. 2.13; John 4.10–15).

'Everything will live where the river goes' (9). *Meditate on this* (*Isa. 44.3; 58.10,11; Psa. 46.4,5*).

*Ezekiel 47.13—48.20   The Holy Land

It is not possible to identify all the places that form the boundaries of the land (13–20). The western border is naturally the Mediterranean (15,20). The northern border starts opposite Cyprus, and runs across to Hamath and to some unidentified places on the boundary of the former territories owned by Hamath and Damascus (15–17). From there the eastern border runs down into the Jordan valley to a place south of the Dead Sea (18). Then it turns west and runs to the Brook of Egypt, which is a small river on the curve of the coast (19).

This is the area which God swore to give to the nation (14, cf. Gen. 15.18–21; Num. 34.1–12), and which was ruled by Solomon (1 Kings 4.24). In the plan for the future this is divided equally among the tribes, whatever their size, in strips from east to west. It is noteworthy that, although the Book warns against contamination of the temple by aliens (44.6–9), it welcomes foreigners who have been integrated into the nation, thus anticipating the equality of Jews and Gentiles in the Christian Church (22; Eph. 2.11–22).

The tribal territory starts with Dan in the north, and runs south to Judah (48.1–7). Then comes the sacred area already described in

45.1-8. The main additions to the description are details about the city and its surroundings (15-20). The city is about a mile and a half square (16), with an open space on each side (17), and land for cultivation to the east and west (18,19). This whole area is regarded as the Lord's property, held in trust for Him (8,20).

How can something belong to God as a holy portion, and still be for our use?

Ezekiel 48.21-35   God is Central

The prince's land (21,22) has already been described in **45.7,8.** The remaining tribes have their territories south of the city. Finally the city is given three gates on each side, named after the tribes (30-34, cf. Rev. 21.12,13). One is named after Levi (31) whose territory was separated from that of the twelve tribes, and who consequently was not counted in the twelve strips in **48.1-7,23-28.** Hence the two Joseph tribes, Manasseh and Ephraim (4,5) have one Joseph gate (32) to form the twelve.

The Book ends magnificently. In the N.T. it corresponds to Emmanuel, *God with us* (Matt. 1.23), and to the Holy Spirit dwelling with us and in us (John 14.17).

'The Lord is there.' How?

This commentary on the new city and temple has not been exciting, but has tried to explain the main points of the description, so that the reader can follow the outline intelligently. Yet we have regarded these visions as intentionally symbolic, setting out permanent truths in O.T. description, and we have noticed applications that are found in the N.T. Thus the brief description of the New Jerusalem in Rev. 21 and 22 has features in common with these chapters, including measurements, and we do not take them literally. Some of them already operate in the Church, although we do not yet see them in their final form. Thus we enjoy the light of God, the benefits of the tree of life and the water of life, and we serve God as those who are marked with His Name (Rev. 21.22-22.5).

Judah and Israel were physically blessed after the return. They rebuilt the temple, and by the time of Christ, even though they were under Rome, they had absorbed the nations that once harassed them, such as Edom and the Philistines, and had full freedom to practise their religion. Yet their history combined both renewal and apostasy. Malachi shows that God's standards were not always observed; and there were many apostates and bitter struggles for the high priesthood, especially during the 2nd century B.C.

Similarly, the Christian Church has known both revival and apostasy, yet God's promises of victory in Christ have not been overthrown. The Jewish nation as a whole was not ready to move into the New Jerusalem and New Temple of the Messiah when He came. Thus they lost the inner reality of the O.T. promises made through Ezekiel and others. We in the Church have inherited these realities, but we must not ignore the warnings that form the other side of the coin.

Questions for further study and discussion on Ezekiel chs. 43–48

1. What is the value, and what is the danger, of separating the sacred from the secular?
2. Having decided this in general, what particular applications are there to our day-to-day lives?
3. How far am I identified with Christ in His death, and how far is His sacrifice unique? How is this indicated in the sacrifices mentioned in these chapters?
4. If you think it profitable, compare the 'furniture' of this temple with that of the Tabernacle and Solomon's Temple. Some things are not mentioned here, e.g. the altar of incense.

Daniel

INTRODUCTION

The Book falls into two main sections: chs. 1–6 are narratives of Daniel and his three friends; chs. 7–12 are a series of visions of the future. A further division, which does not coincide with the former, is the section 2.4–7.28, which is in Aramaic, while the rest of the Book is in Hebrew. Aramaic is a Semitic language, and was widely used as an international means of communication in the Near East. By the time of Christ it had superseded Hebrew as the popular language of Palestine. No theory of the language switch in *Daniel* has commanded universal acceptance. Perhaps the whole Book was translated from Hebrew into Aramaic, and later one section of the Hebrew was lost; as there was no other copy, the lost section was replaced by the Aramaic translation.

The Book professes to be by Daniel (12.4), and, although ob-

394

jections have been raised to this, our commentary will assume that there are good reasons for taking the Book at its face value. We shall not argue about the objections, but, without ignoring any major difficulty, we shall show how they may be integrated into our understanding of the text.

The Hebrew Bible does not include *Daniel* in the section of the Prophets, perhaps because the style of visions that God gave him was so different from normal prophecy. However, the Lord Jesus Christ referred to him as a prophet, and looked for the fulfilment of what he wrote (Matt. **24.15**).

Daniel 1 Under Test

After Nebuchadnezzar had broken Egypt's hold on Palestine at the battle of Carchemish in 605 B.C., he moved south, and, according to the historian Berossus, he took prisoners from the major states, including Judah. 'The third year' (1) is Babylonian reckoning; Jer. **46**.2 gives 'the fourth year' by Jewish reckoning. Probably Jehoiakim was taken to Babylon for a short time, as Manasseh had been (2; 2 Chron. **36**.6; **33**.10–13), and was exhibited in the temple of Marduk.

Assyrian and Babylonian kings appreciated merit, and here the King selected Daniel and his three friends for special training with a view to becoming members of the class of wise advisers at the royal court. They were renamed, as Joseph had been, in Gen. **41.45**. *Belteshazzar* probably means *Protect his life*, or, shall we say, *Lifeguard? Abednego* is usually taken as *Servant of Nebo*. As Nebo was a Babylonian god, the four friends would not have cared to use the name among themselves. The meanings of *Shadrach* and *Meshach* are unknown.

Daniel emerges as the leader (8–10). He was unsuccessful with the head man (10), but managed to persuade the chief steward to give them a different diet for a short test period. The king's food had probably been offered to idols, and the meat would not have been *kosher*, drained of the blood according to the law of Moses (cf. Hos. **9**.3). The steward was delighted to find that his charges did so well on a vegetarian diet. He drew their rations, and he and his family doubtless enjoyed them (16)!

Daniel's confidence was justified, and he and his friends passed their tests with honours (17–20). God had Daniel where He wanted him for a great many years, and the young man lived to see not only the arrival of further exiles from Judah in 597 and 586 B.C., but also the wonderful day when Cyrus captured Babylon and allowed

the exiles to return if they wished. This is the significance of v. 21, but Daniel continued several years longer (e.g. 10.1).
Learn to prove the power of God in small ways before the big tests come (Jer. 12.5; Acts 13.13; 15.37,38).

Daniel 2.1-24   The Lost Dream

Nebuchadnezzar was not yet king when he won the battle of Carchemish, but soon afterwards he was summoned home on the death of his father, followed by his prisoners. We should therefore have expected the events of this chapter to be at least in the third year, not the second year, of his reign (1, cf. 1.5). But the Babylonians generally did not begin to count a king's reign until the New Year after his accession. Thus, putting together this date and the three years of 1.5, we have; first year training—accession year of Nebuchadnezzar; second year training—first year of king; third year training—second year of king. The training need not have taken the whole of three years. The interpretation of the dream faced Daniel almost immediately after his test.

We cannot tell whether Nebuchadnezzar had really forgotten his dream, or whether he was trying out the skill of his wise men to see whether they could read what was in his mind. The wise men are here called *Chaldeans*, which at this date meant *Babylonians*. It is used in this sense in 1.4; 5.30; 9.1, whereas in this chapter and in 3.8 (possibly); 4.7; 5.7,11, it refers to a class of wise men, which became its regular use later. We note that the second use occurs in the Aramaic portions, which were probably translated later, except for vs. 2 and 4 here, where the word was probably put into the Hebrew to make the chapter consistent when the Aramaic version was attached to it (see Introduction). The original Hebrew may have had *galdu*, which occurs in Babylonian writings as a term for *astrologers*.

Nebuchadnezzar was childishly unreasonable in his demand, especially when he began to threaten his wise men with death if they could not tell the dream (8,9), and actually gave orders to kill them (12).

Although Daniel was a member of the group, he obviously kept himself aloof from their magic and astrology. Thus he had not gone in with them to the king (14,15). Now he handles the situation as a man of God. He goes in quietly to the king, and obtains an extension of time (16). Then he appeals to his friends to join him in prayer (18), and in answer God shows him both the dream and its meaning (19). Before he goes in to the king, he lifts up his heart

396

in praise to God (20–23). It is good to see his concern for his colleagues; whatever he thinks of their methods (27), he knows they do not deserve the mad punishment that the king was ready to give.

Compare Daniel's song of praise with other passages in Scripture, such as Prov. 2.1–15; 1 Sam. 2.1–10; 1 Kings 3.5–14.

Daniel 2.25-49 — The Interpretation of the Dream

Daniel assures the king that his discovery of the dream and its interpretation did not depend on his natural wisdom or on magic arts (26–30). He describes and interprets the features of the strange dream of the image, which symbolizes four successive world empires.

Babylon is the gold head. The breast and arms are the joint Medo-Persian empire, initiated by Cyrus. The belly and thighs are Greece, which became the dominant empire when Alexander the Great conquered Persia. The legs and feet are the Roman empire, embracing more scattered peoples than any of the others, but never able to marry them all together into perfect union (43), mixed, but ruthless (41,42).

In the days of the Roman empire a superhuman stone falls on the image (34), and all that had gone to form the four empires is broken and blown away (34,35,44,45). The stone goes on growing until it becomes the size of a mountain (35), and this is the Kingdom of God, which endures for ever (44).

A fair interpretation is that the first coming of Jesus Christ was the falling of the stone on the image. Since then the stone has been growing into a mountain, as the gospel has gone through the world, although the completion will not come before Christ returns again.

Although Daniel is rewarded by being made head of the college of wise men (48), there is no hint of his compromising by becoming a priest or magician. His influence for the true God must have made itself felt; and it may have been what he told the others about the promises of God that was handed down to those wise men who partially understood the message of the Star in the east (Matt. 2.1 ff.).

If, as many suppose, the *Book of Daniel* was really written about 170 B.C. to encourage Jewish resistance against the divine claims of Antiochus Epiphanes (4 syllables), it is strange that the writer makes Nebuchadnezzar offer an oblation and incense to Daniel, as though he were divine (46).

Study other pictures of the Messiah as the Stone, e.g. 1 Pet. 2.6–8; Luke 20.17,18. Note the marginal references in each case.

397

Daniel 3
The Golden Image

Nebuchadnezzar's image was probably of wood, plated with gold. It towered up to 90 feet, but this may have included the plinth, which narrowed to 9 feet at the base of the image itself. The Colossus of Rhodes stood 70 feet. Nelson's Column in Trafalgar Square, London, is 145 feet, and the actual statue of Nelson is 18 feet high on top of the column. The image was presumably of a god, and not of the king himself (12,18). The locality of Dura (1) is unknown.

It was customary to gather large numbers of officials for dedication ceremonies, as Middle East inscriptions show (3). Daniel's three friends were there as governors (2.49), but Daniel himself, as head of the wise men, was evidently exempt from attendance. The word 'satraps' (3) is Persian, not Babylonian, but, since Daniel lived on into the Persian period, he could naturally use the Persian equivalent of the Babylonian word for the head of a province; in any case this is in the Aramaic section, which was probably translated from the Hebrew in the Persian period.

The lyre, trigon, and harp, are stringed instruments, whose names in this passage are basically Greek. Musical instruments travel from country to country in the hands of traders and mercenaries, and Greek traders were in Asia Minor from the 7th century, and there were Greek mercenaries in the Babylonian army.

The three friends are quietly persistent to the end. They do not make any conditions with God; deliverance or martyrdom are equally in His hand (17,18). So they are thrown into the lime kiln furnace through the open door (26). Then a miracle happens. Not only are they unharmed, although the flames roaring out of the door burnt their warders to death, but the fire destroys the ropes that bound them without damaging their clothes. There is good evidence for fire-walking through trenches of glowing ashes without the feet being harmed, but there is no known natural explanation of what happened to the three here.

The intervention of God is confirmed by the presence of one whom Nebuchadnezzar realizes is a supernatural figure (25). We may well recognize Him as the Lord Jesus Christ in one of His pre-incarnation appearances (cf. Gen. 16.11–13; 18.1,2,22).

The fire reveals the presence of the Lord. Consider Acts 18.9,10; 2 Cor. 12.7–10.

Daniel 4.1-18
The Tree Dream

This is Nebuchadnezzar's second recorded dream, but this time the meaning is personal to himself. Secular records describe occasional dreams which kings have felt to be significant, e.g. Xerxes dreamed that he was crowned with an olive shoot, with branches that stretched over the world.

The chapter is a public decree by Nebuchadnezzar. Whereas in 3.28,29 he had sanctioned the worship of the God of Israel as an alternative to other gods, he now admits that there is a supreme God Most High, whom he himself must bow to, since this God is King of kings.

It is not surprising that v. 3 is strongly reminiscent of Psa. 145.5, 13, for in talking to the king about the meaning of his dream, Daniel would certainly have brought out some of the Scriptures, and Psa. 145 is a magnificent hymn of God's rule and providence, which lingered in Nebuchadnezzar's memory.

It is significant that the king did not send immediately for Daniel (6–8), although he had been the only one able to interpret the first dream. No doubt he had an uneasy feeling that this dream had some moral meaning, and he knew that the God of Daniel tended to make severe moral demands. This is a common human failing. People with doubts will often persist in reading sceptical books, and in ignoring authors with sensible Christian answers: if there is no God and no Godward significance in sin, then one can ease up in the demands of life.

The dream is vividly described, and needs only brief notes. The 'watcher' (13,17) is one of the angels who are always watchful to see what God would have them do (Ezek. 1.18; Rev. 4.8; Zech. 4.10). The 'band of iron' (15) is either for restraint (of a madman) or for preservation, so that the stump is not dug up. 'Seven times' (16) in this Book and in the *Revelation* represents seven definite periods fixed by God, possibly years.

The world envies the big man, but he is often a very uneasy man under the surface, especially where God is concerned. Mark 6.20; Acts 24.25.

Daniel 4.19-37   Humbled Greatness

Clearly Daniel was fond of the king, and was appalled at the prediction in the dream (19). At the same time he took the dream to be a warning from God rather than an absolutely fixed destiny. Thus he urges Nebuchadnezzar to set aside his typical oriental despotism, and be a simple benefactor to his people (27), ruling under God (26). Otherwise he will certainly suffer the fate of the tree in the dream.

For twelve months nothing happened. Then one day the king went up to the flat roof of the palace, probably the top terrace of the so-called Hanging Gardens, from which he could see over the city which he had built, and which a modern writer describes as 'a cosmopolitan city, the like of which has never existed since, with the exceptions of Rome and perhaps New York' (Schneider, *Babylon is Everywhere*). As he shouted for the glory of it, a sudden madness fell on him, giving him the awful hallucination of being turned into an animal. He no longer behaved as a man, but insisted on being turned out to pasture, presumably in one of the royal parks where no one would interfere with him (33).

From v. 33 we gather that he must have been in this state for at least a year, but v. 34 does not say that he was mad for seven years, as vs. 16 and 25 might suggest. Just as the 'beast-nature' had been under the surface previously, so now in the depths of his mind he was coming to terms with God and himself, and thus fulfilled the requirement of the end of v. 25.

Note how this section (28–33) is in the third person; Nebuchadnezzar could not describe exactly what was happening. With v. 34 we return to the confession, again paraphrasing Psa. 145, and also bringing in something from Isa. 40.22,26; 43.13. Daniel would certainly have regarded these chapters of *Isaiah* as very precious, since they foretold the ultimate release from Babylon. In talking to the king (27), he would have found plenty of relevant passages about God's·sovereignty there.

Secular records of Nebuchadnezzar's reign are incomplete, but a quotation from Megasthenes (about 300 B.C.) says that Nebuchadnezzar on the roof of his palace was suddenly possessed by a spirit, and, after foretelling the end of the Babylonian empire, suddenly disappeared. This could be a perverted version of the true account in this chapter.

1 Cor. 4.7 is God's corrective for boasting.

Daniel 5.1-16 The Writing on the Wall

Contemporary records say that Nabonidus, the last Babylonian king, 'entrusted the kingship to his son, Bel-shar-usur', while he himself retired to Arabia. Because his father was still the supreme ruler, Belshazzar in this chapter cannot promise a higher position than 'the third ruler in the kingdom' (7).

There are three references to Nebuchadnezzar as the 'father' of Belshazzar (2,11,18). It seems unlikely from the records that Belshazzar was descended from Nebuchadnezzar, but 'father' has several usages in ancient documents. Here it stands for 'predecessor on the throne', as in an Assyrian inscription, which describes Jehu as son of Omri, although in fact Jehu had murdered the last of Omri's line and usurped the throne (2 Kings 9,10). The queen in

v. 10 is unlikely to be one of the wives of Belshazzar, who were already present at the feast (3). She could have been the widow of Nebuchadnezzar, who had died 23 years earlier.

The date now is 539 B.C. Cyrus the Persian is at the gates, but Belshazzar believes that Babylon is easily able to resist him. All the top people join in a dinner of bravado, in which temple cups and bowls are turned to vulgar use (3, cf. 2 Kings 24.13; 25.15; Jer. 27.19–22), and the many idols of Babylon have their praises sung (4).

At this point the party is thrown into a panic by a mysterious hand which writes four words on the wall. We need not suppose that the words were in an unknown language, but they could not be read intelligently. It may be, however, that the letters were in an unusual script, and were mixed up in some way like an anagram in a crossword. The wise men could not make sense of it, but when news of the panic reached the apartments where the elderly ex-queen was living, she was happy to go in and remind the young man, whose father had murdered her grandson and taken the throne from him, of what his predecessor, her husband, had done. He had turned to Daniel for help. So once more God's servant is summoned to meet the crisis.

When the enemy is at the gates bravery is better than bravado, cf. Isa. 22.12–14; Eph. 6.10–18.

Daniel 5.17-31 Found Wanting

The first part of this section (17–23) needs no special comment, apart from noting the powerful conclusion of v. 23.

The meaning of the writing is not easy to follow without a note of explanation. The words are three weights, a mina, a shekel (which is one-sixtieth of a mina), and half minas (*parsin* is the plural of *peres;* Daniel gives the singular in his interpretation in v. 28). The names suggest other words, i.e. numbered, weighed, divided; and *peres* also sounds like the word for 'Persians', *Paras.* A modern parallel would be if the hand had written 'Pound, pound, threepenny bit, and half sovereigns', and Daniel were to interpret as 'God has pounded your kingdom; you are not worth one little bit, and your sovereignty will be shared between the enemy.'

Belshazzar accepted the reading, but had no idea that it was so near fulfilment. That night the troops of Cyrus entered the city. The historian Xenophon says that Cyrus diverted the river, and his troops entered Babylon at night during the celebration of a festival, and killed the king.

There is no archaeological reference to a king called Darius immediately after the fall of Babylon (31). We must therefore assume that this was an alternative name for one of three rulers. (*i*) Cyrus, who had a Median mother, and who is referred to by Nabonidus as king of the Medes. In 6.28 we can translate 'and' by 'even', as in 1 Chron. 5.26, which has 'Pul king of Assyria, *even* the spirit of Tilgath-pilneser', where the two names refer to the same man.

(*ii*) Gubaru, who was appointed governor of Babylon by Cyrus, and who exercised considerable power, even appointing governors.

(*iii*) Cyaxares, the uncle of Cyrus and king of Media. Xenophon suggests that Cyrus made him courtesy king over all his empire. Note that he 'received the kingdom' (31). The Jewish historian Josephus, who had access to writings now lost, says that Darius, 'who had another name among the Greeks', took Daniel to Media. Note that in 10.4 Daniel is by the Tigris, a branch of which rose in Media, and not by the Euphrates, which was Babylon's river.

There are difficulties in each of these identifications, but they are not greater than if we try to explain how the author invented a fictitious king, when he knew all about Cyrus.

Consider the implications of the end of v. 23 for ourselves today.

Daniel 6.1-15 Discipline of Prayer

In the Hebrew Bible 5.31 stands as the opening verse of this chapter. Daniel does not say that Darius captured Babylon, though, if he is the same as Cyrus, he does not deny it. If Josephus is correct, Daniel now writes about his new patron, who had taken him to Media, and who exerted considerable authority from there. Otherwise he is still in Babylon under Cyrus or Gubaru.

By now Daniel was over eighty, but his wisdom and dependability drew from his enemies the striking admission of vs. 4 and 5. Darius was more vulnerable, and was flattered to hear that for a month he should be treated as the only god in the country. The reference in v. 7 is clearly to this, and not to any simple request by one neighbour to another. He is induced to make a binding decree to this effect (8, cf. Esth. 1.19; 8.8).

In v. 10 we see the man of God at his best. He did not stage a special protest, or suddenly do what he had not done before, but simply behaved 'as he had done previously'. The opponents knew what to look for. Daniel opened his western-facing window, looking towards the Jerusalem that his eyes would never see, and there he poured out his heart to God (1 Kings 8.29,30,48; Pss. 5.7; 138.2; Jon. 2.7). This is one of the places in the Bible where a man of God finds it right to defy a decree which the king had no right to make (cf. Acts 5.29. Contrast Rom. 13.1,2).

The three times for prayer were probably the time when the morning burnt offering was offered, when the temple was standing; noon or the afternoon; and sunset, when the evening offering was made (cf. **9.21**).

What is the value in regular times for prayer? Note Pss. 55.17; 119.164; 1 Chron. 23.30; Acts 3.1; 10.9,30.

Daniel 6.16-28   The Lions' Den

We have to decide from the brief description and from common-sense about the form of the den of lions. It cannot have been a dark pit with an entrance only at the top, since lions could neither be lowered into such a pit nor have been kept alive at the bottom. Since, as we saw in ch. 3, the three men were 'cast into' the furnace through an entrance at the side, Daniel was presumably cast into the den through a similar door. The lions would thus be in something like the bear pits at the zoo, though there may well have been a drop inside the door as an additional protection for the keepers (23,24).

It was already dark when Daniel was put in the den (14,15), so it was impossible to see down into the pit from the spectators' gallery at the top. The lower door was habitually closed with a stone, and this was now sealed so that no one could tamper with it during the hours of darkness (17). The king arrived before it was fully light in the morning (19), and called to Daniel before he actually reached the spot where he could look down into the den.

The cruel punishment of v. 24 is typically Persian. Obviously only the ringleaders are meant, and not all the satraps mentioned in v. 1.

The words of praise by Darius in vs. 26,27 are not, like Nebuchadnezzar's (4.3), reminiscent of a psalm, but spontaneously recognize the eternity of God's rule and His supreme power.

Concerning v. 28, if Darius is the same as Cyrus, we translate 'and' by 'even', as explained in note on 5.31. If he is Gubaru or Cyaxares, the reference here is to their joint rule.

Study the way in which Darius progressed in faith.

Questions for further study and discussion on Daniel chs. 1–6

1. What do these chapters teach about the need to stand for our principles? What sort of principles must we stand for?
2. How does the character of Daniel show a proper blend of humility and of complete confidence in God which made him bold?

3. What did Nebuchadnezzar, Belshazzar, and Darius learn through the witness of Daniel and his friends?
4. Find other passages in Scripture that speak of the Lord's deliverance in time of trouble, and also passages where He does not deliver. What then should be our attitude when trouble, or even death, threatens?

Daniel 7.1-18   God on the Throne

With this chapter we begin the description of the visions that God gave to Daniel. They are arranged in chronological order, this one being in 554 B.C., when Nabonidus gave the kingship of Babylon to his son.

The four kings (17) are the rulers of the four world empires that had already been depicted in Nebuchadnezzar's vision of the great image (ch. 2). This time they are symbolized by four wild animals.

(i) The lion (4) is Babylon, but more specifically it symbolizes Nebuchadnezzar, Babylon's greatest king. His eagle wings were plucked when his madness humbled his flight in the face of heaven, but his subsequent confession of God's glory shows that he has the mind of a man, since a true man is one who admits his dependence on God.

(ii) The bear (5) is the Medo-Persian empire. The three ribs in its mouth probably have no special significance other than showing it to be a devouring beast. Its front paw, raised to slash, lifts its body on one side.

(iii) The leopard (6) is Greece, with Alexander the Great flying through Asia in his conquests. After his death his empire became four-headed, i.e. Asia Minor, Mesopotamia, Egypt, and Macedonia (cf. 8.8).

(iv) The terrifying beast, which is Rome, is only partially described (7). Its ten horns, like the ten toes of the image (2.41,42), are its federation of nations, loosely held together. We will leave the consideration of the little horn (8) until the next section.

Daniel, like some of the other prophets, was privileged to have a vision of God (9,10). He is impressed with His shining glorious brightness. This vision may be compared with Ezek. 1, together with the notes there. God is surrounded by the host of heaven. The picture is that of judgement, but probably not of the final judgement day. God's concern is the putting of the rule of the world into the hands of His Messiah. This is done by sending His Son into the Roman Empire, which had incorporated the earlier empires (12), and henceforth superseding it with His new kingdom (14).

If the scene is the final judgement, vs. 13, 14 must refer to the second coming. But in Matt. 26.64 Christ appears to be quoting these words of Himself, and says that the high priest will witness their fulfilment 'from now onwards'. This is the literal Greek, as indicated in the RV's 'henceforth'. Thus this vision begins with the ascension (Heb. 1.3,4; 10.12,13), although it runs through to completion at the second coming (cf. the stone becoming a mountain in 2.35).

Compare other visions of God, remembering that He can be seen only in a form that He chooses, and this must often be 'symbolic' (e.g. Exod. 24.17).

Daniel 7.19-28   Victory after Suffering

It is impossible to be dogmatic about the identity of the 'horn' in this passage. In chs. 8 and 11 Antiochus Epiphanes (4 syllables) is the persecutor, but the persecutor in this chapter is connected with the Roman Empire. The sequence here seems to be the coming of the Messiah in the time of the last of the single world empires, for, since Rome, world rule has been shared by various great powers at one and the same time.

Next comes violent persecution from the little horn, which rises in succession to other horns, and this persecution or war on the saints, continues until the final intervention by God. Some think that this is Antichrist, and, if he arises from Rome, there must be a revival of the Roman Empire still to come.

It is possible to take an intermediate view. Daniel is naturally concerned about the fate of his own people, the Jews. He does not know about the Christian Church, but the vision has the Church in mind, as well as the Jews. Thus Daniel sees a figure who was concerned both with the final destruction of the Jewish nation and also with launching the intense persecution of the Christians. This could be the Emperor Nero. Although he died before the destruction of Jerusalem in A.D. 70, it was he who sent Vespasian with the Roman armies to quell the Jewish rebellion. It was he also who organized the first big persecution of the Christians.

Nero himself did not exhaust the prophecy, any more than Antiochus exhausted other prophecies in *Daniel* (Matt. 24.15). He is like the beast in Rev. 13.3, whose head grows again when it is cut off. Thus the saints down the ages have had to face their Nero again and again, and there may be a final Nero in the person of Antichrist, even though there have been many antichrists (1 John 2.18).

We cannot give an explanation of the 'ten' and the 'three' in

v. 24. They may have reference to assassinations by Nero, or they may be general numbers, as we speak of 'dozens' and 'two or three': i.e. he will not be the first king of this empire, but there will be a number of others before him, and he will put down the few who oppose him.

Nero inaugurates wholesale persecutions of Christians and displays bitter hostility towards the true God; while he tries to force God's people to conform to his pattern (25; Rev. 13.16,17). God's people have to submit to persecution for a specified time, known to God, whether days, weeks, months, or years (25). Yet through suffering we shall share in the victory of God, for Christ's kingdom is ours also (26,27).

Consider the relation between reigning with Christ (Eph. 2.6) and being persecuted for Christ's sake (2 Tim. 2.11–13).

*Daniel 8.1-12   Desecration

Daniel is visiting Susa, east of Babylon and south of Media, and is given a vision on the banks of the river Eulaeus. He sees a ram with two horns that denote Media and Persia (3,4,20). The taller horn is Persia, since Cyrus of Persia had conquered Media and absorbed it into his empire.

Next a goat comes from the west, and overthrows the ram. Greece conquers Persia (5–7,21). Alexander the Great is the goat's horn (5,21), and on his death his empire is divided between four other kings, who were in fact Alexander's generals (8,22). From one of them, Seleucus, who held the eastern part of the empire, another horn appeared after some 125 years (9,23). This was Antiochus Epiphanes, who came to the throne in 175 B.C.

He launches an attack on God, and begins by pulling down some of the stars and trampling on them (10). In the vision these probably represent the loyal people of God, who are put to death for their faith (24; 12.3). Then he makes as direct an attack on God as he can, and desecrates the Temple in Jerusalem, forbidding the daily offering to be made on the altar (11,12). Historically Antiochus plundered the Temple and set up an altar to Zeus in the precincts, offering pig's flesh on it (168 or 167 B.C.).

The meaning of v. 12 may be that from among the people of God ('the host' as in vs. 10,11) there are those who become apostates, and so come under the sway of Antiochus when he takes control of the burnt offering. This links up with 'transgression'. Otherwise, it could be that loyal Jews are killed through the sin of Antiochus.

In what way can anyone attack God today?

406

*Daniel 8.13-27   Restoration

This portion is more or less an interpretation of the vision, but there are several special features to note. In v. 14 we have one of several time-periods in *Daniel*. This one may have in mind the evening and morning sacrifices, which have been suspended by Antiochus. If so, the period is that of 2300 sacrifices, i.e. 1150 days. In actual fact the daily sacrifices were suspended for 1090 days, just over three years.

It is simpler to take the phrase, 'evenings and mornings', in the same sense as in Gen. 1.5, etc. Thus the period is the full 2300 days, and includes the time from the first interference in Jewish affairs in 171 B.C. to the death of Antiochus in 164 B.C.

In the vision Daniel hears a conversation between two angels (13), but the full interpretation comes from the angel Gabriel (16). The phrase, 'the time of the end' (17), must always be interpreted in the light of the context. It may refer to the end of a particular era as well as to the end of world history. There cannot be a reference to Antichrist here, since this vision does not even go as far as the 4th empire, Rome. Thus the 'end' cannot be the second coming. The persecutions by Antiochus were the last of the anti-God persecutions which might have destroyed the Jewish faith, before the coming of the Messiah, and it is in this sense that we may interpret 'the end'.

This time is also referred to as 'the latter end of the indignation', i.e. the conclusion of the persecuting rage of Antiochus and others (19). Daniel is assured that the worship in the Temple will once more be restored (14), and that the boasting Antiochus will die without achieving his aim of crushing the Jewish faith (25). In fact, Antiochus died of an illness, while planning fresh campaigns. The story of this period may be read in 1 Maccabees 1–6, in the Apocrypha.

Daniel is told to keep this record, but not to publish it until the time of the events (26; cf. 12.9).

Somewhere today there is an Antiochus who is trying to stamp out the true faith. We know who will win, but let us pray especially for our brothers and sisters who are being trampled down.

Daniel 9.1-19   Confession of Sin

In 605 B.C. Nebuchadnezzar broke the power of Egypt at the battle of Carchemish. Egypt had to withdraw from Palestine, and the country came under the rule of Babylon. At this point Jeremiah foretold that the dominion of Babylon would last for seventy years, and would include the period of the exile (Jer. 25.1–11). We noticed in ch. 4 that Daniel was familiar with the *Psalms* and *Isaiah*, and here we find him equally familiar with the prophecies of Jeremiah, some of which at least were already being incorporated into the collection of writings recognized as inspired (2).

It is now 538 B.C., approximately seventy years since the Jews came under Babylon (2), and Daniel is naturally anxious for the promised return to come as soon as possible. But he knows that the purpose of the exile was to prepare a repentant nucleus for the future. Hence he takes the lead in this prayer of confession of national sin.

Note the balance and contrast between the sin of the people and the righteousness of God, and between unfaithfulness and faithfulness (4–10). Daniel has also studied the Law of Moses, and admits that God had given full warning and promise in Lev. 26 and Deut. 28–30 (13,14).

He makes his final plea for restoration on the ground of the covenant (implied in v. 15) and for the sake of God's own great Name (17–19). So must we also pray in the Name of the Lord Jesus Christ.

Daniel's prayer embraced all of God's people, both the exiles whom he knew, and also those who were still living in Palestine, near Jerusalem (7). Prayer can easily be too local.

It is worth comparing this prayer with Ezra 9 and Neh. 9.

Daniel 9.20-27   The Messiah

Daniel included himself in his prayer of confession (20). It is dangerous to be critical of others in our prayers without considering ourselves. He had been thinking only of an immediate return from exile, and God was quick to answer his prayer, since almost immediately Cyrus gave permission to the Jews to return (Ezra 1). But just as Isaiah was shown in chs. 40–55 that there would not only be a return from Babylon, but also a return from the exile of sin through the atoning work of God's Servant (especially ch. 53), so Daniel is shown that the climax of Jewish history is not only the return, but the subsequent coming of the Messiah, and that there is a second time-scale for Jeremiah's words. The interpreter is appropriately the same Gabriel who later announced to the virgin Mary that she would be the mother of the Messiah (21; Luke 1.26 ff.).

In this commentary we have room for only one interpretation of the figures and statements in vs. 24–27. The finished work of Christ is described in v. 24. The first four clauses are obvious. 'To seal both vision and prophet' means to set God's seal of fulfilment on the Messianic prophecies of the O.T. 'To anoint a most holy place' is better taken as in the margin of 'a most Holy One', i.e. Christ.

Certain periods are mentioned on a scale of a year for a day (24). In prophecy a year is 360 days, or 12 months of 30 days each (Rev. 11.2,3). The only recorded command to rebuild Jerusalem (25) is in Neh. 2.1 ff., i.e. 446 B.C. In v. 25 the AV and RV margin transliterate 'an anointed one' as 'the Messiah', assuming, probably correctly, that by this time the word was already beginning to be the title of the One who should come.

We are also free to follow the AV and RV margin again with the figures, and punctuate, 'there shall be seven weeks and sixty-two weeks; it shall be built again', i.e. the city will be built, and the Messiah will come after 69 weeks of years, which are 483 years of 360 days, or 476 years, according to our chronology. From 446 B.C. the 476 years would end in A.D. 30, which could be the start of Christ's ministry as Minister of the New Covenant for His people. We thus take the first half of v. 27 as referring to Christ, whose death, when He was cut off after about half a week (3 to 3½ years), ended the Jewish sacrifices. The week ends with the death of Stephen and the opening of the doors to the Gentiles.

His rejection by the nation as a whole resulted in the destruction of Jerusalem by the Romans in A.D. 70 (26,27, cf. Matt. 23.29–39). The final word of v. 27 may be translated 'desolate' (RV margin). The Romans will fly upon the city and bring about the ultimate pollution of the Temple and the scattering of the ruined nation.

Consider v. 24 in the light of Heb. 10.1–22.

Daniel 10.1—11.1 War in Heaven

Daniel has a vision of a conflict (1) which concerns heaven as well as earth. He has been keeping the Passover and Feast of Unleavened Bread, as the date in v. 4 shows, but his private fasting and prayer had lasted longer than the stipulated week (2). He is rewarded by a vision of a glorious being (5,6), who may be Christ Himself (Rev. 1.13–15), but who might be Gabriel or some other angel. V. 7 may be compared with what happened at Paul's conversion (Acts 9.7).

Vs. 12–21 are an O.T. equivalent of what Paul says in Eph. 6.10–18 about the heavenly warfare. It is clear that an evil angel can dominate a nation (13,20), and that there is some power equivalent to a national guardian angel. Michael is spoken of in these terms as the angel who stands behind Israel (13,21; 12.1). The Seventh Day Adventists hold that Michael is the pre-incarnate title of Christ, and this is possible, provided that we also accept His deity, as the Adventists do. Jehovah's Witnesses reject His deity, though they believe that He was Michael and a created being.

The speaker, or speakers, in this chapter speak of the way God had used them and would use them again in the events of history. Note that in **11.1** 'him' is Michael and not Darius.

Consider our warfare in the light of Eph. 6.12,13 and Col. 2.15.

Daniel 11.2-28

The Plan of History

In this chapter we have a most detailed prediction of the course of history. We ourselves would like to see more predictions of our own day, but it was important for the Jewish nation that God should prepare them to face one of the strongest attempts that would ever be made to force them to apostatize. It would be the final attempt before the coming of the Messiah.

The next three kings of Persia (2) were Cambyses, Gaumata, and Darius I. Darius campaigned unsuccessfully against Greece, and his son, Xerxes I, launched a further big attack (3). He also was defeated in 480 B.C. This is the Xerxes of the book of *Esther*. The prophecy now passes to the Greek conquest of Persia under Alexander the Great in 334–330 B.C. (3), though his empire was divided among four of his generals on his death (4).

Ptolemy I ruled Egypt. Seleucus, who had been allotted Babylonia, was forced to escape to Egypt, and served as one of Ptolemy's generals until he could get his kingdom back. Eventually this kingdom stretched from Palestine to India (5). Some fifty years later Ptolemy II gave his daughter in marriage to Antiochus I, a Seleucid, but Antiochus deserted her, and himself was murdered (6). Her brother, Ptolemy III, invaded Syria in 246 B.C. (7,8).

Vs. 9–13 describe the see-saw struggles between the Seleucids of Syria and the Ptolemies of Egypt between 223 B.C. and about 200 B.C. At this point some of the Jews joined in with Antiochus III of Syria, imagining that they were fulfilling some prophecy (14). The Egyptian army was besieged and defeated in Sidon (15), and Antiochus broke the hold of Egypt on Palestine (16). He came to terms with Ptolemy V, and gave him his daughter in marriage, hoping that this would turn out to his own advantage (17). Antiochus III then annexed the coastlands of Asia Minor, and even invaded Greece, but here he was defeated by a Roman commander, and forced to withdraw (18). The Romans followed him, defeated him at Magnesia in 190 B.C., and forced him to pay heavy tribute. He died shortly afterwards (19).

His son, Seleucus IV, exacted tribute from the Jews and others in order to pay the Romans, but he was poisoned not long after an

410

attempt by his agent to seize the Temple treasures (20). His brother, Antiochus IV, known as Epiphanes, succeeded him, and became the great persecutor. By personal influence he managed to be chosen king in place of the son of Seleucus (21). Vs. 22–24 give a sketch of his character and way of life. He despised covenants and alliances, but got his way through a small body of supporters, plundering one area to bribe another.

In 173 B.C. Antiochus defeated Ptolemy VI, captured him, and was crowned as king of Egypt. Some of Ptolemy's courtiers turned traitor (25,26). When the Egyptians set up the brother of Ptolemy VI as king, Antiochus made a half-hearted attempt to restore Ptolemy VI, but this was unsuccessful (27). He therefore retired to Syria, but planned to attack the Jews (28).

These verses have been given contemporary interpretations at various times. Consider how far this is due to invariable factors that lead men to alliances and wars.

Daniel 11.29-45 The End of the Persecutor

Antiochus again invaded Egypt (29), but Roman ambassadors, arriving by ship, forced him to withdraw (30). The Jews were quarrelling over the high priesthood, and the liberal group were glad to have his help (30). However, Antiochus did not rest until he had totally profaned the Temple and its worship (31; see notes on 8.1–12). A number of Jews stood firm, in spite of torture and martyrdom (32,33). They received support from the militant Maccabees, who became powerful enough to frighten some half-hearted Jews into giving nominal support (34). Moreover, in time of persecution even the genuine believers are stimulated to greater devotion (35).

Antiochus had coins struck describing himself as THEOS EPIPHANES (God Manifest) (36), and set aside the traditional gods, including Apollo and Tammuz (or Adonis, the darling god of women) (37), and set up a temple to Jupiter Capitolinus in Antioch (38), and acknowledged him as his guardian (39).

Vs. 40–45 have given rise to various interpretations. They do not describe what actually happened towards the end of Antiochus' life. There are three main lines of interpretation.

(*i*) Antiochus is a type of Antichrist, and in these verses we jump to an attack on the Holy Land before the final coming of Christ.

(*ii*) Since in this chapter there have been various kings of the south and the north, we now have the end of the Syrian empire, when a new king of the north, i.e. Rome under Crassus, subdues the former king, pillages the Temple (54 B.C.), and takes over

Palestine. However, in a war against the Parthians of the north-east, Crassus is killed (44,45).

(*iii*) These verses contain a summary of Antiochus' actions during his whole career, just as vs. 36–39 contain a summary of his methods. He was successful almost everywhere, even apparently against God and His people and holy Temple. Only the Parthians in the north-east remained as a threat (44). The last sentence of the chapter does not say that he died in Palestine. He set himself up as God, but he died like an ordinary man. His death in Persia in 164 B.C. (or 163) was sudden and unexpected. This was the end of the pre-Messianic persecutions, and from now onwards the Roman empire was beginning to take over world power.

Death is the great humiliator. Pss. 49.16–20; 82.6,7; Luke 12.20.

Daniel 12.1-6 Sifting

There is so much to consider in this final chapter, that we divide it into two short portions.

If Antichrist is the subject of the closing verses of the previous chapter, the opening verses here refer to the time of the Lord's return. If, however, Antiochus has been the subject, we have come to the end of the great persecution on account of faith; the Greek empire has given place to the early domination by Rome, which gave the Jews considerable freedom. Now the Jewish nation is to be sifted once again when confronted by the promised Messiah.

The intervention of Michael (1) is then the throwing down of Satan as recorded in Rev. 12.7–12. This victory over Satan is linked with the efficacy of the death of Jesus Christ (Rev. 12.11; John 12.31f.). But for the Jewish nation as a whole, their clinging to nationalism and rejection of the Messiah led to their scattering and tribulation (Luke 21.20–24). However, many among the Jews will accept the Messiah and their names are in the Book of Life (1). If we do not take v. 1 to refer to some special period of trouble shortly before the Lord returns, the meaning is that the continuing sufferings that the Jewish nation has undergone up to the present day are unique in history.

In the reference to the resurrections in v. 2, still to come, it is not clear why the words speak of 'many' rather than 'all'. Probably the verse is singling out Daniel's nation, who are many; it ignores the Gentile dead. Even among God's chosen people there are both sheep and goats.

V. 3 has meant much to many people who are concerned with witness for God by life and speech (cf. 11.33,35; 12.10). Meanwhile Daniel has to keep what he has written, and not disclose it publicly.

During the last persecutions before the Messiah's coming, those who have the book will make it known (cf. Rev. 22.10). Although it is tempting to apply the closing sentence of v. 4 to the present day, it is more likely that it means that many will run to study the book in order to increase their knowledge of God (cf. Amos 8.12; Hab. 2.2).

Compare v. 3 with Mal. 3.16–4.3; Phil. 2.15,16. We do well to examine ourselves.

Daniel 12.7-13 The End

This remarkable book ends with figures and dates that are not easy to decipher. One at least is either absolutely literal or else the most curious coincidence in history. This is the figure in v. 12 of 1335 days. General Allenby captured Jerusalem in the year 1335, according to the Muslim calendar, which was the one used by the Turks who at that time held Jerusalem. This was 1917 in our era, and marked the first step in the liberation of Israel's land.

The other dates are not so clear, unless we throw everything into the future in connection with the events accompanying the second coming. The period of 'a time, two times, and half a time' (7; cf. 7.25) may indicate a literal $3\frac{1}{2}$ years, but since the words that follow, apparently referring to the same period, are general, it may be that the phrase indicates that it will be for a definite period, not known to man, but prescribed by God. (See note on 7.25.)

The reference in v. 11 is to Antiochus, who stopped the daily sacrifices, so v. 7 may also refer to him. As explained in the note on 8.14, the actual desecration lasted for 1090 days (3 years and 10 days). It is reasonable to suppose that the period of 1290 years is the time from the desecration to the death of Antiochus. He died in the same year as the Temple was cleansed, but we do not know how long afterwards.

There is a wider application of v. 10 than to the book of *Daniel* alone. Christ and the Bible are the source both of ultimate wisdom, and of confusion to those who are not prepared to consider their accountability to God (1 Cor. 2.6–16; 2 Cor. 2.15,16). But Daniel would not have us be content with wisdom alone, for God's wisdom is given to lead us to purity (10; 1 John 3.2). Daniel himself sets us this example in his book, and it is a happy thought that we shall share with him in Christ's glorious resurrection (13). Meanwhile we, the people of God, still suffer, and we look for the time of the end when Christ returns. But we stand on the victory side of the cross, which Daniel saw by faith. Christ has broken into history that history which Daniel saw sketched out briefly beforehand

and by a real incarnation, atoning death, resurrection, and ascension, He has wrought our redemption, given us new life, and founded His Kingdom that will supersede all other limited kingdoms, and, unlike the others, will never pass away.

Think out the link between wisdom and purity of life.

Questions for discussion and further study on Daniel chs. 7–12

1. Which passages in the Book indicate that Daniel was told something of the incarnation, atoning death, and enthronement (which would, of course, imply resurrection) of Jesus Christ?
2. Why are the empires depicted as animals?
3. What functions do angels fulfil in the plan of God (e.g. Heb. 1.14)?
4. How far does prediction relieve us of responsibility for our actions (e.g. Matt. 26.24)?

Hosea

Hosea was a Northerner, and he prophesied to Israel shortly after his contemporary, Amos (q.v.). With Isaiah and Micah, these two men make up the quartet of eighth-century prophets who opened up the way for the distinguished line of classical prophets of the succeeding centuries. Of his parentage and family we know only the details given us in ch. 1. Some suppose, on the basis of 7.4–7, that he was a baker by trade, but this is pure conjecture. More than likely he was a professional prophet (which Amos protested that he was not!) and the words in 9.7 may represent a personal attack being made on him by his hostile hearers. He prophesied at the very end of Jeroboam's reign (i.e. before 746 B.C.) and may have continued until about 725 B.C., by which time Hezekiah was already co-regent with Ahaz, but it is unlikely that any of his oracles were uttered after the fall of Samaria and the overthrow of the kingdom of Israel in 722 B.C.

Hosea's uniqueness as a prophet lies in the fact that he learnt his message out of his own personal sufferings. His experience of his wife's unfaithfulness to him and his earnest attempts to woo her back were made by God the means whereby he learnt that Israel's unfaithfulness was being met by just such a love from the God whose covenant she had so flagrantly betrayed. So his message was concerned with the constancy of God's love (Heb. *hesed*) and the persistent unfaithfulness of Israel. These two themes, with suitable variations, run right throughout his book. They are crystallized in the requirements of 6.4–6.

Hosea 1.1—2.1   Hosea's Marriage and Family

The problem of Hosea's marriage is an acute one, and centres initially on the description of Gomer as a 'wife of harlotry' and her children as 'children of harlotry' (2). Three possible explanations are offered: (*i*) Hosea was told by the Lord to go and marry Gomer, who was already known as a prostitute; (*ii*) Gomer was pure when Hosea married her, but she subsequently became unfaithful, and so the description of her in v. 2 is a 'proleptic' idiom, implying that unknown to Hosea she had the potential for harlotry within her; (*iii*) the whole story is an allegory of Israel's unfaithfulness to God and is not to be taken literally. Of these, the first is beset with ethical problems and, even if these could be overcome, it does not provide an accurate analogy with Israel as being originally betrothed to the Lord in purity at Sinai. The last founders because it takes away from the book the very ground on which it is built: Hosea's agony of rejected love becomes simply another aspect of his message and is no longer the personal element out of which the message grew. Moreover, if this were allegory, we would expect the name 'Gomer' to conceal some allegorical meaning, as is usual in such cases. The second explanation is therefore to be preferred, and ch. 1 tells us of a faithful marriage relationship throughout. Some scholars would see the break-up of the marriage after the birth of Jezreel, noticing that the two other children are not born 'to him' (6,8), but this is probably reading too much into the text.

The names of the children speak of judgement—'Jezreel' (4,5), indicating that the bloodbath which brought Jehu's house to power (2 Kings 10.11) would mark its overthrow; 'Not pitied', speaking of the end of God's mercy to Israel; and 'Not my people', representing the final breakdown of the covenant relationship between the Lord and His people. The finality of these messages of doom is tempered, however, by a prospect of mercy for Judah (7) and by a restoration of the united kingdoms, when the covenant mercies would be renewed and Jezreel would become a name to glory in (1.10–2.1).

Hosea 2.2-15 Israel's Unfaithfulness

In the opening verses of this poem there appears to be some deliberate ambiguity as to who is speaking and who are being addressed. At first Hosea seems to be exhorting his children to plead with their mother to give up her harlotries (2) and to return to him, but by v. 8 it is clear that Yahweh is making the plea and is urging the faithful ones among the nation to persuade their mother Israel to return to her former love and loyalty. Certainly the chapter presupposes that Gomer has already sunk deep into adultery, and it oscillates between her husband's longing to have her back and Yahweh's similar longings for Israel (14 f.). This attitude is not the only emotion shown, however, and the speaker (whether Hosea or Yahweh) gives vent to his fury at her unfaithfulness and his determination to divorce, disgrace and punish her (3–6, 9–13). These verses may reflect the ancient custom of stripping the adultress before sending her away (3,10), and may even suggest that Gomer had adopted the prostitute's typical adornments (2b). Hosea vows that he will prevent her from following her evil ways (6), but this only drives her further away after her lovers. Ironically, it is only when she is frustrated in her search for them that she considers returning to her husband (7), and even then her motives have a strong element of selfishness in them, not unlike the returning Prodigal Son (Luke 15.17). Frustration with the sinful pleasures of this life is still the first step which leads many back to God in repentance, and God is gracious enough to receive them on those terms.

Israel's lovers were the Baals, the fertility gods of Canaan, who were thought to be responsible for the agricultural bounties of the land. Little did Israel realize that Yahweh was the Lord of nature (8), and He would prove this to her by withdrawing His blessings (9,12) and causing the joyful feast days to come to an end (11). Then when she had learnt her lesson, He would woo her back to her first love as in the idyllic days of the Exodus before ever she set foot in the land of Canaan (14,15). But this time He will make the entrance-way, the valley of Achor where Achan sinned (Josh. 7.26), into a door of hope. For those who fail and are unfaithful to the Lord, there is a way back and the chance of a new beginning.

Hosea 2.16-23   Restoration and Renewal

It is clear that before Hosea's time the names Yahweh and Baal were sometimes used interchangeably, for the Hebrew word Baal, as well as being the proper name for the Canaanite god of fertility, was also an everyday word meaning 'husband, lord, master'. But if, in Hosea's teaching, the relationship between Israel and Yahweh was to be expressed in terms of a marriage-covenant, the use of the term Baal had to be excised from Israel's religious vocabulary for fear of increased misunderstanding. God tells Hosea, therefore, that Israel is to use instead the term *Ishi*, 'my man' or 'my husband' (16). As a result of this it became customary for some later scribes to replace the word 'Baal' in a person's name with *bosheth*, Hebrew for 'shame' (cf. Ishbosheth, son of Saul, whose original name is retained in the genealogy of 1 Chron. 8.33).

In the day when Israel returns and the covenant is renewed, it will seem as if the Lord is taking her as His bride all over again. It will be like a new creation (18), and it will last for ever (19). The bride-price will be paid in terms of the five abiding covenant qualities of vs. 19 f. These denote conformity to the pattern of God's will (righteousness), consistency in dealing with other people's needs (justice), loyalty to one's covenant obligations and devotion to one's covenant partner (steadfast love), compassion for man in his weakness and frailty (mercy) and reliability, as the recipient of man's trust (faithfulness). The culminating purpose of all this is that Israel should 'know the Lord' (20) in that intimacy of relation-

417

ship which the marriage-bond most effectively represents. Once again, 'knowledge' is a covenant term and is frequently used by Hosea of Israel and the Lord (4.1,6; 5.4; 6.6; 13.4,5).

Finally, all nature responds to the love of God as He directs the heavens to water the earth and the earth to fructify the crops (21 f.). Even the dread name of Jezreel turns into a name of promise and its literal meaning of 'God sows' supersedes its horrifying historical associations of judgement. 'Man's repentance in response to God's call can turn the Jezreel of dread into the Jezreel of blessing' (Snaith).

Hosea 3   Israel on Probation

Opinion is divided whether the unnamed woman of this chapter is Gomer or another woman. The key is in the interpretation of the word 'again' in v. 1, which can be understood in three ways. (i) 'And the Lord said to me again': this merely links ch. 3 with ch. 1, but it is not favoured by the ancient versions. (ii) 'Go again, love a woman' (RSV), which allows the possibility that a new command is being given to love someone else after Gomer has been divorced. (iii) 'Go on loving a woman', which clearly refers to the unfaithful Gomer. Apart from linguistic considerations, however, the analogy of Israel's redemption scarcely allows the intrusion of another woman at this stage, and we must try to understand this of Gomer, by now perhaps divorced and certainly another man's mistress or even slave. Hosea bought her back, partly in cash and partly in kind, for the approximate price of a slave (2; cf. Exod. 21.32). As if to demonstrate his ownership of her, Hosea was to keep her from going astray any more and she was to be deprived of marital relationships, even with Hosea himself (such is the probable meaning of 'so will I also be to you', 3).

The application of this to Israel follows in vs. 1b,4 f. The nation is to undergo a period of deprivation and discipline, without king and prince, and without her objects of religious veneration, both legitimate (sacrifice and ephod) and illegitimate (pillar and teraphim). See the New Bible Dictionary, s.v. for a detailed description of these objects. The reference to king and prince reflects Hosea's view that it was the leadership of Israel which had persistently led them astray from the worship of Yahweh, their true King (cf. 5.1,10; 7.3-7,16; 8.4; 9.15, etc.). Their promised punishment was fulfilled in the overthrow of Samaria in 722 B.C., but Hosea looks forward to a day when Israel will return to the Lord and acknowledge His Davidic king. This may be taken either of a faithful remnant from

418

the north coming to recognize the kings of Judah in Jerusalem (an event of which we have no clear knowledge), or of an eschatological conversion of Israelites to the worship of the Davidic Messiah, Jesus Christ (which the phrase, 'in the latter days', makes a more likely interpretation).

Hosea 4.1-10   Like People, Like Priest

With this section the details of Hosea's marriage become a thing of the past: there are no further references to Gomer or to the children. But the message which his family life conveyed to Hosea lies at the background of everything that now follows, particularly in the description of Israel's sin as spiritual harlotry, though this phrase may have to be interpreted more literally (10). This chapter contains the Lord's accusations against Israel and supplies a reason for their unfaithfulness. It is the priesthood who are corrupt (4) and the people are led astray in consequence (9).

The arraignment of Israel is expressed in forensic terms: the Lord is laying charges in a court of law (1; cf. Isa. 3.13 f.; Jer. 2.9). The accusations are general (absence of the qualities expected of a covenant partner, 1b) and specific (straightforward breaking of the Commandments, 2). But it is no use for people to blame one another. The fault lies with the priests (4), and they are guilty on two counts. (a) They have not imparted the knowledge of God to people because they have forgotten His law (6, Heb. *torah*). Coming after v. 2, this must refer primarily to the Decalogue, that basic body of God's requirements without which no message of love and mercy can be appreciated. (b) They have been thriving on the religious affluence of their day: the greater the prosperity, the more the sacrifices and the greedier were the priests for their portions (7 f.). Instead of acting as a restraining influence upon the people, they indulged their fancies even to the extent of taking part in the licentious rituals of the Canaanite fertility-cult (10). With leadership at that level, what could be expected of their followers?

Upon all who are called to any form of leadership, but particularly in matters of morality or religion, there is an appallingly heavy burden of responsibility. However limited our own sphere of influence may be, in church, community or home, let us ask ourselves whether we are fulfilling our duties to the best of our ability.

Hosea 4.11-19   The Idolatry of Israel

These verses deal with the consequences to the people of the priests' corruption. Verses 11-14 describe the degeneration of popular religion which has set in. Drink-offerings have been turned into occasions for drunkenness (11). Because there are no reliable prophets to turn to, the people have resorted to rhabdomancy, a superstitious form of seeking guidance through wooden rods (12). They perform sacrifices at all kinds of unauthorized local sites, on hilltops and under trees, in the style of the worship of Baal (13). Their young women take part in fertility rituals, though the blame for this is laid not so much on them as on the men who consort with them (14), on the ground that there would be no harlotry if there were not the men who demanded it. And because of all this, the downfall of the nation is assured (14c). This is a frightening verdict, and many modern readers will recognize among their contemporaries the same pattern of religious breakdown and sexual deviation, leading to the same inevitable doom. A people without 'understanding' (essentially a religious term) is as certainly heading for disaster as a ship without a rudder.

Verses 15–19 are a group of statements expressing the hopelessness of Israel's position. She is like a stubborn heifer, which will not accept discipline and so cannot be trusted to roam in the wild; the lamb, on the contrary, by its very weakness is more inclined to be docile (16). Israel is so attached to her idolatry and all her other sins that she is best abandoned to her fate (17 f.). She will be swept away on the wings of the wind and put to shame at the ineffectiveness of her past religious practices (19). The only plea the prophet makes is that Judah will not go the same way, but will steer clear of those idolatrous shrines (15). Gilgal and Beth-aven (lit. 'house of idolatry', a derisory name for Bethel, 'house of God') were northern sanctuaries mentioned in Amos 4.4; 5.5; and swearing by Yahweh suggests a breaking of the third commandment, though others would see in this a reference to the danger of mixing idolatry with even the mention of Yahweh's name (cf. Amos 6.10). If this is so, it underlines the sheer impossibility of serving both God and Mammon. No amount of rationalization can ever make Christ and Belial work in partnership. Sin, like a dangerous virus, has to be isolated if the body is to be treated successfully.

Hosea 5.1-7   The Lord's Withdrawal

It is possible for men to become so inured to sin that they are incapable of repentance. Their sins act like fetters upon their wills, so that they can scarcely raise the inclination to seek after God. They are, in fact, in bondage; as addicted to sin as the 'mainliner' is to his heroin. In the case of Israel, this is because they have the spirit of harlotry within them (4), so completely dominating their every desire and deed that they can no longer be said to be in control of themselves. The only antidote is to be dominated by the Spirit of Christ, who gives life and liberty to men.

Verse 6 does envisage some seeking the Lord, possibly because they have been made to realize their pride and sinfulness (5). But because of their unenlightened hearts they seek the Lord, offering the very things He does not want (6.6), and they find that He has withdrawn Himself and is not to be found (6). This does not mean that He cannot under any circumstances be found, but Jeremiah's condition must first be fulfilled (Jer. **29.**13; cf. Prov. **2.**1–5; Isa. **55.**7), and they show no signs of that degree of sincerity.

In this wholesale condemnation of Israel, none are excluded: priests, commoners and royalty are told to take heed, for the promised judgement concerns them all (1). The place-names in vs. 1,2 probably refer to sanctuaries where idolatrous practices have been leading the people astray. Shittim may have been the shrine of Baal-peor (Num. **25.**1); Mizpah was in Gilead, east of the Jordan (cf. Judg. **11.**11), and is not to be confused with Samuel's town of the same name much further south; Tabor was a hill in Galilee and a natural site for a Canaanite high-place. They had done their deceitful work. The people were ensnared. They had produced a generation of alien children who did not know the Lord (7a). The judgement, however, would not be long in coming: the next new moon would see destruction arrive (7b).

Question: Are there people today who are incapable of repentance? If so, is the cause to be found in their own hard-heartedness or in God's unwillingness to be sought after?

Hosea 5.8-14 The Alarm is Sounded

The historical setting of these verses is probably the time of the Syro-Ephraimite war, known to us from 2 Kings **16.**5–9 and Isa. **7.**1–9. It was a time when the distant pressure of the growing power of Assyria was driving Syria to make a defensive alliance with Israel and to coerce Judah into joining it as well. Despite the threat of invasion, Judah, under Isaiah's influence, refused to get involved. She was attacked, probably on three sides at once, and, this time against Isaiah's advice, appealed to Assyria for help. She thus became more fully involved than ever she had intended and could claim neutrality no more.

Hosea, therefore, was familiar with invading armies and the terrors they aroused. He saw both Ephraim (Israel) and Judah

421

suffering in this way (8 f.), but he looked beyond the actual events to the Lord who was ultimately responsible for them. God's judgement could not be averted by political solutions. Hosea saw that appeals to Assyria would not save Israel, for she had a wound that was too serious to be cured by such means (13). Moral and spiritual sickness needs a moral and spiritual remedy. The maladies within our modern society will similarly not be healed by social and educational reforms, when their origins go much deeper than that. The nation which has neglected God needs to repent and to return to Him, so that He can reform it inwardly. Without that repentance they can expect only what Israel was due to receive: a disaster that was sure (9).

In a strange pair of similes, the Lord represents Himself as being both the enemy within Israel ('like a moth' or 'like dry rot', 12) and the enemy without ('like a lion', 14). All the sufferings of Israel and Judah in this unhappy period of Near Eastern history are thus seen as episodes in the judgement of God. What the historian sees as mere political and military manoeuvres, the prophet sees as the direct activity of the God of history. It would do the Christian good occasionally to read his newspaper through the same prophetic eyes.

Hosea 5.15—6.6   Repentance that is Skin Deep

Despite the strong language of the preceding verses and the apparent finality of God's judgement on Israel, it is clear from 5.15 that this punishment is intended to be corrective. The Lord returns to His seat in heaven and waits to see if His people will repent. They express their repentance in 6.1–3. By introducing these words with the word 'saying', the RSV misleadingly gives the impression that God is putting the statement into Israel's mouth. But in the Hebrew there is a clean break between 5.15 (. . . 'they seek Me') and 6.1 ('Come, let us return . . .'). It is therefore legitimate, and instructive, to compare the quality of repentance that God awaits with the repentance Israel shows.

God requires acknowledgement of guilt and a seeking of His face, but there is little sign of the former in 6.1–3. Cheyne describes it as 'a hasty resolution, from which a full and free confession of sin was fatally absent'. It was a repentance that arose out of distress and not out of a deep sense of the sin which had brought the distress, and as such it lacked genuineness. Many who turn to Christ in times of personal sorrow or trouble show by their lack of perseverance in the faith that theirs was no true repentance in the first place.

This should not inhibit the pastor exhorting people in trouble to turn to Christ for help, but it is only as He becomes to them the Saviour from *sin* that they become members of His Church, the company of the redeemed. Verses 1,2 have an air of optimism and over-confidence about them (they should certainly not be taken as forecasting Christ's resurrection!), but v. 3 shows a true recognition that knowledge of God comes to men gradually and must be persistently sought after by His followers, if blessing is to result.

God sees how transient Israel's love really is, lasting no longer than the morning mist before the rising sun (4), and He adds that this is how it has always been, for they have consistently deserved His punishment (5). But love and knowledge are what He wants, in preference to any number of ritual observances (6). The demand that worship should be the expression of an inward attitude of the heart is no new thing, but as old as the Bible itself.

Hosea 6.7—7.7   A Catalogue of Villainy

(*i*) 6.7–11a. Hosea here lists a number of atrocities that have taken place at individual towns: Adam (7, at the ford on the river Jordan between Gilead and Shechem), Gilead (8, in the hill-country east of the Jordan), Shechem (9, the Israelite centre designated by Moses to be a city of refuge and not of brigandage) and perhaps Bethel, the religious capital, where the most flagrant harlotry is to be found (hinted at in the words 'house of Israel', [Heb. 'Beth Israel'], 10). It seems incredible that these villainies should actually have taken place, especially where priests were involved (9), and some commentators take these statements metaphorically, as spiritual murder and spiritual harlotry. But such was the state of affairs in Israel at the time that a literal interpretation is by no means impossible. Hideous crimes could well have been committed by these profligate priests, for when religion goes to the bad, there is no knowing where it will end up. A final footnote warns Judah that her day of reckoning is also not far away (11a).

(*ii*) 6.11b—7.3. Ephraim's wrongdoings are made worse by the fact that they are committed in defiance of God's attempts to bring her back to Himself, and Hosea reminds the people that God takes note of all their evil deeds. They 'encompass them', like 'a company of witnesses which unite in testifying against them' (Mauchline). Sins do not disappear with the passage of time; they live on to accuse men from the past. Only when there is true repentance and confession can forgiveness and forgottenness be found.

(*iii*) **7.4–7.** Those in Israel who indulge in political intrigue and subversive activity appear to do so with the approval of the king and his nobility (3). But in reality they are like a baker's oven, now blazing angrily, now smouldering quietly until the time is ripe again for action. Then suddenly they will break out and overturn their rulers in a violent coup (7). This was painfully true of Israel's history in the fifteen years after the death of Jeroboam II in 746 B.C. Of the five men who followed him upon the throne, all but one died at the hand of an assassin (see 2 Kings 15.8–31). Small wonder that Hosea had scant regard for Israel's kings.

Hosea 7.8-16   Half-baked and Senseless

The oven referred to in the metaphors of 7.4–7 was the shallow, saucer-like disc of metal that was inverted over the glowing embers of the fire to become a primitive, but very effective, hot-plate for cooking the flat cakes of bread that were the Israelite's daily diet. Hosea could hardly have chosen a more appropriate metaphor. Now, however, he likens Ephraim to the cake that is cooked on the oven: it is badly mixed and cooked only on one side. It is therefore indigestible and valueless as food. Instead of acting as leaven in the world, Ephraim has become submerged by the world (8). The tragic result is that, even though her strength is being sapped from her continually, she fails to realize it (9). 'One of the paradoxes of our time is that while few ages have borne more tragic evidence of sin, few ages have been less conscious of it' (H. C. Phillips). When people are in a state of such sublime self-confidence, they are impervious to the accusations of their conscience and see no need for repentance or for God (10).

A further token of Ephraim's self-sufficiency is the way in which she practises her foreign diplomacy, playing off the rival powers of Egypt and Assyria against each other. Hosea, however, sees this for what it really is: a senseless opportunism which will soon land her in the hunter's snare, and the hunter is none other than the Lord (12). Israel is therefore doomed to destruction, because they have consistently opposed and frustrated God's wishes for them. His intention, even after their backsliding, was to redeem them (13), but everything that they have done has been against this would-be Redeemer (note the repetition of 'against Me' in vs. 13–15). Not even when they pray are they honest: they speak to God in false-hoods; they cry to Him out of insincere hearts. Their only real concern in prayer is 'for grain and wine' (14).

424

Much so-called Christian prayer can be faulted on all these counts. It is dishonest: we use language we do not mean; we make conventional protestations of love and loyalty, but in reality they are empty words. It is not from the heart: we fail to let God see right into the depths of our personalities, and so our prayers are 'surface' prayers. It is 'grain-and-wine' prayer: we want our basic necessities, plus a few luxuries as well, but it is always a demand for *things*, and not for *Him*.

Questions for further study and discussion on Hosea chs. 1–7
1. What other Biblical analogies are there which make use of the marriage relationship?
2. What do chs. 1–3 teach us about the quality of love that God offers to His people?
3. In the light of 4.1–6, what part should the teaching of the Ten Commandments have (*a*) in the Church's life and (*b*) in religious education today?
4. What can be learnt from 5.15—6.6 about the requirements of God in repentance and obedience?
5. What are the good things referred to in chs. 6,7, which the Lord wants to do for His disobedient people?

Hosea 8   False Kings, Gods, Allies and Altars

The Assyrian army, which was a constant threat to Israel's security and which had to be bought off by Menahem (745–738 B.C.) with a heavy tribute, is here typified by an eagle, or griffon vulture, swooping down upon the land. That an invasion by Tiglath-pileser occurred in Pekah's reign (737–732 B.C.) is attested by the record in 2 Kings 15.29, which also shows how successful it was. This may well have been the occasion referred to by Hosea in v. 1. He, however, immediately attributes the invasion, not to political motives, but to the punishment of God upon a nation that had broken their covenant with Him. It was now too late to cry out to God for mercy (2), just as it would be too late for some in the final day of judgement (Matt. 7.22). Israel had made their bed, and now they would have to lie on it (3).

Hosea then enumerates four vanities for which Israel could justly be condemned. (*i*) Her kings were not legitimate (4), a reference either to Israel's breakaway from Judah after Solomon's death or to the chaotic state of kingly government after 746 B.C. (see on 7.4–7). (*ii*) The bull-cult of Samaria was an insult to God and would be utterly crushed (5 f.). This had been instituted by Jeroboam I at

Bethel and Dan, but its antecedents were traceable back to Aaron's golden calf. It had obvious fertility associations and was one of the forms under which the god El was worshipped by the Canaanites. (*iii*) Their attempts to win allies were futile, and would yield disastrous results or no results at all (7). As a nation they have no standing among their contemporaries (8), and in courting Assyria they had acted like a wild ass that goes its own way (9: Heb. *pere'*, a play on words with Ephraim; cf. Gen. 16.12). (*iv*) Their altars had become occasions for stumbling to them and not places where they could meet with God (13). They revelled in sacrificial banquets, but missed completely their spiritual significance and had no knowledge at all of the written law of God, They had forgotten their Maker. But He would remember their sins and reverse their redemption from Egypt (13).

Question: *How does this catalogue of Israel's sins illustrate the truth of Gal. 6.7?*

Hosea 9   Fasting instead of Feasting

The Israelite celebrated three major feasts in the year, all of them connected with agriculture in some way. At Easter time there was Passover, the Feast of Unleavened Bread, when the first-fruits of the ripening ears of barley were offered to the Lord (Lev. 23.10); seven weeks later, at Pentecost, was the Feast of Weeks, the wheat harvest (Exod. 34.22); and at the end of the summer came the Feast of Tabernacles, associated with the gathering in of the grape-harvest. It was probably at this last great festival, when wine flowed like water, that Hosea uttered the words recorded here to the assembled crowds of worshippers. The crops, he said, were going to fail; there would scarcely be enough to provide famine rations for the people; Israel would go into exile and be buried in a foreign land (6).

These words (1–6) were hardly calculated to increase the prophet's popularity, and vs. 7 f. may reflect the reaction of his hearers. They accuse him of being a fool and mad, fit only to be certified (7), but in fact he was the nation's watchman, with a duty to warn them of dangers ahead (8). Such misunderstanding is only to be expected by God's servants, when they speak fearlessly in His name. No one likes to be reminded of the consequences of sin, least of all when he professes not to believe in sin. The fact that so many people today regard God as a dead-letter, morality as a matter of convenience and religion as a quaint but valueless piece of Victoriana, should not deter the Church from issuing stern warnings based on

426

Biblical standards. Anything less than that is dishonouring to God and doing a grave disservice to our fellow men.

In vs. 10–17 Hosea traces the people's treachery, first to Baal-peor in the wilderness days (10), where Israel turned to immorality with the Moabites (cf. Num. 25), and then to Gilgal (15), where they had publicly proclaimed Saul as king (1 Sam. 11.15). The combination of Baal-worship instead of Yahweh's service, and human kings instead of Yahweh as King, had made Ephraim the barren and fruitless nation that she now was. There is another word-play on Ephraim in v. 16 with the word for 'fruit' (Heb. *peri*); cf. also 10.1,12,13; 14.2,8.

Hosea 10.1-8 The Fate of King Bull

The opening words of this chapter are a commentary on 8.11, and explain how it was that Israel developed the penchant for church building projects. It was the result of her affluence, built up through the prosperous days of the Omri dynasty and latterly of Jeroboam II. The figure of Israel as a vine was a time-honoured metaphor (cf. Gen. 49.22; Isa. 5.1–7) and carried on the theme of the previous chapter. But the more of her wealth Israel spent on ecclesiastical buildings and fitments, the more guilty she was becoming. Her heart was false and her allegiance was divided between the Lord and Baal (2). In fact she had reached the point where she no longer trusted in the Lord; He was no longer her King. After all, what use were kings except to utter empty words and make meaningless covenants (4)? The only thing that drew forth Israel's loyalty and anxious concern was the bull-image at Bethel. This was in effect Samaria's king (7). But even that would be carried away as tribute for the Assyrian king, and its altars and sanctuaries would be destroyed and overgrown with weeds and thistles (8). Aven is short for Bethaven, the contemptuous name Hosea gives to Bethel (see on 4.15).

There is a certain irony about the fate of the bull of Bethel. Though some scholars attempt to whitewash Jeroboam's action in installing these images at Bethel and Dan (cf. 1 Kings 12.28 f.), on the altogether plausible grounds that they were intended not to be images of God, but throne-seats for Yahweh, the invisible God (so Albright, etc.), they nevertheless soon came to be regarded as symbols of the deity and were venerated as idols. They were no doubt magnificent pieces of workmanship, made of wood overlaid with gold, and must naturally have evoked admiration from all who saw them. That one day they would float away like a useless sliver of wood on a swollen river represented the ultimate anticlimax. The idols that we worship, the things to which we give our major concern and on which we lavish the greater part of our care and energies, will also likewise come to an end—on the scrapheap, in the breaker's yard, or in a wooden casket. The only God worth worshipping, and worthy of all our adoration, is the eternal King of kings and Lord of lords.

Hosea 10.9-15   'Whatever a man sows . . .'

Hosea is convinced that Israel's sinfulness is no recent phenomenon: it dates back into her early history. So he traces it first to Baal-peor (9.10), then to Gilgal (9.15) and now to Gibeah (10.9). Gibeah was Saul's home town (1 Sam. 10.26), and this may be yet another reference to the evils of the monarchy; but it was also the setting for the hideous crime of the Benjaminites and their subsequent punishment (Judg. 19 f.), and it is more likely that this was in Hosea's mind as he spoke. Alternatively both incidents are recollected in the phrase 'double iniquity' (10). Israel had not changed inwardly since those faraway days of civil war and inter-tribal massacre that marked the break-up of the Judges' rule, and so the Lord's chastisement was as inevitable as the night which follows the day.

Then, in striking contrast to his simile of 4.16, Hosea likens Ephraim to a docile heifer which has been trained to perform the congenial task of treading out the grain on the threshing-floor. She has had an easy time of it in the past, but now she is going to be made to work hard at the plough. Israel must buckle to and make costly efforts to prepare herself for seeking the Lord in repentance and for sowing righteously for the future. The way of repentance and the taking of the yoke of Christ upon one's shoulders *is* costly and demands sweat and sacrifice. It is only because He adds His strength to ours that the yoke becomes easy and the burden light. But the disciple who thinks that the Christian life is a life of effortless passivity has deluded himself and is not walking along the narrow way.

Verse 13 shows that Israel was quickly diverted from God's purpose for her. She trusted in armies and chariots (13), and the crop she sowed would be the crop she would reap. As in recent times Salamanu of Moab had invaded Gilead and cruelly destroyed a city there, so all Israel's fortresses would soon be caught up in the tumult of a disastrous war (14). And she had only herself to blame.

428

Hosea 11

This chapter contains some of the tenderest language in the whole of the book, as it describes the Father's love for His wayward child. The tone does not however remain constant, but fluctuates severely from section to section. (*i*) Verses 1–4. Israel was loved (i.e. chosen) in his infancy as a nation in Egypt. He became God's covenant son (cf. 2 Sam. **7.**14) and was trained gently and lovingly by his Father. Verse 4 reverts to the picture of Israel as the docile heifer and the Lord as her owner, but the relationship is basically the same. God has done everything for His people, and Israel simply has not acknowledged the fact (cf. Isa. **1.**2 f.; Amos **2.**9–12).

(*ii*) Verses 5–7. Therefore all tenderness is gone, and judgement will take its place. The yoke which was eased from the heifer to allow her to eat in comfort (4) will now become a fixture upon her neck (7). The bondage from which the children of Israel were originally delivered will become their lot once more, either in Egypt or Assyria (5).

(*iii*) Verses 8,9. Such a prospect revives God's tender-hearted concern. How could He treat Israel in the same way as the cities of the plain, which had been destroyed with Sodom and Gomorrah (Deut. **29.**23)? Could the Lord ever apply His 'final solution' to the people that He had reared and redeemed? If we find God's judgement a problem, we may be encouraged from this to realize that it is also a problem with God. The tenderness and compassion of God are for ever tempering His justice and it is only in the cross that 'heaven's love and heaven's justice meet'. Peter attributes the delay in the Second Coming to this very quality in the nature of God (2 Pet. **3.**9). The door of God's mercy still stands wide open to all who would return to Him; it has never yet shut . . . but one day it will.

(*iv*) Verses 10–12. Here are two postscripts. The first (10 f.) says that God will finally call His scattered people home. The second (12) is a brief summing-up of the contrast between faithless Ephraim and faithful Judah.

For meditation:
> 'There's a wideness in God's mercy like the
>   wideness of the sea;
> There's a kindness in His justice which is
>   more than liberty.
> For the love of God is broader than the measures
>   of man's mind,
> And the heart of the Eternal is most wonderfully kind.'
>   (F. W. Faber)

429

There are many difficulties in understanding the sequence of thought in the Hebrew text of this chapter (as so often in Hosea's writings), and many emendations and rearrangements of the material have been suggested. Verse 12, put in brackets by the RSV, would go better with the flashback to Jacob's life in vs. 3 f.; v. 7 seems to be suspended in mid-air; and the reference to Judah (2) seems not to be followed through. The general pattern, however, is recognizable. The Lord has a controversy with His people (2; cf. 4.1), and although the brunt of it is directed against Israel-Ephraim, Judah is probably included because he was one of the patriarch Jacob's sons.

Verses 3–6 use the story of Jacob's life to provide a cautionary tale. They play with the names of Jacob ('supplanter', from a word meaning 'heel') and Israel (Gen. 32.28), showing that he developed from being a 'heel' to being a 'prince with God', as he returned to Him at Bethel and God spoke with him face to face. Now the nation named after him and identified with him (Heb. has 'with *us*' in v. 4) must take that same road back to God and demonstrate their repentance with practical morality and submissiveness before Him (6).

Verses 7–9 deal with Israel's affluence. The word for 'a trader' (7) is literally 'a Canaanite', for the Canaanites were a nation of merchants. But here it obviously carries the pejorative sense of all that that word conveys in terms of dishonesty, oppression and religious impurity. Israel had entered Canaan, and Canaan's ways had entered Israel. No amount of protestation that it was all the result of honest effort would save her from the judgement of v. 9; as a nation she would revert to the austerities of wilderness days and be deprived of all her urban prosperity.

Finally (10–14), Hosea makes an unusual reference to the place of prophecy in Israel's history. Moses the prophet had been God's agent in redeeming and preserving Israel (13); and other prophets had been the means whereby God's guidance and help had always been available (10). There may even be a sense in which v. 12 was inserted here to show that the prophet, like the patriarch Jacob, was also the shepherd of his people; but it is more likely that this verse should go with vs. 3–6.

Note: V. 11 is singularly unoriginal: '*if* there is iniquity . . .', when Hosea has been saying over and over again that there was! But there is a typical play on words here between Gilead, Gilgal and 'heaps' (Heb. *gallim*). Probably the verse should be written in quotation marks and taken as a sample of the prophetic 'parables'.

Hosea 13 'No God but Me'

Hosea's message would be a black one indeed if this were the final chapter of his book. It gives a prospect of unalleviated doom and destruction. There are the familiar themes of Israel's idolatry, scornfully decried in v. 2; of a judgement upon Israel by the hand of plundering armies (16). God appears in the role of a wild animal (lion, leopard, bear) lying in wait for Israel and pouncing upon them to rend them limb from limb (7 f.); or coming like the hot east wind (the sirocco or '*hamsin*') and drying up the land and everything green within it (15). In yet other similes (and Hosea's oracles are remarkably rich in these), Israel is likened to the evaporating mist or dew of early morning (cf. **6.**4), to the chaff blown away like dust from the threshing-floor, and like smoke as it curls away through a hole in the roof (3). In every case, be it noted, the stress is on that which is transient, unstable and insubstantial.

As the reader by now scarcely needs to be told, all this is due to Israel's rejection of their only God and Saviour (4). Here is a striking dogmatic assertion of monotheism, comparable to that of Isa. **43–45**. But it is no merely philosophical concept: it is grounded in history. It was Yahweh alone who delivered Israel from Egypt; it was He alone who preserved the people in the wilderness and made them His people. He had no rivals or competitors. The Baals to whom Israel turned (1) were neither gods nor could they save. There could be for Israel 'no other gods before Me' (Deut. **5.**7). But what a nation could believe in adversity she could forget in prosperity (6). Satiety breeds complacency, complacency breeds pride, and pride distracts a people from God. For Ephraim there could be no more mercy (14). The warning of these verses can hardly be repeated too often today, as in Hosea's day.

Hosea 14 A Final Appeal

The finality of the previous chapter, especially the last words of **13.**14, compels some interpreters to regard this section as a later addition. But this reversal of mood, where each successive statement of doom is followed by yet another offer of forgiveness if the people repent, is quite typical of Hosea, and it is entirely in keeping with the oscillation of his own emotions in his domestic life with Gomer, on which his teaching is based. Does this mean that God shares this same inconsistency? In a sense, yes. Hosea's language reflects the unresolved tension that exists between the justice of God and the love of God. It is resolved when, in response to God's love and on the basis of Christ's death, the sinner repents and returns to

Him. But as long as he persists in his rejection, the voice of God persists both in reminding him of the demands of His righteousness and in pleading with him to heed the warning and repent. As long as the prophet has breath to speak and the hearer life to respond, this must be the message. When life is ended, the shutters come down and the judgement of God is the only way in which His love can operate. For there is an element of mercy even in God's act of preventing unrepentant man from seeing the full wonder of the love that he has rejected.

Hosea's final appeal is expressed in the form of a liturgy. The words of repentance are offered for Israel to use (2 f.), and the response of the Lord to that repentance is given in vs. 4–7. Israel will flourish, as it was intended she should; she will be fruitful and prosperous with a fertility that does not come from Baal and that is not expressed in terms of wealth and fortified cities. All this is on offer to Israel, but it is conditional on their genuine response. We know from history that Hosea's words fell on deaf ears. There was no repentance, and judgement came. But in the strange economy of God, Israel has not been cut off for ever (cf. Rom. 11.1 ff.), and many Christians believe that God's purposes of mercy will one day be fulfilled.

Questions for further study and discussion on Hosea chs. 8–14
1. What similes are used in these chapters to describe Israel?
2. Using a concordance, read the O.T. passages which tell of the past history of Gibeah (9.9; 10.9).
3. How many verses in chs. 11–14 illustrate the tenderness of God?
4. Hosea's words are quoted in the N.T. in at least two notable passages, Matt. 2.15 and 1 Cor. 15.55. Study the way in which Matthew and Paul interpret his sayings.
5. Make your own summary of the message of Hosea and mark out the five or six key verses which you consider to be most significant.

Joel

INTRODUCTION

Nothing is known of Joel except his father's name (1.1). Attempts to date him have varied between the eighth and fourth centuries B.C. and have only shown the impossibility of being dogmatic. While one modern scholar, A. S. Kapelrud, argues that he was a contemporary of Jeremiah (c. 600 B.C.) because of the many verbal parallels between them, most commentators feel that he was a post-exilic writer and that he drew upon the language and ideas of predecessors, like Amos, Isaiah, Zephaniah and Ezekiel. Indeed he appears, in 2.32, actually to quote Obad. 17; and if 2.11,31 also reflect Mal. 3.2; 4.5, a date around 400 B.C. would not be out of place. Be that as it may, Joel has a keen interest in the Temple and its rituals, though he does not appear to be a priest, and 'temple-prophet' may not be a bad description of him. His message starts from a contemporary devastating plague of locusts, which he sees as a warning of the coming day of the Lord. This should drive Israel to repentance, and those who do repent will be saved in the judgement and will be recipients of God's Spirit and of the untold blessings of the age to come.

Joel 1   The Locust Disaster

There is no need to understand this chapter symbolically. Its subject is an actual plague of locusts descending on the holy land and devouring everything they find with their customary ferocity. A similar plague which hit Jerusalem in 1915 caused terrible devastation. Trees were stripped of leaves, bark and sometimes even of small limbs (cf. 7); wine prices doubled (cf. 5); and not a sign of any crops was left to be harvested (cf. 10–12). The *National Geographic Magazine* for that year gives graphic photographs which could well illustrate Joel's vivid pen-picture. The size of a typical locust-swarm runs into millions, if not billions, of insects, and so the damage they cause is not to be wondered at. They have always been desperately feared by dwellers in the Middle East and it is only the use of modern insecticides which has made them less of a menace in more recent times. However, Joel clearly regarded what he was describing as a rarity (cf. 2 f.), and that is perhaps why he saw in it a warning of the coming day of judgement.

One of Joel's chief concerns is that the plague has caused a cessation of offerings to the Lord (9,13,16). This may have been due to the fact that the people were husbanding their meagre resources and were not maintaining their priorities towards God (cf. Neh. 13.10; Mal. 3.8 f.), or it may mean simply that there was nothing available to give to God. However, the people are not taken to task for this, but they are reminded that such a catastrophe is an act of God and should be the occasion for national mourning and repentance, under the leadership of the priests (13). Everyone is to be summoned to prayer and a solemn fast is to be proclaimed by them (14).

Verses 15–18 may be a form of words which the people are intended to use. It is reminiscent of Ezek. 30.2 f.; Zeph. 1.7,14. Like many of Joel's statements it contains word-play ('destruction', *shōd*, 'from the Almighty', *Shaddai*, 15). The chapter ends with the prophet himself joining in the lamentation (19), and even the wild beasts are cast in the role of suppliants before God (20). Compare Rom. 8.22 f.

Joel 2.1-11   'The Day of the Lord is Coming'

Ever since Amos warned Israel that the day of the Lord would be a day of darkness and not light, because it would include judgement on Israel as well as upon the heathen (Amos 5.18), this aspect of it had been retained in descriptions like Zeph. 1.15 and here in Joel 2.2. From being a day for Israel to look forward to it had become a day for them to fear. Joel, however, does not keep his hearers in a state of trepidation, for repentance is held out to them as the way to avoid the terrors of judgement. As the people repent of their sins, so the Lord repents of the evil that He was due to inflict upon them (2.13).

The chapter begins with the warning trumpet-blast being sounded, the normal alarm-signal to an Israelite city. The locust plague was not solely the occasion for this, but it was regarded as a foretaste of the coming of the day of the Lord (1). So the language oscillates between the immediate threat of the locusts and the eschatological prospect of God's judgement. The locusts are described in v. 11 as the Lord's army; they are His host, executing His word; and they bring to the day of judgement the same sense of fearfulness and terror as was felt by Malachi (Mal. 3.2).

In vs. 3–10 the invading locust army is described attacking the city (of Jerusalem?). This is the second stage of their onslaught, after the destruction of the vegetation and the denuding of the countryside in ch. 1. They leave in their wake the appearance of 'scorched earth' warfare (3), and they march relentlessly on like a mammoth army of disciplined warriors. Nothing can stand in

434

their way. No weapon is effective against them; no barricade can bar their path. To think that it is possible to avert disaster is as futile as to think that God's judgement can be turned aside by merely human defences. In this way Joel builds up to his climax, that a way of escape does exist and that it is still not too late for the people to do something about it. 'Yet even now return to Me' (12).

For consideration: 'The design of the prophet in these verses is no other than to stir up by fear the minds of the people' (Calvin). Is this a fair assessment of Joel's aim, and is it legitimate for preachers today to play upon the fears of their hearers?

Joel 2.12-27 Repentance and Restoration

Joel's call to repentance (12–14) is one of the finest passages in the prophets. It describes God's character, in language based on Exod. 34.6 (cf. also Jon. 4.2); it stipulates the quality of repentance that God requires (whole-hearted, self-sacrificing, and inward rather than outward in its manifestation); and it holds out the hope not only of mercy but of blessing. Note that the offerings men give to God are gifts *from* God, which the grateful recipient returns to Him as a mark of devotion and thankfulness (14b). This is to be a national occasion, from which no one is exempted (not even newly-weds; contrast Deut. 24.5), and the priests are to lead the people in mourning and intercession from the very steps of the Temple in the inner court (17).

In response to the nation's repentance, the Lord has pity on His people and promises them the produce which the locusts had denied them (19), grain, wine and olive-oil being the basic agricultural products of the land (cf. 24). 'The northerner' is an unusual description of the invading locust army (20), for it is unlikely that the swarm would have approached from that direction. This must probably be taken as an anticipation of the eschatological 'foe from the north' which the locusts were thought to foreshadow. The stench from the locusts' carcasses has been one of the unfortunate aftermaths of other recorded plagues, notably that of 1915.

With the coming of the rains (23) a good crop is assured for the ensuing year, and God promises such abundance as will amply compensate for the losses of earlier years (25). This will not only meet the people's material needs and vindicate them before their heathen neighbours, but it will also give them cause to praise God for His mighty acts and for this further evidence of His uniqueness

(26 f.). The 'never again' of vs. 26,27 is one of the precious promises that God gives to His people. Amos used it twice of judgement (Amos 7.8; 8.2); Joel uses it twice of mercy. It is a phrase that deserves further study and meditation.

Joel 2.28-32   The Outpouring of the Spirit

It had been Moses' wish that all the Lord's people might be prophets and that they all might have His Spirit upon them (Num. 11.29), but it is left to Joel to predict this as a feature of the last days (cf. v. 28, 'afterward'). It was singularly appropriate that the apostle Peter quoted this passage with reference to the events of Pentecost (Acts 2.16-21), but we are so inclined to read it in the light of Pentecost that we miss some of its important features. Joel is in fact saying four things about the last days: (*i*) The gift of the Spirit will be poured out upon all classes in Israel, irrespective of age, sex and status, and will no longer be the privilege of a chosen few. (*ii*) This gift will be the gift of prophecy, and will give its recipients the prophet's insight into the mind and will of God. (*iii*) The outpouring of the Spirit in this way belongs to the climax of history, the end of the age, as witnessed by the portents of v. 30. (*iv*) Salvation in that day will be for those Israelites who trust in Yahweh, the God of Israel, but human faith is nicely balanced by divine election (cf. the two uses of 'call', 32).

The remarkable feature about Peter's use of this passage is not simply its appropriateness to the Day of Pentecost, when an ill-assorted group of Israelites were given the prophetic gift, but his widening of Joel's promise to include non-Israelites who call upon Israel's God. Peter's 'whosoever' is more extensive than Joel's 'whosoever' (AV, KJV), though it is of course implicit in Joel's expression (cf. Rom. 10.13). This may be taken as yet another instance of the O.T. prophet being inspired to 'speak better than he knew'.

The 'portents' are to be interpreted as the normal accompaniments of war (bloodshed and burning, 30), and as the abnormal features of eclipses and supernatural changes in the heavens (31). Both of these were regarded in the N.T. as harbingers of the end-time (Mark 13.7 f., 24 f.; Rev. 6.12). The darkening of the sun at noon on the day of Christ's crucifixion was such a sign that judgement had come into the world and the age of the Messiah had dawned.

Joel 3 Judgement on the Nations

The salvation of those who call upon God and are called by Him is matched, in the last days, by the punishment of the heathen. They are dealt with on the basis of their treatment of God's people. They had scattered them (the Babylonian exile); divided up their land (which was God's land, 2); sold even children into slavery (for the price of a harlot or a bottle of wine, 3); plundered the Temple treasures; and sold Jews as slaves to Greeks (the Philistines and Phoenicians were notorious slave-traders; cf. Amos 1.6,9; Ezek. 27.13). In return for this their descendants would have similar treatment meted out to them (8). This prophecy was fulfilled in 345 B.C. when Artaxerxes III sold the Sidonians into slavery, and in 332 B.C. when Alexander the Great did the same to the people of Tyre and Gaza. Doubtless, Jews were among their purchasers.

In readiness for the day of judgement (the valley of Jehoshaphat is probably a symbolical name, as it means 'Yahweh judges', 2,12), the people are called to arms. The famous prophecy of Isaiah-Micah is parodied and put in reverse (9f.), a clear sign of this being written later than the eighth century, and the nations are called together for the final *dénouement* (12). Here at last is the moment of decision (or 'verdict', 14), when God proclaims His judgement on sinners, and His angel-warriors (11) are commissioned to put in the sickle for the final harvest (cf. Isa. 17.5; Matt. 13.39). The 'valley of decision', which is to be identified with the valley of Jehoshaphat, is not so much the place where men decide about God as where God decides about men. The cross was a valley of decision, when God decided *for* men, not against them. The last judgement will pronounce a verdict on the individual in relation to his response to Calvary. To that extent it will reflect the decision man has made.

After the judgement, with its accompanying darkness and cosmic disturbances (15 f.), the centre of God's blessing will be a purified Jerusalem. With evil overthrown, symbolized by Egypt and Edom (19), God's people will enjoy an abundance of good things and the land will be inhabited for ever. Above all, the Lord will be dwelling in their midst (21; cf. Ezek. 48.35; Rev. 21.3).

Questions for further study and discussion on Joel
1. With the help of a concordance, study the O.T. teaching on 'the day of the Lord'.

2. Are there any events which should serve as reminders to Christians that the day of Christ's coming is imminent?
3. Has the prophecy of Joel 2.28-32 been completely or only partly fulfilled in the events of Good Friday and Pentecost?
4. What does Joel contribute to the Biblical doctrine of the Holy Spirit?

Amos

INTRODUCTION

Amos shared with Hosea the distinction of beginning the great line of Hebrew prophets whose words were written down for posterity. Both men directed their prophecies to the northern kingdom of Israel but, unlike Hosea, Amos was a southerner from Tekoa in the Judean hills, and he travelled north to Bethel to preach on what was virtually foreign soil. He claims not to have been a professional prophet (7.14), but a layman called by God to address His words to a disobedient people. We are not, however, to think of him as an untutored rustic, for there are many indications that he was much more than that. He was a shepherd (1.1), but the Hebrew word *noqed* can mean a 'sheep-breeder', like Mesha, king of Moab (2 Kings 3.4); the fact that he travelled to Bethel, possibly to market the shearings of his sheep, suggests that he may have been a master-shepherd with others in his employ; he was a man of affairs, who was in touch with recent events among the surrounding nations (1.3—2.3); he had sufficient knowledge of liturgical formulae to be able to produce the poetic oracular structures in which most of his messages were couched. His ministry may be dated around 760–750 B.C. The only fixed point in time which he gives us (1.1, 'before the earthquake') must refer to the exceptionally serious tremor which was remembered hundreds of years later (cf. Zech. 14.5), but its actual date is unfortunately not known.

It is interesting to notice the grounds for Amos' condemnation of the northerners. It was not primarily because their worship was interwoven with Canaanite fertility practices (though Hosea makes it clear that this was so), nor was it because of the calf-images set up by Jeroboam I in Bethel and Dan (though this must certainly have been abhorrent to him), nor was it because the northerners failed to attend at the Jerusalem Temple for the great Israelite festivals. He attacks the northern kingdom for their *social evils*, and he lists oppression, violence, sharp practice, debauchery and bribery among the sins which completely invalidate both the worship of the Israelites and their claim to be the covenant people of God. God's covenant, declares Amos, is not a mark of favouritism but an incentive to responsible moral conduct. The two verses which best sum up his teaching, therefore, are 3.2 and 5.24.

439

These seven oracles are a prelude to what is to follow in 2.6–16. Before Amos ventures to utter his scathing attack on Israel, he prepares the way by declaring the sins of Israel's neighbours and pronouncing God's judgement upon them. It is not difficult to imagine Amos in the market-place at Bethel, gathering the crowds with this kind of popular invective, for these countries were all enemies or rivals of Israel. And when he finished up with an attack on the sins of Judah, his homeland, Amos must have captured the hearts of his listeners completely, for there was little love lost between north and south. But Israel's turn was coming, and their condemnation was going to be more severe than anything that had yet been uttered.

The sins of these neighbour States were mainly acts of barbarism, violations not of God's law but of basic humanitarian principles. The Syrians of Damascus had carried out brutal raids on Gilead, probably quite literally mangling the bodies of prisoners under heavily-studded threshing-sledges (the Roman *tribula*, from which we derive the word for 'tribulation'). The Philistines took captive a whole population to sell them into slavery (6). Tyre and Edom both broke faith with nations with whom they had ties by treaty or by kinship (9,11). The Ammonites committed horrible atrocities simply for the sake of territorial aggrandizement (13). The Moabites desecrated the bones of the king of Edom (2.1), an act which in Near Eastern thought meant the elimination of the total personality of a dead victim, making it impossible for him to participate in any life after death. The horror felt at such an act may be judged from the description of a similar occurence in 2 Kings 3.27 (which some regard as having been the basis for Amos' accusation, understanding the words 'his eldest son' as meaning the crown prince of Edom and not of Moab).

For all these atrocities God will punish the nations. Men do not have to know the full revelation of God's law to come under His condemnation: they only have to violate the standards that they in their relatively unenlightened state can yet recognize (cf. Rom. 1.18–20; 2.12). Where, however, revelation has been given, the judgement is related to it and becomes all the more severe. Judah's sin (2.4) was mild in comparison with Edom's, but it was just as much a flouting of God's standards, and so the people merited a similar condemnation. All sin, of whatever sort and by whomever committed, is ultimately sin against God.

At last the pile-driving blows fall upon the ears of the Israelite listeners, as they are treated to a detailed and extended description of their own inhumanities against their fellows (6–8) as well as of their misuse of God's provision for their spiritual needs (12).

Four situations are described in vs. 6–8: (*i*) innocent men are sold up by harsh money-lenders when their debts are only trifling ('a pair of shoes', 6); (*ii*) poor men, with no influence, are trampled underfoot by well-to-do competitors in rigged legal proceedings (7a); (*iii*) young and old alike make use of temple prostitutes (7b; the word 'same' does not appear in the Hebrew); (*iv*) men attend roisterous sacrificial feasts without any scruples about the way the drink was obtained or about the cloaks they are lying on, which ought to have been returned to their rightful owners before nightfall (8; cf. Exod. 22.26). No one could say that these were gross sins, and certainly not in the same class as the atrocities of the other nations; they could easily be excused with the words that 'everyone does this sort of thing these days'. But God's verdict is expressed firmly at the end of v. 7. If morality means anything at all, it must touch the practical details of the way we live and how we treat our neighbours, especially those less fortunate than ourselves. Failure here makes a scandal of our religious profession.

God then recounts some of His unmerited, and apparently unappreciated, gifts to Israel (9–11). He had dispossessed strong enemies from the land ('Amorite' being an umbrella term for all the pre-Conquest inhabitants of Canaan); He had performed the liberating miracle of the Exodus; He had given Israel spiritual leadership to continue the work done by Moses in speaking God's word and witnessing to His holiness. A theocratic community like Israel needed its prophets and its holy men, but Israel's response was to muffle their words and contaminate their consecration (12). Christian workers can be warned that this is the way the natural man still likes to treat those who are dedicated to God.

The punishment is pronounced in vs. 13–16. As Israel's oppressive rulers trampled on their fellow men, so God will trample down these same men, like the threshing-sledge pressing down upon the floor full of sheaves (cf. **1**.3; this is more likely than the 'hay-wagon' figure of most English translations). No one will escape God's judgement, however strong or capable he may be. When God acts, human ability is powerless to frustrate Him.

The last thing Amos wanted to do was to teach a new religion, and it is quite misleading to regard him as the 'founder of ethical monotheism', as some of the older textbooks used to say. Instead he was for ever calling the people back to the faith of the past and to the covenant which the Lord had made with them in the wilderness at Sinai. This was evident in 2.10 and it recurs in 3.1 f. (see also 5.25; 9.7,11,15). The point of Amos' message was that the covenant had been misunderstood by Israel, and that its exclusive demands and ethical implications had been completely neglected by a people who saw in it merely a ground for uncritical self-congratulation. This simply would not do. The election of Israel did not exempt them from punishment; it only deepened their responsibility to live worthily of the Lord of Sinai. A similar danger is faced by Christians who, rightly rejoicing in the assurance of 'once saved, always saved', can be led almost unconsciously into the antinomian way of thinking that personal discipline and practical holiness are somehow less necessary when forgiveness is so freely theirs.

Just as punishment inevitably falls upon the covenant people because of their failure to keep the covenant standards, so Amos goes on to instance a number of other cases of cause and effect (3-6). The effect is seen and heard; the cause can be presumed. For example, travellers journeying together have clearly planned to do so; lions growl only when they have taken prey; snares snap tight when a victim steps inside. Verse 6 brings the examples closer to their intended climax: when the trumpeter sounds the alarm in a city, it is because the people fear an attack, and when calamity comes ('evil' is not to be understood in a moral sense), people know that the Lord is behind it.

The application follows (7,8). God never acts (effect) without first giving warning through the prophets (cause). But He *has* spoken; the prophet *must* prophesy; and the judgement will surely fall.

Meditation: The more God has done for me, the more He expects of me.

Amos 3.9-15   Judgement is Coming

Amos wastes little time in attempting to justify God's intention to punish Israel. To him it is a simple matter of fact: God has spoken, and it will surely happen. But he does give the underlying reason for judgement in v. 10. Israel is both socially corrupt and spiritually ignorant. The former is, of course, the outcome of the latter, and the reason why nations are still plagued with the unhappy manifesta-. tions of social evil (crime, perversion, addiction, racialism, and so on) is usually because they have lost their bearings morally and spiritually: 'they do not know how to do right.' A nation's downward spiral begins with its failure to exercise moral discrimination; and the same can be said to apply to the individual member also.

In v. 12 the prophet makes use of his pastoral knowledge. It was an understood thing that the only evidence a shepherd could bring to his master to excuse the loss of a sheep to a wild beast was a few scraps of the torn carcass (cf. Exod. 22.13). Otherwise there was always the suspicion of a dishonest deal having been done. So Amos declares that when God ravages Israel in judgement there will only be tiny indications left of the luxury that once was hers.

Bethel, too, will suffer the same fate as Samaria, despite its honoured place in patriarchal traditions (Gen. 12.8; 28.18 f.; 35.1). A city cannot live on its past (nor can a church!); it is judged by what it is in the present. Bethel had become a royal sanctuary where the worship of Yahweh, the God of Israel, was contaminated by the presence there of Jeroboam's calf-image (1 Kings 12.29), and its religious trappings were far removed from the simplicity for which it had once stood.

Its most sacred features would therefore be destroyed by the very God who was allegedly worshipped there. The horns (14) were the four corners of the altar on which the blood of the sacrifices was smeared to make atonement for sin (Lev. 4.30), but atonement would no longer be made. The fine houses of the nobility would also come to an end (15). Ornate worship and gracious living were no substitutes for basic morality in the eyes of a righteous God.

Amos 4.1-5   The Cocktail Set

There are very few parts of the Bible where women as a class are criticized. Isa. 3.16–4.1 and Ezek. 13.17–23 are two of the passages which share this distinction with these verses in *Amos*. It was the wives of the rich merchants of Samaria who received the lash of the shepherd's tongue. For it was the unceasing demands that they made upon their husbands that urged them on to more brutal forms of oppression of the poor. All that these women lived for was bigger and better parties, the status symbols of the well-to-do. Amos regarded them with the same suspicious eye that English countryfolk today cast at the cocktail parties of their affluent neighbours. The sin, however, was not in the occasion but in the greed and vanity

443

which caused others to be exploited for mere personal gain. As a punishment these pampered creatures would be dragged out of the city and thrown like so many carcasses upon the city's refuse-heap (3, the meaning of 'Harmon' can only be conjectured).

Such a scathing attack could only come from one who had lived his life out of range of the decadent influence of city life. Caught up in its social whirl, it was all too easy for the people of Samaria to see nothing unusual in their behaviour. But the outsider, reared in the rugged simplicity and equality of the desert, saw this life for what it was. Our effete, western way of life could well be subjected to similar scrutiny by a Christian prophet from a developing country or from behind the Iron Curtain.

Verses 4,5 are a separate oracle and consist of an ironic call to worship on the lines of 'O come, let us *sin* unto the Lord!' This is coupled with 'the caricature of their exaggerated zeal' (G. Adam Smith) in proliferating religious ceremonies and in blazoning abroad the generosity of their freewill offerings. The condemnation of all this is not in the observances themselves but in the motive: for this kind of religion is basically self-centred. It gratifies the feelings of the giver and thinks nothing of the awful majesty of the One who should be worshipped in humble, silent adoration.

Meditation: 'O worship the Lord in the beauty of holiness!
Bow down before Him, His glory proclaim.'

Questions for further study and discussion on Amos chs. 1–4.5
1. Does the Christian Church need to have its counterpart to the Nazirites of the O.T., to bear witness to a deeper quality of holiness and unworldliness? If so, who should they be?
2. Do you think it is still true that God always warns before He acts in judgement? Has the Christian a ministry to warn as well as to reconcile?
3. Is it possible to be involved in too many 'religious activities', to the detriment of true Christian living? What should be the Christian's balance between his social responsibilities as a Christian and his church life?
4. Amos saw the evidence of true repentance in terms of social justice. How should his teaching be applied by the Christian businessman, the Christian trade unionist, the Christian solicitor?
5. What should be the criterion of our forms of worship: what we find satisfying or what is pleasing to God? What does God require of us?

Amos 4.6-13   'Prepare to Meet your God'

Five occurrences which we would describe as natural disasters are
here attributed to God. He sent famine (6), drought (7,8), blight
(9), plague (10), and devastation by fire (11), all with the intention
of bringing Israel to repentance, but the sad refrain tells of Israel's
consistent failure to return to God. The modern mind finds it
difficult to share the Old Testament's readiness to see God's hand
in such tragic happenings. Today only the insurance companies
call them 'acts of God'. But the Hebrew prophet saw past the disaster
to the God who controlled the universe, and who was therefore
ultimately responsible for everything that happened in it. Disaster
did not make him question God's goodness so much as drive him
to ask, 'What has He to teach me through this?' We on the other
hand concentrate on immediate, rather than ultimate, causes with a
view to preventing a repetition of the event. This is a good and proper
reaction, but it is not the whole of the matter. Personal tragedy
can still be 'God's megaphone' to all who will listen to His voice.

Israel did not listen and did not repent. They had become hardened
before a continuous barrage of threats, warnings and misfortunes.
But one day God's forbearance would come to an end. The door
would be shut. The threat of judgement would be replaced by the
fact of judgement. Man would have to face the God described in
v. 13, the One who is the Creator of the massive mountain-ranges
and the Maker of the fickle wind and who can also see into 'the
hidden depths of every heart'. Then excuses would be useless.
What defence can a man put up when he knows that his Judge
can read every thought that is running through his mind? Part of
the horror of the Day of Judgement will be the sheer nakedness of
men before their Maker.

*For self-examination: Is there any recent happening which God has
allowed me to experience and through which He wants to speak to
me? Am I prepared to learn and to repent, or do I try to hide my
real feelings from Him?*

Amos 5.1-15   'Seek Me and Live'

Here is a last-minute call to repentance. It is preceded by two brief
laments which suggest that all is over for Israel. The nation has
been hurled to the ground and has neither the strength to recover
nor an ally to help her up (2). Her armies have been reduced to a
tenth of their former size (3). But it is still not too late for Israel
to repent and seek the Lord. Three times the people are exhorted
to turn to Him (4,6,14). Pilgrimages to holy places will not do any

445

good, however venerable the sanctuaries may be, for they too are going to share in the coming destruction (5). True repentance is a matter not of outward observances but of inward contrition, a personal turning to a personal God. Self-reformation is no substitute for it, but that does not mean that a man's way of life is not to be transformed. Those who seek the Lord must hate evil and do good (14,15), performing deeds worthy of their repentance (Acts 26.20). Notice the sins with which Amos charges his hearers (7,10–12): they are mainly to do with social injustice, and 'the gate' is mentioned three times (10,12,15). This was the Israelite's equivalent of the Greek market-place. It was the open space, usually just outside the city gates, where business was transacted and justice dispensed by the elders.If this became the place where innocent men were oppressed and poor people were cheated of their rights, then no amount of religious profession would be acceptable to God. Repentance had to be accompanied by righteous conduct, or it was not genuine repentance.

Verses 8,9 are a doxology in praise of the God who controls the constellations above, and who orders the succession of night and day, and the ebb and flow of the tide. Verse 9 almost certainly conceals the names of three further constellations, Taurus (the Bull), Capricornus (the Goat) and Vindemiator (the Grape-gatherer), but these were not recognized by the Massoretes who inserted the vowel-points, and so we have to translate them by 'destruction', 'the strong' and 'the fortress'. The point to note is that the God who demands righteousness from His creatures is a God of perfect order and control within His universe.

Amos 5.16-27   The Day of the Lord

We cannot be sure how the concept of the day of the Lord came into being for Israel, but we do know that it represented the beginning of the millennium, the day when righteousness would triumph and God's covenant promises would become a reality. Israel expected that they would be vindicated and their enemies would be judged. It was to be a day of ultimate redemption, a day to be looked forward to by God's people and to be dreaded by His foes. Amos reversed all this. Righteousness would prevail, but it was to be ethical righteousness; and Israel fell far short of this. So Israel would be condemned on that day, and there would be no way of escaping God's final judgement (19f.). It would be a black day for Israel.

To underline his point that judgement is ethical and not religious

Amos goes on to speak disparagingly of all the rites and ceremonies of Israel's religious life (21–23). What God wanted was a spate of justice and righteousness in the land (24). Does this mean that Amos was against the sacrificial system? Was this a case of the prophet totally rejecting established priestly religion as being alien to God's will? Verse 25, with its implication that sacrifice was unknown in the wilderness days, would suggest that this was so. But further consideration points in the opposite direction. Amos must have known that the worship of God was unthinkable without sacrifice and other outward forms. He must have known about the Passover lamb and the altars of the patriarchs; the early traditions of the tent of meeting and its rituals could not have completely passed him by. What he did see, however, was that the *priority* of the Sinai covenant was on obedience to God's laws and not on the carrying out of complicated rituals. Israel, doubtless under Canaanite influence, had developed the latter at the expense of the former, and in so doing had abandoned the basis of their covenant obligations. What Amos saw going on at the shrines of Bethel and Gilgal was a far cry from Sinai religion. There was even a touch of idolatry mixed in with it (26). So God would punish the nation with exile (27), and the day of the Lord would bring them no salvation.

Amos 6.1-7 Beware of Luxury

This passage consists of two more 'woes' against the luxury-loving leaders in Israel. The first (1–3) is addressed to those who by virtue of their nobility dispense justice to the people (1b). They are accused of maintaining an irrational confidence in the security of their cities, whether Jerusalem or Samaria, and Amos has to remind them that other great cities had proved vulnerable, and their self-confidence would be rudely shaken (8,10,14). Gath had fallen to Uzziah in *c.* 760 B.C. (cf. 2 Chron. 26.6); Calneh and Hamath in the north would soon be toppled by Assyria (cf. Isa. 10.9). What right had the little pocket-kingdoms of Israel and Judah to expect immunity when eventually God allowed the storm to break upon them? By fancying that the day of crisis was far away their leaders were in fact only hastening it on (3).

The second woe (4–7) describes vividly the plush elegance of the wealthy men of Israel, whose lives were surrounded by comforts and whose main concerns were food and drink, music and cosmetics. None of these was intrinsically wrong. The sin of these men lay in their carelessness of the awful doom that threatened their country-men (6). When things are going wrong in a community, God does at least expect His people to be concerned, even though they may be unable by themselves to do anything about it. When Jerusalem was on the point of falling, it was this which saved some of her inhabitants from destruction (cf. Ezek. 9.4). Prosperity can be more dangerous to a nation's morale than poverty. It breeds a selfishness and unconcern for the needs of others that can cripple society.

Are we sufficiently aware of the dangers inherent in our own affluent, western way of life? Are we guilty of relying for our security on anything but the mercy of God?

Amos 6.8-14   Pride and its Punishment

Hard on the heels of prosperity comes pride, and Israel developed all the unpleasant characteristics of the self-made man. In fact 'the pride of Israel-Jacob' became almost a byword in these days before the country's overthrow (see Hos. 5.5; 7.10; 12.8; as well as Amos 8.7). It was the attitude of mind which could be traced back to Adam—the attempt to rise above one's station and to think and act like a demi-god. It was the sin of Babel (Gen. 11.4), and of the king of Babylon mentioned in Isa. 14.13 f. It was to bring about the downfall of the wealthy city of Tyre and the flourishing kingdom of Egypt (Ezek. 28.2 ff.; 29.3,9). It still fools men and nations, encouraging them with thoughts of grandeur but actually bringing them down into the dust. The hardest thing a man has to learn is the way of humility.

Israel had been encouraged by two minor military sucesses over towns that can hardly be identified today (13), but God was going to bring against them a real foe, the Assyrians, who would crush them from one end of the land to the other (14). The 'entrance of Hamath' appears frequently as a northern frontier area, and is probably the name of a town in Lebanon (Lebo-Hamath); the Arabah is the dried-up watercourse running south from the Dead Sea to the Gulf of Akaba. Israel's topsy-turvy standards and her futile expectations are nothing short of ridiculous, as Amos makes plain in v. 12a. But there will be nothing amusing about their consequences. Under threat of siege the population of whole cities will be wiped out. The picture of the kinsman, acting as undertaker and collecting up dead bodies to take them away for cremation, suggests the horrors of a plague. So dreadful will things be that men will be terrified of even mentioning the Lord's name in case they too are struck down (10). Such is the awful end of those who persistently profane His name. What a strange contrast to the Christian's delight in Him!

448

Meditation: 'Jesus, the name high over all,
In hell, or earth, or sky;
Angels and men before it fall,
And devils fear and fly.'

Amos 7.1-9

In the first of these visions Amos is shown a swarm of locusts which are on the point of devouring the whole of the spring crop of grass, i.e. the second crop which grows after the latter rains. This was the main crop as far as the people were concerned, because apparently most of the early crop was commandeered by the king as his royal due. The prospect of such a disastrous and irreparable loss moved the prophet to plead with the Lord for mercy on the grounds of Jacob's (i.e. Israel's) insignificance and inability to stand such devastation. The people showed no sign of repentance but, on the basis of Amos' intercession, the Lord relented and stopped the destruction (translating v. 2 as 'when they were on the point of completely eating the grass . . .'; so too in v. 4). The same thing happened in the second vision, which was 'a judgement by fire', i.e. perhaps a drought which had dried up the subterranean sources of water and was devastating the countryside (4). Once again, Amos knew that if this continued unchecked the result would be disastrous for Israel, which for all its boastings and complacency was nothing more than a petty princedom with very limited powers of endurance.

The third time, however, Amos could not see his way to interceding for Israel and God's final words of judgement were pronounced through the vision of the plumbline, a symbol of righteousness and truth. Significantly it was the nation's religious centres and her royal family which were to bear the brunt of the nation's punishment (9), and this was entirely appropriate. When a people degenerates, the responsibility may usually be laid upon its leaders in Church and State.

The visions raise two problems for the reader: (*i*) Why did Amos not go on interceding for Israel? The question could also be asked of Abraham's intercession for Sodom (Gen. **18.**22–33), and the Bible does not give us the answer. Presumably Amos knew that no amount of warnings would bring Israel to repentance: at some stage there had to be a last chance. (*ii*) How can God be said to 'repent'? The word means basically to change one's attitude so as to do something different. When a man repents of sin, he feels more than sorry; he behaves differently. God also changes His mind to suit new circumstances, and we can be thankful that He does.

Amos 7.10-17 Prophet versus Priest

This episode describes in classic form the confrontation between divine authority, represented by the prophet, and human authority, in the person of Amaziah, the royal chaplain. Amos appeals to the God who has called him and given him His message; Amaziah hides behind the authority of his king. It is the perennial clash between the charismatic and the ecclesiastic which the Church's history has seen repeated over and over again. The professional does not understand. He regards the prophet's message as being politically dangerous, and misrepresents him to the king ('Amos has *conspired*': but, as one commentator has said: 'His only fellow-conspirator was God'!). He makes a scathing attack on him, accusing him of being deluded ('O visionary'), of being a foreigner ('Judean, go home'), of being a professional ('sing for your supper there') and of trespass ('Bethel is a royal preserve').

Amos's reply is without rancour. He is not a professional nor is he a member of a prophetic guild (a 'son of a prophet', cf. 2 Kings 2.3,5,7,15). His calling was from a secular occupation (unlike Amaziah the priest), where he had cared for animals and tended fig-trees (the Biblical 'sycamore', which is nothing to do with the tree known by that name today). His message was not of his own invention or construction; it had been given him as a word from God. It carried with it all of God's authority, and he *had* to speak it out because of the inner compulsion he felt (cf. Jeremiah's experience, Jer. 20.9). It was as wrong for him to try to keep silence as it was for anyone like Amaziah to try to silence him (16). Therefore another prophecy, addressed personally but not vindictively to Amaziah, makes it clear that in the coming invasion and overthrow of Israel the priest of Bethel will be able to claim no exemption. His family and property will be treated in the way all conquered peoples must have come to expect, and he himself would die in exile (17). There is more than a hint here that the prophet's calling was not a highly respected one in Israel. Some may have been in it for the money. But the genuine prophet had a profound sense of his holy calling and a fearlessness in proclaiming God's word which set him apart from all lesser men.

Amos 8.1-8 'The End has Come'

After the interlude of Amaziah's encounter with Amos we have a fourth vision, at the heart of which is a play on words (explained in the RSV margin). This is coupled with a repetition of the phrase in 7.8, 'I will never again pass by them'. The artistry and balance of these four visions is worth noting. The first two are of potential disaster-situations, and in response to Amos' plea the Lord repents with the repeated words 'It shall not be' (7.3,6). The second two visions are of apparently innocuous objects, but they both carry a powerful message on the finality of judgement. This is of course expressed in the words spoken, especially in the 'never again' of God's speech, but it may also be concealed in the things seen. *If* the wall of 7.7 was a bowed and sagging wall, Amos would have seen all too clearly the discrepancy between God's standard of uprightness (the plumbline) and the building which should have conformed to it (Israel). Similarly, what are called 'summer fruit' may have been the 'end-of-season' produce whose edible life was strictly limited, and so they naturally suggested speedy deterioration. The horror of the end-time is graphically intensified if we follow G. A. Smith in translating v. 3b as four exclamations: 'Many corpses! Everywhere! Cast them forth! Be silent!'

Verse 4 introduces a further list of sins (4–6) and their condemnation (7,8). Again, not all the sins are serious crimes, e.g. impatience to get on with business after a festival (5); but they are mixed with shady practices involving buying and selling and not giving good value. The merchant was the sole controller both of the scales and containers in which his goods were sold, and of the weights with which the customer weighed out his silver in payment. So an undersized container (ephah, 5) or a heavy shekel weight could bring the merchant double gain in one transaction. It is interesting that of all the weights discovered by archaeologists from O.T. 'digs', no two have tallied exactly. An honest merchant who gave good measure was a rare find (cf. Luke 6.38), and corruption in this realm was all too frequent (cf. Deut. 25.13–15; Prov. 11.1; 20.10). Those who suffered were always the poor and needy, and God was particularly concerned for the under-privileged. So the judgement would fall and it would come like an earthquake and the mighty inundation of the Nile (8). No sin is too 'petty' to pass God's notice.

Amos 8.9-14   The Famine of God's Word

Astronomers tell us that there was a total eclipse of the sun, centred on Asia Minor, in June 763 B.C. Amos would certainly have experienced this and he probably draws on it for his imagery of the last days of God's judgement on Israel (9). In these verses there is unrelieved disaster: Amos can see not the slightest hope for Israel. The day of the Lord will be a bitter day when everyone who is left will have someone to mourn for (10). But the crowning tragedy will be the famine of the word of God. Men who in prosperity neglect, ignore and even deride God's spokesmen will in days of suffering be searching frantically for someone to speak to them in His name. Though we think primarily in terms of God's written word, in Amos' day the word of the Lord was essentially a living message spoken through His servants, the prophets. When there were few original prophets, as against the many professionals who mouthed empty words or quoted second-hand oracles, true religion was at a premium, as had been the case in Samuel's day (1 Sam. 3.1). The very scarcity of a commodity often draws attention to its usefulness, and in days when churches are closed and Bibles confiscated there seems often to be a greater interest in the gospel.

The verb used in v. 12a means to stagger, like a fainting man (cf. 4.8), and men will traverse the whole land from south to west (Dead Sea to Mediterranean), as well as from north to east in a vain search for God. Their youthful strength will not supply their needs (13), nor will any profession of loyalty to any number of local deities (14). The goddess Ashimah was worshipped by the men of Hamath (2 Kings 17.30), and was associated with the worship of Yahweh at the Jewish colony of Elephantine in Upper Egypt many years later. The Elephantine papyri (dateable in the fifth and fourth centuries B.C.) name her as Asham-Bethel, and this affords further evidence of the way in which individual gods were attached to important cult-centres. The word 'way' probably also conceals the name of a deity associated with Beersheba. But like Dagon (1 Sam. 5.3 f.), they have power neither to rise up themselves nor to raise up their followers. *Pray* today for those who suffer from a scarcity of God's word, and for all who try to supply them with copies of the Scriptures.

Amos 9.1-10 The Impossibility of Escape

In his fifth vision Amos sees the Lord, presumably standing in the sanctuary at Bethel, pronouncing judgement upon it and upon all who worship in it. There will be not one person who will be able to escape (cf. 2.14 f.), unless it be specifically within God's purpose (8c). Wherever men try to hide, they will be searched out and taken by God's hand; not even the underworld (Sheol) will be able to conceal them. The only places that God does not actually go are the depths of the sea (3b) and into foreign lands (4). Too much must not be made of this point, but these do represent areas where God's influence was felt by many Israelites to be limited. The deep was where the mythological monster of Canaanite and Babylonian creation myths had its habitation, the epitome of evil, the serpent Leviathan (cf. Isa. 27.1); but even this acted as the instrument of God. Similarly, in heathen lands where it was thought God could neither bless nor punish, exiled Israelites were to find that their captor's swords were still the instruments of His will. For the Lord is the God of the whole earth, the Creator God for whom the earth and the sky, the sea and the dry land, are the sphere of His dominion (5,6).

Verses 7,8 go on to assert that all nations are under God's control, and that Israel's exodus from Egypt was not the only tribal migration that was His responsibility. The Philistines moving from Crete (Caphtor) and the Syrians from Kir (east of Damascus: cf. 1.5) were just as much acting under the motivation of the Lord. This is a rhetorical statement and must not be taken too literally, because the covenant of Sinai set Israel apart from all other nations (3.2), but it is a valuable cautionary word to Israel to prevent them thinking that they are the only people God has an interest in. By their failure to live by the covenant they have reduced themselves to the level of other nations. They are a sinful kingdom (8), and this fact empties the Exodus of all supernatural meaning.

The closing verses present a problem and many scholars regard vs. 8c,9 as the words of a later writer. But it is not unusual in the prophets for a statement of universal judgement to be finally tempered with a glimmer of mercy, and 5.15 has at least held out the possibility of restoration for Israel. Nor are commentators agreed whether v. 9 is a threat in keeping with v. 10 (no one will escape), or a promise linked to 8c (no one will be lost). Probably it is best to take it that in the shake-up of Israel's judgement, every sinner would perish (10) but all the faithful would be preserved.

Amos 9.11-15   Blessings to Come

These verses are commonly denied to Amos on the grounds that they are a complete contradiction of his earlier message, that they would be meaningless if spoken at Bethel and that they refer mainly to the house of David and so to the southern kingdom of Judah. A post-exilic background is postulated for them, when reconstruction work was in progress and the atmosphere was optimistic. If this view is accepted it must at least be separated from the doctrinaire assumption that all the 'happy endings' of the prophets must be late, for such a view is surely suspect. It ought, too, to be challenged

453

on a number of counts: (*i*) Amos has already shown signs of some degree of optimism for the future (5.15; 9.8c, if original); (*ii*) he has shown that his concern is not restricted to Israel, but takes in Judah also (1.2; 2.4 f.; 6.1; cf. too refs. to Beersheba, 5.5; 8.14), and that he sometimes likes to think of all Israel, i.e. Judah and Israel combined (as in 2.10 f.; 3.1 f.); (*iii*) there is no suggestion in the text that all of Amos' prophecies were uttered at Bethel: this could well be 'the prophet's addition as he records his message for posterity' (Ellison).

The language is typically materialistic, in the normal style of such eschatological pronouncements (cf. Isa. 11; Joel 2.21–27; 3.18). The future age of blessing is described in terms of agricultural prosperity, but this is not to be taken literally, as v. 13b indicates. It simply expresses, in as extravagant language as the prophet can muster, a manner of life which is indescribably good. Taken symbolically, this rural setting for the golden age is complemented and not contradicted, by the urban setting of the new Jerusalem in *Ezekiel*. For both prophets, the ultimate future of God's faithful people was beyond man's wildest dreams. What we as Christians enjoy of the blessings of the Messiah are but the foretaste of the joys to come.

Thought: 'Eye hath not seen, nor ear heard, neither have entered into the heart of man, the things which God hath prepared for them that love Him' (1 Cor. 2.9).

Questions for further study and discussion on Amos chs. 6–9
1. With 7.1–6, compare Gen. 18.22–33: what other Biblical examples are there of God's judgement being averted through one man's prayers?
2. Is it possible to distinguish between true and false prophets today? What can be learnt from 7.10–17 about the dangers inherent in being an ordained representative of an established church?
3. Notice the repetition of the words 'never' and 'never again' in chs. 7,8 (RSV). Are we to understand from this that there is a limit to the mercy and forbearance of God? Is this a N.T. doctrine?
4. Summarize the teaching of Amos about the nations of the world with special reference to 1.3–2.3; 3.2; 6.2,14; 9.4,7–10,12.
5. What can we learn from Amos about the privileges and responsibilities of being members of God's chosen people?

Obadiah 1-14   The Treachery of the Edomites

This, the shortest book in the O.T., deals not with Israel or Judah, but with their kinsmen, the Edomites, who inhabited the mountainous region south-east of the Dead Sea. This people was descended from Esau, Jacob's twin, and was always felt to have a real kinship with the Israelites, though this showed itself not so much in mutual assistance as in hostile recriminations and charges of treachery (10). Certainly no love was lost between the two nations, and this can be traced back to Moses' day (Num. 20.14-21). There were frequent battles and occasional massacres in the days of the united monarchy, and later, in Amaziah's reign (c. 796-767 B.C.), 20,000 Edomites were slaughtered in one operation (2 Chron. 25.11 f.). So the fault was not all on one side. Edom's crowning perfidy, however, was to take advantage of Judah's downfall in 587 B.C. and to invade her territory while Jerusalem was being sacked.

This latest episode was the occasion for the accusations of vs. 10-14, and accounts for the bitterness of the anti-Edomite oracles in Jer. 49.7-22; Ezek. 25.12-14; 35.15; cf. also Psa. 137.7; Lam. 4.21 f. Because of this Obadiah warns that Edom will shortly fall (1-4), and her destruction will be complete (5-9). In these verses two features are mentioned for which Edom was renowned. (*i*) Her wisdom would come to an end (8; cf. Jer. 49.7; and there are grounds for thinking that Job originally had an Edomite setting). (*ii*) Her capital city, Sela (3, RSV margin), the modern Petra, perched high up in the mountains, which was fondly thought to be impregnable, would be brought low.

Subsequent history saw the fulfilment of these predictions. The Edomites were driven out of their territory by the Arabs, their former allies, during the fifth century B.C. and had to take refuge in Southern Judah where eventually they became absorbed into Judaism (7). Ironically, it was an Edomite, Herod the Great, who was Jesus' bitterest foe when He was born in Bethlehem, and another Herod who connived at His death.

Notes: 'Teman' (9) was one of the chief cities of Edom and the home of Eliphaz, one of Job's friends; 'Mount Esau' (8 f.) refers to Mount Seir, a prominent landmark in Edom.

Obadiah 15-21   Edom's Punishment on the Day of the Lord

Edom's sins are to be judged according to the law of retribution when the day of the Lord comes, and this is a concept that appears frequently in the Bible. At the last day, wrongs will be righted and the present imbalance between the state of the wicked and the righteous will be rectified. This is well expressed in the song of Mary (the Magnificat: Luke 1.46–55), which shows that the birth of Jesus was thought to be heralding a new age, the beginning of the last days in fact. The retributive principle in the doctrine of judgement has to be understood as a vindication of God's righteousness, and not as vindictiveness against the sinner—a very definite distinction, which is not always recognized.

Edom's total overthrow is expressed also in terms of draining the cup of God's wrath (16; cf. Jer. 25.15–28); and being burnt up like a field of stubble (18; cf. Mal. 4. 1–3). The only place that will survive is the holy Mount Zion (the very antithesis of Mount Esau), where some will find salvation (17, quoted in Joel 2.32). In contrast with the dispossessed Edomites, this remnant of the house of Jacob will then be able to take possession of all their inheritance, everything that by right belongs to them. This is elaborated in vs. 19 f., where the inhabitants of those parts of Palestine in which encroachments had been made will retake their land and overflow into their enemies' territory. (The Negeb is the southern desert; the Shephelah is the low hill country in West Palestine, bordering on Philistia; Ephraim and Samaria comprise the former northern kingdom of Israel; Gilead is east of Jordan from Benjamin's territory). Furthermore, the exiles from Israel, dispossessed in 722 B.C., will occupy the whole of the south. So the Promised Land will belong to God's people once again, from far north to deep south. (Halah is in Mesopotamia, cf. 2 Kings 17.6; Sepharad is Sardis in Asia Minor, though in modern Hebrew it is wrongly taken as Spain—hence the Sephardic Jews.)

Obadiah's final words (21) show that he sees the day of the Lord not simply as a victory for Israelite nationalism, but as the inauguration of God's kingdom upon earth when all enemies will recognize His authority. The verse unconsciously foreshadows the time when the only Saviour would reign as King in Jerusalem, the city of His crucifixion.

Jonah

INTRODUCTION

We know nothing of Jonah, the son of Amittai, except the passing reference to him in 2 Kings **14.**25, which would date him early in the eighth century B.C. The book which bears his name does not profess to be written by him and a number of indications may suggest that it is post-exilic and written about him; e.g. **3.**3 may reflect a time when Nineveh was no more (it was destroyed in 612 B.C.). Most of the argument concerning the book has centred on its historicity and the identification of the 'great fish', misleadingly called a whale by some N.T. translators. The result of this has been to divert attention from the message of the book, which is shot through with hidden meaning and nice innuendos. It is possible to interpret the book either as history or as parable without impugning the infallibility of Christ's words (Matt. **12.**40; Luke **11.**30) and without discarding a high view of Scripture (see *New Bible Dictionary* on 'Jonah, Book of'). If we conclude that the evidence favours the historical interpretation, we nevertheless have to see in the telling of the incident a strong didactic note: it is history with a moral. And the moral is the message that the God of the Hebrews has a concern for the whole world.

Jonah 1.1-10   Running away from God

In his attempt to evade his duty to God and his responsibility to his fellow men, Jonah was being thoroughly human, and so all who read about him see something of themselves in his character. He may also be taken as representing his people, the Jews, who were quite able to produce the correct religious formulae (**1.**9; **4.**2b) but were less willing to fulfil the responsibilities that were theirs under the Abrahamic covenant (cf. Gen. **12.**3; **22.**18) and to act as a light to the nations (Isa. **42.**6). Judaism has always wavered between its concern to maintain its own distinctiveness, with a resultant exclusivism, and its sense of responsibility to the world: it has not often been a missionary force to be reckoned with (see, however, Matt. **23.**15). So the message of Jonah is addressed to the Church as well as to the individual.

It is at first strange that Jonah should have wanted to avoid taking the message of judgement to the people of Nineveh. Later events show that what he baulked at was not the message that God would overthrow Nineveh, but the fact that inherent in the preaching of judgement was the possibility of the people's repentance, with the consequence that God would forgive and the preacher would appear discredited (4.2). The story of Jonah, therefore, probes deep into the preacher's motives and has much to say to Christian workers today.

Notice the subtleties in these opening verses: Jonah's impetuous haste to get away from the Lord (mentioned three times, 3,10); the personal cost involved ('he paid the fare', 3); the fact that when all were praying, Jonah was asleep (5); the way in which Jonah's guilt was identified by heathen men using lots, who are consistently shown in a better light than the prophet (5,6,10,14,16); the hollowness of Jonah's profession of faith (9). In contrast with the Ninevites' wickedness and the mariners' superstitions, Jonah is marked down as the one to whom the real guilt attaches, and he is still a long way from recognizing it himself. Yet the prime need for the man who preaches judgement to others is that he should know himself and his own failings first.

Prayer: Psalm 139. 23f.

Jonah 1.11-17   A Living Sacrifice

The sheer goodness and humanity of these heathen sailors, in not blaming Jonah for bringing such trouble upon them and then in trying their hardest to save his life, are a silent condemnation of Jonah's unwillingness to take the word of the Lord to the heathen Ninevites. The consideration they showed is in marked contrast to Jonah's lack of it. He did, however, see that the only way for them to be saved was by offering his own life as a sacrifice to be thrown into the raging waters. There may be a touch of irony here, in that he was prepared to make the grand gesture but not prepared to obey the call of God to less spectacular service. Alternatively, the offer may represent Jonah's first stage in self-knowledge and repentance, though there is not much contrition in his speech of v. 12. However, the result of his sacrifice is that the wind drops and the sailors are converted! Where words fail to convince, sacrificial action succeeds. But even so the reader cannot help wondering, in the light of 4.1, whether Jonah would have been pleased or sorry at this turn of events, had he known about it.

Meanwhile, he was swallowed up by a passing fish (17). All kinds of attempts have been made to defend the credibility, or at least the feasibility, of this episode, but none with any success. We must frankly admit that if the incident is true and the book of Jonah historical, this is miraculous—as unique in its way as the resurrection, with which our Lord compared it (Matt. 12.40). If the book is taken as a parable, of course, the question does not arise. But we do know that sperm whales and large sharks capable of swallowing a man have been identified in the East Mediterranean, and it is probably one of these creatures that is meant by Jonah's 'great fish'.

It is easy to see that Jonah's offer to die for the safety of the sailors would have been loudly applauded by generations of Jewish readers. The same concept underlay Caiaphas's unconscious prophecy of the death of Christ (John **11**.49 f.). But for one man to die for others, to be preserved in apparent death and to be brought out alive with a commission to take the word of the Lord to the Gentiles, can be paralleled only in the light of Christ's resurrection, and could not have been thought up by anyone but the One who was to fulfil that same pattern in His own experience. This was 'the sign of the prophet Jonah' which the Jews signally failed to understand.

Jonah 2 Out of the Depths

The style of this psalm uttered by Jonah from inside the fish is very similar to that of the psalm of deliverance used by Israelites when they escaped from death or recovered from serious illness. Parallels to it may be found in Pss. **18**.4–6; **88**.1–12; **130**.1 f. Although the sentiments expressed can be taken metaphorically, as they sometimes are in similar language in the *Psalms*, they nevertheless have a remarkably literal appropriateness to Jonah's actual situation (e.g. 'out of the belly of Sheol', which means 'at death's door', v. 2; and the engulfing by the waters, which was a Hebrew metaphor for any kind of death, not just drowning, vs. 3,5; cf. Psa. **42**.7). The result is that Jonah's words can be taken up by any reader who has gone through deep water (metaphorically!) and found the Lord's deliverance from it. Note, incidentally, that Jonah considers his salvation already to have taken place and that the fish's stomach was actually a place of safety from a watery grave! This does not encourage us to follow those who interpret the book allegorically and who see the great fish as a symbol of the Exile, swallowing up Israel and eventually returning him to his own land: Babylon was hardly a haven from which psalms of thanksgiving could be sung (cf. Psa. **137**.1–7).

The psalm well illustrates some basic elements of effective prayer: (*i*) a deep sense of distress in which what is felt most keenly is being far from God's presence (2,4); (*ii*) crying earnestly to God for help (2,4,7); (*iii*) showing one's thankfulness for God's mercy by proclaiming the news to all who will hear, by offering sacrifices to Him and by paying vows (2,9; cf. Psa. **116**.12–14); (*iv*) a resultant conviction that neither men nor idols can do what the Lord can do: only He can be relied upon to save (8,9b).

Jonah 3   Nineveh's Repentance

The terms of Jonah's commission are repeated, but this time the demand on his obedience is extended: before he had simply to denounce Nineveh's wickedness (1.2), but now he is to be completely ready for anything that God may want him to say (3.2). The preacher's calling is to be the servant of God's word, not the exponent of the message he himself would like to preach.

The size of Nineveh has been an acute problem for some. Critics have too readily rejected it as exaggeration, comparing the actual dimensions of the ancient city (roughly $1\frac{1}{2}$ miles by 3 miles in extent, according to Felix Jones's survey in the last century) with the Bible's 60–75 miles breadth ('three days' journey', v. 3). The repeated phrase, 'that great city', however, suggests that we are here dealing with the whole of the administrative district of Nineveh, which incorporated the three cities of Hatra, Nimrud and Khorsabad, as well as the capital itself and which covered an area up to 60 miles across. (Compare the confusion which often exists between the City of London and Greater London.)

The result of Jonah's preaching was an immediate repentance which, even though it is not attested (hardly surprisingly) from ancient secular sources, warranted the commendation of Jesus Christ (Matt. 12.41; Luke 11.32). We cannot say whether other circumstances combined with Jonah's message to condition his hearers to respond in this way, but if this were so, it would be fully in keeping with the Holy Spirit's way of preparing hearts by all manner of means before bringing the word of God to act like a spark to ignite the kindling. The extent of the repentance is shown by its effect on the king, the people and even the livestock of the area! Once again this is told in order to set Jonah's grudging spirit in contrast with the heathen's full-souled responsiveness. Whereas he as a Jew could be confident of God's mercy, they dare not presume on it and can only repent and plead that God may yet relent (9). God does so, and He shows thereby that He is concerned for all men, and not just for the Jew, and that His judgement can always be averted by sincere repentance. He is not so inflexible that He cannot have mercy on the penitent sinner.

Jonah 4   Lack of Sympathy Rebuked

Now at last Jonah is cast in his very worst light. By his displeasure at God's mercy to Nineveh he shows up the falsity of his motives all along the line. Here is Jonah, the 'narrow little nationalist', disappointed that the heathen are not getting their deserts and yet mouthing the pious formula describing God's generous and forgiving nature (2). The fact is that, although he believes in a God who has these qualities, he wants them to be reserved for Israel alone. But God wants to show His love and mercy to all the world, and offers repentance even to the Gentiles. Judaism found this as difficult to accept as Jonah did, and that is why Jesus occasionally harped on O.T. references like this to the blessing of non-Israelites (cf. also Luke 4.24–27), but even so the early Church needed some persuading that the gospel was for any but the Jews (cf. Acts 10.45; 11.1–18).

Jonah's lesson was a sharp one. When Elijah had felt suicidal, God treated him gently (1 Kings 19.4–18). Jonah could be shown no such mercy. By a series of miraculous circumstances he was made to grieve deeply over the loss of a plant that had given him shade from the sun's heat ('gourd' was probably the large-leafed castor oil plant). If he was justified in feeling so upset about the loss of an inanimate object to whose existence he had contributed nothing, was not God permitted to show some concern for thousands of Ninevites who, for all their ignorance of His laws (expressed as not knowing their right hand from their left, i.e. without the basics of knowledge), were His creation?

The book ends with the question, leaving the reader to draw his own conclusion. At its simplest it is asking the reader whether he has any feelings of sympathy or humanity for his fellow men and, if so, whether he cannot attribute at least as much to the heart of God. As soon as this is allowed, exclusiveness is broken down and the extent of God's sympathy is seen to be as wide as His world. In a final touch of irony, the writer adds the words 'and also much cattle', as if to say, 'Even if you can countenance the destruction of thousands of people, just think what a terrible waste of livestock would be involved!'

Questions for further study and discussion on Obadiah and Jonah

1. What is the value of including in the Bible a book like *Obadiah*, which deals mainly with non-Israelites?
2. Contrast the treatment meted out to the Edomites (in *Obadiah*) with that of the Ninevites (in *Jonah*). Did the Edomites have opportunity to repent?
3. Which other O.T. books reflect the Jewish sense of mission to the Gentiles, and which reflect their exclusiveness?
4. Are there any signs in Jon. 3 and 4 that Jonah had learnt anything from his earlier experiences? Was he in any sense a changed man?
5. Relate the message of Jonah to Peter's vision in Acts 10. What similarities can you see?

461

Micah

Micah was a Judean peasant from Moresheth in the south-west of Palestine, not far from Philistine territory. His prophecies dealt mainly with Jerusalem and were probably uttered there on occasional visits. His vigorous championing of the cause of the under-privileged poor against the oppressive rich indicates that the social sins which Amos saw in Israel were to be found in Judah, too. He was also concerned to attack the religious attitudes of his time and, in particular, the view that God would protect Jerusalem irrespective of the people's conduct. So the religious leaders of the nation were marked out for special condemnation for their failure in leadership (3.1–12).

Micah exercised his ministry during the last third of the eighth century and was remembered in Jeremiah's time for his influence on Hezekiah, probably around the time of Sennacherib's siege of Jerusalem in 701 B.C. (cf. Jer. 26.18 f.). Attempts by critical scholars to deny to his authorship everything but the first three chapters are now losing support, and this minor and little-known prophet is being increasingly recognized as the important figure that he was.

Micah 1   A Sad Tale of Two Cities

While Micah predicts the fall of Samaria in 722 B.C. (6), it is clear from this chapter that he is mainly concerned with Judah and Jerusalem (5b,9,12). One of the important themes of his prophecy is that Jerusalem is in danger of suffering the same fate as Samaria. When the armies of Sennacherib actually moved against the Judean capital to besiege it (read the dramatic story in 2 Kings **18**.13–19, 37), it seemed as if all Micah's predictions were about to be fulfilled. By the miracle of the plague which decimated the Assyrian army, a memorable deliverance came to Jerusalem and Micah's warnings came to nothing. The suggestion made by some scholars that he was thus discredited and compelled to retire from prophetic life is hardly borne out by the reputation he acquired within the next hundred years (cf. Jer. **26**.18 f.).

Verses 2–9 describe the Lord as descending from heaven (2: 'His holy temple' is not an earthly dwelling) and treading upon the mountain-tops, to the accompaniment of earthquakes and volcanic eruption (4). The cause of His wrath is the sin of Israel and Judah, and the prophet predicts that Samaria will become a heap of ruins before Him. All her idolatry is going to be stamped out completely

462

(7) and she will no longer be a city, only a place for growing vines (6). Micah mourns for her, but his grief is due chiefly to the fact that the disease of Samaria has infected Jerusalem, and so her turn will come next (9).

A sudden change of style follows (10–16) and we are given a graphic description of the approach of an invading army from the Philistine coastal plain, through the Judean foothills (and Micah's home town) and up to Jerusalem. Gath had been destroyed some years before and Micah's opening words were now proverbial for disaster (cf. 2 Sam. 1.20). Many of the other references to place-names conceal word-plays or echo knowledge which is now lost to us. 'Dust' ('aphar) is found in Beth-le-aphrah (10); Achzib shall become 'achzāb ('a deceitful thing', 14); Mareshah (15) shall have a 'conqueror' (yōrēsh), etc. By this route Sennacherib's army, which has been campaigning against Egypt, will march on Jerusalem, and Judean parents are urged to go into mourning for their children who will be parted from them (16).

Micah 2   Woe to the Oppressor!

In an agricultural community like Israel the possession of land was all-important, and for the small peasant it was a matter of life or starvation. Each citizen had his entitlement to a portion of the city-lands and this had been handed down to him and kept in the family for many generations. This 'portion' (4) or 'inheritance' (2) was regarded as a sacred trust, which he sought to pass on to his children intact. The story of Naboth's vineyard illustrates the Israelite's concern to protect his basic property rights (1 Kings 21.3), as well as the way in which an unscrupulous tyrant could try to dispossess him. The land-grabbing upper classes of Judah used less brutal means, by foreclosing mortgages, for instance (cf. Amos 2.6), but the result was that their peasant victims were reduced to poverty and virtual serfdom.

Micah championed the rights of the working-classes and pro-nounced God's condemnation upon the wealthy ('this family', 3). The men who had without a qualm dispossessed others would be brought under a foreign yoke and would live to bewail the loss of their ill-gotten gains with cries of 'How could God do such a thing?' (4). The city-lands ('fields') would be re-apportioned, and they would get nothing (5).

This was a strong and daring attack on powerful men and it has been suggested that v. 6 was a listener's enraged reply, which Micah takes up and answers (7 f.). In saying 'Is the Spirit of the

Lord impatient?' (lit. 'to be restricted'), he is claiming that nothing is beyond the concern of God: guided by His Spirit the prophet is entitled to investigate and to pronounce on any issue. The upright man will have nothing to fear from his words; only the guilty will react adversely. But then he is the sort who would prefer the prophet to preach under the influence of alcohol rather than of God's Spirit (11)! For their rapacity towards innocent victims (8 f.), these men have defiled the land and will be turned out of it (10). God's land is unclean; it is no longer a place of rest for His people. There is only one solution: the wrongdoer must go, and God has to start again with another 'remnant' (12 f.). The church which is similarly wasted away by dissident elements within it must also take a firm line and part company with them. When the church can no longer be a 'place of rest' for needy men and women, it has ceased to be any use to God.

Micah 3   The Failure of Judah's Leaders

These words were probably spoken at an important civic occasion in Jerusalem where all the leaders of national life were assembled. Micah begins politely enough (1), but then reverses their standards of good and evil and, before his hearers can decide whether it was a slip of the tongue or not, he accuses them of showing as much consideration for their people as butchers showed to carcasses of meat (2 f.). They were not godless men: they prayed to the Lord (4). But no matter how fervently they prayed, they would get no answer. Sin renders prayer completely useless (cf. Pss. 18.41; 66.18).

The prophets receive equally harsh criticism. They are time-servers, and in it for the money (11). They pander to well-to-do clients and have nothing to give to those who are not fee-payers (5). Again, these men are not arrant quacks: they may have been sent by God and known the Spirit's inspiration in days gone by. But now darkness will descend upon them and the genuine prophetic word will be silenced. It is not that God has changed: they have trimmed their sails to the winds of popularity and prosperity. In contrast, Micah claims to have retained the prophetic spirit, which shows itself in divine power, in a sense of justice and in the moral courage to expose the people's sins (8). The true prophet seems always to be aware that he is in the control of the Spirit and is not fully responsible for the words that he speaks (cf. Ezek. 13.2 f.). Micah's final words (9–12) are a comprehensive indictment of Judah's leadership and this time the priesthood also gets a brief mention (11). In every case the fault is measured in terms of financial gain. Apparently everything (and everybody) has its price: mammon is the measure of all things. Salvation is assured through the presence of the Lord in His holy temple: there appears to be nothing whatever to fear. But Micah makes the shattering statement that inviolable Jerusalem will be razed to the ground: God's house will become a ruin. And it will all be 'because of you', Zion's rulers, whose perversion of truth and justice can be ignored no longer. God's judgement cannot be bought off at any price.

Micah 4.1-8   A Glorious Future for Jerusalem

It is very appropriate that the prophecy of Jerusalem's ruin (3.12) should be followed immediately by this oracle about the place of the new Zion in the last days, when it will serve as the religious metropolis of the whole world. From it the Lord will send forth His law, and many nations will come to learn from His teaching. He will act as Judge of the nations and will inaugurate a period of universal peace when there will be neither arms nor the need for men to leave their homesteads at the call to arms (3 f.). Because vs. 1–3 are almost identical with Isa. 2.2–4, endless discussion has gone on to decide which is original and which is the borrower. In view of the similarity (yet real difference) between Mic. 4.5 and Isa. 2.5, many feel that neither is original, but that both prophets have used a contemporary oracle, modifying the ending to suit their own particular needs. For Micah this appears as a vigorous statement of loyalty to the Lord, when other peoples around are going the way of their own religion. We may be thankful to Micah for his bold commitment, and to Judaism for making this their distinctive witness. If there is any truth at all in the revelation of God, it does not allow for the popular view that one man's religion is as good as his neighbour's. Such tolerance, though highly prized by men of few convictions, is the enemy of the truth. Jesus' claim to be the truth was coupled with His claim to exclusiveness (John 14.6), and this is perfectly logical. The contrast between the ideal future hopes of vs. 1–4 and the present realism of v. 5, where what will be has not yet become a reality, is a perfect example of the delicate balance that all believers must learn to strike between their aspirations and the facts of their experience.

Verses 6–8 continue the theme of the Lord's reign from Mount Zion, but now the main concern is with the mutilated, dispersed flock of Israelites who become the chosen remnant and a mighty force for God. These were later seen to be the exiles in Babylon, but the pattern of God choosing the weak things of the world

and making them great has been repeated continually in human history.
Compare 1 Cor. 1.26–29.

Micah 4.9—5.1 Snapshots of Jerusalem

Here are three pictures of life in Jerusalem at different stages in a siege. Each one begins with the introductory 'now' (9,11; **5.1**). In the first (9 f.) the prophet taunts the inhabitants of Jerusalem for their state of panic. They have a king, the puppet Zedekiah, but he is of little use and the nation is virtually leaderless. They are going through torment and their release from the sufferings of siege warfare will only be to go into exile to Babylon. But there they will find redemption (10). The second picture (11–13) shows the nations gloating over Jerusalem's imminent downfall as they gather round for the pickings. Little do they realize, however, that the Lord has a plan in which they are to be the victims. Jerusalem, instead of being a prey, is a bait to lure them around her. Then, like the sheaves piled around the threshing-floor, the nations will find themselves threshed to pulp under the hoofs of the oxen that tread out the corn, and all the booty taken from them will be devoted to the Lord.

The third is a mere sketch (**5.1**) of a siege-wall built against Jerusalem and the humiliation of Judah's king. The Hebrew is obscure, suggesting a call to mobilize armies (cf. KJV, RV), but the versions are very different (as followed by RSV). The striking of the cheek is an insult which can only be administered to a defeated or humiliated foe (cf. Job **16**.10). While it would not be right to see in Christ's mocking a fulfilment of this prophecy (it is not written as a prediction), the incident of Mark **15**.19 bears a remarkable similarity to this verse and it is clearly more than a coincidence. What Scripture appears to be saying is that Christ bore in His own person all the sufferings of Israel's humiliated king and that the whole of His people's history of rejection was summed up in His Messianic experience.

The chief effect of these three snapshots of Jerusalem is to bring to the situation a new dimension. The people crying out under the sufferings of their siege knew nothing of the redemption that would eventually come; the nations gloating over Jerusalem knew nothing of God's plan to deal with them. God always has His plans; and even though we may not have Micah's insight to know what they will be, it is a great comfort to know that His plan is perfect and it will be worked out.

Micah 5.2-6
The Messiah from Bethlehem

Despite its familiarity from the Christmas lessons, this passage needs explanation because its meaning is not at all clear. In v. 2 God is addressing Bethlehem and saying that, despite its insignificance, it will one day produce another David to rule in Israel. Ephrathah (2) was the name of the district in which Bethlehem was situated (cf. Ruth 1.2; 4.11; 1 Sam. 17.12). The clans (KJV, 'thousands') of Judah were the small administrative districts or 'parishes' which made up rural Judah (like the medieval English 'hundreds'). Among these countless villages Bethlehem had only one claim to fame and that was the antiquity of its link with David, who was its greatest son. Until Bethlehem's history repeated itself in the birth of a Messiah, 'He' (i.e. God) was going to give His people up to their enemies (3a). Only when the travailing woman (= Israel, or the young woman of Isa. 7.14, or, in the light of Christian fulfilment, the virgin Mary) brought Him forth would the scattered members of the Hebrew community return to the fold and Israel would be unified once more. This aspect of the Incarnation has not yet been fulfilled, but many believe that one day it will and that our Lord's brethren, the Jews, will yet return and the Church, the whole Israel of God, will then be complete (cf. Rom. 11.23,24,29).

The Messiah's reign will be marked by strength, security, peace and the allegiance of all the earth (4), and in vs. 5 f. Micah gives an example of what this Messianic peace will be like: even the proud Assyrian will be kept at bay and Israel will not lack the leaders to take the war right into the enemy's camp. 'Seven . . . and eight' means an indefinite number of reasonable proportions. To us it seems strange to find the Messianic age of peace expressed in terms of military victory, but for a small nation that was for ever at the mercy of her powerful neighbours this was the only way to security and so to peace. In the coming of Christ, however, we see that this warfare was not against human foes nor was it waged with worldly weapons, but that by the spiritual victory of the cross over His enemies and ours we do indeed find peace.

Micah 5.7-15
Rely only on the Lord

There are two oracles in this section. The first (7-9) consists of two complementary statements about the remnant of Israel and their impact on other nations. They will be like dew, which brings blessing, life and prosperity where it settles (7). They will also be like a lion which destroys and terrifies wherever it goes (8). At first sight contradictory, this pair of similes presents the paradox of Israel's place in the world: a means of blessing and yet a source of judgement; to be welcomed and yet to be feared. The difference between the two aspects is governed by the response of the nations: as they receive the remnant they are blessed, and as they oppose them they are destroyed.

The second oracle (10–15) describes the purifying process which will be applied to Judah in the last days. Everything which could possibly be a substitute for trust in the Lord will be cut off or rooted out: horses and chariots, i.e. military strength; walled cities and fortresses, i.e. military installations; witchcraft and spiritualism, ever-popular alternatives to pure religion (cf. Isa. 8.19 f.). All these were contemporary substitutes for faith in God which were prevalent in Micah's day. Most of all there was idolatry (13 f.), represented by carved images, stone pillars, wooden symbols of the Canaanite fertility goddess Asherah, and sacrificial stones (translated 'cities' in v. 14). All these were the necessary adjuncts of the sex worship of Canaan which was for ever infiltrating the religion of Israel, encouraged no doubt by the fallen nature within every Israelite heart. God saw that the only remedy for this was complete eradication of all evil influences and He promises it to His people 'in that day'. Only then will men be able to trust Him wholly, because 'Satan's sympathizer' will have been finally removed from their hearts.

Snaith points out that all these substitutes for faith reflect what *man* can do; even idols are denounced because they are the work of men's hands (13). This is man's insidious temptation. Trust in his own efforts can frequently hold him back from receiving Christ's salvation by faith, and even the truly converted man can all too easily slip back into forms of self-reliance that cut him off from God's grace. Are we trusting in Him alone—today?

Micah 6.1-8 The Lord's Requirements

Hosea had already used the picture of God bringing a lawsuit against His people (Hos. 4.1; 12.2; cf. Isa. 3.13; 43.26; Jer. 25.31), and here Micah sets the scene with Israel as the defendant and the Lord as both prosecutor and judge. In this cosmic court-room the witnesses are the mountains and the foundations of the earth. Verse 3 begins the prosecution's case, in the form of a survey of Israel's redemption-history from Egypt to the Promised Land. Four aspects only are given a mention: (*i*) the rescue from Egypt, (*ii*) the leadership of Moses, Aaron and Miriam, (*iii*) the reversal of Balaam's intended cursing of Israel and (*iv*) the crossing of Jordan (Shittim being the last main encampment east of Jordan, and Gilgal the first on its western bank). Of particular interest is the Balaam episode, which seems to have had a peculiar fascination for O.T. writers. It occupies three chapters in Num. 22–24 and features in a number of other flashbacks to the wilderness events (e.g. Deut. 23.4 f.; Josh. 13.22; 24.9 f.; Neh. 13.2). Its primary significance seems to be that it showed Israel that God could turn man's evil designs into occasions of blessing, and that neither heathen kings nor hired soothsayers could frustrate God's purposes for His chosen people. For the cult of Balaam in the N.T. (for which a possible Greek translation is 'Nicolaitans'), see a Bible dictionary.

The court-scene now switches to the defendant accepting his guilt and asking what reparation can be made, in terms either of sacrificial offerings or even of the sacrifice of his first-born son (7). But God requires not a gift, but the giver. The good way is expressed in terms of righteous actions, merciful treatment of one's fellow men and living in a humble relationship with one's God. This demands the whole of man: his standards of conduct, his personal relationships and his innermost religious life. Such a fine balance between all three aspects of a man's life could be elaborated, but not improved upon. It is a demand made of every Christian, and to fall short in just one of these items leads to serious spiritual impoverishment. How do we measure up to the Lord's requirements?

Micah 6.9-16   The Merchants of Jerusalem

The Hebrew text of this section is very difficult and the RSV has to make a number of corrections, on the basis of the ancient versions, to make the translation intelligible. The passage is an attack on the traders of Jerusalem who have amassed their 'treasures of wickedness' (10) by dishonest means, viz. with balances that did not weigh fairly and weights that were not up to standard. Micah was not the first to protest against this kind of behaviour (cf. Amos 8.5; see also Deut. 25.13–16; Prov. 20.10), but his words would not have been welcomed. The application of Christian ethical standards to the business-world is rarely appreciated. Many businessmen prefer the Church to keep to the 'spiritual' side of life and to leave them to run their businesses in their own way. Others say that it is impossible to be Christian in the competitive world of modern commerce. The Bible says that God's standards apply everywhere and people who ignore them need not expect to receive His blessing.

The consequences of the dishonesty of Judah and Jerusalem ('O tribe and assembly of the city', 9) are expressed in terms of famine, poverty, death, loss of harvests, devastation of land and being the scorn of other nations (14–16). Moreover, what had already happened to Jerusalem (perhaps in the siege of 701 B.C.) was only the *beginning* of God's punishment (13). Jerusalem's trouble was that she had degenerated so far that she had sunk to the level of Israel in the days of the Omrid dynasty (16). Micah may have been thinking specifically of the incident of Naboth's vineyard (1 Kings 21), but in any case that period had become a byword for apostasy, and now it appeared that Judah was following suit and would therefore merit the prophet's curse on Ahab's house (1 Kings 21.21 f.). When men turn away from the worship of God it is not long before their private lives are affected as well. Religion and personal morality are more closely related to each other than people care to admit.

A Thought: What observations would Micah have to make about our modern society? or about our private lives?

Micah 7.1-10   From Pessimism to Faith

When a nation lacks good leadership it has no sense of purpose, and without that the people live only for themselves. Politicians use their influence to feather their own nests; lesser officials need monetary persuasion before they will perform their necessary duties on behalf of the public; everyone is somehow on the make. Micah saw a situation like that in the Judah of his day. The nation was like a vineyard after the harvest or as barren as the fig-tree which the Lord cursed (Mark 11.13 f.). Try as he would he could find nothing of any worth, no godly man to give a lead to the people. Jeremiah, too, was later to look in vain for the same thing (Jer. 5.1) and the psalmist also despaired over his fellow men (Pss. 14.1–3; 53.1–3). Cf. further Isa. 59.15 f. Micah concluded that the only diligence the leaders of his people showed was to do evil and to take bribes (3). They did not deserve to be reckoned as part of the Lord's vineyard; they were nothing better than highly combustible thorn-bushes that would soon go up in flames (4). So not a soul could be trusted, not even a man's nearest and dearest: the closest family ties were broken in the insane desire for self-advancement.

Had Micah ended at v. 6, we might have suspected him of almost psychopathic pessimism (of the kind that was beginning to infect Elijah in 1 Kings 19.10), but the following verse restores the balance. The best antidote to a bout of depression is to turn away to the Lord and to be absorbed in Him. Micah looks to Him in *faith*, waits for Him in *patient expectation*, and knows Him as the God who *delivers* him and *hears* his prayer. His final words (8–10) are addressed to his people's enemy, who could be the Assyrians, the Edomites or the Babylonians. He identifies himself with his people and uses 'I' and 'my' to represent the nation. For 'when' in v. 8, translate 'though': however low they may fall, vindication will eventually be theirs through the goodness of the Lord, and the tables will be turned on those who gloated over them (10). R. E. Wolfe in *The Interpreter's Bible* comments that vs. 7–9 are 'like three bouncings of a ball. At the beginning of each it is down, but at the end of each there is a rebound, the rebound of faith'.

Micah 7.11-20 God Forgives

Verses 11–13 are addressed by the prophet to Jerusalem. It is 'a forward look through the clouds of exile to the day when devastated Jerusalem and her walls would be rebuilt' (Wolfe). In faith Micah looks forward to an even more extensive city to which men will come from all parts of the world. Very likely Micah's vision in v. 12 was of the return of Jews who had been dispersed throughout Assyria, Egypt and Babylon ('the River' = the Euphrates), but it is easy to see how Christian readers could interpret these verses of the enlarged new Jerusalem, with its population that no man could number coming from every nation upon earth. Verse 13 indicates that 'the earth' (not 'the land', KJV), i.e. the heathen territories, will be suffering the devastation promised in v. 10.

Verses 14–20 are a concluding prayer to God, as the good Shepherd of His people. It has three parts: (*i*) The prayer that the Lord will come and take possession of His inheritance, and lead them out to pasture 'alone', i.e. without fear of molestation, in the fertile lands of Bashan and Gilead: this will be reminiscent of the miraculous days of the Exodus from Egypt (15). (*ii*) Then the nations of the world will come trembling to the Lord, not in faith, but in fear; their tongues will be silenced, they will be humbled in the dust, and they will submit in abject shame before His mighty power (16 f.). This is not to deny that the nations of the world can believe and come to Zion with singing: the O.T. frequently holds out the hope of the Gentiles' free and spontaneous conversion. Micah, however, was referring to the humiliation of the Gentiles after they had seen (16) the glory of the Lord in His final vindication of His people, when His truth and power would be so forcefully demonstrated that they would have no choice but to acknowledge it. (*iii*) Supremely, God is a God of forgiveness, who loves His children and removes their sins far away, out of *His* sight and out of *theirs* (19). When He punishes, it is only short-lived (18b):but His favour is for a lifetime (cf. Psa. 30.5). This is no new theology, however, but merely the fulfilment of His promises to earlier generations (20). The book that began with the faithlessness of men ends on the note of the faithfulness and goodness of the Lord.

Meditate on vs. 18–20 and make them your own expression of worship.

Questions for further study and discussion on Micah
1. What can we learn from ch. 3 about prayer which is not answered? See especially vs. 4,7; and then turn to 7.7.
2. What does Micah have to contribute to a doctrine of the remnant?
3. With the help of a concordance examine the place of Bethlehem in the O.T. and N.T.
4. What, according to Mic. 3, is the difference between true and false prophets?
5. How did Jesus apply 7.5 f. to the effect of discipleship on His own followers? Study Matt. 10.21,34–38; Mark 13.12; Luke 12.49–53.

Nahum 1   Vengeance and Comfort

Nineveh, the proud capital of the Assyrian empire, fell to the armies of the Babylonians and Medes in the summer of 612 B.C. From that time onwards it became nothing but a heap of ruins, silted up with the sandy deposits of the desert. The modern name for it is Tell Kuyunjik ('mound of many sheep'), which is an unconscious fulfilment of the prophecy of Zeph. 2.13–15.

Nahum probably wrote shortly before this event, predicting it in some of the most graphic poetry the O.T. possesses. He was a Judean, and the suggested location of Elkosh in S. W. Judah is preferable to the traditional association of his tomb with Al-Qûsh near Nineveh. His name means 'comforter' and some have taken this as a kind of *nom de plume* in that, interspersed with his devastating predictions for Nineveh, he incorporates occasional words of comfort for Judah.

Part of ch. 1 consists of an acrostic poem (2–10), but it is not at all easy to disentangle this, and it may be that the author has freely used an older poem without being too concerned to retain its acrostic form. The theme is the avenging wrath of the Lord, though this is interwoven with balancing statements about His patience, justice and goodness to those who trust in Him (3,7).

The presence of both these aspects of God's nature is in itself a reminder to the preacher that his portrait of God must never be overweighted in any one direction. So Nahum looks towards arrogant Nineveh and towards believing Judah at one and the same time.

Comfort for Judah comes out more strongly in vs. 12,13,15. Nineveh, or one of its kings, is addressed in vs. 11,14. (Verse 11 may even be a flashback to the notorious Sennacherib, cf. Isa. 36,37.) The joyful sequel to Nineveh's fall will be the coming of the messenger of peace, whose arrival in Jerusalem will be the signal for the people to offer the sacrifices that they had promised against the day of their deliverance (15). If the end of an earthly kingdom was to bring such relief and jubilation, how much more welcome should be the good news of the destruction of Satan's empire?

Nahum 2   Storming the Citadel

These verses describe the onslaught of the armies of God upon the ramparts of Nineveh. The troops arrayed for battle present a striking sight with their red shields, scarlet uniforms, gleaming chariots and prancing horses (3, RSV). Before long the outer defences are breached and the battle continues on the city's streets (4). The last stronghold is the temple of Ishtar in the heart of the city, and the attackers are regrouped for the final assault on its walls, using the 'tortoise' siege-engine (known from Assyrian bas-reliefs) as they batter at the defences (5). Then the river-gates are breached and the temple ('palace', AV, RSV) is flooded with torrents of water from the Tigris (6).

Huzzab (7; RSV, 'its mistress') has been taken to be a reference to an Assyrian deity, or the image of one, from its literal meaning of 'that which is set up', but many prefer to emend the text. The associated verbs are feminine and so the idea of a goddess (Ishtar?) being led out in captive procession, followed by her mourning devotees, cannot be discounted. The city (v. 8 is the first mention of Nineveh in the oracle; 1.1 is the title) is emptied of its teeming population (cf. Jon. 4.11) like a lake drained of its waters, and it becomes a vast treasury of spoil for the conquering army (9).

So ends the glory of Assyria. A final lament over Nineveh makes play upon Assyria's fondness for lion-symbolism in her descriptions of her imperial might. Ishtar herself was often depicted as a lioness or as riding upon a lion's back. But now the lion's den, to which the prey of other nations had often been taken (Israel included; cf. 2 Kings 17.6), is to be a danger no more. For the Lord is really in control among the nations of the earth. It is His might and His armies which will destroy Assyria. The Babylonian troops who were so soon to invade Nineveh would be His agents, as Habakkuk also observed (Hab. 1.5–11). God is in command and no power on earth can stand against Him. Imagine what a comfort this message was to the little principality of Judah, surrounded as she was by the giant empires of the near eastern world. The struggling community of the Christian Church takes her comfort from the self-same truth.

Nahum 3 Nineveh's Utter Destruction

This chapter consists of a cycle of prophecies dealing with different aspects of Nineveh's downfall. Verses 1–4 give a fresh description of the battle for the city, in an unusual staccato rhythm that almost catches the sound of the galloping hoofbeats of the attacking chariotry. With this is incorporated a new feature, namely, the reason why she is being treated thus (4). She has seduced other nations by her charms until they are in her power and so, like the harlot that she is, she will receive a harlot's punishment (5–7). She will be exposed and pilloried, and such will be the hatred that she has earned that no one will be found to lament her loss. This is the reward of the prostitute: even her conquests and her customers turn against her in revulsion. Lust knows nothing of loyalty.

Verses 8–13 compare the coming doom of Nineveh with the fate of No-amon, or Thebes, the great city of Upper Egypt, sacked by the Assyrians in 663 B.C. Both cities were founded beside great rivers and both relied partly upon them for defence. Both had vassal territories to turn to for support (9). But Thebes fell and endured the cruel treatment which the Assyrians were notorious for meting out to their enemies; and what could happen to Thebes would happen also to Nineveh (11). The Assyrians would drink deeply of the Lord's cup of wrath; they would reel about drunkenly, seeking a refuge in vain. Their resistance would collapse completely: strongholds would fall and troops would lose their morale (13).

Finally, Nahum ironically exhorts Nineveh to prepare for the siege with supplies of water and bricks (like filling sandbags!). But it will be no use, because fire and sword will do their work no matter what resistance is offered (15). The vast imperial machine of Assyria may appear to be as infinitely powerful as a locust-swarm, but even locusts can disappear overnight (15b–17). There remains nothing more except to pronounce a brief funeral elegy over the Assyrian king, whose generals sleep the sleep of death, whose people are scattered and whose doom is greeted with delight and derision by all (19).

Habakkuk 1

A Faith that Questions

The abiding value of this little prophecy is that it presents the picture of a man who believes and yet questions. That this is a healthy and not an unspiritual exercise is borne out by the way in which the concluding psalm closes with a towering expression of faith which is scarcely equalled anywhere else in the O.T. (3.17 f.). The key to this outcome is that the prophet questions from a standpoint of initial faith; he takes his questions to God honestly and openly; and he waits upon God for the answers to his problems.

The first question (2–4) deals with God's toleration of oppression. This is similar to the psalmist's 'why do the wicked prosper?' (e.g. Pss. 13; 22; 73). It may refer to the social evils within Judah in Jehoiakim's reign (609–598 B.C.), or it may spring from the time when Assyrian power was at its height under Ashurbanipal (669–626 B.C.). In either case the ability of godless men to tyrannize others unchecked seemed to Habakkuk to be a denial of all the principles of law and justice by which God's world was supposed to be governed. How long could this go on?

The reply comes in the form of an oracle from God (5–11). God's justice is going to be administered by a new power, the Chaldeans, who will trample down oppressors and give them their deserts. This is interpreted variously of Nabopolassar's campaigns of 625 B.C. (freeing Babylon from Assyrian domination) and 612 B.C. (the fall of Nineveh), or of the battle of Carchemish against the Egyptians, in 605 B.C. If Habakkuk's statement was genuinely predictive, this oracle must come from before 625 B.C., and its fulfilment may account for the pro-Babylon sentiments of Jeremiah (Jer. 27.6 f.).

God's reply and the report of its fulfilment raise a second question (12–17): How can a pure God use an instrument as cruel and idolatrous as the Chaldeans? The agents of punishment are even worse than those they are sent to punish (13b). They treat their foes as a fisherman does his catch and they venerate their weapons of destruction (14–16). Is this also to go on for ever? Habakkuk's answer, as we shall see, is that God is entitled to use any means at His disposal to work His sovereign will, but that in the last resort only the man who by faith is righteous will live before Him.

Note: The original in v. 12 has 'Thou shalt not die', corrected by later Hebrew scribes to the more reverent 'we shall not die'. With the following verse this gives us Habakkuk's basic creed: the eternal holiness, goodness and justice of God.

The prophet sees himself as the spokesman both for the questionings of his fellow Israelites and for the response of God. He does not, however, shoulder the burden of his own complaint. He waits upon God to see what vision will come to him and what answer he is to give (1). Eventually, with a build-up that commits God to the fulfilment of what is to follow (2 f.), the crucial statement comes (4). It deals, not so much with international politics as with the individual's destiny. The wicked man, inflated with his own importance, is not right with God; he is inwardly bent and this will bring about his condemnation and destruction. The righteous man, however, will live (i.e. enjoy abundance of life) through his fidelity.

The word for 'faith' is the Hebrew *'emunah*, meaning 'moral steadfastness' (it is related to 'amen' and to *'emeth*, truth). It is the quality of reliability and loyalty to God's covenant. The person who has *'emunah* is both a man who trusts and a man who is to be trusted. It therefore has both the meanings which can be attached to the Greek equivalent, *pistis*. Paul, in Rom. 1.17; Gal. 3.11, concentrates on the aspect of personal reliance upon God's word which brings justification, but he does not twist the meaning of the Hebrew as some have supposed. In the N.T., as well as in the O.T., life comes through a relationship of faith between man and God.

Verses 6–20 consist of a series of 'woes' addressed to five different classes of evil-doer: the greedy capitalist (6–8), the man who feathers his own nest and imagines himself secure from all retribution (9–11), the ruler who builds cities with the blood and sweat of others less fortunate (12–14), the lascivious man who uses alcohol as a prelude to perversion (15–17), the idolator who worships inanimate objects (18 f.). All these could be veiled attacks on the Assyrians, but it is more natural to see them as denunciations of Judah's sins in the typical prophetic tradition. Verse 20 is probably a liturgical cry which Habakkuk uses to contrast with the sins and idolatry which have gone before, and to prepare the way for the concluding hymn of praise.

For meditation: What place does silent waiting upon God have in your devotional life? Consider the first and last verses of this chapter.

Habakkuk 3   Triumphant Faith

The heart of this psalm consists of a theophany (3–15), as God appears from the southern deserts surrounded by all the awesome features of a violent thunder-storm. Lightning, dark clouds, thunderclaps, torrential rain, all these follow in His wake and bring terror to all mankind. The language is reminiscent of the Sinai appearance to Moses, though Ezekiel was also to use the image of a storm-cloud to introduce his vision of the Lord in Babylon (Ezek.1.4). Other poetical passages which bear comparison with Habakkuk's psalm are Deut. 33.2; Judg. 5.4 f.; Pss. 68.7–16; 77.16–20. It could be that the prophet is using well-worn symbolism or even an older composition and adapting it to his own needs.

Teman (3) was a district in Edom; Paran was the mountainous area between Edom and Sinai. God was coming from the south, from His Sinai haunts. The fact that the annual rains were usually preceded by the scorching heat of the sirocco, also from the south-eastern deserts, has encouraged some to see the Lord here as the initiator of the annual cycle of fertility—but if so, He is not to be identified with it. The O.T. teaches a God who brings fertility, but not a fertility-god. Traces of ancient mythological figures have been seen in v. 5, named Deber ('pestilence') and Resheph ('plague'; a deity known from Ugaritic texts), but these need not be regarded as anything more significant than literary echoes from the past. (Compare, too, vs. 13 f. with the Babylonian myth of the slaying of Tiamat by Marduk.)

Surrounding this poem are (i) the prophet's plea to God to act as Deliverer, as He has done in times past (2), and (ii) his terrified reaction to the coming of the Lord in majesty (16). This soon gives way, however, to the affirmation of faith (17–19) that God will be trusted and praised irrespective of the fertility of the crops: He is to be adored for His own sake and not simply for the blessings He brings. If, as some suppose, Habakkuk was a cult prophet, attached to the Temple and taking part in its regular worship, much of his book can be interpreted liturgically. This would explain the question and answer pattern in ch. 1; the prophetic oracle in 2.1–4 and the rubric 2.20; and this psalm as a composition designed for use by the whole community at an agricultural festival. If so, the author's faith would have become the vehicle for strengthening the faith of all the people as they recited it together in the Temple. In this sense we can share with Habakkuk and all Israel in the same expression of trust in God.

Zephaniah 1 The Day of the Lord is Near

The prophet Zephaniah lived in the latter part of the seventh century B.C. and was probably a slightly older contemporary of Jeremiah. His long genealogy (1) suggests noble birth and his

477

great-great-grandfather may well have been the king Hezekiah. To judge from his knowledge of the locality (10 f.), he was a Jerusalemite and he may have been attached to the staff of the Temple. His strictures on idolatry (4–6) suggest that his words were uttered before Josiah's reforms in 621 B.C., which removed most of these abuses from Jerusalem.

The theme running through *Zephaniah* deals with the day of the Lord. This has a long history in Israelite thought, but it was Amos who first confounded his hearers by warning them that it would be a bad day for Israel and not a day of rejoicing. The popular idea that God's people would be blessed abundantly, irrespective of their deserving, was shattered by him once and for all (Amos 5.18–20). Zephaniah speaks in the same tradition: the day of the Lord's judgement is both imminent (7,14) and ruinous (15; cf. too, the frequency of 'I will punish', 8,9,12).

Like Amos, Zephaniah specifies the sins in Judah which merit God's displeasure, e.g. syncretistic worship (4–6), adoption of foreign culture (8), deceit and violence (9), carelessness and complacency (12). As he makes these charges he conducts his hearers on a tour of Jerusalem, beginning with the Temple and the roof-top shrines (4–7), then to the royal palace (8 f.), the commercial centres (10 f.) and finally, roaming the streets, lantern in hand, to those who in their prosperity are indifferent to God (12). The Mortar (11), like 'the hills' (10), is the name of a district of Jerusalem; it was probably a low-lying area, like the 'hollow' of the Tyropoeon valley, where one of the main markets was situated.

The description of men 'thickening upon their lees' (12) implies slothfulness; the phrase relates to wine-making, in which the wine has to be stirred and kept moving by continual pouring from one vat to another or it loses its potency and taste (cf. Jer. 48.11). G. A. Smith comments on this verse: 'God's causes are never destroyed by being blown up, but by being sat upon.' Indifference is the greatest enemy of goodness. Could it have affected you, or your church? If you no longer expect the Lord to do great things, it has.

Zephaniah 2   God's Wrath upon the Nations

Before the prophet turns to pronounce the fate of the heathen he utters a brief, scornful oracle against Judah, the 'shameless nation' (1 f.; this is better than supposing vs. 1–3 to refer to the Philistines). At the same time he exhorts the faithful ('the humble of the land', 3) to seek the Lord's mercy in humble obedience. Clearly there is a chance that the day of the Lord may not be total darkness for everybody. Some in Judah may be saved—'perhaps'. This uncertain prospect becomes more definite later, as a remnant are given specific privileges in vs. 7,9; and a full programme of blessing for them is described in 3.12–20.

The first to experience God's wrath are Israel's age-old enemies, the Philistines (4–7). Only four of the five cities of the Pentapolis are mentioned, Gath having been overpowered in the previous century by Uzziah (2 Chron. 26.6) and later destroyed by Sargon of Assyria. Cherethites (5) are etymologically the same as Cretans; the Philistines originated from the Aegean islands.

The next oracle is addressed eastwards to the Moabites and Ammonites (8–11), whose arrogance and pride, especially as shown against God's people (and therefore against that people's God), earn them the same fate as the Philistines: devastation and spoliation at the hands of the remnant of Israel. The remaining points of the compass, south and north, are dealt with in vs. 12–15, as Ethiopians and Assyrians are addressed with God's word. In this last oracle Zephaniah augments Nahum's prophecy about the overthrow and utter desolation of the Assyrian capital. From being the pride of a huge empire it will become a place for pasturing flocks, and all kinds of desert creatures (mostly unclean by the standards of Lev. 11) will haunt its ruins (14). A closing funeral dirge over Nineveh ironically spells out her epitaph in terms, not of her achievements, but of her downfall (15).

These are not simply vindictive predictions of the destruction of Israel's foes. They are to be read as a theological assessment of the world, as seen by God. To the human observer it was chaotic: Israel was weak politically and did little credit either morally or religiously to the faith she stood for. God could not allow this to last for ever. On His day all would be put right: He would be vindicated as sole Ruler of the universe and this meant the overthrow of the mighty, the punishment of unfaithful Israel and the glorification of the righteous remnant. Only so could God be seen to be God. This was what the day of the Lord would achieve.

Zephaniah 3   Corrupt but Purified

There is a marked contrast between the beginning and the end of this chapter. The introductory 'woe' (1) turns to the exhortation to sing aloud for joy (14). In both cases Jerusalem is being addressed. In vs. 1–7, her moral and spiritual breakdown is pronounced in words which show that God must justly punish her guilt. In vs. 11–20, the day of the Lord is seen to produce, not a total overthrow, but only a removal of the guilty members of the community, leaving a righteous remnant to enjoy the salvation and peace of the future Messianic age. Between these two contrasting sections are a pair of shorter oracles, in the first of which (8) the nations of the world are to be destroyed, but this changes in the second (9 f.) to a prediction of their conversion!

It is no solution to this apparent paradox to assume, as many scholars do, that vs. 9–20 are late and not the work of Zephaniah. The combination of the themes of judgement, deliverance of a remnant, and a new life of blessing for the faithful is as old as the story of the Flood. It comes out particularly in the eschatology of the prophets. The day of the Lord has of necessity the two aspects of punishment and purification. If it were only judgement, God's purposes would be utterly frustrated. The remnant *had* to be saved and promised a life of peace and blessing, if God was to remain consistent with Himself. To see any of the O.T. prophets *purely* as a prophet of doom would reflect so badly on his doctrine of God as to be tantamount to denying him his place in the canon. Judgement without mercy is never an attribute of the God of the Hebrews (cf. 5).

For Zephaniah, salvation is for the humble and lowly. This is the quality of quiet dependence on God demanded in Mic. 6.8 and, of course, supremely in *Isaiah* (Isa. 7.9; 10.20; 12.2; 26.3; 30.15). It is not far from the faith that Habakkuk looked for (Hab. 2.4) and the N.T. demanded. Its antithesis is always self-reliance ('your proudly exultant ones', 11), though this may take various forms (e.g. reliance on armies, alliances with other nations, idolatry, etc.). The whole Bible speaks with one voice in saying that salvation is not of works; it is all of God's grace.

Questions for further study and discussion on Nahum, Habakkuk and Zephaniah

1. Summarize the qualities of God which are mentioned in Nah. 1: how complete is the picture of God given here?
2. What spiritual value is to be derived from the book of Nahum?
3. Examine closely the use made of Hab. 2.4 in Rom. 1.17; Gal. 3.11; and Heb. 10.37 f.
4. What has Habakkuk to teach us, in each of his three chapters, about faith?
5. According to Zephaniah, what will the day of the Lord mean to Judah, to heathen nations, and to 'the humble of the land'?
6. Study the hymn of praise in Zeph. 3.14–20. Do you see its fulfilment in the experience of the Christian Church, or could it still have meaning for the Jewish people?

480

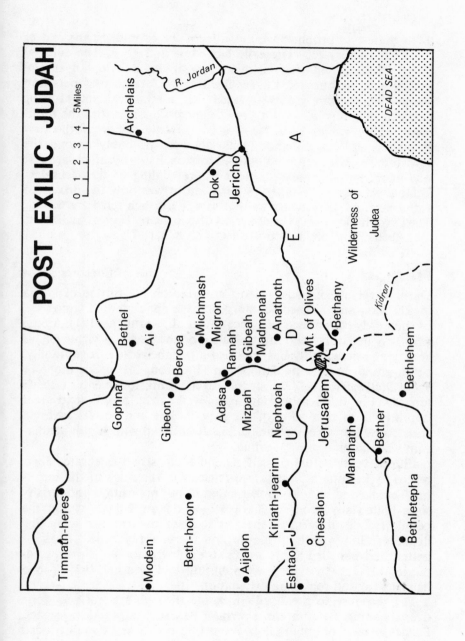

POST EXILIC JUDAH

0 1 2 3 4 5 Miles

R. Jordan

DEAD SEA

Archelais

Dok

Jericho

A

Wilderness of Judea

Kidron

Bethel

Ai

Michmash

Migron

Beroea

Ramah

Gibeah

Madmenah

Anathoth

Mt. of Olives

Bethany

D

E

Gophna

Gibeon

Adasa

Mizpah

Nephtoah

Jerusalem

U

Bethlehem

Manahath

Bether

Kiriath-jearim

Eshtaol

Chesalon

Bethletepha

Timnath-heres

Modein

Beth-horon

Aijalon

Haggai and Zechariah

With these two prophets we move from the seventh to the end of the sixth century B.C. The exile has come and gone. The edict of Cyrus, promulgated after his overthrow of the Babylonian empire in 539 B.C., encouraged the repatriation of foreign prisoners and assisted them with grants towards the re-establishment of their national religious life. The Cyrus Cylinder confirms that the sentiments expressed in Ezra 1.2–4 were the true policy of the new Persian ruler. Haggai and Zechariah were probably among the Jewish exiles who returned with Zerubbabel shortly afterwards. It was many years, however, before the rebuilding of the Jerusalem Temple was seriously taken in hand and it was only the drive and enthusiasm of these two men that saw it through (cf. Ezra 5.1 f.). They prophesied over a brief period of two years, Haggai in 520 B.C. and Zechariah from 520 to 518 B.C. (Zech. 1.1; 7.1).

Haggai 1   The Prophet of Encouragement

Darius I (Hystaspis) succeeded Cambyses on the throne of Persia in 522 B.C., and reigned for 36 years. He appointed, as 'governor' of the newly-constituted province of Judah, Zerubbabel (1), a man who was not only the natural leader of the Jews by virtue of his energy and personality but was also a member of the royal family, being grandson of king Jehoiachin (1 Chron. 3.19). See the *New Bible Dictionary*, s.v. 'Zerubbabel', on the confusion over his father's identity. For this reason Haggai, as well as the people, had great hopes for him as a scion of the Davidic line and he was invested with near-Messianic honours (2.23). Associated with him in leadership was the high priest, Joshua.

Fifteen years before, in 537 B.C., the exiles had celebrated their return by keeping a feast of Tabernacles in the ruins of the burnt-out Temple and had begun to rebuild it, but opposition and apathy soon halted any progress (Ezra 3.2–4.5). Now Haggai chides the people for devoting their energies to their own houses while the house of God is without a roof and in ruins (4; 'ceiled', KJV, is better than 'panelled'). It is because they have ignored their responsibilities to God that they are suffering bad weather (10 f.), bad harvests (6) and rocketing prices (6b).

The response to the Lord's message through Haggai was quite overwhelming. Seldom has a sermon had such a practical impact. Parties were no doubt organized to get timber from the well-wooded hill country to the south of Jerusalem (8) and this was shaped to provide the spars, rafters and decorative panelling for the Temple, to replace the woodwork destroyed in the fires of 587 B.C. Stonework would have been readily available nearer at hand but this would still need cleaning and re-shaping to any new design (14). Haggai recognized, however, that this was not his doing, but the Lord's; he took no credit for the success of his preaching (12,14). Instead, he encouraged the people with the briefest of oracles (13) to assure them that God was on their side and that they were fellow labourers with Him.

Thought: Christian people need to be reproved and rebuked when they fall short, but they need the ministry of encouragement just as much.

Haggai 2.1-9 The Glory of the New Temple

The number of those in Jerusalem who remembered the glory of Solomon's Temple must have been small. By 520 B.C. many of the older men who were involved in the emotional scenes described in Ezra 3.10–13 would have died. Perhaps it was disillusionment over the delays that prompted the handful that remained to be slightly scornful of the new efforts being made to rebuild God's house (3). Perhaps it was just that greybeards (they must all have been septuagenarians) have a habit of idealizing the past, and these men had forgotten the degradation of Temple worship which Ezekiel had described (Ezek. 8). In any event the criticism of older men can be very dispiriting (and you don't have to be over seventy to live in the past!), and Haggai is prompted to give further incentive to the builders by the promise of God's Spirit among them (4 f.; note the threefold 'take courage'). The promise referred to in v. 5 is not specified and these words are omitted in the Septuagint version, but Exod. 19.5 or 33.14 could be in the prophet's mind; alternatively this is intended to be a general parallel between the Exodus from Egypt and the great new age that is about to dawn.

Verses 6–9 clearly put the immediate future of the new Temple in the context of the end-time. There is the 'shaking of the nations' (6,7; cf. 21 f. and Isa. 13.13; Mic. 1.4), followed by the conversion of the heathen and an era of peace and prosperity (9, where there is probably a play on the meaning of Jeru*salem*, city of peace/*shalom*). The God of the Hebrews is daringly described as the One who owns the riches of the whole world, and these will pour into Jerusalem from all sides so that nothing will be able to rival the new Temple for splendour. That such a claim bore so little resem-

483

blance to the actual resources of the struggling Jewish community did not apparently daunt Haggai. He had learnt, as every Christian must, to reckon on God's unseen riches that were available for His people.

The so-called 'Messianic' interpretation of v. 7 ('the Desire of all nations') is based on the Vulgate translation, and is properly abandoned now. The Hebrew demands a plural, 'the desirable things', i.e. the riches of the Gentiles, and in a sense this adds lustre to the overall Messianism of these treasured verses.

Haggai 2.10-23   A Question of Contamination

Within three months of the encouragements offered by Haggai in 1.13—2.9, he appears to be rebuking 'this people' for their uncleanness (14). This seems incongruous to some and they therefore interpret vs. 10–14 as a self-contained oracle relating to the Samaritans, whose offer to assist with the rebuilding of the Temple is rejected by Haggai on the grounds that their uncleanness would be contagious (cf. Ezra 4.1–5). Attractive as this suggestion is, it is unlikely that 'this people' and 'this nation' (14) could refer to any but the Jews, without its being specifically stated, and the addition of vs. 15–19 implies that the writer was thinking of the troubles suffered by the Jewish people before the rebuilding began in earnest. The Samaritan interpretation demands that vs. 15–19 be transposed to just after 1.11 or 1.15 and that the final editor of the book either concealed or failed to realize that the Samaritans were the original subject of the prophecy. In view of this it is probably better to seek another explanation for these words.

The occasion of the oracle is a question put to the priests regarding the relative contagion of holiness ('holy flesh' being the meat of a sacrificed animal) and uncleanness, through contact with a corpse. The answer that the latter is more contagious is turned by Haggai into a parable to show how Israel has been contaminated through her neglect of the ruined Temple. It was like a dead thing in the midst of the city, and it brought upon Israel the troubles described in vs. 16 f. But the point of Haggai's message is that 'from this day on' blessing will come to the people. It is not a rebuke that he is administering so much as an assurance that the days of Israel's chastisement are over. This is followed up by a further message, given the same day (20) and addressed to Zerubbabel, in which he is described as God's servant, His chosen one, and His personal representative ('signet ring'; cf. Jer. 22.24). In view of the military expectations of v. 22 and the expressed hope that in Zerubbabel the Davidic monarchy would be revived, it is not impossible that Zerubbabel's disappearance from the scene shortly after this time was due to Persian suspicions of his loyalty, which brought about his removal from office or an untimely death.

Zechariah 1.1-17   The Four Horsemen

Like John the Baptist, Zechariah began his ministry with a call to repentance. Speaking between the last two prophecies of Haggai (cf. Hag. 2.1 and 2.10), he reminded the people of Judah that all their troubles had been due to their fathers' persistent rejection of the message of pre-exilic prophets like Isaiah and Jeremiah (4). So what they needed to do was not simply to rebuild a new Temple: they had to rebuild the foundations of a new society, based on repentance towards God and the sound moral values that the prophets had taught. Zechariah's insistence on these standards of behaviour is one of his chief contributions to the history of his time (cf. Zech. 1.4; 7.8–10; 8.16 f., 19).

In vs. 7–17 we have the first of a series of eight visions. Much of their symbolism is lost on us now, but it is still possible to understand their general import. The background to this first vision could well have been the sight of Persian mounted patrols who acted as the eyes and the ears, as well as the postal service, of the Persian empire. If there was any original meaning in the colour of the four horses, it is lost to sight. We are not justified in reading the interpretation given in Rev. 6 back into this vision. Zechariah has the assistance of a divine messenger, 'the angel who talked with me', who acts as the mouthpiece of God Himself in interpreting to the prophet what he sees. The horsemen are God's patrols reporting that all is peaceful upon earth (11).

This news dismays 'the angel of the Lord', presumably yet another angelic figure, who appears to be disappointed that nothing more spectacular is happening to Jerusalem after the seventy years prophesied by Jeremiah (Jer. 25.12) have nearly come to an end (i.e. 587 B.C. to the present, 520 B.C.). It looks as if the upheavals in the Persian empire which followed the death of Cambyses and the accession of Darius I (522 B.C.) had been interpreted as signs of the inauguration of the Messianic era (cf. the shaking of the nations, Hag. 2.6, 21 f.). Darius' success in subjugating his empire was a real disappointment. However, this is compensated by a series of favourable statements ('gracious and comforting words', 13) about God's concern for Jerusalem (14), His displeasure with

Jerusalem's enemies (15), the promise of the city's rebuilding (16) and her eventual prosperity (17).
Let all our disappointments lead us to the promises of God.

Zechariah 1.18—2.5   Jerusalem's Protection

There are two separate visions here, but both of them relate to the Lord's protection of Jerusalem. In the first (1.18–21) the four horns represent heathen powers hostile to Judah. Their number signifies completeness, as if coming from the four corners of the earth (cf. the four horsemen of 1.10 and the four chariots of 6.5 f.). For the horn as a symbol of power, compare 1 Kings 22.11; Jer. 48.25. To meet these the Lord produces four smiths, who are meant to represent His agents of destruction upon the oppressor nations. Commentators refer to Ezek. 21.31 where the phrase 'skilful to destroy' translates what is literally 'smiths of destruction'. These will 'terrify' the nations, thus repaying them in their own coin, and render them powerless.

Note that this is entirely the Lord's provision for His people. He intervenes on their behalf and provides His own agents and weapons against their foes. The number of the smiths is also intended to be a reminder that God's resources exactly match the needs they are meant to satisfy. He does not have to be extravagant in His provision for our needs, but He never underestimates them. His power is 'sufficient for every need'.

The second vision is reminiscent of the angel in Ezekiel's vision of the new temple (Ezek. 40.3); but it is doubtful whether Zechariah meant the man with a measuring-line to be understood as an angelic figure. This would mean that there were three angels in this one brief scene (cf. 2.3). Possibly this is a self-conscious autograph (in the same way as the young man of Mark 14.51 f. probably was), and the prophet is addressing the message to himself. Alternatively, it could be Zerubbabel.

The message is that the city of Jerusalem needs no walls to protect it; partly because it will be so populous that it will overflow them anyway, and partly because the Lord is going to dwell in the midst and be her Protector (cf. Rev. 21.23,25). This is a great spiritual truth which the builders of Jerusalem took to heart, but the pressing need for protection against outside interference eventually led Nehemiah to fortify Jerusalem in c. 444 B.C. Perhaps it is no accident that the period of Ezra–Nehemiah moulded Judaism into a religion of exclusiveness from which it has never been released.

Walls can imprison those within, as well as keeping others out. *Meditation: Are we in danger of building walls around God?*

Zechariah 2.6-13   A Call to Return Home

It is clear from v. 7, as well as from the narrative in *Ezra–Nehemiah*, that many Jews stayed in Babylon after the decree of Cyrus and failed to take advantage of the offer of repatriation which was held out to them. Many of them had, of course, been born in exile and had so come to terms with their environment that they would not face the upheaval of the journey and the uncertainties of settling into a completely new way of life in Judah. An enthusiastic call from one who had made the effort, like Zechariah's plea in these verses, might have swayed the minds of some. The situation has its parallel in the unwillingness shown by the Israelites to venture out of Egypt into the Promised Land and, in Christian terms, of the slowness of many an unbeliever to be persuaded to step out into faith and eternal life.

Zechariah first appeals to the exiles still in Babylon to return to Jerusalem and to escape the judgement which is about to fall on that country (6–9). The 'land of the north' (6) is a vague reference to their land of exile and may carry echoes of the mythological Saphon, the home of the Canaanite gods, which is a cognate of the Hebrew for 'north'. Evil nearly always struck from that direction; it was the direction from which the sun never shone. The original reading of v. 8 had 'My eye', but this was altered to 'His eye' because it was thought to represent too anthropomorphic a picture of God. The thought that anyone who harmed God's people was touching God in His most sensitive part is a very striking one.

In vs. 10–12 the people living in Jerusalem are addressed. For them there will be nothing but blessing. The Lord will dwell in their midst and heathen peoples will come and share their allegiance to Him. Their land will be 'the holy land' (12), the only time, incidentally, in the O.T. when this name is given to Palestine. Verse 13 looks like a liturgical formula (cf. Hab. 2.20), borrowed for the occasion to show that God is about to take action very soon to reveal His glory. When that happens and these predictions are fulfilled, Zechariah's prophetic calling will be authenticated (9,11). How many people know that the Lord has sent us?

Zechariah 3   The Vision of Joshua's Cleansing

The fourth and fifth visions are concerned with Judah's leadership, in the persons of Joshua and Zerubbabel. In this chapter it looks as if charges had been made against Joshua concerning his unfitness for high priestly office. This may have come from those who had remained in Judah and who felt that Joshua had been polluted by his residence in Babylon. Equally, Joshua may have stayed in Judah during the exile and been accused of compromise by those who returned. Certainly there was a deep rift which Zechariah's vision was intended to heal.

The vision is of the Lord's tribunal (cf. Job 2.1), with Satan (lit. 'the accuser') fulfilling his customary role as the prosecutor of God's people. By command of the angel of the Lord (who appears to be the personification of the Lord Himself) Joshua's filthy robes are removed and he is clothed in clean garments and invested with clean priestly headgear. This symbolical authentication of Joshua's status is confirmed by the words that follow (6–10). In these Joshua and his fellow priests are given 'right of access' to God's heavenly court on condition that they observe God's moral laws ('walk in My ways') and follow the priestly duties ordained by Him ('keep My charge' being a cultic term, cf. Ezek. 44.15 f.). If they do this they are given jurisdiction in the renewed Temple, and God will establish His Messianic servant, the Branch, a title which must obviously refer to Zerubbabel (based on Isa. 11.1; Jer. 23.5 f.; 33.14–16).

The stone with seven 'eyes' or facets has been variously interpreted (9). The least improbable suggestions are that this was (a) a jewel in the Messiah's diadem on which would be inscribed Zerubbabel's name; (b) a symbol of the completed Temple in the form of an inscribed coping-stone; (c) a precious stone to be worn on the high priest's person, similar to the breast-plate jewels or the turban inscription of Exod. 28.9–12,36–38. That these events will genuinely herald the Messianic age is borne out by the closing references to the removal of sin (9b) and the idyllic life of peace and security, borrowed from Mic. 4.4.

It need not deter us that Zechariah's expectation that the new age was about to dawn was not fulfilled. An imminent Messianism has always been the mark of a healthy church, in both O.T. and N.T. times, as well as in the present day. God frequently allows us to have our hopes, but then shows that the best is yet to be.

Zechariah 4   The Lamp and the Olive Trees

In order to understand the meaning of this vision one must first separate off the paragraph from 'This is the word of the Lord' (6) to 'in the hand of Zerubbabel' (10a). The rest of the chapter then flows in an intelligible sequence. If we look at the two sections separately we can then see how they relate to each other.

The vision proper (1–6a, 10b–14) is of a gold, seven-branched lampstand, the seven lamps being supplied with oil from a central bowl or reservoir (2). The seven lips are the nozzles which hold the wicks. Flanking this are two olive trees which appear to be supplying the oil to the reservoir by means of two golden pipes (12). Alternatively, the pipes are simply the channels by which the central bowl feeds the lamps, and the olive trees are worked in gold on either side of the bowl just beside its two outlets.

The interpretation is not without its difficulties. Some see the lampstand (which has many similarities with the one described in Exod. 25.31–37) as a symbol of the Lord, and this is attested by the comparison of the lamps with the seven eyes of the Lord in v. 10b. If this is correct, it would be impossible to interpret the olive trees as if they were *supplying* the oil for the lampstand. God does not need His anointed ones as much as that! They would have to be thought of as His servants, standing by His side and dependent upon Him. Another interpretation makes the lampstand a symbol of the Jewish community, through whom God surveys the whole earth (10b) and who are supported and sustained by God's two appointed and anointed leaders, Joshua and Zerubbabel, who act as the channels of divine grace to His people. A third alternative, based on the cultic significance of the lampstand, is to see it as a symbol of the Temple, which is sustained by the Spirit of God through His two servants and which serves as the eyes of God in the earth. The passage in Rev. 11.4, based upon these verses, develops a symbolism of its own and does not help with the interpretation of Zechariah's vision.

The parenthetic passage (6b–10a) relates to Zerubbabel and the Temple, assuring him that his problems will be overcome and that the building will be completed amid general acclamation (7,9). The plummet (10) will be in his hand as he lays the last stone straight and true. These verses have only a general connection with the vision, though their concern with the Temple suggests the third alternative interpretation as the likeliest. They also link the supply of oil to the lampstand with the resource of God's Spirit (6b) and this is a significant identification. To displace this section to after 3.10 or 6.15, as many would wish to do, does not make things any easier, and it seems best to keep it in its context, either as a large parenthesis or as following on from 4.14.

Meditate on v. 6 in relation to your Christian service.

Zechariah 5

The Removal of Sin

These two visions are an elaboration of the promise made in 3.9b, that God will remove the iniquity of the land. They follow naturally upon the visions which deal with the purifying and authorization of the nation's leadership. Two methods of purging are reflected in the visions. In the first (1–4), evil men are exterminated by means of a curse written upon a huge flying scroll, measuring 30 ft. by 15ft., which hovers over the land of Judah and settles upon individual habitations. This is a strange figure to our minds, but it reflects the Hebrew concept of the effective power of the curse in dealing with the individual wrongdoer. Other judgements affected groups of people, but the terms of a curse could be specific and it would therefore touch only those specified. Compare the cursings (or 'sanctions') which were an integral part of ancient covenants, e.g. Deut. 27.15–26; 28.15–19.

The measurements of the scroll do not have any recognizable significance, except to show that it was unrolled and of tremendous size. No reader of *Zechariah*, for instance, would remember that it had the same dimensions as the porch of Solomon's Temple. Comparisons of this sort can only lead to fanciful exegesis. The two kinds of wrongdoer mentioned in vs. 3 f. are representative of those who commit sins against their fellow men rather than against God.

The second vision (5–11) envisages the physical deportation of wickedness, personified as a woman, in a large measuring-bowl or barrel ('ephah') with a leaden lid. She is carried off by two other women with stork-like wings and deposited in Babylon (Shinar), where a temple is built for her. The context suggests that the woman represents the sin of idolatry, which is to be cleared out of Judah and banished (appropriately) to Babylon, where a suitable welcome will await her. The word 'base' (11) is normally used for the pedestal of an idol or altar. Taken this way this vision complements the previous one and promises the removal of religious as well as social sins.

Meditate on Psa. 51.1–4.

Zechariah 6

The Four Chariots

The series of eight visions concludes with one reminiscent of the first (cf. 1.8–17). The horsemen are replaced by chariots, because whereas the former were patrols reporting back with information about the state of affairs on earth, the chariots are hostile agents with the task of executing God's wrath upon the people of the north country, i.e. upon Babylon (8). Once again there are problems over the colours of the horses, and occasional inconsistencies if they are compared too closely with 1.8, but it is better that we admit our inability to understand it all than that we follow the Greek version in harmonizing everything into a pleasing kaleidoscope. The only clear meaning is that given in v. 8, namely that God's anger against Babylon has been satisfied in the punishment of its inhabitants, and so the wrongs done to His people in the exile have now been fully avenged. 'Spirit' (8) has the meaning of 'anger', as in Judg. 8.3; Prov. 16.32.

Verses 9–15 represent the symbolic crowning of Joshua the high priest, as a kind of historical appendix to the visions. But there are problems: (a) why should Joshua and not Zerubbabel be crowned? (b) why is Joshua now called the Branch (12)? (c) what is the meaning of 'between them both' (13)? The fact that the Hebrew has 'crowns' instead of the singular in vs. 11,14 suggests to most commentators that this was originally written with the names of both Joshua and Zerubbabel in v. 11. Then vs. 12,13a would describe the coronation of Zerubbabel, the Messianic ruler and builder of the Temple, and v. 13b would refer to Joshua, who would be Zerubbabel's religious counterpart and would govern harmoniously with him. The very writing down of this prophecy would have been like an act of treason against the Persian authorities and it may even have contributed to Zerubbabel's downfall. If this was indeed so it is not surprising that his name had been removed from the book for political reasons, but traces of the original prophecy were left behind so that the perceptive could read between the lines. Verse 10 suggests that recent reinforcements had arrived from Babylon (cf. 2.6 f.), bringing with them these offerings for the new Temple.

For consideration: How can you 'help to build the temple of the Lord' (15)? See Eph. 2.22; 1 Pet. 2.4–6.

Zechariah 7   A Question about Fasting

By 518 B.C. the work on the Temple must have been making real headway. At this point a deputation arrived from Bethel to ask about the necessity for continuing the fasts which commemorated the sack of Jerusalem. The fifth month (3) was the month in which the city had been burnt by the Babylonians (Jer. 52.12 f.). In the seventh month (5) Gedaliah, the Babylonian nominee, had been murdered by Ishmael (2 Kings 25.25). Bethel was in the northern province, though only twelve miles north of Jerusalem, and its inhabitants would have been the mixed population, settled there by the Assyrians, who were later called Samaritans. Zerubbabel showed them no great friendliness (see Ezra 4.1–3) and this may be why Zechariah rebuffed the deputation. It is not easy to see why Bethel, which had long set itself up as a rival to Jerusalem, should have sought the authoritative ruling of the priests and prophets of that city. Perhaps their intentions were not wholly sincere.

In his reply (4–7) the prophet questions the value of the fasts, implying that they had been directed manwards and not Godwards. Fuller consideration of the teaching of the pre-exilic prophets might have saved the people of Bethel from their concentration on matters of ceremonial at the expense of moral righteousness (7.9–12). The fast which God was pleased with is that described in Isa. 58.6–10. Moreover, these fasts (and two more are mentioned in 8.19) were initiated to enable the people to lament their losses, i.e. they were for their own satisfaction and they had been occasioned by their own disobedience (11 f.). T.C. Speers (Interpreter's Bible) comments: 'A fast is a means to an end. . . . Religion and all religious practices exist for the sole purpose of establishing a closer, more meaningful relationship between people and God.' This should be the criterion by which everything we do in God's name is to be measured.

Verses 9 f. summarize the O.T. standard of justice. This is very different from Roman *iustitia*, represented by the blindfold goddess with a balance and a sword. It meant fair dealings for all men, but with a particular element of consideration for the deprived member of the community. To the Hebrew mind, justice and mercy were bound up with each other, a fact demonstrated supremely in the cross, where God could be 'just and the justifier' (Rom. 3.26).

Question: What part should fasting play in the Christian's life, and what safeguards should be applied?

Zechariah 8.1-13   Bright Hopes for Jerusalem

This chapter consists of ten prophecies concerning the era of salvation which is about to dawn upon Jerusalem. All are introduced with 'Thus says the Lord (of hosts)', as in vs. 2, 3, 4, 6, 7, 9, 14, 19, 20, 23. Most of them make reference to the glorious future of the holy city, and several echo earlier statements made by Zechariah.

(*i*) Verse 2 is virtually a repeat of 1.14: God's jealousy includes His ardent zeal *for* Jerusalem and His anger *against* her enemies.

(*ii*) Verse 3 is similar to 1.16; 2.10, and echoes Isa. 2.2: God would return to Jerusalem and inhabit it once again, as envisaged in Ezek. 43.1–5.

(*iii*) Verses 4 f. present the combined blessings of ripe old age for the inhabitants of Jerusalem and of many children playing freely in the streets (cf. Isa. 65.20, 23). This symbolizes freedom from war, sickness and famine, which were the great decimators of human life. In O.T. times, when there was no bright prospect of an after life, longevity was a blessing greatly to be prized (cf. 2 Chron. 1.11).

(*iv*) Verse 6 reflects the doubts that some felt about Zerubbabel's ability to carry through his ambitious plans (cf. Hag. 2.3; Zech. 4.10). What they thought to be too wonderful to be true, however, God could regard as wonderful *and* true.

(*v*) Verses 7 f. are a well-used statement of God's intention to restore the scattered community of Judah from their various places of exile. 'East' and 'west' mean more than just Babylon and Egypt. All will return to become once again God's covenant people in a relationship of mutual trust ('faithfulness' = reliability) and harmony ('righteousness' is the word used when both parties to a covenant are keeping it properly).

(*vi*) Verses 9–13 are a more elaborate exhortation, designed to encourage the work of building by showing the change in the fortunes of Judah since the work began. The economic distress of the early days is giving way to fruitfulness and fertility (12), and even the nations will bless themselves by Israel (cf. Gen. 12.2 f.; 22.18). It is a striking thought that, when God really blesses those who put their trust in Him, even unbelievers will notice and appreciate it.

Zechariah 8.14-23   The Question Answered

(*vii*) Verses 14–17: Zechariah is emphatic that in the good days that are coming the ethical demands of God are not to be forgotten. There is no sense in which he is thinking of an age where sin is a human impossibility. Even though God gives His people peace, they are still to make judgements that 'make for peace' (16). This reduces the level of Zechariah's expectation from the full Messianic 'golden age', described in Isa. 11.1–9, for instance, to that of an age of salvation. We would compare it with the post-Pentecostal era, when salvation is a reality and God is with His people by His Spirit, as against the sin-free perfection of heaven, which is yet to come.

(*viii*) With vs. 18 f. we come at last to the answer to the deputation's enquiry (7.3). The two fasts that are added probably commemorated the date when the siege of Jerusalem had begun, in the tenth month (i.e. January 588 B.C.; cf. 2 Kings 25.1); and the date when the Babylonian army breached the walls some eighteen months later, in the fourth month (2 Kings **25**.4). In the spirit of the new age, Zechariah advocates turning these into feast days, because rejoicing is in future to be the hallmark of the Hebrew community. One wonders whether his words were consciously in our Lord's mind when He made some of His observations on fasting, e.g. Matt. **9**.14 f. Jesus was very aware that He was ushering in the age of salvation that had long been expected.

(*ix*) Verses 20–22 fill out the statement in **2**.11a about the influx of Gentiles into the saved community. All men will enthusiastically want to share in the Lord's blessings upon Jerusalem and will encourage each other to take part. Gentiles will be the evangelists to lead other Gentiles to God. They will not come patronizingly, for they will see that they have no claim upon the God of the Hebrews; they will come, as they rightly should, to seek His favour.

(*x*) The last of this decalogue of prophecies foretells the tenfold expansion of the Jewish faith as every Jew brings with him ten Gentiles who are anxious to accept his way of life. The phrase 'God is with you' recalls the Immanuel prophecy (Isa. **7**.14; cf. **45**.14), and looks forward to the day when a Jew will draw all men to Himself (John **12**.32).

Questions for further study and discussion on Haggai and Zechariah 1–8

1. What does Haggai **1**.4 have to say to us on the relative priorities of our home and our church?
2. What incentives did Haggai give to the people to encourage them to work for God?
3. What place does the Holy Spirit have in the writings of these two prophets?
4. From what sins did Zechariah feel his people needed to be cleansed? See **1**.1–6; **3**.1–9; **5**.1–11; **7**.1–7.
5. Consider the passages which attach Messianic status to Zerubbabel, e.g. Hag. **2**.23; Zech. **3**.8–10; **4**.7–10; **6**.11–13. Do these justify us in regarding him as a type of Christ?
6. With the help of a concordance, collect all the O.T. references to Satan. What does his chief role appear to be?
7. How did Zechariah draw upon the teachings of his predecessors, the prophets before the exile?

Zechariah 9-14

INTRODUCTION

The last ten chapters of the O.T. consist of three groups of material, each beginning with the word 'Oracle' (Zech. 9.1; 12.1; Mal. 1.1). The third is named after Malachi (lit. 'my messenger') which may simply be the subject of the oracle (see Mal. 3.1) and not a personal name. The others are added on to the end of *Zechariah* without any explicit mark of identification. To assume that they are *not* by Zechariah, as many critics do, and to attribute them to a supposed 'Deutero–Zechariah' does not help at all. It glosses over the real similarities that exist between chs. 1–8 and 9–14 (for a list of these see the *New Bible Dictionary*, s.v. 'Zechariah, Book of', p. 1356), and it is never satisfactory to argue from a change of style to different authorship. Certainly, Zech. 9–14 are in a markedly different literary category from 1–8: they are apocalyptic, and they do not deal with the rebuilding of Jerusalem or the progress of the Persian empire. But they are virtually impossible to date from internal evidence alone, and that is all there is to go on. They do, however, contain an effective message, which will be our main interest in the comments that follow. On the question of authorship we can only say that they could be by Zechariah, they have traditionally been attributed to him, but they do not claim to be and it does not matter greatly if they are not his work.

Zechariah 9 The Triumph of the Messiah

One of the strongest marks of similarity between the two halves of *Zechariah* is in their concept of the Messianic age: both of them concentrate their attention on its imminence, and chs. 9–14 lead on from many of the expectations of chs. 1–8. The main difference is that Zerubbabel is well out of the picture in chs. 9–14, and these chapters must have been written after he had been discredited (presuming that was his fate). The Messianic hope still burns brightly, however, and in ch. 9 we see the awaited King's triumphal march on Jerusalem (9).

This is preceded in vs. 1–7 by a description of an army invading from the north, defeating first Syria (Hadrach, Damascus and Hamath), then Phoenicia (Tyre and Sidon), and finally Philistia (Ashkelon, Gaza, Ekron and Ashdod). Some would see this as a prophecy relating to Alexander's march southwards after defeating the Persians at the battle of Issus (333 B.C.). But in view of the expectation that Philistia would become a satellite of Judah, embracing the Jewish faith and sharing the remnant's privileges (7), this interpretation is most unlikely. While other nations would be overrun, God would see to it that His house was protected by His own presence (8). The Jebusites (7) were the ancient inhabitants of Jebus (= Jerusalem) who were assimilated after David's victory (2 Sam. 5.6 ff.).

The triumph of God's anointed King reaches its climax as He enters Jerusalem, not on a prancing charger surrounded by His men of war, but in lowly dignity riding upon an ass (9). His reign is going to be marked by compulsory disarmament, by a rule of peace (10) and by release for all Hebrew captives (11 f.). The justification for this is to be found in the covenant of Sinai, which was sealed by the sprinkled blood (Exod. 24.6–8), and is therefore binding upon God as well as upon His people (11). So the Lord will give His people superiority over their foes, protection from all troubles and prosperity and honour in their new life (13–17). The reference to Javan (Greece, v. 13) has been thought to be a gloss, added after the Greeks came to power under Alexander, but Greece appears in earlier passages (e.g. Isa. 66.19; Ezek. 27.13; Joel 3.6) as a distant power to be reckoned with.

Summarize the blessings which come to the Christian through the triumph of Christ, and claim them for yourself.

Zechariah 10   The Need for Proper Leadership

Our Lord's pity for the multitude because they were 'like sheep without a shepherd' (Matt. 9.36; Mark 6.34) recalls sentiments expressed in several O.T. passages (e.g. Num. 27.17; Ezek. 34.5) where God saw the need of His people for strong spiritual leadership. Because they were leaderless, the Jewish people in the time of which Zechariah was speaking were being led astray to seek the blessing of rain and fertility for the crops through all kinds of superstition (2). Clearly Zerubbabel, and probably Joshua, too, were by now no longer at the helm. Teraphim were the household gods, highly prized from ancient times (Gen. 31.19; Judg. 17.5, etc.) but frequently associated with divination (2 Kings 23.24; Ezek. 21.21). Despite the O.T. prohibitions of these and other forms of spiritualism, the fact that Hebrew had an extensive vocabulary of words relating to its practice and its practitioners suggests that it was much more widespread than would otherwise appear. Its fault was that it interposed magical or demonic powers between the inquirer and God, who alone should be approached and consulted direct (1; cf. Isa. 8.19).

The shepherds and leaders of v. 3 may well be foreign overlords, but God promises to overthrow them (11) and to make Judah strong under native leadership ('out of them', 4). At that time all the pre-exilic threats would be reversed; instead of Israel's rejection there would be acceptance (6); instead of defeat, victory (5,7); instead of dispersion, return and redemption (8–10). As with a number of other similar passages (e.g. Isa. 43.16–19; 48.20 f.), Israel's return, whether from the Babylonian exile or from the dispersion which followed Alexander's conquests, is seen in terms of a second Exodus from Egypt through the waters of the Red Sea (11). This great act of redemption was as definitive for Israel as the cross is for the Christian Church. It is no accident that in the N.T. Christ's ministry and death are frequently understood in 'Exodus' terms (Luke 9.31, etc.).

Zechariah 11   The Shepherd of the Flock

The opening verses (1–3) continue the theme of the previous chapter and are a mock lamentation over the fall of the tyrants who had been dominating Israel. Cedars of Lebanon and oaks of Bashan were symbols of great powers, as in Isa. 2.13; 10.33 f.; Ezek. 31.1–18. Similarly their rulers were described as shepherds and lions (3).

Verse 4, however, introduces a new theme. The prophet is bidden to act the part of shepherd of God's flock, but he in turn is in the employ of unscrupulous master-shepherds who care nothing for the flock and exploit it for their own profit (5). He takes on the job and his intentions are symbolized by the two staffs named 'Grace' (i.e. God's covenant with the flock) and 'Union' (i.e. harmony between Israel and Judah). His destruction of three shepherds in one month (8, a historical allusion which has been variously interpreted) does not win him the loyalty of the flock, who apparently prefer being exploited to being cared for. So the covenant is annulled (10) and the prophet asks to be paid off (12). The 'lordly price' of thirty silver shekels changes hands (surely said scornfully—it was a slave's value, Exod. 21.32) and he deposits it in the Temple treasury where, as he was acting in God's name, it rightly belonged.

There is a variant reading in v. 13, recognized by RSV margin, and it is interesting that in the Gospel narrative where this is applied to the betrayal price of Jesus, both traditions are remembered (Matt. 27.5–7). So the money is both offered to 'the treasury' (Heb. *hā'ōtsar*) and used to buy the field of 'the potter' (Heb. *hayyōtser*).

The prophet is here representing God, who comes to His people with the twin blessings of covenant and unity. The people, however, reject His offer and so the cancellation of these gifts must be their responsibility. Finally, the prophet is told to play the role of a worthless shepherd, for that is the kind of leadership the people are going to have to endure (15 f.).

A dogmatic interpretation of these words is impossible. They cannot refer to the Messianic age and they appear to have no real link with what has gone before. They do, however, have remarkable similarities with the coming of Jesus Christ, His rejection by the people He came to shepherd, His betrayal by Judas. But details must not be pressed or Jesus will be found to be His own betrayer. Probably the original meaning had to do with an immediate historical situation which our scanty knowledge of the period prevents us from understanding in any detail.

Thought: 'Grace and Union—two of Christ's most precious gifts to His people.' How would you interpret them?

Zechariah 12   The Martyred Messiah

With these closing chapters we meet with the apocalyptic style of writing for the first time in *Zechariah*. Notice the frequency of the phrase 'On that day' (3, 4, 6, 8, 9, 11; 13.1, etc.), found previously only in 9.16. This sort of writing is futuristic, symbolical and often cryptic. It deals with the last days but is often addressed to the present. One commentator describes it as 'a pep-talk to the faithful and a nightmare to the sober expositor'.

The main theme is the inviolability of Jerusalem. The Lord is on her side and will strengthen her inhabitants so that they will be able to devastate the hostile peoples round about (2–6). In the final battle with the nations of the world, which is a recurrent theme in apocalyptic writings (cf. Ezek. 38,39; Rev. 12, etc.), the tribes of Judah will realize that supernatural forces are at work on behalf of the people of Jerusalem (5) and will fight more ferociously and successfully than they (7). In this way Jerusalem and her Davidic house will be rebuked for their arrogance, but this is to be only temporary: a Davidic ruler of semi-divine status will arise to lead the people to final victory and the nation will become strong and glorious (8 f.).

At the height of the triumph, however, there is introduced a note of sombreness. Mourning and lamentation will fill the land like the mourning at the first Passover (if that is the meaning of 'over a first-born' in v. 10) or like the ritual weeping of the heathen over their dying vegetation-gods (11; cf. Ezek. 8.14). The reference to the plain of Megiddo has been associated with Josiah's untimely death there (2 Kings 23.29), but it may simply have been the site of this Canaanite ritual. Nathan and Shimei were sub-clans of David and Levi.

The cause of this mourning is the violent death of an unnamed hero, who could be the prophet himself but is more likely the Davidic king, over whom the people feel remorse as well as sorrow, inasmuch as they had been responsible for his death (10). Numerous attempts have been made to find a historical context for this prophecy, but none is so apt as that which sees in it a prediction of the cross. Could it be that one day the Jewish people will feel remorse and come to repentance and faith in their crucified Messiah?

Let your prayers today include a prayer for the conversion of the Jews.

Zechariah 13   Cleansing for God's People

If, as seems likely, these verses follow on from the end of ch. 12, it appears that Zechariah intended us to see a relationship between the Messiah's martyrdom and the cleansing of the house of David from its sin (1). There is also more than an echo of the language of Isa. 53, quite sufficient indeed to make these parts of *Zechariah* a regular treasure-chest for the prophetic interpreters of the apostolic Church. To judge from Matt. 26.31 (= Mark 14.27), this was a lesson they learned direct from our Lord, who must have used these Scriptures, alongside Isa. 53, to develop His own sense of being the Shepherd of His flock, the King of peace, the pierced Messiah and the means of His people's cleansing. All of these crucial concepts lie concealed in chs. 9–14 of *Zechariah*.

Verses 2–6 show that in the last days even prophecy will have become discredited. It will be classed with idolatry (2); prophets will disavow their calling (5) and be disowned by their families (3); and they will avoid wearing their distinctive uniform (4; cf. 2 Kings 1.8; Matt. 3.4). Verse 6 probably means that prophets who have suffered lacerations in an ecstatic frenzy (cf. 1 Kings 18.28) will pretend that they were simply scratches received in a friendly brawl. This is, of course, not true prophetism, but a totally false phenomenon which is a parody of the real thing. An alternative interpretation is to regard the prophet in v. 6 as a true prophet who has been persecuted by his friends for following his vocation, and whose injuries thus received belie his claim to be a simple tiller of the soil. This explanation fits in better with attempts to read back Christ's scourging into this verse, but it agrees less readily with the context of discredited prophets.

Verses 7–9 deal with the Messianic testing, i.e. the purificatory sufferings which precede the dawn of the age of Messianic bliss. The shepherd is here a good leader (unlike 11.15–17), who is smitten in order that the flock may be scattered and subjected to the fires of persecution. Only a third will survive, but they will be the remnant who will inherit the covenant blessing-of being God's special possession (9). So when Christ came He was at pains to show that the reign of universal peace was *not* imminent. There would be wars, persecutions and suffering (e.g. Matt. 10.34).

For study: what does the Bible say about the value of persecution? See Job 23.10; Isa. 48.10; Mal. 3.3; 1 Pet. 1.7.

Zechariah 14   A Glimpse of the Age to Come

Again, in typical apocalyptic style, the curtain that hides the future from sight is drawn back for a few brief glimpses into the happenings of the last days. The chapter has little cohesion apart from this, and it ranges over an onslaught on Jerusalem (2), with the inhabitants escaping through a rift in the Mount of Olives (4 f.); a transformation of nature (6–8); the establishment of God's kingdom (9); the levelling of the hill-country around Jerusalem (10 f.); a plague on Jerusalem's enemies (12–15), and the enforced conversion of those who survive it (16–19).

Verses 1–5 are a parallel to the battle-scene described in 12.1–9: the last great siege of Jerusalem. After human defeat (2a), the Lord will intervene with supernatural acts until the moment when He comes for His final victory (5b). The earthquake is that referred to in Amos 1.1, though the escape from Jerusalem is reminiscent of Zedekiah's flight in 587 B.C. (2 Kings 25.4).

Then will come the ending of winter and night, and it will be an era of continuous daylight. As the mountains are turned into a plain, so the city of Jerusalem, rebuilt as in ancient times (Jer. 31.38), will be all the more visibly exalted above it. Geba, ten miles north of Jerusalem, and Rimmon, ten miles north of Beersheba, were the approximate limits of Judah before the exile (2 Kings 23.8). 'Over all the earth' (not just over this land) the Lord will be King, and all men will acknowledge the basic creed of Jewish monotheism (9). These will be the survivors of God's judgements and they will be expected, under threat of drought, to worship annually at Jerusalem at the Feast of Tabernacles, the celebration of the Lord's enthronement as King of the universe. Special sanctions are threatened against Egypt because lack of rain would be no loss to them (18 f.)!

Finally, the prophet's concern for Temple ritual is reflected in vs. 20 f.: sacrifice in abundance is envisaged (cooking pots the size of huge cauldrons, 20b); there will be no need of special utensils, for everything will be sacred to the Lord for all to use (21a); no one will need to trade in the Temple, i.e. to exchange secular for sacred goods (cf. Matt. **21.12**). In the great day that is coming, everything will be sacred to the Lord—right down to the bells on the harness of the horses! Thus is expressed in priestly terms the acme of perfection which is to be found in the new Jerusalem.

Questions for further study and discussion on Zechariah chs. 9–14

1. Study the way in which Jesus fulfilled the prophecy of Zech. **9.9** (cf. Matt. **21.1–11**; John **12.12–19**). What other predictions in this chapter can He be said to have fulfilled?
2. What is the meaning of the phrase 'the blood of My covenant' (**9.11**)?
3. What light is thrown by these chapters on the meaning of Christ's death?
4. How is the Lord's Kingship described in ch. **14,** in relation to (*a*) the nations, and (*b*) His own people?

Jerusalem in the time of Nehemiah

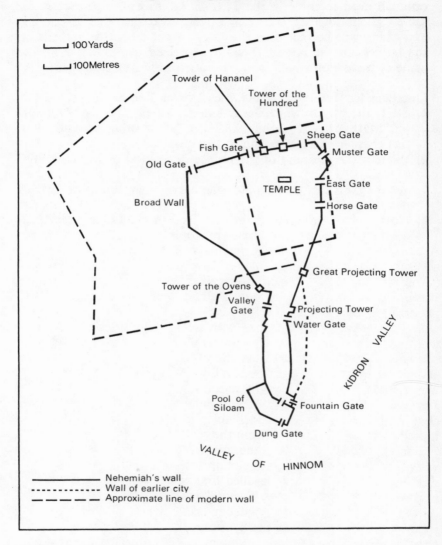

100 Yards

100 Metres

Tower of Hananel

Tower of the Hundred

Fish Gate

Sheep Gate

Muster Gate

Old Gate

TEMPLE

East Gate

Broad Wall

Horse Gate

Great Projecting Tower

Tower of the Ovens

Valley Gate

Projecting Tower

Water Gate

KIDRON VALLEY

Pool of Siloam

Fountain Gate

Dung Gate

VALLEY OF HINNOM

———————— Nehemiah's wall
·············· Wall of earlier city
— — — — Approximate line of modern wall

   Nehemiah's nocturnal survey of the walls (Neh. **2**.12-15) extended from the Valley Gate to a point near the Great Projecting Tower. This was the area of acute destruction, accentuated by the steep slope in this region. As a result of this reconnaissance he made no attempt to follow the old line of the wall in the south-east, but rebuilt the wall along the ridge of the hill, thus *reducing* the internal dimensions of the city.

Malachi

INTRODUCTION

Whether Malachi (lit. 'my messenger') was the author's name or a *nom de plume* based on **3.1**, the book he wrote has a consistency and pattern which assures its unity. Its background is of lax Temple worship (**1.7**), failure to pay tithes (**3.8**), frequent marriage with foreign women (**2.11**): all this at a time when a Persian governor was ruling Judah (**1.8**). Our knowledge of conditions during the Persian period is very limited, but as these were among the evils that Nehemiah tried to rectify (Neh. **13.**10, 23 f.), most commentators date Malachi either just before Nehemiah's governorship (i.e. about 450 B.C.) or in the interval between his first and second periods of administration (i.e. between 444 and 433 B.C.). The message of Malachi may be summed up in the phrase in **1.6**: 'If I am your Master, where is the honour due to Me?'

Malachi 1   Injured Innocence

A recurring pattern is seen throughout *Malachi* consisting of an accusation by the prophet, followed by a reply of injured innocence ('How have we . . . ?'), which in turn is followed by a more explicit statement of the fault with which the people are charged. This pattern is found in **1.**2,6,7; **2.**17; **3.**7,8,13.

In this chapter it begins not with an accusation but with the announcement of the Lord's love for Israel. When taxed for evidence of this, the prophet points to the fate of Edom, the nation who had earned such hatred by their betrayal of Jerusalem in 587 B.C., and whose history went back to the rejection of Esau and the choice of Jacob as the heir of the promises to Abraham (Gen. **25.**23). 'Love' clearly means election-love, and 'hate' is its opposite (not an immoral hatred so much as rejection from the position of honour).

If Israel has been chosen to the covenantal father–son relationship with God, he is charged with failing to show his 'senior partner' due respect. The charge is levelled first at the priesthood for their slovenly ways in the Temple. They take the view that anything will do for God, an attitude not peculiar to their day. God could wish that one of the priests saw the hypocrisy of it and had the courage to close down Temple services altogether (10). In comparison with this so-called worship, God was getting better and purer offerings at heathen sanctuaries from Gentile congregations (11). This is a far better interpretation of a difficult verse than to attribute universalism to Malachi or the popular contemporary notion that 'everybody worships the same God under different names'. Such an idea would have been abhorrent to any O.T. writer, and Malachi plays on the incredibility of his statement to shock his readers, or hearers, into seeing the utter unworthiness of their worship.

Verse 13 caricatures the professionalism of the priest who finds his routine duties tedious, and v. 14 castigates the layman who gives God the second best when he has promised Him the best. It is a case of 'like priest, like people': the fault in both cases is that they have lost sight of the greatness of the King, the Lord of hosts (14).

Thought: Only the best is good enough for God.

Malachi 2.1-9 Irresponsible Clergy

The accusation made in 1.6 receives now its condemnation. The duty of the priesthood is made clear: it consists of (*i*) giving true instruction (Heb. *torah*), a word meaning oral direction on matters of ritual, moral and spiritual importance, given in response to an inquiry (6a); (*ii*) unimpeachable conduct, which combines qualities of moral rectitude (righteousness), good relations with others (peace), and awareness of the presence of God (walking with Him); (*iii*) influencing the lives of others positively for good, inducing repentance and true conversion (6b). As he does all this, the priest is fulfilling his intended role as God's messenger and the guardian of God's truth (7). 'Knowledge' (7) is not academic learning, but personal experience of the living God: books are no substitute for this kind of wisdom, though they can, and do, enhance it.

God's expectations of the priesthood are expressed in the phrase, 'My covenant with Levi' (4,8), the patriarch standing for the whole priestly family descended from him. This was intended to be a means of bringing life (= 'blessing'; what the N.T. calls 'abundant life') and peace (social, religious and inner harmony). As with the covenant with Moses on Sinai, it had its sanctions in the form of blessings and curses. The priests, having themselves departed from the requirements of God, were misleading others and thus failing in their duties (8). There was therefore nothing for it but that God should turn the blessings into curses, desecrate the priestly order and remove them from His presence (2 f.).

The passage highlights the crucial influence, for good as well as for harm, that the clergy can exercise through their office; and this applies to the lay preacher who is invested with ministerial responsibilities as well as the ordained clergyman. If their ministry is grounded in the fear of God (5) and their sole concern is to glorify

Him (2), there should be no cause for anxiety. But as soon as they show partiality to those they are called to serve (9), they are on the way to making shipwreck.

Question: Are you fulfilling your responsibilities as a priest (Rev. 5.10)? Could God call you Malachi ('My messenger'; cf. v. 7)?

Malachi 2.10-16 Marriage and Divorce

Quite apart from the failure of the priesthood, Malachi felt that the troubles his people were going through could be attributed to a number of particular points in which they were all falling short. These were (a) the general disregard for the sanctity of marriage (2.10–16); (b) the carelessness about maintaining the ministry through regular tithing (3.8–12); and (c) the general attitude of contempt for God of which these were symptomatic (2.17; 3.13–15).

The question of marriage and divorce he relates to the ineffectiveness of their public worship (13). A man's prayers, as well as his preaching, can all too easily be vitiated by the inconsistency of his marriage relationship. Two evils were prevalent in Malachi's time. The first was contracting marriages with foreign women, whom he describes as daughters of a foreign god (11). To do this was to deny the covenant of Sinai and the Jewish doctrine of election (10). Jews were God's own people, His creation, His offspring (unless we take the 'one father' of v. 10 to be referring to Abraham or Jacob; cf. 3.6). In any event v. 10 means the integral unity of the children of Abraham: it does not teach the 'universal fatherhood of God and brotherhood of man'. That concept is flatly contradicted by what follows. Malachi was in fact saying exactly what Paul was to enlarge upon in 2 Cor. 6.14–18. A chosen people must marry within the community.

The second evil was that of divorcing Jewish wives in order to make these liaisons with foreigners, thus adding to the guilt of the enterprise. The phrase, 'the wife of your youth' (14,15), suggests that it was as the husbands grew older that they put aside their maturing wives in favour of younger and more shapely foreign girls. This practice is attacked on three counts: (a) it is a sin against God, for He was the unseen witness to the original marriage covenant (14); (b) it frustrates the purpose of God, which is that children are brought up to serve Him in the community of faith (15); and (c) it is abhorrent to God because it constitutes cruelty against the rejected wife (16); 'covering one's garment with violence' being a figurative expression for treating one's wife with cruelty.

Note the repetition of 'faithfulness': God expects us to be faithful to our partners, both in marriage and in the faith, and supremely to Himself.

Malachi 2.17-3.5 The God of Justice

The days after the exile saw an age of increasing rationalism. As new patterns were being built up, old values were being questioned and often rejected. Many were sceptical of the old prophetic faith in a righteous God who rewarded the good and punished the wicked. The inequalities of life did not seem to fit into this tidy pattern and so God's justice was frequently called in question. This was no new revolt against the beliefs of past generations: Israel had always had her questioners. But the upheaval of the exile had brought it to the surface and scepticism was on the increase. By Malachi's time even God was tired of it (2.17)! His message was that God was going to act to remedy the injustices of which men were complaining.

3.1 brings together the persons of the forerunner ('My Messenger' = Malachi) and of the Lord who comes to purify the Temple and the priesthood. It seems best to understand 'the messenger of the covenant' as belatedly in apposition to the forerunner, and to take vs. 2 f. as being the activity of the Lord Himself. This does not leave much for the messenger to do, but possibly that was the writer's intention. The forerunner's task is simply to prepare the way and to call attention to the great One who is following behind. He is described in 4.5 as Elijah restored to life again and, of course, in the N.T. as John Baptist.

When the Lord comes, He will (a) purify the priesthood so that the worship of Israel may be acceptable (Jesus' action in cleansing the Temple was only a symbolic fulfilment of this and cannot be said to have exhausted its meaning); and (b) He will then, and only then, take punitive action against individuals for their acts of injustice (5). The sins mentioned are a combination of infringements of the Ten Commandments and the inhumanities against which the eighth-century prophets preached. The only 'religious' sin is that of sorcery: all the others are anti-social, but in committing them men do in fact show their disrespect for God ('do not fear Me', 5).

Malachi 3.6-18 Giving to God

The first verse of this section presents a problem of interpretation. As it stands in the RSV it means that only God's unchanging mercy prevents the people from being punished with destruction. This is true enough, but it is strange to find a word of mercy following hard on the heels of God's justice (5) and immediately preceding a statement of Israel's persistent disobedience (7). There is something to be said therefore for translating v. 6: 'I the Lord do not change; and you do not cease to be sons of Jacob', i.e. you are inveterate deceivers like your forefather.

When challenged to be specific in His call for repentance, the Lord refers to the issue of paying tithes. A man's money is often a barometer of his whole outlook on life. His treasure goes where his heart goes (Matt. 6.21). No protestation of piety carries weight when it is contradicted by a failure to give sacrificially.

Tithing was a duty more than an option. It involved handing over a tenth of one's produce or income to God as a token of recognition that all increase came from Him and belonged to Him. To pay tithes was not an act of generosity: it was an act of self-deprivation. To the Israelite, giving only began when tithes had been paid. The tithe was a kind of ecclesiastical income-tax, which went to the maintenance of the Temple and its staff; giving was done additionally through hospitality, aid to the poor and the 'free will offering', which was usually given through Temple funds for a special need. It is impossible to apply the same pattern rigorously to present-day Christian needs, but there are obviously basic principles which should be related to our giving, as Christians, to God's work and the needs of others.

The nation's failure to tithe produced the results found in Neh. 13.10–13: Nehemiah the administrator appears to have been more successful than Malachi the preacher! However, despite their withholding of God's dues and their serious questioning of the value of religion (13–15), there was a nucleus of faithful men who had a regard for God and whom He would remember and acknowledge (16 f.).

> *'Take my silver and my gold,*
> *Not a mite would I withhold. . . .'*

True or false?

Malachi 4   The Day of the Lord

In the final analysis the only answer to the perennial question of the inequality of life, and especially to the complaint expressed in 3.14 f., has to be left to the day of judgement. This is described by Malachi in terms of a consuming fire which will annihilate the wicked as quickly and easily as a farmer burns off a field of stubble when he has harvested the corn. The righteous, on the other hand, will enjoy the sunshine of God's blessing and will rejoice with all the exuberance of calves which have been set free from their stalls to go prancing over the now-blackened stubble-fields (3). The figure of the sun of righteousness with healing in its wings (2) is probably derived from Egyptian or Persian art, which often represents the Sun-god as a winged disc, affording protection and blessing to those who worship it. Malachi saw no harm in borrowing the imagery without taking over the theology that went with it.

Verses 4-6 consist of two postscripts, which could be regarded as rounding off the minor prophets, the Hebrew 'Book of the Twelve', or even as suitable finales to the whole O.T. The first looks back to the beginning of the story: Moses, the covenant, and the commandments (4). The second looks forward to the beginning of a new era: Elijah, heralding the coming of the Messianic age and preparing men's hearts for it. One represents the law and its demands; the other stands for prophecy and its promises. Here were the two main strands of O.T. teaching, sometimes mutually critical but never mutually incompatible. In the years which separated Malachi from the birth of Christ, Judaism developed in different directions. In the religion of the rabbis and the scribes the Law was paramount; but there were other sections of Judaism where the spirit of prophecy was never forgotten (as evidenced by the Qumran community's writings). The period between the Testaments spoke with many conflicting voices, but when Jesus came it was with Moses and Elijah that He appeared on the Mount of Transfiguration, and with whom He discussed the details of His Messiahship. In Him, therefore, as both Prophet and Priest, the two elements of Judaism find their perfect unity.

Questions for further study and discussion on Malachi
1. What may be learnt from 1.6—2.9 about the Christian minister's chief areas of temptation?
2. Is divorce always contrary to the will of God? Cf. 2.16; and see also Deut. 24.1; Matt. 5.31 f.; 19.3–9; Luke 16.18; 1 Cor. 7.10–16.
3. What principles of Christian giving may be deduced from 3.8–12?
4. In what way does the book of *Malachi* prepare the reader for the N.T. dispensation?

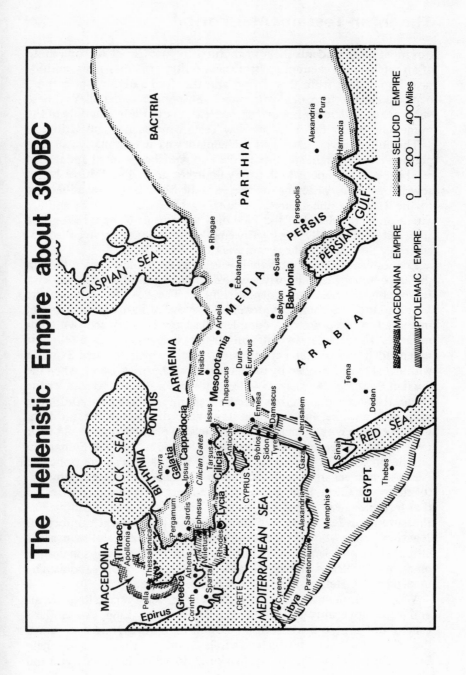

The Hellenistic Empire about 300BC

MACEDONIA
Epirus
Greece
Thrace
BLACK SEA
BITHYNIA
PONTUS
Ancyra
Pergamum
Galatia
Ipsus Cappadocia
Sardis
Ephesus
Athens
Corinth Sparta
Miletus
Rhodes
Lycia
CRETE
MEDITERRANEAN SEA
CYPRUS
Cilician Gates
Tarsus
Issus Cilicia
Antioch
Byblos
Sidon
Tyre
Gaza
Alexandria
Paraetonium
Cyrene
Libya
Memphis
Thebes
EGYPT
RED SEA
Sinai
Jerusalem
Damascus
Emesa
ARMENIA
Mesopotamia
Nisibis
Thapsacus
Dura-Europus
Arbela
MEDIA
Ecbatana
Babylon
Babylonia
Susa
ARABIA
Tema
Dedan
PERSIAN GULF
PERSIS
Persepolis
Rhagae
CASPIAN SEA
PARTHIA
BACTRIA
Alexandria
Pura
Harmozia

Pella
Apollonia
Thessalonica

MACEDONIAN EMPIRE
PTOLEMAIC EMPIRE
SELUCID EMPIRE

0   200   400 Miles

The Inter-Testamental Period

For most Bible students the four centuries before Christ are something of an intellectual vacuum. With the exception of Ecclesiastes, no biblical books date from this period and the books of the Apocrypha, neglected as they are, deal with only a few periods in detail. Yet these years are considerably important, not least in our understanding of the immediate background of the New Testament parties and attitudes.

The influence of Ezra and Nehemiah was determinative in this period. They brought stability to the impoverished state of Judah and established its religious faith firmly upon the Law. The Temple-based Jewish community became the people of the Book, and loyal adherence to the Law became their distinguishing characteristic. The minute attention to the detail of the Law may seem to us to be a retrograde step, but undoubtedly this loyalty enabled Judaism to survive the considerable pressures of these centuries.

Economically and politically it was a day of small things, although the Jews enjoyed certain privileges and a degree of autonomy under a reasonably tolerant Persian government. The hostility between the Jews and the Samaritans, evident in the books of Ezra and Nehemiah, increased to the point of a complete cleavage between the two communities. However, it was difficult for the Samaritans to gain religious independence under the Persian government, which included Samaria within an area controlled by the Jerusalem authorities. Later, when the Persian Empire was crushed by the victorious armies of Alexander the Great, the Samaritans seized their opportunity. In 332 B.C., Alexander occupied Palestine, and the Samaritans, according to reliable tradition, welcomed him with open arms and requested permission to build their own temple. There can be no reasonable doubt that the Samaritan temple on Mt. Gerizim dates from this period. It was the policy of Alexander to set up Greek colonies in strategic areas, and Samaria, together with Gaza, Ptolemais and Damascus, formed such centres, so that Jerusalem was ringed in by areas of powerful Hellenistic influence. Pressure upon Jerusalem was also increased by the large numbers of Jewish pilgrims who would come up for the principal feasts from areas influenced by Hellenism. Within Jerusalem itself a party, including many of the rich and influential, was in favour of modifying Judaism by incorporating Hellenistic ideas and institutions.

When Alexander died in 323 B.C., his empire fell apart as his generals and local governors fought for power. Ptolemy Lagi, Alexander's general in Egypt, quickly secured himself in this area, and established the Ptolemaic kingdom which was to last until c. 31 B.C. With his help Seleucus was able to gain power in a kingdom which included Syria and much of Mesopotamia. The Seleucid kingdom, thus established, lasted until c. 64 B.C. It will be apparent that Judah lay between these two great kingdoms, and being a strategic area, it became a bone of contention between the two. During the entire third century the Ptolemies had little difficulty in retaining control of Judah, in spite of the minor friction detailed so accurately in Daniel ch. 11. But in 198 B.C. the Seleucids gained the upper hand, and Judah became one of the spoils of her victory—the Jews had new masters.

For a while there was no perceptible disadvantage in this, but gradually the situation changed. The Seleucids were defeated in conflict with Rome, and from this point on their Empire began to crumble; their subject peoples started to revolt and Rome kept an unrelenting financial pressure on them. When Antiochus Epiphanes became king in 175 B.C., he believed that Hellenism could provide a unifying bond to cement together his disintegrating Empire, and he encouraged cities to conform to this policy by granting them special privileges. There were many in Jerusalem who were attracted, and a considerable Hellenist group was established. At this time there was trouble over the appointment of the High Priest, regarded as hereditary by the Jews, but as a civil appointment by the Seleucids and therefore open to the highest bidder. The conservative High Priest, Onias III, was supplanted by his brother Joshua, who adopted the Greek name of Jason, an appointment which greatly displeased the traditionalists.

The acute crisis came in 168 B.C. when Antiochus was frustrated, in a campaign against Egypt, by Roman intervention. Humiliated and resentful, he determined that the Jews would conform to his policies, and instituted a period of savage persecution to stamp out everything which was distinctively Jewish. The first book of Maccabees accurately details this period. Surprisingly, however, it was the ultimate salvation of the Jewish faith. A minority of traditionalists, the Chasidim, had long withstood the insidious inroads made by Hellenism, but the bulk of the population was unaware of the danger. It did, however, understand the barbarities of Antiochus, and a powerful reaction was provoked, spearheaded by an old priest, Mattathias, and his five sons. One of these, Judas Maccabeus (the hammer) was to give his name to the (Maccabean) uprising. The revolt was singularly, some would say, miraculously, successful, but there is no doubt that it was aided by acute divisions within the Seleucid kingdom.

The first objective of the revolt was religious freedom, and this was obtained by 163 B.C. when Lysias, the Seleucid general, who was poised to capture Jerusalem and crush the Maccabees, was forced to withdraw his forces to meet a threat to his authority in the Syrian capital of Antioch. He negotiated a treaty with the Jews which, whilst not grant-

511

ing them political freedom, was distinctly favourable to them. The religious group, the Chasidim, were satisfied with this agreement, but the Maccabees, with popular support, continued their campaign with a new objective, i.e. national independence. It can be argued that this policy was a fundamental mistake, for Judah was in no position to sustain her independence in a world situation where she was no more than a minor power. Certainly it involved her in almost three centuries of bloodshed, culminating in the Roman devastation of A.D. 70 and 132.

However, the Maccabeans, or Hasmoneans as they were known in the late period (after Hashmon, a remote ancestor), achieved full independence in 141 B.C. Simon, the last survivor of the five sons of Mattathias, was elected 'general, leader and high priest for ever', i.e. he was king in all but name. It is not surprising that Messianic expectations became attached to the house of Levi, the priestly family, in this period. Simon's son, John Hyrcanus (135–104 B.C.), further developed this 'priest-king' concept but it was not until the reign of John's eldest son, Aristobulus (104–103 B.C.) that the term 'king' was used publicly. The Jewish historian, Josephus, notes that Aristobulus was 'the first to put a diadem on his head', although in Jewish domestic affairs he diplomatically retained the title of high-priest. The Jews were able to maintain their independence until the Romans entered the land in 63 B.C. After a period of intrigue and counter-intrigue for power within Judah the Romans backed Herod (the Great), an Idumean, and the power of the Hasmoneans gradually declined, although it was not until 37 B.C. that the Romans were able to establish Herod in Jerusalem.

It is against this background that we may see the rise of the Jewish religious parties. The Sadducees were, by and large, the successors of the Hellenists, although of a less blatant kind than those who were in favour of modifying Judaism during the Maccabean crisis. Broad in their sympathies, they were prepared to co-operate with the ruling power and so provided the high priests during the period of Roman supremacy. For them the Law (i.e. the Pentateuch) alone was inspired.

The Pharisees were the successors of the Chasidim, the strongly traditionalist and pious group whose resistance to Antiochus Epiphanes was so decisive. They were deeply attached to the Law, but unlike the Sadducees, they also accepted as inspired the prophets and most of the other books now found in the Old Testament. Historically, there is much to be commended in the Pharisees, they were popular with the people and were the religious leaders and teachers of the nation. They accepted the settlement which vested civil and religious power in the Hasmonean family.

However, there were groups which strongly resented the pretensions of the Hasmoneans, and who became markedly separatist and ascetic,

512

often withdrawing from contemporary life into small, self-supporting communities. They were strongly critical of the Pharisees, calling them 'seekers after smooth things', and the Temple worship. The Essenes are the best known of such groups, and the Qumran community provides an excellent illustration of this type.

The Zealots (or Canaaneans) were a small but influential party whose affinities were with the Chasidim but who were strongly nationalistic. They resented any outside interference and viewed the payment of tribute to Rome as treason. Whereas the Pharisees submitted to Roman domination as just retribution for the sin of the nation, until God should remove it, the Zealots regarded themselves as God's chosen instrument to throw off the Roman yoke. It is likely that Simon, one of Christ's disciples, was originally a Zealot (Luke 6.15; Acts 1.13).

The only party sufficiently virile to survive the wars with Rome was the Pharisees, and theirs has been the enduring and distinctive impress upon Judaism.

NOTES

NOTES

NOTES

NOTES

NOTES